Southern Literary Studies

SOUTHERN LITERARY STUDIES

edited by

Louis D. Rubin, Jr.

A Season of Dreams: The Fiction of Eudora Welty
Alfred Appel, Jr.

The Hero with the Private Parts
Andrew Lytle

Hunting in the Old South: Original Narratives of the Hunters
Clarence Gohdes, Editor

Joel Chandler Harris: A Biography
Paul M. Cousins

John Crowe Ransom: Critical Essays and a Bibliography
Thomas Daniel Young, Editor

A Bibliographical Guide to the Study of Southern Literature
Louis D. Rubin, Jr.

A BIBLIOGRAPHICAL GUIDE
TO THE STUDY OF
SOUTHERN LITERATURE

A BIBLIOGRAPHICAL GUIDE
TO THE STUDY OF
SOUTHERN LITERATURE

ecimus

EDITED BY LOUIS D. RUBIN, JR.

_With an Appendix
Containing Sixty-eight Additional Writers
of the Colonial South
by J. A. Leo Lemay_

LOUISIANA STATE UNIVERSITY PRESS   BATON ROUGE

Z
1225
R8

THIS BOOK IS DEDICATED
TO THE MEMORY OF

Edd Winfield Parks

1906–1968

INTRODUCTION

The present volume is an attempt to bring together, within the covers of a single book, a compilation of some of the most useful material available for the student who would begin work in the field of Southern literary study.

The idea of a Southern literature dates back at least to the 1830s, and the study of the South's literature as Southern, both in order to understand the literature and the region which nurtured it, goes well into the nineteenth century. From the work of the earliest important scholars in the field—William Malone Baskervill, William Peterfield Trent, Carl Holliday, Charles Alphonso Smith, and others—up to the present day, the assumption has existed that, whether for better or worse, the experience of life in the South has marked its writers in important ways, and has produced a recognizably and identifiably *Southern* literature, so that the failure to take this factor into account in any consideration of the work of the South's writers must result in an impoverishment of understanding.

Customarily, there has been little hesitation, either on the part of Southern critics or of others, to discuss the South's writers as "Southern," but such discussion has typically consisted of a few cliches and some facile generalization. Anything more thoroughgoing is apt to be branded "insular" and "sectional." Especially because of the South's particular history, of course, there are manifest dangers inherent in the attempt to study the work of its writers as regional expression. The very idea of a distinct Southern literature arose as an expression of the growing sectionalism of the ante-bellum period, and then and afterward the study of Southern literature has too often tended to involve a strident sectionalism. The tendency to view literature as a form of patriotic propaganda, and to judge it in accordance with such standards, has always been present, and likewise the tendency to exalt second-rate literature because it satisfies one's patriotic pride. In particular a great deal of the late nineteenth and early twentieth century writing about Southern literature by Southerners has suffered from sectionalism at the expense of literary judgment and taste.

Nevertheless, it seems superfluous to debate, as I have heard it debated, whether Southern literature *should* be studied in terms of regional origins. The test is, after all, pragmatic; the obvious fact is that there has been and continues to be important American literature which is distinctively and importantly Southern, and which exists in the form and content that it does *because* it is Southern. To attempt to study it, therefore, without proper consideration of its regional identity would be to fail to that extent in understanding it. No amount of patriotism can make a Sidney Lanier into the literary equal of a Walt Whitman; but, at the same time, no analysis of Lanier which fails to include the consideration of his origins can succeed in properly explaining Lanier.

Not a few good Southern writers have made vigorous efforts to dissociate themselves from any consideration as being in any important sense "Southern" writers. Their concern is understandable, when one considers how much futile chauvinism and defiant insularity has in the past gone hand in hand with the self-conscious assertion of Southern uniqueness and Southern virtue. The very word "Southern" has itself too often seemed an assertion of smallness. Yet such abuse of regional identity need not and should not be a concomitant of the useful recognition of such identity. No one would contend that the consideration of James Joyce as being importantly a product of Irish society has the inevitable effect of reducing the stature and relevance of his fiction to a level with that of Charlotte O'Connor Echols and John Francis O'Connor. Similarly, the approach to the fiction of William Styron in terms of Styron's Southern origins should in no sense constitute an assertion of limitation. It should not reduce Styron to the status of a present-day counterpart of Henry Sydnor Harrison.

I say that it *should* not; I am aware that all too often that is in effect what has happened. No one familiar with the scholarship in the field of Southern literary study can avoid the recognition that too much of it has been a mediocre business. All too much of it has been slipshod, superficial, unimaginative, chauvinistic. The same is perhaps true of the study of American literature as a whole, but it has been especially so for the literature of the South. There has been all too much generalizing, and a paucity both of reliable fact and of sound taste and judgment. Until 1954, when Jay B. Hubbell published his monumental study *The South in American Literature, 1607–1900*, there did not exist a single competent overall historical account of Southern writing, based on solid scholarly research. And despite the brilliance of the Souther.. literary achievement in the years following the conclusion of the First World War, no thoroughgoing unitary study of the modern Southern writers as a group, relating their fiction and poetry to the life and times of the region, has as yet been produced. Of good formal criticism of the modern Southern writers there has been aplenty, while for the Southern writers of the nineteenth century and before, good historical and biographical work has been produced. But what is still very much needed is imaginative critical scholarship dealing with the earlier work, and informed historical and cultural scrutiny of the more recent writers.

Happily, there are signs that past deficiencies are beginning to be remedied. In recent years the publication of such books as William R. Taylor's *Cavalier and Yankee: The Old South and the National Character* and Cleanth Brooks's *William Faulkner: The Yoknapatawpha Country*, to select but two examples, has shown what can be accomplished when the literature of the South is subjected to first-rate imaginative scholarship. Neither of these books satisfies everyone; legitimate criticism has been made of both. But in their very different ways, both of them, in their imaginativeness and perceptiveness, are models of what is possible in the disciplined study of the literature of the South.

It is to further such study that the present volume was conceived. The editor, preparing to offer graduate courses and seminars in the literature of the South, was struck by the fact that, despite the widespread interest in Southern literary study, both in Southern colleges and universities and elsewhere, and despite the mass of critical and historical scholarship that has grown up in the field, there was no single work to which the beginning or the advanced student of Southern literature could turn to discover what was available to him. The critical bibliography in Professor Hubbell's invaluable book covered a great deal of the material about Southern literature before 1900 and especially that before 1865, to be sure, but it was already fifteen years old. To learn of any of the scholarship in Southern literature since 1954, and of all of the scholarship about writers of the twentieth century, the student must search among myriad individual checklists, partial compilations, general bibliographies, and the like. It seemed obvious that if continued study in Southern literature was to be desirable, such work would be greatly facilitated by a volume which brought together compilations of some of the principal scholarship concerned with a number of the South's writers and some of the more pervasive themes and areas of investigation having to do with Southern literature. Such a work must necessarily be selective. For some of the writers involved, a staggering amount of critical and historical commentary existed, so that the principal use of a checklist would be to note some of the best work and to indicate precisely where more inclusive bibliographical information could be found.

To accomplish this task, therefore, the help of some one hundred scholars was enlisted. In each instance the editor sought to find contributors whose knowledge of the assigned topic would permit them to choose intelligently from among the available scholarship those items which would be of most use to the beginning student. For the individual writers to be included, an approximate limit was placed on the number of items to be listed. Beyond that, the choice was left to the bibliographer himself, with the single exception that the editor has inserted mention of occasional material published during the months preceding the printing of this checklist.

The editor's first thought had been to aim at a comprehensive descriptive and critical checklist, of which each section would constitute a considered bibliographical essay. On reflection, however, this appeared impracticable for a number of reasons. The preparation of elaborate interpretive checklists would necessarily be a task of several years' duration, and the need for an overall checklist of Southern literature existed right now, not four or five years from now. Furthermore, the field was so extensive, and the scholarship so uneven, that it would be extremely difficult to secure very much uniformity of judgment among the contributors and about the material, so that the result might be, in the present stage of Southern literary scholarship, all too misleading to the beginning student. The question came down to this: what did the beginning student in Southern literature need most, a series of carefully organized critical bibliographical essays about some of the major aspects of the field, or a much more inclusive, less integrative compilation, which would show him in general what was available, with minimal editorial guidance and a maximum of coverage? Given these considerations, then, the decision was made to proceed along the present lines. Perhaps at some future date it would be possible to produce a different kind of work, of the sort previously noted.

The contributors to this volume, then, were asked to draw up selective checklists about their assigned subjects. They were given the option of preceding the checklists, if they wished, with some paragraphs of critical comment on the scholarship. Minimum descriptive phrases in brackets could accompany each entry, if desirable. Contributors assigned general topics, and a few of the most written-about individual authors, could arrange their entries in such groupings as they saw fit, but otherwise the lists were to be alphabetical and not subdivided into genres. Items with useful bibliographical material were to be preceded with an asterisk. The chief task would lie in the decision of what to include and what to omit. No work by the individual authors being covered was to be included within the checklists unless specifically of an autobiographical or demonstrably self-analytical nature. A bibliography of the writings of Southern authors themselves might be a very desirable thing to have, but to attempt to combine it with the selective checklist planned here would result in a volume of such length that the publication of it would constitute a considerable problem, and the completed work would of necessity have to be priced so high that most of the beginning students for whom it was designed could not afford to purchase it.

From the outset, one problem immediately became apparent. Most scholars are reasonably modest individuals, reluctant to call attention to their own writings. Yet to be the reasonably authoritative volume that this one was designed to be, it was obviously desirable to secure as contributor, for each general topic and for each individual author, scholars who knew the material from having worked with it. Yet how, for example, was a Louis B. Wright to select the best scholarship on William Byrd, or the late Edd Winfield Parks on Henry Timrod, without including what to an uninformed observer might seem a disproportionate amount of work by Louis B. Wright or Edd Winfield Parks? The editor felt impelled, therefore, to insist that each contributor was not to let scholarly modesty prevent him from directing attention to his own work.

The selective checklist that has resulted from all these considerations is not, as the editor and the contributors are the first to recognize, an entirely satisfactory volume. For one thing, it is necessarily uneven. The scholar given the task of selecting approximately fifty of the best items on, for example, William Gilmore Simms or Katherine Anne Porter faced a vastly different task from another who must select from ten to fifteen items on Edward Coote Pinkney or Shirley Ann Grau. The guidelines given to contributors of the various sections on general topics were necessarily somewhat vague, what with the variety of subjects and the disparity between the accessibility of material on various topics. Thus considerable responsibility was placed on the individual contributor's judgment, and there is some latitude in the extent to which the individual contributors felt at liberty to attempt coverage of their topics. For all such disparities, and for the choice of which general topics and which particular authors were to be included in this volume, the editor assumes full responsibility. Doubtless there are authors not included whom some readers will think ought to have been, and others who are included whom readers will think might well have been omitted. The editor can only say that in his judgment the usefulness of this volume, in the general condition of Southern literary scholarship, would be greatest if a large number of authors, some of them admittedly very minor, were to be included. It seemed preferable to err on the side of inclusiveness.

One other caveat ought to be entered. There is a great deal of overlap in this volume. The individual contributors were *encouraged* to list the works of scholarship they felt most relevant to an understanding of their subjects, without any concern for possible duplication by other contributors. The objective was a volume to the various sections of which the student could refer in order to discover the most useful scholarship now available, without the necessity of having to consult the full listings. Again, considering the uneven state of present scholarship in Southern literature and the absence of clearly defined areas of subject matter, this seemed the most feasible course to pursue.

Given all these limitations, the editor hopes that the volume will prove a useful reference guide for students in the field of Southern literature, and he is grateful to the individual contributors for their willingness, especially upon such short notice, to take part in this cooperative effort.

Because bibliographical checklists, especially in so active a field of study as Southern literature, go out of date as soon as they are compiled, blank pages have been appended to this book so that scholars may add additional items as they appear. To facilitate such reference, these pages have been numbered; thus the page on which additional items are listed may be noted on the relevant checklist.

LOUIS D. RUBIN, JR.
June 15, 1968
Chapel Hill

CONTENTS

PART II INDIVIDUAL WRITERS

xvii

APPENDIX

SHORT TITLES
AND ABBREVIATIONS

Short Titles for Works Frequently Cited

Because of the frequency with which they contain material about the Southern writers, the following works are listed by short title as the first entry for each of the checklists of individual writers. For the general topics entries they are cited under name of authors or editors.

DAB—Johnson, Allen (later Dumas Malone, Robert Livingston Schuyler), ed., *Dictionary of American Biography*, 20 vols (New York, 1927–37), First Supplement 1946, Second Supplement 1958.

Duyckinck—Duyckinck, Evert A., and George L. Duyckinck, eds., *Cyclopedia of American Literature*, rev ed, 2 vols (Philadelphia, 1875).

Hubbell—Hubbell, Jay Broadus, *The South in American Literature, 1607–1900* (Durham, 1954).

LHUS I, II, Supp—Spiller, Robert E., Willard Thorp, Thomas H. Johnson, Henry Seidel Canby, Richard M. Ludwig, eds., *Literary History of the United States*, 3rd ed rev, 2 vols (New York, 1963). [vol I contains the material included in vols I and II of the 1st ed of 1948, and an enlarged and expanded section covering additional material added to the one volume, 2nd ed of 1953. Vol II contains all the material included in vol III: *Bibliography* of the first ed of 1948, plus that in the *Bibliographical Supplement* of 1959, ed. Richard M. Ludwig, which is separately paginated]

LSL—Alderman, Edwin A., and Joel Chandler Harris, eds., *A Library of Southern Literature*, 17 vols and supplement (Atlanta, 1908–23).

Other Works Frequently Cited

The following titles are among those which appear most frequently throughout the individual checklists, and are cited there in shorter form:

Blanck, Jacob, comp., *Bibliography of American Literature*, 8 or 9 vols planned (New Haven, 1955 ——).

Bradbury, John M., *Renaissance in the South: A Critical History of the Literature, 1920–1960* (Chapel Hill, 1963).

Cantrell, Clyde H., and Walton R. Patrick, *Southern Literary Culture: A Bibliography of Masters' and Doctors' Theses* (University, Ala., 1955).

Cohen, Hennig, and William B. Dillingham, eds., *Humor of the Old Southwest* (Boston, 1964).

Cowie, Alexander, *The Rise of the American Novel* (New York, 1949; 1951).

Gossett, Louise Y., *Violence in Recent Southern Fiction* (Durham, 1965).

Hennemann, John Bell, et al, eds., *The South in the Building of a Nation*, 12 vols (Richmond, 1909–1913).

Hoffman, Frederick J., *The Art of Southern Fiction: A Study of Some Modern Novelists* (Carbondale and Edwardsville, Ill., 1967).

Jackson, David K., ed., *American Studies in Honor of William Kenneth Boyd* (Durham, 1940).

Kunitz, Stanley J., and Howard Haycraft, *A Biographical Dictionary of American Literature, 1600–1900* (New York, 1938).

Quinn, Arthur Hobson, *American Fiction: An Historical and Critical Survey* (New York, 1936).

Rubin, Louis D., Jr., *The Curious Death of the Novel: Essays in American Literature* (Baton Rouge, 1967).

————, *The Faraway Country: Writers of the Modern South* (Seattle, 1963). Repr as *Writers of the Modern South: The Faraway Country* (Seattle, 1966).

————, and Robert D. Jacobs, eds., *Southern Renascence: The Literature of the Modern South* (Baltimore, 1953; 1966).

————, *South: Modern Southern Literature in Its Cultural Setting* (New York, 1961).

Simonini, Rinaldo C., Jr., ed., *Southern Writers: Appraisals in Our Time* (Charlottesville, 1964).

Walker, William E., and Robert L. Welker, eds., *Reality and Myth: Essays in American Literature in Memory of Richmond Croom Beatty* (Nashville, 1964).

Periodicals

AL—American Literature

AQ—American Quarterly

BB—Bulletin of Bibliography

CL—Contemporary Literature (formerly *Wisconsin Studies in Contemporary Literature*)

Crit—Critique

GaR—Georgia Review

HudR—Hudson Review

JSH—Journal of Southern History

KR—Kenyon Review

MFS—Modern Fiction Studies

MinnR—Minnesota Review

MissQ—Mississippi Quarterly
PMLA—Publications of the Modern Language Association of America
PubW—Publishers Weekly
SAQ—South Atlantic Quarterly
SatR—Saturday Review of Literature
SB—Studies in Bibliography
SeR—Sewanee Review
SFQ—Southern Folklore Quarterly
Shen—Shenandoah
SLM—Southern Literary Messenger
SP—Studies in Philology
SoR—Southern Review
SWR—Southwest Review
TLS—Times Literary Supplement, London
TQ—Texas Quarterly
TSLL—Texas Studies in Literature and Language
VMHB—Virginia Magazine of History and Biography
VQR—Virginia Quarterly Review
WMQ—William and Mary Quarterly
WR—Western Review
WSCL—Wisconsin Studies in Contemporary Literature (Now *CL—
     Contemporary Literature*)

Throughout the volume, individual titles and sections of checklists which contain extensive bibliographical material are preceded by an asterisk (*).

Abbreviations

The following abbreviations are used throughout the checklist:

Acad—academy, academics
Aesth—aesthetic, aesthetics
Amer—American
Assn—association
Bibl—bibliography, bibliographies
Biog—biography, biographical
Bk—book
Bull—bulletin

Cent—century, centennial
Chron—chronicle, chronicles
Coll—college
Comp—compiler, compiled
Crit—critical, criticism
Ed—editor, editors, edited, edition
Eng—English

Folkl—folklore
Gaz—gazette
Hist—history, historical, historian
Hum—humanities
Illus—illustrated, illustrations
Inst—institute, institution
Intern—international
Interv—interview
Intro—introduction
Jour—journal
Lib—library, libraries
Lit—literary, literature
Mag—magazine
Misc—miscellany
Mod—modern
Month—monthly
Nat—national
Newsp—newspaper
No—North, northern
n.s.—new series
o.s.—old series
Pamph—pamphlet

Phil—philological
Philos—philosophical
Proc—proceedings
Pub—publication, publications
Q—quarterly
R—review, reviewed
Rec—record
Repr—reprint, reprinted
Res—research
Rev—revised, revision
Schol—scholar, scholastic
Ser—series
So—South, southern
Soc—society, social
Sociol—sociology, sociological
Stud—studies
SW—Southwest, southwestern
Trans—transactions
U—university
W—West, western
Wk—weekly

PART I

GENERAL TOPICS

GENERAL WORKS
ON THE SOUTH

Any study of Southern literature in terms of its being specifically Southern must involve, by definition, a consideration of the relationship of works of literature to a time and a place. And however difficult it might be to define exactly what the South was or is, few will deny that a specific historical and cultural entity is involved, with a recognizable impact upon the work of many writers who by reason of birth or residence may be called Southern.

For the student who would work in the field of Southern literature, therefore, it would seem appropriate to provide a checklist of material which, not itself of a specifically literary nature, provides an introduction to the South's history and society. That such material is voluminous goes without saying; for well over a century and a half historians, economists, sociologists, journalists, political scientists, and others have been writing about the South, and any bibliography of such work would be volumes in length. One can only, therefore, note a few of the most obvious works.

Two very different books are likely to prove invaluable for anyone who would study the life of the South. One is W. J. Cash's *The Mind of the South* (New York, 1941). Brilliant, penetrating, opinionative, at times erratic, often oversimplified, it is by far the best, and indeed almost the only, attempt to look at the Southern mind as a whole, to analyze its fundamental components, to interpret its evolutions from colonial times to the New Deal. It should be used with caution, for it is not factual history, but no one who would write about the South should fail to read it.

A quite different work is a remarkable festschrift, *Writing Southern History: Essays in Historiography in Honor of Fletcher M. Green*, edited by Arthur S. Link and Rembert W. Patrick (Baton Rouge, 1965). This volume consists of a set of bibliographical essays by Southern historians, in which scholarship about the South is interpreted and evaluated, so that the student who wishes to learn more about almost any phase of Southern life at a particular period can turn to the relevant essay and there find a discussion of the chief work available.

The authoritative history of the South is the series of books published by the Louisiana State University Press and the Littlefield Fund for Southern History, under the general editorship of Wendell Holmes Stephenson and E. Merton Coulter, and entitled *A History of the South*. Though the individual volumes vary in quality, the general level is very high, in particular C. Vann Woodward's *Origins of the New South, 1877-1913* (Baton Rouge, 1951), and George Brown Tindall's *The Emer-*

3

gence of the New South, 1913-1945 (Baton Rouge, 1967). Both of these volumes contain good historical chapters on Southern literature of the period; Tindall's is especially good in this respect. All but one of the ten volumes of this series have now been published.

The best single-volume history of the South is Francis Butler Simkins' *A History of the South* (New York, 1953). Another good study is William B. Hesseltine and David L. Smiley, *The South in American History* (Englewood Cliffs, N. J., 1960). Clement Eaton's *History of the Old South* (New York, 1966) covers the period from colonial times to the Civil War. Thomas D. Clark and A. D. Kirwan, *The South Since Appomattox* (New York, 1967), and John S. Ezell, *The South Since 1865* (New York, 1963), are useful histories of the region from the end of the Civil War to the present day.

Among good studies of the Old South are Carl Bridenbaugh's *Myths and Realities: Societies of the Colonial South* (Baton Rouge, 1952); T. J. Wertenbaker's *The Old South: The Founding of American Civilization* (New York, 1942); Clement Eaton's *The Freedom-of-Thought Struggle in the Old South* (New York, 1964), and *The Mind of the Old South,* rev ed (Baton Rouge, 1967); Rollin G. Osterweis' somewhat fanciful yet insightful *Romanticism and Nationalism in the Old South* (New Haven, 1949; Baton Rouge, 1967); U. B. Phillips' *Life and Labor in the Old South* (Boston, 1929); Verner W. Crane's *The Southern Frontier, 1676-1732* (Philadelphia, 1929); W. E. Dodd's *The Cotton Kingdom* (New Haven, 1917); Louis B. Wright's *The Cultural Life of the American Colonies, 1607-1763* (New York, 1957) and *Culture on the Moving Frontier* (Bloomington, Ind., 1955); Howard R. Floan's *The South in Northern Eyes, 1831-1861* (Austin, Tex., 1957); and Francis Pendleton Gaines's *The Southern Plantation* (New York, 1924).

The literature on slavery is voluminous; next to the Reconstruction era, this subject is probably the most controversial topic in the field of Southern history. Ulrich B. Phillips' *American Negro Slavery* (New York, 1918; the best edition is that with Eugene Genovese's new foreword, Baton Rouge, 1967) presents the matter from the traditonal Southern point of view. Two recent studies, Kenneth M. Stampp's *The Peculiar Institution* (New York, 1956) and Stanley M. Elkins' *Slavery: A Problem in American Institutional and Intellectual Life* (Chicago, 1959) take a very different position.

The causes of the Civil War have been the subject of much historical controversy. Thomas Pressly's *Americans Interpret Their Civil War* (Princeton, 1954) views the changing theories and schools of interpretation. Among the more important modern studies are Avery Craven, *The Coming of the Civil War* (Chicago, 1957); Edwin C. Rozwenc, ed., *The Causes of the Civil War* (Boston, 1961); Kenneth M. Stampp, ed.,

The Causes of the Civil War (Englewood Cliffs, N.J., 1959) and Stampp, *And the War Came* (Baton Rouge, 1950); James G. Randall, *Civil War and Reconstruction* (Boston, 1937); Roy F. Nichols, *The Disruption of American Democracy* (New York, 1948); David Donald, *An Excess of Democracy: The American Civil War and the Social Process* (Oxford, 1960); John Hope Franklin, *The Militant South, 1860-1861* (Cambridge, Mass., 1956); Louis Filler, *The Crusade Against Slavery, 1830-1860* (New York, 1960); and Bruce Catton, *The Coming Fury* (New York, 1961). Obviously this is no territory for the beginning student to venture into without considerable caution, for the interpretations differ widely from historian to historian and from historical school to historical school. A good, brief bibliographical introduction is that of Charles E. Cauthen and Lewis P. Jones, "The Coming of the Civil War," in *Writing Southern History.*

As for the Civil War itself, and the condition of the Confederacy during it, the recent centennial was the occasion of the publication of so many shelfloads of books in a field already consisting of thousands of titles that it is impossible to comment intelligently on it. I can only suggest a few recent one-volume general histories: Clement Eaton, *A History of the Southern Confederacy* (New York, 1954); Roy F. Basler, *A Short History of the American Civil War* (New York, 1967); Clifford Dowdey, *The Land They Fought For* (New York, 1955); and E. Merton Coulter, *The Confederate States of America, 1861-1865* (Baton Rouge, 1950). The military aspects of the war have been exhaustively treated. Most readers are familiar with the work of such scholars as Douglas S. Freeman, T. Harry Williams, Bruce Catton, Frank Vandiver, Clifford Dowdey, Bell Wiley, James I. Robertson, Jr., and others. Shelby Foote's two volumes, *The Civil War: A Narrative* (1958, 1963) are outstanding. Hundreds of contemporary diaries, journals, and personal accounts have been reissued; among the best are Mary Boykin Chesnut's *A Diary from Dixie,* ed. Ben Ames Williams (Boston, 1949); C. G. Chamberlayne, ed., *Ham Chamberlayne: Virginian* (Richmond, 1932), the letters of a Confederate artillery officer; the *Mason-Smith Family Letters,* ed. D. E. H. and Alice R. Huger Smith and Arney R. Childs (Columbia, S.C., 1950); and John Q. Anderson, ed., *Brokenburn: The Diary of Kate Stone* (Baton Rouge, 1955). The student ought not to overlook Robert Penn Warren's excellent little book, *The Legacy of the Civil War* (New York, 1961), a provocative discussion of the meaning of the centennial observance.

The nature and meaning of the Reconstruction era is something about which historians today are sharply divided. For many years the traditional Southern interpretation as advanced by William A. Dunning in *Reconstruction, Political and Economic, 1865-1877* (New York and London, 1907), Walter L. Fleming in *Sequel of Appomattox* (New Haven, 1921), and Claude G. Bowers in *The Tragic Era* (Boston, 1929) was generally accepted, but within the last several decades that position has been severely challenged. In 1935, the Negro historian W. E. B. DuBois produced his *Black Reconstruction: An Essay Toward a History of the Part Which Black Folk Played in the Attempt to Reconstruct Democracy, 1860-1888* (New York, 1935), which took a very different view. His lead has been followed by Carl N. Degler, *Out of Our Past: The Forces That Shaped Modern America* (New York and Evanston, Ill., 1959); John Hope Franklin, *Reconstruction: After the Civil War* (Chicago, 1961); Eric Louis McKitrick, *Andrew Johnson and Reconstruction* (Chicago, 1960); Kenneth M. Stampp, *The Era of Reconstruction* (New York, 1965); and David Donald, *The Politics of Reconstruction, 1863-1867* (Baton Rouge, 1965). The last-named is an interesting attempt to apply behavioral science techniques to a very much disputed subject. Perhaps the best study of Reconstruction so far, however, is Donald's revision of James G. Randall's *Civil War and Reconstruction* (Boston, 1961). A good survey of the problems of historiography involved is Vernon L. Wharton's chapter, "Reconstruction," in Link and Patrick, eds., *Writing Southern History*.

An interesting study of the latter half of the nineteenth century is Paul S. Buck's *The Road to Reunion, 1865-1900* (Boston, 1937), which interprets the move toward sectional reconciliation, with much attention paid to the role of the local color movement in the process. Woodward's *Origins of the New South, 1876-1912* is a brilliant account of the period. Another useful book is Thomas D. Clark's *The Emerging South* (New York. 1961). For the problems of the Populist period, John D. Hicks's *The Populist Revolt* (Minneapolis, 1931) discusses the South in detail; C. Vann Woodward, *Tom Watson, Agrarian Rebel* (New York, 1938), Francis Butler Simkins, *Pitchfork Ben Tillman* (Baton Rouge, 1943), Stuart Noblin, *Leonidas LaFayette Polk, Agrarian Crusader* (Chapel Hill, 1949), and Dewey W. Grantham, *Hoke Smith and the Politics of the New South* (Baton Rouge, 1958), are excellent biographies of agrarian reformers; and Theodore Saloutos, *Farmer Movements in the South, 1865-1933* (Berkeley, 1960), is a good general analysis. W. W. Ball's *The State That Forgot* (Indianapolis, 1932) is a vigorous old conservative's view of South Carolina history of the period.

The thirteen-volume set entitled *The South in the Building of the Nation,* edited by John Bell Hennemann and others (Richmond, 1909-13) is full of material about the New South. Edgar Gardner Murphy's *Problems of the Present South* (New York, 1904) is a perceptive critique. Holland Thompson's *The New South* (New Haven, 1919) is a general interpretation of the region during the period. A look at the South through rose-tinted glasses is Edwin Mims's *The Advancing South* (New York, 1926). But by far the best study of the South since 1912 through the Second World War is George B. Tindall's *The Emergence of the New South, 1913-1945;* it describes and interprets the Southern scene in authoritative fashion, and its bibliographical essay is an outstanding survey of writings about the region during this period.

Much has been written about the Negro in the late nineteenth-and twentieth-century South. C. Vann Woodward's *The Strange Career of Jim Crow* (New York, 1955) is an excellent account of the coming of segregation. Victor DeSantis describes the Republican Party's attitude toward the freedman in *Republicans Face the Southern Question: The New Departure Years, 1877-1897* (Baltimore, 1959). Earlie E. Thorpe's *The Mind of the Negro* (Baton Rouge, 1961) is an intellectual history. Rayford W. Logan's *The Negro in American Life and Thought: The Nadir, 1877-1901* (New York, 1954) studies the post-Reconstruction years. August O. Meier, *Negro Thought in America, 1880-1915: Racial Ideologies in the Age of Booker T. Washington* (Ann Arbor, 1963) is an authoritative work. Louis R. Harlan's *Separate and Unequal: Public School Campaigns and Racism in the Southern Seaboard States, 1901-1915* (Chapel Hill, 1958) tells the story of discrimination in education. Gunnar Myrdal's *An American Dilemma: The Negro Problem and Modern Democracy* (New York, 1944) is a seminal study of segregation. John Hope Franklin's *From Slavery To Freedom* (New York, 1956) is a useful general account. E. Franklin Frazier's *The Negro in the United States* (New York, 1949) is a sociological analysis. J. Saunders Redding's *No Day of Triumph* (New York, 1942) is an eloquent personal commentary. In *Segregation* (New York, 1957) and *Who Speaks for the Negro?* (New York, 1965) Robert Penn Warren deals with the changing status of the Negro. James W. Silver's *Mississippi: The Closed Society* (New York, 1964) describes events in that state. Carl T. Rowan's *South of Freedom* (New York, 1952) is a report on a trip through the South. Finally, Arlin Turner's edition of George W. Cable's writings on the status of the Negro in the South during the 1880s, entitled *The Negro Question* (New York, 1958) shows how a discerning Southern novelist produced some prophetic work on the Negro in the South almost three-quarters of a century before the *Brown v. Board of Education* decision of the Supreme Court that ended legal segregation in schools.

The authoritative study, now somewhat dated, of politics in the South is V. O. Key's *Southern Politics in State and Nation* (New York, 1949). Other good studies in the field are Alexander Heard, *A Two-Party South?* (Chapel Hill, 1952); T. Harry Williams, *Romance and Realism in*

Southern Politics (Athens, Ga., 1961); Dewey Grantham, *The Democratic South* (Athens, Ga., 1963); Frank Friedel, *F.D.R. and the South* (Baton Rouge, 1965); and Taylor Cole and John H. Hallowell, eds., *The Southern Political Scene, 1938-1948.*

Sociologists have written importantly and influentially about Southern society. Among the best of such books are Howard W. Odum's monumental *Southern Regions of the United States* (Chapel Hill, 1936) and his *The Way of The South* (New York, 1947); Rupert P. Vance's *Human Geography of the South* (Chapel Hill, 1932) and, with Nadia Danilevsky, *All These People: The Nation's Human Resources in the South* (Chapel Hill, 1954); John M. MacLachlan and Joe S. Floyd, Jr., *This Changing South* (Gainesville, 1954); John Dollard, *Caste and Class in a Southern Town* (New York, 1937); Arthur F. Raper, *Preface to Peasantry: A Tale of Two Black Counties* (Chapel Hill, 1936) and *Tenants of the Almighty* (New York, 1943); Morton Rubin, *Plantation Country* (Chapel Hill, 1951); John Kenneth Morland, *Millways of Kent* (Chapel Hill, 1958); and, finally, an important volume of essays edited by Rupert Vance and Nicholas J. Demarath, *The Urban South* (Chapel Hill, 1954).

General economic studies of the South are Emory Q. Hawks, *Economic History of the South* (New York, 1934), a rather dated critique; Broadus and George Sinclair Mitchell, *The Industrial Revolution in the South* (Baltimore, 1930); Calvin B. Hoover and Benjamin U. Ratchford, *Economic Resources and Policies of the South* (New York, 1958); and William H. Nicholls, *Southern Tradition and Regional Progress* (Chapel Hill, 1960). There are hundreds of specialized regional studies of agriculture, industry, and commerce.

In addition to W. J. Cash's *The Mind of the South*, there are numerous other works dealing with the way Southerners think and behave. For the Old South there are Clement Eaton's *The Mind of the Old South* and *The Freedom-of-Thought Struggle in the Old South* and Rollin Osterweis' *Romanticism and Nationalism in the Old South*, mentioned earlier. For the post-Civil War South, the student can consult Virginius Dabney, *Liberalism in the South* (Chapel Hill, 1932), and *Below the Potomac: A Book About the New South* (New York, 1942); Harry Ashmore, *Epitaph for Dixie* (New York, 1958); John Temple Graves, *The Fighting South* (New York, 1943); Benjamin B. Kendrick and Alex M. Arnett, *The South Looks at Its Past* (Chapel Hill, 1935); Howard W. Odum, *An American Epoch* (New York, 1930); William Alexander Percy, *Lanterns on the Levee* (New York, 1941); James McBride Dabbs, *The Southern Heritage* (New York, 1958) and *Who Speaks for the South?* (New York, 1964); James Jackson Kilpatrick,

The Sovereign States: Notes of a Citizen of Virginia (New York, 1957);
Henry Savage, Jr., *Seeds of Time: The Background of Southern Think-
ing* (New York, 1959); Jonathan Daniels, *A Southerner Discovers the
South* (New York, 1938); William Peters, *The Southern Temper* (New
York, 1959); Brooks Hays, *A Southern Moderate Speaks* (Chapel Hill,
1959); Hodding Carter, *Southern Legacy* (Baton Rouge, 1950); Clar-
ence Cason, *90° in the Shade* (Chapel Hill, 1935); Lillian Smith, *Kill-
ers of the Dream* (New York, 1949); Stetson Kennedy, *Southern Ex-
posure* (New York, 1946); William T. Polk, *Southern Accent: From
Uncle Remus to Oak Ridge* (New York, 1953); Ben Robertson, *Red
Hills and Cotton: An Upcountry Memory* (New York, 1942); Katherine
DuPre Lumpkin, *The Making of a Southerner* (New York, 1947);
Ralph McGill, *The South and The Southerner* (Boston, 1963); Wilma
Dykeman and James Stokely, *Neither Black Nor White* (New York,
1957); Francis B. Simkins, *The Everlasting South* (Baton Rouge, 1963);
and C. Vann Woodward, *The Burden of Southern History,* rev ed
(Baton Rouge, 1968). A recent study, David Bertelson's *The Lazy
South* (New York, 1967), uses economic, philosophical, and even theo-
logical history to "prove" that the region is less social-minded and more
addicted to *laissez-faire* than the more socially responsible North.

Among important books about religion in the South are Hunter D.
Farish, *The Circuit Rider Dismounts* (Richmond, 1938); Kenneth K.
Bailey, *Southern White Protestantism in the Twentieth Century* (New
York, 1964); James Grier Sellers, *The South and Christian Ethics* (New
York, 1962); Archibald T. Robertson, *That Old-Time Religion* (Boston,
1950); and S. S. Hill, Jr., *Southern Churches in Crisis* (New York,
1967).

Architecture has always been an important aspect of Southern society.
Among useful books on Southern architecture are: Henry Chandlee For-
man, *The Architecture of the Old South: The Medieval Style, 1585-1850*
(Cambridge, Mass., 1948); Thomas J. Waterman and J. A. Barrows,
Domestic Colonial Architecture of Tidewater Virginia (Chapel Hill,
1947); Lewis Mumford, *The South in Architecture* (New York, 1941);
Talbot Hamlin, *Greek Revival Architecture in America* (New York,
1944); Joseph Frazer Smith, *White Pillars: Early Life and Architecture
of the Lower Mississippi Valley* (New York, 1941); and Edward and
Elizabeth Waugh, *The South Builds* (Chapel Hill, 1960).

Important material on education in the South is contained in Edgar
W. Knight, *A Documentary History of Education in the South Before
1860* (Chapel Hill, 1949-53) and *Public Education in the South* (Boston, 1922); E. Merton Coulter, *College Life in the Old South* (New
York, 1928); Albea Godbold, *The Church College of the Old South*

(Durham, 1944); Charles William Dabney, *Universal Education in the South* (Chapel Hill, 1936); Horace M. Bond, *The Education of the Negro in the American Social Order* (New York, 1934); Louis R. Harlan, *Separate and Unequal*, previously noted; and D. O. W. Holmes, *The Evolution of the Negro College* (New York, 1934).

Almost all the work cited in this essay is of a general nature. There are voluminous works on almost all the topics mentioned written about individual states. There are also hundreds of excellent biographies of Southerners, travel accounts, memoirs, and the like. The student will also find the W.P.A. Guides to the various states published during the New Deal period quite informative.

Finally, a number of symposia have been published in recent years which comment on various aspects of Southern life and problems. In addition to the two Agrarian books, *I'll Take My Stand* and *Who Owns America?*, discussed elsewhere in this book, these include: W. T. Couch, ed., *Culture in the South* (Chapel Hill, 1935); Louis D. Rubin, Jr., and James Jackson Kilpatrick, eds., *The Lasting South* (Chicago, 1957); Charles Grier Sellers, ed., *The Southerner as American* (Chapel Hill, 1960); Robert B. Highsaw, ed., *The Deep South in Transition* (University, Ala., 1964); Frank E. Vandiver, ed., *The Idea of the South* (Chicago, 1964); Allan P. Sindler, ed., *Change in The Contemporary South* (Durham, N.C., 1963); John C. McKinney and Edgar T. Thompson, eds., *The South in Continuity and Change* (Durham, 1965); and Thompson, ed., *Perspectives on the South: Agenda for Research* (Durham, 1967).

LOUIS D. RUBIN, JR.
University of North Carolina
Chapel Hill, North Carolina

GENERAL WORKS ON
SOUTHERN LITERATURE

The study of Southern literature has produced a great quantity of material ranging from the lush and unfactual celebrations of the Lost Cause, like La Salle C. Pickett's *Literary Hearthstones of Dixie* (Philadelphia, 1912), to detailed, precise, and carefully documented studies of special subjects, like Edd Winfield Parks's *Ante-Bellum Southern Literary Critics* (Athens, Ga., 1962). But general studies of Southern literature have not very often been distinguished by both completeness and perception. They have tended toward historical-biographical treatment marked too frequently by local piety or toward attempts to understand and define the unique aspects of Southern culture as it reflects itself in the writing of the region. I shall briefly discuss a group of books that appear to me not to be without distinction and which will bring the student of Southern literature into contact with fact presented with accuracy and ideas that are fresh and potentially fruitful.

Of the bibliographies, in addition to *Literary History of the United States,* II, pp. 308–16, and Supplement, p. 59, a number are particularly useful. The discursive essay on general studies in Jay B. Hubbell's *The South in American Literature,* pp. 883–92, is informed and generous; the listings in Clarence Gohdes' *Literature and Theater of the States and Regions of the U.S.A.* (Durham, 1967), pp. 200–19, are detailed and accurate; the bibliographies in Gregory L. Paine, ed., *Southern Prose Writers* (New York, 1947), and Edd Winfield Parks, ed., *Southern Poets* (New York, 1936), are judiciously made and succinctly annotated. Paine's is particularly rich in cultural and historical materials. There is also much useful bibliographical data with a cultural and historical emphasis in Rollin G. Osterweis, *Romanticism and Nationalism in the Old South* (New Haven, 1949; Baton Rouge, 1967) and C. Hugh Holman, *Three Modes of Modern Southern Fiction* (Athens, Ga., 1966).

There is no up-to-date general history of Southern writing from its beginning to the present. Hubbell's *The South in American Literature* is a detailed, authoritative, historical, and biographical account of the literature of the region to 1900. It has general chapters and biographies of individual writers and is an indispensable compendium of facts—the fruits of a lifetime of scholarly inquiry. It is very inclusive to 1860 and much more selective (and less useful, therefore) between 1860 and 1900. Of the several attempts at a literary history of the South before Hubbell, Montrose J. Moses, *The Literature of the South* (New York, 1910), is still useful, although it is sometimes eccentric and always dated. The long introductions to the two American Writers Series volumes dealing with Southern writing, Paine's *Southern Prose Writers* (pp. xiii–cxvii) and Parks's *Southern Poets* (xvii–cxxix), taken together, form a careful, well-documented, and astute history.

There are several fine books about the culture and intellectual life of the region which contain pertinent commentaries on its literature. W. J. Cash, *The Mind of the South* (New York, 1941), has been, along with Vernon L. Parrington, *Main Currents in American Thought* (New York, 1927, 1930), I, 131–48, 327–57; II, 3–179, a major cultural re-assessment of the region, a germinative force for much which has followed it. Both Cash and Parrington, with fundamentally liberal orientations, should be seen against *I'll Take My Stand*, by "Twelve Southerners," which sets forth a conservative, "Agrarian" view of Southern history and tradition, a view which has been powerfully effective in Southern writing in our century. C. Vann Woodward, *The Burden of Southern History*, rev ed (Baton Rouge, 1968), in a group of incisive essays, states a philosophy of Southern history with emphasis on literary materials. William T. Couch, ed., *Culture in the South* (Chapel Hill, 1934), contains essays by thirty-one specialists on all aspects of Southern life. Rollin G. Osterweis, *Romanticism and Nationalism in the Old South*, is a provocative but oversimplified treatment of certain Romantic aspects of the Southern tradition, with emphasis on material from literature and periodicals. Volume VII of *The South in the Building of the Nation*, entitled *History of the Literary and Intellectual Life of the South*, contains excellent material. William R. Taylor, *Cavalier and Yankee: The Old South and American National Character* (New York, 1961), is a brilliant study and one of almost endless usefulness to the student of Southern literature or culture.

Four historians in formal histories have given unusual attention to literary matters: Clement Eaton in *The Growth of Southern Civilization, 1790–1860* (New York, 1961) and *The Mind of the Old South*, rev ed (Baton Rouge, 1967); Francis B. Simkins in *A History of the South* (New York, 1953); C. Vann Woodward in *Origins of the New South, 1877–1913* (Baton Rouge, 1951); and George B. Tindall in *The Emergence of the New South, 1913–1945* (Baton Rouge, 1967). To fail to explore these historians' efforts to relate Southern literature to Southern experience is to shut one's self off from a valuable and illuminating source of knowledge.

A number of studies have attempted to explore special themes and subject matters in Southern literature. Francis Pendleton Gaines, *The Southern Plantation: A Study in the Development and Accuracy of a Tradition* (New York, 1924), is a landmark and model for such studies. Of special value as a complementary study is Shields McIlwaine, *The*

Southern Poor White from Lubberland to Tobacco Road (Norman, Okla., 1939). The role of the Civil War has been explored in two useful and radically different works: Robert A. Lively, *Fiction Fights the Civil War* (Chapel Hill, 1957) and Edmund Wilson, *Patriotic Gore: Studies in the Literature of the Civil War* (New York, 1962), especially chapters 12 and 13. The Negro has been a recurrent subject which is treated in detail elsewhere in this bibliography.

A number of contemporary critics have concerned themselves with efforts to define the distinguishing characteristics of Southern literature. Several of these essays appear in two books edited by Louis D. Rubin, Jr., and Robert D. Jacobs, *Southern Renascence: The Literature of the Modern South* (Baltimore, 1953) and *South: Modern Southern Literature in Its Cultural Setting* (Garden City, N.Y., 1961). Rubin also pursues the subject in *The Faraway Country: Writers of the Modern South* (Seattle, 1963). Frederick J. Hoffman analyzes Southern qualities in *The Art of Southern Fiction* (Carbondale, Ill., 1967). Ellen Glasgow has illuminating things to say about the writer and the South in obiter dicta interspersed through the essays on her own work in *A Certain Measure* (New York, 1943). C. Hugh Holman has attempted to define and qualify the nature of Southern writing, past and present, in "The Southerner as American Writer," in *The Southerner as American* (Chapel Hill, 1960), in "A Cycle of Change in Southern Literature," in *The South in Continuity and Change*, ed. John C. McKinney and Edgar T. Thompson (Durham, 1965), and in *Three Modes of Modern Southern Fiction*.

Arthur Palmer Hudson explores the frontier tradition in Southern culture in *Humor of the Old Deep South* (New York, 1936). Cleanth Brooks examines the issue of regionalism in two essays: "Regionalism in American Literature," *Journal of Southern History* (Fall 1960), and "Southern Literature: The Wellsprings of Its Vitality," *Georgia Review* (Fall 1962). Two symposia published in the *Georgia Review* are helpful: "Agrarianism as a Theme in Southern Literature," ed. Louis D. Rubin, Jr. (Summer 1957), with essays by Edd Winfield Parks, Allen W. Becker, Virginia Rock, and C. Hugh Holman; and "Rhetoric in Southern Writing," ed. C. Hugh Holman (Spring 1958), with essays by Robert D. Jacobs, Floyd C. Watkins, and William Van O'Connor. Edd Winfield Parks, *Ante-Bellum Southern Literary Critics,* is detailed and thorough, and his essays on various topics connected with Southern literature in *Segments of Southern Thought* (Athens, Ga., 1938) are provocative and always useful.

One of the few efforts to give the Southern writer in the nineteenth century an appropriate place in the literary history of the larger nation (something which the LHUS almost totally failed to do) was that of Van Wyck Brooks in his five-volume *Makers and Finders: A History of the Writer in America, 1800–1915* (New York, 1936–52). Most of the Southern material from this large work is conveniently assembled in Brooks, *A Chilmark Miscellany* (New York, 1948).

One of the works which anyone approaching the serious study of Southern literature should always examine is Allen Tate, *Collected Essays* (Denver, 1959), containing *On the Limits of Poetry* and *The Forlorn Demon*, for almost every idea which has proved fruitful for the serious critic is at least adumbrated in an essay in this volume.

*Alderman, E. A., et al, eds., *The Library of Southern Literature*. [inclusive selections, adulatory comment, good bibl in vol XIV]

Barksdale, Richard K., "White Tragedy—Black Comedy: A Literary Approach to Southern Race Relations," *Phylon*, XXII (1961), 226–33.

Baskervill, William Malone, *Southern Writers: Biographical and Critical Studies*, I (Nashville, 1897); II (Dallas, 1903). [vol II mostly by others, publ posthumously; both vols primarily on late 19th century writers; contains good crit]

Beatty, Richmond Croom, Floyd C. Watkins, and T. Daniel Young, eds., *The Literature of the South*, rev ed (Chicago, 1968). [anthol with intro chaps and head notes]

Brevard, Caroline M. *Literature of the South* (New York, 1908). [superficial]

Brooks, Cleanth, "Regionalism in American Literature," *JSH*, XXVI (1960), 33–43.

———, "Southern Literature: The Wellsprings of Its Vitality," *GaR*, XVI (1962), 238–53.

Brooks, Van Wyck, *A Chilmark Miscellany* (New York, 1948). [materials on So writing and writers from his *Makers and Finders: A History of the Writer in America, 1800–1915*, 5 vols (New York, 1936–52)]

*Cantrell and Patrick, *Southern Literary Culture*.

Cardwell, Guy A., Jr., "On Scholarship and Southern Literature," *SAQ*, XL (1941), 60–72.

Cash, W. J., *The Mind of the South* (New York, 1941).

Clark, Emily, *Innocence Abroad* (New York, 1931). [casual reflections on So lit and authors]

*Collins, Carvel E., "Nineteenth Century Fiction of the Southern Appalachians," *BB*, XVII (1942–43), 186–90; 215–18.

Cowan, Louise, "The Communal World of Southern Literature," *GaR*, XIV (1960), 248–57.

Couch, William T., ed., *Culture in the South* (Chapel Hill, 1934). [31 specialists discuss many phases of So life and culture]

Current–Garcia, Eugene, "Southern Literary Criticism and the Sectional Dilemma," *JSH* (1949), 325–41.

Davidson, Donald, *The Attack on Leviathan: Regionalism and Nationalism in the United States* (Chapel Hill, 1938). [Agrarian defense of So regionalism]

———, *Still Rebels, Still Yankees, and Other Essays* (Baton Rouge, 1957).

———, *Southern Writers in the Modern World* (Athens, Ga., 1958). [Lamar Lectures]

Davidson, James Wood, *The Living Writers of the South* (New York, 1869). [often inexact and inaccurate biog and crit treatments of over 200 writers]

Davis, Richard Beale, "Spadework, American Literature, and the Southern Mind:

Opportunities," *So Atl Bull*, XXXI, (1966).

Eaton, Clement, *The Growth of Southern Civilization, 1790–1860* (New York, 1961).

———, *The Mind of the Old South*, rev ed (Baton Rouge, 1967).

Gaines, Francis Pendleton, *The Southern Plantation: A Study in the Development and the Accuracy of a Tradition* (New York, 1924).

Glasgow, Ellen, *A Certain Measure* (New York, 1943). [prefaces to her novels but containing much comment on So lit]

*Gohdes, Clarence, *Literature and Theater of the States and Regions of the U.S.A.: An Historical Bibliography* (Durham, 1967), pp. 200–19. [excellent bibl of gen stud of the So region]

Green, Claud B., "The Rise and Fall of Local Color in Southern Literature," *MissQ*, XV (1965), 1–6.

*Harkness, David J., ed., *Literary Profiles of the Southern States: A Manual for Schools and Clubs*, University of Tennessee Extension News-Letter, XXXII, No. 1 (Jan 1953). [listing of So writers by state and town]

Harwell, Richard B., "Gone with Miss Ravenel's Courage; or Bugles Blow So Red: A Note on the Civil War Novel," *New Eng Q*, XXXV (1962), 253–61.

Hayne, Paul H., "Ante-Bellum Charleston," *So Bivouac*, n.s., I (1885), 193–202; 257–68; 327–36.

Henneman, et al, *The South in the Building of the Nation*. [esp vol VII, *History of the Literary and Intellectual Life of the South*, and vol VIII, *History of Southern Fiction*, which contains selections, with intro by Edwin Mims]

Hoffman, *The Art of Southern Fiction*. [mostly on contemporary writers, but contains much comment on gen qualities of So writing]

Holliday, Carl, *A History of Southern Literature* (New York, 1906). [inaccurate but quite readable]

Holman, C. Hugh, "A Cycle of Change in Southern Literature," in *The South in Continuity and Change*, ed. John C. McKinney and Edgar T. Thompson (Durham, 1965), pp. 384–403.

———, "European Influences on Southern American Literature: A Preliminary Survey," in *Comparative Literature: Proceedings of the Second Congress of the International Comparative Literature Association*, 2 vols (Chapel Hill, 1959), II, pp. 444–54.

———, "The Novel in the South," in *A Time of Harvest: American Literature, 1910–1960*, ed. Robert E. Spiller (New York, 1962), pp. 83–94.

———, "The Southerner as American Writer," in *The Southerner as American*, ed. Charles G. Sellers, Jr. (Chapel Hill, 1960), pp. 180–99, 215–16.

*———, *Three Modes of Modern Southern Fiction: Ellen Glasgow, William Faulkner, Thomas Wolfe* (Athens, Ga., 1966). [on the differing characteristics of So fict in different sections of the region; Lamar Lectures]

———, ed., "Rhetoric in Southern Writing," *GaR*, XII (1958), 74–86. [intro plus essays by Robert D. Jacobs, Floyd C. Watkins, and Willam Van O'Connor]

Hubbell, Jay B., "Literary Nationalism in the Old South," in *American Studies in Honor of William Kenneth Boyd*, ed. Jackson, pp. 175–220. [a richly informed study]

———, "The Old South in Literary Histories," *SAQ*, XLVIII, (1949), 452–67. [statement of the gen inadequacy of most such treatments, with particular emphasis on the weaknesses of LHUS]

———, *South and Southwest: Literary Essays and Reminiscences* (Durham, 1965).

———, *Southern Life in Literature* (Athens, Ga., 1960). [Lamar Lectures]

*———, *The South in American Literature*. [indispensable]

Hudson, Arthur Palmer, *Humor of the Old Deep South* (New York, 1936).

Lewisohn, Ludwig, "The Books We Have Made," *Charleston* [S.C.] *News and Courier,* July 5–September 20, 1903. [valuable but not always accurate hist of S.C. writers]

Lively, Robert A., *Fiction Fights the Civil War* (Chapel Hill, 1957). [on the hist novels about the Civil War]

Link, Samuel Albert, *Literary Pioneers of the South,* 2 vols (Nashville, 1899–1900). [mediocre Victorian crit]

McDowell, Tremaine, "The Negro in the Southern Novel Prior to 1850," *Jour of Eng and Ger Phil,* XXV (1926), 455–73.

*McIlwaine, Shields, *The Southern Poor–White from Lubberland to Tobacco Road* (Norman, Okla., 1939).

Manly, Louise, *Southern Literature from 1579 to 1895* (Richmond, 1895). [superficial]

Mims, Edwin, *The Advancing South* (Garden City, N.Y., 1926). [a study of new forces in So culture, with special reference to lit]

Moses, Montrose J., *The Literature of the South* (New York, 1910). [best gen hist before Hubbell]

*Osterweis, Rollin G., *Romanticism and Nationalism in the Old South* (New Haven, 1949; Baton Rouge, 1967). [thesis that Scott-like Romanticism led to Civil War is oversimplified; good bibl]

Paine, Gregory L., *Southern Prose Writers: Representative Selections* (New York, 1947). [132 pp. intro excellent, as is selective bibl]

Parks, Edd Winfield, *Ante-Bellum Southern Literary Critics* (Athens, Ga., 1962). [detailed and well-documented]

————, *Segments of Southern Thought* (Athens, Ga., 1938). [thoughtful essays on varied aspects of So culture]

————, *Southern Poets: Representative Selections* (New York, 1936). [141-page intro is best single gen hist treatment of So poetry; bibl good]

————, "Three Streams of Southern Humor," *GaR,* IX (1955), 147–59.

*Parrington, Vernon Louis, *Main Currents in American Thought,* 3 vols (New York, 1927–30). [landmark in study of So lit in relation to liberal tradition]

Pickett, La Salle C., *Literary Hearthstones of Dixie* (Philadelphia, 1912). [so sentimental and inaccurate that it gives an insight into hist attitudes]

Riley, Susan B., "The Hazards of Periodical Publishing in the South during the Nineteenth Century," *Tenn Hist Q,* XXI (1962), 365–76.

Rubin, Louis D., Jr., ed., "Agrarianism as a Theme in Southern Literature," *GaR,* XI (1957), 145–64. [intro plus essays by Edd W. Parks, Allen Becker, Virginia Rock, and C. Hugh Holman]

————, *The Faraway Country.* [essays on the nature of So experience and on selected So writers; paperback reprint, 1966, reverses the elements of the title]

————, *The Curious Death of the Novel.* [essays on several So novelists among others and on the quality of the experience of being So]

————, *The Teller in the Tale* (Seattle, 1967). [essays on problems of technique in fict with comments on So novelists]

Rubin and Jacobs, eds., *Southern Renascence.* [an essential vol]

————, eds., *South.*

Rubin and James J. Kilpatrick, eds., *The Lasting South* (Chicago, 1957).

Rutherford, Mildred L., *The South in History and Literature* (Atlanta, 1907) [elementary and sentimental]

Simkins, Francis B., *A History of the South* (New York, 1953).

Simonini, ed., *Southern Writers.* [essays selected from the following vols growing out of the Longwood Coll Inst of So Culture: R. C. Simonini Jr., ed. *Virginia* in *History and Tradition* (Farmville, Va., 1958); Francis B. Simkins, ed., *The South in Perspective* (Farmville, Va., 1959); Richard K. Meeker, ed., *The Dilemma of the Southern Writer* (Farmville, Va., 1961).]

Smith, C. Alphonso, *Southern Literary Studies: A Collection of Literary, Biographical, and Other Studies* (Chapel Hill, 1927). [good—but old-fashioned—crit]

Snyder, Henry N., "The Reconstruction of Southern Literary Thought," *SAQ*, I (1902), 145–55. Repr in *Fifty Years of the South Atlantic Quarterly*, ed. William B. Hamilton (Durham, 1952), pp. 28–52.

*Spiller, et al, eds., *LHUS*, I, II, Supp. [weak on treatment of So writing; bibl is indispensable tool]

Stewart, Randall, *Regionalism and Beyond: Essays of Randall Stewart*, ed. George Core (Nashville, 1968). [part 3 (pp. 219–65) consists of four essays on So lit]

Stone, Edward, "Usher, Poquelin, and Miss Emily: The Progress of Southern Gothic," *GaR*, XIV (1960).

Tate, Allen, *Collected Essays* (Denver, 1959). [contains both *On the Limits of Poetry* and *The Forlorn Demon*]

Taylor, William R., *Cavalier and Yankee: The Old South and American National Character* (New York, 1961).

Thorp, Willard, ed., *A Southern Reader* (New York, 1955). [anthol with perceptive intro and head notes]

Tindall, George B., "The Benighted South: Origins of a Modern Image," *VQR*, XL (1965).

———, *The Emergence of the New South, 1913–1945* (Baton Rouge, 1967). [contains perhaps the best gen hist of lit for its period]

Turner, Arlin, ed., *Southern Stories* (New York, 1961). [intro and head notes are useful; an anthol of short stories by So writers]

Twelve Southerners, *I'll Take My Stand* (New York, 1930). [essays on So and Agrarian tradition; Twelve Southerners are John Crowe Ransom, Donald Davidson, Frank L. Owsley, John Gould Fletcher, Lyle H. Lanier, Allen Tate, H. C. Nixon, Andrew Lytle, Robert Penn Warren, John D. Wade, Henry Blue Kline, and Stark Young; there is Harper Torchbook repr, 1962 with useful intro by Louis D. Rubin, Jr., and biog notes by Virginia Rock]

Weatherford, W. D., and Wilma Dykeman, "Literature Since 1900," in *The Southern Appalachian Region*, ed. Thomas R. Ford (Lexington, Ky., 1962), pp. 259–70.

Wilson, Edmund, *Patriotic Gore: Studies in the Literature of the Civil War* (New York, 1962). [chaps 12 and 13 are esp on So lit]

Wilson, Louis R., and Robert B. Downs, "Special Collections for the Study of History and Literature in the Southeast," *Pub of Bibl Soc of Amer*, XXVIII (1934), 97–131.

Woodward, C. Vann, *The Burden of Southern History*, rev ed (Baton Rouge, (1968).

———, *Origins of the New South, 1877–1913* (Baton Rouge, 1951).

C. Hugh Holman
University of North Carolina
Chapel Hill, North Carolina

THE COLONIAL PERIOD

I have omitted many books and articles with passing references to Southern writers and have even omitted whole categories (e.g., foreign influences on early American literature) that do not exclusively pertain to Southern writing. My reason is simply that, even so, my checklist is larger than suggested.

*1. Bibliographical Aids

For bibliographies of poetry and travel literature, see the sections devoted to these special topics. Because of the inadequacy of existing literary bibliographies, the various state bibliographies are extremely useful to literary historians. Professor Richard Beale Davis' volume, *American Literature Through Bryant*, scheduled to appear in the Goldentree bibliography series in 1969, will be of especial value.

Adams, Thomas R., *American Independence: The Growth of an Idea. A Bibliographical Study of the American Political Pamphlets Printed Between 1764 and 1776* (Providence, R.I., 1965).

Baer, Elizabeth, *Seventeenth Century Maryland: A Bibliography* (Baltimore, 1949).

Bell, Whitfield J., Jr., *Early American Science: Needs and Opportunities for Study* (Chapel Hill, 1955).

Brantly, William T., "The English in Maryland, 1632–1691," in Justin Winsor, ed., *Narrative and Critical History of America*, III (Boston, 1884), pp. 517–53, and "Critical Essay on the Sources of Information," pp. 553–62.

Brock, Robert A., "Virginia, 1606–1689," in Winsor, ed., *Narrative and Critical History of America*, III, pp. 127–53, and "Critical Essay on the Sources of Information," pp. 153–66.

Cohen, Hennig, *Articles in Periodicals and Serials on South Carolina Literature and Related Subjects, 1900–1955* (Columbia, S.C., 1956).

Davis, Richard Beale, *American Literature Through Bryant* (New York, 1969).

———, "Literature to 1800," in James Woodress, ed., *American Literary Scholarship: An Annual* (Durham, 1965, 1966, 1967, etc.). [ALS is a crit assessment of the year's work in Amer lit scholarship, and Professor Davis has written chap 9, "Literature to 1800," in each of the first three vols of this annual]

Evans, Charles, *American Bibliography*, 14 vols (Chicago, 1903–59).

Gohdes, Clarence, *Bibliographical Guide to the Study of the Literature of the U.S.A.*, rev ed (Durham, 1963).

———, *Literature and Theater of the States and Regions of the U.S.A.: An Historical Bibliography* (Durham, 1967).

Guerra, Francisco, *American Medical Bibliography, 1639–1783* (New York, 1962).

Jones, Charles C., "The English Colonization of Georgia, 1733–1752," in Windsor, ed., *Narrative and Critical History of America*, V (Boston, 1887), pp. 357–92, and "Critical Essay on the Sources of Information," pp. 392–405.

Manross, William Wilson, *The Fulham Papers in the Lambeth Palace Library: American Colonial Section. Calendar and Indexes* (Oxford, Eng., 1965).

Rivers, William J., "The Carolinas," in Winsor, ed., *Narrative and Critical History of America*, V, pp. 285–335, and "Critical Essay on the Sources of Information," pp. 335–56.

Sabin, Joseph, *A Dictionary of Books Relating to America from its Discovery to the Present Time*, 29 vols (New York, 1868–1936).

Spiller, et al, eds., *LHUS*, II, with Supp.

Swem, Earl Greg, et al, eds., *A Selected Bibliography of Virginia, 1607–1699* (Williamsburg, 1957; Jamestown 350th Anniversary Historical Booklet No. 2).

Thornton, Mary Lindsay, *A Bibliography of North Carolina, 1589–1956* (Chapel Hill, 1958).

Torrence, William Clayton, *A Trial Bibliography of Colonial Virginia*, 2 vols (Richmond, 1908–10; Va. State Library, Annual Reports, Nos. 5 [1907–1908] and 6 [1908–1909]).

Turnbull, Robert J., *Bibliography of South Carolina, 1563–1950*, 6 vols (Charlottesville, 1956–60).

Winsor, Justin, ed., "Maryland and Virginia," *Narrative and Critical History of America*, V (Boston, 1887), pp. 259–70, and "Critical Essay on the Sources of Information," pp. 270–84.

Wroth, Lawrence C., *A History of Printing in Colonial Maryland, 1686–1776* (Baltimore, 1922).

II.   General Studies

Moses Coit Tyler's volumes on the literary history of colonial and revolutionary America (published in 1878 and 1897, respectively) are, unfortunately, still standard. Little work on Southern colonial and revolutionary American literature has been done. Presently, the best general study is Jay B. Hubbell, *The South in American Literature*. In progress is a major work by Professor Richard Beale Davis, *Cultural Life in the South, 1585–1763*. A revised and expanded version of Howard Mumford Jones, *The Literature of Virginia in the Seventeenth Century*, was published early in 1968; this replaces his earlier (1946) work as the best survey of seventeenth century Virginia literature. J. A. Leo Lemay's "A Literary History of Colonial Maryland" is the only present attempt to study in sufficient detail the literary life of any Southern colony. No attempt to survey the literature of the American Revolution in any Southern state has ever been made.

Bowes, Frederick P., "Literature and the Arts," *The Culture of Early Charleston* (Chapel Hill, 1942), pp. 92–114.

Boynton, Percy H., *Literature and American Life* (Boston, 1936), esp pp. 26–34, 118–26.

Brown, Alexander, *The Genesis of the United States*, 2 vols (London, 1890).

Davidson, Philip, *Propaganda and the American Revolution, 1763–1783* (Chapel Hill, 1941).

Davis, Richard Beale, *The Colonial Virginia Satirist: Mid–Eighteenth-Century Commentaries on Politics, Religion, and Society* (Philadelphia, 1967; *Trans.* of the Am. Philos. Soc., part I, n.s., LVII).

Engdahl, Bonnie Thoman, "Paradise in the New World: A Study of the Image of the Garden in the Literature of Colonial America," California at Los Angeles, 1967, esp pp. 8–54, 149–270. [diss]

Flanders, Bertram H., "Reading and Writing in Early Georgia," *GaR*, I (1947), 209–17.

Grabo, Norman S., "The Veiled Vision: The Role of Aesthetics in Early American Intellectual History," *WMQ*, 3rd ser, XIX (1962), 493–510.

Granger, Bruce Ingham, *Political Satire in the American Revolution, 1763–1783* (Ithaca, N.Y., 1960).

Heimert, Alan, *Religion and the American Mind from the Great Awakening to the Revolution* (Cambridge, Mass., 1966).

Hindle, Brooke, *The Pursuit of Science in Revolutionary America, 1735–1789* (Chapel Hill, 1956).

Hirsch, Leota K., "The Literary Milieu of the Seventeenth Century South," Minnesota, 1967. [diss]

Holliday, Carl, *The Literature of Colonial Virginia, 1607–1750* (New York, 1909).

*Hubbell, *The South in American Literature*.

Jones, Howard M., "American Prose Style: 1700–1770," *Huntington Lib Bull*, VI (1934), 115–151. Repr in Jones, *Ideas in America* (Cambridge, Mass., 1944), pp. 70–106.

―――, "Desiderata in Colonial Literary History," *Pub Colonial Soc of Mass*, XXXII (1933–37), 428–39. Repr in *Ideas in America* (Cambridge, Mass., 1944), pp. 12–27.

―――, *The Literature of Virginia in the Seventeenth Century* (Boston, 1946; rev ed, 1968).

―――, *O Strange New World. American Culture: The Formative Years* (New York, 1964).

Lemay, J. A. Leo, "A Literary History of Colonial Maryland," *DA*, XXV, 7,246 (Pennsylvania).

Marx, Leo, "The Garden," *The Machine in the Garden* (New York, 1964), pp. 73–144. [nature in So writing in 18th century]

Miller, Perry, "Religion and Society in the Early Literature of Virginia," *Errand into the Wilderness* (Cambridge, Mass., 1956), pp. 99–140. [repr of two complementary essays from *WMQ*, 3rd ser, V (1948), 492–522; and VI (1949), 24–41]

Moses, Montrose J., *The Literature of the South* (New York, 1910), esp pp. 17–90.

*Murdock, Kenneth B., "The Colonial and Revolutionary Period," in Arthur Hobson Quinn, ed., *The Literature of the American People* (New York, 1951), pp. 3–171, and bibl, pp. 991–1019.

Piercy, Josephine K., *Studies in Literary Types in Seventeenth Century America (1607–1710)* (New Haven, 1939).

Purcell, James S., Jr., "Literary Culture in North Carolina before 1820," Duke, 1950. [diss]

Tyler, Moses Coit, *A History of American Literature, 1607–1765* (New York, 1878).

―――, *The Literary History of the American Revolution, 1763–1783* (New York, 1897).

Wood, Gordon S., "Rhetoric and Reality in the American Revolution," *WMQ*, 3rd ser, XXIII (1966), 3–32.

Wooley, Mary E., "The Development of the Love of Romantic Scenery in America," *AHR*, III (1897), 56–67.

Wright, Louis B., *The First Gentlemen of Virginia: Intellectual Qualities of the Early Colonial Ruling Class* (San Marino, Calif., 1940).

―――, "Intellectual History and the Colonial South," *WMQ*, 3rd ser, XVI (1959), 214–27.

―――, "Literary Production: North and South," *The Cultural Life of the American Colonies, 1607–1763* (New York, 1957), pp. 154–75.

_____, "Literature in the Colonial South," *Huntington Lib*, X (1946–47), 297–315. Repr (without footnotes) as "Writers of the South," in *LHUS*, I, pp. 40–53.

III. Poetry

The paucity of studies of Southern poetry during the Colonial and Revolutionary periods is surpassed only by the absence of reliable editions of the poetry. Roger E. Stoddard of the Houghton Library, Harvard University, has in hand a bibliography of additions to Wegelin.

Boys, R. C., "The English Poetical Miscellany in Colonial America," *Stud Phil*, XLII (1945), 114–30.

_____, "General Oglethorpe and the Muses," *Ga Hist Q*, XXXI (1947), 19–30.

Cohen, Hennig, "An Early Example of French Poetry in America [Charleston, 1706?]," *Mod Lang Notes*, LXVII (1952), 187–88.

_____, "A Southern Colonial Elegy," *WMQ*, 3rd ser, X (1953), 628–29. [in S.C. *Gaz*, Apr 19, 1773]

_____, "Two Colonial Poems on the Settling of Georgia," *Ga Hist Q*, XXXVII (1953), 129–36.

_____, "Two Poems from English Magazines on the Naming of Georgia," *Ga Hist Q*, XXXV (1951), 319–23.

Counsell, E. M., "Latin Verses presented by Students of William and Mary College to the Governor of Virginia, 1771, 1772, 1773, and 1774," *WMQ*, 2nd ser, X (1930), 269–74.

Gordon, Armistead C., *Virginian Writers of Fugitive Verse* (New York, 1923), pp. 18–64, 137–82.

Hubbell, Jay B., "'On Liberty Tree': A Revolutionary Poem from South Carolina," *S.C. Hist Mag*, XLI (1940), 117–22. [from *S.C. Gaz*, Sept 21, 1769]

Hudson, Arthur P., "Songs of the Regulators," *WMQ*, 3rd ser, IV (1947), 470–85.

Johnson, Robert C., "A Poem on the Late Massacre in Virginia [1622] by Christopher Brooke," *VMHB*, LXXII (1964), 259–92.

Moore, Frank, *Songs and Ballads of the American Revolution* (New York, 1856).

Moses, Montrose J., "Revolutionary Literature: Poetry and Poets," *The Literature of the South* (New York, 1910), pp. 143–59.

*Otis, William Bradley, *American Verse, 1625–1807: A History* (New York, 1909).

Powell, William S., "A Swift Broadside from the Opposition," *VMHB*, LXVII (1959), 164–69. [argues that Swift wrote the poem *The Loyal Address of the Clergy of Virginia* (1702)]

Reece, Frances R., "A Revolutionary War Rhyme," *S.C. Hist Mag*, XLVI (1945), 103. [by Francis Lee, dated Charleston, S.C., 16 March 1782]

Salley, A. S., "The Independent Company from South Carolina at Great Meadows," *Bull Hist Com S.C.*, No. 11 (1932). [repr memorial poem, 1754]

*Schlesinger, Arthur M., "A Note on Songs as Patriot Propaganda 1765–1776," *WMQ*, 3rd ser, XI (1954), 78–88. ["the first attempt at a comprehensive list"]

Silverman, Kenneth Eugene, *Colonial American Poetry: An Anthology* (New York, 1968).

Smythe, Augustine T., "The Hibernian Society: The Song and the Toast," *Charleston Year Book, 1901*, pp. 39–40.

Stephens, John Calhoun, Jr., ed., *Georgia, A Poem, Tomo Chachi, An Ode. A Copy of Verses on Mr. Oglethorpe's Second Voyage to Georgia* (Atlanta, 1950; Emory U Sources and Repr. Ser VI, No. 2).

Untermeyer, Louis, *Early American Poets* (New York, 1952).

*Wegelin, Oscar, *Early American Poetry: A Bibliography, 1650–1820* (New York, 1930).

IV.   Travel and Promotion Literature

The dominance of travel and promotion literature with its influence upon American literature and culture is still an unexplored subject.

Adams, Percy G., *Travelers and Travel Liars, 1660–1800* (Berkeley and Los Angeles, 1962).

Adams, Randolph G., "Reports and Chronicles," in *LHUS*, I, pp. 24–39.

Barbour, Philip L., ed., *The Jamestown Colony under the First Charter, 1606–1609* (London, 1969?). [forthcoming from the Hakluyt Soc]

*Carson, Jane, *Travelers in Tidewater Virginia, 1700–1800: A Bibliography* (Williamsburg, 1965).

*Clark, Thomas D., *Travels in the Old South: A Bibliography*, 2 vols (Norman, Okla., 1956).

*Cole, George Watson, "Elizabethan Americana," in *Bibliographical Essays: A Tribute to Wilberforce Eames* (Cambridge, Mass., 1924), pp. 161–78.

*Cox, Edward G., *A Reference Guide to the Literature of Travel*, Vol. II, *The New World* (Seattle, 1938).

*Crane, Verner W., "The Promotion Literature of Georgia," in *Bibliographical Essays: A Tribute to Wilberforce Eames*, pp. 281–98.

Jones, Howard M., "The Colonial Impulse: An Analysis of the 'Promotion' Literature of Colonization," *Proceed of the Amer Philos Soc*, XC (1946), 131–61.

———, "The Image of the New World," in *Elizabethan Studies and Other Essays in Honor of George F. Reynolds* (Boulder, Colo., 1945), pp. 62–84.

Kane, Hope Frances, "The Colonial Promotion and Promotion Literature of Carolina, 1660–1700," Brown, 1930. [diss]

Milling, Chapman A., ed., *Colonial South Carolina: Two Contemporary Descriptions. By Governor James Glen and Doctor George Milligen–Johnston* (Columbia, S.C., 1951).

Morse, Jarvis Means, *American Beginnings* (Washington, D.C., 1952).

*Parker, John, *Books to Build an Empire: A Bibliographical History of English Overseas Interests to 1620* (Amsterdam, Holland, 1965).

Pennington, Loren Earl, "The Origins of English Promotional Literature for America, 1553–1625," *DA*, XXIII (1963), 3336 (Michigan).

Quinn, David Beers, ed., *The Roanoke Voyages, 1584–1590*, 2 vols (Cambridge, Eng., 1955; Hakluyt Soc, 2nd ser, vols CIV-CV).

*Vail, Robert W. G., *The Voice of the Old Frontier* (Philadelphia, 1949).

Wright, Louis B., *Religion and Empire: The Alliance between Piety and Commerce in English Expansion, 1558–1625* (Chapel Hill, 1943).

*Wroth, Lawrence C., "The Maryland Colonization Tracts, 1632–1646," in *Essays Offered to Herbert Putnam* (New Haven, 1929), pp. 539–55.

V.   Miscellaneous Prose

Aldridge, Alfred Owen, "George Whitfield's Georgia Controversies," *JSH*, IX (1943), 357–80.

Beirne, Francis F., "Sam Chase, 'Disturber,'" *Md Hist Mag*, LVII (1962), 78–89. [lit war in 1766]

Bridenbaugh, Carl, "Violence and Virtue in Virginia, 1766: Or, The Importance of the Trivial," *Proceed of Mass Hist Soc*, LXXVI (1966), 1–29. [casts light on lit quarrels in *Va Gaz*, 1766]

Cohen, Hennig, "Literary Reflections of Slavery in the *South Carolina Gazette*," *Jour Negro Hist*, XXXVII (1952), 188–93.

Davis, Richard Beale, "The Gentlest Art in Seventeenth Century Virginia," *Tenn Stud in Lit*, No. 2 (1957), 51–63.

Kraus, Michael, "Literary Relations Between Europe and America in the Eighteenth Century," *WMQ*, 3rd ser, I (1944), 210–35.

Lehmer, Derrick Norman, "The Literary Material in the Colonial Records of North Carolina," *U of Calif Chron*, XXX (1928), 125–39.

Powell, J. H., "The War of the Pamphlets," in *LHUS*, I, pp. 131–61.

Ryan, Frank Winkler, "Travelers in South Carolina," *Charleston Year Book, 1945*, pp. 184–256. [Tony Aston, 1682–1750?, and John Bernard, 1774–1854, actors]

Smith, Glenn Curtis, "Pamphleteers and the American Revolution in Virginia, 1752–1776" (Virginia, 1941). [diss]

Strawser, Neil, "Samuel Chase and the Annapolis Paper War," *Md Hist Mag*, LVII (1962), 177–94. [lit war in 1766]

Vancura, Zdenek, "Baroque Prose in America," *Studies in English by Members of the English Seminar of Charles University*, IV (Prague, 1933), pp. 39–58.

Webber, Mabel L., "South Carolina Almanacs to 1800," *S.C. Hist Mag*, XV (1914), 73–81.

VI.   Newspapers

Hennig Cohen's *The South Carolina Gazette* is the only full study of a colonial newspaper, and the *Virginia Gazette Index* is a useful, though unique, tool. Few of the poems and essays that appeared in the colonial newspapers have been reprinted. Surely the "Humorist" essay series from *The South Carolina Gazette* should be edited and published, and the author should be identified. Calendars of the prose and poetry of the colonial newspapers should be compiled. The newspapers were the primary place to publish in colonial and revolutionary America, and the newspapers—and, consequently, the writers—have been ignored.

Aldridge, Alfred Owen, "Benjamin Franklin and the *Maryland Gazette*," *Md Hist Mag*, XLIV (1949), 177–89. [Franklin's borrowings from William Parks's *Md Gaz*]

———, "The Poet's Corner in Early Georgia Newspapers," *GaR*, III (1949), 45–55.

Bond, Beverley Waugh, Jr., "A Colonial Sidelight," *SeR*, XIX (1911), 87–107; and XX (1912), 213–34. [poetry in *Md Gaz* and *Va Gaz*]

Cappon, Lester J. and Stella F. Duff, *Virginia Gazette Index, 1736–1780*, 2 vols (Williamsburg, 1950).

Castles, William H., Jr., "The *Virginia Gazette,* 1736–1766: Its Editors, Editorial Policies and Literary Content," *DA,* XXIII, 3350 (Tennessee).

Cohen, Hennig, *The South Carolina Gazette, 1732–1775* (Columbia, S.C., 1953).

*Cook, Elizabeth Christine, "Colonial Newspapers and Magazines, 1704–1775," in William Peterfield Trent, et al, eds., *The Cambridge History of American Literature,* I (New York, 1917), pp. 111–23, and bibl, pp. 452–54.

——, *Literary Influences in Colonial Newspapers, 1704–1750* (New York, 1912).

Corbitt, D. L., "The North Carolina Gazette," *N.C. Hist R,* XII (1936), 45–61.

Crittenden, Charles Christopher, "North Carolina Newspapers before 1790," *James Sprunt Historical Studies,* XX (1928), 7–83.

Gibson, George H., and Judith C. Gibson, "The Influence of the *Tatler* and the *Spectator* on the 'Monitor,'" *Furman Studies Issue of the Furman U Bull,* XIV, No. 1 (1966), 12–23.

Howard, Martha C., "*The Maryland Gazette:* An American Imitation of the *Tatlér* and the *Spectator,*" *Md Hist Mag,* XXIX (1934), 295–98.

Hubbell, "The South Carolina Gazette," *The South in American Literature,* pp. 76–79.

——, "The Virginia Gazette," *The South in American Literature,* pp. 35–40.

Joost, Nicholas, "Plain-Dealer and Free-Thinker: A Revaluation," *AL,* XXIII (1951), 31–37.

——, "William Parks, Benjamin Franklin, and a Problem in Colonial Deism," *Mid-America,* XXXIV (1952), 3–13.

Myers, Robert M., "The Old Dominion Looks to London: A Study of the English Literary Influences upon *The Virginia Gazette,* 1736–1766," *VMHB,* LIV (1946), 195–217.

Pilcher, George W., "Virginia Newspapers and the Dispute over the Proposed Colonial Episcopate, 1771–1772," *The Historian,* XXIII (1960–61), 98–113.

Skaggs, David C., "Editorial Policies of the *Maryland Gazette,* 1765–1783," *Md Hist Mag,* LIX (1964), 341–49.

J. A. LEO LEMAY
University of California
Los Angeles, California

THE EARLY NATIONAL PERIOD, 1789-1830

Literary scholarship about the Early National period in the South is somewhat scattered and fragmented. Excellent studies of individual figures or locales have been written, but no one has yet synthesized the scholarship now available into a historical survey comparable to Jay B. Hubbell's *The South in American Literature, 1607–1900* (Durham, 1954). Richard Beale Davis, in his "Spadework, American Literature, and the Southern Mind: Opportunities," *South Atlantic Bulletin*, XXXI (March, 1966), suggests that much more work must be done before an adequate survey of the period can be written. And he calls upon scholars to do additional "spadework" on the literary character of the South in both the Colonial and the Early National periods.

Since 1960, however, several significant books have appeared, indicating that Davis' "spadework" is under way. Clarence Gohdes' *Literature and Theater of the States and Regions of the U.S.A.: An Historical Bibliography* (Durham, 1967) lists books and articles on each of the Southern states, plus more than 1,200 items under the heading "South." Many of these items are relevant to the Early National period. Among literary and cultural studies are Richard Beale Davis' *Intellectual Life in Jefferson's Virginia, 1790–1830* (Chapel Hill, 1964) and Edd W. Parks's *Ante-Bellum Southern Literary Critics* (Athens, Ga., 1962). Davis' book includes material on the literary culture of Virginia, and the early chapters of Parks's volume deal with figures of the Early National era. Russel B. Nye's *The Cultural Life of the New Nation, 1776–1830* (New York, 1960) provides a survey of the cultural life in all regions, while Clement Eaton's *The Growth of Southern Civilization, 1790–1860* (New York, 1961) and his *The Mind of the Old South*, rev ed (Baton Rouge, 1967) focus upon the distinctly Southern culture and contain sections dealing specifically with the Early National period. In *The Lazy South* (New York, 1967), David Bertelson examines Southern attitudes towards work, with chapters on both the Colonial and Early National eras. Winthrop D. Jordan's *White Over Black: American Attitudes Toward the Negro, 1550–1812* (Chapel Hill, 1968) pays considerable attention to Southern attitudes. James H. Dormon's *Theater in the Ante-Bellum South, 1815–1861* (Chapel Hill, 1967) treats extensively the theatrical activity in Southern cities and towns towards the end of the Early National period.

In addition, a number of doctoral dissertations, dealing in whole or in part with the period, have been written. Among the more recent studies are those by Julian D. Mason, Jr., Charles S. Watson, Thomas L.

Robertson, Clyde H. Cantrell, and others (see below).

Professor Davis is correct in saying that much work remains to be done, but students of the Early National era now have at hand significant "spadework" that was non-existent just a few years ago.

*I.   Bibliographical Aids and Special Checklists

Although no extensive bibliography of the Early National period is now available, four bibliographical guides are particularly relevant to the period. Clarence Gohdes' *Literature and Theater of the States and Regions of the U.S.A.* is particularly valuable. Gohdes has arranged his material under headings for each of the states, as well as for the major regions. Under each state are listed general items, plus a separate section on the theater. Still one of the most useful guides is Jay B. Hubbell's bibliography in *The South in American Literature.* Also useful are the *Literary History of the United States,* II, with Supplement, and Clyde H. Cantrell and Walton R. Patrick, *Southern Literary Culture: A Bibliography of Masters' and Doctors' Theses* (University, Ala. 1955), which lists more than 2,500 items.

Alderson, William T., and Robert H. White, *A Guide to the Study and Reading of Tennessee History* (Nashville, 1959). [folkl, biog, the press, social and cultural hist]

Bristol, Roger P., *Maryland Imprints, 1801–1810* (Charlottesville, 1953).

Brockett, O. G., "The Theatre of the Southern United States from the Beginnings Through 1865: A Bibliographical Essay," *Theatre Research,* II (1960), 163–74.

Cantrell and Patrick, *Southern Literary Culture.* [indexed by subject and author]

Clark, Thomas D., ed., *Travels in the Old South: A Bibliography,* 3 vols (Norman, Okla., 1956–59). [vol II lists entries for 1750–1825; part 1 of vol III continues through 1840s]

Ellison, Rhoda, *A Check List of Alabama Imprints, 1807–1870* (University, Ala., 1946).

———, *History and Bibliography of Alabama Newspapers in the Nineteenth Century* (University, Ala., 1954). [arranged by cities and towns]

Gohdes, Clarence, *Literature and Theater of the States and Regions of the U.S.A.: An Historical Bibliography* (Durham, 1967).

Gilmer, Gertrude, *Checklist of Southern Periodicals to 1861* (Boston, 1934). [some 178 periodicals between 1800–30]

Hoole, William S., *A Check-List and Finding-List of Charleston Periodicals, 1732–1864* (Durham, 1936).

Hubbell, *The South in American Literature,* pp. 893–914. [see also entries on individual authors]

Jillson, Willard R., *Early Kentucky Literature, 1750–1840* (Frankfort, Ky., 1931). [intro, pp. 17–67; checklist, pp. 67–112]

Leary, Lewis, *Articles on American Literature, 1900–1950* (Durham, 1954).

McMurtrie, Douglas C., *A Bibliography of Mississippi Imprints, 1798–1830* (Beauvoir Community, Miss., 1945). [McMurtrie comp many checklists and wrote much on early printing]

———, *Early Printing in Tennessee, with a Bibliography of Issues of the Tennessee Press, 1793–1830* (Chicago, 1933).

———, *Eighteenth Century North Carolina Imprints, 1749–1800* (Chapel Hill, 1938).

———, *Louisiana Imprints, 1768–1810* (Hattiesburg, Miss., 1942).

———, "Some Nineteenth Century South Carolina Imprints, 1801–1820," *S.C. Hist & Gen. Mag*, XLIV (1943), 87–106, 155–72, 228–46.

Spiller, et al, eds., *LHUS*, II with Supp. [arranged by periods and by individual authors]

Swem, Earl G., ed., *A Bibliography of Virginia*, 5 vols (Richmond, 1916–55). [vol I arranged alphabetically and with many items from Early National era; vol II arranged chronologically and mostly state papers]

Tennessee Historical Records Survey, *List of Tennessee Imprints, 1793–1840, in Tennessee Libraries* (Nashville, 1941).

Thornton, Mary L., *A Bibliography of North Carolina, 1589–1956* (Chapel Hill, 1958). [arranged alphabetically, with index]

Turnbull, Robert J., *Bibliography of South Carolina, 1563–1950*, 6 vols (Charlottesville, 1955–60). [vols I and II arranged chronologically and with many relevant items; vol VI is index]

Weistert, John J., *The Curtain Rose: A Checklist of Performances at Samuel Drake's City Theatre and Other Theatres at Louisville from the Beginnings to 1843* (Louisville, 1958).

Woodress, James, ed., *American Literary Scholarship: An Annual* (Durham, 1965, 1966, 1967). [the three annuals cover the years 1963, 1964, 1965; reviews of year's scholarship by prominent scholars; for 1963, see pp. 95–106, 213–17; for 1964, pp. 91–108; for 1965, pp. 107–28, 278–81]

———, *Dissertations in American Literature, 1891–1955, with Supplement, 1955–1961* (Durham, 1962).

Wyllie, John C., and Randolph W. Church, eds., *Virginia Imprint Series* (Richmond, 1947–49).

See below: III, Ellison; V, Cardwell, Lewis, Minick, Wheeler.

II. Cultural Backgrounds and Histories

Books mentioned above by Nye, Eaton, Bertelson, Davis, and Jordan all provide comments on cultural backgrounds and include extensive bibliographies and notes. Two somewhat similar volumes are Daniel J. Boorstin's *The Americans: The National Experience* (New York, 1965, 1967) and William R. Taylor's *Cavalier and Yankee: The Old South and American National Character* (New York, 1957, 1961), the latter of which quotes extensively from literary documents.

On the Southern mind, W. J. Cash's *The Mind of the South* (New York, 1941) remains one of the standard studies, as does the first section of Vernon L. Parrington's *The Romantic Revolution in America, 1800–1860* (New York, 1927). Eaton's *The Mind of the Old South*, rev ed (Baton Rouge, 1967), primarily about the period 1820–60, examines the lives of several representative Southerners, many of whom matured during the Early National period. Arthur K. Moore's *The Frontier Mind* (Lexington, Ky., 1957; New York, 1963) treats Kentucky life. Two other volumes on the frontier are Louis B. Wright's *Culture on the Moving Frontier* (Bloomington, Ind., 1955; New York, 1961) and Everett Dick's *The Dixie Frontier* (New York, 1948).

*Abernethy, Thomas P., *The South in the New Nation, 1789–1819* (Baton Rouge, 1961). [hist background]

*Bertelson, David, *The Lazy South* (New York, 1967).

Binder, Frederick M., "The Color Problem in Early National America as Viewed by John Adams, Jefferson, and Jackson," *DA*, XXIV, 1,987 (Columbia). [both the Negro and the Indian discussed]

*Boorstin, Daniel J., *The Americans: The National Experience* (New York, 1965, 1967), pp. 169–218.

*_____, *The Lost World of Thomas Jefferson* (New York, 1948).

Cash, W. J., *The Mind of the South* (New York, 1941). [chaps 1–3]

*Chase, Gilbert, *America's Music, From the Pilgrims to the Present* (New York, 1955), pp. 41–282; 679–706.

*Curti, Merle, *The Growth of American Thought*, 3rd ed (New York, 1964). [first publ in 1943, rev in 1951; chaps 6–11 and 16–17]

*Dangerfield, George, *The Awakening of American Nationalism, 1815–1828* (New York, 1965).

*_____, *The Era of Good Feelings* (New York, 1952), pp. 199–245.

*Davenport, F. Garvin, *Ante-Bellum Kentucky: A Social History, 1800–1860* (Oxford, Ohio, 1943). [chap 10 on lit culture]

*_____, *Cultural Life in Nashville, 1825–1860* (Chapel Hill, 1941). [chaps 1–2]

*Davidson, Philip, *Propaganda and the American Revolution, 1763–1783* (Chapel Hill, 1941). [sections on So background for pamph lit of Early National era]

*Davis. Richard Beale, *Francis Walker Gilmer: Life and Learning in Jefferson's Virginia* (Richmond, 1939), esp pp. 267–74.

*_____, *Intellectual Life in Jefferson's Virginia, 1790–1830* (Chapel Hill, 1964). [chaps 2, 3, 7, 8]

*Dick, Everett, *The Dixie Frontier* (New York, 1948).

*Eaton, Clement, *The Freedom-of-Thought Struggle in the Old South* (New York, 1964); rev version of *Freedom of Thought in the Old South* (Durham, 1940).

*_____, *The Growth of Southern Civilization, 1790–1860* (New York, 1961).

*_____, *The Mind of the Old South*, rev ed (Baton Rouge, 1967).

*Fossier, Albert E., *New Orleans: The Glamour Period, 1800–1840* (New Orleans, 1957), pp. 467–84.

Gaines, Francis P., *The Southern Plantation: A Study in the Development and the Accuracy of a Tradition* (New York, 1924). [chaps 1–2]

Horton, Rod W., and Herbert W. Edwards, *Backgrounds of American Literary Thought*, 2nd ed (New York, 1967), pp. 365–95.

Hubbell, Jay B., *South and Southwest: Literary Essays and Reminiscences* (Durham, 1965), pp. 228–49, 269–84 for background.

_____, *Southern Life in Fiction* (Athens, Ga., 1960). [lecture II]

*Jensen, Merrill, *The New Nation: A History of the United States During the Confederation, 1781–1789* (New York, 1950).

*Jones, Howard Mumford, *O Strange New World: American Culture: The Formative Years* (New York, 1964). [chaps 7–10]

*_____, *America and French Culture, 1750–1848* (Chapel Hill, 1927).

*Jordan, Winthrop D., *White Over Black: American Attitudes Towards the Negro, 1550–1812* (Chapel Hill, 1968). [parts 3, 4, and 5 deal with 1775–1812; much attention to Jefferson and Early National era]

Kohn, Hans, *American Nationalism* (New York, 1957). [chaps 2–3]

*Moore, Arthur K., *The Frontier Mind* (Lexington, Ky., 1957; New York, 1963).

*Nagel, Paul C., *One Nation Indivisible: The Union in American Thought, 1776–1861* (New York, 1964).

*Nye, Russel B., *The Cultural Life of the New Nation, 1776–1830* (New York, 1960).

*Parrington, Vernon L., *The Romantic Revolution in America, 1800–1860* (New York, 1927), pp. 2–179.

Pearce, Roy H., *The Savages of America: A Study of the Indian and the Idea of Civilization* (rev ed, Baltimore, 1965). [So attitudes discussed in part 2]

Potter, David M., and Thomas G. Manning, eds., *Nationalism and Sectionalism in America, 1775–1877* (New York, 1949). [a textbook-anthol of primary documents; see pp. 65–93, 125–81]

Simkins, Francis B., *A History of the South* (New York, 1953), originally publ as *The South, Old and New: A History, 1820–1947* (New York, 1947). [chaps 6–13 are relevant]

*Smith, James Ward, and A. Leland Jamison, eds., *Religion in American Life*, 4 vols (Princeton, 1961). [extensive bibl esp vol IV, part 4, p. 851, "Religion in Literature"]

*Sonne, Niels H., *Liberal Kentucky, 1780–1828* (New York, 1939). [religion and educ at Transylvania Coll, "The Harvard of the South"]

*Sydnor, Charles S., *The Development of Southern Sectionalism, 1819–1848* (Baton Rouge, 1948).

*Taylor, Rosser H., *Ante–Bellum South Carolina: A Social and Cultural History* (Chapel Hill, 1942).

*Taylor, William R., *Cavalier and Yankee: The Old South and American National Character* (New York, 1957, 1961).

Tinker, Edward Larocque, *Creole City: Its Past and Its People* (New York, 1953). [hist of New Orleans to 1877]

Wright, Louis B., *Culture on the Moving Frontier* (Bloomington, Ind., 1955; New York, 1961).

III. Literary Backgrounds and Histories

The standard literary history is Jay B. Hubbell, *The South in American Literature, 1607–1900*. Hubbell's "Literary Nationalism in the Old South," in *American Studies in Honor of William Kenneth Boyd* (Durham, 1940), is still one of the most important brief statements on that topic. A full-length study is Rollin G. Osterweis' *Romanticism and Nationalism in the Old South* (New Haven, 1949; Baton Rouge, 1967). In *Ante-Bellum Southern Literary Critics* (Athens, Ga., 1962), Edd W. Parks devotes early chapters to Jefferson, Richard Henry Wilde, and Hugh S. Legaré.

*Blair, Walter, ed., *Native American Humor* (New York, 1937; San Francisco, 1960). [intro, pp. 16–36, 62–101; bibl, 183–96]

Birnbaum, Henry, "American Literary Nationalism after the War of 1812: 1815–1825," George Washington, 1954. [diss]

Calhoun, Richard J., "Literary Criticism in Southern Periodicals, 1828–1860," *DA*, XX, 2,286 (North Carolina).

*Clark, Thomas D., *The Rampaging Frontier* (New York and Indianapolis, 1939). [folk humor and culture of Ohio and Tenn River Valleys]

*Charvat, William, *The Origins of American Critical Thought, 1810–1835* (Philadelphia, 1936). [background; not much about the So; see p. 205]

Coberly, James H., "The Growth of Nationalism in American Literature, 1800–1815," George Washington, 1950. [diss]

*Dorson, Richard, *American Folklore* (Chicago, 1959), pp. 39–74, 166–98.

*Ellison, Rhoda C., *Early Alabama Publications* (University, Ala. 1947). [see esp chap 1, "Publishing Conditions"]

*Fisher, Miles Mark, *Negro Slave Songs in the United States* (Ithaca, N.Y., 1953; New York, 1963). [intro by Ray A. Billington; extensive notes and bibl]

Guilds, John C., "Simms's Views on National and Sectional Literature, 1825–1845," *N.C. Hist R*, XXXIV (1957), 393–405.

Hayne, Paul H., "Ante-Bellum Charleston," *So Bivouac*, IV (1885), 199–202, 257–68, 327–36.

Howard, Leon, *Literature and the American Tradition* (Garden City, N.Y., 1960). [some material in parts 1 and 2]

Hubbell, Jay B., "Literary Nationalism in the Old South," in *American Studies in Honor of William Kenneth Boyd*, ed. Jackson, pp. 175–220.

*———, *The South in American Literature*, pp. 89–323.

Hudson, A. P., ed., *Humor of the Old Deep South* (New York, 1936). [intros and head notes]

*Loggins, Vernon, *The Negro Author: His Development in America to 1900* (New York, 1931; Port Washington, N.Y., 1964). [chaps 1–3]

McIlwaine, Shields, *The Southern Poor-White from Lubberland to Tobacco Road* (Norman, Okla., 1939), pp. xiii–xxv, 17–32.

Mason, Julian D. Jr., "The Critical Reception of American Negro Authors in American Magazines, 1800–1885," *DA*, XXIII, 4677 (North Carolina).

Miles, Guy S., *Literary Beginnings in Nashville, 1815–1825: A Summary of a Thesis* (Nashville, 1942). [also Vanderbilt diss of same title, 1941]

Moses, Montrose J., *The Literature of the South* (New York, 1910). [an early hist, to be used with caution]

*Osterweis, Rollins G., *Romanticism and Nationalism in the Old South* (New Haven, 1949; Baton Rouge, 1967).

Page, Thomas N., "Authorship in the South Before the War," in *The Old South* (New York, 1927), pp. 52–97. [repr in several editions with different pagination]

*Parks, Edd W., *Ante-Bellum Southern Literary Critics* (Athens, Ga., 1962).

———, "The Three Streams of Southern Humor," *GaR*, IX (1955), 147–59.

Pattee, Fred L., *The First Century of American Literature, 1770–1870* (New York, 1935), pp. 247–59, 420–37.

Quinn, Arthur Hobson, et al, *Literature of the American People* (New York, 1951).

Reid, Alfred S., et al, *The Arts in Greenville, 1800–1960*, in *Furman U Bull*, VII (Nov 1960), 97 ff.

Richey, Ish, *Kentucky Literature, 1784–1963* (Tompkinsville, Ky., 1963), pp. 1–23.

Rion, Mary, "Civilization of the Frontier: Literary Activity in Kentucky before 1830," Johns Hopkins, 1957. [diss]

Robertson, Thomas L., Jr., "The Unfolding Magnolia: A Literary History of Mississippi until 1876," *DA*, XXI, 628 (Vanderbilt). [before 1830, mostly "devotional or practical writing"]

*Rourke, Constance, *American Humor* (New York, 1931). [chaps 2–3]

Simpson, Lewis P., "Federalism and the Crisis of Literary Order," *AL*, XXXII (1960), 253–66. [background; focus on New Eng]

Smelser, Marshall, "The Federalist Period as an Age of Passion," *AQ*, X (1958), 391–419.

Spiller, et al, eds., *LHUS*, I, pp. 115–241, 306–20.

Thorp, Willard, "The Writer as Pariah in the Old South," in *Southern Writers: Appraisals in Our Time*, ed. Simonini, pp. 3–18.

Trent, W. P., et al, *The Cambridge History of American Literature*, 4 vols (New York, 1917–21). [vol I, pp. 185–244, 307–25]

Tyler, Moses C., *The Literary History of the American Revolution, 1763–1783*, 2 vols (New York, 1897). [background; still a standard work]

IV. Books, Reading, and Education

Bogner, Harold F., "Sir Walter Scott in New Orleans, 1818–1832," *La Hist Q*, XXI (1938), 420–517.

Cantrell, Clyde H., "The Reading Habits of Ante-Bellum Southerners," *DA*, XXI, 1,573 (Illinois).

Clark, Thomas D., "Arts and Sciences on the Early American Frontier," *Nebr Hist*, XXXVII (1956), 247–68. [1810 to 1840]

*Come, Donald R., "The Influence of Princeton on Higher Education in the South before 1825," *WMQ*, 3rd ser, II (1945), 359–96. [notes]

Davis, Richard Beale, "Literary Tastes in Virginia before Poe," *WMQ*, 2nd ser., XIX (1939), 55–68.

*Godbold, Albea, *The Church College in the Old South* (Durham, 1944).

Houlette, W. D., "Plantation and Parish Libraries of the Old South," Iowa, 1933. [diss]

———, "Sources of Books for the Old South," *Lib Q*, XXVIII (1958), 194–201.

*Knight, Edgar K., ed., *A Documentary History of Education in the South before 1860*, 5 vols (Chapel Hill, 1949–53). [vol II, *Toward Educational Independence*; III, *The Rise of the State University*; IV, *Private and Denominational Schools*]

*———, *Public Education in the South* (Boston, 1922).

Krumpelmann, John T., *Southern Scholars in Goethe's Germany* (Chapel Hill, 1965). [full notes; Legaré, Calvert, and others discussed]

Lancaster, E. R., "Books Read in Virginia in Early Nineteenth Century, 1806–1823," *VMHB*, XLVI (1938), 56–59.

Landrum, Grace W., "Sir Walter Scott and His Literary Rivals in the Old South," *AL*, II (1930), 256–76.

Leonard, Irving A., "A Frontier Library, 1799," *Hispanic-Amer Hist R*, XXIII (Feb, 1943), 21–51. [lib of Don Manuel Gayoso de Lemos]

McCutcheon, Roger P., "Books and Booksellers in New Orleans, 1730–1830," *La Hist Q*, XX (1937), 606–18.

McDermott, John F., *Private Libraries in Creole St. Louis* (Baltimore, 1938).

McMullen, Haynes, "Social Libraries in Ante-Bellum Kentucky," *Ky Hist Soc R*, LVIII (1960), 97–128. [1794–1860]

Napier, James, "Some Book Sales in Dumfries, Virginia, 1794–1796," *WMQ*, 3rd ser X (1953), 441–45.

Norton, Elizabeth, "The Old Library of Transylvania College," *Filson Club Hist Q*, I (1927), 123–33.

Orians, G. Harrison, "The Romance Ferment after *Waverley*," *AL*, III (1932), 408–31.

Sherman, Stuart C., "The Library Company of Baltimore, 1795–1854," *Md Hist Mag*, XXXIX (March 1944), 6–24.

Silver, Rollo G., "The Baltimore Book Trade, 1800–1825," *Bull N.Y. Pub Lib*, LVII (1953), 114–25, 182–201, 248–51, 297–305, 349–57.

Spruill, Julia C., "The Southern Lady's Library, 1700–1776," *SAQ*, XXXIV (1935), 23–41.

Wilson, James S., "Best-Sellers in Jefferson's Day," *VQR*, XXXVI (1960), 222–37.

V. Periodicals, Publishing, and the Press

Bentley, George F., "Printers and Printing in the Southwest Territory, 1790–1796," *Tenn Hist Q*, VIII (1949), 332–44.

Cardwell, Guy A., "Charleston Periodicals, 1795–1860: A Study in Literary Influences," North Carolina, 1936. [diss]

———, "The Influence of Addison on Charleston Periodicals, 1795–1860," *SP*, XXXV (1938), 456–70.

Cohen, Hennig, *The South Carolina Gazette, 1732–1775* (Columbia, S.C., 1953). [good background]

*Elliott, Robert N., Jr., *The Raleigh Register, 1799–1863* (Chapel Hill, 1955).

Gilmer, Gertrude, "Maryland Magazines—Ante-Bellum, 1793–1861," *Md Hist Mag*, XXIX (1934), 120–31.

Goff, Frederick R., "Early Printing in Georgetown (Potomak), 1789–1800," *Proceed of Amer Antiq Soc*, LXVIII (Apr 16, 1958), 107–34.

Hyslop, Beatrice F., "The American Press and the French Revolution of 1789," *Proceed of Amer Philos Soc*, CIV (Feb 1960), 54–85.

Lewis, Benjamin M., *An Introduction to American Magazines, 1800–1810* (Ann Arbor, 1961). [lists 15 So mags]

———, *A Register of Editors, Printers, and Publishers of American Magazines, 1741–1810* (New York, 1957).

McFarland, Daniel M., "North Carolina Newspapers, Editors, and Journalistic Politics, 1815–1835," *N.C. Hist R*, XXX (1953), 376–414.

*Minick, Amanda R., *A History of Printing in Maryland, with a Bibliography* (Baltimore, 1949).

Morrison, Alfred J., "The Virginia Literary and Evangelical Magazine, 1818–1828," *WMQ*, 1st ser, XIX (1911), 266–72.

Mott, Frank L., *American Journalism*, 3rd ed (New York, 1961; also New York, 1941), pp. 133–211 of rev ed.

———, *A History of American Magazines, 1741–1850* (Cambridge, Mass., 1930), pp. 204–205, 380–84. [also see individual hist in part 2 (1794–1825) and part 3 (1825–50); this is vol I of 4-vol work]

Stearns, Bertha-Monica, "Southern Magazines for Ladies, 1819–1860," *SAQ*, XXXI (1932), 70–87.

Wiley, Edwin, "Eighteenth Century Presses in Tennessee," *Pub Bibl Soc Amer*, II (1907), 70–83.

*Wheeler, Joseph T., *The Maryland Press, 1777–1790* (Baltimore, 1938).

Woodward, F. G., "An Early Tennessee Almanac and Its Maker: Hill's Almanac, 1825–1862," *Tenn Folkl*, XVIII (March 1952), 9–14.

See above: I, Ellison, Gilmore, Hoole; III, Ellison.

VI.   Poetry, Fiction, Drama

Southern verse and prose fiction in the Early National period are comparatively small in output. There were a considerable number of verse writers, but most wrote for their own amusement, and scholars agree that much of this verse is amateurish. One must remember, however, that Poe had published two volumes of poetry before 1830. Even fewer writers attempted prose fiction early in the period, but by the 1830s Southern fiction had achieved national recognition in the works of such writers as Simms and Kennedy. Hubbell's discussions of individual authors in *The South in American Literature* provide a survey of both verse and prose fiction in the period. Introductions to Edd W. Parks's *Southern Poets* (New York, 1936) and Gregory Paine's *Southern Prose Writers* (New York, 1947) are also helpful.

Southerners gave considerably more attention to theatrical activities during the period. Innumerable theatrical studies are available, among them James H. Dormon's *Theater in the Ante-Bellum South, 1815–1861* (Chapel Hill, 1967).

Poetry

*Bigelow, Gordon E., *Rhetoric and American Poetry of the Early National Period* (Gainesville, 1960). [focus on No writers; presents background material]

Bradshaw, Sidney E., *On Southern Poetry Prior to 1860* (Richmond, 1900). [brief, early study superseded by later work]

Huddleston, Eugene L., "Topographical Poetry in the Early National Period," *AL*, XXXVIII (1966), 303–22. [mentions Jefferson, John Filson, and some So poems]

*Parks, Edd W., ed., *Southern Poets* (New York, 1936). [intro and bibl; see pp. 9–25 for selections by So poets of the period]

Roth, George L., "Verse Satire on 'Faction,' 1790–1815," *WMQ*, 3rd ser, XVII (1960), 473–85.

Snyder, Henry N., "Characteristics of Southern Poetry from the Beginnings to 1865," in *The South in the Building of the Nation*, VII, pp. 1–24.

Fiction

*Brown, Herbert Ross, *The Sentimental Novel in America, 1789–1860* (Durham, 1940; New York, 1959).

*Cowie, *The Rise of the American Novel*. [pp. 165–326 give background material and some relevant comments]

Duvall, Severn P. C., Jr., "The Legend of the South in Southern Historical Fiction, 1820–1861," *DA*, XV, 2204 (Princeton, 1955).

Hilldrup, Robert L., "Cold War against the Yankees in the Ante-Bellum Literature of Southern Women," *N.C. Hist R*, XXXI (1954), 370–84. [mentions Anne Royall's *The Tennessean: A Novel* (1827)]

Holman, C. Hugh, "Diversity Within Unity," *Three Modes of Southern Fiction* (Athens, Ga., 1966), pp. 1-10. [deals with 20th century, but distinctions are important to student of earlier periods]

*Leisy, Ernest E., *The American Historical Novel* (Norman, Okla., 1949). [chaps 1–2]

McDowell, Tremaine, "The Negro in the Southern Novel Prior to 1850," *Jour of Eng and Ger Phil*, XXV (1926), 455–73.

Mims, Edwin, intro to *History of Southern Fiction,* in *The South in the Building of the Nation,* VIII, pp. xi–xlvii.

*Paine, Gregory, ed., *Southern Prose Writers* (New York, 1947). [intro and notes]

Drama

*Adams, Henry W., *The Montgomery Theatre, 1822–1835,* in *U of Ala Stud,* IX (University, Ala., 1955).

Armistead, Margaret Beauchamp, "The Savannah Theater—Oldest Theater in America," *GaR,* VII (1953), 50–56. [built 1818]

*Dormon, James H., *Theater in the Ante-Bellum South, 1815–1861* (Chapel Hill, 1967). [chaps 1–5]

Free, Joseph M., "The Ante-Bellum Theatre of the Old Natchez Region," *Jour Miss Hist,* V (1943), 14–27. [1806–40]

*Graham, Philip, *Showboats: The History of an American Institution* (Austin, Tex., 1951). [chaps 1–2]

Henderson, Archibald, "Early Drama and Amateur Entertainment in North Carolina," *The Reviewer,* V (July 1925), 47–57. [to 1825]

Hoole, William S., *The Ante-Bellum Charleston Theatre* (University, Ala., 1946). [chaps 1–3; also checklist of plays arranged alphabetically and by season]

———, "Two Famous Theatres of the Old South," *SAQ,* XXXVI (1937), 273–77.

Kendall, John S., *The Golden Age of the New Orleans Theater* (Baton Rouge, 1952). [parts 1 and 2]

*Le Gardeur, René J., *The First New Orleans Theatre, 1792–1803* (New Orleans, 1963).

*Patrick, J. Max, *Savannah's Pioneer Theater from Its Origins to 1810* (Athens, Ga., 1953). [1781–1810; index of plays and actors]

Roppolo, Joseph P., "Local and Topical Plays in New Orleans, 1806–1865," *Tulane Stud in Eng,* IV (1954), 91–124. [includes checklist]

Rulfs, D. J., "The Ante-Bellum Professional Theater in Fayetteville," *N.C. Hist R,* XXXI (1952), 125–33.

Sherman, Susanne K., "Thomas Wade West, Theatrical Impressario, 1790–1799," *WMQ,* 3rd ser, IX (1952) 10–28.

Shockley, Martin S., "American Plays in the Richmond Theatre, 1819–1838," *SP,* XXXVII (1940), 100–19. [lists plays performed]

———, "First American Performance of English Plays in Richmond before 1819," *JSH,* XIII (1947), 91–105.

———, "The Proprietors of Richmond's New Theatre of 1819," *WMQ,* 2nd ser, XIX (1939), 302–308.

———, "The Richmond Theatre, 1780–1790," *VMHB,* LX (1952), 421–36.

Smither, Nelle, *A History of the English Theatre at New Orleans, 1806–1842* (Philadelphia, 1944). Also enlarged in *La Hist Q,* XXVII (1945), 85–276, 361–572, Repr Bronx, N.Y., 1966, with index.

Walser, Richard, "Negro Dialect in Eighteenth-Century American Drama," *AS,* XXX (1955), 269–76.

Watson, Charles S., "Early Dramatic Writing in the South: Virginia and South Carolina Plays, 1798–1830," *DA,* XXVII, 3435-A (Vanderbilt, 1966).

See also the listings under checklist on eighteenth- and nineteenth-century Southern Drama elsewhere in this volume.

ROBERT BAIN
University of North Carolina
Chapel Hill, North Carolina

ANTE-BELLUM SOUTHERN WRITERS

As the following listing will show, there have been comparatively few general studies of the ante-bellum writers, and most of these few studies were published half a century ago. Notable among the scholars and critics who have helped revive interest in Southern literature have been Jay B. Hubbell, Edd Winfield Parks, and Richard Beale Davis, whose work has superseded that of Montrose Moses, Carl Holliday, and Edwin Mims. The histories of Southern literature written by Moses and Holliday are still worth examining, but indispensable to the modern student is Jay B. Hubbell's *The South in American Literature, 1607–1900.* The writings of Edd Winfield Parks, listed below, are valuable for ante-bellum literary theory; and Richard Beale Davis' *Intellectual Life in Jefferson's Virginia* is a model of scholarship devoted to a single period and region.

Early compilations, such as the *Library of Southern Literature* and Davidson's *The Living Writers of the South,* are inclusive rather than critical, but have value in providing selections from little-known authors. The scholarship of that ambitious work *The South in the Building of the Nation* has been largely superseded, but Volume VIII, edited by Edwin Mims, for many years an influential professor at Vanderbilt University, is still worth consulting for its account of Southern fiction. A fairly recent bibliography of writings about Southern fiction may be found in Paine's *Southern Prose Writers,* in the American Writers Series. The bibliography in Parks's *Southern Poets* should be supplemented by the more recent listings in Hubbell's *The South in American Literature.* A selection of the few general studies published since the date of Hubbell's history is included in the following bibliography. A very useful listing of materials pertaining to Southern culture is *Southern Literary Culture: A Bibliography of Masters' and Doctors' Theses,* ed. Clyde H. Cantrell and Walton R. Patrick. (University, Ala., 1955). This descriptive bibliography lists theses on every aspect of Southern literature and culture as well as studies of individual authors.

*Alderman, et al, eds., *LSL.* [anthol; vols XV–XVI include biog and bibl]
Bradshaw, S. E., *On Southern Poetry Prior to 1860* (Richmond, 1900).
Brevard, Caroline M., *Literature of the South* (New York, 1908).
Brooks, Van Wyck, *The Times of Melville and Whitman* (New York, 1947).
―――, *The World of Washington Irving* (New York, 1944).
Calhoun, Richard J., "Literary Criticism in Southern Periodicals," North Carolina, 1959. [diss]
Davidson, James W., *The Living Writers of the South* (New York, 1869).

Davis, Richard Beale, *Intellectual Life in Jefferson's Virginia* (Chapel Hill, 1964), pp. 253–351.

Duvall, Severn P., Jr., "The Legend of the South in Southern Historical Fiction, 1820–1861," Princeton, 1954. [diss]

Eaton, Clement, *The Freedom-of-Thought Struggle in the Old South* (New York, 1964). [contains comments on writers]

Gordon, A. C., Jr., *Virginian Writers of Fugitive Verse* (New York, 1923). [anthol; contains good crit essay]

Holliday, Carl, *A History of Southern Literature* (New York, 1906).

Hubbell, Jay B., "Literary Nationalism in the Old South," in *American Studies in Honor of William Kenneth Boyd*, ed. Jackson.

*_____, *Southern Life in Fiction* (Athens, Ga., 1960). [Lamar Lectures]

*_____, *The South in American Literature*.

Hubner, Charles W., *Representative Southern Poets* (New York, 1906). [essays on various poets]

Jillson, Willard R., *Early Kentucky Literature 1750–1840* (Frankfort, Ky., 1931).

Johnson, James G., *Southern Fiction Prior to 1860: An Attempt at a First-Hand Bibliography* (Charlottesville, 1909).

Link, S. A., *Pioneers of Southern Literature,* 2 vols (Nashville, 1899–1900). [essays on various writers]

Miller, Perry, *The Raven and the Whale* (New York, 1956). [So writers in N.Y. lit politics]

Mims, Edwin, *History of Southern Fiction,* vol VIII of *The South in the Building of the Nation*.

Minor, Benjamin Blake, *The Southern Literary Messenger* (New York and Washington, 1905).

*Moses, Montrose J., *The Literature of the South* (New York, 1910). [hist]

Osterweis, Rollin G., *Romanticism and Nationalism in the Old South* (New Haven, 1949; Baton Rouge, 1967). [contains comments on lit]

Page, Thomas Nelson, "Authorship in the South Before the War," *The Old South* (New York, 1912), pp. 67–109. [1st ed, 1896]

*Paine, Gregory, ed., *Southern Prose Writers: Representative Selections* (New York, 1947). [intro and bibl]

Painter, F. V. N., *Poets of the South* (New York, 1903). [biog and crit essays with selections]

Parks, Edd Winfield, *Ante-Bellum Southern Literary Critics* (Athens, Ga., 1962).

_____, *Segments of Southern Thought* (Athens, Ga., 1938), pp. 43–74, 75–128. [essays on poetry and poetic theory]

*_____, ed., *Southern Poets: Representative Selections* (New York, 1936). [intro and bibl]

Parrington, Vernon Louis, *Main Currents in American Thought,* II (New York, 1927), pp. 3–125.

Rogers, Edward R., *Four Southern Magazines* (Richmond, 1902). [concerns *De Bow'sR, SoR, SoQR,* and *SLM,* the most important lit mags of the ante-bellum So]

Rutherford, Mildred L., *The South in History and Literature: A Hand-Book of Southern Authors from the Settlement of Jamestown, 1607, to Living Writers* (Atlanta, 1907). [biog sketches, not always reliable]

Simms, William Gilmore, "Southern Literature: Its Conditions, Prospects and History . . .," *Magnolia,* III (Jan, Feb, 1841), 1–6, 69–74. [essay by an ante-bellum writer]

Snyder, Henry N., "Characteristics of Southern Poetry from the Beginning to 1865," in *The South in the Building of the Nation*, VII, pp. 1–24.

Spiller, Robert E., et al, eds., *LHUS*, I. [see esp chaps 22, 23, 36]

Taylor, William R., *Cavalier and Yankee: The Old South and American National Character* (New York, 1961). [image of regional life in various writers]

Thorp, Willard, ed., *A Southern Reader* (New York, 1955). [anthol designed to interpret So]

————, "The Writer as Pariah in the Old South," in *Southern Writers*, ed. Simonini, pp. 3–18.

Timrod, Henry, "Literature in the South," *Russell's Mag*, V (1859), 385–95. [essay by an ante-bellum writer]

Trent, William P., *Southern Writers: Selections in Prose and Verse* (New York, 1905). [anthol; brief biog notes].

Wilson, Edmund, *Patriotic Gore: Studies in the Literature of the American Civil War* (New York, 1962). [see esp chap 12]

ROBERT D. JACOBS
University of Kentucky
Lexington, Kentucky

THE NEW SOUTH AND ITS WRITERS

The most comprehensive descriptive treatment of the literature of the New South, and the starting point for any study of it, is that of Professor Hubbell in *The South in American Literature*. More analytical treatments of the period are found in Cash's *The Mind of the South* and Woodward's *Origins of the New South*, but neither of these is intended as literary history. There would seem to be an opportunity in the area of literary history, or intellectual history approached through literature, for more analytical study of the period. This is particularly true of the relations between the New South and the present century. One often gets the impression that the literature of the New South represents a dead end, that it simply terminates at about World War I in a fragmentation of the culture, and that the Renascence of the twenties represents a rebuilding of the literary community along different lines than those of the pre-1914 literary South. For example, in the foreword to the initial number of *The Fugitive*, there appears the metaphor of Southern literature as a stream whose source is stopped up. This discontinuity may be the case, but as yet the belief has not been very critically examined. The articles by Professors Holman and Rubin suggest that modern critics are beginning to explore these relations.

Because the New South was an economic and social movement as well as being literary, this check list includes some historical and sociological works as desirable for an understanding of the literary culture of the period. The student should also examine the checklists on individual writers of the period 1865–1900.

Atchison, Ray M., "*The Land We Love*: A Southern Post-Bellum Magazine of Agriculture, Literature and Military History," *N.C. Hist R*, XXXVII (1960), 506–15.

———, "*Scott's Monthly Magazine*: A Georgia Post-Bellum Periodical of Literature and Military History," *Ga Hist Q*, XLIX (1965), 294–305.

———, "Southern Literary Magazines, 1865–1887," Duke, 1956. [diss]

Baker, Carlos, "Delineation of Life and Character," in *LHUS*, I, pp. 843–61.

Baskervill, William M., "Southern Literature," *PMLA*, VII (1892), 89–100.

———, *Southern Writers: Biographical and Critical Studies*, 2 vols (Nashville, 1897–1903).

Bassett, John S., "The Bottom of the Matter," *SAQ*, I (1902), 99–106.

———, "Editor's Announcement," *SAQ*, I (1902), 1–3.

———, "The Problems of the Author in the South," *SAQ*, I (1902), 201–208.

Beasley, William, "The New South in Southern Fiction, 1900–1950," *DA*, XVIII, 210 (Vanderbilt).

Berthoff, Warner, *The Ferment of Realism* (New York, 1965), pp. 61–89.

Brawley, Benjamin G., *Negro Genius* (New York, 1937), pp. 100–23, 143–70.

Brooks, Van Wyck, *The Confident Years, 1885–1915* (New York, 1952), pp. 41–61, 337–52.

———, *The Times of Melville and Whitman* (New York, 1947), pp. 323–94.

Buck, Paul, *The Road to Reunion* (Boston, 1937), pp. 196–235.

Bush, Robert, "Louisiana Prose Fiction, 1870–1900," *DA*, XVII, 2000 (Iowa).

Calverton, Vernon F., *The Liberation of American Literature* (New York, 1932), pp. 89–148. [interesting as Marxist view of the development of So letters]

Cash, W. J., *The Mind of the South* (New York, 1941), pp. 113–242.

Cate, Wirt A., *Lucius Quintus Cincinnatus Lamar, Secession and Reunion* (Chapel Hill, 1935). [useful study of politician, orator, and minor lit figure noted for efforts toward No-So reconciliation]

*Clark, Thomas D., and Albert D. Kirwin, *The South Since Appomattox* (New York, 1967).

Couch, W. T., ed., *Culture in the South* (Chapel Hill, 1935). [symposium, partly in answer to *I'll Take My Stand*]

Cowie, *The Rise of the American Novel*, pp. 536–98.

Davidson, Donald, *Still Rebels, Still Yankees* (Baton Rouge, 1957), pp. 180–212.

Dillon, Sister Mary I., "The Influence of the South on American Fiction, 1870–1921," Fordham, 1922. [diss]

Gaines, Francis P., *The Southern Plantation: A Study in the Development and Accuracy of the Tradition* (New York, 1924).

Gloster, Hugh M., *Negro Voices in American Fiction* (Chapel Hill, 1948), pp. 3–100.

*Gross, Seymour L., and John E. Hardy, eds., *Images of the Negro in American Literature* (Chicago, 1966).

*Hall, Wade, *The Smiling Phoenix: Southern Humor from 1865 to 1914* (Gainesville, 1965).

Henneman, John B., "The National Element in Southern Literature," *SeR*, XI (1903), 345–66.

———, ed., *History of the Literary and Intellectual Life of the Southern States*, vol VII of *The South in the Building of the Nation.*

Herron, Ima H., *The Small Town in American Literature* (Durham, 1939), pp. 321–33.

*Holliday, Carl, *A History of Southern Literature* (New York, 1906).

———, "One Phase of Literary Conditions in the South," *SeR*, XI (1903), 463–66.

Holman, C. Hugh, "A Cycle of Change in Southern Literature," in *The South in Continuity and Change*, ed. John C. McKinney and Edgar T. Thompson (Durham, 1965), pp. 384–403.

*Hubbell, *The South in American Literature*, pp. 695–836.

Howells, William D., "American Letter: The Southern States in Recent American Literature," *Literature* (London), Sept 10, 1898, pp. 231–32; Sept 17, 1898, pp. 257–58; Sept 24, 1898, pp. 280–81.

Hubner, Charles W., *Representative Southern Poets* (New York, 1906), pp. 55–82.

I'll Take My Stand: The South and the Agrarian Tradition, by Twelve Southerners. Intro by Louis D. Rubin, Jr.; biog essays by Virginia Rock (New York, 1962). [most important single book expressing reaction against New So values]

Kent, Charles W., *The Revival of Interest in Southern Letters* (Richmond, 1900).

King, James K., "George Washington Cable and Thomas Nelson Page: Two Literary Approaches to the New South," *DA*, XXV, 2493–94 (Wisconsin).

Mabie, Hamilton W., "The New North," *SAQ*, IV (1905), 109–14.

———, "The Poetry of the South," *International Monthly*, V (1902), 200–23.

McIlwaine, Shields, *The Southern Poor White from Lubberland to Tobacco Road* (Norman, Okla, 1939), pp. 75–162.

Martin, Jay, *Harvests of Change: American Literature, 1865–1914* (Englewood Cliffs, N.J., 1967), pp. 88–104.

*Miles, Dudley, "The New South," in *Cambridge History of American Literature,* ed. William P. Trent et al (New York, 1921), II, pp. 314–46.

Mims, Edwin, *The Advancing South* (Garden City, N.Y., 1926).

———, "The Function of Criticism in the South," *SAQ,* II (1903), 334–45.

———, *History of Southern Fiction,* intro to vol VIII of *The South in the Building of the Nation,* pp. xlviii–lxv.

Moore, Rayburn S., "Southern Writers and Northern Literary Magazines, 1865–1890," Duke, 1956. [diss]

*Moses, Montrose J., *Literature of the South* (New York, 1910), pp. 358–474.

Mott, Frank L., *American Journalism* (New York, 1962), pp. 446–58.

———, *A History of American Magazines* (Cambridge, Mass., 1938–57), III, pp. 45–49; IV, pp. 90–94.

Nelson, John H., *The Negro Character in American Literature* (Lawrence, Kans., 1926), pp. 93–138.

Nixon, Raymond B., *Henry W. Grady, Spokesman of the New South* (New York, 1943).

Ormond, John R., "Some Recent Products of the New School of Southern Fiction," *SAQ,* III (1904), 285–89.

*Paine, Gregory L., *Southern Prose Writers* (New York, 1947), pp. lxxxvii–cxvii.

*Parks, Edd W., *Southern Poets* (New York, 1936), pp. xvii–cxlvii.

Pattee, Fred L., *A History of American Literature Since 1870* (New York, 1915).

*———, "The Short Story," in *Cambridge History of American Literature,* II, pp. 367–95.

*Quinn, *American Fiction,* pp. 305–73, 427–83, 670–82.

*———, ed., *Literature of the American People* (New York, 1951), pp. 569–97, 622–60.

Rubin, Louis D., Jr., "A Looking Two Ways," *Shen,* VI (Summer 1955), 19–28. [useful in relating New So and So Renascence]

*Simkins, Francis B., *A History of the South* (New York, 1953), chap 27, pp. 426–54. [good bibl notes, but erroneously headed chap 26]

*Smith, C. Alphonso, "The Dialect Writers," in *Cambridge History of American Literature,* II, 347–66.

———, "The Possibilities of Southern Literature," *SeR,* VI (1898), 298–305.

*———, *Southern Literary Studies* (Chapel Hill, 1927), pp. 48–82, 128–57. [good bibl of Smith appears pp. 185–92, and is of interest because of his role as one of principal academic critics espousing New So position]

Snyder, Henry N., "The Reconstruction of Southern Literary Thought," *SAQ,* I (1902), 145–55.

Smith, Henry N., "The Second Discovery of America," in *LHUS,* I, pp. 639–51.

Thompson, Holland, *The New South,* Chronicles of America, XLII (New Haven, 1921).

Tourgée, Albion W., "The South as a Field for Fiction," *Forum,* VI (1888), 404–13.

Van Doren, Carl, *The American Novel* (New York, 1940), pp. 203–24.

Wade, John D., "Old Wine in New Bottles," *VQR,* XI (1935), 239–52. [on conservative oppostion to growth of New So ideology]

Weaver, Richard M., "The Confederate South, 1865–1910: A Study in the Survival of a Mind and Culture," Louisiana, 1943. [diss]

Weissbuch, Theodore N., "Literary and Historical Attitudes Toward Reconstruction

Following the Civil War," *DA*, XXV, 4710–11 (Iowa).
*Woodward, C. Vann, *Origins of the New South, 1877–1913* (Baton Rouge, 1951).

*Bibliographies

Cantrell and Patrick, *Southern Literary Culture: A Bibliography of Masters' and Doctors' Theses.*

Collins, C. E., "Nineteenth Century Fiction of the Southern Appalachians," *BB*, XVII (1942–43), 186–90, 215–19.

Hawley, Edith, "Bibliography of Literary Geography," *BB*, X (1918–19), 34–38, 58–60, 76, 93–94, 104–105.

LHUS, II, 133ff; 308–16. See also *Supp.*

Smith, R. W., "Catalogue of the Chief Novels and Short Stories by American Writers Dealing with the Civil War and Its Effects, 1861–99," *BB*, XVI (1935), 193–94; XVII (1940–41), 10–12, 33–34, 53–55, 72–75.

Otis B. Wheeler
Louisiana State University
Baton Rouge, Louisiana

EARLY TWENTIETH CENTURY SOUTHERN LITERATURE

The years from 1900 to 1920 constitute an interregnum in Southern literature between the achievement of the local color writers during the last quarter of the nineteenth century and what was to be the renascence of Southern letters following the First World War. As usual with such periods, there were writers who continued in the tradition of the past and others who gave intimations and promises of what was to come. James Lane Allen and Madison Cawein were primarily local colorists writing after local color fiction had already passed its zenith in the South and in the nation. But James Branch Cabell and Ellen Glasgow were establishing for themselves in the early years of the twentieth century the solid reputation which continued to be theirs after they were joined by the younger Southern writers who came to prominence after 1920.

Other Southern writers during these first two decades of the twentieth century followed their individual predilections and wrote according to their talents and abilities. Thomas Dixon and John Fox, Jr., exploited with a mixture of romance and realism certain aspects of Southern life which interested them—interracial matters and the Southern mountaineer. In periodical fiction O. Henry perfected a formula for writing the short story which brought him fame for a season. With less recognition at the time than many of his contemporaries were receiving, William Alexander Percy in Mississippi was producing a small but select quantity of poetry whose quality merits greater consideration than it has yet received.

The Southern Negro writer emerged during this period with the work of James Weldon Johnson and Charles W. Chesnutt.

Two university-oriented periodicals, the *Sewanee Review* (1892) and the *South Atlantic Quarterly* (1902), which have continued their existence to the present time, provided a means by which the South could evaluate and encourage its own literature during the early years of the twentieth century. The fact that the quantity and the quality of this evaluation are not greater is as much a commentary on the times as it is on the editorial policies of the two quarterlies.

Barr, Stringfellow, "The Uncultured South," *VQR*, V (1929), 192–200.

Baskervill, W. M., "Southern Literature," *PMLA*, VII (1892), 89–100.

Bassett, J. S., "An Exile from the South," *SAQ*, IV (1905), 82–90. [on Moncure Daniel Conway]

Batson, Essie Beatrice, "The Treatment of American History in the American Novel 1890–1910," *DA*, XVII, 619–20 (Peabody).

Becker, Allen W., "Ellen Glasgow and the Southern Literary Tradition," *MSF*, V (1959), 295–303.

Blackstock, Walter, "Corra Harris: An Analytical Study of her Novels," in *Writers and Their Critics: Studies in English and American Literature* (Tallahassee, 1955), pp. 39–92.

Blair, Walter, "Traditions in Southern Humor," *AQ*, V (1953), 132–42.

Bloomfield, Maxwell, "Dixon's *The Leopard's Spots:* A Study in Popular Racism," *AQ*, XVI (1964), 387–401.

*Bontemps, Arna, "The James Weldon Johnson Memorial Collection of Negro Arts and Letters," *Yale U Lib Gaz*, XVIII (Oct 1943), 19–26.

Brooke, Tucker, "Afoot in Alsace-Virginia," *SeR*, XXII (1914), 358–65. [the author walks in West Virginia]

Bushby, D. M., "Poets of our Southern Frontier," *Overland Monthly*, LXXXIX (Feb 1931), 41–52, 58.

Cabell, James Branch, "Relative to My Grandmother," *GaR*, VII (1953), 260–66.

———, "Vitality en Vogue: A Plea of an Average Novel-Reader," *SeR*, XXIII (1915), 66–74.

Cardwell, G. A., Jr., "On Scholarship and Southern Literature," *SAQ*, XL (1941), 60–72.

Carlisle, Jean Todd, "*The State's* Editorial Policy Relative to South Carolina 1903–1913," *S.C. Hist Assn Proceed* (1951), 29–40.

Carter, Everett, "Cultural History Written with Lightning: The Significance of *The Birth of a Nation*," *AQ*, XII (1960), 347–57.

*Cohen, Hennig, *Articles in Periodicals and Serials on South Carolina Literature and Related Subjects, 1900–1955* (S.C. Bibl No. 4), Columbia, S.C. Archives Dept, 1956.

Collins, Carvel, "Faulkner and Certain Earlier Southern Fiction," *Coll Eng*, XVI (1954), 92–97.

Conway, A.M., "Art for Art's Sake in Southern Literature," *SeR*, XXIV (1916), 81–87. [prediction that "America's purest literature is to come out of the Southland"]

Couch, W. T., "Reflections on the Southern Tradition," *SAQ*, XXXV (1936), 284–97.

Davidson, Donald, *Southern Writers in the Modern World: Eugenia Dorothy Blount Lamar Memorial Lectures, 1957* (Athens, Ga., 1958).

———, "The 43 Best Southern Novels for Readers and Collectors," *Publ W*, CXXVII (Apr 27, 1935), 167–76.

Daviess, Maria T., "American Backgrounds for Fiction, III—Tennessee," *Bookman*, XXXVIII (1913), 394–99.

Dickey, C. H., "Something about the Circuit Rider by the Circuit Rider's Wife," *Richmond Times-Dispatch*, Feb 24, 1935, pp. 3, 12.

Dillon, Sister Mary I., "The Influence of the South on American Fiction, 1870–1921," Fordham, 1922. [diss]

Dixon, Thomas, "American Backgrounds for Fiction, IV—North Carolina," *Bookman*, XXXVIII (1914), 511–21.

Durham, Frank, "South Carolina's Poetry Society," *SAQ*, LII (1953), 277–85.

Edwards, C. H., "The Early Literary Criticism of Corra Harris," *GaR*, XVII (1963), 449–55.

Fletcher, J. G., "The Modern Southern Poets," *Westminster Mag*, XXIII (1935), 229–51.

Glasgow, Ellen, "The Novel in the South," *Harper's*, CXLIII (1928), 93–100.

Glasson, William H., "Ten Years of the *South Atlantic Quarterly*," *SAQ*, XI (1912), 1–2.

Gohdes, Clarence, "On the Study of Southern Literature," *WMQ*, XVI (1963), 81–87.

Going, William T., "Samuel Minturn Peck, Late Laureate of Alabama," *GaR*, VIII (1954), 190–200.

Green, Claud B., *John Trotwood Moore: Tennessee Man of Letters* (Athens, Ga., 1957).

──────, "Old Books: *The Bishop of Cottontown,* by John Trotwood Moore," *GaR,* XI (1957), 345–48.

Guess, William Francis, "South Carolina's Incurable Aristocrats," *Harper's,* CCXIV (Feb 1957), 44–48.

Harben, W. N., "American Backgrounds for Fiction, I—Georgia," *Bookman,* XXXVIII (1913), 186–92.

Harris, Mrs. L. H., "Fiction North and South," *Critic,* XLIII (1903), 273–75.

*Hartin, John S., "The Southeastern United States in the Novel Through 1950: A Bibliographic Review," Michigan, 1957. [diss]

Hartsock, Ernest, "Roses in the Desert: A View of Contemporary Southern Verse," *SeR,* XXXVII (1929), 328–35.

Hardwood, W. S., "New Orleans in Fiction," *Critic,* XLVII (1905), 426–35.

Heald, William F., "The Appeal of Southern Literature," *MissQ,* XVII (1964), 208–18.

Heilman, Robert B., "The Southern Literary Temper," in Rubin and Jacobs, eds., *Southern Renascence,* pp. 3–13.

Henderson, Archibald, "Democracy and Literature," *SAQ,* XII (1913), 97–108.

Henneman, John Bell, "Ten Years of the *Sewanee Review:* A Retrospect," *SeR,* X (1902), 477–92.

──────, "The National Element in Southern Literature," *SeR,* XI (1903), 345–66.

Hibbard, Addison, ed., *The Lyric South: An Anthology of Recent Poetry from the South* (New York, 1928).

Holliday, Carl, "One Phase of Literary Conditions in the South," *SeR,* XI (1903), 463–66.

──────, "Southern Poets of Today," *SAQ,* IX (1910), 63–67.

Holman, C. Hugh, "Ellen Glasgow and the Southern Literary Tradition" in *Southern Writers: Appraisal in Our Time,* ed. Simonini, pp. 103–23.

──────, "The Novel in the South" in *A Time of Harvest: American Literature, 1910–1960,* ed. Robert E. Spiller (New York, 1962).

Holman, Harriet R., "Chivalry's Last Stand: Some Comment on American Fiction, 1900–1920," *GaR,* X (1956), 161–67.

Howells, William Dean, "In Charleston," *Harper's,* CXXXI (1915), 747–57.

Hubbell, Jay B., "The Decay of the Provinces: A Study of Nationalism and Sectionalism in American Literature," *SeR,* XXXV (1927), 473–87.

──────, "The Passing of the New South, 1901–1920," *The South in American Literature,* pp. 839–46.

"John Bennett [Autobiography]" *Carolinian,* XLVII (1939), 4.

Johnson, G. W., "Southern Image-Breakers," *VQR,* IV (1928), 508–19.

──────, "The South Takes the Offensive," *Amer Mercury,* II (May 1924), 70–78.

Jones, H. M., "Is There a Southern Renaissance?" *VQR,* VI (1930), 184–97.

Knickerbocker, William S., "Asides and Soliloquies: *The Sewanee Review,*" *SeR,* XXXVIII (1930), 1–4.

──────, "Trent at Sewanee," *SeR,* XLVIII (1940), 145–52.

──────, "Up from the South," *WR,* XIII (1949), 168–78. [comment on the *SeR*]

Lee, C. P., "Decline and Death of the Southern Gentlemen [in fiction]," *SWR,* XXXVI (1951), 164–70.

Lit Digest, "Slighting Southern Literature," XLVI (1913), 1224–26.

McCormick, Virginia Taylor, "Is Poetry a Live Issue in the South?" *SeR,* XXXVII (1929), 399–406.

Mabie, H. W., "The Poetry of the South," *International Monthly,* V (1902), 200–23.

Marcosson, I. F., "The South in Fiction: Kentucky and Tennessee," *Bookman*, XXXII (1910), 360–70.

Markham, Edwin, "Archibald Henderson," *SeR*, XXVI (1918), 468–73.

Maurice, Arthur Bartlett, "Irvin S. Cobb," *Bookman*, LXIX (1929), 511–14.

Mazyck, William G., "The Charleston Museum, Its Genesis and Development," *Charleston Year Book* (1907), pp. 13–36.

Mims, Edwin, "Early Years of the *South Atlantic Quarterly*," *SAQ*, LI (1952), 33–63.

———, "The Function of Criticism in the South," *SAQ*, II (1903), 334–45; XXXI (1932), 133–49.

Monroe, Harriet, "Southern Shrines," *Poetry*, XVIII (1921), 91–96.

———, "This Southern Number," *Poetry*, XX (1922), 31–34.

Moss, Margaret Anne, "Miss Millie Rutherford, Southerner," *GaR*, VII (1953), 57–66.

Moses, Montrose J., "The South in Fiction: The Trail of the Lower South," *Bookman*, XXXIII (1911), 161–72.

Morrison, M. B., "Poetry of the Southern United States," *Westminster R*, CLXXVI (July 1911), 61–72.

Munson, Gorham, "*The Sewanee Review* from 1892 to 1930," *SeR*, XL (1932), 1–4.

O'Connor, Norreys J., "Ireland's Literary Revival and Regional Writing," *GaR*, I (1947), 420–26.

Peckham, H. Houston, "Some Recent Southern Verse," *SAQ*, XIV (1915), 181–85.

Peterkin, Julia, "One Southern View-Point," *NoAmerR*, CCXLIV (1937–38), 389–98.

Pratt, Julius W., "Recent Poetry by North Carolina Writers," *SAQ*, XVII (1918), 40–43.

———, "The Cumberland Mountains in Verse," *SAQ*, XVII (1918), 217–21.

Rawlings, Marjorie Kinnan, "Regional Literature of the South," *Coll Eng*, I (1940), 381–89.

Rea, Paul Marshall, "Our First American Museum [Charleston]," *Museum Work*, V (1923), 87–88.

Richardson, E. R., "The South Grows Up," *Bookman*, LXX (1930), 545–50.

Rollins, Hyder E., "The Negro in the Southern Short Story," *SeR*, XXIV (1916), 42–60.

Rubin, Louis D., Jr., "A Looking Two Ways," *Shen*, VI, iii (1955), 19–28.

———, "H. L. Mencken and the National Letters," *SeR*, LXXIV (1966), 723–38. Repr in *The Curious Death of the Novel*, pp. 100–19.

———, *No Place on Earth: Ellen Glasgow, James Branch Cabell and Richmond-in-Virginia* (Austin, Tex., 1959).

———, "The Historical Image of Modern Southern Writing," *JSH*, XXII (1956), 147–66.

Shearin, Hubert G., "British Ballads in the Cumberland Mountains," *SeR*, XIX (1911), 313–27.

Sherman, C. B., "Farm Life Fiction in the South," *SLM, n.s.*, I (1939), 203–10.

———, "Rural Poetry in the South," *SLM, n.s.*, I (1939), 461–65.

Shyrock, R. H., "Cultural Factors in the History of the South," *JSH*, V (1939), 333–46.

Simkins, Francis Butler, "The Everlasting South," *JSH*, XIII (1947), 307–22.

Smith, C. Alphonso, "The Possibilities of the South in Literature," *SeR*, VI (1908), 298–305.

Smythe, Augustine T., "The Hibernian Society: The Song and the Toast," *Charleston Year Book* (1901), 39–40.

Snyder, Henry N., "The Matter of 'Southern Literature,' " *SeR*, XV (1907), 218–26.

———, "The Reconstruction of Southern Literary Thought," *SAQ*, I (1902), 145–55.

Spencer, Benjamin T., "Nationality During the Interregnum (1892–1912)," *AL*, XXXII (1961), 434–45.

————, "Wherefore This Southern Fiction?" *SeR*, XLVII (1939), 500–13.

Stephenson, Wendell H., "William P. Trent as a Historian of the South," *JSH*, XV (1949), 151–77.

Strong, Katherine H., "The Poetry Society of Georgia," *GaR*, VIII (1954), 29–40.

Talmadge, John E., "Corra Harris Goes to War," *GaR*, XVIII (1964), 150–56.

Tate, Allen, "The Profession of Letters in the South," *VQR*, XI (1935), 161–76.

Tate, William, "A Neighbor's Recollections of Corra Harris," *GaR*, V (1951), 22–33.

Thompson, Lawrence S., "Bluegrass and Bourbon: The Colonel of Kentucky Fiction," *GaR*, VII, (1953), 107–15.

————, "Books in Foreign Languages about South Carolina, 1900–1950," *S.C. Hist Mag*, LIV (1953), 70–74.

Tindall, George B., "The Benighted South: Origins of a Modern Image," *VQR*, XL (1964), 281–94.

Townsend, John W., "A History of Kentucky Literature Since 1913," *Filson Club Hist Q*, XIII (1939), 21–26.

*Turnbull, Robert J., *Bibliography of South Carolina,1563–1950*, 5 vols (Charlottesville, 1956).

Turner, Arlin, "The Southern Novel," *SWR*, XXV (1940), 205–12.

Van Auken, Sheldon, "The Southern Historical Novel in the Early Twentieth Century," *JSH*, XIV (1948), 157–91.

Walcutt, Charles C., "Regionalism—Practical or Aesthetic?" *SeR*, XLIX (1941), 165–72.

Whittington, Joseph Richard, "The Regional Novel of the South: The Definition of Innocence," *DA*, XXIV (1964), 4202–203 (Oklahoma).

Wilcox, L. C., "The South in Fiction: Virginia," *Bookman*, XXXIII (1911), 44–58.

*Woodward, C. Vann, *Origins of the New South* (Baton Rouge, 1951), pp. 162–69, 429–36, *513–15.

Wright, Louis B., "Myth-Makers and the South's Dilemma," *SeR*, LIII (1945), 544–58.

Zucker, A. E., "Southern Critics of 1903 on Ibsen's *Ghosts*," *PhilQ*, XIX (1940), 392–99.

CLAUD B. GREEN
Clemson University
Clemson, South Carolina

THE SOUTHERN RENASCENCE, 1925-1945

Scholarship on the literature of the Southern Renascence might well be classified by decades. In the 1920s there was an attempt, often uncritical and amateurish, to list Southern writers in order to show that there was significant literary activity in the South. Undoubtedly motivating these early commentators was the desire to correct the prevailing view, promulgated by H. L. Mencken's classic attack, "The Sahara of the Bozart," that the South was a literary wasteland. It is with this indictment of Southern culture and with the first attempts to reply to it that a survey of the scholarship on the Southern literary Renascence must begin. The essay by Hershel Brickell (*Bookman*, 1927) was one of the first to pose the question as to whether an actual renascence in Southern letters was occurring. Most of the writers mentioned in these early articles would now be regarded as minor, but there was, surprisingly, some awareness as early as the late 1920s of the first works of William Faulkner and of the poetry of the Nashville Fugitives. For the intentions of the Nashville group during this period, Louise Cowan's study is basic.

From the early 1930s down to World War II, one of the chief concerns of commentators on Southern literature was with the concept of regionalism and the contributions of Southern writers to an authentic regional literature. The writings of the University of North Carolina sociologists (although anathema to the Vanderbilt Agrarians), especially those of Howard W. Odum, are essential to an understanding of regionalism. For the Southern Agrarians the chief spokesman exalting regionalism was Donald Davidson. But the best article cautioning against the dangers of extreme regionalism in writing was written by Robert Penn Warren ("Some Don'ts for Literary Regionalists").

Since World War II, discussions of Southern writing during the 1920s, 1930s, and 1940s have been more concerned with discerning shared characteristics and attitudes among Southern writers and describing distinctive Southern qualities in their writings than in merely enumerating Southern authors and books. The most significant articles illustrating this new interest in Southern writing were published in *Southern Renascence* (1953) and in *South* (1961), both edited by Louis D. Rubin, Jr., and Robert D. Jacobs.

Another scholarly concern has been with the Nashville Group, as Fugitives, Agrarians, and New Critics. Basic studies of these writers by John Bradbury, Louise Cowan, and John L. Stewart are essential. But a disproportionate share of this concern has been with their social agrarianism rather than with their literary contributions.

It should be added that although Faulkner items *per se* are excluded
from this list, there is a considerable body of literature (listed elsewhere
in this volume) on Faulkner and the South and on the influence,
direct and indirect, of Faulkner on other Southern writers which should
not be ignored by anyone interested in the Southern Renascence.

Allen, Hervey, and DuBose Heyward, "Poetry South," *Poetry*, XX (April 1922), 35–37.
Allen, Walter, *The Modern Novel in Britain and the United States* (New York, 1964),
    pp. 138–87, 293–332.
Angoff, Allan, ed., *American Writing Today: Its Independence and Vigor* (New York,
    1957), pp. 71–80. Repr of "The Southern Revival: A Land and Its Interpreters,"
    in [London] *TLS* issue on Amer writing.
Bamberg, Robert Douglas, "Plantation and Frontier: A View of Southern Fiction,"
    DA, XXII 1973–74 (Cornell).
Barr, Stringfellow, "The Uncultured South," *VQR*, V (1929), 192–200.
Basso, Hamilton, "Letters in the South," *New Rep*, LXXXIII (June 19, 1935), 161–63.
Beasley, William M., "The New South and Five Southern Novelists (1920–1950)," *DA*,
    XVIII, 210–11 (Vanderbilt).
Bishop, John Peale, "The South and Tradition," *VQR*, IX (1933), 161–74.
*Bonner, John W., Jr., "Bibliography of Georgia Authors," *GaR* (Winter 1950——).
Bowyer, J. W., "Conflict in the South," *SWR*, XXVIII (1943), 252–66.
Boynton, Percy H., *America in Contemporary Fiction* (Chicago, 1940), pp. 103–12.
*Bradbury, John M., *The Fugitives: A Critical Account* (Chapel Hill, 1958).
*———, *Renaissance in the South*. [appendix lists So authors by states]
Bradley, Sculley, "The Renaissance in Poetry," in *A Time of Harvest: American Lit-
    erature, 1910–1960*, ed. Robert E. Spiller (New York, 1962), pp. 21–32.
Brickell, Hershel, "The Literary Awakening in the South," *Bookman*, LXVI (1927),
    138–43. [one of first statements that there was a So Renascence, citing Faulkner,
    Stark Young, Ransom, Tate, Cabell as proof]
Brooks, Cleanth, "The Modern Southern Poet and Tradition," *VQR*, XI (1935), 305–20.
———, "What Deep South Literature Needs," *SatR*, XXV (Sept 19, 1942), 8–9, 29.
———, "The New Criticism: A Brief for the Defense," *Amer Schol*, XIII (1944),
    285–95.
———, "Regionalism in American Literature," *JSH*, XXVI (1960), 35–43.
———, "Southern Literature: The Wellsprings of Its Vitality," *GaR*, XVI (1962),
    238–53.
Burger, N. K., "Story to Tell: Agee, Wolfe, Faulkner," *SAQ*, LXIII (1964), 32–43.
Calhoun, Richard James, "The New Criticism: Ten Years After," *SoAtlBull*, XXVII
    (Nov 1961), 1–7.
Calverton, V. F., "The Bankruptcy of Southern Culture," *Scribner's*, XCIX (1936),
    294–98.
Campbell, Harry M., "Notes on Religion in the Southern Renascence," *Shen*, V (Win-
    ter 1953), 10–18.
Carter, Hodding, "The South and Writing, 1953," *Shen*, V (Winter 1953), 9–12. [relates
    So writing to frontier spirit and to importance given the spoken word]
———, "Why We Write in the South," in *Literature in the Modern World: Lectures
    Delivered at George Peabody College for Teachers, 1951–1954*, ed. John Mason
    Brown, et al (Nashville, 1956), pp. 135–44.
Cash, W. J., "Literature and the South," *Sat R*, XXIII (Dec. 28, 1940), 3–4, 18–19.

Cater, Catherine, "Myth and the Contemporary Southern Novelist: A Note," *Midw Jour*, II (Winter 1949), 1–8.

Clark, Emily, *Innocence Abroad* (New York, 1931). [on editing *The Reviewer*]

Couch, W. T., "Reflections on the Southern Tradition," *SAQ*, XXXV (1936), 284–97.

Cowan, Louise, *The Fugitive Group: A Literary History* (Baton Rouge, 1959). [definitive hist of mag]

———, "The Communal World of Southern Literature," *GaR*, XIV (1960), 248–57.

———, "The Pietas of Southern Poetry," in *South*, pp. 95–114.

Cox, H. Morris, "The Charleston Poetic Renascence, 1920–1930," *DA*, XVIII, 1797 (Pennsylvania).

Daiches, David, "The New Criticism," in *A Time of Harvest: American Literature, 1910–1960*, pp. 95–110.

Davidson, Donald, "A Mirror for Artists," in *I'll Take My Stand: The South and the Agrarian Tradition*, by Twelve Southerners (New York and London, 1930), pp. 28–60. Repr with intro by Louis D. Rubin, Jr. (New York, 1962). [discussion of "special blessings" of So artist as provincial]

———, "The Trend of Literature," in *Culture in the South*, ed. W. T. Couch (Chapel Hill, 1934), pp. 183–210.

———, "The Southern Poet and His Tradition," *Poetry*, XL (May 1932), 94–103. Repr in *The Attack on Leviathan: Regionalism and Nationalism in the United States* (Chapel Hill, 1938), pp. 339–48.

———, "Sectionalism in America," *Hound and Horn*, VI (July 1933), 561–89.

———, "Regionalism and Nationalism in American Literature," *Still Rebels, Still Yankees* (Baton Rouge, 1957), pp. 267–78. [important attempt to define function of regional lit]

———, "Regionalism in the Arts," *The Attack on Leviathan* (Chapel Hill, 1938), pp. 65–101.

———, "The Talking Oaks of the South," *Shen*, V (Winter 1953), 3–8. [on characteristics of So writing]

———, "Why the Modern South Has a Great Literature," *Still Rebels, Still Yankees*, pp. 159–79.

———, *Southern Writers in the Modern World* (Athens, Ga., 1958). [Lamar Lectures]

Davis, R. G., "New Criticism and the Democratic Tradition," *Amer Schol*, XIX (1950), 9–19.

Durham, Frank, "South Carolina's Poetry Society," *SAQ*, LII (1953), 277–85.

Durrett, Frances B., "The New Orleans Double Dealer," *Reality and Myth*, pp. 212–36.

Elton, William, "A Glossary of the New Criticism," *Poetry*, LXXIII (1948–49), 153–62, 232–45. Repr as *A Guide to the New Criticism* (Chicago, 1951). [best definitions of the crit terminology of New Crit]

England, Kenneth, "The Decline of the Southern Gentleman Character as He Is Illustrated in Certain Novels by Present-Day Southern Novelists," *DA*, XVII, 2594 (Vanderbilt).

Ezell, John Samuel, *The South Since 1865* (New York, 1963), pp. 277–95. [chap on "The Southern Literary Renaissance"]

Feibleman, James K., "Literary New Orleans Between the World Wars," *SoR*, n.s., I (1965), 702–19.

Fletcher, J. G., "The Modern Southern Poets," *Westminster Mag*, XXIII (1935), 229–51.

Fletcher, Marie, "The Southern Heroine in Fiction of Representative Southern Women Writers 1850–1960," *DA*, XXIV, 1159–60 (Louisiana).

Foster, Richard J., *The New Romantics: A Reappraisal of the New Criticism* (Bloomington, Ind., 1962). [attempt to point out hidden romanticism in important New Crit]

Frazier, Annie C. M., "The South Speaks Out," *SeR*, XXXV (1927), 313–24. [renascence of lit activity in So periodicals]

Garlington, Jack, "The Decadent South," *ColoQ*, IX (Summer 1960), 59–62. [crit of tradition of lit of decadence]

Glasgow, Ellen, "The Novel in the South," *Harper's*, CLVIII (1928), 93–100. [early attempt to define distinctive qualities of So writers]

———, "Heroes and Monsters," *SatR*, XII (May 4, 1935), 3–4. [So Gothic in mod So writers]

———, *A Certain Measure* (New York, 1943). [description of how Va. materials were used by lit artist]

Glenn, Eunice, "Southern Writing Today," *Amer Ltrs*, I (June 1949), 2–10.

*Grantham, D. W., Jr., "Interpreters of the Modern South," *SAQ*, LXIII (1964), 521–29.

Gregory, Horace, and Marya Zaturenska, *A History of American Poetry, 1900–1940* (New York, 1942), pp. 360–86. [Ransom, Tate, Warren, Laura Riding]

Handy, William J., "Science, Literature, and Modern Criticism," *TQ*, I, No. 2 (1958), 147–56. [discusses Ransom, Tate, Brooks]

*———, *Kant and the Southern New Critics* (Austin, Tex., 1963).

Hardy, John Edward, "Poets and Critics," *South*, pp. 260–75.

Harrington, Catherine Steta, "Southern Fiction and the Quest for Identity," *DA*, XXV, 1210–11 (Washington).

Hazel, Robert, "The Southern Writer and His Region," in *The Lasting South: Fourteen Southerners Look at Their Home*, ed. Louis D. Rubin, Jr., and James Jackson Kilpatrick (Chicago, 1957), pp. 171–80.

Heald, William F., "The Appeal of Southern Literature," *MissQ*, XXVII (1964), 208–18.

Heilman, Robert B., "The Southern Temper," in *Southern Renascence*, pp. 3–13. Repr also in *South*, both ed. Rubin and Jacobs, pp. 48–54.

Heyward, DuBose, "Contemporary Southern Poetry," *Bookman*, LXII (1926), 561–64. [Charleston's interest in a So Renascence]

*Hoffman, Frederick J., Charles Allen, and Carolyn Ulrich, *The Little Magazine: A History and a Bibliography* (Princeton, 1946). [survey of 500 little mags of the 20th cent, with extensive bibl]

Hoffman, *The Art of Southern Fiction*.

*———, *The Modern Novel in America 1900–1950* (Chicago, 1951), pp. 155–70. ["Violence and Rhetoric"—brief discussion of these elements in mod So lit]

———. "The Sense of Place," in *South*, pp. 60–75.

———, "The Southern Past" and "The Affair of Dayton, Tenn.," *The Twenties: American Writing in the Postwar Decade*, rev ed (New York, 1965), pp. 172–81, 309–15.

Holman, C. Hugh, "The Defense of Art: Criticism since 1930," in *Development of American Literary Criticism*, ed. Floyd Stovall (Chapel Hill, 1955), pp. 199–245.

———, "The Southerner as American Writer," in *The Southerner as American*, ed. Charles Grier Sellers, Jr. (Chapel Hill, 1960), pp. 180–99.

———, "The Novel in the South," in *A Time of Harvest: American Literature, 1910–1960*, ed. R. E. Spiller, pp. 83–94.

———, "Ellen Glasgow and the Southern Literary Tradition," in *Southern Writers:* ed. Simonini, pp. 103–23.

*———, *Three Modes of Southern Fiction: Ellen Glasgow, William Faulkner, Thomas Wolfe* (Athens, Ga., 1966).

Howe, Irving, "The South and Current Literature," *Amer Mercury*, LXVII (1948), 494–503.

Hubbell, Jay B., "Southern Magazines," in *Culture in the South*, pp. 159–82.

———, "The Southern Literary Renaissance," *South and Southwest: Literary Essays and Reminiscences* (Durham, 1965), pp. 73–89.

Jarrell, Randall, "Fifty Years of American Poetry," *Prairie Schooner*, XXXVII, No. 1 (1963), 1–27.

Johnson, G. W., "The Horrible South," *VQR*, XI (1935), 201–17.

Jones, H. M., "Is There a Southern Literary Renaissance?" *VQR*, VI (1930), 184–97.

———, "The Future of Southern Culture," *SWR*, XVI (1931), 141–65.

Kazin, Alfred, *On Native Grounds: An Interpretation of Modern American Prose Literature* (New York, 1942), pp. 453–84. [chap 15, "The Rhetoric and the Agony"]

*Krieger, Murray, *The New Apologists for Poetry* (Minneapolis, 1956).

*Kunitz and Haycroft, eds., *Twentieth Century Authors: A Bibliographical Dictionary of Modern Literature*. [see also 1st supp, 1952]

Lewis, C. L., "What Is a Southern Book?" *SLM*, n.s., III (1941), 194–96.

*Lively, Robert A., *Fiction Fights the Civil War: An Unfinished Chapter in the Literary History of the American People* (Chapel Hill, 1957), pp. 166–88.

Lytle, Andrew, "The Working Novelist and the Myth-making Process," *Daedalus*, LXXXVIII (1959), 326–38. [how *The Velvet Horn* came to present its picture of the So]

McIlwaine, Shields, *The Southern Poor-White from Lubberland to Tobacco Road* (Norman, Okla., 1939), pp. 169–240. [poor-white as treated in mod So lit]

McLuhan, H. M., "The Southern Quality," in *A Southern Vanguard*, ed. Allen Tate (New York, 1947), pp. 100–21.

Matthiessen, F. O., "American Poetry 1920–1940," *SeR*, LV (1947), 24–55. Repr in *LHUS*, I, pp. 1335–57.

Mencken, J. L., "The Sahara of the Bozart," *A Mencken Chrestomathy, Edited and Annotated by the Author* (New York, 1949), pp. 184–94. Also in *Prejudices: Second Series* (New York, 1920), pp. 136–54.

*Meriwether, James B., "For Further Reading: A Selected Checklist," in *South*, pp. 392–433.

Montesi, A. J., "*The Southern Review* (1935–1942)," *Chicago R*, XVI, No. 4 (1964), 201–12.

Montgomery, Marion, "The Sense of Violation: Notes Toward a Definition of 'Southern Fiction," *GaR*, XIX (1965), 278–87.

Odum, Howard W., and Harry Estill Moore, *American Regionalism: A Cultural-Historical Approach to National Integration* (New York, 1938), pp. 168–87. [summary of arguments in 1930s for and against concept of regional lit, with emphasis on So lit]

———, *Southern Regions of the United States* (Chapel Hill, 1936), pp. 207–44. [classic social survey of So during 1930s]

———, and John Maclachlan, "Literature in the South: An Exchange of Views," in *Southern Renascence*, pp. 83–111.

Ong, W. J., "The Meaning of the 'New Criticism,'" *Mod Schoolman*, XX (1943), 192–209.

*Parks, Edd Winfield, *Southern Poets* (New York, 1936), pp. xxviii–lxxxii, cxxiii–cxxix.

———, *Segments of Southern Thought* (Athens, Ga., 1938), pp. 70–74, 113–20, 129–35.

Peden, William, *The American Short Story: Front Line in the National Defense of Literature* (Boston, 1964), pp. 162–78. [on regional writers, including So]

Polk, William T., *Southern Accent: From Uncle Remus to Oak Ridge* (New York,

1953), pp. 201–27. [chap on "Main Currents in Southern Thought"]

*Pratt, William, *The Fugitive Poets: Modern Southern Poetry in Perspective*, pp. 13–46.

Purdy, Rob Roy, ed., *Fugitives' Reunion: Conversations at Vanderbilt, May 3–5, 1956.* Intro by Louis D. Rubin, Jr. (Nashville, 1959).

*Quinn, Arthur Hobson, et al, eds., *The Literature of the American People: An Historical and Critical Survey* (New York, 1951), pp. 914–26.

Raiziss, Sona, *The Metaphysical Passion: Some Modern American Poets and the Seventeenth-Century Tradition* (Philadelphia, 1952), pp. 184–211. [The Fugitives]

Raleigh, John Henry, "The New Criticism as an Historical Phenomenon," *Comp Lit*, XI (1959), 21–28.

Ransom, John Crowe, "Modern with the Southern Accent," *VQR*, XI (1935), 184–200. [chiefly on fict but last two pages on So poetry]

Rawlings, Majorie Kinnan, "Regional Literature of the South," *Coll Eng*, I (1940), 381–89.

Richardson, E. R., "The South Grows Up," *Bookman*, LXX (1930), 545–50. [Glasgow, Cabell, Heyward, Green, Stribling, Peterkin cited as examples of lit flowering in So]

Rovit, Earl H., "The Region Versus the Nation: Critical Battle of the Thirties," *MissQ*, XIII (1960), 90–98.

Rubin, Louis D., Jr., "The Historical Image of Modern Southern Writing," *JSH*, XXII (1956), 147–66. Also in *South*, pp. 29–47. [how So writers judge present by view of past]

―――, "The Concept of Nature in Southern Poetry," *AmerQ*, LXIII (1957), 63–71.

―――, "The Southern Muse: Two Poetry Societies," *AmerQ*, XIII (1961), 365–75. [comparison of Fugitives and Poetry Soc of S.C. during 1920s]

―――, "The South and the Faraway Country," *VQR*, XXXVIII (1962), 444–59. [perspective gained by So writers as they leave and return to So]

―――, *The Faraway Country:* [essays on Cable, Faulkner, Wolfe, Warren, Welty, Styron, and Agrarian poets]

―――, "The Literature of the Changing South," in *The Deep South in Transformation*, ed. Robert B. Highsaw (Lexington, Ky., 1964), pp. 147–61. Also comments by Carl Benson, Hudson Strode, and Walter Sullivan, pp. 161–75.

―――, "The Image of an Army: The Civil War in Southern Fiction," in *Southern Writers*, ed. Simonini, pp. 124–41.

―――, "Notes on the Literary Scene: Their Own Language," *Harper's*, CCXXX (Apr 1965), 173–75. [primarily on literature of 1960s but attempts to show how younger So novelists differ from older contemporaries]

―――, "Four Southerners," in *American Poetry*, ed. J. R. Brown, B. Harris, Irwin Ehrenpreis (London, 1963; New York, 1966), pp. 11–43. [Ransom, Davidson, Tate, Warren]

Rubin and Jacobs, intro to *South*, pp. 11–28.

Scholes, Robert E., "The Modern American Novel and the Mason-Dixon Line," *GaR*, XIV (1960), 193–204. [No and So approaches to novel contrasted]

Simkins, Francis Butler, *A History of the South*, 3rd ed (New York, 1965), pp. 426–54. [very gen survey of So lit since Civil War]

Spencer, B. T., "Wherefore This Southern Fiction?" *SeR*, XLVII (1939), 500–13.

*Spiller, et al, eds., *LHUS*. See bibl in II, 149–72, 308–16, and *Supp*. pp. 23–28, 63.

Stallman, Robert Wooster, "The New Criticism and the Southern Critics," in *A Southern Vanguard*, ed. Allen Tate (New York, 1947), pp. 28–51.

Stewart, John L., *The Burden of Time: The Fugitives and Agrarians* (Princeton, 1965). [critique of philos assumptions of New Crit]

Stewart, Randall, ed., "The Southern Literary Renascence: A Symposium," *Shen*, VI (Spring, 1955), 3–36. [intro and four papers: Louise Cowan, "The Fugitive Poets in Relation to the South"; Harry M. Campbell, "Notes on Religion in the Southern Renascence"; Louis D. Rubin, Jr., "A Looking Two Ways"; Andrew N. Lytle, "A Summing Up"]

———, "Outlook for Southern Writing: Diagnosis and Prognosis," *VQR*, XXXI (1955), 252–63. Repr in George Core, ed., *Regionalism and Beyond: Essays of Randall Stewart* (Nashville, Tenn., 1968), pp. 255–66. [Writers of 1950s viewed in relation to So Renascence]

———, "Tidewater and Frontier," *GaR*, XIII (1959), 296–307. [two traditions evidenced in writings of So Renascence]

Sullivan, Walter, "Southern Novelists and the Civil War," in *Southern Renascence*, pp. 112–25. [Tate, Lytle, Gordon, Young, Faulkner]

Tate, Allen, "American Poetry Since 1920," *Bookman*, LXVIII (1929), 503–508.

———, "The Profession of Letters in the South," *VQR*, XI (1935), 161–76. Repr in *Collected Essays* (Denver, 1959), pp. 265–81.

*———, *Sixty American Poets—1896–1944* (Washington, D.C., 1945; rev ed, 1954).

———, "The New Provincialism," *VQR*, XXI (1945), 262–72. Repr in *Collected Essays*, pp. 282–93.

———, "Random Thoughts on the 1920's," *MinnR*, I (Fall 1960), 45–56. [includes observations on So lit and culture of period]

———, "A Southern Mode of the Imagination, Circa 1918 to the Present," *Carleton Misc*, I, No. 1 (1960), 9–23. Repr in *Studies in American Culture: Dominant Ideas and Images*, ed. Joseph J. Kwiat and Mary C. Turpie (Minneapolis, 1960).

*Thornton, Mary Lindsay, et al, "North Carolina Bibliography," *N.C. Hist R* (1934—).

*Thorp, Willard, *American Writing in the Twentieth Century* (Cambridge, Mass., 1960), pp. 233–75.

———, "The Southern Mode," *SAQ*, LXIII (1964), 576–82. [r essay with pertinent comments on So Renascence]

Tindall, George B., "The Benighted South: Origins of a Modern Image," *VQR*, XL (1964), 281–94. [image of So in the 1920s]

*———, *The Emergence of the New South, 1913–1945* (Baton Rouge, 1967), pp. 285–317, 650–86.

Turner, Arlin, "The Southern Novel," *SWR*, XXV (1940), 205–12.

Vance, Rupert B., *Human Geography of the South* (Chapel Hill, 1932), pp. 20–76. [sect on environmental and cultural backgrounds in classic study of people of So]

Warren, Robert Penn, "Not Local Color," *VQR*, VIII (1932), 153–60.

———, "Note on Three Southern Poets," *Poetry*, XL (May 1932), 103–13.

———, "Some Don'ts for Literary Regionalists," *AmerR*, VIII (Dec 1936), 142–50.

Weaver, Richard M., "Aspects of the Southern Philosophy," in *Southern Renascence*, pp. 14–30.

———, "Contemporary Southern Literature," *TQ*, II (Summer 1959), 126–44.

Wells, Henry W., *The American Way of Poetry* (New York, 1943), pp. 161–73.

Westbrook, John T., "Twilight of Southern Regionalism," *SWR*, XLIII (1957), 231–34.

Wittemore, Reed, *Little Magazines* (Minneapolis, 1963). [Minn pamph]

Whittington, Joseph Richard, "The Regional Novel of the South: The Definition of Innocence," *DA*, XXIV, 4202–203 (Oklahoma). [Faulkner, Warren, Welty, Gordon, others]

Woodward, C. Vann, "The Historical Dimension," *VQR*, XXXII (1956), 258–67.

[historian's interest in hist consciousness of So writers after 1930]

————, "The Irony of Southern History," in *The Burden of Southern History*, rev ed (Baton Rouge, 1968), pp. 187–242; also in *Southern Renascence*, pp. 63–82.

Wright, Louis B., "Myth-Makers and the South's Dilemma," *SeR*, LIII (1945), 544–58. [myths created by So writers]

RICHARD JAMES CALHOUN
Clemson University
Clemson, South Carolina

SOUTHERN WRITING SINCE 1945

Although 1940 or 1945 is regularly accepted as the dividing year between the first and second generations of the Southern Renascence, studies of writers belonging to either generation reflect similar concerns: What influences—literary or non-literary—account for Southern creativity? What qualities identify Southern writing? What use do writers make of time and place? What themes may the presence or the absence of manners stimulate? Now questions being raised specifically about younger writers ask how they respond to swift social changes, how they incorporate or reject the influence of William Faulkner, and how they qualify as important artists.

The standard access to modern Southern writing remains *Southern Renascence*, edited by Louis D. Rubin, Jr., and Robert D. Jacobs. The essays attempting to define the mind of the South and its literary expression provide background for considering the merits of subsequent literature. These essays are supplemented by *South: Modern Southern Literature in Its Cultural Setting*, which includes four essays originally in *Southern Renascence*. An extension of these considerations is Rubin's *The Faraway Country*, with introductory and concluding chapters which discuss the detachment of Southern writers from their community and speculate briefly on future directions. In these three books the authors who are examined are those generally included in the Southern canon.

Frederick Hoffman in *The Art of Southern Fiction* considers Southern writers from 1925 to 1960 as a single generation. In addition to dealing with writers already widely studied, such as Robert Penn Warren, Eudora Welty, and Katherine Anne Porter, he devotes a chapter to history in Southern fiction (Lytle, Humphrey, etc.) and to fantasy (Capote, Goyen, etc.).

John Bradbury in *Renaissance in the South* classifies and evaluates fiction, poetry, and drama by some five hundred Southerners substantial enough to be published by reputable presses. In two hundred pages, he includes abbreviated biographical references, summaries, and judgments in a running commentary of literary history. A list of Southern Renascence authors by states precedes the index.

The only book-length discussion specifically about the post-1945 writers as such is Louise Y. Gossett, *Violence in Modern Southern Fiction*, in which a number of authors are discussed as Southern writers.

Current essays about Southern writing increasingly reflect an interest in the relationship between the regional context and international literature.

Bradbury, *Renaissance in the South*, pp. 107–202.

Breyer, Bernard R., "A Diagnosis of Violence in Recent Southern Fiction," *MissQ*, XIV (1961), 59–67.

Brooks, Cleanth, "Regionalism in American Literature," *JSH*, XXVI (1960), 35–43.

Calhoun, Richard J., "Southern Voices: Past and Present," *SoR*, n. s., IV (1968), 482–490.

Carter, Hodding, "Why We Write in the South," in *Literature in the Modern World: Lectures Delivered at George Peabody College for Teachers, 1951–1954*, ed. John Mason Brown et al (Nashville, 1954), pp. 135–44.

_____, "The South and Writing, 1953," *Shen*, V (Winter 1953), 9–12.

Cater, Catherine, "Myth and the Contemporary Southern Novelist: A Note," *Midw Jour*, II (Winter 1949), 1–8.

Corrington, John William, and Miller Williams, eds., *Southern Writing in the Sixties: Fiction* (Baton Rouge, 1966). [anthol includes work of 20 younger writers, intro interesting but controversial]

_____, eds., *Southern Writing in the Sixties: Poetry* (Baton Rouge, 1967). [anthol]

Dabbs, James M., *Who Speaks for the South?* (New York, 1965).

Davidson, Donald, "The Southern Writers and the Modern University," *GaR*, XII (1957), 18–28.

_____, *Southern Writers in the Modern World* (Athens, Ga., 1958). [Lamar Lectures]

*Eisinger, Chester E., *Fiction of the Forties* (Chicago, 1963), pp. 146–283.

Ford, Jesse Hill, "To a Young Southern Writer," *SoR*, n.s., IV (1968), 291–98.

Fuller, Edmund, *Man in Modern Fiction: Some Minority Opinions on Contemporary American Writing* (New York, 1958).

Gossett, *Violence in Recent Southern Fiction*.

Grantham, Dewey W., Jr., "Interpreters of the Modern South," *SAQ*, LXIII (1964), 521–29. [cultural hist and autobiog]

Harrington, Catherine Steta, "Southern Fiction and the Quest for Identity," *DA*, XXV, 1, 210–11 (Washington).

Hassan, Ihab H., "The Victim: Images of Evil in Recent American Fiction," *Coll Eng*, XXI (1959), 140–46.

Hazel, Robert, "The Southern Writer and His Region," in *The Lasting South*, ed. Louis D. Rubin, Jr., and James J. Kilpatrick (Chicago, 1957), pp. 171–80.

*Hoffman, *The Art of Southern Fiction*.

Holman, C. Hugh, "The Southerner as American Writer," in *The Southerner as American*, ed. Charles G. Sellers, Jr. (Chapel Hill, 1960), pp. 180–99.

Howe, Irving, "The South and Current Literature," *Amer Mercury*, LXVII (1948), 494–503.

Lawson, Lewis Allen, "The Grotesque in Recent Southern Fiction," *DA*, XXV, 2514 (Wisconsin).

Leatherman, LeRoy, "The Artist as Southerner," *SatR*, LXX (1962). 164-69. [r essay]

Malin, Irving, *New American Gothic* (Carbondale, Ill., 1962).

Meeker, Richard K., ed., *The Dilemma of the Southern Writer: Institute of Southern Culture Lectures* (Farmville, Va., 1961).

Montgomery, Marion, "The Sense of Violation: Notes Toward a Definition of 'Southern' Fiction," *GaR*, XIX (1965), 278–87.

O'Connor, William Van, *The Grotesque: An American Genre and Other Essays* (Carbondale, Ill., 1962), pp. 3–19.

Peden, William, *The American Short Story: Front Line in the National Defense of Literature* (Boston, 1964).

Prescott, Orville, *In My Opinion: An Inquiry into the Contemporary Novel* (Indianapolis, 1952), pp. 110–21.

Recent Southern Fiction: A Panel Discussion, (Macon, Ga., 1961; Bull Wesleyan College). [participants Katherine Anne Porter, Flannery O'Connor, Caroline Gordon, Madison Jones, Louis D. Rubin, Jr.]

Rubin, Louis D., Jr., "The Difficulties of Being a Southern Writer Today; or How to Get Out from under William Faulkner," *JSH*, XXIX (1963), 486–94. Repr in *The Curious Death of the Novel*, pp. 282–93.

———, *The Faraway Country*.

———, "The Historical Image of Modern Southern Writing," *JSH*, XXII (1956), 147–66.

———, "The Literature of a Changing South," in *The Deep South in Transformation*, ed. Robert B. Highsaw (University, Ala., 1964), pp. 147–75. [added commentary by Carl Benson, Hudson Strode, and Walter L. Sullivan]

———, "Their Own Language: Notes on the Literary Scene," *Harper's*, CCXXX (April 1965), 173–75.

*———, and Jacobs, eds., *South*.

———, eds., *Southern Renascence*.

Simonini, ed., *Southern Writers*.

Steele, Frank, intro to Steele, ed., *Poetry Southeast, 1950–1970* (Martin, Tenn., 1968), pp. 7–8.

Stewart, Randall, "The Outlook for Southern Writing: Diagnosis and Prognosis," in George Core, ed., *Regionalism and Beyond: Essays of Randall Stewart* (Nashville, 1968), pp. 255–66.

———, et al, "The Southern Literary Renascence: A Symposium," *Shen*, VI (Summer 1955), 3–36. [foreword and four essays: Louise Cowan, "The Fugitive Poets in Relation to the South"; Harry M. Campbell, "Notes on Religion in the Southern Renascence"; Louis D. Rubin, Jr., "A Looking Two Ways"; Andrew Lytle, "A Summing Up"]

Sullivan, Walter, "The Continuing Renascence: Southern Fiction in the Fifties," in *South*, pp. 376–91.

———, "In Time of the Breaking of Nations: The Decline of Southern Fiction," *SoR*, n.s., IV (1968), 299–305.

Tate, Allen, "The New Provincialism: With an Epilogue on the Southern Novel," *VQR*, XXI (1945), 262–72. Repr in *Collected Essays (Denver, 1959)*, pp. 182–93.

———, "A Southern Mode of the Imagination," in *Studies in American Culture: Dominant Ideas and Images*, ed. Joseph Kwiat and Mary C. Turpie (Minneapolis, 1960), pp. 96–108.

Thorp, Willard, *American Writing in the Twentieth Century* (Cambridge, Mass., 1960), pp. 233–63.

Weaver, Richard, "Contemporary Southern Literature," *TQ*, II (1959), 126–44.

White, Ellington, "The View from the Picture Window: The Southern Writer Today," *Provincial*, I (1957), 2–5. Repr in Louis D. Rubin, Jr., and J. J. Kilpatrick, eds., *The Lasting South* (Chicago, 1957), pp. 163–70.

Woodward, C. Vann, "The Search for Southern Identity," *VQR*, XXXIV, (1958), 321–38. Repr in *The Burden of Southern History*, enlarged ed (Baton Rouge, 1968), pp. 3–25.

LOUISE Y. GOSSETT
Salem College
Winston-Salem, North Carolina

THE NEGRO IN SOUTHERN LITERATURE

The checklist which follows does not rigidly adhere to its title. Although relevance to the study of the Negro in Southern literature has been the primary principle of selection, to limit the checklist only to studies of the Southern Negro writer and to portrayals of the Negro in the literature of the South would be, in the opinion of the compiler, to limit its usefulness.

Serious Negro literature, from whatever part of the country, has in one way or another been at least partially motivated by a desire to counteract the image of the Negro projected by earlier Southern literature. The studies listed in Part I (Negro American Literature) should therefore have some contextual value to any critical or historical exploration of the Negro in Southern literature. In this section I have listed all the book-length studies of the Negro as American writer, many of the (in my opinion) most interesting essays, as well as some of the most significant statements in print on what the posture of the Negro writer should be. I have not, however, included studies which focus on a single Negro author, since this would have expanded this section of the checklist disproportionately.

Part II (The Negro in American Literature) is comprised of studies of the depiction of the Negro in the various genres and/or epochs of our literary history; many of these items include in their survey the Negro's image in the literature of the South, but none do so exclusively. Part III (The Negro and the Literature of the South) is of course the heart of the matter; it is composed of studies of the Southern Negro writer and the portrayal of the Negro in the literature of the South. I have not included in this section discussions of writers from other sections of the country whose work deals with the Negro in the South, except where the critic is chiefly concerned with establishing a direct relationship to Southern life or literature. That is, an essay on *Uncle Tom's Cabin* would find no place in the checklist unless, for example, it addressed itself to the reaction to the novel in the South or discussed the novel's debt to the slave narrative. Nor have I included material on Negro writers covered elsewhere in this volume. Part IV (Bibliographies) is a compilation of further primary and secondary bibliographical aids.

I. Negro American Literature

Barton, Rebecca, *Race Consciousness and the American Negro* (Copenhagen, 1934). [correlates Negro experience and fict, 1900–30]

Bland, Edward, "Social Forces Shaping the Negro Novel," *NegroQ*, I (1945), 328–33.

*Blue, Ila Jacuith, "A Study of Literary Criticism by Some Negro Writers, 1900–1950," *DA*, XXI, 342 (Michigan).

Bone, Robert A., *The Negro Novel in America* (New Haven, 1958; rev ed 1965).

Bontemps, Arna, "Recent Writing by Negroes," in *Literature in the Modern World*, ed. John Mason Brown et al (Nashville, 1956), pp. 113–23.

_____, "The Negro Contribution to American Letters," in *The American Negro Reference Book*, ed. John P. Davis (Englewood Cliffs, N.J., 1966), pp. 850–78.

*Brawley, Benjamin, *The Negro Genius* (New York, 1937).

*_____, *The Negro in Literature and Art* (New York, 1929).

_____, "The Promise of Negro Literature," *Jour of Negro Hist*, XIX (1934), 53–59.

*Bronz, Stephen H., *Roots of Negro Racial Consciousness: The 1920s* (New York, 1964).

Brown, Sterling, "Negro Folk Expression," *Phylon*, XI (1950), 318–27.

*_____, *Negro Poetry and Drama* (Washington, D.C., 1937).

Butcher, Philip, "The Younger Novelists and the Urban Negro," *CLA Jour*, IV (1961), 443–56.

Calverton, V. F., ed., "The Growth of Negro Literature," *Anthology of American Negro Literature* (New York, 1929), pp. 1–17.

*Chapman, Abraham, *The Negro in American Literature and a Bibliography of Literature by and about Negro Americans* (Stevens Point, Wis. 1966). [pamph publ by Wis. Council of Eng Teachers]

_____, "The Harlem Renaissance in Literary History," *CLA Jour*, XI (1967), 38–58.

Davis, Arthur P., "Integration and Race Literature," *Phylon*, XVII (1965), 141–46.

Davis, John A., ed., *The American Negro Writer and His Roots* (New York, 1960). [Samuel Allen, "Negritude and Its Relevance to the American Negro Writer"; John Henrik Clarke, "Reclaiming the Lost African Heritage"; Julian Mayfield, "Into the Mainstream and Oblivion"; Loften Mitchell, "The Negro Writer and His Materials"; J. Saunders Redding, "The Negro Writer and His Relationship to His Roots"]

*Dowd, Jerome, "The Negro in Literature and Art," *The Negro in American Life* (New York, 1926), pp. 261–354.

Dreer, Herman, *American Literature by Negro Authors* (New York, 1950).

Ellison, Ralph, and Stanley Edgar Hyman, "The Negro Writer in America," *PartisanR* XXV (1958), 197–222.

Ellison, Ralph, *Shadow and Act* (New York, 1964).

*Farrell, Harold A., "Theme and Variation: A Critical Evaluation of the Negro Novel, 1919–1947," Ohio State, 1949. [diss]

Ford, Nick Aaron, *The Contemporary Negro Novel* (Boston, 1936). [1914-34]

*Frazier, E. Franklin, "Negro Press and Literature," *The Negro in the United States*, rev ed (New York, 1957), pp. 492–519.

Fuller, Hoyt W., "Contemporary Negro Fiction," *SWR*, L (1965), 321–35.

Gérard, Albert, "Humanism and Negritude: Notes on the Contemporary Afro-American Novel," *Diogenes*, XXXVII (1962), 115–33.

Glicksberg, Charles I., "The Alienation of Negro Literature," *Phylon*, XI (1950), 49–58.

_____, "Negro Fiction in America," *SAQ*, XLV (1946), 477–88.

_____, "The Negro Cult of the Primitive," *AntiochR*, IV (1944), 47–55.

_____, "Negro Poets and the American Tradition," *AntiochR*, VI (1946), 243–53.

*Gloster, Hugn M., *Negro Voices in American Fiction* (Chapel Hill, 1948).

Hill, Herbert, ed., *Anger, and Beyond: The Negro Writer in the United States* (New York, 1966). [intro, 11 essays, and a symposium: Saunders Redding, "The Negro

Writer and American Literature"; Arna Bontemps, "The Negro Renaissance: Jean Toomer and the Harlem Writers of the 1920s"; Horace R. Cayton, "Ideological Forces in the Work of Negro Writers"; LeRoi Jones, "Philistinism and the Negro Writer"; Harvey Swados, "The Writer in Contemporary American Society"; Nat Hentoff, "The Other Side of the Blues"; Robert Bone, "Ralph Ellison and the Uses of the Imagination"; Albert Murray, "Something Different, Something More"; M. Carl Holman, "The Afternoon of a Young Poet"; Ossie Davis, "The Wonderful World of Law and Order"; Melvin B. Tolson, "A Poet's Odyssey" (interview); and "Reflections on Richard Wright: A Symposium on an Exiled Native Son"]

Howe, Irving, "Black Boys and Native Sons," *A World More Attractive* (New York, 1963), pp. 98–122.

Hughes, Carl Milton, *The Negro Novelist: A Discussion of the Writings of American Negro Novelists, 1940–1950* (New York, 1953).

Isaacs, Harold R., "Five Writers and Their African Ancestors," *Phylon*, XXI (1960), 243–65, 317–36. [Baldwin, Ellison, Hansberry, Hughes, Wright]

Jackson, George Blyden, "Of Irony in Negro Fiction: A Critical Study," *DA*, XIII, 388 (Michigan).

———, "Faith Without Works in Negro Literature," *Phylon*, XII (1951), 378–88.

———, "A Golden Mean for the Negro Novel," *CLA Jour*, III (1959), 81–87.

———, "The Negro's Image of the Universe as Reflected in His Fiction," in *Images of the Negro in America*, ed. Darwin T. Turner and Jean M. Bright (Boston, 1965), pp. 85–90. Repr from *CLA Jour*, IV (1960), 22–31.

———, "The Negro's Negro in Negro Literature," *MichQR*, IV (1965), 290–95.

Johnson, James Weldon, "Race Prejudice and the Negro Artist," *Harper's*, CLVII (1928), 769–76.

Kaiser, Ernest, "The Literature of Negro Revolt," *Freedomways*, III (1963) 36–47.

Knickerbocker Mag, "Who Are Our National Poets?" XXVI (1845), 331–41.

Lash, John S., "What is Negro Literature?" *Coll Eng*, IX (1947), 37–42.

———, "The Race Consciousness of the American Negro Author," *Social Forces*, XXVIII (1949), 24–34.

Littlejohn, David, *Black on White: A Critical Survey of Writing by American Negroes* (New York, 1966).

*Locke, Alain, *A Decade of Negro Self-Expression* (Charlottesville, 1928).

———, "The Negro's Contribution to American Art and Literature," *Annals of Amer Acad of Pol and Soc Science*, CXL (1928), 234–47.

*———, *The Negro in America* (Chicago, 1933).

*Loggins, Vernon, *The Negro Author* (New York, 1931). [1760–1900]

Marcus, Steven, "The American Negro in Search of Identity," *Commentary*, XVI (1953), 456–63.

Mays, Benjamin E., *The Negro's God as Reflected in His Literature* (Boston, 1938).

Park, Robert E., "Negro Race Consciousness as Reflected in Race Literature," *AmerR*, I (1923), 505–17.

Putnam's Mag, "Negro Minstrelry—Ancient and Modern," V (1855), 72–79.

Redding, J. Saunders, "American Negro Literature," *Amer Schol*, XVIII (1949), 137–48.

———, "The Problems of the Negro Writer," *MassR*, VI (1964), 57–70.

———, *To Make a Poet Black* (Chapel Hill, 1939). [study of Negro poetry from 18th century to 1930s]

———, "Since Richard Wright," *African Forum*, I, No. 4 (1966), 21–31.

Rourke, Constance, "Tradition for a Negro Literature," *Roots of American Culture* (New York, 1942), pp. 262–75.

Shapiro, Karl, "The Decolonization of American Literature," *Wilson Lib Bull, XXXIX* (1956), 843–53.

Turner, Darwin T., "The Negro Dramatist's Image of the Universe, 1920–1960," in *Images of the Negro in America,* ed. Darwin T. Turner and Jean M. Bright (Boston, 1965), pp. 91–99. [repr from *CLA Jour,* V (1961), 106-20]

Turpin, Waters E., "The Contemporary Negro Playwright," *CLA Jour,* IX (1965),12–24.

*Wagner, Jean, *Les Poètes Nègres des Etats-Unis* (Paris, 1963). [Dunbar to Hughes]

White, Newman, "American Negro Poetry," *SAQ,* XX (1921), 304–22.

———, "Racial Feeling in Negro Poetry," *SAQ,* XXI (1922), 14–29.

White, Walter, "Negro Literature," in *American Writers on American Literature,* ed. John Macy (New York, 1931), pp. 442–51.

Wright, Richard, "Blueprint for Negro Writing," *New Challenge,* I (1937), 53–65.

———, "Littérature noir américain," *Les Temps Modernes,* III (1948), 193–221.

———, "The Literature of the Negro in the United States," *White Man, Listen!* (Garden City, N.Y., 1957), pp. 105–50.

II.   The Negro in American Literature

*Bailey, Dale S., "Slavery in the Novels of Brazil and the United States," *DA,* ⋏˙˙II, 1973 (Cornell).

Baldwin, James, "Everybody's Protest Novel," *PartisanR,* XVI (1949), 578–85. Repr in *Notes of a Native Son* (Boston, 1955), 13–23. [*Uncle Tom's Cabin*]

———, Alfred Kazin, Lorraine Hansberry, Langston Hughes, "The Negro in American Culture: A Symposium," in *The New Negro,* ed. M. H. Ahmann (Notre Dame, 1961), pp. 109–45.

Beja, Morris, "It Must Be Important: Negroes in Contemporary Fiction," *AntiochR,* XXIV (1964), 323–36.

Bond, Frederick W., *The Negro and the Drama* (Washington, D.C., 1940).

Bradley, Gerald, "Goodbye Mr. Bones: The Emergence of Negro Themes and Character in American Drama," *Critique,* VII (1964), 79–86.

Braithwaite, William, "The Negro in American Literature," in *The New Negro,* ed. Alain Locke (New York, 1925), pp. 29–44.

———, "The Negro in Literature," *Crisis,* XXVIII (1924), 204–10.

Brawley, Benjamin, "The Negro in American Fiction," *Dial,* LX (1916), 445–50.

———, "The Negro in American Literature," *Bookman,* LVI (1922), 137–41.

Brown, Sterling, "The American Race Problem as Reflected in American Literature," *Jour of Negro Educ,* VIII (1939), 275–90.

———, "A Century of Negro Portraiture in American Literature," *MassR,* VII (1966), 73–96.

———, "Negro Character as Seen by White Authors," *Jour of Negro Educ,* II (1933), 179–203.

*———, *The Negro in American Fiction* (Washington, D.C., 1937).

Bullock, Penelope, "The Mulatto in American Fiction," *Phylon,* VI (1945), 78–82.

*Butcher, Margaret Just, *The Negro in American Culture* (New York, 1956).

Cantor, Milton, "The Image of the Negro in Colonial Literature," in *Images of the Negro in American Literature,* ed. Seymour L. Gross and John Edward Hardy (Chicago, 1966), pp. 29–53. Repr from *New EngQ,* XXXVI (1963), 452–77.

Clay, Edward, "The Negro in Recent American Literature," *American Writers Congress* (New York, 1935), pp. 145–53.

Couch, William, Jr., "The Problem of Negro Character and Dramatic Incident," *Phylon,* XI (1950), 127–33.

Damon, S. Foster, "The Negro in Early American Songsters," *Papers of Bibl Soc of Amer*, XXVIII (1934), 132–63.

David, Leona King, "Literary Opinions on Slavery in American Literature after the American Revolution to the Civil War," *Negro Hist Bull*, XXIII (1960), 99-104.

Daykin, Walter I., "Negro Types in American White Fiction," *Sociol and Soc Research*, XXII (1937), 45–52.

Dempsey, David, "Uncle Tom's ·Ghost and the Literary Abolitionists," *AntiochR*, IV (1946), 442–8.

Fiedler, Leslie, "The Jig is Up," *Waiting for the End* (New York, 1964), pp. 118-37.

Fontaine, W. T., "The Mind and Thought of the Negro of the United States as Revealed in Imaginative Literature, 1876–1940," *So U Bull*, VIII (1942), 5–50.

Furnas, Joseph C., *Goodbye to Uncle Tom* (New York, 1956).

Gaines, Francis P., "The Racial Bar Sinister in American Romance," *SAQ*, XXV (1926), 396–402.

Glicksberg, Charles I., "Bias, Fiction, and the Negro," *Phylon*, XII (1952), 127–35.

Goldman, Hannah S., "The Tragic Gift: The Serf and Slave Intellectual in Russian and American Fiction," *Phylon*, XXIV (1963), 51–63.

Gross, Seymour L., "Stereotype to Archetype: The Negro in American Literary Criticism," *Images of the Negro in American Literature* (Chicago, 1966), pp. 1–26.

Jackson, Esther Merle, "The American Negro and the Image of the Absurd," *Phylon*, XXIII (1962), 359–71.

*Johnson, Beulah V., "The Treatment of the Negro Woman as a Major Character in the American Novel, 1900–1950," *DA*, XVI, 528 (New York University).

Knox, George, "The Negro Novelists' Sensibility and the Outsider Theme," *WHumR*, XI (1957), 137–48.

*Lawson, Hilda J., "The Negro in American Drama," Illinois, 1939. [diss]

*Liedel, Donald E., "The Anti-Slavery Novel," *DA*, XXII, 1965 (Michigan).

*Linnehan, Edward G., "We Wear the Mask: Life and Character of the Negro in American Drama," Pennsylvania, 1949. [diss]

Locke, Alain, "American Literary Tradition and the Negro," *ModQ*, III (1926), 215–22.

———, "The Negro in American Literature," *New World Writing*, No. 1 (New York, 1952), 18–33.

*Logan, Rayford W., "The Negro as Portrayed in the Leading Literary Magazines," *The Negro in American Life and Thought: The Nadir, 1877–1901* (New York, 1954), pp. 239–74.

Mitchell, Loften, *Black Drama: The Story of the Negro in the American Theatre* (New York, 1967).

*Nelson, John Herbert, *The Negro Character in American Literature* (Lawrence, Kan., 1926).

*Nilon, Charles, "The Treatment of Negro Characters by Representative American Novelists: Cooper, Melville, Tourgee, Glasgow, Faulkner," Wisconsin, 1952. [diss]

Nolen, W., "The Colored Child in Contemporary Literature," *Horn Book*, XVIII (1942), 348–55.

Patterson, Cecil L., "A Different Drum: The Image of the Negro in the Nineteenth Century Songster," *CLA Jour*, VIII (1964), 44–50.

*Poag, Thomas E., "The Negro in Drama and the Theatre," Cornell, 1943. [diss]

Roth, Philip, "Channel X: Two Plays on the Race Conflict," *N.Y. R of Bks*, II (May 28, 1964), 10–13. [r of Baldwin's *Blues for Mr. Charlie* and Jones's *The Dutchman*]

*Smith, Helena M., "Negro Characterization in the American Novel: An Historical Survey of Work by White Authors," *DA*, XX, 3284 (Pennsylvania State).

*Starke, Juanita, "Negro Stock Characters, Archetypes, and Individuals in American Literature," *DA*, XXIV, 228 (Columbia).

_____, "Symbolism of the Negro College in Three Recent Novels," *Phylon*, XI (1950), 297–303.

*Turner, Lorenzo Dow, *Anti-Slavery Sentiment in American Literature Prior to 1865* (Port Washington, N.Y., 1966; orig pub 1929).

*Wiley, Electa Campbell, "A Study of the Noble Savage Myth in Characterizations of the Negro in Selected American Literary Works," *DA*, XXV, 5914 (Arkansas).

Wilson, Edmund, *Patriotic Gore: Studies in the Literature of the Civil War* (New York, 1962), *passim*.

Zanger, Jules, " 'The Tragic Octoroon' in Pre-Civil War Fiction," *AQ*, XVIII (1966), 63–70.

III. The Negro and the Literature of the South

Altenbernd, Lynn, "Huck Finn, Emancipator," *Criticism*, I (1959), 298–307.

Backman, Melvin, "The Wilderness and the Negro in Faulkner's 'The Bear,' " *PMLA*, LXXVI (1961), 595–600.

Barksdale, Richard K., "White Tragedy—Black Comedy: A Literary Approach to Southern Race Relations," *Phylon*, XXII (1961), 226–33. [suggests comic lit approach to white treatment of Negro in So]

Bloomfield, Maxwell, "Dixon's *The Leopard's Spots:* A Study in Popular Racism," *AQ*, XVI (1964), 387–401.

Bradford, Melvin E., "Faulkner, James Baldwin, and the South," *GaR*, XX (1966), 431–43.

*Brawley, Benjamin, *Paul Laurence Dunbar: Poet of His People* (Chapel Hill, 1936).

Burch, Charles E., "Negro Characters in the Novels of William Gilmore Simms," *So Workman*, LII (1923), 192–95.

Butcher, Philip, "George Washington Cable and Booker T. Washington," *Jour of Negro Educ*, XVII (1948), 462–68.

_____, "George Washington Cable and Negro Education," *Jour of Negro Hist*, XXXIV (1949), 119–34.

_____, "Mark Twain Sells Roxy Down the River," *CLA Jour*, VIII (1965), 225–33.

Campbell, Killis, "Poe's Treatment of the Negro and Negro Dialect," *U of Tex Stud in Eng*, XVI (1936), 107–14.

Chamberlain, John, "The Negro as Writer," *Bookman*, LXX (1930), 603–11. [Dunbar]

Cox, James M., "*Pudd'nhead Wilson*: The End of Mark Twain's American Dream," in *Images of the Negro in American Literature*, pp. 181–93. Repr from *SAQ*, LVIII (1959), 351–63.

Cunningham, Virginia, *Paul Laurence Dunbar and His Song* (New York, 1948).

Daniel, Bradford, "William Faulkner and the Southern Quest for Freedom," *Black, White and Gray: Twenty-one Points of View on the Race Question*, ed. Bradford Daniel (New York, 1964), pp. 291–308.

Doherty, Herbert J., "Voices of Protest from the New South," *Miss Val Hist R*, XLII (1955), 45–66. [Cable]

*Doster, William C., "William Faulkner and the Negro," *DA*, XX, 1094 (Florida).

Drake, B. M., *The Negro in Southern Literature Since the War* (Nashville, 1898).

Durham, Frank M., *DuBose Heyward's Use of Folklore in His Negro Fiction* (Charleston, S.C., 1961).

Duvall, Severn, "*Uncle Tom's Cabin*: The Sinister Side of the Patriarchy," in *Images of the Negro in American Literature*, pp. 163–80. Repr from *NewEngQ*, XXXVI

(1963), 3–22. [discusses So reactions to the novel]

Edmonds, Irene C., "Faulkner and the Black Shadow," in *Southern Renascence,* ed. Rubin and Jacobs, pp. 192–206.

Faulkner, Seldon, "*The Octoroon* War," *Educ Theatre Jour,* XV (1963), 33–8.

Fiedler, Leslie A., "The Blackness of Darkness: E. A. Poe and the Development of the Gothic," *Love and Death in the American Novel* (New York, 1960), 370–414.

———, " 'Come Back to the Raft Ag'in Huck Honey!' " *PartisanR,* XV (1948), 664–71. Repr in *An End to Innocence* (Boston, 1955), 142–51.

Fishwick, Marshall, "Uncle Remus vs. John Henry: Folk Tension," *WFolkl,* XX (1961), 77–85.

Geismar, Maxwell, "William Faulkner: The Negro and the Female," *Writers in Crisis* (Boston, 1942). pp. 143–83.

Gérard, Albert, "William Faulkner ou le fardeau de l'homme noir," *La Revue Nouvelle,* XXIV (1956), 331–38.

Gilbert, Roland B., "The Negro in Southern Fiction and Social Studies, 1932–1952," *DA,* XIII, 794 (Vanderbilt).

Glicksberg, Charles I., "William Faulkner and the Negro Problem," *Phylon,* X (1949), 153-60.

Gloster, Hugh, "The Negro Writer and the Southern Scene," *So Packet,* IV (1948), 1–3.

Greer, Dorothy, "Dilsey and Lucas: Faulkner's Use of the Negro as Gauge of Moral Character," *Emporia St Research Stud,* XI (1962), 43–61.

Gross, Theodore L., "The Negro in the Literature of the Reconstruction," *Images of the Negro in American Literature,* pp. 71–83. Repr from *Phylon,* XXII (1961), 5–14.

Hamblen, Abigail, "Uncle Tom and Nigger Jim: A Study in Contrasts and Similarities," *Mark Twain Jour,* XI (1961), 13–17.

Hardy, John Edward, "Eudora Welty's Negroes," in *Images of the Negro in American Literature,* pp. 221–32.

Hansen, Chadwick, "The Character of Jim and the Ending of *Huckleberry Finn,*" *MassR,* V (1963), 45–66.

Howe, Irving, "Faulkner and the Negroes," in *Images of the Negro in American Literature,* pp. 204–20. Repr from *William Faulkner: A Critical Study,* rev ed (New York, 1956), 116–37.

Jackson, Blyden, "Some Negroes in the Land of Goshen," *Tenn Folkl Soc Bul,* XIX (1953), 103–7. [Zora Neale Hurston]

James, Stuart Burke, "Race Relations in Literature and Sociology," *DA,* XXI, 1565 (Washington). [incl Welty and Faulkner]

Kaplan, Sidney, intro to *The Narrative of Arthur Gordon Pym* (New York, 1960), pp. vii–xxv.

———, "*The Octoroon*: Early History of the Drama of Miscegenation," *Jour of Negro Educ,* XX (1951), 547–57.

Klaus, Rosemarie, "Mark Twain und die Negerfrage—*Huckleberry Finn,*" *Zeitschrift für Anglistik und Amerikanstik* (East Berlin), V (1957), pp. 166–81.

Law, Robert A., "Mrs. Peterkin's Negroes," *SWR,* XIV (1929), 455–61.

McDowell, Tremaine, "The Negro in the Southern Novel Prior to 1850," in *Images of the Negro in American Literature,* pp. 54–70. Repr from *Jour of Eng and Ger Phil,* XXV (1926), 455–73.

Marley, Harold, "The Negro in Recent Southern Literature," *SAQ,* XXVII (1928), 29–41.

*Moreland, Agnes Louise, "A Study of Faulkner's Presentation of Some Problems that Relate to Negroes," *DA,* XX, 1192 (Columbia).

Nichols, Charles H., "The Origins of *Uncle Tom's Cabin*," *Phylon*, XIX (1958), 328–34. [sources of the novel in slave narratives]
_____, "Slave Narratives and the Plantation Legend," *Phylon*, X (1949), 201–10.
_____, "Who Read the Slave Narratives?" *Phylon*, XX (1959), 149–62.
*Nilon, Charles, *Faulkner and the Negro* (New York, 1965).
*Odum, Howard, and Guy B. Johnson, *The Negro and His Songs, A Study of Typical Negro Songs in the South* (Chapel Hill, 1925).
*Player, Raleigh Preston, Jr., "The Negro Character in the Fiction of William Faulkner," *DA*, XXVII, 483A (Michigan)
Reeves, W. Paschal, Jr., "Race and Nationality in the Works of Thomas Wolfe," *DA*. XXIV, 4, 195 (Duke).
Rollins, Hyder E., "The Negro in the Southern Short Story," *SeR*, XXIV (1916), 42–60.
Rousseve, Charles B., *The Negro in Louisiana: Aspects of His History and His Literature* (New Orleans, 1937).
Sakae, Morioka, "*Pudd'nhead Wilson* and the Racial Problem," *Stud in Eng Lit and Lang* (Fukuoka, Japan), No. 12 (1962), 1–11.
Seiden, Melvin, "Faulkner's Ambiguous Negro," *MassR*, IV (1963), 675–90.
Shelton, Austin J., "African Realistic Commentary on Culture Hierarchy and Racistic Sentiment in *The Yemassee*," *Phylon*, XXV (1964), 72– 78.
*Steinberg, Aaren, "Faulkner and the Negro," *DA*, XXVII, 1385A (New York University).
Tandy, Jeanette Reid, "Pro-Slavery Propaganda in American Fiction of the Fifties," *SAQ*, XXII (1922), 41–50, 170–78.
Taylor, Walter F., Jr., "Let My People Go: The White Man's Heritage in *Go Down Moses*," *SAQ*, LVIII (1959), 20–32.
*_____, 'The Roles of the Negro in William Faulkner's Fiction," *DA*, XXV, 2990 (Emory).
Tischler, Nancy P., "William Faulkner and the Southern Negro," *Susquehanna U Stud*, VII (1965), 261–65.
Tourgée, Albion W., "The South as a Field for Fiction," *Forum*, VI (1888), 405–12.
Turner, Arlin, ed., intro to *The Negro Question: A Selection of Writings on Civil Rights in the South by George W. Cable* (Garden City, N.Y., 1958).
Warren, Robert Penn, "Faulkner: The South and the Negro," *SoR*, n.s., I (1965), 501–27.
Whipple, James B., "Southern Rebel," *Phylon*, XX (1959), 345–57. [Cable]
*Wormley, Margaret J., "The Negro in Southern Fiction, 1920–1940," Boston University, 1948. [diss]

*IV.   Bibliographies

A Catalogue of Books in the Moorland Foundation (Washington, D.C., 1939). [Howard U's collection of 70,000 vols on the Negro]
Dictionary Catalogue of the Schomburg Collection of Negro Literature and History (Boston, 1962). [9 vols, to be supplemented]
Du Bois, W. E. B., *Encyclopedia of the Negro* (New York, 1945; rev ed, 1946).
Dumond, Dwight L., *A Bibliography of Antislavery in America* (Ann Arbor, 1961).
Gross, Seymour L., "The Negro in American Literature: A Checklist of Criticism and Scholarship," *Images of the Negro in American Literature*, pp. 289–315.
A Guide to Negro Periodical Literature (Winston-Salem, 1941–46) [superseded in 1950 by *Index to Selected Periodicals*, Ohio Central State Coll Lib]

Homer, Dorothy R., *The Negro: A List of Significant Books*, 8th rev ed (New York, 1960).

Kessler, S. H. "American Negro Literature, A Bibliographic Guide," *BB*, XXI (1955), 181–85. [lists 93 bibl]

Lash, John S., "The American Negro and American Literature," *BB*, XIX (1946), 12–15, 33–36.

Lawson, Hilda, "The Negro in American Drama (bibliography of contemporary Negro drama)," *BB*, XVII (1940), 7–8, 27–30.

Miller, Elizabeth, comp., *The Negro in America: A Bibliography* (Cambridge, Mass., 1966).

Porter, Dorothy B., "Early American Negro Writings: A Bibliographical Study," *Papers of Bibl Soc of Amer*, XXXIX (1945), 192-268.

———, *North American Negro Poets: A Bibliographical Check List of Their Writings, 1760–1944* (Hattiesburg, Miss., 1945).

Schomburg, Arthur A., *A Bibliographical Checklist of American Negro Poetry* (New York, 1916).

Thompson, Edgar T., *The Plantation: A Bibliography* (Washington, D.C., 1957).

——— and Alma M. Thompson, *Race and Region: A Descriptive Bibliography Compiled with Special Reference to the Relations Between Whites and Negroes in the United States* (Chapel Hill, 1949).

Welsch, Edwin K., *The Negro in the United States: A Research Guide* (Bloomington, Ind., 1965).

Whiteman, Maxwell, ed., *A Century of Fiction by American Negroes: A Descriptive Bibliography* (Philadelphia, 1955).

Work, Monroe, *A Bibliography of the Negro in Africa and America* (New York, 1965).

SEYMOUR L. GROSS
University of Notre Dame
Notre Dame, Indiana

HUMORISTS OF THE OLD SOUTHWEST

From Andrew Jackson's time to the Civil War, the trans-Appalachian frontier in the South produced a vigorous body of narrative fiction which has come to be called the humor of the Old Southwest. The area was fringed by cities such as Charleston and New Orleans, crossed by waterways, the Tennessee and the Mississippi, and traversed by trails such as the Natchez Trace. The land opened inward to a new settlement as the Civilized Tribes were driven out and transported westward in the great Indian Removal of the 1830s. The land was settled or exploited, plantations and villages grew or disappeared, frontier became backwoods, and the area's variety of human creatures flourished or decayed in dramatic juxtaposition. Writers from within and without felt they were preserving oddities of character and speech, exciting adventure, describing strange new settings, and offering for contemplation peculiar or wonderful or terrible human deeds and ways.

These narratives ordinarily appeared in local newspapers and a few national journals, such as the New York *Spirit of the Times, Yankee Notions,* and others. A few of its best writers collected their sketches in books which were widely circulated. Among its first devotees, it numbered European and American sportsmen, military officers, and a wide variety of readers, usually male, with an interest in the American frontier and backwoods character. Modern scholarly and critical assessment began about 1930 with Franklin Meine's anthology, *Tall Tales of the Southwest,* with Bernard DeVoto's *Mark Twain's America,* with Walter Blair's essays on its forms and quality, with Constance Rourke's study of the Crockett myth, and particularly with her brilliant and never superseded *American Humor,* which Lewis Mumford calls "the most original piece of investigation and interpretation that has appeared in American cultural history."

Study of the forms and meanings of humor is difficult. Therefore a few titles outside the area of Southwestern humor might be mentioned for the beginning scholar. Formidably difficult, but really illuminating, is Northrop Frye's *Anatomy of Criticism,* particularly those chapters titled "Comic Fictional Modes," "The Mythos of Spring: Comedy," and "The Mythos of Winter: Irony and Satire." Wylie Sypher's essay "The Meanings of Comedy," in his *Comedy,* and Johan Huizinga's *Homo Ludens: A Study of the Play Element in Culture* offer useful insights and broad theory. Certain works of classical scholarship, particularly Francis M. Cornford's *The Origins of Attic Comedy,* study the ancient roots and meanings of comic ritual. The forms and psychological functions of jokes are studied in Freud's *Jokes and Their Relation to the Unconscious*, and the nature of humor in his essay "Humour," *Collected Papers*, edited by James Strachey (London, 1950), Volume V. José Ortega y Gasset's *Meditations on Quixote* is a seminal philosophical work. Richard Dorson's *American Folklore* is indispensable. Finally, Brom Weber's *An Anthology of American Humor* concludes with an elegantly selected and highly pertinent general bibliography.

Adkins, N. F., "James K. Paulding's *Lion of the West*," *AL*, III (1931), 249–58.

Anderson, John Q., "Scholarship in Southwestern Humor—Past and Present," *MissQ*, XVII (1964), 67–86.

———, intro to *With the Bark On: Popular Humor of the Old South* (Nashville, 1967). [anthol with valuable commentary and notes]

Bettersworth, John K., "The Humor of the Old Southwest: Yesterday and Today," *MissQ*, XVII (1964), 87–94.

Blair, Walter, *Horse Sense in American Humor* (Chicago, 1942).

*———, *Native American Humor* (San Francisco, 1960), pp. 62–101, 188–90, 191–96, 279–389.

———, "The Popularity of Nineteenth-Century American Humorists," *AL*, III (1931), 175–94.

———, "Traditions in Southern Humor," *AQ*, V (1953), 132–42.

*———, and Franklin J. Meine, *Half Horse, Half Alligator: The Growth of the Mike Fink Legend* (Chicago, 1956).

———, *Mike Fink, King of Mississippi Keelboatmen* (New York, 1933).

Boatright, Mody C., *Folk Laughter on the American Frontier* (New York, 1942).

———, "Frontier Humor: Despairing or Buoyant?" *SWR*, XXVII (1942), 320–34.

Bolton, Theodore, "The Book Illustrations of Felix Octavius Carr Darley," *Proceed of Amer Antiq Soc*, n.s., LXI (Apr 18, 1951), 137–82. [includes a catalogue of all bks illus by Darley]

Brinley, Francis, *Life of William T. Porter* (New York, 1860).

British Quarterly Review, r of *The Americans at Home*, XXI (Jan 1855), 60–78.

Budd, Louis J., "Gentlemanly Humorists of the Old South," *SFQ*, XVII (1953), 232–40.

Chittick, V. L. O., intro to *Ring-Tailed Roarers* (Caldwell, Idaho, 1946), pp. 13–25.

———, *Thomas Chandler Haliburton ("Sam Slick"): A Study in Provincial Toryism* (New York, 1924).

Clark, Thomas D., "Humor in the Stream of Southern History," *MissQ*, XIII (1960), 176–88.

———, *The Rampaging Frontier: Manners and Humors of Pioneer Days in the South and the Middle West* (New York, 1939).

Clemens, Samuel Langhorne, comp., *Mark Twain's Library of Humor* (New York, 1888).

*Cohen and Dillingham, eds., *Humor of the Old Southwest*, pp. ix–xxiv.

Collins, Carvel, "Faulkner and Certain Earlier Southern Fiction," *Coll Eng*, XVI (1954), 92–97.

Colville, Derek, "History and Humor: The Tall Tale in New Orleans," *La Hist Q*, XXXIX (1956), 153–67.

Covici, Pascal, Jr., *Mark Twain's Humor: The Image of a World* (Dallas, 1962), pp. 3–109.

Current-Garcia, Eugene, "Alabama Writers in the *Spirit*," *AlaR*, X (1957), 243–69.

———, " 'Mr. Spirit' and *The Big Bear of Arkansas*: A Note on the Genesis of Southwest Sporting and Humor Literature," *AL*, XXVII (1955), 332–46.

―――, "Newspaper Humorists in the Old South, 1835–1855," *AlaR*, II (1949), 109–21.

DeVoto, Bernard, *Mark Twain's America* (Boston, 1932).

Dick, Everett, *The Dixie Frontier: A Social History of the Southern Frontier from the First Transmontane Beginnings to the Civil War* (New York, 1948).

*Dobie, J. Frank, *Guide to Life and Literature of the Southwest* (Dallas, 1952). [chap 8, "Backwoods Life and Humor," is most germane, but other chaps should be consulted. "Southwest" here refers to the mod SW]

Dondore, Dorothy A., "Big Talk! The Flyting, the Gabe, and the Frontier Boast," *AS*, VI, (Oct 1930), 45–55.

Dorson, Richard M., "America's Comic Demigods," *Amer Schol*, X (1941), 389–401.

*―――, *American Folklore* (Chicago, 1959), pp. 39–73.

―――, "Davy Crockett and the Heroic Age," *SFQ*, VI (1942), 95–102.

―――, "The Identification of Folklore in American Literature," *Jour of Amer Folkl*, LXX (1957), 1–8. [part 2 of a symposium on "Folklore in Literature," pp. 1–24 of this issue]

Eaton, Clement, "The Humor of the Southern Yeoman," *SeR*, XLIX (1941), 173–83.

―――, "The Southern Yeoman: The Humorists' View and the Reality," *The Mind of the Old South*, rev ed (Baton Rouge, 1967), pp. 130–51.

Ferguson, J. DeLancey, "The Roots of American Humor," *Amer Schol*, IV (1935), 41–49.

Flanders, B. H., "Humor in Ante-Bellum Georgia," *Emory UQ*, I (1945), 149–59.

Foster, Ruel E., "Kentucky Humor: Salt River Roarer to Ol' Dog Tray," *MissQ*, XX (1967), 224–30.

Haliburton, Thomas C., intro to *The Americans at Home*, 3 vols (London, 1854).

―――, intro to *Traits of American Humor by Native Authors*, 3 vols (London, 1852).

Harris, Joel Chandler, "Georgia Wit and Humor," in *Stories of Georgia* (New York, 1896), pp. 240–51.

Hoffman, Daniel G., *Form and Fable in American Fiction* (New York, 1961), esp pp. 33–82, 317–42.

*Hubbell, Jay B., *The South in American Literature*.

Hudson, Arthur Palmer, intro to *Humor of the Old Deep South* (New York, 1936), pp. 1–25 and elsewhere.

Hyde, Stuart W., "The Ring-Tailed Roarer in American Drama," *SFQ*, XIX (1955), 171–78.

Ives, Sumner, "A Theory of Literary Dialect," *Tulane Stud in Lit*, II (1950), 137–82.

Jordan, Philip D., "Humor of the Backwoods, 1820–1840," *Miss Val Hist R*, XXV (June, 1938), 25–38.

Lang, Andrew, "American Humour," and "Western Drolls," in *Lost Leaders* (London, 1889), pp. 70–77, 181–88.

Legman, G., "Toward a Motif-Index of Erotic Humor," *Jour of Amer Folkl*, LXXV (1962), 227–48. [issue devoted to obscenity in folkl; abundant sexual and scatological elements in SW humor (which Mr. Legman does not specifically discuss) have received little analysis]

Link, Samuel A., "Southern Humorists: Longstreet, Baldwin, Hooper, W. T. Thompson, Davy Crockett and Others," in *Pioneers of Southern Literature* (Nashville, 1900), II, 465–545.

Lynn, Kenneth, *Mark Twain and Southwestern Humor* (Boston, 1959).

McIlwaine, Shields, *The Southern Poor-White from Lubberland to Tobacco Road* (Norman, Okla., 1939), pp. 40–74.

Maclachlan, John M., "Southern Humor as a Vehicle of Social Evaluation," *MissQ*, XIII (1960), 157–62.

*Masterson, James R., *Tall Tales of Arkansaw* (Boston, 1942).

*Meine, Franklin J., intro to *Tall Tales of the Southwest: An Anthology of Southern and Southwestern Humor 1830–1860* (New York, 1930), pp. xv–xxxii. [also under Walter Blair]

*Meriwether, Frank T., "The Rogue in the Life and Humor of the Old Southwest," Louisiana, 1952. [diss]

Moore, Arthur K., "Specimens of the Folktales from Some Ante-Bellum Newspapers of Louisiana," *La Hist Q*, XXXII (1949), 723–58.

Mott, Frank Luther, "Human Nature in Some Folks," *Golden Multitudes: The Story of Best Sellers in the United States* (New York, 1947), pp. 198–204.

Parks, Edd Winfield, *Ante-Bellum Southern Literary Critics* (Athens, Ga., 1962), pp. 60–65.

―――, "The Intent of the Ante-Bellum Southern Humorists," *MissQ*, XIII (1960), 163–68. [on relationship of oral to publ tales, see Parks's quotation of Simms, p. 165]

―――, "The Three Streams of Southern Humor," *GaR*, IX (1955), 147–59.

Parrington, Vernon L., *The Romantic Revolution in America, 1800–1860* (New York, 1927), pp. 166–79.

Pearce, James T., "Folk Tales of the Southern Poor-Whites, 1820–1860," *Jour of Amer Folkl*, LXIII (1950), 398–412.

Penrod, James H., "Characteristic Endings of Southwestern Yarns," *MissQ*, XV (1961–62), 27–35.

―――, "The Folk Hero as Prankster in the Old Southwestern Yarns," *Ky Folkl Rec*, II (Jan–March, 1956), 5–12.

―――, "The Folk Mind in Early Southwestern Humor," *Tenn Folkl Soc Bull*, XVIII (June 1952), 49–54.

―――, "Folklore Motifs in Old Southwestern Humor," *SFQ*, XIX (1955), 117–24.

―――, "Minority Groups in Old Southern Humor," *SFQ*, XXII (1958), 121–28.

―――, "Teachers and Preachers in the Old Southwestern Yarns," *Tenn Folkl Soc Bull*, XVIII (Dec 1952) 91–96.

―――, "Two Types of Incongruity in Old Southwest Humor," *K Folkl Rec*, IV (1958), 163–73.

Rickels, Milton, "The Humorists of the Old Southwest in the London *Bentley's Miscellany*," *AL*, XXVII (1956), 557–60.

*Rourke, Constance, *American Humor: A Study of the National Character* (New York, 1931). [effectively analyzes traditional char types, functions, and meanings of comic fantasy]

*―――, *Davy Crockett* (New York, 1934). [contains bibl of Crockett almanacs]

Smither, Nelle, "Library of Humorous American Works," Columbia, 1936. [MA thesis]

Spotts, Carle Brooks, "The Development of Fiction on the Missouri Frontier (1830–1860)," *Mo Hist R*, XXIX (1935) 17–26; 100–108; 186–96. [careers of Alphonse Wetmore, John S. Robb, and Joseph M. Field]

Stewart, Randall, "Tidewater and Frontier," *GaR*, XIII (1959), 296–307.

*Tandy, Jennette, *Crackerbox Philosophers in American Humor and Satire* (New York, 1925), pp. 65–96.

*[Thompson, Harold W.] "Humor," in *LHUS*, I, 728–57. See also bibl "Folk Tales and Humor" in II, 202–11, and *Supp*, pp. 47–49.

Thompson, William F., "Frontier Tall Talk," *AS*, IX (Oct 1934), 187–99.

*Thorp, Willard, *American Humorists* (Minneapolis, 1964). [Minn pamph]

Tidwell, James N., intro to *The Lion of the West by James Kirke Paulding* (Stanford, 1954), pp. 7–14.

Turner, Arlin, "Realism and Fantasy in Southern Humor," *GaR*, XII (1958), 451–57.

———, "Seeds of Literary Revolt in the Humor of the Old Southwest," *L Hist Q*, XXXIX (1956) 143–51.

Walser, Richard, "Ham Jones: Southern Folk Humorist," *Jour of Amer Folkl*, LXXVIII (1965), 295–316.

Watterson, Henry, "The South in Light and Shade," *The Compromises of Life* (New York, 1903), pp. 59–101.

———, ed., *Oddities of Southern Life and Character* (Boston and New York, 1882). [valuable interpretive notes]

Weber, Brom, "American Humor and American Culture," *AQ*, XIV (1962), 503–507. [r essay]

*———, Preface to *An Anthology of American Humor* (New York, 1962), pp. xi–xiv.

*Yates, Norris W., *William T. Porter and the Spirit of the Times* (Baton Rouge, 1957).

MILTON RICKELS
University of Southwestern Louisiana
Lafayette, Louisiana

THE CIVIL WAR IN SOUTHERN LITERATURE

No matter how the study of the South is divided into periods, the Civil War—like it or not—remains the fulcrum of Southern history and, therefore, of the literary history of the South. The effect of the war on Southern literature was both real and immediate on the one hand, and emotional and inspirational, even insidious, on the other.

This list of bibliographical references attempts to cover, selectively at least, the several kinds of effects of the Civil war on Southern literature. In bibliographical items such as Crandall's *Confederate Imprints* the record of the war as it related to literature in its largest sense—the whole range of publishing—is indicated. In items relating to such individual authors as John Esten Cooke, John Hill Hewitt, and Henry Timrod, the war's effect on individual authors is demonstrated. In general, however, biographical material has been left to appear in this volume simply under the name of the biographee. The effect of the war is on the whole literature of the South since 1860, not just on the literature contemporaneous with the war.

There is considerable emphasis in this list on the war in historical novels, but there are also references to its place in Southern literature in biography, drama and the theater, historiography, humor, poetry, and the short story. Because the Civil War permeates virtually all aspects of Southern life since the war and because it has deeply influenced the attitudes of all non-Southerners who have written about the South, the topic is impossible to cover in a brief list of articles and books. But this list can start a reader toward wider coverage—much of which will eventually have to be built from sections of literary histories and of general histories of the South, much of which will have to come from bits incidental to other subject or biographical coverage, and much, in the long run, from a growing grasp and feel for the topic as the interested reader's experience in reading in the area broadens.

Abel, Darrel, "The American Renaissance and the Civil War: Concentric Circles," *Emerson Soc Q*, No. 44 (1966), 86–91.

Allen, Hervey, "History and the Novel," *Atlantic*, CLXXIII (1944), 119–21.

Atchison, Ray M., "*Our Living and Our Dead*: A Post-Bellum North Carolina Magazine of Literature and History," *N.C. Hist R*, XL (1963), 423–33.

Baro, Gene, *After Appomattox: The Image of the South in Its Fiction, 1865–1900* (New York, 1963).

Bradbury, *Renaissance in the South*.

Bridgers, Emily, *The South in Fiction* (Chapel Hill, 1948).

Brockett, O. G., and Lenyth Brockett, "Civil War Theater: Contemporary Treatments," *Civil War Hist*, I (1955), 229–50.

Brooks, Cleanth, "Southern Literature: The Wellsprings of Its Vitality," *GaR*, XVI (1962), 238–53.

Christie, Anne M., "Civil War Humor: Bill Arp," *Civil War Hist*, II (1956), 103–19. [about Charles Henry Smith]

Cooke, John Esten, "War Diary of John Esten Cooke," *JSH*, VII (1941), 526–40.

_____, *Outlines from the Outpost* (Chicago, 1961).

*Crandall, Marjorie Lyle, *Confederate Imprints*, 2 vols ([Boston] 1955).

Crawford, Bartholow V., "The Civil War and American Literature," *Emerson Soc Q*, No. 44 (1966), 91–94.

Davidson, Donald, *Still Rebels, Still Yankees, and Other Essays* (Baton Rouge, 1957).

*Davidson, James Wood, *The Living Writers of the South* (New York, 1869).

Davidson, Nora F. M., *Cullings from the Confederacy: A Collection of Southern Poems* (Washington, D.C., 1903).

Daviess, Maria T., "American Backgrounds for Fiction, III—Tennessee," *Bookman*, XXXVIII (1913), 394–99.

De Leon, Thomas Cooper, *Belles, Beaux and Brains of the 60s* (New York, 1907).

_____, *Four Years in Rebel Capitals* (Mobile, 1890).

_____, *South Songs: From the Lays of Later Days* (New York, 1866).

Derby, James Cephas, *Fifty Years Among Authors, Books and Publishers* (New York, 1886).

DeVoto, Bernard, "Fiction Fights the Civil War," *SatR*, XVII (Dec 18, 1937), 3–4.

Dixon, Thomas, "American Backgrounds for Fiction, IV—North Carolina," *Bookman*, XXXVIII (1914), 511–14.

Ellinger, Esther P., *The Southern War Poetry of the Civil War* (Philadelphia, 1918).

Fife, Iline, "The Confederate Theater," *So Speech Jour*, XX (1955), 224–31.

_____, "The Confederate Theater in Georgia," *GaR*, IX (1955), 305–15.

Ford, Paul Leicester, "The American Historical Novel," *Atlantic*, LXXXI (1897), 721–28.

*Freeman, Douglas Southall, *The South to Posterity* (New York, 1939).

Hall, Wade H., *Reflections on the Civil War in Southern Humor* (Gainesville, 1962).

_____, *The Smiling Phoenix: Southern Humor from 1865 to 1914* (Gainesville, 1965).

Harben, Will N., "American Backgrounds for Fiction, I—Georgia," *Bookman, XXXVIII* (1913), 186–92.

Harrison, Constance Cary, *Recollections Grave and Gay* (New York, 1911).

Harwell, Richard B., "Civil War Theater: The Richmond Stage," *Civil War Hist*, I (1955), 295–304.

*_____, *Confederate Belles-Lettres* (Hattiesburg, Miss., 1941).

_____, "Gone with Miss Ravenel's Courage; or Bugles Blow So Red: A Note on the Civil War Novel," *New Eng Q*, XXXV (1962), 253–62.

_____, "John Esten Cooke, Civil War Correspondent," *JSH*, XIX (1933), 501–16.

_____, *More Confederate Imprints*, 2 vols (Richmond, 1957).

_____, "The Stream of Self-Consciousness," in Frank Vandiver, ed., *The Idea of the South* (Chicago, 1964), pp. 17–25.

Hazel, Robert, "The Southern Writer and His Region," in Louis D. Rubin, Jr., and James Jackson Kilpatrick, eds., *The Lasting South* (Chicago, 1957), pp. 171–80.

Hewitt, John Hill, *King Linkum the First, a Musical Burletta* (Atlanta, 1947).

_____, *Shadows on the Wall; or, Glimpses of the Past* (Baltimore, 1877).

Hoole, William Stanley, "Charleston Theatricals During the Tragic Decade, 1860-1869," *JSH*, XI (1945), 538–47.

_____, "*Jeremiah Clemens, Novelist*," *AlaR*, XVIII (1965), 5–36.

Howell, Elmo, "William Faulkner and the Andrews Raid in Georgia, 1862," *Ga Hist Q*, LXIX (1965), 187–92.

Hubbell, Jay B., *The Last Years of Henry Timrod, 1864–1867, Including Letters of Timrod to Paul Hamilton Hayne and Letters about Timrod by William Gilmore Simms, John R. Thompson, John Greenleaf Whittier, and Others* (Durham, 1941).

Hubner, Charles W., *War Poets of the South and Confederate Camp-Fire Songs* (Atlanta, 1896).

Jones, Katharine M., *New Confederate Short Stories* (Columbia, S.C., 1954).

Lanux, Pierre de, "Le roman du Sud; Tableaux de l'Amérique en guerre, 1861–1865," *R Hebdomadaire*, XL (1941), 13–28, 176–96,·315–31, 456–80.

Leisy, Ernest E., *The American Historical Novel* (Norman, Okla., 1950).

*Lively, Robert A., *Fiction Fights the Civil War* (Chapel Hill, 1957).

Miller, Douglas T., "Faulkner and the Civil War: Myth and Reality," *AQ*, XV (1963), 200–209.

Mims, Edwin, *The Advancing South* (Garden City, N.Y., 1926).

Page, Thomas Nelson, "Literature in the South Since the War," *Lippincott's*, XLVIII (1891), 740–56.

Painter, Franklin Verzelius Newton, *Poets of the South* (New York, 1903).

Reardon, William, and John Foxen, "Civil War Theater: The Propaganda Play," *Civil War Hist*, I (1955), 281–93.

Rubin, Louis D., Jr., *The Faraway Country.*

———, "The Historical Image of Modern Southern Writing," *JSH*, XXII (1956), 147–66. Repr in *South*, pp. 29–47.

———, "The Image of an Army: Southern Novelists and the Civil War," *TQ*, I (1958), 17–34. Repr rev in *The Curious Death of the Novel*, pp. 183–206, and in Simonini, ed., *Southern Writers*. pp. 57–70.

———, "An Image of the South," in Rubin and James Jackson Kilpatrick, eds., *The Lasting South* (Chicago, 1957), pp. 1–15.

*Rudolph, Earl Leighton, *Confederate Broadside Verse* (New Braunfels, Tex., 1950).

Rutherford, Mildred Lewis, *The South in History and Literature* (Atlanta, 1907).

*Smith, Rebecca Washington, *The Civil War and Its Aftermath in American Fiction, 1861–1899* (Chicago, 1934).

Simms, William Gilmore, ed., *War Poetry of the South* (New York, 1867).

Sullivan, Walter, "The Decline of Regionalism in Southern Fiction," *GaR*, XVIII (1964), 301–308.

———, "Southern Novelists and the Civil War," in *Southern Renascence*, pp. 112–25.

[Tardy, Mrs. Mary T.] *The Living Female Writers of the South*, ed. by the author of "Southland Writers" (Philadelphia, 1872).

[———,] *Southland Writers . . . by Ida Raymond* [pseud], 2 vols (Philadelphia, 1870).

Taylor, Alastair MacDonald, "The Historical Novel as a Source in History," *SeR*, XLVI (1938), 459–79.

Thompson, Lawrence S., "The Civil War in Fiction," *Civil War Hist*, II (1956), 83–95.

———, "The War Between the States in the Kentucky Novel," *State Hist Soc Register*, L (1952), 26–34.

———, and Algernon D. Thompson, *The Kentucky Novel* (Lexington, Ky., 1953).

Tourgée, Albion Winegar, "The South as a Field for Fiction," *Forum*, VI (1888), 404–13.

Van Auken, Sheldon, "The Southern Historical Novel in the Early Twentieth Century," *JSH*, XIV (1948), 157–91.

Waal, Carla, "The First Original Confederate Drama: *The Guerillas*," *VMHB*, LXX (1962), 459–67.

Webb, William A., "Southern Poetry: 1849–1881," *SAQ*, II (1903), 35–50.

Welsh, Willard, "Civil War Theater: The War in Drama," *Civil War Hist*, I (1955), 251–80.

Westbrook, John T., "Twilight of Southern Regionalism," *SWR*, XLII (1957), 231–34.

Williams, Benjamin B., "Thomas Cooper DeLeon: Alabama's First Professional Man-of-Letters," *Ala Hist Q*, XXIV (1962), 40–51.

Wilmer, Richard H., "Collecting Civil War Novels," *Colophon*, n.s., III (1938), 513–18.

Wilson, Edmund, *Patriotic Gore: Studies in the Literature of the Civil War* (New York, 1962).

Woodberry, George E., "The South in American Letters," *Harper's*, CVII (1903), 735–41.

Woodward, C. Vann, "The Historical Dimension," *VQR*, XXXII (1956), 258–67. Repr in Woodward, *The Burden of Southern History*, rev ed (Baton Rouge, 1968), pp. 27–39.

RICHARD HARWELL
Smith College
Southampton, Massachusetts

THE SOUTH IN NORTHERN EYES

The checklist is highly selective; it is intended to be a guide to a historical survey of the subject and is limited, in general, to primary sources of special or representative significance. Since the Northern conception of the South is reflected vividly and dramatically in the fiction of the period (early nineteenth to early twentieth centuries), representative novels are included as primary sources. The voluminous polemical writing of the Abolitionists in the thirty-year period before 1860 is represented only by characteristic example; the reader is referred to Howard Floan, *The South in Northern Eyes* (listed below), for a detailed guide to the literature of this period. Some of the writings discussed in this book are also cited in Jay B. Hubbell, *The South in American Literature.*

Adams, Henry, *The Education of Henry Adams* (New York, 1930), pp. 57–59.

Anderson, Charles R., "James's Portrait of the Southerner," *AL*, XXVII (1955), 309–31.

Anderson, Sherwood, *The South: The Black and White and Other Problems Below the Mason and Dixon Line* (New York, 1925).

Bryant, William Cullen, *The Letters of William Cullen Bryant* (New York, 1871), pp. 71–88, 90–94, 100–10, 126–27, 341.

Cash, Wilbur J., *The Mind of the South* (New York, 1941).

Colvert, James B., "Views of Southern Character in Some Northern Novels," *MissQ*, XVIII (1965), 59–68.

Cooper, James Fenimore, *The American Democrat* (Cooperstown, 1838), pp. 173–76.

———, *Notions of the Americans: Picked up by a Travelling Bachelor* (Philadelphia, 1836).

———, *The Spy: A Tale of the Neutral Ground* (New York, 1821). [portrait of a So cavalryman, Capt Jack Lawton]

Dabney, Virginius, "The Emancipation of Women," in *Contemporary Southern Prose*, ed. R. C. Beatty and W. P. Fidler (Boston, 1940), pp. 67–77. [on So chivalry]

DeForest, John W., *Kate Beaumont* (Boston, 1872). [novel]

———, *Miss Ravenel's Conversion from Secession to Loyalty* (New York, 1867). [novel]

Dunham, Chester Forrester, *The Attitude of the Northern Clergy toward the South, 1860–1865* (Toledo, Ohio, 1942).

Emerson, Ralph Waldo, *Journals of Ralph Waldo Emerson*, ed. Edward W. Emerson and Waldo Emerson Forbes (Boston, 1910), p. 275. [on So as a savage]

Fitzgerald, F. Scott, *The Great Gatsby* (New York, 1925).

Floan, Howard R., *The South in Northern Eyes, 1831–1861* (Austin, Texas, 1958).

Franklin, John Hope, *The Militant South, 1800–1861* (Cambridge, Mass., 1956).

Gaines, Francis Pendleton, *The Southern Plantation: A Study in the Development and the Accuracy of a Tradition* (New York, 1924).

Garrison, William Lloyd, *The New "Reign of Terror" in the Slaveholding States, for 1859–1860* (New York, 1860).

Gilden, K. B., *Hurry Sundown* (New York, 1965). [novel on Ga. after World War II]

Griffin, Max Liles, "Bryant and the South," *Tulane Stud in Eng*, I (1949), 53–80.

_____, "The Relations with the South of Six Major Northern Writers, 1830–1861," North Carolina, 1944. [diss]

Hale, Sarah Josepha, *Northwood or Life North and South; Showing the True Character of Both* (New York, 1852). [novel]

Hawthorne, Nathaniel, *The Complete Works of Nathaniel Hawthorne* (Boston, 1903), XVII, pp. 398–402.

Helper, Hinton R., *The Impending Crisis of the South: How to Meet It* (New York, 1860). [So abolitionist summarizing No sentiment]

Howells, William Dean, *A Hazard of New Fortunes* (New York, 1890).

Hubbell, Jay B., *The South in American Literature*.

Irving, Washington, *The Works of Washington Irving* (New York, 1881), VIII, 124–30; X, 441–74, 529–37. [commentary on So]

James, Henry, *The American Scene* (New York, 1907). [essay]

_____ *The Bostonians* (New York, 1886). [novel]

_____, *A Small Boy and Others* (London, 1913), pp. 159–265.

King, Edward, *The Great South* (New York, 1874).

Longfellow, Henry Wadsworth, "Poems on Slavery," in *The Pioneer, A Literary Magazine*, ed. James Russell Lowell, intro by Sculley Bradley (Scholars' Facsimiles and Reprints, New York, 1947), I.

Lowell, James Russell, *The Anti-Slavery Papers of James Russell Lowell* (Boston, 1902).

Melville, Herman, *Mardi* (New York, 1849). [allegory of So in description of Vivenza]

Nims, John Frederick, *A Fountain in Kentucky* (New York, 1950). [poetry]

Olmsted, Frederick L., *The Cotton Kingdom* (New York, 1861).

_____, *A Journey in the Seaboard Slave States* (New York, 1856).

Paulding, James Kirke, *The Diverting History of John Bull and Brother Jonathan* (New York, 1812). [summarizes No stereotype of Southerner]

_____, *Letters from the South* (New York, 1817). [observations on Va]

_____, *Westward Ho! A Tale* (New York, 1832). [Tidewater aristocrat as hero]

Paulding, William I., *Literary Life of James K. Paulding* (New York, 1867), pp. 287–88. [on Jackson as So]

Rhodes, James Ford, *History of the United States from 1850–1877* (New York, 1892–1895), I, 70; III, 355, 381, *passim*. [summarizes No concept of So]

Sampson, F. A., "Washington Irving. Travels in Missouri and the South," *Mo Hist R* (Oct 1910) 26–38.

Stowe, Harriet Beecher, *Uncle Tom's Cabin, or, Life Among the Lowly* (Boston, 1852).

Sumner, Charles, "Crime Against Kansas," in *The Works of Charles Sumner* (Boston, 1871), IV, pp. 141 *ff*.

Taylor, William R., *Cavalier and Yankee* (New York, 1961).

Thoreau, Henry David, *The Writings of Henry David Thoreau* (Boston, 1906). [comments *passim*]

Tindall, George B. "The Benighted South: Origin of a Modern Image," *VQR*, LX (1964), 281–94.

Tourgee, Albion W., "The South as a Field for Fiction," *Forum*, VI (1888), 404–13.

_____, *A Fool's Errand* (New York, 1879). [novel]

Trowbridge, John T., *The South: A Tour of Its Battlefields and Ruined Cities* (New York, 1866).

Whitman, Walt, *Franklin Evans; or the Inebriate: A Tale of the Times* (New York, 1929). [novel]

Whittier, John Greenleaf, *The Narrative of James Williams, An American Slave*

(Boston, 1838). [purported true account of slave life in the So with comment by Whittier]

Wilson, Edmund, *Patriotic Gore: Studies in the Literature of the Civil War* (New York, 1962).

JAMES B. COLVERT
University of Georgia
Athens, Georgia

LOCAL COLOR

Because local color is not a genre or a distinct sub-genre, it has not often been treated separately by anthology makers or by writers of literary history and criticism. The two collections of local color stories listed below, one edited by Claude M. Simpson and the other by Harry R. Warfel and G. Harrison Orians, have introductions which place the Southern writings in the national movement. The term is normally applied to the period from 1870 to 1900, and in particular to fiction. Of those listed below who have written significantly on local color, several lived within this period: Charles W. Coleman, Jr., John Bell Henneman, J. H. Morse, Thomas Nelson Page, and Albion W. Tourgee. Important later works on the subject have been written by Carvel Collins, Claud B. Green, Jay B. Hubbell, and Fred Lewis Pattee.

The local color movement had roots in the humor of the Old Southwest, and it contributed to the rise of realism, as demonstrated in the works by Walter Blair, Constance Rourke, and Henry Watterson. Likewise the local writings which flourished in the 1930s, generally labeled literary regionalism, had a lineal connection with the earlier local color movement. See the works below by Joseph E. Baker, Paul Robert Beath, Carey McWilliams, Walter Sullivan, Charles Child Walcutt, and Robert Penn Warren.

I. Background

Buck, Paul H., *The Road to Reunion, 1865–1900* (Boston, 1937), pp. 196–219.

Cash, W. J., *The Mind of the South* (New York, 1941), pp. 103–44.

*Clark, Thomas D., *The Rampaging Frontier: Manners and Humors of Pioneer Days in the South and the Middle West* (Indianapolis, 1939), bibl, pp. 343–50.

Gaines, Francis Pendleton, *The Southern Plantation: A Study in the Development and the Accuracy of a Tradition* (New York, 1924).

Odum, Howard W., *The Southern Regions of the United States* (Chapel Hill, 1936).

Owsley, Frank L., *Plain Folk of the Old South* (Baton Rouge, 1949).

*Simkins, Francis Butler, "The South," in *Regionalism in America*, ed. Merrill Jensen (Madison, Wis., 1951), pp. 147–72.

_____, *A History of the South* (New York, 1953).

*Spencer, Benjamin T., "Regionalism in American Literature," in *Regionalism in America*, pp. 219–60.

Woodward, C. Vann, *Origins of the New South, 1877–1913* (Baton Rouge, 1951).

II. Collections

Blair, Walter, *Native American Humor, 1800–1900* (New York, 1937; San Francisco, 1960).

Boatright, Mody C., ed., *Tall Tales from Texas* (Dallas, 1934).

Burke, T. A., ed., *Polly Peablossom's Wedding; and Other Tales* (Philadelphia, 1851).

McVoy, Lizzie C., ed., *Louisiana in the Short Story* (Baton Rouge, 1940).

Meine, Franklin J., ed., *Tall Tales of the Southwest: An Anthology of Southern and Southwestern Humor, 1830–1860* (New York, 1930).

Porter, William T., ed., *The Big Bear of Arkansas and Other Sketches Illustrative of Characters and Incidents in the South and South-West* (Philadelphia, 1845, 1855).

————, ed., *A Quarter Race in Kentucky* (Philadelphia, 1846, 1847).

Simpson, Claude M., ed., *The Local Colorists: American Short Stories, 1857–1900* (New York, 1960).

Turner, Arlin, ed., *Southern Stories* (New York, 1960).

Warfel, Harry R. and G. Harrison Orians, eds., *American Local-Color Stories* (New York, 1941).

Watterson, Henry, ed., *Oddities in Southern Life and Character* (Boston, 1882).

III. Literary Studies

[Baker, Carlos,] "Delineation of Life and Character," in *LHUS*, I, pp. 843–61.

Baker, Joseph E., "Four Arguments for Regionalism," *SatR*, XV (Nov 28, 1936), 3–4, 14.

Beath, Paul Robert, "Four Fallacies of Regionalism," *SatR*, XV (Nov 28, 1936), 3–4, 14, 16.

*Campbell, Walter S. [Stanley Vestal], *The Book Lover's Southwest: A Guide to Good Reading* (Norman, Okla., 1955).

Coleman, Charles W., Jr., "The Recent Movement in Southern Literature," *Harper's Monthly Mag*, LXXIV (1887), 837–55.

Collins, Carvel E., "Nineteenth-Century Fiction of the Southern Appalachians," *BB*, XVII (1942–43), 186–90, 215–19.

Fiske, Horace S., *Provincial Types in American Fiction* (New York, 1903).

Green, Claud B., "The Rise and Fall of Local Color in Southern Literature," *MissQ*, XVIII (1964–65), 1–6.

Hall, Wade, *The Smiling Phoenix: Southern Humor from 1865 to 1914* (Gainesville, 1965).

Harris, Isabella Deas, "The Southern Mountaineer in American Fiction, 1824–1910," Duke, 1948. [diss]

Henneman, John Bell, "The National Element in Southern Literature," *Shakespearean and Other Papers* (Sewanee, 1911), pp. 199–220. First publ in *SeR*, XI (1903), 345–66.

*Herron, Ima H., *The Small Town in American Literature* (Durham, 1939).

Hubbell, Jay B., "Literary Nationalism in the Old South," in *American Studies in Honor of William Kenneth Boyd*, ed. Jackson, pp. 175–220.

————, *The South in American Literature*.

-————, *Southern Life in Fiction* (Athens, Ga., 1960).

Johnson, R. B., "The Tyranny of Local Color," *Critic*, XLVIII (1906), 266–68.

McIlwaine, Ardrey Shields, *The Southern Poor-White from Lubberland to Tobacco Road* (Norman, Okla., 1939).

McWilliams, Carey, *The New Regionalism in American Literature* (Seattle, 1930).

Martin, Jay, *Harvests of Change: American Literature, 1865–1914* (Englewood Cliffs, N.J., 1967), pp. 88–105.

Masterson, James R., *Tall Tales of Arkansaw* (Boston, 1942).

Mims, Edwin, intro to *History of Southern Fiction*, VIII, *The South in the Building of the Nation*, pp. xi–lxiv.

Morse, J. H., "The Native Element in American Fiction," *Century*, IV (1883), 288–98, 362–75.

*Moses, Montrose J., *The Literature of the South* (New York, 1910), pp. 417–74; bibl, 475–511.

Page, Thomas Nelson, "Literature in the South Since the War," *Lippincott's*, XLVIII (1891), 740–56.

Pattee, Fred Lewis, *The Development of the American Short Story* (New York, 1923).

*———, *A History of American Literature Since 1870* (New York, 1915), pp. 1–24, 294–320, 355–84.

Pizer, Donald, *Realism and Naturalism in 19th Century American Literature* (Carbondale, Ill., 1966).

Rourke, Constance M., *American Humor: A Study of the National Character* (New York, 1931).

———, "The Significance of Sections," *New Rep*, XXVI (Sept 20, 1933), 148–51.

Sherman, C. B., "Farm-Life Fiction in the South," *SLM*, n.s., I (1939), 203–10.

Smith, Charles Foster, "Southern Dialect in Life and Literature," *So Bivouac*, n.s. I, (1885), 343–51.

Sullivan, Walter, "The Decline of Regionalism in Southern Fiction," *GaR*, XVIII (1964), 300–308.

Tourgee, Albion W., "The South as a Field of Fiction," *Forum*, VI (1888), 404–13.

Turner, Arlin, "Fiction of the Bayou Country," *SatR*, XVIII (Apr 30, 1938), 3–4, 16.

Walcutt, Charles Child, "Regionalism—Practical or Aesthetic?" *SeR*, XLIX (1941), 165–72.

Warren, Robert Penn, "Some Don'ts for Literary Regionalists," *AmerR*, VIII (1936), 142–50.

ARLIN TURNER
Duke University
Durham, North Carolina

SOUTHERN LITERARY PERIODICALS
1732-1967

No one studying the mind of the South can afford to overlook the numerous literary periodicals published between the eighteenth century and the present. Yet the standard histories of American literature largely ignore these periodicals. One can acquire little more than a nodding acquaintance with them even when he examines books which attempt nationwide coverage, such as James Playsted Wood's *Magazines in the United States*. An exception, however, is Frank Luther Mott's *A History of American Magazines*, which covers the period to 1905; Mott includes sketches of a few important Southern magazines and gives penetrating, though brief, comments about others.

A better introduction to this topic may be obtained by reading Jay B. Hubbell's discussions in *The South in American Literature* and his chapter "Southern Magazines" in *Culture in the South*. If one adds to these Edwin Mims's and Gregory Paine's essays and *Little Magazines* by Reed Whittemore (see below, Part II), he will gain an overall view of trends in Southern magazine publishing from the eighteenth century to the present.

For fuller information, though, the student must turn to the special studies which focus upon the field: a small number of doctoral dissertations and published books; a substantial list of masters' theses; and an impressive array of articles. A large number of the articles discuss the twentieth-century so-called "little" magazines, the epithet being a description of their limited circulation, not of their importance.

Scholars have studied various aspects of periodical writing, editing, and publishing; the wide range of their interests is indicated in the checklist. Locating the files, uncloaking contributors' pseudonyms, evaluating contents of individual magazines, and studying editorial problems—these are some of the topics that have engaged the attention of investigators. Among the more important editors who have been subjects of studies are Hugh Swinton Legaré, Edgar Allan Poe, William Gilmore Simms, George W. Bagby, John R. Thompson, and Albert Taylor Bledsoe. Rayburn S. Moore's forthcoming *Paul Hamilton Hayne* (TUSAS) will recount Hayne's editorship of *Russell's Magazine* (Charleston, 1857–60). Of interest, also, are reminiscences by contributors and editors, including Jay B. Hubbell (*Southwest Review, American Literature*); Donald Davidson and Allen Tate (*The Fugitive*); and John Bell Henneman (*Sewanee Review*). Biographical information about other editors may be found in national and regional biographical dictionaries and in county histories.

Richard B. Harwell, Bertram Holland Flanders, and a few others have searched for and evaluated the ephemeral Civil War periodicals. The compiler of this checklist is continuing to publish sketches of post-Civil War literary magazines, and he has in manuscript "A Reconstruction Reader" of representative essays, poems, and short stories selected from these periodicals.

In the twentieth century there have been two main categories of Southern literary periodicals: 1) the academic or critical reviews, beginning with the *Sewanee Review* (1892———) and including the *South Atlantic Quarterly* (1902———), the *Virginia Quarterly Review* (1925———), and *American Literature* (1929———), which have found financial sustenance from universities; and 2) the little or experimental magazines. By bulk alone, if not for their role in fostering the careers of new writers, the little magazines have been frequently spotlighted, even earning for themselves indexes, a book-length history, and a periodical, *Trace*, which since 1952 has reported their births and deaths.

Because Southerners have been negligent until recent years in collecting their magazines and preserving them, there is no single depository which contains files of all these periodicals. The chief depositories are various state libraries, state and private university libraries, and state and local historical society libraries. However, sometimes one will find scattered issues of short-lived ventures gathering dust in small public libraries throughout the South (see Ralph B. Flanders' article, checklist, part II). Libraries which have extensive holdings and long runs of files include the Library of Congress and the libraries of Duke University, University of North Carolina, University of Virginia, Louisiana State University, and the University of Texas. The New York Public Library and the library of the University of Wisconsin have two of the largest collections of twentieth-century magazines. AMS, Johnson, Kraus, and William Dawson are among corporations which specialize in reprinting periodicals; and many of the issues are also available on microfilm.

Published guides to library holdings are indispensable aids to researchers. Of first importance is a combination of Edna Brown Titus's *Union List of Serials*, 3rd ed (1965) and *New Serial Titles: A Union List of Serials Commencing Publication After December 31, 1949*. Because some magazines are difficult to distinguish from newspapers, one should not overlook Winifred Gregory's *American Newspapers 1821–1936*. For example, the *Southern Opinion* (Richmond, 1867–69), an important literary weekly, is listed only in *American Newspapers*. Other nationwide and regional guides are given in the checklist, part I. For an annotation of these, see Contance Winchell's *Guide to Reference Books*, 8th ed (1967). Many of the special studies, especially the doctoral dissertations, include finding lists of periodicals.

This checklist is selective; additional studies of Southern literary periodicals are listed in the following published works. James Woodress' *Dissertations in American Literature* covers the period 1891 through 1961. *Southern Literary Culture*, compiled by Clyde H. Cantrell and Walton R. Patrick, lists dissertations and theses written through 1948. Continuing coverage is provided by *Dissertation Abstracts*, a monthly compilation of abstracts of doctoral dissertations submitted to University Microfilms, Ann Arbor, Michigan; its companion *Index to American Doctoral Dissertations*; and the *South Atlantic Bulletin* (under "Theses for the Year").

In addition to selective book reviews, *American Literature* publishes a quarterly bibliography of doctoral dissertations and articles appearing in current periodicals. The annual bibliography in *PMLA* contains books and articles, some of which give listings of dissertations.

Articles on American Literature Appearing in Current Periodicals, compiled by Lewis Leary, is comprehensive for the years 1900 through 1950. Thomas F. Marshall's *Analytical Index* to the first thirty volumes of *American Literature*, 1929–59, is helpful.

The entries in part II of the checklist are arranged alphabetically by author and grouped within periods according to the publication dates of the periodicals, with an occasional overlapping. The beginning date is arbitrarily set at 1732, for there is some question about the title and date of the earliest Southern magazine. With the demise of the *Southern Bivouac* (Louisville) in 1887, there was no longer an intense effort to establish and sustain major literary periodicals devoted to the Lost Cause. The modern era, therefore, logically began in 1892 with the launching of the *Sewanee Review*.

I.   General Studies
*GUIDES TO LIBRARY HOLDINGS OF PERIODICALS

Downs, Robert B., *American Library Resources: A Bibliographical Guide* (Chicago, 1951).

———, *Resources of Southern Libraries: A Survey of Facilities for Research* (Chicago, 1938).

Freitag, Ruth S., comp., *Union List of Serials: A Bibliography* (Washington, D.C., 1964).

Gregory, Winifred, ed., *American Newspapers 1821–1936, A Union List of Files Available in the United States and Canada* (New York, 1937).

New Serial Titles: A Union List of Serials Commencing Publication After December 31, 1949 (Washington, D.C., January 1953———).

Roberts, Edward Graham, ed., *A Southeastern Supplement to the Union List of Serials* (Atlanta, 1959).

Skaggs, Alma S., ed., *Serials Currently Received in Southern Libraries: A Union List* (Chapel Hill, 1936).

Titus, Edna Brown, ed., *Union List of Serials in Libraries of the United States and Canada*, 3rd ed (New York, 1965).

Wilson, Louis R., and R. B. Downs, "Special Collections for the Study of History and Literature in the Southeast," in *Papers of the Bibl Soc of Amer*, XXVIII (1934), 97–131.

*Sources for Locating Studies of Southern Literary Periodicals

American Literature, bibl, 1929——.

Cantrell, and Patrick, *Southern Literary Culture: A Bibliography of Masters' and Doctors' Theses*.

Dissertation Abstracts (Ann Arbor, 1957——).

Gohdes, Clarence, comp., "Indexes to Contents of Magazines," "Magazines," in *Bibliographical Guide to the Study of the Literature of the U.S.A.*, 2nd ed (Durham, 1963), pp. 17–18; 31–32.

Hubbell, "Bibliography, Important Topics: Magazines," in *The South in American Literature*, pp. 902–903.

Index to American Doctoral Dissertations (Ann Arbor, 1957——).

Leary, Lewis, comp., *Articles on American Literature Appearing in Current Periodicals, 1900–1950* (Durham, 1954).

Marshall, Thomas F., *An Analytical Index to American Literature, Volumes I–XXX, March 1929–January 1959* (Durham, 1963).

PMLA, annual bibl.

SoAtlBull, "Theses for the Year."

Winchell, Constance M., *Guide to Reference Books*, 8th ed (Chicago, 1967).

Woodress, James, comp., *Dissertations in American Literature, 1891–1955, With Supplement, 1956–1961* (Durham, 1962).

II. Studies of Southern Literary Periodicals: A Selected Checklist

Studies of Periodicals Published 1732–1860

Abney, Beth, "The *Orion* as a Literary Publication," *Ga Hist Q*, XLVIII (1964), 411–24. [ed. at Penfield, Ga., by William C. Richards]

Agnew, Virginia Miller, "*Russell's Magazine*," Duke, 1937. [MA thesis]

Calhoun, Richard James, "Literary Criticism in Southern Periodicals: 1828–1860," North Carolina, 1959. [diss]

*Cardwell, Guy Adams, Jr., "Charleston Periodicals, 1795–1860: A Study in Literary Influences, with a Descriptive Checklist of Seventy-five Magazines," North Carolina, 1936. [diss]

———, "The Influence of Addison on Charleston Periodicals, 1795–1860," *SP*, XXXV (1938), 456–70.

———, "*The Quiver* and *The Floral Wreath*: Two Rare Charleston Periodicals," *N.C. Hist R*, XVI (1939), 418–27.

Carson, Clements, "Four Magazine Centers of the Old South," Vanderbilt, 1933. [MA thesis]

Cohen, Sidney J., *Three Notable Ante-Bellum Magazines of South Carolina* (Columbia, S.C., 1915). [*Russell's*, *Magnolia*, *SLM*]

Dempsey, Ray, "The History and Influence of Major Southern Literary Magazines Prior to the Civil War," Georgia, 1947. [MA thesis, includes *Orion*, *Russell's*, *So Ladies' Bk*, *SoR*, and *SQR*]

*Ellison, Rhoda Coleman, "Periodicals," in *A Checklist of Alabama Imprints 1807–1870* (University, Ala., 1946), pp. 23–26.

*———, "Literary Interests Reflected in Periodicals," in *Early Alabama Publications: A Study in Literary Interests* (University, Ala., 1947), pp. 88–132.

Ferry, Robert M., "Early Literary Magazines in Kentucky," Western Kentucky, 1934. [MA thesis]

*Flanders, Bertram Holland, *Early Georgia Magazines: Literary Periodicals to 1865* (Athens, Ga., 1944).

Flanders, Ralph B., "Newspapers and Periodicals in the Washington Memorial Library, Macon, Georgia," *N.C. HistR*, VII (1930), 220–23.

Gibbs, John Ernest, Jr., "William Gilmore Simms and *The Magnolia*," Duke, 1931. [MA thesis]

*Gilmer, Gertrude, *Checklist of Southern Periodicals to 1861* (Boston, 1934).

*———, "A Critique of Certain Georgia Ante-Bellum Literary Magazines Arranged Chronologically, and a Checklist," *Ga. Hist Q*, XVIII (1934), 293–334.

*———, "Maryland Magazines—Ante Bellum, 1793–1861," *Md Hist Mag*, XXIX (1934), 120–31.

*Griffin, Max L., "A Bibliography of New Orleans Magazines," *La Hist Q*, XVIII (1935), 493–556. [includes only periodicals of lit interest of the "past 100 years."]

Guilds, John C., Jr., "Simms as a Magazine Editor, 1825–1845: With Special Reference to His Contributions," Duke, 1954. [diss]

*Hoole, William Stanley, *A Checklist and Finding List of Charleston Periodicals, 1732–1864* (Durham, 1936).

———, "The Gilmans and the *Southern Rose*," *N.C. Hist R*, XI (1934), 116–28.

———, "William Gilmore Simms's Career as Editor," *Ga Hist Q*, XIX (1935), 47–54.

*Hubbell, "Newspapers and Magazines [1789–1830]," "Southern Magazines, [1830–1865]," *The South in American Literature*, pp. 218–19, 366–69.

*Jackson, David K., *The Contributors and Contributions to The Southern Literary Messenger (1834–1864)* (Charlottesville, 1936).

———, "An Estimate of the Influence of *The Southern Literary Messenger*, 1834–1864," *SLM*, n.s., I (1939). 508–14.

———, *Poe and the Southern Literary Messenger* (Richmond, 1934).

Kennedy, Fronde, "*Russell's Magazine*," *SAQ*, XVIII (1919), 125–44.

Long, Edgar, "*Russell's Magazine* as an Expression of Ante-Bellum South Carolina Culture," South Carolina, 1932. [diss]

*McLean, Frank, "Periodicals Published in the South Before 1880," Virginia, 1928. [diss; checklist with brief annot]

*Mims, Edwin, "Southern Magazines," in *The South in the Building of the Nation*, VII, 437–69.

Minor, Benjamin Blake, *The Southern Literary Messenger, 1834–1864* (New York, 1905). [assessment by ed., 1843–47]

*Mott, Frank Luther, "Southern Magazines," in *A History of American Magazines*, 1741–1850 (Cambridge, Mass., 1957), pp. 204–205, *passim*. [consult Mott's 3 other vols: II, 1850–65; III, 1865–85; IV, 1885–1905]

Paine, Gregory, "Magazines," in *Southern Prose Writers* (New York, 1947), pp. lxxix–lxxxvii.

Rhea, Linda, *Hugh Swinton Legaré* (Chapel Hill, 1934). [ed. and chief contributor to important *SoR*, 1828–32]

Riley, Susan B., "The Hazards of Periodical Publishing in the South During the Nineteenth Century," *Tenn Hist Q*, XXI (1962), 365–76.

_____, "Southern Literary Magazines of the Mid-Nineteenth Century," *Tenn Hist Q*, XXIII (1964), 221–36.

Rogers, Edward Reinhold, *Four Southern Magazines* (Richmond, 1902). [*De Bow's R*, *SoR*, *SoQR*, *SLM*]

Simpson, Francis Willard, "William Gilmore Simms and the *Southern Quarterly Review*," Furman, 1946. [MA thesis]

*Stearns. Bertha-Monica, "Southern Magazines for Ladies (1819–1860)," *SAQ*, XXXI (1932), 70–87.

*Terwilliger, W. Bird, "A History of Literary Periodicals in Baltimore," Maryland, 1941. [diss]

Trent, William P., *William Gilmore Simms* (Boston, 1892).

*Uhler, John Earle, "Literary Taste and Culture in Baltimore: A Study of the Periodical Literature of Baltimore from 1815 to 1833," Johns Hopkins, 1927. [diss]

STUDIES OF PERIODICALS PUBLISHED 1861–1865

*Atchison, Ray M., "Intellectual Life of the South During the War: Magazines," in "Southern Literary Magazines, 1865–1887," Duke, 1956, 17–24. [diss]

*Brantley, Rabun Lee, *Georgia Journalism of the Civil War Period* (Nashville, 1929). [discusses newsps, bks, and mags]

Cousins, Paul, *Joel Chandler Harris* (Baton Rouge, 1968). [much material on J. A. Turner's *The Countryman*]

Flanders, Bertram Holland, "*Bugle-Horn of Liberty*: A Confederate Humorous Magazine," *Emory U Q*, IX (1953), 79–85.

_____, "Third Period: 1859–65," *Early Georgia Magazines: Literary Periodicals to 1865* (Athens, Ga., 1944), pp. 129–78. [sketches of eight war-time periodicals]

*Harwell, Richard B., "Magazines and Newspapers," *Confederate Belles-Lettres: A Bibliography and a Finding List of the Fiction, Poetry, Drama, Songsters, and Miscellaneous Literature Published in the Confederate States of America* (Hattiesburg, Miss., 1941), pp. 78–79.

_____, "A Confederate View of the Southern Poets," *AL*, XXIV (1952), 51–61. [facts about the *So Illus News* and Paul H. Hayne's contributions]

*Hubbell, "The Civil War," *The South in American Literature*, pp. 455–56.

*Huff, Lawrence, "The Literary Publications of Joseph Addison Turner," *Ga Hist Q*, XLVI (1962), 223–36. [Turner's *Countryman*, 1862–66, launched career of Joel Chandler Harris]

*King, Joseph Leonard, Jr., "Richmond—Literature and War," in *Dr. George William Bagby: A Study of Virginian Literature, 1850–1880* (New York, 1937), pp. 70–95. [Bagby was war-time ed. of *SLM*]

Linneman, William R., "*Southern Punch*: A Draught of Confederate Wit," *SFQ*, XXVI (1962), 131–36.

STUDIES OF PERIODICALS PUBLISHED 1865–1891

Adams, Raymond William, "A Study of the Chief Literary Magazines of the South During the Years 1865 to 1880," North Carolina, 1921. [MA thesis]

Atchison, Ray M., "*The Land We Love*: A Southern Post-Bellum Magazine of Agriculture, Literature, and Military History," *N.C. Hist R*, XXXVII (1960), 506–15.

_____, "*Our Living and Our Dead*: A Post-Bellum North Carolina Magazine of Literature and History," *N.C. Hist R*, XL (1963), 423–33.

_____, "*Scott's Monthly Magazine*: A Georgia Post-Bellum Periodical of Literature and Military History," *Ga Hist Q*, XLIX (1965), 294–305.

*———, "Southern Literary Magazines, 1865–1887," Duke, 1956. [diss; surveys 11 states of Confederacy and 4 border states]

Bennett, John Boyce, "Albert Taylor Bledsoe: Social and Religious Controversialist of the Old South," Duke, 1942. [diss; Bledsoe was chief ed. of *SoR*, 1867–79]

High, Thomas O'Connor, "[Albert Taylor] Bledsoe's *Review:* A Southern Apologia," Vanderbilt, 1942. [MA thesis]

*Hubbell, "Southern Magazines [1865–1900]," *The South in American Literature*, pp. 716–26. [summarizes accomplishments of post-Civil War mags]

*Johnson, Aliene, "Southern Literary Magazines of the Reconstruction Period," Duke, 1935. [MA thesis]

Moore, L. Hugh, [Jr.], "Poetry in *The Sunny South*, 1882," Emory, 1959. [MA thesis]

———, "*The Sunny South* and Its Literature," *GaR*, XIX (1965), 176–85. [Atlanta wkly, 1875–1907, superseded by *Uncle Remus's Mag*]

*Young, Laura Newell, "Southern Literary Magazines, 1865–1887: With Special Reference to Literary Criticism," Duke, 1940. [MA thesis]

STUDIES OF PERIODICALS PUBLISHED 1892–1967

Allen, Charles, "*The Fugitive*," *SAQ*, XLIII (1944), 382–89.

Angoff, Charles, "The Little Magazines," *Amer Mercury*, LXIII (1946), 370–74. [primarily r of Hoffman, Allen, and Ulrich's history, 1st ed 1946]

*Bentley, Imogene, "Texas Literary and Educational Magazines: Their History and Educational Content," Peabody, 1941. [diss; includes *Corona, Dixieland, Guardian, Gulf Messenger, Frontier Times*]

*Carter, Virginia, "Literary Periodicals of the Southwest, Especially as Shown by a Detailed Study of the *Southwest Review*," Oklahoma, 1933. [MA thesis]

Cline, John, "Thirty-Eight Years of the *South Atlantic Quarterly:* A Chapter in the Progress of Liberalism in the South," Duke, 1940. [MA thesis]

Cowan, Louise, "The Birth of *The Fugitive*: Spring, 1922," *The Fugitive Group: A Literary History* (Baton Rouge, 1959), pp. 43–62.

Davidson, Donald, "The Thankless Muse and Her Fugitive Poets," *Southern Writers in the Modern World* (Athens, Ga., 1958), pp. 1–30. [reminiscence by member of Nashville group which publ *The Fugitive*, 1922–25, one of most important little mags]

Durett, Frances Bowen, "The New Orleans *Double Dealer*," in *Reality and Myth*, pp. 212–36.

*French, Warren, "The Little Magazines in the Fifties," *Coll Eng*, XXII (1961), 547–52. [lib holdings listed and accomplishments cited]

Green, Claud B., "Novelist and Magazinist of the New South," *John Trotwood Moore: Tennessee Man of Letters* (Athens, Ga., 1957), pp. 66–81. [Moore as ed. and chief contributor to *Trotwood's Monthly* and its successor, *The Taylor-Trotwood Magazine*, 1905–10]

Hamilton, William Baskerville, "Fifty Years of Liberalism and Learning," *Fifty Years of the South Atlantic Quarterly* (Durham, 1952), pp. 1–27. [sketch of *SAQ*; see Cline, above]

Henneman, John Bell, "Ten Years of the *Sewanee Review*: A Retrospect," *SeR*, X (1902), 477–92.

Hodge, Llewellyn Bush, "A Descriptive and Critical Analysis of *Uncle Remus's Magazine*," Georgia, 1948. [MA thesis; mag ed. by Joel Chandler Harris]

*Hoffman, Frederick J., "The Little Magazines: Portrait of an Age," *SatR*, XXVI (Dec 25, 1943), 3–5.

*_____, Charles Allen, and Carolyn F. Ulrich, *The Little Magazine: A History and a Bibliography*, 2nd ed (Princeton, 1947).

Hubbell, Jay B., "*American Literature, 1928–1954*," in *South and Southwest: Literary Essays and Reminiscences* (Durham, 1965), pp. 22–48. [information by founding ed.]

_____, "*Southwest Review, 1924–1929*," in *South and Southwest: Literary Essays and Reminiscences* (Durham, 1954), pp. 3–21. [information by early ed.]

*_____, "Southern Magazines," in *Culture in the South*, ed. W[illiam] T. Couch (Chapel Hill, 1935), pp. 159–82. [trends in So mag pub to 1932]

*Miles, Virginia, "Kentucky Literary Magazines since 1900," Western Kentucky, 1935. [MA thesis]

*O'Connor, William Van, "Little Magazines in the Third Generation," *Poetry*, LXXIII (1949), 367–69.

Tate, Allen, "*The Fugitive, 1922–1925: A Personal Recollection Twenty Years After*," *Princeton U Lib Chron*, III, No. 3 (1942), 75–84.

*Troy, William, "The Story of the Little Magazines," *Bookman*, LXX (1930), 476–81, 657–63.

Turner, Alice Lucille, "A Study of the Contents of *The Sewanee Review*, with Historical Introduction," Peabody, 1931. [diss]

*Webb, Vina Wadlington, "A Study of the Negro Magazine: With Special Reference to Its Literary Value," North Carolina College, 1946. [MA thesis; *Phylon, So Workman, Southland, Stylus, Voice of the Negro*]

*Whittemore, Reed, *Little Magazines* (Minneapolis, 1963). [Minn pamph]

*Williford, Lyde Gwynne, "Provincial Literary Magazines in America, 1915 to 1932," Southern Methodist, 1932. [MA thesis; includes *TexR* (later *SWR*), *VQR*]

RAY M. ATCHISON
Samford University
Birmingham, Alabama

SOUTHERN POPULAR LITERATURE

Studies of popular literature (dime novels, mysteries, best sellers, and the like) usually have placed little emphasis on the regional backgrounds. Most of the items listed here, therefore, are actually studies of other topics which also discuss Southern popular literature in passing.

Information about popular writing may also be found in items listed under other topics in this checklist (the Civil War, local color, periodicals) and in studies of individual authors (such as Margaret Mitchell).

The popularity or the sales of a book, according to the critic who rightfully decries mass advertising of literature and mass taste, should be one of the last factors in evaluating it. For this reason, when this topic overlaps with others (the Civil War, local color, periods of Southern literature, periodicals), this category has been the first to yield.

*Agnew, Janet Margaret, *A Southern Bibliography: Fiction 1929–1938* (LSU Lib School, Bibl Ser No. 1, 1939).

*———, *A Southern Bibliography: Historical Fiction 1929–1938* (LSU Lib School, Bibl Ser No. 2, 1940).

Bode, Carl, *The Half-World of American Culture: A Miscellany* (Carbondale, Ill., 1965). [see esp "Adversity's Favorite Son," pp. 121–24, on Hervey Allen's *Anthony Adverse,* and "The Buxom Biographies," pp. 158–69, partly on Harnett Kane]

Bradbury, *Renaissance in the South.* [discusses many minor writers; see esp extensive list of So writers in appendix]

Brown, Herbert Ross, *The Sentimental Novel in America, 1789–1860* (Durham, 1940). [esp chap 3, Bk 2, "Uncle Tom's and Other Cabins," and ff]

Buck, Paul H., *The Road to Reunion, 1865–1900* (New York, 1937). [esp chaps 8 and 9, "The South Begins to Write" and "The North Feels the Power of the Pen"]

Coleman, Charles W., Jr., "The Recent Movement in Southern Literature," *Harper's New Monthly Mag,* LXXIV (1887), 837–55.

Cowie, *The Rise of the American Novel.* [esp chap 10, "The Domestic Sentimentalists and Other Popular Writers"]

Davis, Richard Beale, "The 'Virginia Novel' Before *Swallow Barn,*" *VMHB,* LXXI (1963), 278–93.

English, Thomas H., "On Choosing a Southern Hundred," *Princeton U Lib Chron,* XXVII (1965), 45–52.

———, "One Hundred Famous Southern Books," *SoAtlBull,* XIII (May 1947), 1, 12–13.

Forrest, Mary, *Women of the South Distinguished in Literature* (New York, 1866). [provides biog sketches and selections from 34 authors and "writers not yet authors"]

Gaines, Francis Pendleton, *The Southern Plantation: A Study in the Development and the Accuracy of a Tradition* (New York, 1924). [esp chaps 3 and 4]

Gross, Theodore L., "The South in the Literature of Reconstruction," *MissQ,* XIV (1961), 68–78.

Hackett, Alice P., *Sixty Years of Best Sellers, 1895–1955* (New York, 1956).

Hart, James D., *The Popular Book: A History of America's Literary Taste* (New York, 1950).

Hilldrup, Robert LeRoy, "Cold War Against the Yankees in the Ante-Bellum Literature of Southern Women," *N.C. Hist R*, XXXI (1954), 370–84.

Leisy, Ernest E., *The American Historical Novel* (Norman, Okla., 1950). [four chaps contain discussions of hist novels about So in different hist periods]

Mims, Edwin, *The Advancing South* (New York, 1926). [esp pp. 128–30 and chaps 8 and 9; writers as they progress from popular and stereotyped subjects]

———, intro to *History of Southern Fiction*, vol VIII of *The South in the Building of the Nation*, ed. John Bell Henneman. [esp "Southern Fiction After the War of Secession," pp. xlviii–lxv]

Mott, Frank Luther, *Golden Multitudes* (New York, 1947). [hist of best sellers, many So]

Odum, Howard W., "On Southern Literature and Southern Culture," in *Southern Renascence*, ed. Rubin and Jacobs, pp. 84–100. [lists best-sellers, Pulitzer Prizes; gives statistics on articles by So writers in mags]

Osterweis, Rollin G., *Romanticism and Nationalism in the Old South* (New Haven, 1949; Baton Rouge, 1967). [see esp chap 6, "Richmond and Southern Romantic Literature," which studies mainly the *SLM*]

Paine, Gregory, *Southern Prose Writers* (New York, 1947). [see esp "The Plantation Tradition" and "Local Color," pp. lxxxvii–cxvii, for discussion of popular So lit]

Papashvily, Helen Waite, *All the Happy Endings: A Study of the Domestic Novel in America, the Women Who Wrote It, the Women Who Read It, in the Nineteenth Century* (New York, 1956).

Pilkington, John, "History and Literature in Mississippi Since 1900," *Jour of Miss Hist*, XX (1958), 234–43.

Robertson, Thomas Luther, "The Unfolding Magnolia: A Literary History of Mississippi Until 1876," *DA*, XXI, 628–29 (Vanderbilt).

Rosenberg, Bernard, and David M. White, eds., *Mass Culture: The Popular Arts in America* (Glencoe, Ill., 1957).

Thompson, Lawrence S., "Bluegrass and Bourbon: The Colonel of Kentucky Fiction," *GaR*, VII (1953), 107–15.

Turner, H. Arlin, "The Southern Novel," *SWR*, XXV (1940), 205–12. [plea for novelists to "picture the So whole" rather than follow stereotyped view of Old So]

Van Auken, Sheldon, "The Southern Historical Novel in the Early Twentieth Century," *JSH*, XIV (1948), 157–91.

FLOYD C. WATKINS
Emory University
Atlanta, Georgia

EIGHTEENTH AND NINETEENTH CENTURY DRAMA

Though Southern drama before 1900 has received inadequate attention, the work already done and the materials now available for study present a challenge to future scholarship. The theater of the antebellum South was a vital institution, as the theatrical histories attest, and not surprisingly its existence was accompanied by dramatic composition, a practice which continued after the Civil War. Considering the present state of scholarship in this area, the following objectives have the best claims for priority: to determine which plays comprise Southern drama before 1900; to make these plays available in modern printings or microtext, or, at the least, to make known their locations; to provide studies of individual dramatists and their plays; and, finally, to complete more general treatments of the subject.

The goal of determining the body of plays and of making them readily accessible to the scholar is the first order of business. Owing to the collection of all extant American plays from the beginning through 1830 in *Three Centuries of Drama: American*, edited by Henry W. Wells (New York: Readex Microprint), the early period is in the best state by far, though a number of extant plays are missing from the microprint collection, and others will probably turn up from time to time. For the plays through 1830, then, it is fair to state that the list supplied here contains the body of Southern drama that the scholar can reliably concentrate on for that period.

After 1830, it is much more difficult to procure plays for examination. In the three decades preceding the Civil War, some authors of plays wrote primarily in other literary forms, as did Poe and Simms. Their plays have received some attention and in certain cases are readily available, but the dramas of lesser known writers often cannot be conveniently obtained, and little study of them has been made. Thus, it cannot be stated with any finality which plays make up the drama of this period, nor can its nature be described at this time. From the Civil War to 1900, the main source for determining and securing the body of plays is *Dramatic Compositions Copyrighted in the United States 1870 to 1916*, a listing issued by the Library of Congress. For this period, Professor Paul T. Nolan has almost single-handedly provided the only scholarship, through his articles, checklists of drama for states, and editions of the plays in modern printings or microtext.

Scholarship so far has treated most adequately a few dramatists and theatrical activities. Plays by Robert Munford, George Washington Parke Custis, and Poe have elicited a considerable number of studies.

There is a need for more critical biographies such as *Robert Munford: America's First Comic Dramatist*, by Rodney M. Baine. Numerous studies of the theater in the South have appeared. Much material exists on the Colonial and Ante-bellum periods and, in special studies, on the theater in Charleston, Richmond, Savannah, and New Orleans. The scholar should check these historical accounts for the valuable information they contain on the dramas and dramatists and for descriptions of the milieu in which the writers composed. Clarence Gohdes' *Literature and Theater of the States and Regions of the U.S.A.* and James H. Dormon's *Theater in the Ante-Bellum South* provide excellent bibliographies on the Southern theater. No attempt has been made at a comprehensive listing of the scholarship on the theater in this bibliography, which concentrates on the drama.

This checklist includes plays, as well as scholarly studies of the drama, because work cannot proceed successfully until it is determined which plays in fact constitute Southern drama, where they can be read and examined, and which are the most significant. Only those plays are given which are readily available or which have a location verified by this compiler. The most complete body of plays, that from the beginning through 1830, can be easily identified in the division devoted to ante-bellum plays by noting the first publication date. Only four entries represent the drama for the remaining decades before the Civil War. For several dramas, more than one printing of the text is listed in order to provide information on its availability and to specify important introductory essays. All of the modern printings include introductions by the editors. Southern drama in this bibliography is to be understood as plays composed by natives of the South (the eleven states of the Confederacy) or by writers who spent an important part of their careers in the South, and is restricted to dramas in English.

In addition to the entries given below see the listings under "Drama" in the checklist for the Early National period elsewhere in this volume.

I.   From the Beginning to the Civil War

PLAYS

Note: "RM" in brackets designates those plays included in the Readex Microprint collection: *Three Centuries of Drama: American*, ed. Henry W. Wells.

Burk, John Daly, *Bethlem Gabor* (Petersburg, Va., 1807). [RM]

_____, *Bunker-Hill; or, The Death of General Warren* (New York, 1797). [RM]

_____, *Female Patriotism; or, The Death of Joan of Arc* (New York, 1798). [RM]

Crafts, William, *The Sea-Serpent* (Charleston, S.C., 1819). [RM]

Custis, George Washington Parke, *The Indian Prophecy* (Georgetown, 1828). [RM]

_____, *Pocahontas; or, The Settlers of Virginia* (Philadelphia, 1830). [RM]

————, *Pocahontas; or, The Settlers of Virginia*, in *Representative American Plays*, ed. Arthur Hobson Quinn (New York, 1953).

Darling, David, *Beaux Without Belles; or, Ladies We Can Do Without You* (Charlottesville, 1820). [RM]

Doddridge, Joseph, *Logan, The Last of the Race of Shikellemus* (Buffaloe Creek, Brooke County, Va., 1823). [RM]

Grice, C. E., *Battle of New Orleans* (Baltimore, 1815). [RM]

Hall, Everard, *Nolens Volens; or The Biter Bit* (Newbern, N.C., 1809). [RM]

Harby, Isaac, *Alberti*, in *Selections from the Miscellaneous Writings of Isaac Harby*, ed. Henry L. Pinckney and Abraham Moise (Charleston, 1829). [RM]

————, *The Gordian Knot* (Charleston, 1810). [RM]

Holland, E. C., *The Corsair* (Charleston, 1818). [RM]

Ioor, William, *The Battle of Eutaw Springs* (Charleston, 1807). [RM]

————, *Independence* (Charleston, 1805). [RM]

Kennicott, James H., *Irma; or, the Prediction* (New York, 1830). [RM]

Maxwell, William Bulloch, *The Mysterious Father*, ed. Gerald Kahan (Athens, Ga., 1965). [Maxwell's play was first publ in Savannah, 1807]

Munford, Robert, *The Candidates; or, The Humours of a Virginia Election*, in *A Collection of Plays and Poems* (Petersburg, Va., 1798). [RM]

————, *The Candidates; or, The Humours of a Virginia Election*, ed. Jay B. Hubbell and Douglass Adair, *WMQ*, 3rd ser, V (1948), 217–57.

————, *The Candidates; or, The Humours of a Virginia Election*, in *Dramas from the American Theatre, 1762–1909*, ed. Richard Moody (Cleveland, 1966).

————, *The Patriots*, in *A Collection of Plays and Poems* (Petersburg, Va., 1798). [RM]

————, *The Patriots*, ed. Courtlandt Canby, *WMQ*, 3rd ser, VI (1949), 437–502.

Munford, William, *Almoran and Hamet*, in *Poems and Compositions in Prose on Several Occasions* (Richmond, 1798). [RM]

Nature and Philosophy (New York, 1830). [RM—play by "a citizen of Richmond"]

Oscar Fitz-James (Richmond, 1819). [RM—play by "a native of Virginia"]

Pinckney, Maria, *The Young Carolinians; or, Americans in Algiers, A Tyrant's Victims*, and *The Orphans* in *Essays, Religious, Moral, Dramatic, and Poetical* (Charleston, 1818). [RM—three closet dramas]

*Poe, Edgar Allan, *Politian*, in *The Poems of Edgar Allan Poe*, ed. Floyd Stovall (Charlottesville, 1965). [scenes from play first publ 1835, *SLM*]

Sawyer, Lemuel, *Blackbeard* (Washington, D.C., 1824). [RM]

————, *Blackbeard*, ed. Richard Walser (Raleigh, 1952).

————, *The Wreck of Honor* (New York, 1824). [RM]

Simmons, James Wright, *Manfredi* (Philadelphia, 1821). [RM]

————, *Valdemar; or, the Castle of the Cliff* (Philadelphia, 1822). [RM]

Simms, William Gilmore, *Michael Bonham; or, The Fall of Bexar*, *SLM*, XVIII (1852), 89–96, 145–49, 234–40, 296–304, 342–49.

————, *Norman Maurice: or, The Man of the People* (Philadelphia, 1853).

Tayleure, Clifton W., *Horseshoe Robinson*, in *Representative Plays by American Dramatists from 1765 to the Present Day*, ed. Montrose J. Moses (New York, 1918–25), II, 765–823. [Tayleure's play first publ in 1858]

Tucker, St. George, "The Wheel of Fortune," in "A Critical Edition of St. George Tucker's 'The Wheel of Fortune,'" by Hal Laughlin, William and Mary, 1960. [MA thesis. This unpubl play was composed in 1796–97]

White, John Blake, *The Forgers*, in *So Lit Jour*, n. s., I (1837), 118–25, 218–26, 354–62, 435–43, 509–18.

————, *The Forgers: A Dramatic Poem*, repr from *So Lit Jour* of 1837 by order of his son, Octavius A. White, 1899. [copy in Charleston Library Soc, Charleston, S.C.]
————, *Foscari* (Charleston, S.C. 1806). [RM]
————, *Modern Honor* (Charleston, S.C. 1812). [RM]
————, *The Mysteries of the Castle* (Charleston, S.C., 1807). [RM]
————, *The Triumph of Liberty, or Louisiana Preserved* (Charleston, S.C., 1819). [copy in The Library Co of Philadelphia]
Workman, James, *Liberty in Louisiana* (Charleston, S.C., 1804). [RM]

Scholarship on the Plays and Playwrights

Bass, Robert Duncan, "The Plays and Playwrights of South Carolina," South Carolina, 1927. [MA thesis]
*Baine, Rodney M., *Robert Munford: America's First Comic Dramatist* (Athens, Ga., 1967).
*Bergquist, G. William, ed., *Three Centuries of English and American Plays: A Checklist, England: 1500–1800, United States: 1714–1830* (New York, 1963). [checklist for *Three Centuries of Drama: American*, RM]
Brown, T. Allston, "Clifton W. Tayleure," *History of the American Stage* (New York, 1870), p. 354.
Cairns, William B., *British Criticisms of American Writings, 1783–1815*, U of Wis Stud in Lang and Lit, No. 1 (Madison, Wis., 1918).
*Cauble, Frank P., "William Wirt and His Friends: A Study in Southern Culture," North Carolina, 1933. [diss; information on playwriting of Wirt, others in Va]
Custis, George Washington Parke, *Recollections and Private Memoirs of Washington* with "A Memoir of the Author" by his daughter (New York, 1860).
*Damon, S. Foster, *Thomas Holley Chivers, Friend of Poe* (New York, 1930). [comments on and passages from Chivers' plays *Conrad and Eudora* and *Leoni*, pp. 76–84, 110–19]
*Davis, Richard Beale, "Plays and the Theater," *Intellectual Life in Jefferson's Virginia, 1798–1830* (Chapel Hill, 1964), pp. 239–52.
Duyckinck, *Cyclopaedia of American Literature*. [on William Crafts, Isaac Harby, Robert and William Munford, others]
Harby, Isaac, *A Selection from the Miscellaneous Writings of the Late Isaac Harby*, ed. Henry L. Pinckney and Abraham Moise, with "A Memoir of His Life," by Abraham Moise (Charleston, S.C., 1829).
*Hill, Frank P., *American Plays, Printed 1714–1830* (Stanford, 1934). [gives locations in libraries for plays; draws on bibl by Oscar Wegelin; RM collection based on Hill's bibl]
Hoole, W. Stanley, "Simms's *Michael Bonham*, A 'Forgotten Drama' of the Texas Revolution," *SW Hist Q*, XLVI (1942), 255–61.
*Hubbell, "Robert Munford," in *The South in American Literature*, pp. 142–48, 950–51; "Theater and Drama," pp. 911–12.
Lewisohn, Ludwig, "Books We Have Made: A History of Literature in South Carolina," *Charleston* (S.C.) *News and Courier*, Sunday News, July 5—Sept 20, 1903. [part 3 for early drama in S.C.]
Lynn, Kenneth S., *Mark Twain and Southwestern Humor* (Boston, 1959). [Robert Munford's plays as part SW tradition, pp. 47–50]
McGowan, Clelia P., "Louisa M'Cord" and passages from her play, *Caius Gracchus*, in *Library of Southern Literature,* ed. E. A. Alderman et al, VIII, 3505–30.
Moise, L. C., *Biography of Isaac Harby* (n.p., 1931).

Moody, Richard, *America Takes the Stage: Romanticism in American Drama and Theatre, 1750–1900* (Bloomington, Ind., 1955).

*_____, ed., *Dramas from the American Theatre, 1762–1909* (Cleveland, 1966).

Moses, Montrose J., *The American Dramatist* (Boston, 1925).

_____, *The Literature of the South* (New York, 1910).

Nelligan, Murray H., "American Nationalism on the Stage: The Plays of George Washington Custis (1781–1857)," *VMHB*, LVIII (1950), 299–324.

Parks, Edd Winfield, "Urban Influences on Ante-Bellum Writers of the Southeast," *Segments of Southern Thought* (Athens, Ga., 1938), pp. 136–55. [comments on dramatists, theaters in S.C. and Va.]

_____, "On Dramas and Dramatists," *William Gilmore Simms as Literary Critic*, U. of Ga. Monographs, No. 7 (Athens, Ga., 1961).

Parrington, Vernon Louis, "William Crafts," *Main Currents in American Thought* (New York, 1927), II, 112–14.

Quinn, Arthur Hobson, *Edgar Allan Poe: A Critical Biography* (New York, 1941). [analysis of *Politian*, pp. 231–34]

*_____, *A History of the American Drama from the Beginning to the Civil War* (New York, 1943). [early Charleston dramatists, pp. 187–94, 198 and bibl, p. 411]

Reed, Perley I., *The Realistic Presentation of American Characters in Native American Plays Prior to Eighteen Seventy*, *Ohio State U Bull*, XXII (May 1918).

Roppolo, Joseph Patrick, "American Themes, Heroes, and History on the New Orleans Stage, 1806–1865," *Tulane Stud in Eng*, V (1955), 151–81.

_____, "Local and Topical Plays in New Orleans, 1806–1865," *Tulane Stud in Eng*, IV (1954), 91–124.

Sawyer, Lemuel, *Auto-Biography* (New York, 1844).

Shulim, Joseph I., "Joseph Daly Burk, Playwright of Libertarianism: From 1796 to 1807," *Bull N.Y. Public Lib*, LXV (1961), 451–63.

Simms, William Gilmore, "Our Early Authors and Artists," *XIX Century*, I (1869), 273–83. [includes comments on early dramatists of S.C.]

Snowden, Yates, *South Carolina Plays and Playwrights*, in the series *The Carolinian* (Nov 1909).

Sowerby, E. Millicent, ed., *Catalogue of the Library of Thomas Jefferson* (Washington, D.C., 1953), III, 330–31. [information on James Workman]

Trent, William P., *William Gilmore Simms* (Boston, 1892). [comments on Simms's plays, pp. 214–17]

Walser, Richard Gaither, ed., *North Carolina Plays* (Richmond, 1956).

*Watson, Charles S., "Early Dramatic Writing in the South: Virginia and South Carolina Plays, 1798–1830," *DA*, XXVII, no. 10, 3,435–A (Vanderbilt).

_____, "Jeffersonian Republicanism in William Ioor's *Independence*, the First Play of South Carolina," *S.C. Hist Mag*, LXIX (July 1968).

_____, "Stephen Cullen Carpenter: First Drama Critic of the Charleston *Courier* and Supporter of the First Plays of South Carolina," *S.C. Hist Mag*, LXIX (Oct 1968).

Watts, Charles Henry, *Thomas Holley Chivers, His Literary Career and His Poetry* (Athens, Ga., 1956).

*Wegelin, Oscar, *Early American Plays, 1714–1830* (New York, 1905).

Weidner, Paul R., ed., "The Journal of John Blake White," *S.C. Hist and Geneal Mag* XLII (1941), 55–71, 99–117, 169–86; XLIII (1942), 35–46, 103–17, 161–74.

Wyatt, E. A., IV, *John Daly Burk; Patriot—Playwright— Historian* (Charlottesville, 1936).

II.   From the Civil War to 1900

PLAYS

Arthur, Lee, *The One Act Plays of Lee Arthur: The Sardou of Shreveport*, ed. Paul T. Nolan, U of Ky Microcards, ser A (Lexington, Ky., 1962). Republ without documentation and with rev intro, *The One Act Plays of Lee Arthur* (Cody, Wyo., 1962).

Bien, Herman M., *The Feast of Lights; or Chanukoh*, ed. Paul T. Nolan, U of Ky Microcards, ser A, No. 145 (Lexington, Ky., 1963).

Williams, Espy, *The Atheist*, in "A Southerner's Tribute to Illinois' 'Pagan Prophet,' " by Paul T. Nolan, *Jour of Ill Hist Soc*, LI (1958), 268–83. [text of *The Atheist*, one-act play by Williams; discussion of its form]

———, *Marlowe: The Buried Name, A Romantic Melodrama*, ed. Paul T. Nolan, U of Ky Microcards, ser A, No. 31, (Lexington, Ky., 1960).

———, *Morbid Versus Quick* in "A Farcial View of the New Orleans Gallant: Williams's *Morbid Versus Quick*," by Paul T. Nolan, *SW La Jour*, V (1961), 2–22.

———, *Parrhasius* in *Espy Williams: Parrhasius: A Southerner Returns to the Classics*, ed. Paul T. Nolan, U of Ky Microcards, ser A, No. 26 (Lexington, Ky., 1958).

———, *The Selected Works of Espy Williams: Southern Playwright*, ed. Paul T. Nolan, U of Ky Microcards, ser A, No. 45 (Lexington, Ky., 1960).

SCHOLARSHIP ON THE PLAYS AND PLAYWRIGHTS

Dramatic Compositions Copyrighted in the United States 1870 to 1916, 2 vols (Washington, D.C., 1918).

*Finley, Katherine P., and Paul T. Nolan, "Mississippi Dramas Between Wars, 1870–1916: A Checklist and an Argument," *Jour of Miss Hist*, XXVI (1964), 219–28, 299–306.

*Nolan, Paul T., "Alabama Drama, 1870–1916: A Checklist," *AlaR*, XVIII (1965), 65–72.

———, "Almost: Marshall Thompson," *SW Mag*, II (Apr—May, 1960), 3, 19. [La playwright]

*——— and Amos E. Simpson, "Arkansas Drama Before World War I," *Ark Hist Q*, XXII (1963), 61–75.

———, "Arthur Lee Kahn of Louisiana," *So Israelite*, XXXVI (Sept 1961), 27–31.

———, "Arthur Lee Kahn: 'The Sardon of Shreveport,' " *Bull of La Lib Assn*, XXIV (Summer 1961), 55–58, 83.

———, "Bright American Minds, British Brains, and Southern Drama," *So Speech Jour*, XXIV (1959), 129–34. [Espy Williams and producer Clarence Brune]

———, "The Case for Louisiana Drama," *SW La Jour*, IV (1960), 35–42.

———, "Classical Tragedy in the Province Theater," *AQ*, XIII (1961), 410–13. [about play by Espy Williams]

———, "Drama in the Lower Mississippi States," *MissQ*, XIX (1965–66), 20–28.

*———, "Espy Williams: New Orleans Playwright," *Bull of La Lib Assn*, XXI (1958), 137–39.

———, "Felix Voorhies – Judge – Playwright – Actor – Writer," *SW Mag*, II (Feb 1960), 3, 24.

*———, "Georgia Drama Between the Wars (1870–1916): A Checklist," *Ga Hist Q*, LI (1967), 216–30.

———, "Journal of a Young Southern Playwright: Espy Williams of New Orleans, 1874–75," *La Stud*, I (Fall—Winter 1962), 30–50, 33–54.

_____, "The Life and Death of a Louisiana Play: Espy Williams' 'Unorna,'" *La Hist,*
V (1964), 143–60.

_____, "Patience Lesson: Lee D. Freeman, Louisiana Playwright," *SW Mag,* II (Aug—
Sept 1960), 4–5.

_____, ed., *Provincial Drama in America, 1870–1916* (Metuchen, N.J., 1967). [contains
articles previously publ by Nolan; several on Espy Williams]

_____, "The Sacrifice of Poucha-Houmma," *Amer Indian,* VI (Winter 1966), 42–44.
[first La play publ, 1814]

_____, "A Shakespeare Idol in America," *MissQ,* XII, (1959), 64–74. [crit of Shake-
speare by Espy Williams]

_____, "South Carolina Drama: The Lost Years Between the Wars," *S.C. Mag,* XXVI
(Spring 1962), 20–29.

_____, "A Southern Playwright: Arthur Lee Kahn," *So Speech Jour,* XXVII (1962),
202–12.

_____, "Victor H. Smalley (Louisiana Playwright, 1880–1910)," *SW Mag,* II (June—
July 1960), 12.

_____, "Williams' *Dante:* The Death of Nineteenth Century Heroic Drama," *So Speech
Jour,* XXV (1960), 255–63.

III.   Theatrical History

Adams, Henry W., *Montgomery Theater, 1822–1835* (Montgomery, Ala., 1955).

*Brockett, O. G., "The Theatre of the Southern United States from the Beginnings
Through 1865: A Bibliographical Essay," *Theatre Research,* II (1960), 163–74.

Carpenter, Stephen Cullen, reviews by "Thespis," *Charleston* (S.C.) *Courier,* 1803–1806.
[dramatic crit, giving information on early theater and dramatists of Charleston]

*Dormon, James H., Jr., *Theater in the Ante-Bellum South, 1815–1861* (Chapel Hill,
1967).

Dunlap, William, *History of the American Theater* (New York, 1963).

Free, Joseph Miller, "The Ante-Bellum Theatre of the Old Natchez Region," *Jour of Miss
Hist,* V (1943), 14–27.

*Gohdes, Clarence, *Literature and Theater of the States and Regions of the U.S.A.: An
Historical Bibliography* (Durham, 1967).

Henderson, Archibald, "Early Drama and Amateur Entertainment in North Carolina,"
The Reviewer, V (Oct 1925), 68–77.

Hoole, W. Stanley, *The Ante-Bellum Charleston Theatre* (University, Ala., 1946).
[unpubl vol by Hoole, "A History of the Charleston Theatres, 1800–1875," deposited
at U of Ala Lib, contains information on period after Civil War]

_____, "Charleston Theatricals During the Tragic Decade, 1860–1869," *JSH,* XI
(1945), 538–47.

_____, "Two Famous Theatres of the Old South," *SAQ,* XXXVI (1937), 273–77.

Hunt, Douglas L., *The Nashville Theater, 1830–1840,* Birmingham-Southern Coll Bull,
XXVIII (May 1935).

Johnson, Guion Griffis, *Ante-Bellum North Carolina, A Social History* (Chapel Hill, 1937).
[information on theater, pp. 175–80]

Kendall, John S., *The Golden Age of the New Orleans Theatre* (Baton Rouge, 1952).

Ludlow, Noah M., *Dramatic Life as I Found It* (St. Louis, 1880).

Patrick, J. Max, *Savannah's Pioneer Theater from Its Origins to 1810* (Athens, Ga., 1953).

*Rankin, Hugh S., *The Theater in Colonial America* (Chapel Hill, 1965).

Robinson, Emmett, ed., "Dr. Irving's Reminiscences of the Charleston Stage," *S.C. Hist and Geneal Mag*, LI (1950), 125–31, 195–215; LII (1951), 26–33, 93–106, 166–79, 225–32; LIII (1952), 37–47.

Sherman, Susanne K., "Thomas Wade West, Theatrical Impresario, 1790–1799," *WMQ*, 3rd ser, IX (1952), 10–28.

Shockley, Martin Staples, "American Plays in the Richmond Theatre, 1819–1838," *SP*, XXXVII (1940), 100–19.

————, "A History of the Theatre in Richmond, Virginia, 1819–1838," North Carolina, 1938. [diss]

Smith, Solomon F., *Theatrical Management in the West and South for Thirty Years* (New York, 1868).

Smither, Nelle, "A History of the English Theatre in New Orleans, 1806–1842," *La Hist Q*, XXVIII (1945), 85–276, 361–572.

Sonneck, O. G., *Early Opera in America* (New York, 1915).

Willis, Eola, *The Charleston Stage in the XVIII Century* (Columbia, S.C., 1924).

Wyatt, E. A., IV, "Three Petersburg Theaters," *WMQ*, 2nd ser, XXI (1941), 83–110.

CHARLES S. WATSON
University of Alabama
Tuscaloosa, Alabama

TWENTIETH CENTURY SOUTHERN DRAMA

In the twentieth century some individual Southern playwrights have distinguished themselves, but there has been no significant theatrical movement or coterie of dramatists from the South expressing similar ideas and techniques. New York is still the center of the American theater, and most plays produced there reflect the tastes of urban audiences. Perhaps the South's chief contribution to the theater has been the experiments in folk drama and outdoor "symphonic" drama. Showboats were for many years an important means of bringing plays to Southerners. Next the university drama departments attempted to fill the need for theater. Recently independent theater groups have been formed in many Southern cities, but so far the Southern experience has not provided material for playwrights commensurate with what it has offered novelists. The list below reveals the need for a Southern dramatic renascence.

Adler, Jacob H., "The Rose and the Fox: Notes on the Southern Drama," in *South*, ed. Rubin and Jacobs, pp. 349–75.

Anderson, John, "Look Away, Dixieland," *Theatre*, LII (Dec 1930), 47, 62.

Bailey, J. O., "Negro Players in Southern Theatres," *New Theatre*, II (July 1935), 24–25.

Cimnaghi, Mario R., *Il Teatro in America 1900–1950* (Rome, 1954), pp. 106–13.

Clark, Barrett H., and George Freedly, *A History of Modern Drama* (New York, 1957).

Connor, L. R., "Southern Plays on the Gotham Stage," *SLM*, n.s., I (1939), 407–11.

Cooke, Anne M., "The Little Theatre Movement as an Adult Education Project Among Negroes," *Jour of Negro Educ*, XIV (1945), 418–24.

Downer, Alan S., *50 Years of American Drama: 1900–1950* (Chicago, 1951), pp. 76–91.

Dusenburg, Winifred L., *The Theme of Loneliness in Modern American Drama* (Gainesville, 1960), pp. 134–54.

*Eubanks, Ralph T., V. L. Baker, et al, "A Bibliography of Speech and Theatre in the South for the Year . . ." *So Speech Jour*, XX (Summer 1955———).

Field, L. M., "The South on Broadway," *SLM*, n. s., II (1940), 174–76.

Gagey, Edmond M., *Revolution in American Drama* (New York, 1947), pp. 92–99.

Gallaway, Marian, "Southern Materials for Graduate Research in the Theatre." *So Speech Jour*, XVII (1951), 125–29.

Gassner, John, "Outdoor Pageant Drama: Symphony of Sight and Sound," *Theatre Arts*, XXXVIII (July 1954), 80–83, 89.

———, "Theatre Arts in a Free Society," *Educ Theatre Jour*, VI (1954), 191–200.

Getchell, Charles M., "Southern Graduate Study in Speech and Theatre: 1951—, *So Speech Jour*, XVIII (Dec 1952———).

*Gohdes, Clarence, *Literature and Theatre of the States and Regions of the U.S.A.: An Historical Bibliography* (Durham, 1967). [bibl for individual So states]

Graham, Philip, "Showboats in the South." *GaR*, XII (1958), 174–85.

Green, Paul, "Symphonic Drama," *Eng Jour*, XXXVIII (1949), 177–83.

Harkness, David J., "Cumberland Gap in Literature," *So Observer*, III (1955), 107–15.

Hughes, Glenn, *A History of American Theatre, 1700–1950* (New York, 1951).
Koch, Frederick H., "Making a Regional Drama," *Bull Amer Drama Assn* (Aug 1932), 1–8.
———, "Drama in the South," *National Theatre Conference Bull*, II (Apr 1940), 9–11.
Mayorga, Margaret, *A Short History of American Drama* (New York, 1932), pp. 357–472.
Miller, Jordan Y., *American Drama Literature* (New York, 1961), pp. 251–61, 307.
Mitchell, Joseph, "The New Theatre in the New South," *Carolina Play-Book*, I (June 1928), 14–17.
Nolan, Paul T., 'Drama in the Lower Mississippi States," *MissQ*, XIX (1965–66), 20–28.
Pryor, William L., "An Examination of the Southern Milieu in Representative Plays by Southern Dramatists, 1923–1956," Florida State, 1959. [diss]
Quinn, Arthur H., *A History of the American Drama: From the Civil War to the Present Day*, II (New York, 1945), pp. 240–49.
Sper, Felix, *From Native Roots: A Panorama of Our Regional Drama* (Caldwell, Idaho, 1948), pp. 79–171.
Upshaw, Lois, "Footlight Trails: The Progress of the Little Theatre Movement in the South," *Drama*, XIX (Oct 1928), 15–16.
Wentz, John C., "American Regional Drama 1920–40: Frustration and Fulfillment," *Mod Drama*, VI (1963), 286–93.

KIMBALL KING
University of North Carolina
Chapel Hill, North Carolina

FOLKLORE

Of the varying definitions of the term *folklore*, the one most appropriate to the present volume restricts its range to traditional beliefs and oral artistic expression. Commentary on such topics as folk material culture or instrumental music is therefore omitted from the following checklist, as are all basically sociological or anthropological studies of Indian, Negro, or white society. Southern speech and humor, which are treated elsewhere in this book, are omitted here except when a particular study directly illuminates folklore. The checklist includes representative major book-length collections of Southern folklore and bibliographical guides that will lead the student to slighter volumes or to the hundreds of compilations published in periodicals. Emphasis has been placed, however, upon works that treat most informatively and thoughtfully the form, the history, and the social implications of folklore in the South. This criterion results in the virtual absence of entries relating to such types as the riddle, the proverb, and the superstition, which have been extensively collected but have received little interpretive comment.

I.   The Collection and Study of Southern Folklore

The history of the study of Southern folklore, like that of the rest of the nation, falls into three overlapping phases. In the first, tales and songs and superstitions were casually recorded in the accounts of travelers or in books of local history or reminiscence. Fugitive scraps appeared in newspapers and almanacs. Actual bearers of the traditional lore also set down their store in manuscript collections of fiddle tunes or "song ballets" or printed them in hymnals. In the second phase, amateurs like Joel Chandler Harris made happy discoveries and were imitated, and teachers bestirred themselves in answer to the American Folklore Society's call for the establishment of state societies to undertake active collecting. In this period the pearls of greatest price were the archaic survivals: Negro animal tales and spirituals and the Child ballad. In the third phase, collectors like Guy B. Johnson, Newman I. White, John Lomax and his son Alan, George P. Jackson, and Richard Dorson began to disclose the creativity exhibited in other genres of folklore which had flourished or were still evolving in the region. Such men also initiated the effort to study the development of the genres and to examine their function in Southern society or in the lives of the informants.

No one work surveys the whole range of these activities. The overviews are usually confined to a genre, a race, a region, or an occupation. For folksong, however, a comprehensive and judicious guide is D. K.

Wilgus' *Anglo-American Folksong Scholarship Since 1898*. Dorson's essays on Negro and Cajun folklore are essentially surveys of scholarship, though he gives fewer details than Wilgus. A collection of brief accounts of the collecting activities of most of the state folklore societies was edited by Wayland D. Hand for the *Journal of American Folklore*. More extended accounts of the work of these societies can often be found in their journals or prefaced to volumes published under their auspices. One can sample the full range of lore sought by the state societies in the most ambitious publication to emerge from their efforts, *The Frank C. Brown Collection of North Carolina Folklore*. Its seven volumes were edited with great care by a group of distinguished scholars. The collection is characteristic of the work of the state societies in stressing the traditions brought from the British Isles and in showing lack of system or thoroughness in the collecting, inadequate documentation of the sources, and virtual omission of contextual commentary. In the absence of extensive scholarship on the folklore of occupational groups, one can gather an idea of the range of some of this material from the popular anthologies of B. A. Botkin. To complete his picture of the general developments in the collection and study of Southern folklore, the student must extrapolate from the more comprehensive bibliographies of the field. The largest is that of Charles D. Haywood, which contains a state-by-state listing and other subject groupings. It is both widely used and widely lamented.

Boswell, George W., "Progress Report: Collection of Tennessee Folksongs in Recent Years," *Tenn Folkl Soc Bull*, XXV (June 1959), 31–79.
Botkin, B. A., *A Treasury of Mississippi River Folklore* (New York, 1955).
_____, and Alvin F. Harlow, *A Treasury of Railroad Folklore* (New York, 1953).
Brewer, J. Mason, "South Carolina Negro Folklore Guild" in "North American Folklore Societies: A Supplement," *JAF*, LIX (1946), 493–94.
*Brewton, John E., "Scholarship in Tennessee Folklore," *Tenn Folkl Soc Bull*, XX, (Dec 1954), 91–97.
Buermann, T. Barry, "A History of the North Carolina Folklore Society," *N.C. Folklore*, XI (Dec 1963), 1–23.
Claudel, Calvin, "History of the Louisiana Folklore Association," *SFQ*, VIII (1944), 11–21.
*Davis, Arthur K., Jr., *Folk-Songs of Virginia: A Descriptive Index and Classification of Material Collected under the Auspices of the Virginia Folklore Society* (Durham, 1949).
*Dorson, Richard, "Louisiana Cajuns," *Buying the Wind: Regional Folklore in the United States* (Chicago, 1964), pp. 229–34.
*_____, "The Negro," *American Folklore* (Chicago, 1959), pp. 166–98.
Hand, Wayland, ed., "North American Folklore Societies," *JAF*, LVI (1943), 161–91.
*Haywood, Charles, *A Bibliography of North American Folklore and Folksong*, 2 vols, 2nd rev ed (New York, 1962).
*Jackson, Bruce, "Appendix II: Further Reading, A.[general], B. 'Articles in the

Journal of American Folklore, 1888–1900,' " *The Negro and His Folklore in Nineteenth-Century Periodicals* (Austin, Tex., 1967), pp. 353–67.

Kirkland, Edwin C., "A Check List of the Titles of Tennessee Folksongs," *JAF*, LIX (1946), 423–76.

*Lawless, Ray M., *Folksingers and Folksongs in America: A Handbook of Biography, Bibliography, and Discography*, rev ed (New York, 1965).

Randolph, Vance, and Frances Emberson, "The Collection of Folk Music in the Ozarks," *JAF*, LX (1947), 115–25.

*White, Newman I., "The Negro Song in General" and "Bibliography," *American Negro Folk-Songs* (Cambridge, Mass., 1928), pp. 3–30, 469–80.

————, et al, *The Frank C. Brown Collection of North Carolina Folklore*, 7 vols (Durham, 1952–64).

*Wilgus, D. K., *Anglo-American Folksong Scholarship Since 1898* (New Brunswick, N.J., 1959).

II.   Periodicals and Serials

Literary and family journals of the late nineteenth century published many articles concerning Southern folklore, particularly that of the Negro. The first periodical specifically devoted to folklore, however, was the *Journal of American Folklore*, established in 1888 as the organ of the American Folklore Society. Its pages and its memoir series were long the place where much of the serious collecting and discussion of Southern folklore found publication. In recent years the *Southern Folklore Quarterly* has been the journal most hospitable to Southern materials. The journals of the state societies have largely confined themselves to collectanea from their states. The journal *Sing Out*, which pronounces itself "partial to songs of protest and topical comment," is worth consulting for its transcriptions of taped interviews with recorded folk performers and other information about them.

Bibliographies of articles on folklore appearing in current periodicals can be found in three journals: *Journal of American Folklore*, annual Supplement; *Southern Folklore Quarterly*, March issue; and *PMLA*, June issue. *Abstracts of Folklore Studies*, published quarterly, includes bibliographical notes on some books and recordings as well as brief abstracts of periodical articles. Current doctoral dissertations can be followed in *Dissertation Abstracts*.

Abstracts of Folklore Studies, 1962——
Dissertation Abstracts, 1938——
Kentucky Folklore Record, 1955——
Journal of American Folklore, 1888——
North Carolina Folklore, 1953——
Publications of the Texas Folklore Society, 1916——
Sing Out, 1950——
Southern Folklore Quarterly, 1937——
Tennessee Folklore Society Bulletin, 1935——

III. The Folktale

The enthusiastic reception given *Uncle Remus: His Songs and Sayings* in 1880 stimulated the first serious compilations of the Southern folktale. Harris himself told in the preface to his next volume how the public interest encouraged his own in the traditional elements of his tales, and the bibliography of Richard Dorson's *Negro Folktales of Michigan* shows the numerousness of Harris' imitators. However delightful Harris' own gifts as a raconteur, his influence also worked harm by focusing too much attention upon the animal tale and by setting the model of rather free adaptation of traditional material. Of the early collectors, only Elsie Clews Parson was straightforward in her transcriptions of the tales. Even such a recent collector as J. Mason Brewer candidly admits that except in his latest volume, *Worser Days and Better Times*, the renditions he has published have been "something of others and mostly of me."

However free in their transcriptions and however undocumented their sources, the work of such collectors as Brewer, Zora Neale Hurston, and the WPA writers showed how small a segment the animal tale was of the total range of the Negro folktale. Further confirmation of this is the chapter entitled "The Astonishing Repertoire of James Douglas Suggs" in Dorson's *Negro Tales from Pine Bluff, Arkansas, and Calvin, Michigan.* This volume and Dorson's Michigan collection, which includes an excellent chapter on "The Art of the Negro Story Telling," are composed of materials largely gathered from emigrant Southern Negroes, and they are the two most thoughtful studies of the Negro folktale.

Abrahams, Roger, "The Changing Conception of the Negro Hero," in *The Golden Log*, ed. Mody C. Boatright et al, *Pub of Tex Folkl Soc*, No. 31 (Dallas, 1962), pp. 119–34.

Botkin, B. A., *Lay My Burden Down: A Folk History of Slavery* (Chicago, 1945). [WPA]

Brewer, J. Mason, *Dog Ghosts, and Other Texas Negro Folk Tales* (Austin, Tex., 1958).

———, *The Word on the Brazos: Negro Preacher Tales from the Brazos Bottoms of Texas* (Austin, Tex., 1953).

———, *Worser Days and Better Times: The Folklore of the North Carolina Negro* (Chicago, 1965).

*Dorson, Richard M., *Negro Folktales in Michigan* (Cambridge, Mass., 1956).

———, *Negro Tales from Pine Bluff, Arkansas, and Calvin, Michigan* (Bloomington, Ind., 1958).

Duncan, Eula G., *Big Road Walker, Based on Stories Told by Alice Cannon* (New York, 1940).

Espinosa, Aurelio M., "Notes on the Origin and History of the Tar-Baby Story," *JAF*, XLIII (1930), 129–209.

Harris, Joel Chandler, *Nights with Uncle Remus: Myths and Legends of the Old Plantation* (Boston, 1883).

_____, *Uncle Remus: His Songs and Sayings. The Folk-Lore of the Old Plantation* (New York, 1880).

Hendricks, W. C., ed., *Bundle of Troubles and Other Tarheel Tales* (Durham, 1943). [WPA]

Hurston, Zora N., *Mules and Men* (Philadelphia, 1935).

Parsons, Elsie Clews, *Folk Lore of the Sea Islands, South Carolina*, Memoirs of Amer Folkl Soc, No. 16 (Cambridge, Mass., 1923).

South Carolina Folk Tales: Stories of Animals and Supernatural Beings (Columbia, S.C., 1941). [WPA]

Weldon, Fred O., Jr., "Negro Folktale Heroes," in *And Horns on the Toads*, ed. Mody C. Boatright, *Pub of Tex Folkl Soc*, No. 29 (Dallas, 1959), pp. 170–89.

Interest in Negro folktales preceded by many years interest in the tales of the whites. The first field collection of the latter was published in the *Journal of American Folklore* in 1925, and subsequent efforts have uncovered considerable caches of material. Richard Chase's *The Jack Tales*, though edited more for a popular than a scholarly reader, presents a valuable cycle of tales. Chase discovered that certain mountain families were important bearers of these tales, and the pattern has been corroborated by later field study. This fact has enabled editors like Marie Campbell and Leonard W. Roberts to present their Kentucky collections with a wealth of contextual information. The fullest body of such materials is Roberts' *Up Cutshin and Down Greasy*, which was issued in conjunction with one family's entire repertory on the Kentucky Microcard series.

In recent years there has been increasing interest in recovering early printed folktales from the nineteenth-century newspapers, almanacs, and books in which they have lain hidden. The most significant collection yet drawn together from such sources is Richard Dorson's *Davy Crockett, American Comic Legend*. Walter Blair and Franklin J. Meine compiled a similar though more literary collection of tales about Mike Fink. A good list of articles reporting other research on folk tales in early newspapers is to be found in the "Bibliographical Notes" to Dorson's *American Folklore*.

Blair, Walter, and Franklin J. Meine, *Half Horse, Half Alligator: The Growth of the Mike Fink Legend* (Chicago, 1956).

Boatright, Mody C., "The Family Saga as a Form of Folklore," *The Family Saga and Other Phases of American Folklore* (Urbana, Ill., 1958), pp. 1–19.

Campbell, Marie, *Tales from Cloud Walking Country* (Bloomington, Ind., 1958).

Chase, Richard, ed., *The Jack Tales, Told by R. M. Ward and His Kindred in the Beech Mountain Section of Western North Carolina* . . . (Cambridge, Mass., 1943).

*Dorson, Richard M., "Bibliographical Notes," *American Folklore* (Chicago, 1959), pp. 288–90.

_____, ed., *Davy Crockett, American Comic Legend* (New York, 1939).

_____, "Oral Styles of American Folk Narrators," in *Style in Language*, ed. Thomas A. Sebeok (Cambridge, Mass., 1960), pp. 27–51.

_____, "The Sources of *Davy Crockett, American Comic Legend*," *Midw Folkl*, VIII (1958) 143–49.

Roberts, Leonard, "The Cante Fable in Eastern Kentucky," *Midw Folkl*, VI (1956), 68–88.

_____, ed., *South from Hell-fer-Sartin: Kentucky Mountain Tales* (Lexington, Ky., 1955).

_____, ed., *The Tales and Songs of the Couch Family*, Kentucky Microcards, ser A, No. 30 (Lexington, Ky., 1959).

_____, ed., *Up Cutshin and Down Greasy: Folkways of a Kentucky Mountain Family* (Lexington, Ky., 1959).

Smaller ethnic groups have also received some attention. Among the early officers of the American Folklore Society was Alcée Fortier, whose collection of Louisiana French folktales was the second volume of the society's memoir series. Fifty years elapsed, however, before other significant collections of these materials began to appear.

Brandon, Elizabeth, "La Paroisse de Vermillon: Moeurs, Dictons, Contes et Légendes," *Le Bayou*, XIX (1955), 449–68; XX (1956), 64–86, 164–80, 269–81; XXI (1957), 358–67, 420–31.

Carrière, Joseph M., *Tales from the French Folk-Lore of Missouri*, Northwestern U Stud in Humanities, No. 1 (Evanston, Ill., 1937).

Claudel, Calvin, "Spanish Folktales from Delacroix, Louisiana," *JAF*, LVIII (1945), 208–24.

Fortier, Alcée, *Louisiana Folk-Tales in French Dialect and English Translation*, Memoirs of Amer Folkl Soc, II (Boston, 1895).

Saucier, Corinne, *Folk Tales from French Louisiana* (New York, 1962).

_____, *Traditions de la Paroisse des Avozelles en Louisiane*, Memoirs of Amer Folkl Soc, XLVII (Philadelphia, 1956).

For the folktales of Southeastern Indians the major collections are those of John R. Swanton and James Mooney, both published by the Bureau of American Ethnology. Other collections and studies can be found listed in Charles Haywood's bibliography, which groups its materials by tribe and genre.

Hatfield, Dorothy B., and Eugene Current-Garcia, "William Orrie Tuggle and the Creek Indian Folk Tales," *SFQ*, XXV (1961), 238–55.

*Haywood, Charles, "The Southeastern Area," *A Bibliography of North American Folklore and Folksong*, 2nd rev ed, II (New York, 1962), pp. 892–915.

Mooney, James, *Myths of the Cherokee*, 19th Annual Report of the Bureau of American Ethnology, part 1 (Washington, D.C., 1900).

Swanton, John R., *Myths and Tales of the Southeastern Indians*, Bureau of American Ethnology, Bull 88 (Washington, D.C., 1929).

IV. Secular Song

The earliest records of secular folk song in the South are "song ballets" and dance-tune manuscripts compiled by the bearers of the live tradition and a scattering of texts in newspapers, journals, books, and sheet music. Many of the song ballets have been gathered into archives and transcribed in publications. The other materials remain largely unrecovered, and few efforts have been made to find or catalogue them.

After a few weak and scattered individual efforts, collecting of secular song began in earnest in the second decade of this century with the Appalachian tour of the prestigious English collector Cecil Sharp. For all the haste and superficiality of his field work, Sharp's collection, especially in its revised edition, remains the best compilation of the older songs. Much of value is to be found, however, in the major state collections. D. K. Wilgus has ably summarized the strengths and weaknesses of their compilers: though more open than English collectors to new and indigenous types of folksong, they were men of literary training eager to pluck the last fruits of the failing ballad tree. They were preoccupied with the gathering of the songs, and even the Child ballad has received little attention from scholars seeking to determine or interpret regional preferences in general repertory or in the reshaping of traditional songs. The tools for such studies exist, however, in B. H. Bronson's monumental four-volume collection *Traditional Tunes of the Child Ballads* (which prints the texts as well as tunes, excluding only variants newly published in books and recordings) and Tristram Coffin's classified finding list, *The British Traditional Ballad in North America*. The service Coffin provides for the study of the Child ballads is rendered for later ballads in G. Malcolm Laws's two books, *American Balladry from British Broadsides* and *Native American Balladry*. Other song types of the older tradition, such as the lullaby, the love lyric, the play-party song, and the dance tune, have been less interesting to collectors and interpreters. Some of the newer forms have received study. John Greenway included chapters on songs of the Southern white textile workers, miners, and farmers, as well as of Negroes, in his *American Folksongs of Protest*. The hillbilly issue edited by D. K. Wilgus for the *Journal of American Folklore* is an indispensable introduction to this new concern of folklorists. Outside the Anglo-American tradition relatively little collecting has been done. The small amount of material available on Louisiana French folksongs is summarized in the opening chapter of Irène Whitfield's collection.

Abrahams, Roger D., "Patterns of Structure and Role Relationships in the Child Ballad in the United States," *JAF*, LXXIX (1966), 448–62.

Arnold, Byron, *Folksongs of Alabama* (University, Ala., 1950).

Boswell, George W., "Some Characteristics of Folksongs in Middle Tennessee," *Tenn Folkl Soc Bull*, XV (Dec 1949), 63–69.

Bronson, Bertrand H., *The Traditional Tunes of the Child Ballads with Their Texts,*

According to the Extant Records of Great Britain and America, 4 vols (Princeton, 1959——),

Coffin, Tristram P., *The British Traditional Ballad in North America*, rev ed (Philadelphia, 1963).

Davis, Arthur K., Jr., *Traditional Ballads of Virginia Collected under the Auspices of the Virginia Folk-Lore Society* (Cambridge, Mass., 1929).

————, *More Traditional Ballads of Virginia, Collected with the Cooperation of Members of the Virginia Folklore Society* (Chapel Hill, 1960).

Greenway, John, *American Folksongs of Protest* (Philadelphia, 1953).

————, "Aunt Molly Jackson and Robin Hood: A Study in Folk Re-creation," *JAF*, LXIX (1956), 23–38.

————, "Jimmie Rodgers—A Folksong Catalyst," *JAF*, LXX (1957), 231–34.

Hudson, Arthur Palmer, *Folksongs of Mississippi and Their Background* (Chapel Hill, 1936).

————, and George Herzog, *Folk Tunes from Mississippi* (New York, 1937).

*Laws, G. Malcolm, *American Balladry from British Broadsides: A Guide for Students and Collectors of Traditional Song* (Philadelphia, 1957).

*————, *Native American Balladry: A Descriptive Study and a Bibliographical Syllabus*, rev ed (Philadelphia, 1964).

*McLendon, Altha L., "A Finding List of Play-Party Games," *SFQ*, VIII (1944), 201–34.

Mason, Wilton, "The Music of the Waldensians in Valdese, North Carolina," *N.C. Folkl*, (July 1960), 1–6.

Morris, Alton C., *Folksongs of Florida* (Gainesville, 1950).

Powers, Doris C., "The American Variants of 'Earl Brand,' Child No. 7," *W Folkl*, XVII (1958), 77–96.

Randolph, Vance, *Ozark Folksongs*, 4 vols (Columbia, Mo., 1946–50).

Sharp, Cecil J., *English Folk Songs from the Southern Appalachians*, rev ed, 2 vols (London, 1932).

Smith, Reed, ed., *South Carolina Ballads, with a Study of the Traditional Ballad Today* (Cambridge, Mass. 1928).

Stamper, Frances C., and William H. Jansen, "'Water Birch': An American Variant of 'Hugh of Lincoln,'" *JAF*, LXXI (1958), 16–22.

Whitfield, Irène T., *Louisiana French Folk Songs* (Baton Rouge, 1939).

Wilgus, D. K., et al, eds., "Hillbilly Issue," *JAF* (1965), LXXVIII, 195–286.

Negro secular song, in which the ballad plays a relatively minor role, has been extensively collected and has received considerable thoughtful commentary. Some of the early references to Negro work and dance songs are compiled in Dena J. Epstein's "Slave Music in the United States before 1860" and somewhat later texts and descriptions are assembled in Bruce Jackson's *The Negro and His Folklore in Nineteenth-Century Periodicals*. Beginning in the 1920s considerable collecting of Negro secular song was undertaken by what might loosely be called a North Carolina "school": Newman Ivey White, Guy B. Johnson, Howard Odum, and Louis Chappell. Each of these men discussed the nature of the materials he collected, White being led to this by the question of Negro creativity and Johnson and Odum by their role as professional sociologists. The two books written on the Negro ballad "John Henry" by Johnson and Chappell make it indeed the most carefully studied American folksong, though their work needs to be supplemented by a reading of Richard Dorson's article "The Career of 'John Henry'" and by MacEdward Leach's recent account of his discovery of a Jamaican prototype.

The field trips undertaken by John Lomax and his son Alan in the middle thirties prepared the way for even greater study of Negro lore. Extraordinarily open to all forms of American folklore, the Lomaxes made recordings of field hollers, gang songs, reels, blues, and other types of Negro song. They conceived of the numerous books that grew from these trips as written for the people rather than the pedant, and they consequently took liberties with text and documentation. But the variety, extensiveness, and musical quality of the performances they recorded for the Library of Congress served as both a stimulus and a standard for later collectors. The best introduction to the whole range of such materials is Harold Courlander's *Negro Folk Music U.S.A.*, though it cannot be called a profound study.

Courlander's discussion of at least one form, blues, can be supplemented by a number of other useful works. Studies of an interpretive nature, such as Samuel Charters' *The Poetry of the Blues* or Paul Oliver's *Blues Fell This Morning* are good beginnings but less authoritative than Charters' *The Country Blues*, which conveys a great deal of information about the development of the genre by means of biographical accounts of the major singers. Urban backgrounds are provided in the study of New Orleans by Henry Kmen and by Wilfred Mellers.

Charters, Samuel B., *The Country Blues* (New York, 1959).
———, *The Poetry of the Blues* (New York, 1963).
*Courlander, Harold, *Negro Folk Music U.S.A.* (New York, 1963).
———, *Negro Songs from Alabama*, rev ed (New York, 1963).
Dorson, Richard M., "The Career of 'John Henry,'" *WFolkl* XXIV (1965), 155–63.
Epstein, Dena J., "Slave Music in the United States before 1860, a Survey of Sources," Music Lib Assn *Notes*, 2nd ser, XX (1963), 195–212, 377–90.
*Jackson, Bruce, ed., *The Negro and His Folklore in Nineteenth-Century Periodicals* (Austin, Tex, 1967).
Jones, LeRoi, *Blues People: Negro Music in White America* (New York, 1963).
Kmen, Henry A., "Negro Music," *Music in New Orleans: The Formative Years, 1791–1841* (Baton Rouge, 1966), pp. 226–45.
Leach, MacEdward, "John Henry," in *Folklore and Society: Essays in Honor of Benjamin A. Botkin*, ed. Bruce Jackson (Hatboro, Pa., 1966), pp. 93–106.
Lee, Hector, "Leadbelly's 'Frankie and Albert,'" *JAF*, LXIV (1951), 314–17.
Mellers, Wilfrid, "Heterophony and Improvisation: The New Orleans Jazz Band and King Oliver; Bessie Smith and the Urban Blues" and "Orgy and Alienation: Country Blues, Barrelhouse Piano, and Piano Rag." *Music in a New Found Land: Themes and*

Developments in the History of American Music (New York, 1965),
Odum, Howard, and Guy B. Johnson, *Negro Workaday Songs* (Chapel Hill, 1926).
Oliver, Paul, *Blues Fell this Morning: The Meaning of the Blues* (New York, 1960).
Parrish, Lydia, *Slave Songs of the Georgia Sea Islands* (New York, 1942).
Wheeler, Mary, *Steamboatin' Days; Folk Songs of the River Packet Era* (Baton Rouge, 1944).

V. Religious Song

Rural "New Light" revivalism was the matrix in which the American folk spiritual developed. All sections of the young country contributed to the movement, as the admirable bibliographical and historical studies of Irving Lowens make clear. In the South, the spiritual first surfaced in print about 1815. From that time to the present, the "shape-note" hymnals that are the vehicle of much of the white tradition have been continuously in print and in use. Antipathy to revivalism, however, long discouraged scholarly attention to their contents. It was in 1933 (after Ransom had defended the country religion of the up-country white in *God Without Thunder*) that George Pullen Jackson of Vanderbilt University published the first history of the movement, *White Spirituals in the Southern Uplands*. His subsequent studies progressively elaborated upon aspects of this history, explored the bibliography, and documented the folk song sources and analogues of the melodies of the spirituals. The most distinctive feature of the shape-note spiritual, its three- and four-part settings, has yet to receive thorough examination. A few of the camp meeting songs not recorded in hymnals may be found in such collections as that of Lucien McDowell, and some of the songs of the Kentucky Shakers were included in Edward D. Andrews' *The Gift to be Simple*.

Andrews. Edward D., *The Gift to be Simple: Songs, Dances and Rituals of the American Shakers* (New York, 1940).

Horn, Dorothy D., "Quartal Harmony in the Pentatonic Folk Hymns of the Sacred Harps," *JAF*, LXXI (1958), 564–81.

*Jackson, George Pullen, *Spiritual Folk-Songs of Early America: Two Hundred and Fifty Tunes and Texts* (New York, 1937).

*_____, *White Spirituals in the Southern Uplands: The Story of the Fasola Folk, Their Songs, Singings, and "Buckwheat Notes"* (Chapel Hill, 1933).

Lowens, Irving, "John Wyeth's *Repository of Sacred Music, Part Second* (1813): A Northern Precursor of Southern Folk-Hymnody," *Music and Musicians in Early America* (New York, 1964), pp. 138–55.

[Parker, W. A., ed.], *Directory and Minutes of Annual Sacred Harp Singings 1966–1967, Alabama, Florida, Georgia, Tennessee and Mississippi* (Birmingham, 1966).

*Stevenson, Robert, "Bibliography," *Protestant Church Music in America: A Short Survey of Men and Movements from 1564 to the Present* (New York, 1966), pp. 113–51.

Traywick, Linda, "Some Contemporary Builders of *The Sacred Harp*," *Tenn Folkl Soc Bull*, XXX (June 1964), 57–61.

By contrast, the Negro spirituals received earlier acceptance and fuller study. To some Southern whites, the songs were pleasing for their evocation of "befo' de war" conditions. To Northern whites they were the voice of a downtrodden people. To some Negroes they were evidence of Negro creativity. Publication of a significant collection, *Slave Songs of the United States*, came as early as 1867. Other collections rapidly followed, many issued in conjunction with the fund-raising activities of such schools as Fisk, Tuskegee, Hampton, Penn, and Utica. These collections sometimes ran into numerous editions, with new pieces added in each republication. Serious field collecting of Negro spirituals began in the 1920s with the research of Guy B. Johnson on St. Helena Island, South Carolina. In the 1960s excellent collections continue to appear, notably those of Guy Carawan and Harold Courlander.

Although the rich possibilities for collecting both white and Negro spirituals remain largely unexploited, the field has been an arena for bitter infighting. An excellent summary of these disputes is included in D. K. Wilgus' *Anglo-American Folksong Scholarship*. One of the issues raised has been whether the texts of the early Negro spirituals contain hidden commentary on the institution of slavery. The point is controvertible only when carried to injudicious extremes by such Negro apologists as Miles M. Fisher. A more significant issue was the question of whether the Negro spiritual was derived from the white spiritual or from African sources. Jackson's *White and Negro Spirituals* documents most fully the kinship of the two traditions. Contentious interpretations of the relationship began to subside as scholars came to a clearer understanding of the nature of African, European, and Afro-American folksong styles and as sociologists developed understanding of the processes of acculturation (see Section VIII below). Basic research into secondary historical documents may further illuminate the relationship, but this has only recently begun in such publications as those of Dena J. Epstein and Bruce Jackson.

The Negro sermon seems to have interested literary men like Styron, Faulkner, and James W. Johnson more than it has the folklorists. Johnson's preface to *God's Trombones* is a brief but useful discussion of the form, and one lengthy transcription of a Negro sermon comprises the last chapter of Alan Lomax's *The Rainbow Sign*. A few recordings are available. But the sermon and related genres such as the prayer, the testimony, and other rituals have been insufficiently collected or considered.

[Allen, William F., Charles P. Ware, and Lucy M. Garrison], *Slave Songs of the United States* (New York, 1867).
Epstein, Dena J., "Slave Music in the United States before 1860, A Survey of Sources,"

Music Lib Assn *Notes*, 2nd ser, XX (1963), 195–212, 377–90.

Fisher, Miles M., *Negro Slave Songs in the United States* (Ithaca, N.Y., 1953).

*Jackson, Bruce, ed., *The Negro and His Folklore in Nineteenth-Century Periodicals* (Austin, Tex., 1967).

*Jackson, George P., *White and Negro Spirituals: Their Life Span and Kinship . . . With 116 Songs as Sung by Both Races* (New York, 1943).

Johnson, Guy B., *Folk Culture on St. Helena Island, South Carolina* (Chapel Hill, 1930).

Johnson, James W., "Preface," *God's Trombones: Seven Negro Sermons in Verse* (New York, 1927), pp. 1–11.

Lomax, Alan, "The Meeting—There Is a Hell," *The Rainbow Sign: A Southern Documentary* (New York, 1959).

Marsh, J. B. T., *The Story of the Jubilee Singers, with Their Songs*, rev ed, seventy-fifth thousand (Boston, Mass., n.d.).

Seale, Lea, and Marianna Seale, "Easter Rock: A Louisiana Negro Ceremony," *JAF*, LV (1942), 212–18.

*Stevenson, Robert, "Negro Spirituals: Origin and Present-Day Significance," *Protestant Church Music in America: A Short Survey of Men and Movements from 1564 to the Present* (New York, 1966), pp. 92–105.

Tallmadge, William H., "Dr. Watts and Mahalia Jackson—The Development, Decline, and Survival of a Folk Style in America," *Ethnomusicology*, V (Jan 1961), 95–99.

*Wilgus. D. K., "The Negro-White Spiritual," *Anglo-American Folksong Scholarship Since 1898* (New Brunswick, N.J., 1959), pp. 345–64.

VI.   Studies of the Cultural Context and Miscellaneous Beliefs and Practices

In comparison with the scholarly effort to collect and edit texts or even with efforts to trace the history or define the nature of genres like the spiritual or the blues, little attention has been given to the study of the relation between oral lore and other Southern folk beliefs and practices or to its psychological or social functions. Some materials pertinent to the topic are scattered through works cited above. Newbell N. Puckett's study of Negro superstitions was a notable early work, but Guy Johnson's *Folk Culture on St. Helena Island* (cited in Section V) was the first to attempt to study the Negro songs in a social context. When read in conjunction with T. J. Woofter's *Black Yeomanry*, it provides the best picture yet drawn. Two other good, recent studies of the role of folklore in Negro communities of the Deep South are Frederic Ramsey's *Been Here and Gone* and Guy and Candie Carawan's *Ain't You Got a Right to the Tree of Life*, both of which were issued in conjunction with phonograph recordings (listed in Section VII). John Lomax's *Autobiography of a Ballad Hunter* is rich in information about the singers from whom he collected. Biographical material is also included in *Negro Folk Songs as Sung by Leadbelly*, edited by John and Alan Lomax, and the latter edited tapes of reminiscences by two other Negro informants into a moving volume, *The Rainbow Sign*. A

valuable background for all of these studies is Melville J. Herskovits'
The Myth of the Negro Past.

For white informants and communities, there are fewer good studies.
Vance Randolph has written interestingly of the Ozarks, and Jean
Ritchie of her family traditions in the Appalachians. The folktale studies
of Marie Campbell and Leonard W. Roberts (cited in Section III)
provide considerable information about both the individual raconteurs
and the role of the family in the preservation of folklore. In recent
years, however, one of the best sources of information about the folk
performer's attitudes and background has been the phonograph recording. A number of commercial discs attempting to provide such information are discussed in Section VII.

Anderson, John Q., "The New Orleans Voodoo Ritual Dance and Its Twentieth-
   Century Survivals," *SFQ*, XXIV (1960), 135–43.
Broonzy, William, and Yannick Bruynoghe, *Big Bill Blues: William Broonzy's Story*
   (London, 1955).
Browne, Ray B., "Some Notes on the Southern 'Holler,' " *JAF*, LXVII (1954), 73–77.
Campbell, Marie, "Survivals of Old Folk Drama in the Kentucky Mountains," *JAF*,
   LI (1938), 10–24.
Carawan, Guy, and Candie Carawan, *Ain't You Got a Right to the Tree of Life: The
   People of Johns Island, South Carolina—Their Faces, Their Words and Their Songs*
   (New York, 1966).
Drums and Shadows: Survival Studies among the Georgia Coastal Negroes (Athens,
   Ga., 1940). [WPA]
Green, Archie, "The Carter Family's 'Coal Miner's Blues,' " *SFQ*, XXV (1961), 226–37.
Greenway, John, "The Song Makers: Ella May Wiggins, Aunt Molly Jackson, Woody
   Guthrie," *American Folksongs of Protest* (Philadelphia, 1953), pp. 243–302.
*Herskovits, Melville J., *The Myth of the Negro Past*, rev ed (Boston, 1958).
Hurston, Zora, "Hoodoo in America," *JAF*, XLIV (1931), 317–417.
James, Willis L., "The Romance of the Negro Folk Cry in America," *Phylon*, XVI
   (1955), 15–30.
Kaimen, Audrey A., "The Southern Fiddling Convention—A Study," *Tenn Folkl Soc
   Bull*, XXXI, (March 1965), 7–16.
Lomax, Alan, *Mister Jelly Roll, The Fortunes of Jelly Roll Morton, New Orleans
   Creole and "Inventor of Jazz"* (New York, 1950).
———, *The Rainbow Sign: A Southern Documentary* (New York, 1959).
Lomax, John A., *Adventures of a Ballad Hunter* (New York, 1947).
———, and Alan Lomax, *Negro Folk Songs as Sung by Lead Belly* (New York, 1936).
Puckett, Newbell N., *Folk Beliefs of the Southern Negro* (Chapel Hill, 1926).
Saxon, Lyle, et al, *Gumbo Ya-Ya: A Collection of Louisiana Folktales* (Boston, 1945).
   [superstitions and cults]
Ramsey, Frederic, Jr., *Been Here and Gone* (New Brunswick, N.J., 1960).
Randolph, Vance, *Ozark Superstitions* (New York, 1947).
———, *The Ozarks: An American Survival of Primitive Society* (New York, 1931).
Ritchie, Jean, *Singing Family of the Cumberlands* (New York, 1955).
Whiting, B. J., intro, "Proverbs and Proverbial Sayings," *The Frank C. Brown Collec-*

tion of North Carolina Folklore, ed. Newman I. White, et al, I (Durham, 1952), pp. 331–54.
Whitten, Norman E., Jr., "Contemporary Patterns of Malign Occultism among Negroes in North Carolina," *JAF,* LXXV (1962), 311–25.
Woofter, T. J., Jr., *Black Yeomanry: Life on St. Helena Island* (New York, 1930).

VII.   Discography, and Its Bibliography

Extensive recording of authentic folk performers was first undertaken in the 1920s when Ralph S. Peer of Okeh Records realized the potential market for what he labeled "race" and "hillbilly" music. This development is recounted best in Archie Green's article "Hillbilly Music: Source and Symbol." A three-volume anthology of re-recordings of these early performances was edited by Harry Smith under the title *American Folk Music,* unfortunately with skimpy notes. In the field of blues, Samuel Charters' albums are only two of many re-recordings now available, but they can be used in conjunction with his books and do give a broad sampling. He includes a discography in his book, *The Country Blues.*

In the early 1930s John A. Lomax commenced an enterprising career recording folk performers in the field. His greatest find was the singer Leadbelly, but the series of recordings issued by the Library of Congress is a monument to the breadth of his interests. Although accoustically inferior to later recordings, these albums contain much excellent material; the entry *Folk Music: A Catalogue of Folk Songs* below is a price list describing the contents of the entire series and can be obtained at nominal cost from the Music Division of the Library of Congress.

The tape recorder and the long-playing disc of the 1950s and 1960s have made available for study an even more remarkable range of authentic folk materials. Some of the discs provide a wealth of information about folk attitudes through printed or spoken interviews with the performers (see below, the recordings of Blind Willie Johnson, Big Bill Broonzy, Leadbelly, Buell Kazee, and Dock Boggs). John Cohen's three albums devoted to Roscoe Holcomb are even more enterprising. The first "deals with the sociological, physical, and geographical setting of his music," the second "the idea of a folk aesthetic," and the third "his thoughts about music, religion, work, and life." Guy Carawan's *Been in the Storm So Long* takes the opposite tack, presenting the life of a Negro community through its songs, tales, and religious services.

The two recent general series, listed below, differ greatly in scope and approach. Frederic Ramsey's *Music from the South* confines itself to the Negro tradition of the deep South and studies it in some depth (the book *Been Here and Gone* complements the recordings). Alan Lomax's *Southern Journey* series is, on the other hand, provided with the scantiest of commentaries. Its strength is the great variety of materials and the geographical range of his field work. His purpose will be well served if he awakens his Southern listeners to the richness of the folk traditions still thriving about them.

As an addendum to the discussion of two of the recordings above, brief mention should be made of two films. Samuel Charters' *The Blues* (1963) supplements his books and discs with a film record of many of the great Negro blues singers of the rural and urban South. The singing and the world of Roscoe Holcomb are further documented in John Cohen's *The High Lonesome Sound, Kentucky Mountain Music* (1963). Both films can be bought or rented from Brandon Films, Inc., of New York City.

Almeda Riddle: Songs and Ballads of the Ozarks, Vanguard VRS–9158 (New York, 1964).

Bluestein, G., ed., *Buell Kazee Sings and Plays*, Folkways FS–3810 (New York, 1965).

Carawan, Guy, ed., *Been in the Storm So Long: Spirituals and Shouts, Children's Game Songs*, Folkways FS–3842 (New York, 1967).

Charters, Samuel B., ed., *Blind Willie Johnson: His Story Told, Annotated, and Documented by Samuel B. Charters in Louisiana and Texas*, Folkways FG–3585 (New York, 1957; 1962).

————, *The Country Blues*, Record, Book, and Film Sales RF–1 (New York, 1959).

————, *The Country Blues: Volume Two*, Record, Book, and Film Sales RFB–9 (New York, 1964).

*————, "Recorded Blues Backgrounds" and "The Blues Recordings," *The Country Blues* (New York, 1959), pp. 269–78.

Cohen, John, ed., *Mountain Music of Kentucky*, Folkways FA–2317 (New York, 1960).

————, *The Music of Roscoe Holcomb & Wade Ward*, Folkways FA–2363 (New York, 1962).

————, *Roscoe Holcomb: The High Lonesome Sound*, Folkways FA–2368 (New York, 1965).

Cohn, Lawrence, ed., *Leadbelly: The Library of Congress Recordings, 1933–1942*, Electra EKL–301/2 (New York, n.d.).

*Courlander, Harold, "Discography," *Negro Folk Music, U.S.A.* (New York, 1963), pp. 302–308.

————, ed., *Negro Folk Music of Alabama*, 6 vols, Folkways P–417/418, P–471/474 (New York, 1956).

Folk Music: A Catalogue of Folk Songs, Ballads, Dances, Instrumental Pieces, and Folk Tales of the United States and Latin America on Phonograph Records . . . Library of Congress (Washington, D.C., 1958).

Gott, Peter, and John Cohen, eds., *Old Love Songs & Ballads from the Big Laurel, North Carolina*, Folkways FA–2309 (New York, 1964).

[Green, Archie, ed.], *Babies in the Mill: Carolina Traditional, Industrial, Sacred Songs. Sung by Dorsey, Nancy, and Howard Dixon*, Testament T–3301 (Chicago, [1964]).

*————, "Hillbilly Music: Source and Symbol," *JAF*, LXXVIII (1965), 204–28.

Greenway, John, ed., *The Songs and Stories of Aunt Molly Jackson. Stories Told by Aunt Molly Jackson, Songs Sung by John Greenway*, Folkways FH–5457 (New York, 1961).

*Haywood, Charles, *A Bibliography of North American Folklore and Folksong*, 2nd rev ed, 2 vols (New York, 1962). [discography *passim*]

*A *List of American Folksongs Currently Available on Records, Compiled by The Archive of American Folksong of the Library of Congress* (Washington, D.C., 1953).

Lomax, Alan, ed., *Negro Prison Songs from the Mississippi State Penitentiary*, Tradition TLP–1020 (New York, n.d.).

————, ed., *Southern Journey*, 12 vols, Prestige International 25001/25012 (Bergenfield, N.J., n.d.).

Original Sacred Harp Singing in the Traditional Style by Sacred Harp Singers, Sacred Harp Publ Co., S.H.–101 ([Cullman, Ala.], 1965).

Oster, Harry, ed., *A Sampler of Louisiana Folksongs: Negro, Negro French, Cajun, Creole French, and Anglo-Saxon*, Louisiana Folklore Society, LSF–1201 ([Baton Rouge], n.d.).

Paton, Sandy, ed., *Frank Proffitt of Reese, North Carolina*, Folk-Legacy FSA–1 (Huntington, Vt., 1962).

————, *Horton Barker, Traditional Singer, Recorded in Beech Creek, North Carolina*, Folkways FA–2362 (New York, 1962).

————, *Ray Hicks Telling Four Traditional "Jack Tales,"* Folk-Legacy FTA–14 (Huntington, Vt., 1964).

————, *The Traditional Music of Beech Mountain, North Carolina*, 2 vols, Folk-Legacy FSA–22/23 (Huntington, Vt., 1964, 1965).

Ramsey, Frederic, Jr., ed., *Leadbelly's Last Sessions*, 2 vols, Folkways FP–2941/2942 (New York, 1953; 1962).

————, ed., *Music from the South*, 10 vols, Folkways FP–650/659 (New York, 1956).

Seeger, Mike, ed., *Dock Boggs, Volume 2*, Folkways FA–2392 (New York, 1965).

————, *Excerpts from Interviews with Dock Boggs*, Folkways FH–5458 (New York, n.d.).

Smith, Harry, ed., *American Folk Music*, 3 vols, Folkways FP–251/253 (New York, 1952).

Terkel, Studs, ed., *Big Bill Broonzy, Interviewed by Studs Terkel, Introduction by Charles E. Smith*, Folkways FG–3586 (New York, 1966).

*Whitfield, Irène T., "Work Done in the Field of Louisiana French Folk Songs," *Louisiana French Folk Songs* (Baton Rouge, 1939), pp. 1–11.

*Wilgus, D. K., "Current Hillbilly Recordings: A Review Article," *JAF*, LXXVIII (1965), 267–86.

VIII.   Song Style and Its Implications

The mechanical means for recording sounds have made it possible to study with care subtle features of folk singing ranging from melodic structure to vocal quality. Phonophotography, as applied to Negro singing by Metfessel in the 1920s, was the first use of such a tool, but the phonograph has been far more significant to research in folklore. To it we owe Schinhan's discussion of scale patterns in North Carolina songs and Lomax's two articles, which show by both analytical and comparative methods that the singing styles in the Anglo- and Afro-American traditions are more profoundly complex and dissimilar than had been supposed. Although Lomax's efforts to correlate style of performance to the subject matter of the songs and to the larger attitudes and structures of a culture are premature, it is clear that the elements are indeed organically related. In their *Anglo-American Folksong Style* (which draws its illustrative material largely from the South) Roger Abrahams and George Foss are working toward such an all-inclusive definition of the term *song style*. The field needs more workers.

Abrahams, Roger D., and George Foss, *Anglo-American Folksong Style* (Englewood Cliffs, N.J., 1968).

Herzog, George, "African Influences in North American Indian Music," *Papers Read at the International Congress of Musicology . . . 1939* (New York, 1944), pp. 130–43.

Lomax, Alan, "Folk Song Style," *American Anthropologist*, LXI (1959), 927–54.

————, Intro to *The Folk Songs of North America in the English Language* (Garden City, N.Y., 1960), pp. xv–xxx.

————, "Song Structure and Social Structure," *Ethnology*, I (1962), 425–51.

Metfessel, Milton, *Phonophotography in Folk Music: American Negro Songs in New Notation* (Chapel Hill, 1928).

Rosenberg, Neil V., "From Sound to Style: The Emergence of Bluegrass," *JAF*, LXXX (1967), 143–50.

Schinhan, Jan P., Intro and Appendices to *The Frank C. Brown Collection of North Carolina Folklore*, ed. Newman I. White, et al, IV (Durham, 1957), pp. xviii–xxxviii; 361–402.

Slotkin, J. S., "Jazz and Its Forerunners as an Example of Acculturation," *Amer Soc R*, VIII (1943), 570–75.

Waterman, Richard A., "African Influence on the Music of the Americas," in *Acculturation in the Americas: Proceedings and Selected Papers of the XXIXth International Congress of Americanists*, ed. Sol Tax (Chicago, 1952), pp. 207–18.

————, "On Flogging a Dead Horse: Lessons Learned from the Africanisms Controversy," *Ethnomusicology*, VII (1963), 83–87.

DANIEL W. PATTERSON
University of North Carolina
Chapel Hill, North Carolina

AGRARIAN THEMES AND IDEAS IN SOUTHERN WRITING

To my knowledge, no bibliography on Agrarianism as a theme, a movement, or a philosophy has been published, although many lists have included sections concerned with economic or practical aspects of agriculture and the problems of the Southern farmer, while some have given attention to the subject through a focus on the group who called themselves the Southern Agrarians (e.g., Alexander Karanikas' study *Tillers of a Myth* contains an extensive bibliography, but it is frequently inaccurate, and it omits important primary sources).

The problems inherent in compiling a comprehensive list—to include relevant statements from the Colonial period to the present—are evident when the implications of definition through selection are considered. For Agrarianism is characterized and limited by whatever the bibliographer chooses to include; a quick check through the list below will reveal that I found it impossible to select *only* statements reaffirming or denying in one way or another that "an agrarian society is one in which agriculture is the leading vocation . . . —a form of labor that is pursued with intelligence and leisure, and that becomes the model to which the other forms approach as they may." [*I'll Take My Stand*, p. xxix]. Had this definition been the only touchstone, many works reflecting a political expression, economic difficulties or historical or sociological implications and emphases might have been discarded. I have included a selection of such titles, although certainly not a comprehensive one; these are primarily relevant to the practical concerns in farming, to the larger area of the economic state of agriculture, to political expressions (e.g., the Populist Party or the Farmers' Alliance), to sociological implications (e.g., the issue of race, the problems of the poor whites and tenant farmers), to questions concerned with regionalism and a consciousness of the "Southernness" of Southern experience.

I have not, however, included in the checklist selections of fiction, drama, and poetry; these forms of expression I chose to eliminate for several reasons: for one thing, because of the difficulties inherent in deciding just how many characteristics of agrarian belief have to be evident and how extensively they are developed before a literary work qualifies as agrarian; and for another, because of my unwillingness to suggest that a work of the creative imagination be labeled as an expression of a particular point of view—including it in such a checklist might seem to imply that it is merely social document or propaganda. (Students of the subject, though, whether their interest is literary, cultural, or historical, ought to be aware of such works as William Grayson's "The

Hireling and the Slave," William Caruthers' *The Cavaliers of Virginia*, Ellen Glasgow's *Barren Ground*, Elizabeth Madox Roberts' *The Time of Man*, Robert Penn Warren's "The Patented Gate and the Mean Hamburger," Allen Tate's *The Fathers*, and Stark Young's *So Red the Rose*, of Ransom's "Antique Harvesters" and Tate's "Ode to the Confederate Dead"—all these are informed by assumptions which have come to be recognized as "agrarian" in part.)

This checklist, then, is chiefly a selection of secondary sources (with a few exceptions—e.g., contemporary works by Southern writers clearly concerned with matters now definable as "agrarian"). At this point, perhaps another explanation about the absence of a group of evidently relevant works is in order—those travel or personal accounts by non-Southerners who visited the South. Interpreting the descriptive label of this checklist quite precisely, I have discarded such titles as *Journal and Letters of Philip Vickers Fithian, 1773–1774: A Plantation Tutor of the Old Dominion*; James Kirke Paulding's *Letters from the South*, and Frederick Law Olmsted's *A Journey in the Seaboard Slave States in the Years 1853–1854*, although these non-Southern observers react unmistakably to the agrarian character of Southern society and culture. Also eliminated were special bibliographies, relevant to particular expressions of this theme, on the grounds that they are easily discovered by anyone seriously engaged in an investigation of the area—e.g., Everett Edwards' *A Bibliography of the History of Agriculture in the U.S.* (1930), or Louise Bercaw's *Rural Standards of Living: A Selected Bibliography* (1931).

My failure to include a particular work or writer which scholars have found relevant or useful can only be explained by my ignorance of the work, its unavailability for examination, or my bad judgment; my first selected checklist was twice as long as this one.

I.   General

Cash, Wilbur J., *The Mind of the South* (New York, 1941).
*Clark, Thomas D., and Albert D. Kirwan, *The South Since Appomattox: A Century of Regional Change* (New York, 1967), pp. 395–420.
Clay, Cassius M., *The Mainstay of American Individualism: A Survey of the Farm Question* (New York, 1934).
Couch, W. T., ed., *Culture in the South* (Chapel Hill, 1934). [see essays by Vance, Pinckney, Hubbell, Davidson, Nixon, Poe, Botkin, Wade]
Govan, Thomas P., "Agrarian and Agrarianism: A Study in the Use and Abuse of Words," *JSH*, XXX (1964), 35–47.
Griswold, A. Whitney, *Farming and Democracy* (New York, 1948).
*Hubbell, *The South in American Literature*, pp. 853–974.
Johnstone, Paul H., "Turnips and Romanticism," *Agricultural Hist*, XII (1938), 224–55.
Key, V. O., Jr., *Southern Politics in State and Nation* (New York, 1949).

Lively, Robert, *Fiction Fights the Civil War: An Unfinished Chapter in the Literary History of the American People* (Chapel Hill, 1957).

McConnell, Grant, *The Decline of Agrarian Democracy* (Berkeley, 1953).

McIlwaine, Shields, *The Southern Poor-White: From Lubberland to Tobacco Road* (Norman, Okla., 1939).

Odum, Howard, *Folk, Region, and Society: Selected Papers of Howard W. Odum*, ed. Katharine Jocher et al (Chapel Hill, 1964).

_____, *Southern Regions of the United States* (Chapel Hill, 1936).

*_____, and Harry E. Moore, *American Regionalism: A Cultural-Historical Approach to National Integration* (New York, 1938), pp. 643–75.

Saloutos, Theodore, *Farmer Movements in the South, 1865–1933* (Berkeley and Los Angeles, 1960).

Thorp, Willard, ed., *A Southern Reader* (New York, 1955).

Woodward, C. Vann, *The Burden of Southern History*, rev ed (Baton Rouge, 1968).

Young, Thomas D., F. C. Watkins, and R. C. Beatty, eds., *The Literature of the South*, rev ed (Glenview, Ill., 1968).

II. To 1865
PRIMARY SOURCES

The Arator: Devoted to Agriculture and Its Kindred Arts, 2 vols (Raleigh, Apr 1855; March 1857).

Baldwin, Joseph, *The Flush Times of Alabama and Mississippi* (New York, 1853), pp. 72–105.

Byrd, William, *The Prose Works of William Byrd: Narratives of a Colonial Virginian*, ed. Louis B. Wright (Cambridge, Mass., 1966).

Fitzhugh, George, *Sociology for the South, or the Failure of the Free Society* (Richmond 1854; New York, 1965).

Helper, Hinton, *The Impending Crisis of the South*, intro by Earl Schenck Miers (New York, 1963).

Jefferson, Thomas, *Notes on the State of Virginia*, ed. William Peden (Chapel Hill, 1955). [see Queries XI, XIV, XIX, XXII]

_____, *Thomas Jefferson's Farm Book with Commentary and Relevant Extracts from Other Writings*, intro by Francis L. Berkeley, Jr.; ed. Edwin M. Betts (Princeton, 1953).

Ruffin, Edmund, *Essays and Notes on Agriculture* (Richmond, 1855).

Taylor, John, *Arator, being a Series of Agricultural Essays, Practical and Political* (Georgetown, 1813).

SECONDARY SOURCES: BOOKS AND MONOGRAPHS

Abernethy, Thomas P., *From Frontier to Plantation in Tennessee* (Chapel Hill, 1932).

Buck, Solon J., *Agrarian Crusade: A Chronicle of the Farmer in Politics* (New Haven, 1921).

Davis, Richard Beale, *Intellectual Life in Jefferson's Virginia, 1790–1830* (Chapel Hill, 1964). [Chap 5, "Agrarian Economy, Theory and Practice," pp. 147–73]

Demaree, A. L., *The American Agricultural Press, 1819–1860* (Montgomery, Ala., 1933).

*Eaton, Clement, *A History of the Old South*, 2nd ed (New York, 1966), pp. 512–41.

_____, *The Mind of the Old South*, rev ed (Baton Rouge, 1967). [chap 7—"The Southern Yeoman: The Humorists' View," pp. 130–51]

*Edwards, Everett E., comp. and ed., *Jefferson and Agriculture* (Washington, D.C., Agric. Hist. Ser., 1943).

Gaines, Francis P., *The Southern Plantation: A Study in the Development and the Accuracy of a Tradition* (New York, 1924).

Gates, Paul W., *The Farmer's Age, 1815–1860* (New York, 1960).

*Genovese, Eugene, *The Political Economy of Slavery: Studies in the Economy and Society of the Slave South* (New York, 1965).

*Gray, Lewis C., *History of Agriculture in the Southern United States to 1860*, 2 vols (Washington, D.C. 1933, 1958) II, 943–1016.

Lytle, Andrew, *Bedford Forrest and His Critter Company*, rev ed (New York, 1960).

*Osterweis, Rollin, *Romanticism and Nationalism in the Old South* (Baton Rouge, 1967), pp. 240–60.

Phillips, Ulrich B., *Life and Labor in the Old South* (Boston, 1930).

Tate, Allen, *Stonewall Jackson* (New York, 1928).

Taylor, William R., *Cavalier and Yankee: The Old South and the American National Character* (New York, 1961).

Vance, Rupert B., *Human Geography of the South* (Chapel Hill, 1932).

Warren, Robert Penn, *John Brown, The Making of a Martyr* (New York, 1929).

SECONDARY SOURCES: ESSAYS AND REVIEWS

Eisinger, Chester, "Land and Loyalty: Literary Expressions of Agrarian Nationalism in the Seventeenth and Eighteenth Centuries," *AL*, XXI (1949), 160–78.

Lytle, Andrew, "John Taylor and the Political Economy of Agriculture," *AmerR*, III (1933), 432–47, 630–43; IV (1934), 84–99.

*Miller, August C., Jr., "Jefferson as an Agriculturalist," *Agric Hist*, XVI (1942), 65–78.

Quinn, Patrick F., "Agrarianism and the Jeffersonian Philosophy," *R of Politics*, II (1940), 87–104.

III.   1865–1920
PRIMARY SOURCES

Cable, George Washington, *The Silent South* (New York, 1885).

Grady, Henry, *The New South* (New York, 1890).

Kelsey, Carl, *The Negro Farmer* (Chicago, 1903).

Lanier, Sidney, "The New South," *Centennial Edition of the Works of Sidney Lanier*, ed. Charles R. Anderson (Baltimore, 1945), V, pp. 334–58.

Otken, Charles, *The Ills of the South or Related Causes Hostile to the General Prosperity of the Southern People* (New York, 1894).

Percy, William Alexander, *Lanterns on the Levee: Recollections of a Planter's Son* (New York, 1941).

SECONDARY SOURCES

Buck, Paul H., *The Road to Reunion, 1865–1900* (Boston, 1937).

Clark, Thomas, *The Emerging South* (New York, 1961).

Ezell, John, *The South Since 1865* (New York, 1963).

*Franklin, John Hope, *From Slavery to Freedom: A History of Negro Americans*, 3rd ed (New York, 1967), pp. 653–86.

*Hicks, John D., *The Populist Revolt: A History of the Farmer's Alliance and the People's Party* (Minneapolis, 1931), pp. 445–64.

Owsley, Frank, "The Historical Philosophy of Frederick Jackson Turner," *AmerR*, V (1935), 368–75.

Shankle, George E., "Poetry of American Farm Life," Peabody 1926. [diss; Harris, Lanier, Page, Russell, Stanton]

*Shannon, Fred A., *The Farmer's Last Frontier: Agriculture, 1860–1897* (New York, 1945). [esp "The Literature of the Subject," pp. 379–414]

*Woodward, C. Vann, *Origins of the New South, 1877–1913* (Baton Rouge, 1951), pp. 485–515.

IV. Since 1920

THE CULTURAL, LITERARY CONTEXT: BOOKS AND MONOGRAPHS

Bishop, John Peale, *Collected Essays*, ed with intro by Edmund Wilson (New York, 1948).

Bradbury, *Renaissance in the South.*

Carter, Hodding, *Southern Legacy* (Baton Rouge, 1950).

Cowan, Louise, *The Fugitive Group: A Literary History* (Baton Rouge, 1959).

Daniels, Jonathan, *A Southerner Discovers the South* (New York, 1938).

Highsaw, Robert, ed., *The Deep South in Transformation* (University, Ala., 1964). [see essays by Patrick and Rubin, and commentaries, pp. 111–75]

Hollis, Christopher, *The American Heresy* (London, 1927).

Mims, Edwin, *The Advancing South: Stories of Progress and Reaction* (Garden City, N.Y., 1926)

Ransom, John Crowe, *God Without Thunder: An Unorthodox Defense of Orthodoxy* (New York, 1930).

*Rubin and Jacobs, *South*, pp. 392–433.

_____, *Southern Renascence.* [see essays by Heilman, Lytle, Jacobs, Donahoe, Odum, Maclachlan, Rubin]

Rubin, Louis D., Jr., and James J. Kilpatrick, eds., *The Lasting South: Fourteen Southerners Look at Their Home* (Chicago, 1957). [see essays by Rubin, Hazel, Dabbs]

Tate, Allen, *Collected Essays* (Denver, 1959).

_____, ed., *A Southern Vanguard: The John Peale Bishop Memorial Volume* (New York, 1947). [see essays by Cowley, Stallman, O'Connor, McLuhan, Heilman]

Wade, John Donald, *Selected Essays and Other Writings of John Donald Wade,* ed., with intro by Donald Davidson (Athens, Ga., 1966).

Walker and Welker, eds., *Reality and Myth.* [see essays by Haun and Cowan]

Weaver, Richard. *Life Without Prejudice and Other Essays,* intro by Eliseo Vivas (Chicago, 1965).

Young, Stark, *The Pavilion: Of People and Times Remembered, of Stories and Places* (New York, 1951).

THE CULTURAL, LITERARY CONTEXT: ESSAYS AND REVIEWS

Burgess, R. L. "Farming: A Variety of Religious Experience," *AmerR,* III (1934) 591–607.

Clark, Thomas D., "The South in Cultural Change," in *Change in the Contemporary South,* ed. Allan P. Sindler (Durham, 1963), pp. 3–25.

Cowley, Malcolm, "The Meriwether Connection," *SoR,* n.s., I (1965), 46–56.

Douglas, Wallace, "Deliberate Exiles: The Social Sources of Agrarian Poetics," in *Aspects of American Poetry,* ed. Richard Ludwig (Columbus, 1962), pp. 273–300.

Fletcher, John Gould, "Regionalism and Folk Art," *SWR,* XIX (1934), 429–34.

Govan, Thomas, "Americans Below the Potomac," in *The Southerner as American,* ed. Charles G. Sellers, Jr. (Chapel Hill, 1960), pp. 19–39.

Hoffman, "The Mark of Time: Society and History in Southern Fiction," *The Art of Southern Fiction,* pp. 96–114.

Holman, C. Hugh, "Ellen Glasgow and the Southern Literary Tradition," in *Southern*

Writers, ed. Simonini, pp. 103–23.

Kazin, Alfred, "Criticism at the Poles," *On Native Grounds: An Interpretation of Modern American Prose Literature* (Garden City, N.Y., 1956), pp. 311–49.

Lytle, Andrew, "The Working Novelist and the Mythmaking Process," *The Hero with the Private Parts* (Baton Rouge, 1966), pp. 178–92.

Mencken, H. L., "The Sahara of the Bozart," *Prejudices, Second Series* (New York, 1920), pp. 136–54. Repr in *A Mencken Chrestomathy* (New York, 1949), pp. 184–95.

———, "The South Astir," *VQR,* XI (1935), 47–60.

O'Connor, Flannery, "The Fiction Writer in His Country," in *The Living Novel,* ed. Granville Hicks (New York, 1957), pp. 157–64.

Parks, Edd Winfield, "The Background of Southern Thought," *Segments of Southern Thought* (Athens, Ga., 1938), pp. 20–42.

Ransom, John Crowe, "The Most Southern Poet" [Davidson], *SeR,* LXX (1962), 202–207. [r essay]

Rubin, Louis D., Jr., "The Concept of Nature in Modern Southern Poetry," *AQ,* IX (1957), 63–71.

———, "The Poetry of Agrarianism," *The Faraway Country,* pp. 155–84.

———, et al., "Agrarianism as a Theme in Southern Literature," *GaR,* XI (1957), 145–64. [intro and four papers; Edd Winfield Parks, "The Ante-Bellum Period"; Allen W. Becker, "The Period 1865–1925"; Virginia Rock, "The Period Since 1925"; C. Hugh Holman, "Summary: The Utility of Myth"]

———, mod., *Recent Southern Fiction: A Panel Discussion:* Bulletin of Wesleyan College (Macon, Ga.), XLI (Jan 1961). [participants: Katherine Anne Porter, Flannery O'Connor, Caroline Gordon, Madison Jones]

Sherman, Caroline B., "Farm-Life Fiction in the South," *SLM,* n.s., I (1939), 203–10.

———, "Rural Poetry in the South," *SLM,* n.s., I (1939), 461–65.

Stewart, Randall, et al, "The Southern Literary Renascence," [symposium], *Shen,* VI (Summer 1955), 3–36. [foreword and four papers: Louise Cowan, "The Fugitive Poets in Relation to the South"; Harry M. Campbell, "Notes on Religion in the Southern Renascence"; Louis D. Rubin, Jr., "A Looking Two Ways"; Andrew Lytle, "A Summing Up"]

Watkins, Floyd C., "Thomas Wolfe and the Nashville Agrarians," *GaR.* VII (1953), 410–23.

Economic, Political, Social Context: Books and Monographs

Agee, James, *Let Us Now Praise Famous Men,* photog by Walker Evans (Boston, 1941; 1960).

Caldwell, Erskine, *You Have Seen Their Faces,* photog by Margaret Bourke-White (New York, 1937).

Cauley, T. J., *Agrarianism: A Program for Farmers* (Chapel Hill, 1935).

Dabbs, James McBride, *Who Speaks for the South?* (New York, 1964).

Ford, Thomas R., ed., *The Southern Appalachian Region: A Survey* (Lexington, Ky, 1962). [see essays by Vance, Ford, Proctor and White]

*Fulmer, John L., *Agricultural Progress in the Cotton Belt Since 1920* (Chapel Hill, 1950), pp. 215–25.

Maclachan, John, and Joe S. Floyd, Jr., eds., *This Changing South* (Gainesville, 1956).

Odum, Howard, *An American Epoch: Southern Portraiture in the National Picture* (New York, 1930).

*Tindall, George B., *The Emergence of the New South, 1913–1945* (Baton Rouge, 1967), pp. 733–68.

Turner, Frederick Jackson, *The Significance of Sections in American History,* intro by

Max Farrand (New York, 1950).
Vance, Rupert B., *Human Factors in Cotton Culture* (Chapel Hill, 1929).
Warren, Robert Penn, *The Legacy of the Civil War: Meditations on the Centennial* (New York, 1961).

ECONOMIC, POLITICAL, SOCIAL CONTEXT: ESSAYS, REVIEWS

Cauley, T. J., "The Integration of Agrarian and Exchange Economics," *AmerR*, V (1935), 584–602.
Couch, W. T., "An Agrarian Programme for the South," *AmerR*, III (1934), 313–26.
Gee, Wilson, "The Effects of Urbanization on Agriculture," *So Econ Jour*, II (1935), 3–15.
*Going, Allen J., "The Agrarian Revolt," in *Writing Southern History*, ed. Arthur S. Link and Rembert W. Patrick (Baton Rouge, 1965), 362–82.
Matherly, Walter L., "Rural Yesterdays in the Upper South," *SAQ*, XXXV (1936), 237–50.
Rawe, John C., "Agrarianism: The Basis for a Better Life," *AmerR*, VI (1935), 176–92.
Simkins, Francis B., "The South," in *Regionalism in America*, ed. Merrill Jensen (Madison, Wis., 1951), pp. 147–72.
Vance, Rupert, "Is Agrarianism for Farmers?" *SoR*, o.s., I (1935), 41–57.

V.   Southern Agrarians and Agrarianism

PRIMARY SOURCES: BOOKS AND MONOGRAPHS

Davidson, Donald, *The Attack on Leviathan: Regionalism and Nationalism in the United States* (Chapel Hill, 1938).
_____, *Still Rebels, Still Yankees and Other Essays* (Baton Rouge, 1957).
Fugitives Reunion: Conversations at Vanderbilt, ed. Rob Roy Purdy (Nashville, 1959), pp. 156–218.
I'll Take My Stand: The South and the Agrarian Tradition, by Twelve Southerners (New York, 1930; 1962).
Nixon, Herman Clarence, *Forty Acres and Steel Mules* (Chapel Hill, 1938).
_____, *Lower Piedmont Country* (New York, 1946).
_____, *Possum Trot, Rural Community, South* (Norman, Okla., 1941).
Owsley, Frank L., *Plain Folk of the Old South* (Baton Rouge, 1949).
Tate, Allen and Herbert Agar, eds., *Who Owns America? A New Declaration of Independence* (Boston, 1936).

PRIMARY SOURCES: ARTICLES AND REVIEWS

Davidson, Donald, "An Agrarian Looks at the New Deal," *Free America*, II (June, 1938), 3–5, 17.
_____, "Agrarianism and Politics," *R of Politics*, I (1939), 114–25.
_____, "r of *American Regionalism* by Howard Odum and Harry E. Moore, *Free America*, II (Oct 1938), 19–20.
_____, "Counterattack, 1930–1940: The South Against Leviathan," *Southern Writers in the Modern World* (Athens, Ga., 1958), pp. 31–62.
_____, "The First Agrarian Economist," *AmerR*, V (1935), 106–12. [r of T. J. Cauley's *Agrarianism: A Program for Farmers*]
_____, "*I'll Take My Stand*: A History," *AmerR*, V (1935), 301–21.
_____, "The 'Mystery' of the Agrarians: Facts and Illusions about Some Southern Writers," *SatR*, XXVI (Jan 23, 1943), 6–7.

———, "Regionalism as a Social Science," *SoR*, o.s., III (1937), 209–24.

———, "The Restoration of the Farmer," *AmerR*, III (1934), 96–101. [r of C.M. Clay's *The Mainstay of American Individualism: A Survey of the Farm Question*]

Fletcher, John Gould, "Cultural Aspects of Regionalism," Round Table on Regionalism. Institute of Public Affairs, U of Va, July 9, 1931, III, 707–13 (Charlottesville, 1931). [mimeo]

———, "Is Folk Art Property?" *NMexQ*, V (Spring 1935), 77–80.

———, "Section versus State," *AmerR*, I (1933), 483–89. [r of F. J. Turner's *The Influence of Sections in American History*]

Nixon, Herman Clarence, "Farewell to 'Possum Trot'?" in *The Urban South*, ed. Rupert Vance and Nicholas J. Demerath (Chapel Hill, 1954), pp. 283–92.

———, "A Thirty Years' Personal View," *MissQ*, XIII (1960), 76–79.

Owsley, Frank L., "The Old South and the New," *AmerR*, VI (1936), 475–85. [r of B. B. Kendrick and A. M. Arnett, *The South Looks at Its Past*]

———, "The Pillars of Agrarianism," *AmerR*, IV (1935), 529–47.

Ransom, John Crowe, "Art and the Human Economy," *KR*, VII (1945), 683–88.

———, "Happy Farmers, *AmerR*, I (1933), 513–35.

———, "Hearts and Heads," *AmerR*, II (1934), 554–71.

———, "Land!" *Harper's*, CLXV (1932), 216–24.

———, "The South Is a Bulwark," *Scribner's*, XCIX (1936), 299–303.

———, "The State and the Land," *New Rep*, LXX (1932), 8–10.

"A Symposium: The Agrarians Today," *Shen*, III, (Summer 1952) 14–33. [responses from Ransom, Davidson, Owsley, Tate, Nixon, Lytle, Wade]

[Tate, Allen], "An Interview with Allen Tate," by Michael Millgate. *Shen*, XII (Spring 1961), 27–34.

———, "A Traditionist Looks at Liberalism," *SoR*, o.s., I (1936), 731–44.

———, "A View of the Whole South," *AmerR*, II (1934), 411–32. [r W. T. Couch's *Culture in the South*]

Warren, Robert Penn, "The Art of Fiction, XVIII," *ParisR*, 16 (Spring-Summer 1957). 113–40. [interv by Ralph Ellison, Eugene Walter]

Young, Stark, "Communications," *Shen*, III (Autumn 1952), 39.

SECONDARY SOURCES: BOOKS AND THESES

*Bradbury, John, "Critics and Agrarians," *The Fugitives: A Critical Account* (Chapel Hill, 1958), pp. 88–101, 274–94.

Casper, Leonard, "The New Agrarianism," *Robert Penn Warren: The Dark and Bloody Ground* (Seattle, 1960), pp. 24–32.

*Karanikas, Alexander, *Tillers of a Myth: Southern Agrarians as Social and Literary Critics* (Madison, Wis., 1966).

Linenthal, Mark, "Robert Penn Warren and the Southern Agrarians," Stanford, 1957. [diss]

*Rock, Virginia, "The Making and Meaning of *I'll Take My Stand*: A Study in Utopian Conservatism, 1925–1939," Minnesota, 1961, pp. 592–634. [diss]

Stewart, John L., "Toward Agrarianism," "Agrarianism and After," *The Burden of Time: The Fugitives and Agrarians* (Princeton, 1965), pp. 91–205.

SECONDARY SOURCES: ARTICLES AND REVIEWS

Amacher, Anne Ward, "Myths and Consequences: Calhoun and Some Nashville Agrarians," *SAQ*, LIX (1960), 251–64.

Auerbach, M. Morton, "The Illusion of a Southern Conservative Revival," *The Conservative Illusion* (New York, 1959), pp. 104–27.

Carmichael, Peter A., "Jeeter Lester, Agrarian Par Excellence," *SeR*, XLVIII (1940), 21–29.

Connelly, Thomas L., "The Vanderbilt Agrarians: Time and Place in Southern Tradition," *Tenn Hist Q*, XXII (1963), 22–37.

Couch, W. T., "The Agrarian Romance," *SAQ*, XXXVI (1937), 419–30.

Current-Garcia, Eugene, et al, "The Fugitive-Agrarian Movement: A Symposium: Introduction," *MissQ*, XIII (1960), 53–98. [intro and six papers: Randall Stewart, "The Relation between Fugitives and Agrarians"; Theodore C. Hoepfner, "Economics of Agrarianism"; Ruel E. Foster, "Flight from Mass Culture"; H. C. Nixon, "A Thirty Years' Personal View"; Virginia Rock, "Dualisms in Agrarian Thought"; Earl H. Rovit, "The Region versus The Nation: Critical Battle of the Thirties"]

Fishwick, Marshall, "They Took Their Stand," *WR*, XI (1947), 234–40.

Hesseltine, W. B., "Look Away, Dixie," *SeR*, XXXIX (1931), 97–103.

Holland, Robert B., "The Agrarian Manifesto—A Generation Later," *MissQ*, X (1957), 73–78.

Holman, C. Hugh, "Literature and Culture: The Fugitive-Agrarians," *Social Forces*, XXXVII (Oct 1958), 15–19.

Irish, Marian, "Proposed Roads to the New South, 1941: Chapel Hill Planners vs. Nashville Agrarians," *SeR*, XLIX (1941), 1–27.

Knickerbocker, W. S., "Mr. Ransom and the Old South," *SeR*, XXXIX (1931), 222–39.

McGill, Ralph, "Agrarianism *vs.* Industrialism—Question Skillfully Debated by Anderson and Dr. Ransom," *Atlanta Constitution* (Feb 12, 1931). [newsp art]

Mencken, H. L., "Uprising in the Confederacy," *Amer Mercury*, XXII (1931), 379–81.

Moore, Edward, "The 1930 Agrarians," *SeR*, LXXI (1963), 134–42.

Newby, Idus A., "The Southern Agrarians: A View after Thirty Years," *Agric Hist*, XXXVII (1963), 143–55.

Nicholls, William H., "The New Southern Agrarianism: Progress Condemned," *Southern Tradition and Regional Progress* (Chapel Hill, 1960), pp. 27–42.

Pressly, Thomas J., "Agrarianism: An Autopsy," *SeR*, XLIX (1941), 145–63.

Rock, Virginia, "The Fugitive-Agrarians in Response to Social Change," *So Hum R.*, I (1967), 170–81.

Rubin, Louis D., Jr., intro to the Torchbook Edition, *I'll Take My Stand: The South and the Agrarian Tradition* by Twelve Southerners (New York, 1962), pp. vi–xviii.

Smith, Henry Nash, "The Dilemma of Agrarianism," *SWR*, XIX (1934), 215–32.

Stewart, Randall, "The Relation Between Fugitives and Agrarians," in George Core, ed., *Regionalism and Beyond: Essays of Randall Stewart* (Nashville, 1968), pp. 234–40.

Ward, C. A., "The Good Myth"; "Myths: Further Vanderbilt Agrarian Views," *U Kan Cy R*, XXV (1958), 53–56, 272–76.

Weaver, Richard, "Agrarianism in Exile," *SeR*, LVIII (1950), 586–606.

Westbrook, John T., "Twilight of Southern Regionalism," *SWR*, XLII (1957), 231–34.

Wilson, Edmund, "Tennessee Agrarians," *New Rep*, LXVII (1931), 279–81.

VIRGINIA ROCK
York University
Toronto, Ontario

SOUTHERN SPEECH

The study of Southern American English has had three modes which have overlapped in time: (1) the recording of provincialisms, (2) exact phonetic description, and (3) linguistic geography.

First was the collection of localisms, much like natural history museum collection, beginning with Adiel Sherwood's and Robley Dunglison's glossaries of the 1820s and culminating in the word lists in *Dialect Notes* (1889–1937) and the first fifteen issues of *Publication of the American Dialect Society* (1944–51). The principal word lists are recorded in the bibliography in Wentworth's *American Dialect Dictionary* and in the *PMLA* annual bibliography.

The second mode, the detailed study of Southern phonetics, flourished from the 1920s through the 1940s. Standard works on American pronunciation, which include Southern speech, are Arthur Bronstein, *The Pronunciation of American English* (1960), John S. Kenyon, *American Pronunciation* (10th ed, 1950), and Charles K. Thomas, *The Phonetics of American English* (2nd ed, 1958). Representative special studies of Southern pronunciation are listed below in part II.

The currently dominant mode is linguistic geography, with its carefully selected informants (native speakers) and uniform work sheets or questionnaires. Interviewing in the South Atlantic states for a linguistic atlas of the United States and Canada was completed in 1949. Although the atlas has not been published, a number of studies based on the field records have been written. Interviewing in the central South has not yet begun. However, various surveys using modified atlas methodology have been made from Georgia to East Texas, and the subregional patterns made by the overlapping of Lowland Southern and Mountain Southern in the Gulf states (reflecting past population movements) are beginning to emerge.

The newest concern of dialect geographers is social dialectology, made possible by the educational, ethnic, occupational, and age criteria used in selecting representative informants. Just as phonetic studies of 1925–45 produced accurate descriptions of Southern sounds and their occurrence, so dialect geography is producing accurate accounts of the areal and social distribution of Southern speech forms.

Lowland Southern and Mountain Southern (the English used from Maryland to East Texas south of the Ohio River) are represented in the studies listed, in four categories: (1) general and historical, (2) phonology, (3) linguistic geography, and (4) bibliography.

Because the reviews of books in the field are often as important as the books themselves, references to selected reviews are listed after each title when appropriate.

Abbreviations

AJP	*American Journal of Philology*
AS	*American Speech*
DN	*Dialect Notes*
Lang.	*Language*
PADS	*Publication of the American Dialect Society*
QJS	*Quarterly Journal of Speech*
SIL	*Studies in Linguistics*
So Speech Jour	*Southern Speech Journal*

I. General and Historical

Berrey, Lester V., "Southern Mountain Dialect," *AS*, XV (1940), 45–54. [phonology, morphology, syntax, subregions]

Brooks, Cleanth, Jr., *The Relation of the Alabama-Georgia Dialect to the Provincial Dialects of Great Britain*, LSU Stud, No. XX (Baton Rouge, 1935). [r by G. T. Flom, *JEGP*, XXXV (1936), 614; G. W. Gray, *QJS*, XXIII (1937), 146; R. J. Menner, *AS*, X (1935), 304–307; S. S. Smith, *Amer Oxonian*, XXIV (1937), 177–80; K. Malone, *Mod Lang Notes*, LIII (1938), 39–40; C. L. Wrenn, *Year's Wk in Eng Stud*, XVI (1935), 62–63]

Clarke, Mary W., "Jesse Stuart's Writings Preserve Passing Folk Idiom," *SFQ*, XXVIII (1964), 157–98.

Cohen, Hennig, "Slave Names in Colonial South Carolina," *AS*, XXVII (1952), 102–12. [see G. W. Williams, *AS*, XXXIII (1958), 294, and N. N. Puckett, in *Studies in the Science of Society Presented to Albert Galloway Keller* (New Haven, 1937), pp. 471–94]

Combs, Josiah H., "The Language of the Southern Highlander," *PMLA*, XLVI (1931), 1302–22. [idioms, names, pronunciation, syntax]

Dingus, L. R., "A Word List from Virginia," *DN*, IV (1915), 177–93. [includes notes on phonology, morphology, and syntax]

Dunglison, Robley, see M. M. Mathews, 1931.

Eliason, Norman E., *Tarheel Talk: An Historical Study of the English Language in North Carolina to 1860* (Chapel Hill, 1956). [r by D. E. Baughan, *AS*, XXXII (1957), 283–86; H. Galinsky, *Anglia*, LXXVI (1958), 452–60; J. R. Gaskin, *CarolinaQ*, IX (1957), 58–59; M. M. Bryant, *Midw Folkl*, VIII (1958) 53–56; W. C. Greet, *Mod Lang Notes*, LXXIII (1958), 64–67; S. Potter, *Mod Lang R*, LII (1957), 624; R. I. McDavid, Jr., *JEGP*, LVII (1958), 160–65; T. Pyles, *Lang*, XXXIII (1957), 256–61; R. H. Spiro, Jr., *JSH*, XXIII (1957), 375–76; R. Walser, *N.C. HistR*, XXXIV (1957), 86–87; C. K. Thomas, *QJS*, LXIV (1958), 196; Paul Christophersen, *Eng Stud*, XXXIX (1958), 183–85; R. W. Burchfield, *R of Eng Stud*, IX (1958), 458]

Greet, W. Cabell, "Southern Speech," in *Culture in the South*, ed W. T. Couch (Chapel Hill, 1934), pp. 594–615.

Harrison, James A., "Negro English," *Anglia*, VII (1884), 232–75. [phonetics, morphology, lexicon, neologisms, interjections, linguistic change; based on personal observation and dialect writings]

Holmes, Urban T., "A Study in Negro Onamastics," *AS*, V (1930), 463–67.

Howren, Robert, "The Speech of Okracoke, North Carolina," *AS*, XXXVII (1962), 163–75. [Okracoke is a village in the isolated Outer Banks of N.C.]

Johnson, Guy B., "Gullah: The Dialect of the Negroes of St. Helena Island," *Folk Culture on St. Helena Island, South Carolina* (Chapel Hill, 1930), pp. 3–62. [description of Gullah by a sociologist]

Kephart, Horace, "The Mountain Dialect," *Our Southern Highlanders* (New York, 1913), pp. 276–304. [anecdotal account; some phonology and grammar, mostly lexicon]

Lumiansky, Robert M., "New Orleans Slang in the 1880s," *AS*, XXV (1950), 28–40, [evidence from *The Lantern*, a wk jour]

McDavid, Raven I., Jr., "Postvocalic /-r/ in South Carolina: A Social Analysis," *AS*, XXIII (1948), 194–203.

————, and Virginia Glenn McDavid, "The Relationship of the Speech of American Negroes to the Speech of Whites," *AS*, XXVI (1951), 3–17.

McJimsey, George D., *Topographic Terms in Virginia*, *AS* Reprints and Monographs, No. 3 (New York, 1940); also in *AS*, XV (1940), 1–38, 149–79, 262–300, 381–419; Columbia. [diss; r by H. B. Woolf, *Lang.*, XVII (1941), 275–77]

McMullen, E. Wallace, *English Topographic Terms in Florida, 1563–1874* (Gainesville, 1953). [r by M. Bryant, *Names*, II (1954), 142–43; R. I. McDavid, Jr., *AS*, XXX (1955), 53–54; M. M. Mathews, *AS*, XXX (1955), 58–60]

Mathews, M. M., *The Beginnings of American English* (Chicago, 1931). [includes "Mrs. Anne Royall (1769–1854)," pp. 88–98; Robley Dunglison, "Americanisms in the Virginia Literary Museum," pp. 99–112; Adiel Sherwood, "Provincialisms," pp. 118–21; and "Southwestern Vernacular," pp. 151–63; see *DN*, V (1927), 415–21, for Sherwood's first (1827), list of Georgia provincialisms]

————, *Some Sources of Southernisms* (University, Ala. 1948). [popular treatment of So Amer words from Muskogean, Nahuatl, and African sources; r by N. E. Eliason, *AS*, XXIV (1949), 123–24; T. A. Kirby, *JEGP*, XLVIII (1949), 422–24; R. I. McDavid, Jr., *SIL*, VII (1949), 71–74; L. D. Turner, *Lang.*, XXVI (1950), 167–70] ·

Payne, L[eonidas] W., "A Word-List from East Alabama," *DN*, III (part 4, 1908), 279–328 (part 5, 1909), 343–91. [lexicon, phonology, morphology; repr in *Bull of U of Tex*, No. 113, repr ser No. 8 (Austin, Tex., 1909)]

Primer, Sylvester, "Charleston Provincialisms," *Trans Mod Lang Assn*, III (1887), 84–99; *AJP*, IX (1888), 198–213; *Phonetische Studien*, I (1887), 227–43. [see MLA *Transactions* (1887), pp. xix–xxv, for discussion of this pioneer paper at the MLA meeting; cf. Raven I. McDavid, Jr., 1955, for a modern study of the same dialect]

Pyles, Thomas, "Bible Belt Onomastics, or Some Curiosities of Anti-Pedobaptist Nomenclature," *Names*, VII (1959), 84–101.

*Randolph, Vance, and George P. Wilson, *Down in the Holler: a Gallery of Ozark Folk Speech* (Norman, Okla., 1953). Bibl pp. 303–14. [r by E. H. Criswell, *AS*, XXVIII (1953), 285–88; C. W. Garbutt, *QJS*, XXXIX (1953), 374–75; see also A. H. Orrick, *PADS*, No. 23 (Apr. 1955), 49–50]

Read, Allen Walker, "The Rebel Yell as a Linguistic Problem," *AS*, XXXVI (1961), 83–92.

————, "The Speech of Negroes in Colonial America," *Jour of Negro Hist*, XXIV (1939), 247–58.

Royall, Mrs. Anne, see M. M. Mathews, 1931.

Sawyer, Janet B., "Aloofness from Spanish Influence in Texas English," *Word*, XV (1959), 270–81.

Sherwood, Adiel, see M. M. Mathews, 1931.

*Smith, Reed, "The Black Border Series," *AS*, I (1926), 559–62. [r of Gullah stories by Ambrose E. Gonzales; bibl of writings in Gullah]

Stephenson, Edward A., "Early North Carolina Pronunciation," *DA*, XIX (1958), 2342–43 (North Carolina).

*Turner, Lorenzo D., *Africanisms in the Gullah Dialect* (Chicago, 1949). [r by R. A. Hall, Jr., *AS*, XXV (1950), 51–54; R. I. McDavid, Jr., *Lang.*, XXVI (1950), 323–33; J. B. McMillan, *AlaR* III (1950), 148–50; M. Swadesh, *Word*, VII (1951), 82–84; G. P. Wilson, *QJS*, XXXVI (1950), 261–62; see also H. P. Blok, *Lingua*, VIII (1959), 306–21.]

_____, "Notes on the Sounds and Vocabulary of Gullah," *PADS*, No. 3 (May 1945), 13–28.

Walser, Richard, "Negro Dialect in Eighteenth-Century American Drama," *AS*, XXX (1955), 269–76.

Wilson, George P., ed., "Folk Speech," in *The Frank C. Brown Collection of North Carolina Folklore*, I (Durham, 1952), pp. 503–618. [extensive word list]

II. Phonology

Atwood, E. Bagby, "Some Eastern Virginia Pronunciation Features," in *English Studies for James Southall Wilson*, ed. Fredson Bowers, *U of Va Stud*, IV (Charlottesville, 1951), 111–24.

Caffee, N. M., "Some Notes on Consonant Pronunciation in the South," in *Studies for William A. Read*, ed. N. M. Caffee and Thomas A. Kirby (Baton Rouge, 1940), pp. 125–32.

Greet, W. Cabell, "Delmarva Speech," *AS*, VIII (1933), 56–63.

_____, "A Phonographic Expedition to Williamsburg, Virginia," *AS*, VI (1931), 161-172.

*Hall, Joseph S., *The Phonetics of Great Smoky Mountain Speech*, *AS* Reprints and Monographs, No. 4 (New York, 1942); also in *AS*, XVII (1942, part 2), Columbia, 1942, [diss; r by R. I. McDavid, Jr., *Lang*, XIX (1943), 184–95; A. H. Marckwardt, *QJS*, XXVIII (1942), 487]

Howren, Robert R., "The Speech of Louisville, Kentucky," *DA*, XIX (1958), 527 (Indiana).

Ives, Sumner, "The Phonology of the Uncle Remus Stories," *PADS*, No. 22 (Nov., 1954). [systematic description of the dialect, and verification from records of So Atl atlas]

Jaffe, Hilda, "The Speech of the Central Coast of North Carolina: the Carteret County Version of the Banks 'Brogue,'" *DA*, XXVII (1966), 1355–56A (Michigan State).

Kurath, Hans, *A Phonology and Prosody of Modern English* (Ann Arbor, 1964). [based on atlas records, including those from the Southeast; r by J. H. Sledd, *AS*, XL (1965), 201–205; C. L. Laird, *Eng Lang Notes*, IV (1966), 315; R. I. McDavid, Jr., *Mod Phil*, LXIV (1966), 182]

La Ban, Frank Kenneth, "Phonological Study of the Speech of the Conchs, Early Inhabitants of the Florida Keys, at Three Age Levels," *DA*, XXVI (1965), 3318–19 (Louisiana).

McMillan, James B., "Vowel Nasality as a Sandhi-Form of the Morphemes -*nt* and -*ing* in Southern American," *AS*, XIV (1939), 120–23.

Primer, Sylvester, "The Pronunciation of Fredericksburg, Virginia," *PMLA*, V (1890), 185–99.

*Read, William A., "Some Variant Pronounciations in the New South," *DN*, III (1911), 496–536. Repr *LSU Bull*, III, No. 5 (1912).

Shewmake, Edwin F., "Distinctive Virginia Pronunciation," *AS*, XVIII (1943), 33–38. [see Argus Tresidder, 1943, for disagreement]

————, *English Pronunciation in Virginia* (Charlottesville, 1927). [Va., 1920 diss; r by H. Kurath, *AS*, III (1928), 478–79]

Sledd, James H., "Breaking, Umlaut, and the Southern Drawl," *Lang.*, XLII (1966), 18–41. [generative phonological rules to account for So features]

Stanley, Oma, "Negro Speech of East Texas," *AS*, XVI, (1941), 3–16.

————, *The Speech of East Texas*, American Speech Monograph No. 2 (New York, 1937). [Columbia, 1937, diss; also in *AS*, XI (1936), 3–36; 145–66; 232–52; 327–53. r by C. K. Thomas, *QJS*, XXIV (1938), 693]

Todd, Julia M., "A Phonological Analysis of the Speech of Aged Citizens of Claiborne County, Mississippi," *DA*, XXVI (1965), 4894 (Louisiana).

Tresidder, Argus, "The Sounds of Virginia Speech," *AS*, XVIII (1943), 261–72. [analysis of passage of 195 words rec by 254 college students representing all sections of Va; some disagreement with Shewmake]

Wheatley, Katherine E., and Oma Stanley, "Three Generations of East Texas Speech," *AS*, XXXIV (1959), 83–94.

Williamson, Juanita, "A Phonological and Morphological Study of the Speech of the Negro of Memphis, Tennessee," *DA*, XXI (1961) 3777–78 (Michigan).

Wilson, George P., "Some Unrecorded Southern Vowels," *AS*, IX (1934), 209–13.

Wise, C. M., "Negro Dialect," *QJS*, XIX (1933), 522–28.

————, "Southern American Dialect," *AS*, VIII (1933), 37–43.

————, W. Scott Nobles, and Herbert Metz, "The Southern American Diphthong [aɪ]," *So Speech Jour*, XIX (1954), 304–12.

Zimmerman, Jane Dorsey, ed., *Phonetic Transcriptions from 'American Speech' AS* Reprints and Monographs, No. 1, rev ed (New York, 1939). [includes IPA transcriptions of speech from Va., N.C., S.C., Ga., and Tex.; see annual indexes through 1945 in *AS* for other transcriptions]

III. Linguistic Geography

Atwood, E. Bagby, "*Grease* and *greasy*; a Study of Geographical Variation," in *Readings in Applied English Linguistics*, ed. H. B. Allen, 1st ed (1958), pp. 158–67; 2nd ed (1964), pp. 242–51. Repr from *U of Tex Stud in Eng*, XXIX (1950), 249–60. [cf. C. K. Thomas, 1958]

————, *The Regional Vocabulary of Texas* (Austin, Tex., 1962). [lexical survey based on standard interv; includes 125 maps and some study of border areas of Louisiana, Oklahoma, and Arkansas; r by W. Labov, *Word*, XIX (1963), 266–72; D. M. McKeithan, *SW Hist Q*, LXVII (1963), 158–63; C. E. Reed, *Lang.*, XL (1964), 296–98; G. R. Wood, *AS*, XXXVIII (1963), 220–23; J. N. Tidwell, *Jour Amer Folkl*, LXXVII (1964), 163–64]

————, *A Survey of Verb Forms in the Eastern United States* (Ann Arbor, 1953). [based on atlas rec including the Mid and So Atl states; r by A. L. Davis, *AS*, XXX (1955), 120–23; N. E. Eliason, *Mod Lang Notes*, LXIX (1954), 282; A. H. Marckwardt, *Lang.*, XXX (1954), 426–28; C. M. Wise, *So Speech Jour*, XIX (1954) 341–42; C. K. Thomas, *QJS*, XL (1954), 81–82]

Avis, Walter S., "'Crocus Bag': A Problem in Areal Linguistics," *AS*, XXX (1955), 5–16.

————, "The Mid-Back Vowels in the English of the Eastern United States," *DA*, XVII (1956), 140 (Michigan). [includes So Atl states]

Babington, Mima, and E. Bagby Atwood, "Lexical Usage in Southern Louisiana," *PADS*, No. 36 (Nov 1961), 1–24.

Folk, Mary Lucile, "A Word Atlas of North Louisiana," *DA*, XXII (1961), 3653–54 (Louisiana).

Foscue, Virginia Oden, "Background and Preliminary Survey of the Linguistic Geography of Alabama," *DA*, XXVII (1966), 214–A (Wisconsin).

George, Albert Donald, "Graduate Study and Research in Linguistic Geography," *So Speech Jour*, XVIII (1952), 87–95. [La isoglosses on 13 maps]

Ives, Sumner, "Pronunciation of 'Can't' in the Eastern States," *AS*, XVIII (1953), 149–57. [based on atlas rec; includes maps]

Kurath, Hans, *A Word Geography of the Eastern United States* (Ann Arbor, 1949). [first study of dialect geography of Atl states based on atlas rec; first documented description of principal east-coast regions and subregions; r by E. B. Atwood, *Word*, VI (1950), 194–97; A. L. Davis, *JEGP*, XLIX (1950), 431–32; N. E. Eliason, *Mod Lang Notes*, LXVI (1951), 478–89; J. B. McMillan, *Lang.*, XXVII (1951), 423–29; R. J. Menner, *AS*, XXV (1950), 122–26; H. L. Smith, Jr., *SIL*, IX (1951), 7–12; C. K. Thomas, *QJS*, XXXVI (1950), 262]

———, and Raven I. McDavid, Jr., *The Pronunciation of English in the Atlantic States* (Ann Arbor, 1961). [demarcation of dialect areas on phonological criteria; r by W. S. Avis, *Canad Jour Ling*, XI (1965), 63–70; A. J. Bronstein, *QJS*, XLVIII (1962), 440–41; R. M. Dorson, *Ohio Hist*, LXXII (1963), 73–75; N. E. Eliason, *SAQ*, LXI (1962), 121–22; T. Hill, *Mod LangR*, LVII (1962), 624–25; S. J. Keyser, *Lang*, XXXIX (1963), 303–16; J. Y. Mather, *R of Eng Stud*, XIV (1963), 216–18]

Lowman, Guy S., "The Treatment of [au] in Virginia," *Proceed Second Int Cong Phon Sci* (Cambridge, Eng., 1936), pp. 122–25. [7 types of [au] described, with well-defined areal boundaries, from atlas evidence]

McDavid, Raven I., Jr., "Derivations of Middle English [o:] in the South Atlantic Area," *QJS*, XXXV (1949), 496–504.

———, "The Position of the Charleston Dialect," *PADS*, No. 23 (Apr 1955), 35–50.

McDavid, Virginia, "*To* as a Preposition of Location in Linguistic Atlas Materials," *PADS*, No. 40 (Nov 1963), 12–19. [includes Mid and So Atl usage]

Nixon, Phyllis J., "A Glossary of Virginia Words," *PADS*, No. 5 (May 1946), 3–43. [r by R. I. McDavid, Jr., *SIL*, V (1947), 21–24; see also *PADS*, No. 6 (Nov 1946), 44–46; No. 8 (Nov 1947), 11–38]

Norman, Arthur M. Z., "Migration to Southeast Texas; People and Words," *SW Soc Sci Q*, XXXVII (1956), 149–58.

Tarpley, Fred A., "A Word Atlas of Northeast Texas," *DA*, XXI (1960), 2289 (Louisiana).

Thomas, Charles K., "The Linguistic Mason and Dixon Line," in *The Rhetorical Idiom*, ed. Donald C. Bryant (Ithaca, N.Y., 1958), pp. 251–55. [includes map with isoglosses for *on*, *greasy*, and *grease*; cf E. B. Atwood, 1950]

———, "Notes on the Pronunciation of 'hurry'," *AS*, XXI (1946), 112–15. [data and map showing New Eng and the SE differing from the rest of the country]

Van Riper, William R., "The Loss of Post-Vocalic *R* in the Eastern United States," *DA*, XIX (1958), 806 (Michigan). [includes Mid and So Atl states]

Walker, Saunders, "A Dictionary of the Folk Speech of the East Alabama Negro," (abst.) Western Reserve U *Bibl of Pub and Abstracts of Diss*, 1956–58, 403. [based on information from standard work sheets]

Wetmore, Thomas H., "The Low-Central and Low-Back Vowels in the English of the Eastern United States," *PADS*, No. 32 (Nov 1959). [incl western N.C., eastern Va., and eastern S. C.; r by M. L. Gateau, *Words*, XVIII (1963), 362; C. K. Thomas, *AS*, XXXVI (1961), 201–203]

Wood, Gordon R., "Dialect Contours in the Southern States," *AS*, XXXVIII (1963), 243–56. [isoglosses in the interior So based on mail questionnaires; includes maps]

——, *Sub Regional Speech Variations in Vocabulary, Grammar, and Pronunciation*, Coöperative Research Project No. 3046, So Ill U (Edwardsville, Ill., 1967). [computer mapping of isoglosses in the interior So]

——, "Word Distribution in the Interior South," *PADS*, No. 35 (Apr 1961), 1–16.

*IV. Bibliography

"Bibliography," *AS*, q, 1925——.

Cantrell and Patrick, *Southern Literary Culture*. [bibl of theses and diss to the end of 1948, indexed]

"Folkspeech" [1938–48], "Speech [1949——]" in "Folklore Bibliography for [1937——]" *SFQ*, annually in March issue, 1938——.

Kennedy, Arthur G., *Bibliography of Writings on the English Language* [to the end of 1922] (Cambridge and New Haven, 1927; New York, 1961). [see esp "American Sectional Dialects," pp. 413–16]

Krapp, George Philip, *The English Language in America*, 2 vols (New York, 1925; 1960). [bibl in II]

"Language and Phonetics" in "A Bibliography of Speech and Theater in the South for the Year [1955——]," annually in *So Speech Jour.*, 1956——.

Mencken, H. L., *The American Language*, 4th ed (New York, 1936), pp. 358–64; *Supplement One* (1945); *Supplement Two* (1948), pp. 115–235. One-vol abr ed, abr by Raven I McDavid, Jr., with assistance of David W. Maurer (1963), pp. 448–78. [bibl in footnotes]

Northup, Clark S., "A Bibliography of the English and French Languages in America from 1894 to 1900," *DN*, II (1900–1904), 151–78; supp bibl in I (1890–96), 13–16, 80–83, 254–58, 344–47. [of chiefly antiq interest]

"Theses for the Year," annually in *So Atl Bull* (Fall 1936——).

Wentworth, Harold, *American Dialect Dictionary* (New York, 1944). [bibl pp. 737–47, lists important lexical collections in *DN* and *AS* to 1940]

Woodbridge, Hensley C., "A Tentative Bibliography of Kentucky Speech," *PADS*, No. 30 (Nov., 1958), 17–37.

JAMES B. McMILLAN
University of Alabama
University, Alabama

MANUSCRIPT COLLECTIONS AND HOLDINGS

Authoritative general surveys of library resources include Robert B. Downs, *American Library Resources: A Bibliographical Guide* (Chicago, 1951) and its *Supplement, 1950–1961* (Chicago, 1962), and Lee Ash, *Subject Collections,* 4th ed (New York, 1967). Because college and university libraries in the South tend to specialize in literature of the region, the student of Southern literature will find helpful Downs's earlier survey, *Resources of Southern Libraries* (Chicago, 1938). The resources of a single state are surveyed in John Hammond Moore's *Research Materials in South Carolina: A Guide* (Columbia, S.C., 1967), which includes a 75-page listing of manuscripts in the South Caroliniana Library of the University of South Carolina.

For the location and description of Southern literary manuscripts, as for American literary manuscripts generally, there are three basic sources:

American Literary Manuscripts: A Checklist of Holdings in Academic, Historical and Public Libraries in the United States, Joseph Jones et al, comp (Austin, Tex., 1960). [*ALM*]
Hamer, Philip M., ed., *A Guide to Archives and Manuscripts in the United States* (New Haven, 1961). [Hamer]
The National Union Catalog of Manuscript Collections, 1959———, 6 vols to date (1962———). [*NUCMC*]

Of the three, Hamer alone permits an overall view of the holdings of a particular library, although a repository index to *NUCMC* enables a researcher to reconstruct such a view in part. *NUCMC* alone provides substantial descriptive information about individual manuscript collections, including names of principal correspondents, subject areas, and titles of literary manuscripts. *ALM* provides a breakdown of types of manuscripts and cumulates the number of an author's manuscripts, letters, etc., which may be in several different collections in one library. Because Hamer and *NUCMC* focus on *collections,* they are less likely than *ALM* to locate an isolated manuscript or small group of papers. The student of Southern literary manuscripts, in short, will find all three reference works of complementary value.

NUCMC, which alone has an apparatus for continuation in annual volumes, may be expected to supersede Hamer and *ALM,* although the sponsoring organizations of the latter are giving consideration to revising or supplementing both. One proposal is to store *ALM* information, suitably revised, on magnetic tape and to supply it on demand.

The earliest comprehensive attempt to provide information about manuscript sources is the Library of Congress' *Manuscripts in Public and Private Collections in the United States,* rev ed (Washington, 1924). It remains of some value. Information about primary resources for major American writers was also included in the bibliography volume II, of *Literary History of the United States,* including the *Supplement.* A new venture is a series of calendars of American literary manuscripts (CALM). The first volume in the series is Kenneth Lohf, *The Literary Manuscripts of Hart Crane* ([Columbus, Ohio,] 1967). The next volume in the series is to be devoted to Nathaniel Hawthorne. It is probable that, as the CALM series continues, a number of major Southern writers will be included.

Special collections for individual Southern writers, including sizable groups of manuscripts, are likely to exist in a principal university library or manuscript repository in their native states. It is not surprising, therefore, that Emory University has a notable collection of Joel Chandler Harris material; that a special collection of James Lane Allen exists at the University of Kentucky; that the Tennessee State Library and Archives should include Mary N. Murfree papers; that the South Carolina Historical Society should report DuBose Heyward papers; that Eudora Welty manuscripts should be in the Mississippi Department of Archives and History; that Marjorie Kinnan Rawlings papers should be housed at the University of Florida; and that important collections of George W. Cable and Lafcadio Hearn exist at Tulane University. In addition, Southern university archives usually contain material pertaining to distinguished graduates.

On the other hand, important holdings for Southern writers exist elsewhere than in the South. The papers of Erskine Caldwell, for example, are in Baker Library, Dartmouth College; those of Samuel L. Clemens, in the University of California (Berkeley); those of James Dickey in Washington University (St. Louis); and the major collection of Thomas Wolfe papers is in Houghton Library, Harvard University.

Despite the variety suggested by the examples listed, the student of Southern literary history is well advised to give first priority to acquainting himself with the holdings of a few principal research libraries in the South: those of Duke University, the University of North Carolina, the University of Texas, Vanderbilt University, and the University of Virginia.

Duke University is particularly strong in nineteenth- and early twentieth-century materials, including substantial holdings in papers of Paul Hamilton Hayne, George Frederick Holmes, and Thomas Nelson Page. Notable also is Duke's vast collection of Confederate imprints. Other Southern writers well represented in Duke's manuscript collections are

Thomas Holley Chivers, John Esten Cooke, Henry Timrod, and William Gilmore Simms. However, the whole—in this case the George Washington Flowers Collection relating to Southern literature and history—is greater than the sum of its parts.

The principal published descriptions of manuscript and other primary resources at Duke are:

Tilley, Nannie M., and Noma Lee Goodwin, *Guide to Manuscript Collections in the Duke University Library*. Historical Papers of the Trinity College Historical Society, Nos. 27–28 (Durham, 1947).

The Centennial Exhibit of the Duke University Library . . . from the George Washington Flowers Collection . . . [comp. William Goodfellow Land] (Durham, 1930).

These may be supplemented by *Library Notes* (Duke), 1936——.

The counterpart to Duke's Flowers Collection at the nearby University of North Carolina in Chapel Hill is the Southern Historical Collection, much more extensive but less rich in literary materials. At Chapel Hill there is also a substantial collection of Confederate imprints and a sizable collection of Civil War fiction. Manuscripts of books by North Carolina authors range from the almost unknown to those of major Southern authors such as Paul Green and Thomas Wolfe.

A description of the Southern Historical Collection, which, because of its early publication date, covers fewer than one-third of the separate collections, is:

Guide to the Manuscripts in the Southern Historical Collection . . . . James Sprunt Studies in History and Political Science, XXIV, No. 2 (Chapel Hill, 1941).

This may be supplemented by:

"Archives and Manuscripts in North Carolina," *North Carolina Libraries*, XIX (Winter 1961), 2–29.

Lively, Robert A., *Fiction Fights the Civil War* (Chapel Hill, 1957).

Resources of North Carolina Libraries, ed. Robert B. Downs (Raleigh, 1965).

Wilkinson, Billy Rayford, "The Thomas Wolfe Collection of the University of North Carolina Library," North Carolina, 1960. [MA thesis]

Over the past decade few if any American institutions have been more productively active than the University of Texas in acquiring manuscripts and other research materials in the field of recent American literature. These include important single items and entire collections of literary manuscripts and papers. There is no general guide to the literary holdings, but there are occasional notices in *The Library Chronicle of the University of Texas* and in publications of the University's Humanities Research Center. The following are representative examples:

Kramer, Victor A., "James Agee Papers at the University of Texas," *Lib Chron of U of Tex*, VIII (Spring 1966), 33–36.

Triesch, Manfred, "The Lillian Hellman Collection," *Lib Chron of U of Tex*, VIII (Spring 1965), 17–20.
William Faulkner: An Exhibition of Manuscripts, intro by James B. Meriwether ([Austin, Tex.] 1959).

Strong and continuing interest in the work of the Fugitives and Agrarians at Vanderbilt University insures that the Joint University Libraries in Nashville will remain a center for study of Southern literature. There the files of *The Fugitive* and official Fugitive correspondence are supplemented by the personal papers of Donald Davidson, the only major Fugitive who remained at Vanderbilt throughout his active professional life. A description of unpublished documents relating to the Fugitives appears in *"The Fugitive*: A Critical History," a 1953 Ph.D. dissertation by Louise Cowan, but not in Miss Cowan's published book, *The Fugitive Group* (1960).

The Alderman Library of the University of Virginia is a treasure-house of manuscripts for the study of Southern literature. Virginia authors such as Edgar Allan Poe, Ellen Glasgow, and James Branch Cabell are represented by sizable special collections, including the Ingram collection of Poe. The magnificent C. Waller Barrett collection insures continued growth of the university's resources for advanced research, of which the Barrett library already represents a major segment, including manuscripts of Simms, Wolfe, John Esten Cooke, and Mark Twain, among others.

There are excellent published descriptions of some of the principal collections at Virginia. The University of Virginia Bibliographical Series (not to be confused with *Studies in Bibliography*) contains several numbers on Southern writers: Poe (No. 4), Jefferson (No. 8), and John Randolph (No. 9). In addition, the first number, *A Survey of Research Materials in Virginia Libraries, 1936–1937*, comp. Harry Clemons (Charlottesville, 1941), is valuable to the date of compilation. Other listings are:

Annual Report on Historical Collections (1930–1950). [originally titled *Report of the Archivist*, comp. for many years by Lester J. Cappon]
Bruccoli, Matthew J., *Notes on the Cabell Collection at the University of Virginia* (Charlottesville, 1957). [forms vol II of Frances J. Brewer, *James Branch Cabell: A Bibliography*, 2 vols]
[Cahoon, Herbert,] *A Brief Account of the Clifton Waller Barrett Library* (Charlottesville, 1960).
Kelly, William W., *Ellen Glasgow: A Bibliography* (Charlottesville, 1964).
Meriwether, James B., *The Literary Career of William Faulkner: A Bibliographical Study* (Princeton, 1961). [This study, which originated as catalog of exhibit at Princeton in 1957, describes Faulkner mss later deposited at the U of Va]

Massey, Linton, comp., *William Faulkner: "Man Working, 1919–1962"* (Charlottesville, 1968).

The separate publications describing segments of the Barrett collection have not yet been devoted to Southern writers.

Outside the South three research libraries require special mention: those of Princeton University and Yale University, and the Library of Congress—if indeed the last-named institution is "outside the South."

At Princeton the principal collections for Southern literary history are the John Peale Bishop papers, the papers of Allen Tate and Caroline Gordon, and material relating to William Faulkner acquired from his literary agent Harold Ober. It is also natural to expect that the Scribner's and Holt editorial files at Princeton will yield scattered manuscripts and papers relating to Southern literature. See Alexander Clark, *The Manuscript Collections of the Princeton University Library: An Introductory Survey*, rev ed (Princeton, 1960) and *Princeton University Library Chronicle* (1939———).

The John Gould Fletcher, Hamilton Basso, and Robert Penn Warren papers and the James Weldon Johnson Memorial Collection of Negro Arts and Letters strengthen the claims of Yale University as a center for studies in Southern literature. See:

Gallup, Donald, "The Yale Collection of American Literature," *Yale U Lib Gaz*, XXXVIII (Apr 1964), 151–59.
Pearson, Norman Holmes, "The John Gould Fletcher Collection," *Yale U Lib Gaz*, XXX (January 1956), 120–25.

The Library of Congress Manuscript Division has significant collections of manuscripts and papers of Richard Henry Wilde, George Frederick Holmes, Douglas Southall Freeman, Elizabeth Madox Roberts, Merrill Moore, William Styron, and Truman Capote. In addition, its papers of George Washington, Thomas Jefferson, James Madison, and Woodrow Wilson (and other national leaders of Southern origin) are not without interest to the student of Southern literature. The *Handbook of Manuscripts in the Library of Congress* (Washington, D.C., 1918) should be supplemented by the *Annual Report* of the Librarian of Congress and the annual report on acquisitions which appears in the Library's *Quarterly Journal* (1943———).

For Southern literature of the Colonial period, the principal repositories, in addition to those already mentioned, are the Henry E. Huntington Library (San Marino, California), the Virginia Historical Society, and the mutually supporting collections of Colonial Willamsburg and the Earl G. Swem Library of the College of William and Mary. Helpful published descriptions include:

Adcock, Lynette, comp., *Guide to the Manuscript Collections of Colonial Williamsburg* (Williamsburg, 1954).

Schulz, Herbert C., "American Literary Manuscripts in the Huntington Library," *Huntington Lib Q,* XXII (May 1959), 209–50.

A final source of published information, likely to be overlooked, is institutional histories. Two of the more recent containing relevant information about research library holdings are listed below.

English, Thomas H., *Emory University 1915–1965: A Semicentennial History* (Atlanta, 1966).

Dyer, John P., *Tulane: The Biography of a University, 1834–1965* (New York, 1966).

Despite an abundance of published guides, it is likely that the greater amount of descriptive information about manuscript and other special collections exists in unpublished form. To secure control over large groups of manuscript material, research libraries prepare calendars, indexes, registers, and other descriptive tools, which are available on the spot and may sometimes be photocopied for the use of scholars at other institutions. Moreover, much of interest in Southern literature is so recent that important manuscript materials have not yet come to rest permanently. Consequently, the student of Southern literary manuscripts is well-advised to keep in touch by correspondence with major research centers and to add the periodical publications of research libraries to his routine scholarly reading.

JOHN C. BRODERICK
Library of Congress
Washington, D.C.

*BIBLIOGRAPHICAL WORKS

The list of titles which follows is by no means a complete and definitive compilation of bibliographical titles for Southern literary studies. Various compilers would provide titles not listed here, and perhaps they would delete some of these titles. It is believed, however, that this brief bibliography is a practical collection of material for the purpose, and it is presented with this in mind.

In 1949 Professor Clarence Gohdes wrote that "the bibliographical study of American letters is still in its infancy." Although much has been done in this field since 1949, the opportunities for further study are almost limitless.

For convenience, titles listed here are grouped under the following headings:

I. Bibliographies, Book Lists, Collections

II. Selected Critical-Cultural Works

III. Periodicals

The entire list of titles is suggestive and should be used according to individual needs. Researchers are referred to the various sections of this bibliography for in-depth information on specific subjects or authors. Errors of omission or commission found here are purely the fault of this compiler, who will be grateful for any comments and suggestions.

I. Bibliographies, Book Lists, Collections

Agnew, Janet Margaret, *A Southern Bibliography . . ., 1929–1938*, 4 vols: Fiction, Historical Fiction, Poetry, Biography, *LSU Bull*, n.s., XXXI, No. 7; XXXII, Nos. 8, 11; XXXIV, No. 7 (1939–42).
Altick, Richard Daniel, and Andrew Wright, *Selective Bibliography for the Study of English and American Literature*, 3rd ed (New York, 1967).
American Newspapers, 1821–1936: A Union List of Files Available in the United States and Canada . . ., ed. Winifred Gregory (New York, 1937).
Basler, Roy Prentice, et al, *A Guide to the Study of the United States of America: Representative Books Reflecting the Development of American Life and Thought* (Washington, D.C., 1960).
Beers, Henry P., *Bibliographies in American History: Guide to Materials for Research*, rev ed (New York, 1942).
Best American Short Stories of 1915——, and *The Yearbook of the American Short Story*, ed. Edward J. O'Brien (1915–41) and Martha Foley (1942——) (Boston, 1916——).

141

Blanck, *Bibliography of American Literature*. [eight to ten volumes planned; locates copies in libraries]

The Book Review Digest (Minneapolis and New York; 1905———). [annual comp; evaluative comments]

Books in Print (New York, 1938———). [issued annually]

Collins, Carvel Emerson, "Nineteenth-Century Fiction of the Southern Appalachians," *BB*, XVII (1942–43), 186–90; 215–18. [chron, with author index]

Cumulative Book Index (Minneapolis and New York, 1898———).

Dobie, James Frank, *Guide to Life and Literature of the Southwest*, rev ed (Dallas, 1952).

Early American Periodicals Index to 1850, microform (New York, 1964). [an index of about 650,000 cards]

Evans, Charles, *American Bibliography* . . ., 14 vols (New York, 1941–42; 1955). [includes books printed up to 1820]

Gohdes, Clarence, *Bibliographical Guide to the Study of the Literature of the U.S.A.*, 2nd ed (Durham, 1963).

———, *Literature and Theater of the States and Regions of the U.S.A.: An Historical Bibliography* (Durham, 1967).

Harwell, Richard Barksdale, *Confederate Belles-Lettres: A Bibliography and a Finding List* (Hattiesburg, Miss., 1941).

Hockey, Dorothy C., "The Good and the Beautiful: A Study of the Best-Selling Novels in America, 1895–1920," Western Reserve, 1947. [diss; includes many So novels]

Hoole, William Stanley, *A Check-List and Finding-List of Charleston Periodicals, 1732–1864* (Durham, 1936).

Houlette, William Dale, "Plantation and Parish Libraries in the Old South," Iowa, 1933. [diss]

Johnson, Merle De Vore, *American First Editions*, 4th ed, rev and enl (Cambridge, Mass., 1962).

Jones, Howard Mumford, and Richard M. Ludwig, *Guide to American Literature and Its Backgrounds Since 1890*, 3rd ed (Cambridge, Mass., 1964).

Leary, Lewis G., *Articles on American Literature, 1900–1950* (Durham, 1954). [after 1950, see PMLA annual bibl and q check-lists in *AL*; Gohdes, *supra*, 54]

———, comp., "Doctoral Dissertations in American Literature, 1933–1948," *AL*, XX (1948), 169–230.

Leisy, Ernest E., and Jay B. Hubbell, comps., "Doctoral Dissertations in American Literature," *AL*, IV (1933), 419–65.

A Library of Southern Literature, 17 vols. [crit intros uneven but selections usually good; vol XV devoted to biog sketches of writers, many little-known figures]

Literary Market Place: A Directory of Publishers, Broadcasters and Advertisers . . . (New York, 1940———).

Marshall, Thomas F., *An Analytical Index to American Literature* (Durham, 1963). [I–XXX, March 1929–Jan 1959]

Modern Language Association of America, *MLA International Bibliography of Books and Articles on the Modern Languages and Literatures, 1921———* (New York, 1963———). [repr of annual bibl (1919–55 called *Amer Bibl*) issued in each vol of *PMLA*]

Northup, Clark S., *A Register of Bibliographies of the English Language and Literature* . . . (New York, 1962). [includes some topics in So lit]

O. Henry Memorial Award Stories (New York, 1919———).

PMLA, "Research in Progress in the Modern Languages and Literatures." [in this jour beginning with 1948]

————, Supp (New York, 1923————).

Paperbound Books in Print (New York, 1955————).

Powell, Benjamin E., "The Development of Libraries in Southern State Universities to 1920," Chicago, 1946. [diss]

Publishers' Weekly, I (1872————). [lists new bks as publ]

Roberts, Edward Graham, ed., *A Southern Supplement to the Union List of Serials* (Atlanta, 1959).

Roorbach, Orville A., *Bibliotheca Americana: Catalogue of American Publications, Including Reprints of Original Works, from 1820 to 1852 Inclusive* (New York, 1939). [see also Supp, 1855, 1858, 1861]

Sabin, Joseph, et al, *Bibliotheca Americana: A Dictionary of Books Relating to America, from Its Discovery to the Present Time*, 29 vols (New York, 1868–1936).

Stratman, Carl J., *Bibliography of the American Theatre, Excluding New York City* (Chicago, 1965).

Swem, Earl Gregg, comp., *Virginia Historical Index*, 2 vols in 4 (Gloucester, Mass., 1965). [repr indexes, bks, and several periodicals to 1930]

Union List of Serials in Libraries of the United States and Canada, 3rd ed, 5 vols (New York, 1965).

The United States Catalog: Books in Print, 1899–1928 (Minneapolis and New York, 1899–1928).

U.S. Library of Congress, *A Catalog of Books Represented by Library of Congress Printed Cards, Issued to July 31, 1942*, 167 vols (Ann Arbor, 1942–46). [Supp, Aug 1, 1942—Dec 31, 1947, 42 vols (Ann Arbor, 1948). See later continuations]

U.S. Library of Congress, *The National Union Catalog, 1952–1955 Imprints* (Ann Arbor, 1961). [see later continuations]

U.S. Works Projects Administration, *Index to Early American Periodical Literature, 1728–1870* (New York, 1940).

Wilson, Louis R., and Robert B. Downs, "Special Collections for the Study of History and Literature in the Southeast," *Papers of Bibl Soc of Amer*, XXVIII (1934), 97–131.

Woodress, James L., *Dissertations in American Literature, 1891–1955, With Supplement, 1956–1961* (Durham, 1962). [includes diss from some 100 Amer and foreign U]

Wright, Lyle Henry, *American Fiction, 1774–1850; 1851–1875; 1876–1900; a Contribution Toward a Bibliography*, 3 vols (San Marino, Calif., 1948, 1957, 1966).

II. Selected Critical-Cultural Works

Boger, Lorise C., *The Southern Mountaineer in Literature* (Morgantown, W. Va., 1964).

Bradbury, John M., *The Fugitives: A Critical Account* (Chapel Hill, 1958).

————, *Renaissance in the South*. [So renaissance authors by states, pp. 203–13]

Bradshaw, Sidney Ernest, *On Southern Literature Prior to 1860* (Richmond, 1900). [chron and bibl, pp. 135–57]

Brigham, Clarence Saunders, *History and Bibliography of American Newspapers, 1690–1820*, 2 vols (Worcester, Mass., 1947).

Brown, Herbert Ross, *The Sentimental Novel in America, 1789–1860* (Durham, 1940). [bibl, pp. 371–80]

Cambridge History of American Literature, ed. William P. Trent et al, 4 vols (New York, 1917–21). [repr of 1944, no bibl]

Cantrell, Clyde H., "The Reading Habits of Ante-Bellum Southerners," Illinois, 1960. [diss]

———, and Patrick, *Southern Literary Culture*.

Cowan, Louise, *The Fugitive Group: A Literary History* (Baton Rouge, 1959). [chron index to *The Fugitive*, I–IV, pp. 258–67]

Dickinson, A.T., *American Historical Fiction*, 2nd ed (New York, 1963).

Ellison, Rhoda C., *Early Alabama Publications: A Study in Literary Interests* (University, Ala., 1947).

Fisher, Miles Mark, "The Evolution of Slave Songs of the United States," Chicago, 1948. [diss; bibl, leaves 305–50]

Flanders, Bertram Holland, *Early Georgia Magazines: Literary Periodicals to 1865* (Athens, Ga., 1944). [valuable bibl]

Hubbell, *The South in American Literature*. [detailed study, excellent bibl, pp. 883–974]

Hughes, Glenn, *A History of the American Theatre, 1700–1950* (New York, 1951).

Leisy, Ernest E., *The American Historical Novel* (Norman, Okla., 1950). [additional novels chron listed, pp. 219–59]

Loshe, Lillie Deming, *The Early American Novel, 1789–1830* (New York, 1958). [lists novels to 1830, pp. 106–20; gen bibl, pp. 120–24]

Mott, Frank Luther, *A History of American Magazines*, 4 vols (Cambridge, Mass., 1938–57). [chron list of mags at end of each vol]

Moses, Montrose J., *The Literature of the South* (New York, 1910). [bibl, pp. 475–99]

Parrington, Vernon L., *Main Currents in American Thought*, 3 vols (New York, 1927–30).

Pattee, Fred Lewis, *The Development of the American Short Story: An Historical Survey* (New York, 1923).

———, *A History of American Literature Since 1870* (New York, 1915). [more important New So writers stud]

Quinn, *American Fiction*. [bibl, pp. 725–72]

———, *A History of the American Drama from the Beginning to the Civil War*, 2nd ed (New York, 1943). [note list of American plays, pp. 423–77]

———, *A History of the American Drama from the Civil War to the Present Day* (New York, 1936). [gen bibl and list of Amer plays, 1860–1936, pp. 303–402]

———, et al, *The Literature of the American People: An Historical and Critical Survey* (New York, 1951). [120-page bibl good for chief So authors]

Redding, Jay Saunders, *To Make a Poet Black* (Chapel Hill, 1939).

Rubin. Louis D., Jr., and John Rees Moore, eds., *The Idea of an American Novel* (New York, 1961).

Spiller et al, eds., *LHUS*, II, *Supp*.

Tyler, Moses Coit, *A Literary History of the American Revolution, 1763–1783*, 2 vols (New York, 1897). [bibl, pp. 429–83]

III. Periodicals

American Literature, I (1929———).

American Quarterly, I (1949———).

Bulletin of Bibliography, I (1897———).

Critique: Studies in Modern Fiction, I (1956———). [supersedes *Faulkner Studies*, q.v.]

De Bow's Review, I–XXXIV (1846–64), I–VIII (1866–70), n.s., I (1879–80).
The Double-Dealer, I–VIII (1921–26).
Faulkner Studies, I–III (1952–54).
The Fugitive, I–IV (1922–25).
Georgia Review, I (1947———).
Journal of American History, I (1914———). [publ as *Miss Valley Hist R*, 1914–64]
Journal of Southern History, I (1935———).
The Masses, a Monthly Magazine Devoted to the Interests of the Working People, I (1911———).
Mississippi Quarterly, I (1948———).
Mississippi Valley Historical Review. [see *Jour of Amer Hist*]
Modern Fiction Studies, I (1955———).
Modern Language Association of America, Publications (PMLA) I (1884———).
Russell's Magázine, I–VI (1857–60).
Sewanee Review, I (1892———).
Shenandoah, I (1950———).
South Atlantic Bulletin, I (1935———).
The South Atlantic Quarterly, I (1902———).
The Southern Literary Messenger, I–XXXVI (1834–64), n.s., I–VII (1939–45).
Southern Quarterly Review, I–XXX (1842–57). [some anon contributions are identified in Duyckinck]
Southern Review, I–VIII (1828–32). [Charleston, S.C.]
Southern Review, I–XXVI (1867–79). [Baltimore]
Southern Review, I–VII (1935–42), n.s., I (1965———). [Baton Rouge]
Southwest Review, I (1915———).
Studies in Bibliography, I (1948–49———).
The Texas Quarterly, I (1958———).
The Texas Review, I–IX (1915–24). [continued as *SWR*]
Texas Studies in Literature and Language: A Journal of the Humanities, I (1959———).
The Virginia Quarterly Review, I (1925———).
William and Mary Quarterly, I–XXVII (1892–1919); 2nd ser, I–XXIII (1921–43); 3rd ser, I (1944———).
Wisconsin Studies in Contemporary Literature, I (1960———). [After 1967, *Contemporary Literature*]

CLYDE HULL CANTRELL
Auburn University Library
Auburn, Alabama

PART II

INDIVIDUAL WRITERS

JAMES AGEE (1909-1955)

It was not until the publication of James Agee's novel, *A Death in the Family*, in 1957, two years after his death, that there was any widespread attention paid to the writings of this talented Tennessean who for more than two decades on the literary scene had never seemed to find the proper metier for his literary talents. The novel, published by his long-time friend David McDowell, made it obvious that Agee was indeed an important writer. It focused renewed interest on his earlier novella, *The Morning Watch* (1951), and on that remarkable and totally unclassifiable book "about" sharecropping in Alabama, *Let Us Now Praise Famous Men* (1941). Subsequently the latter was reprinted (1960), and there followed volumes of Agee's movie writings and of his film scripts and, in 1962, an edition of his letters to Father Flye, which became widely popular. A reprinting of Agee's early book of poems, *Permit Me Voyage* (1934), together with what must surely be additional unpublished poetry has been announced. Peter Ohlin has produced a creditable critical study of Agee, and McDowell is working on a biography.

Agee, James, "James Agee, By Himself," *Esquire*, LX (May 1963), 149, 289, 290.

*Behar, Jack, "James Agee: The World of His Work," *DA*, XXIV (1964), 4690 (Ohio State).

Burger, Nash K., "A Story to Tell: Agee, Wolfe, Faulkner," *SAQ*, LXIII (1964), 32–43.

Da Ponte, Durant, "James Agee: The Quest for Identity," *Tenn Stud in Lit*, VIII (1963), 25–37.

Dupee, F. W., "The Prodigious James Agee," *New Leader*, XL (Dec 9, 1957), 20–21.

Evans, Walker, "James Agee in 1936," *Atlantic*, CCVI (July 1960), 74–75. Repr in Agee and Evans, *Let Us Now Praise Famous Men* (Boston, 1960).

*Fabre, Genevieve, "A Bibliography of the Works of James Agee," *BB*, XXIV (1965), 145–48, 163–66.

Frohock, W. M., "James Agee—The Question of Wasted Talent," *The Novel of Violence in America*, rev ed (Dallas, 1957).

Grossman, James, "Mr. Agee and the New Yorker," *PartisanR*, XII (1945), 111–19.

Holland, Norman, "Agee on Film: Reviewer Re-Viewed," *HudR*, XII (1959), 148–51.

Huston, John, intro to *Agee on Film, Volume II: Five Film Strips* (New York, 1960).

Kazin, Alfred, "Goodby to James Agee," *Contemporaries* (Boston, 1962), 185–86.

*Kramer, Victor A., "James Agee Papers at the University of Texas," *Lib Circular of U of Tex*, VIII (1966), 33–36.

Larsen, E., "Let Us Not Now Praise Ourselves," *Carleton Miscellany*, II (Winter 1961), 86–96.

Macdonald, Dwight, "Death of a Poet," *New Yorker*, XXXIII (Nov 16, 1957), 224–41. Repr in Macdonald, *Against the American Grain* (New York, 1962).

*Ohlin, Peter H., *Agee* (New York, 1966).

Phelps, Robert, "James Agee," in *The Letters of James Agee to Father Flye* (New York, 1962).

Phillipson, J. S., "Character, Theme, and Symbol in *The Morning Watch*," *WHumR*, XV (1961), 359–67.

Roe, Michael Morris, Jr., "A Point of Focus in James Agee's *A Death in the Family*," *Twentieth Cent Lit*, XII (1966), 149–53.

Rosenberg, Harold, "The New as Value," *New Yorker*, XXXIX (Sept 7, 1963), 136–46.

Ruhe, Edward, r of *A Death in the Family*, in *Epoch*, XXVIII (Spring 1963), 247–51.

Louis D. Rubin, Jr.
University of North Carolina
Chapel Hill, North Carolina

JAMES LANE ALLEN (1849-1925)

James Lane Allen had a wide popularity among general readers, reviewers, and literary critics in the 1890s and during the first few years of this century. After 1903 his productivity was suspended, and when he resumed the writing of fiction in 1909 he was unable to recover his reputation. Since that time he has been largely glossed over as a second-rank local colorist or as an apologist for the genteel tradition in American culture. Though his works have more worth than this, and in spite of the recent critical work and reprint of some of his best things, today he is virtually unknown. That the commentary on Allen in Robert E. Spiller et al, eds., *Literary History of the United States* sees his stories as too contrived and sentimentalized, whereas earlier critics had favorably likened him to Hawthorne, is a measure of his decline in critical esteem. And this reveals that romance in fiction, except when handled by one of the few great masters such as Hawthorne, is out of fashion in present-day America; there is no tolerance for the minor master who is not in the realist tradition.

The most recent study (1964), the only wholly critical one, recognizes Allen's contribution as a latter-day romanticist, who built on the tradition and example of both Hawthorne and Thoreau, to create for American fiction stories where romance and realism (as human impulses) are in tension, and to resolve the tension in myth, "the romance of reality." This study utilizes the approach of the New Criticism in combination with archetypal or myth criticism. The Knight book, cited below, still contains the fullest bibliography of primary and secondary sources; the present checklist supplies most other critical and scholarly titles to date. Knight, Townsend, and the *Dictionary of American Biography*, ed. Allen Johnson et al, offer the only biographical treatments beyond mere sketches.

DAB, I, pp. 195–97; *LSL*, I, pp. 40–45; *LHUS*, *II, p. 386.

*Bottorff, William K., *James Lane Allen* (New York, 1964), [TUSAS crit]

_____, intro to *A Kentucky Cardinal, Aftermath, and Other Selected Works by James Lane Allen* (New Haven, 1967).

Clemens, Cyril, "An Unpublished Letter from James Lane Allen," *AL*, IX (1937), 355–56.

Finley, John H., "James Lane Allen," *Amer R of R*, LXXI (1925), 419–20. [eulogy]

Hancock, Albert E., "The Art of James Lane Allen," *Outlook*, LXXIV (1903), 953–55. [mag art]

Henneman, John Bell, "James Lane Allen: A Study," *Shakespearean and Other Papers* (Sewanee, 1911), pp. 115–66.

*Knight, Grant C., *James Lane Allen and the Genteel Tradition* (Chapel Hill, 1935). [biog crit]

Marcosson, Isaac F., "The South in Fiction," *Bookman*, XXXII (1910), 360–70. [illus]

Maurice, A. B., "James Lane Allen's Country," *Bookman*, XII (1900), 154–62. [illus]

Payne, Leonidas W., Jr., "The Stories of James Lane Allen," *SeR*, VIII (1900), 45–55.

Sherman, Ellen Burns, "The Works of James Lane Allen," *Book Buyer*, XX (1900), 374–77. [mag art]

Toulmin, Harry Aubrey, Jr., "James Lane Allen," *Social Historians* (Boston, 1911), pp. 101–30.

*Townsend, John Wilson, *James Lane Allen: A Personal Note* (Louisville, 1928). [biog; Allen's poems, letters]

WILLIAM K. BOTTORFF
University of Toledo
Toledo, Ohio

WASHINGTON ALLSTON (1779-1843)

Literary histories give scant attention, if any at all, to Allston's writings, and little has been published in recent years in any form on this subject, despite Allston's prominence in his own time.

Edgar P. Richardson's biography, *Washington Allston: A Study of the Romantic Artist in America* (1948), is the most informative book-length study and corrects most of the errors in Jared B. Flagg's *Life and Letters* (1892). Although Richardson centers critical attention mostly upon Allston's painting, there is a short treatment of the writings and their relationship to the paintings. William Dunlap's *History of the*

Rise and Progress of the Arts of Design in the United States (1834; 1918) has interesting biographical detail. Jay B. Hubbell's essay in *The South in American Literature* is valuable as a succinct biographical-critical summation, and the *Georgia Review* article (1967) by John R. Welsh treats Allston's literary friendships and influence.

In the nineteenth century, Allston and his work (both painting and writing) were the subject of numerous journal and newspaper reviews and essays. Unfortunately, these writers used Allston as an example to prove the thesis that the young nation could produce the cultivated man and artist, and their praise was fulsome. C. C. Felton's two *North American Review* essays (1842; 1850) most clearly demonstrate this tendency. Simms's 1843 *Southern Quarterly Review* article is the most objective, especially in regard to Allston's poetry, which he treats at some length.

To understand the esteem in which Allston was held and how, in one way or another, he stimulated others to creativity in the arts, the student should consult the letters, journals, notebooks, and biographies of eminent contemporaries who knew him. Important among these were Coleridge, Wordsworth, Southey, S. F. B. Morse, Irving, Hawthorne, Emerson, and Charles R. Leslie.

DAB, I, pp. 224–25; *Duyckinck*, II, p. 12; *Hubbell*, pp. 274–83, *915–16; *LSL*, I, pp. 87–91.

B., "The Sylphs of the Seasons, with Other Poems, by Washington Allston," *Analectic Mag*, VI (1815), 151–58. [r essay signed "B"]

Dana, Richard Henry, "Allston's Sylphs of the Seasons," *NoAmerR*, V (1817), 365–89. Repr in Dana's *Poems and Prose Writings* (New York, 1850), II, 101–31. [r essay]

Dunlap, William, "Washington Allston," in *A History of the Rise and Progress of the Arts of Design in the United States* (New York, 1834), II, 152–88. Repr Boston, 1918, II, 296–335.

Felton, C. C., "Allston's Poems and Lectures on Art," *NoAmerR*, LXXI (1850), 149–68. [r essay]

————, "Monaldi: a Tale," *NoAmerR*, LIV (1842), 397–419. [r essay]

Flagg, Jared B., *The Life and Letters of Washington Allston* (New York, 1892).

[Fuller, Margaret], "A Record of Impressions Produced by the Exhibition of Mr. Allston's Pictures in the Summer of 1839," *The Dial*, I (July 1840), 73–84. Repr in *Literature and Art* (New York, 1852), part 2, pp. 108–21.

[Holmes, Oliver Wendell], "Exhibition of Pictures Painted by Washington Allston at Harding's Gallery," *NoAmerR*, L (1840), 358–81.

Jameson, Mrs. A. B. M., "Memoir of Washington Allston, and His Axioms on Art," *Memoirs and Essays Illustrative of Art, Literature, and Social Morals* (London, 1846), pp. 159–205.

Peabody, Elizabeth P., *Last Evening with Allston, and Other Papers* (Boston, 1886), pp. 1–61. [biog details and crit of paintings]

*Richardson, Edgar P., *Washington Allston: A Study of the Romantic Artist in America* (Chicago, 1948). [best bibl, pp. 220–28]

[Simms, William Gilmore], "The Writings of Washington Allston," *So Q R*, IV (1843), 363–414. [crit essay]

Sweetser, Moses F., *Allston* (Boston, 1879).

Ware, William, *Lectures on the Works and Genius of Washington Allston* (Boston, 1852). [Three lectures on paintings]

Welsh, John R., "Washington Allston: Expatriate South Carolinian," *S.C. Hist Mag*, LXVII (1966), 84–98. [biog essay detailing relationships with native state]

———, "Washington Allston, Cosmopolite and Early Romantic," *GaR*, XXI (1967), 491–502. [biog, crit essay]

JOHN R. WELSH
University of South Carolina
Columbia, South Carolina

GEORGE WILLIAM BAGBY (1828-1883)

There is little recent scholarly activity on Bagby to record. Wade Hall cites his sketches frequently and discusses several briefly in *The Smiling Phoenix* (1965), but never deals with his humor fully. In "Southern Writers and Northern Literary Magazines, 1865–1890" (Duke University dissertation, 1956), Rayburn S. Moore discusses Bagby's forthright and unreconstructed contributions to *Lippincott's Magazine* (1869–73). The fullest recent treatment of Bagby is in Hubbell, *The South in American Literature*. Joseph L. King's biography (1927) remains the only book-length study to date.

The Old Virginia Gentleman and Other Sketches (5th ed., 1948) is generally a selection from Bagby's best and most popular pieces, and many of his writings are still uncollected. A scholarly edition selected from the whole range of his work and a full critical discussion of his humor and humorous writings are much to be desired.

DAB,I, pp. 492–93; *Hubbell*, pp. 680–83, *916; *LSL*, I, pp. 141–46.

*Bagby, Ellen M. ed., "Bibliography," in George W. Bagby, *The Old Virginia Gentleman and Other Sketches*. 5th ed (Richmond, 1948), pp. 315–18. [Bagby's own writings; also: Kate B. Bowyer, "Personal Reminiscences of Dr. George W. Bagby"; Thomas Nelson Page, "A Virginia Realist"; and Douglas Southall Freeman, "Introduction: George W. Bagby, Patriot"]

Gregory, Edward S., "George William Bagby," in *Selections from the Miscellaneous Writings of Dr. George W. Bagby* (Richmond, 1884), I, xiii–xxxvii. [biog sketch by old friend]

Hall, Wade, *The Smiling Phoenix: Southern Humor from 1865 to 1914* (Gainesville, 1965). [Bagby mentioned frequently but not discussed fully]

Jackson, David K., *The Contributors and Contributions to the Southern Literary Messenger* (Charlottesville, 1936). [Bagby's contributions to *SLM*]

*King, Joseph L., Jr., *Dr. George William Bagby: A Study of Virginian Literature, 1850–1880* (New York, 1927). [only full-length study; bibl lists Bagby's work only]
Moore, Rayburn S., "Southern Writers and Northern Literary Magazines, 1865–1890." Duke, 1956, [diss; disc Bagby's contributions, esp those under name of Richard B. Elder, to *Lippincott's Mag* (1869–73); see esp pp. 60–63]
Page, Thomas Nelson, "A Virginia Realist," in *The Old Virginia Gentleman and Other Sketches*, ed. Thomas Nelson Page (New York, 1910), pp. v–xiii. Repr in 5th ed, 1948, cited above.
Pickett, La Salle C., " 'Bacon and Greens,' Dr. George William Bagby," *Literary Hearthstones of Dixie* (Philadelphia, 1912), pp. 225–50.

RAYBURN S. MOORE
University of Georgia
Athens, Georgia

JOSEPH GLOVER BALDWIN (1815-1864)

In 1918, Will D. Howe called Baldwin's *Flush Times* "perhaps the most significant volume of humor by a Southerner before the Civil War" (*Cambridge History of American Literature*, II). Baldwin has been rated lower by most commentators, but a recent rise of interest in his work is manifest in the re-editing of *Flush Times in Alabama and Mississippi* and in the first printing in book form of two fugitive pieces by Baldwin (one previously unpublished) under the single title *The Flush Times of California*. Detailed examination of Baldwin's style and ideas is still needed.

DAB, I, pp. 538–39; *Hubbell*, pp. 675–78, *916–17; *LSL*, I, pp. 175–81.
Amacher, Richard E., and George W. Polhemus, intro to Joseph Glover Baldwin, *The Flush Times of California* (Athens, Ga., 1966), pp. 1–10. See also [George W. Polhemus], "Biographical Sketch of Joseph Glover Baldwin," pp. 65–78.
*Cohen and Dillingham, "Joseph Glover Baldwin." in *Humor of the Old Southwest*, pp. 250–51. See also p. 414.
Current-Garcia, Eugene, "Joseph Glover Baldwin: Humorist or Moralist?" *AlaR*, V (April 1952), 122–41.
Farish, H. D., "An Overlooked Personality in Southern Life," *N.C. Hist R*, XII (1935), 341–53. [Samuel Hale, an Ala ed., may be original of "Samuel Hele, Esquire" in *Flush Times of Alabama*. . .]
Kitch, John C., "Dark Laughter: A Study of the Pessimistic Tradition in American Humor," Northwestern, 1964, 54–56. [diss]
*Kunitz and Haycraft, "Joseph Glover Baldwin," in *A Biographical Dictionary of American Literature*, pp. 48–49.
Lynn, Kenneth S., *Mark Twain and Southwestern Humor* (Boston, Toronto, 1959), pp. 115–24.

*McDermott, John Francis, "Baldwin's *Flush Times of Alabama and Mississippi*—a Bibliographical Note," *Papers of the Bibl Soc of Amer*, XLV (1951), 251–56. [Baldwin's contributions to *SLM*]

McMillan, Malcolm C., "Joseph Glover Baldwin Reports on the Whig National Convention of 1848," *JSH*, XXV, (1959), 366–82.

*Meine, Franklin J., intro to *Tall Tales of the Southwest 1830–1860* (New York, 1930), pp. xxi–xxii. See also pp. 69, 183, 207, 451.

Mellen, George Frederick, "Joseph G. Baldwin and the 'Flush Times,'" *SeR*, IX (1901), 171–84. [rev of author's "Joseph Glover Baldwin," in *LSL*]

Owens, William A., intro to Baldwin, *The Flush Times of Alabama and Mississippi* (New York, 1957), pp. v–ix.

*Paine, Gregory, "Joseph Glover Baldwin," *Southern Prose Writers* (New York, 1947), pp. 107–108. See also pp. lxxvi, cxxiv–cxxv.

Stewart, Samuel Boyd, "Joseph Glover Baldwin," Vanderbilt, 1941. [diss]

Norris W. Yates
Iowa State University
Ames, Iowa

JOHN BARTH (1930–)

Barth, John, "The Literature of Exhaustion," *Atlantic*, CCXX (Aug 1967), 29–34.

———, "Muse, Spare Me from Social-Historical Responsibility," *Bk Wk* (Sept 26, 1965), 29–30.

Bryer, Jackson R., "John Barth," *Crit*, VI (Fall 1963), 86–89.

Enck, John, "John Barth: An Interview," *WSCL*, VI (Winter; Spring 1965), 3–14.

Fiedler, Leslie, *The Return of the Vanishing American* (New York, 1968), pp. 150–52.

Garis, Robert, "What Happened to John Barth," *Commentary*, XLII (Oct 1966), 89–95.

Keily, Benedict, "Ripeness Was Not All: John Barth's *Giles Goat-Boy*," *Hollins Crit*, III (Dec 1966), 1–12. [r essay]

Kennedy, Mopsy Strange, "Roots of An Author," *Washington* (D.C.) *Post*: "Potomac Magazine," Sept 3, 1967, pp. 17–19. [interv with Barth's family]

Miller, Russell H., "*The Sot-Weed Factor*: A Contemporary Mock Epic," *Crit*, VIII (Winter 1966), 88–100.

Noland, Richard W., "John Barth and the Novel of Comic Nihilism," *WSCL*, VII (Autumn 1966), 239–57.

Rovit, Earl, "The Novel as Parody: John Barth," *Crit*, VI (Fall 1963), 77–85.

Rubin, Louis D. Jr., "Notes on the Literary Scene: Their Own Language," *Harper's*, CCXXX (Apr 1965), 173–75.

Schickel, Richard, "The Floating Opera," *Crit*, VI (Fall 1963), 53–67.

Scholes, Robert, *The Fabulators* (New York, 1967). [last chapter]

———, "George Is My Name," *N.Y. Times Bk R*, Aug 7, 1966, pp. 1, 22. [r of *Giles Goat-Boy*]

Smith, Herbert F., "Barth's Endless Road," *Crit*, VI (Fall 1963), 68–76.

Stubbs, John C., "John Barth as a Novelist of Ideas: The Themes of Value and Identity," *Crit*, VIII (Winter 1966), 101–16.
Thomas, Charles S., "John Barth: A Buoyant Denial of Relevance," *Commonweal*, XXXV (Oct 1966), 80–81.
Trachtenberg, Alan, "Barth and Hawkes: Two Fabulists," *Crit*, VI (Fall 1963), 4–18.

DOUGLAS COLLINS
University of North Carolina
Chapel Hill, North Carolina

HAMILTON BASSO (1904-1964)

Although John M. Bradbury, in *Renaissance in the South*, writes that "the most extensive criticism in fiction of the South's manners and mores has been that of Hamilton Basso," not very much has yet been written about him. Except for his essays and a novel (*Sun in Capricorn*) dealing with Huey Long demagoguery and, of course, the once-popular *View from Pompey's Head*, his works, which speak with a liberal voice, are relatively unknown to critics and readers alike of Southern literature. Despite the lack of a broad assessment, some good criticism of individual novels appears in book reviews.

Aaron, Daniel, *Writers on the Left: Episodes in American Literary Communism* (New York, 1961), pp. 339–40.
Basso, Hamilton, "Huey Long Legend," *Life*, XXI (Dec 9, 1946), 106–108 ff.
———, "Letters in the South," *New Rep*, LXXXIII (June 19, 1935), 161–63.
———, "A New Orleans Childhood," *New Yorker*, XXX (Oct 9, 1954), 97–98 ff. [autobiog essay]
———, "William Faulkner, Man and Writer," *SatR*, XLV (July 28, 1962), 11–14. [reminiscences of Faulkner]
Blotner, Joseph, *The Modern American Political Novel, 1900–1960* (Austin, Tex., 1966), pp. 205, 214–15.
Bradbury, *Renaissance in the South*, pp. 11, 159, 161–62, 176, 200.
Cowley, Malcolm, "The Writer as Craftsman: The Literary Heroism of Hamilton Basso," *Sat R*, XLVII (June 27, 1964), 17–18.
Durrett, Frances Bowen, "The New Orleans Double Dealer," in Walker and Welker, eds., *Reality and Myth*, pp. 212–36.
Eisinger, Chester E., *Fiction of the Forties* (Chicago, 1963), pp. 113*n*, 114.
*Hoffman, Frederick J., "The Sense of Place," in Rubin and Jacobs, *South*, pp. 72–73.
Milne, Gordon, *The American Political Novel* (Norman, Okla., 1966), pp. 132–34, 136.
Rubin, Louis D., Jr., "All the King's Meanings," *GaR*, VIII (1954), 422–34. Repr in Rubin, *The Curious Death of the Novel*, pp. 222–38.
———, *The Faraway Country*, pp. 107–108, 244.

Thorp, Willard, *American Writing in the Twentieth Century* (Cambridge, Mass., 1960), pp. 115, 234, 255, 259.

JAMES E. ROCKS
Tulane University
New Orleans, Louisiana

ROBERT BEVERLEY (ca 1673-1722)

No full-length study of Robert Beverley exists, but three short essays give biographical information and comment on Beverley as historian. Jay B. Hubbell's *The South in American Literature* provides a brief sketch, plus a bibliography. Louis B. Wright discusses Beverley at some length in *The First Gentlemen of Virginia* (San Marino, Calif., 1940) and in the introduction to his edition of Beverley's *The History and Present State of Virginia* (Chapel Hill, 1947).

DAB, II, p. 233; *Hubbell*, pp. 26–30, *917; *LSL*, I, pp. 375–78.

Campbell, Charles, ed., *The History and Present State of Virginia* (Richmond, 1855). [based on the 1722 text; includes intro]

Harrison, Fairfax, "Robert Beverley, the Historian of Virginia," *VMHB*, XXXVI (1928), 333–44.

Stanard, William G., "Major Robert Beverley and His Descendants," *VMHB*, II (1895), 405–13; III (1895), 42–52, 169–76.

Tyler, Moses Coit, *A History of American Literature During the Colonial Period*, rev ed, II (New York, 1897), pp. 264–67.

Wright, Louis B., "Beverley's *History* . . . (1705): A Neglected Classic," *WMQ*, 3rd ser, I (1944), 49–64.

———, *The First Gentlemen of Virginia* (San Marino, Calif., 1940). Chap 10, "Robert Beverley II: Historian and Iconoclast," pp. 286–311. Repr Charlottesville, 1964).

———, ed., *The History and Present State of Virginia* (Chapel Hill, 1947). [intro, pp. xi–xxxv, and notes, pp. 349–59; text based on 1705 ed]

ROBERT BAIN
University of North Carolina
Chapel Hill, North Carolina

JOHN PEALE BISHOP (1892-1944)

The checklist which follows is just barely selective; its fifteen items all but exhaust the pertinent scholarly and critical commentary on John Peale Bishop. A couple of mediocre essays have been excluded from the list, along with a couple of *Explicator* notes; students interested in contemporaneous reviews of Bishop's work and in reviews of the post-humously published *Collected Poems* and *Collected Essays* should consult footnote citations in Stallman's essay.

Bishop's name is encountered frequently enough in critical discussions of such of his contemporaries as Hemingway and Fitzgerald, and frequently enough in discussions of modern poetry and the literature of the American South; almost always, however, his name merely crops up—most often in a footnote or at the end of a summary paragraph—and in such discussions little is ever actually said of him or his work. During his lifetime Bishop was never at the center of the cliques and movements of modern literature, and in contemporary criticism he continues to be a shadowy and peripheral figure.

A perusal of the checklist, however, may suggest that future critical attention given Bishop will not be so limited and fragmentary—that his stature and significance will not always be so dimly perceptible to the average student of American literature. First of all, it may be remarked that Bishop's worth as a writer has been attested by some of our most trenchantly independent critics. Friendship may have partly prompted the good words for Bishop spoken by Tate and Wilson, but critical respect for his gifts had no less a role to play in their verdicts than it had in the cases of such men as Arrowsmith, Hyman, Stallman, Frank, and Fiedler. Second, one may observe that during the 1960s there has been at least a minor resurgence of critical interest in Bishop. During these recent years, there has also been an increasing awareness of Bishop's gifts as a critic and author of fiction. If the critical trend continues, perhaps Bishop will be more widely recognized as the good, if not great, writer he was; possibly more of his work will be more permanently reprinted; and perhaps his place in modern Southern literature will be better made out.

LHUS, II, *Supp.* p. 219.

Arrowsmith, William, "An Artist's Estate," *HudR*, II (1949), 118–27.

Bier, Jessie, "John Peale Bishop: The Memory Lingers On," *WHumR*, IX (1955), 243–48.

Eby, Cecil D., Jr., "The Fiction of John Peale Bishop," *Twentieth Cent Lit*, VII (1961), 3–9.

Fiedler, Leslie, "John Peale Bishop & the Other Thirties," *Commentary*, XLIII (Apr

1967), 74–82. Repr as Afterword to Avon Books ed of *Act of Darkness* (New York, 1967), pp. 305–19.

Frank, Joseph, "Force and Form: A Study of John Peale Bishop," *SeR*, LV (1947), 71–107.

———, "The Achievement of John Peale Bishop," *MinnR*, II (1962), 325–44, Repr in *The Widening Gyre: Crisis and Mastery in Modern Literature* (New Brunswick, N.J., 1963), pp. 203–28.

Haun, Eugene, "John Peale Bishop: A Celebration," in *Reality and Myth*, pp. 80–97.

Hyman, Stanley, E., "Notes on the Organic Unity of John Peale Bishop," *Accent*, IX (1949), 102–13. Repr in *The Promised End* (Cleveland, 1963), pp. 49–62.

Moore, S. C., "The Criticism of John Peale Bishop," *Twentieth Cent Lit*, XII (1966), 66–77.

*Patrick, J. Max, and Robert W. Stallman, "John Peale Bishop: A Checklist," *Princeton U Lib Chron*, VII (1946), 62–79. [bibl of Bishop's publ writings]

Stallman, Robert W., "The Poetry of John Peale Bishop," in Rubin and Jacobs, *Southern Renascence*, pp. 368–91.

Tate, Allen, intro to *The Collected Poems of John Peale Bishop* (New York, 1948), pp. xi–xvi.

———, "A Note on Bishop's Poetry," *SoR*, o.s., I (1935), 357–64. Repr in *Collected Essays* (Denver, 1959), pp. 238–47.

*White, Robert L., *John Peale Bishop* (New York, 1966). [TUSAS]

Wilson, Edmund, intro to *The Collected Essays of John Peale Bishop* (New York, 1948), pp. vii–xiii. Repr in *The Bit Between My Teeth: A Literary Chronicle of 1950–1965* (New York, 1965), pp. 6–15.

ROBERT L. WHITE
York University
Toronto, Ontario

ROARK BRADFORD (1896-1948)

Roark Bradford's fame did not survive his death, and, it would seem from a check of bibliographical listings, no one now takes any interest in his life or his stories. Following the method of Irwin Russell, Bradford, in his famous *Ol' Man Adam an' His Chillun* (the basis of Marc Connelly's long lived play, *Green Pastures*), tells biblical stories through what seems to be their authenic perception in the thought and language of the Negroes of Louisiana and Mississippi. He ·pursued the same method in other stories, or else, in other ways, followed his interest in Negro lore. Today, it would seem that he was the last of a line of Southern storytellers who more or less invented a Negro folk culture. The relationship of this pseudo-folk culture to the whole ambiguous area of American pseudo-folk culture is of much literary, political, and sociological significance. For this reason serious students of Southern letters would do well not to neglect Bradford altogether.

Adams, Marjorie, "Roark Bradford's Negro Characters," Texas, 1948. [MA thesis]
Cohn, David L., "Roark Bradford's Revenge," SaR, XXVII (June 24, 1944), 13–14. [personal reminiscence]
————, "Straight to Heaven," SatR, XXXI (Dec 4, 1948), 20–21. [memoir and eulogy]
Durrett, Ruth Louise, "Roark Bradford's Portrayal of the Negro," Louisiana, 1950. [MA thesis]
Frost, Meigs O., "The Man Who Put God in a Role on the Stage," New Orleans States, May 18, 1930, pp. 1–2.
Jones, Elizabeth Frances, "The Background of the Louisiana Short Story," Louisiana, 1936. [MA thesis]
Knoblock, Kenneth Thomas, "Uncle Roark," The New Orleanian, II (Jan 15, 1931), 19–20, 38–39.
Leake, Grace, "Old Man Fortune and the Bradford Boy," Holland's, XLIX (Nov 1930), 18, 34. [Bradford's career]
Moore, Opal, "The Development of the Negro Character in Louisiana Fiction," Louisiana, 1942. [MA thesis]
Richardson, Rupert Norval, Jr., "Roark Bradford: An Analysis of His Works and Technique," Texas, 1941. [MA thesis]
"Roark Bradford," (New Orleans) Times-Picayune, Nov 15, 1948, p. 12. [editorial on Bradford's significance]
Smith, Harrison, "Roark Bradford," SatR, XXXI (Nov 27, 1948), 20.

LEWIS P. SIMPSON
Louisiana State University
Baton Rouge, Louisiana

CLEANTH BROOKS (1906–)

Cleanth Brooks has not received the critical attention he deserves. The principal discussions of his contribution to modern American criticism are included in general treatments of the New Criticism or of the Southern Renascence. The general works in which Brooks is given extensive individual treatment are included in this checklist; those in which he is not adequately distinguished from his fellow critics have been excluded. Some of the most interesting commentary on Brooks's critical theories still lies buried in reviews of his principal works or in unpublished dissertations. Because of space limitations only the most helpful of these works can be included in this checklist.

Auden, W. H., New Rep, CII (1940), 87. [r of Modern Poetry and the Tradition]
Blackmur, R. P., NY Times Bk R (June 8, 1947), p. 6. [r of The Well-Wrought Urn]
Bush, Douglas, "Marvell's Horatian Ode," SeR, LX (1952), 363–76. [disputes Brooks's interpretation of the Marvell poem in The Well-Wrought Urn]

Crane, R. S., "Cleanth Brooks: Or, the Bankruptcy of Critical Monism," *Mod Phil*, XLV (1948), 226–45.

Daniel, R. W., *SeR*, LXXIII (1965). 119–24. [r *Yoknapatawpha Country*]

Empson, William, *Poetry*, LV (1939), 154–57. [r of *Modern Poetry and the Tradition*]

———, *SeR*, LV (1947), 691–97. [r of *The Well-Wrought Urn*]

Fitts, Dudley, *KR*, IX (1947), 612–16. [r of *The Well-Wrought Urn*]

Fogle, Richard H., "Romantic Bards and Metaphysical Reviewers," *Eng Lit Hist*, XII (1945), 221–50. [sec 4 is on Brooks, 239–46]

Graff, G. E., "The Dramatic Theory of Poetry," Stanford, 1964. [diss]

Hardy, John Edward, "The Achievement of Cleanth Brooks," *Hopkins R*, VI (1953), 148–61; repr in Rubin and Jacobs, *Southern Renascence*, pp. 413–26. Also included as part of essay, "Poets and Critics," in Rubin and Jacobs, *South*, pp. 260–75.

Hart, Sister M. J., "Cleanth Brooks and the Formalist Approach to Metaphysical and Moral Values in Literature," Southern California, 1963. [diss]

Hecht, Roger, "Paradox and Cleanth Brooks," *Bard R*, II (1947), 47–51.

Krieger, Murray, *The New Apologists for Poetry* (Minneapolis, 1956). [extensive discussion of Brooks, pp. 123–55, 185–88]

Mizener, Arthur, *SeR*, LV (1947), 460–69. [r of *The Well-Wrought Urn*]

Muller, H. J., "The New Criticism in Poetry," *SoR*, o.s., VI (1941), 811–39. [discussion of Brooks, 820–27]

Pulos, C. E., "Cleanth Brooks," in *The New Critics and the Language of Poetry*, U Nebraska Stud, No. 19 (Lincoln, Nebr., 1958), 72–82.

Ransom, John Crowe, "Poetry: I, The Formal Analysis," *KR*, IX (1947), 436–56. [Ransom begins a theoretical discussion with interesting remarks about Brooks]

———, *KR*, II (1940), 247–51. [r of *Modern Poetry and the Tradition*]

Scholes, Robert, *Yale R*, LIII (1964), 431–35. [r of *Yoknapatawpha Country*]

*Stallman, Robert W., "Cleanth Brooks: A Checklist of His Critical Writings," *U of Kan Cy R*, XIV (1948), 317–24.

Strauss, Albrecht B., "The Poetic Theory of Cleanth Brooks," *Centenary R*, I (1949), 10–22.

Sutton, Walter, *Modern American Criticism* (Englewood Cliffs, N.J., 1963). [Individual discussion of Brooks, pp. 116–23, 237–43.]

Tassin, A. G., "The Phoenix and the Urn: The Literary Theory and Criticism of Cleanth Brooks," Louisiana, 1966. [diss]

Woodward, Barbara, "Theories of Meaning in Poetry,. 1915–1940: A Critical History," Michigan, 1946. [diss]

THOMAS DANIEL YOUNG
Vanderbilt University
Nashville, Tennessee

WILLIAM BYRD (1674-1744)

Biographical information about William Byrd will be found in the introductions to editions of Byrd's works by Louis B. Wright and John Spencer Bassett. A full-length biography, now out of date, is that by Richmond C. Beatty. Further bibliographical information about Byrd will be found in Jay B. Hubbell's *The South in American Literature*.

DAB, III, pp. 383–84; *Duyckinck*, I p. 74; *Hubbell*, pp. 40–51, *919–21; *LHUS*, I, pp. 45–46; *II, 429–31, *Supp*, 88; *LSL*, II, pp. 583–85.

Bassett, John Spencer, ed., *The Writings of "Colonel William Byrd of Westover in Virginia Esqr."* (New York, 1901).

Beatty, Richmond C., *William Byrd of Westover* (New York, 1932).

———, and W. J. Mulloy, eds., *William Byrd's Natural History of Virginia* (Richmond, 1940).

Boyd, William K., ed., *William Byrd's Histories of the Dividing Line* (Raleigh, 1929).

Bruce, Philip A., *The Virginia Plutarch* (Chapel Hill, 1929).

Byrd, William, "Letters of William Byrd II, and Sir Hans Sloane Relative to Plants and Minerals of Virginia," *WMQ*, 2nd ser, I (1921), 186–200.

———, "Letters of William Byrd II, of Westover, Virginia," *VMHB*, IX (1901). 113–30; 225–31.

———, *William Byrd Esqr Accounts as Solicitor General . . . Letters Writ to Facetia by Veramour* [Byrd] (Privately printed for Thomas F. Ryan, ca. 1913).

Cannon, Carl L., "William Byrd II of Westover," *Colophon*, n.s., III (1938), 201–302. [Byrd's private lib]

Houlette, W. D., "The Byrd Library," *Tyler's Q Hist and Geneal Mag*, XVI (1934), 100–109.

Leary, Lewis, "A William Byrd Poem," *WMQ*, 3rd ser, IV (1947), 356.

Lonn, Ella, *The Colonial Agents of the Southern Colonies* (Chapel Hill, 1945).

Lyle, G. R., "William Byrd, Book Collector," *Amer Bk Collector*, V (1934), 163–65, 208–11.

The Orrery Papers, ed. Countess of Cork and Orrery, 2 vols (London. 1903). [Byrd correspondence with Orrery]

Weathers, Willie T., "William Byrd: Satirist," *WMQ*, 3rd ser, IV (1947), 27–41.

Woodfin, Maude H., "The Missing Pages of William Byrd's Secret History of the Line," *WMQ*, 3rd ser, II (1945), 63–70.

———, "William Byrd and the Royal Society," *VMHB*, XL (1932), 23–34.

———, and Marion Tinling, eds., *Another Secret Diary of William Byrd of Westover, 1739–1741: With Letters and Literary Exercises, 1696–1726* (Richmond, 1942).

Wright, Louis B., "The Byrds' Progress from Trade to Genteel Elegance," *The First Gentlemen of Virginia* (San Marino, Calif., 1940), pp. 312–48.

———, ed., *An Essay upon the Government of the English Plantations on the Continent of America* [1701] (San Marino, Calif., 1945). [2 memoranda by Byrd]

———, ed., *The Prose Works of William Byrd of Westover* (Cambridge, Mass., 1966). [new ed based on collation of original mss]

———, "A Shorthand Diary of William Byrd of Westover," *Huntington Lib Q*, II (1939), 489–96.

———, "William Byrd: Citizen of the Enlightenment," *Anglo-American Cultural Re-*

lations in the Seventeenth and Eighteenth Centuries (Los Angeles, 1958), pp. 26–40. [paper delivered at Fourth Clark Lib Seminar]

————, "William Byrd II . . . a Virginia Planter of the Upper Class," in *The Unforgettable Americans*, ed. John A. Garraty (New York, 1960), pp. 36–40.

————, "William Byrd's Defense of Sir Edmund Andros," *WMQ*, 3rd ser, II (1945), 47–62.

————, "William Byrd's Opposition to Governor Francis Nicholson," *JSH*, XI (1945), 68–79.

————, and Marion Tinling, eds., *The Great American Gentleman: The Secret Diary of William Byrd of Westover in Virginia, 1709–1712* (New York, 1963). [abr previously publ diary]

————, eds., *The Secret Diary of William Byrd of Westover, 1709–1712* (Richmond, 1941).

————, ed., *William Byrd of Virginia: The London Diary (1717–1721) and Other Writings* (New York, 1958).

————, "William Byrd of Westover, an American Pepys," *SAQ*, XXXIX (1940), 259–74.

Wynne, T. H., ed., *A History of the Dividing Line and Other Tracts*, 2 vols (Richmond, 1866).

LOUIS B. WRIGHT
Folger Shakespeare Library
Washington, D.C.

JAMES BRANCH CABELL (1879-1958)

Critical opinion on the work of James Branch Cabell has varied with the times. The note of disillusionment in *Jurgen* (1919) hit the fancy of the post-war period. When this book was suppressed in 1920, many of the most significant writers and critics of the day rushed to its defense. Some of these writers, men such as H. L. Mencken and Carl Van Doren, continued to champion the cause of the Virginian throughout most of the 1920s. To the 1930s and 1940s, however, his work had little appeal; his style seemed overly ornate and his philosophy, repetitious. During this period the work of Cabell was subjected to scathing criticism; perhaps the most devastating was that of Oscar Cargill in *Intellectual America* (1941). In the late 1940s and 1950s, however, the tide began to turn once again in Cabell's favor. When Edmund Wilson called for a reopening of the Cabell case in the pages of the *New Yorker* (April 21, 1956), in an article which has since been republished in *The Bit Between My Teeth* (1965), Cabell's work was subjected to a more careful scrutiny than it had ever been in the past. The first of these more thoroughgoing analyses was Louis Rubin's *No Place on Earth* (1959), which was followed by Joe Lee Davis' biographical study in the Twayne series (1962), and by Arvin R. Wells's *Jesting Moses* (1962), the most profound critical study of Cabell yet produced. In 1967 appeared Desmond Tarrant's *James Branch Cabell: The Dream and the Reality,* the latest and longest study to date—but somewhat unreliable in its details.

Much information on the life and works of James Branch Cabell has been provided by the author himself, in prefaces, afterwords, and sometimes in entire books. The prefaces to the works contained in the Storisende edition of the *Biography of the Life of Manuel,* 18 volumes (New York, 1927–30), have been reprinted in a separate volume, *Preface to the Past* (New York, 1936). The best statements of the critical theories which have guided Cabell in his own writing are contained in the prologue and epilogue of the biography, entitled respectively *Beyond Life* and *Straws and Prayerbooks* (volumes I and XVII of the Storisende edition). Biographical material is in *These Restless Heads* (New York, 1932), *Special Delivery* (New York, 1933), *Quiet, Please* (Gainesville, 1952), and *As I Remember It* (New York, 1955).

Hubbell, pp. 945–46; *LSL,* II, pp. 609–10; *LHUS,* I, pp. 1219–22, *II, pp. 1431–33; *Supp,* pp. 88–89.

*Brewer, Frances Joan, *James Branch Cabell: A Bibliography of His Writings, Biography and Criticism,* foreword by James Branch Cabell (Charlottesville, 1957).

*Bruccoli, Matthew J., *James Branch Cabell: A Bibliography, Part II: Notes on the Cabell Collections at the University of Virginia* (Charlottesville, 1957).

Cargill, Oscar, "The Intelligentsia," *Intellectual America: Ideas on the March* (New York, 1940), pp. 495–503.

Colum, Padraic, and Margaret Freeman Cabell, eds., *Between Friends: Letters of James Branch Cabell and Others.* intro by Carl Van Vechten (New York, 1962).

Davis, Joe Lee, *James Branch Cabell* (New York, 1962). [TUSAS]

Hergesheimer, Joseph, "James Branch Cabell," *Amer Mercury,* XIII (Jan 1928), 38–47. [mag art]

Himelick, Raymond, "Figures of Cabell," *MFS,* II (1956–57), 214–20. [mag art]

Klinefelter, Walter, *Books about Poictesme: An Essay in Imaginative Bibliography* (Chicago, 1937).

McNeil, Warren A., *Cabellian Harmonics* (New York, 1928).

Mencken, Henry L., *James Branch Cabell* (New York, 1927).

Parks, Edd Winfield, "James Branch Cabell," in Rubin and Jacobs, *Southern Renascence,* pp. 251–61.

Parrington, Vernon Louis, "The Incomparable Mr. Cabell," *Main Currents in American Thought* (New York, 1930), III, pp. 335–45.

Peter, Emmett B., "Cabell: The Making of a Rebel," *CarolinaQ,* XIV (Spring, 1962), 74–81. [mag art]

Richardson, Eudora Ramsay, "Richmond and Its Writers," *Bookman,* XVIII (1928), 449–53. [mag art]

Rothman, Julius Lawrence, "A Glossorial Index to the *Biography of the Life of Manuel,*" Columbia, 1954. [diss]

Rubin, Louis D., Jr., "A Southerner in Poictesme," *No Place on Earth: Ellen Glasgow,*

James Branch Cabell and Richmond-in-Virginia (Austin, Tex., 1959), pp. 50–81.

————, "Two in Richmond: Ellen Glasgow and James Branch Cabell," Rubin and Jacobs, *South*, pp. 115–41. Repr in Rubin, *The Curious Death of the Novel*, pp. 152–82.

Schlegel, Dorothy B., "Cabell and His Critics," in *The Dilemma of the Southern Writer*, Inst. of So Culture Stud, 1961, ed. Richard K. Meeker (Farmville, Va., 1961), pp. 119–40.

————, "James Branch Cabell and Southern Romanticism," in *Southern Writers*, ed. Simonini, pp. 124–41.

Tarrant, Desmond, *James Branch Cabell: The Dream and the Reality* (Norman, Okla., 1967).

Van Doren, Carl, *James Branch Cabell* (New York, 1932).

Wagenknecht, Edward, "James Branch Cabell: The Anatomy of Romanticism," *Cavalcade of the American Novel* (New York, 1952), pp. 339–53.

Walpole, Hugh, "The Art of James Branch Cabell," *YaleR*, IX (1919–20), 264–98.

*Wells, Arvin R. *Jesting Moses: A Study in Cabellian Comedy* (Gainesville, 1962).

Wilson, Edmund, "The James Branch Cabell Case Reopened," *The Bit Between My Teeth* (New York, 1965), pp. 291–321.

Dorothy B. Schlegel
Norfolk Division, Virginia State College
Norfolk, Virginia

GEORGE WASHINGTON CABLE (1844-1925)

DAB, III, pp. 392–93; *Hubbell*, pp. 804–22, *920–21; *LSL*, II, pp. 619–24; *LHUS*, I, pp. 855–58, *II, pp. 432–34, *Supp*, pp. 89–90.

Arvin, Newton, intro to *The Grandissimes* (New York, 1957), pp. v–xi.

Barrie, James M., "A Note on Mr. Cable's 'The Grandissimes,'" *Bookman*, VII (1898), 401–403.

Berthoff, Warner, *The Ferment of Realism: American Literature, 1884–1919* (New York, 1965), pp. 83–88, 208–209.

*Biklé, Lucy Leffingwell Cable, *George W. Cable: His Life and Letters* (New York, 1928).

*Blanck, *Bibliography of American Literature*, II, pp. 1–12.

Bourne, Randolph, "From an Older Time," *Dial*, LXV (1918), 363–65. [r of *Lovers of Louisiana*]

Bowen, Edwin W., "George Washington Cable: An Appreciation," *SAQ*, XVIII (1919), 145–55.

Brooks, Van Wyck, *The Times of Melville and Whitman* (New York, 1947), pp. 385–94.

*Butcher, Philip, *George W. Cable* (New York, 1962). [TUSAS]

*————, "George Washington Cable," *Amer Lit Realism, 1870–1910*, No. I (1967), 20–25.

*————, *George W. Cable: The Northampton Years* (New York, 1959).

Cardwell, Guy A., *Twins of Genius* ([East Lansing, Mich.] 1953). [Twain-Cable reading tour of 1884–85]

Chase, Richard, "Cable and His *Grandissimes*," *KR*, XVIII (1956), 373–83. Repr in Chase, *The American Novel and Its Tradition* (Garden City, N.Y., 1957), pp. 167–76.

Coleman, Charles W., "The Recent Movement in Southern Literature," *Harper's Mag*, LXXIV (1887), 837–55.

Cowie, *The Rise of the American Novel*, pp. 556–67.

Dart, Henry P., "George W. Cable," *La Hist Q*, VIII (1925), 647–53.

*Ekström, Kjell, *George Washington Cable: A Study of His Early Life and Work* (Uppsala, Sweden; Cambridge, Mass., 1950).

Fulweiler, Howard W., "Of Time and the River: 'Ancestral Nonsense' vs. Inherited Guilt in Cable's 'Belles Demoiselles Plantation,'" *Midcont Amer Stud Jour*, VII (1966), 53–59.

Grau, Shirley Ann, foreword to *Old Creole Days* (New York, 1961), pp. vii–xiii.

Johnson, Robert Underwood, "George Washington Cable," in *Commemorative Tributes to Cable, . . . Sargent, . . . Pennell* (New York, American Academy of Arts and Letters, Pub No. 57, 1927), pp. 1–6.

Martin, Jay, *Harvests of Change: American Literature, 1865–1914* (Englewood Cliffs, N.J., 1967), pp. 100–105, *et passim*.

*Pugh, Griffith T., "George Washington Cable," *MissQ*, XX (1967), 69–76.

_____, *George Washington Cable, A Biographical and Critical Study* (Nashville, Tenn., 1947). [summary of diss]

Quinn, Arthur H., "The Passing of a Literary Era," *SatR*, I (March 21, 1925), 609–10.

Rubin, Louis D., Jr., "The Road to Yoknapatawpha: George W. Cable and 'John March, Southerner,'" *VQR*, XXXV (1959), 119–32. Repr in Rubin, *The Faraway Country*, pp. 21–42.

Stone, Edward, "Usher, Poquelin, and Miss Emily: The Progress of Southern Gothic," *GaR*, XIV (1960), 433–43.

Tinker, Edward Larocque, "Cable and the Creoles," *AL*, V (1934), 313–26.

Turner, Arlin, intro to *Creoles and Cajuns: Stories of Old Louisiana by George W. Cable* (Garden City, N.Y., 1959), pp. 1–19.

*_____, *George W. Cable: A Biography* (Durham, 1956).

*_____, *Mark Twain and George W. Cable: The Record of a Literary Friendship* ([East Lansing, Mich.] 1960).

_____, intro to *The Negro Question: A Selection of Writings on Civil Rights in the South by George W. Cable* (Garden City, N.Y., 1958), pp. xi–xx.

Wilson, Edmund, "Citizen of the Union," *New Rep*, LVII (Feb 13, 1929), 352–53. [r Biklé's *George W. Cable: His Life and Letters*]

_____, "The Ordeal of George Washington Cable," *New Yorker*, XXXIII (Nov 9, 1957), 172, 174–84, 189–96, 199–206, 209–16. Repr in *Patriotic Gore* (New York, 1962), pp. 548–87. [r essay on Turner's biography]

PHILIP BUTCHER
Morgan State College
Baltimore, Maryland

ERSKINE CALDWELL (1903–)

There is no full-length study of the life or works of Erskine Caldwell. In the light of his undeniable popularity and productiveness, this seems surprising. Caldwell's own autobiography is not satisfactory.

Sections of works by W. M. Frohock and Louise Y. Gossett are devoted to Caldwell. Both of these books are concerned with more than their titles suggest. Shields McIlwaine places Caldwell in a tradition of Southern writers. Of the few good critical articles, Kenneth Burke's, John Donald Wade's, and Malcolm Cowley's are the best. Burke considers "balked religiosity" the underlying· theme in Caldwell, and the scrambling of priorities a central technique. He sees Caldwell's characters as "grotesques" or automatons, and not realistic. Wade's rather sarcastic article insists that Caldwell panders to "detached, nervous, thrill-goaded metro-cosmopolitans" and Europeans who enjoy feeling superior to the depraved inhabitants of the Southern United States. Cowley suggests that the sociologist-moralist and the imaginative humorist in Caldwell battle for supremacy, with the sociologist often ruining the work of the humorist.

Carmichael and Cantwell, among others, discuss the relationship of the characters to the land. Cantwell likens the played-out land in the novels to the weak popular fiction which Caldwell's success helped to spawn.

Dr. Lawrence S. Kubie's study is one of the few pieces devoted to a single work. Some of his suggestions concerning the sex fantasies and imagery are quite provocative.

John M. Maclachlan has for his central concern a matter many others also touch upon: Caldwell as a recorder of folkways.

As Robert Hazel has noted, there has been little substantial criticism of Caldwell, and almost none of his later work. Also, much of the existing criticism has been concerned with peripheral matters. Until someone can explain the artistic reasons for his success, the articles berating Caldwell for commercialism will be more influential than they ought to be.

*LHUS, II, pp. 434–35, Supp, pp. 90.

Bode, Carl, "Erskine Caldwell: A Note for the Negative," Coll Eng, XVII (1956), 357–59.

Burke, Kenneth, "Erskine Caldwell: Maker of Grotesques," New Rep, LXXXII (Apr 10, 1935), 232–35.

Caldwell, Erskine, Call It Experience (New York, 1951). [autobiog]

———, Deep South: Memories and Observations (New York, 1968).

Cantwell, Robert, "Caldwell's Characters: Why Don't They Leave?" *GaR*, XI (1957), 252–64.

Carmichael, Peter A., "Jeeter Lester, Agrarian Par Excellence," *SeR*, XLVIII (1940), 21–29.

Couch, W. T., "Landlord and Tenant," *VQR*, XIV (1938), 309–12.

Cowley, Malcolm, "The Two Erskine Caldwells," *New Rep*, CXI (Nov 6, 1944), 599–600.

Cross, Carlyle, "Erskine Caldwell as a Southern Writer," *DA*, XXIV, 4, 696–97 (Georgia).

Frohock, W. M., "Erskine Caldwell—The Dangers of Ambiguity," *The Novel of Violence in America 1900–1950*, rev ed (Dallas, 1957), pp. 106–23.

Gossett, "The Climate of Violence: Wolfe, Caldwell, Faulkner," in *Violence in Recent Southern Fiction*, pp. 16–29.

Hazel, Robert, "Notes on Erskine Caldwell," in Rubin and Jacobs, *Southern Renascence*, pp. 316–24. Repr in Rubin and Jacobs, *South*, pp. 323–32.

Kubie, Lawrence S., M.D., "*God's Little Acre*: An Analysis," *SatR*, XI (Nov 24, 1934), 305–306, 312.

McIlwaine, Shields, "Naturalistic Modes: The Gothic, The Ribald, and the Tragic: William Faulkner and Erskine Caldwell," *The Southern Poor-White from Lubberland to Tobacco Road* (Norman, Okla., 1939), pp. 217–40.

Maclachlan, John Miller, "Folk and Culture in the Novels of Erskine Caldwell," *SFQ*, IX (1945), 93–101.

Wade, John Donald, "Sweet Are the Uses of Degeneracy," *SoR*, o.s., I (1936), 449–66.

DONALD R. NOBLE, JR.
University of North Carolina
Chapel Hill, North Carolina

TRUMAN CAPOTE (1924–)

Capote as stylist is treated by John W. Aldridge and Paul Levine, who have defined the major boundaries of Capote's idiom. Capote as personality—and writer—appears in statements recorded by Harvey Breit and Pati Hill. His experimentation in the concept and form of fiction is considered by George Garrett. Comparisons between Capote and other American writers have been made by Mark Schorer and Alberto Moravia. Criticism of Capote's work will be found in periodicals or within sections of books, no full-length study having appeared.

Aldridge, John W., *After the Lost Generation: A Critical Study of the Writers of Two Wars* (New York, 1951), pp. 194–230.

———, "The Metaphorical World of Truman Capote," *WR*, XV (1951), 247–20.

Baldanza, Frank, "Plato in Dixie," *GaR*, XII (1958), 150–67.

Berger, Yves, "Truman Capote," *Crit*, XV (1959), 491–507.

Breit, Harvey, *The Writer Observed* (Cleveland, 1956), pp. 235–37.

Bucco, Martin, "Truman Capote and the Country Below the Surface," *Four Quarters*, VII (1957), 22–25.

Garrett, George, "Crime and Punishment in Kansas: Truman Capote's *In Cold Blood*," *Hollins Crit*, III, No. 1 (1966), 1–12. [r essay]

*Goad, Craig M., "Daylight and Darkness, Dream and Delusion: The Works of Truman Capote," *Emporia (Kan) State Res Stud*, XVI (Sept 1967), 1–57.

Hassan, Ihab H., "Birth of a Heroine," *Prairie Schooner*, XXXIV (1960), 78–83.

———, *Radical Innocence: Studies in the Contemporary American Novel* (Princeton, 1961), pp. 230–58.

Hill, Pati, "Truman Capote," in *Writers at Work, The Paris Review Interviews*, ed. Malcolm Cowley (New York, 1958), pp. 283–99.

Levine, Paul, "Truman Capote: The Revelation of the Broken Image," *VQR*, XXXIV (1958), 600–17.

Malin, Irving, *New American Gothic* (Carbondale, Ill., 1962).

Mengeling, Marvin E., "*Other Voices, Other Rooms*: Oedipus Between the Covers," *Amer Imago*, XIX (1962), 361–74.

Moravia, Alberto, "Two American Writers (1949)," *SeR*, LXVIII (1960), 473–81.

Schorer, Mark, "McCullers and Capote: Basic Patterns," in *The Creative Present: Notes on Contemporary American Fiction*, ed. Nona Balakian and Charles Simmons (Garden City, N.Y., 1963), pp. 83–107.

Louise Y. Gossett
Salem College
Winston-Salem, North Carolina

WILLIAM ALEXANDER CARUTHERS
(1802-1846)

Publication in 1953 of the first full-length study of this pioneering, but very obscure, author has had the predictable results. Early in 1955 the Georgia Historical Commission erected a marker near the site of Caruthers' home in Savannah. A few months later his work shared the spotlight with that of two other early romancers in a special exhibition staged by the Atlanta Public Library. In 1957 the reported discovery of a copy of his last novel, *The Knights of the Horse-Shoe* (1845), became a newspaper feature. In 1967, facsimile reprints of his first two novels, *The Kentuckian in New-York* . . . (1834), and *The Cavaliers of Virginia*. . . (1834–35), appeared in the "Americans in Fiction" series of the Gregg Press.

DAB, III, pp. 551; *Duyckinck*, II, pp. 436; *Hubbell*, pp. 495–502, *923–24; *LSL*, II, pp. 753–57.

*Davis, Curtis Carroll, *Chronicler of the Cavaliers: A Life of the Virginia Novelist, Dr. William A. Caruthers* (Richmond, 1953). [illus]

————, "That Daring Young Man," *Va Cavalcade*, IX (Summer 1959), 11–15. [career of Caruthers' friend, James H. Piper, glorified by the novelist as first climber of the Natural Bridge of Virginia; illus]

Davis, David B., *Homicide in American Fiction, 1798-1860: A Study in Social Values* (Ithaca, N.Y., 1957), pp. 213, 277–78.

Davis, Richard Beale, *Intellectual Life in Jefferson's Virginia, 1790–1830* (Chapel Hill, 1964), pp. 298, 309, 311–12.

Henry, Harley, "Book Collector's Search Uncovers Rare Volumes" (Jacksonville) *Florida Times-Union*, June 16, 1957, p 2. [bibliophile's discovery of title from Caruthers' lib, John D. Burk's *History of Virginia*....]

Parks, Edd Winfield, *Ante-Bellum Southern Literary Critics* (Athens, Ga., 1962), pp. 71–76, 283–85, *passim*.

Taylor, William R., *Cavalier and Yankee: The Old South and The American National Character* (New York, 1961), pp. 149, 151, 205–24.

CURTIS CARROLL DAVIS
Baltimore, Maryland

MADISON CAWEIN (1865-1914)

A traditional poet, imitative in most of his work but with occasional flashes of inspiration, Madison Cawein had a strong appeal to conventional readers and to students of regional literature around the turn of the century. The late "Uncle Otto" Rothert, a devoted servant of the Filson Club and of Louisville cultural life for more than a half century, pulled together the basic facts about Mr. Cawein in *The Story of a Poet* (1921). A perceptive obituary appeared in the *Boston Transcript*, December 8, 1914.

Several essays by graduate students have penetrated deeply into Mr. Cawein's prosody and the traditions he represents (*e.g.*, the Arthurian). In the Ohio Valley he still enjoys a reputation as a nature poet without a peer. We still have no retrospective or critical appraisal which may be considered definitive. Source material may be found in the Louisville Free Public Library (*e.g.*, the "Kentucky Authors Scrapbooks"), the Filson Club (Louisville), the University of Virginia Library, and the University of Kentucky Library.

DAB, III, pp. 578–80; *LSL*, II, pp. 785–89.

Briney, Melville O., "Madison Cawein, Louisville's Poet of Nature," *Louisville* (Ky.) *Times*, Dec 3, 1959, p. 14.

Covi, Madeline, "Madison Cawein," *Louisville* (Ky.) *Courier-Journal*, May 6, 1962, Sec. 4, p. 6 [in the same issue, Sec. 5, p. 103, art on the Cawein home at 1436 St. James Court]

*Davis, Frank John, "Madison Cawein and His Poetry," Virginia, 1935. [MA thesis]

*Ferguson, Donald Elias, "An Appraisal of the Life and Work of Madison Cawein," Ohio State, 1934. [MA thesis]

Gillis, Everett A., "American Prosody in the Eighteen Nineties with Special Reference to Magazine Verse," Texas, 1948. [diss; substantial portions devoted to Cawein]

Guthrie, William Norman, "A Southern Poet," *SeR*, I (1892–93), 290–308.

*Harrison, Richard Clarence, "Studies in the Poetry of Madison Cawein," Texas, 1917. [MA thesis]

*King, Julia C., "Some Aspects of the Poetry of Madison Cawein," Louisville, 1916. [MA thesis]

Rittenhouse, Jessie B., "Memories of Madison Cawein Incident to Otto Rothert's *The Story of a Poet*," *Bookman*, LVI (1922), 305–12.

*Rothert, Otto Arthur, *The Story of a Poet: Madison Cawein*, (Louisville, 1921; *Filson Club Pub No. 30*).

*Swank, Albert Lee, "Madison Cawein, a Poet of Kentucky," Pittsburgh, 1933. [MA thesis]

*Townsend, John Wilson, *Kentucky in American Letters 1784–1912*, intro by James Lane Allen (Cedar Rapids, Iowa, 1913), 2 vols. [biog and crit comment, short bibl, II, 187–98]

_____, "Has Kentucky Produced a Poet?" *Kentuckians in History and Literature* (New York, 1907), pp. 135–52.

Tyree, Mabel Irene, "The Arthurian Legend as Treated by Four American Poets, James Russell Lowell, Richard Hovey, Madison Cawein, Edwin Arlington Robinson," Kentucky, 1938. [MA thesis]

U.S. Works Progress Administration, "Madison Julius Cawein," *Kentucky Biography: Biographical and Critical Materials Pertaining to Kentucky Authors* (Louisville, 1941), II, pp. 69–75. [Louisville Lib Biog Ser]

LAWRENCE S. THOMPSON
University of Kentucky
Lexington, Kentucky

CHARLES W. CHESNUTT (1858-1932)

After his death in 1932, there was little significant scholarly or critical attention given the fiction of Chesnutt until the fine biography by his daughter Helen in 1952 stimulated a renewed interest which has been slowly, but surely, increasing since. This biography made good use of her memories and his letters and journal, and is indispensable to anyone interested in Chesnutt. From the earlier period, two reviews by William Dean Howells have been listed which should be considered together, one showing his almost excessive enthusiasm for Chesnutt and the other his later tempering of that enthusiasm.

Two articles by Chesnutt have been included here, one primarily concerned with his writing and publication, and the other very revealing concerning the folk material which pervades his stories.

Although his fiction has been out of print for almost forty years, a recent announcement by The Gregg Press that *The Conjure Woman, The Wife of His Youth,* and *The House Behind the Cedars* are to be among the new facsimile editions in its "Americans in Fiction" series is but one of several signs of Chesnutt's having come into serious consideration once more. Certainly the best scholarly work on Chesnutt now being done is that of Sylvia Render of North Carolina College, whose dissertation has made very good use of the various materials in the Chesnutt Collection at Fisk University. This work contains the best and most complete bibliography of Chesnutt's writings to date. Mrs. Render is currently working on a book on Chesnutt for the Twayne *United States Authors Series.*

LHUS, II, p. 440, *Supp*, p. 93.

Ames, Russell, "Social Realism in Charles W. Chesnutt," *Phylon*, XIV (1953), 199–206.

Cary, Elisabeth L., "A New Element in Fiction," *Book Buyer*, XXIII (1901), 26–28. [crit essay]

Chamberlain, John, "The Negro As Writer," *Bookman*, LXX (1930), 603–605.

Chesnutt, Charles W., "Post-Bellum—Pre-Harlem," *The Colophon*, part 5, lead essay, 8 pages (1931). Repr in Elmer Adler, ed., *Breaking into Print* (New York, 1937), pp. 47–56. [autobiog and bibl essay]

———, "Superstitions and Folk-lore [sic] of the South," *Mod Cult*, XIII (1901), 231–35.

Chesnutt, Helen M., *Charles Waddell Chesnutt: Pioneer of the Color Line* (Chapel Hill, 1952). [biog]

*Freeney, Mildred, and Mary T. Henry, comps, *A List of the Manuscripts, Published Works and Related Items in the Charles Waddell Chesnutt Collection of the Erastus Milo Cravath Memorial Library, Fisk University* (Nashville, 1954).

Gloster, Hugh M., "Charles W. Chesnutt: Pioneer in the Fiction of Negro Life," *Phylon*, II, (1941), 57–66. Repr in Sylvestre C. Watkins, ed., *An Anthology of American Negro Literature* (New York, 1944), pp. 295–307; and only slightly adapted for Hugh M. Gloster, *Negro Voices in American Fiction* (Chapel Hill, 1948, repr New York, 1965), pp. 34–46.

Howells, William Dean, "Mr. Charles W. Chesnutt's Stories," *Atlantic*, LXXV (1900), 699–701. [r essay]

———, "A Psychological Counter-Current in Recent Fiction," *NoAmerR*, CLXXIII (1901), 881–83. [r essay]

Hubert, Julia M., "*The Marrow of Tradition*: Studies in the Fiction of Charles W. Chesnutt," Ohio State, 1948. [MA thesis]

*Keller, Dean H., "Charles Waddell Chesnutt," *Amer Lit Realism*, No. 3 (1968), 1–4.

Loggins, Vernon, *The Negro Author* (New York, 1931, repr Port Washington, N.Y., 1964), pp. 310–13, 318–20, 326–31.
Mason, Julian D., Jr., "Charles W. Chesnutt As Southern Author," *MissQ*, XX (1967), 77–89.
Parker, John W., "Chesnutt As a Southern Town Remembers Him," *The Crisis*, LVI (1949), 205–206, 221.
*Render, Sylvia Lyons, "Eagle with Clipped Wings: Form and Feeling in the Fiction of Charles Waddell Chesnutt," Peabody, 1962. [diss]
———, "Tar Heelia in Chesnutt," *CLA Jour*, IX (1965), 39–50.
Smith, Robert A., "A Note on the Folktales of Charles W. Chesnutt," *CLA Jour*, V (1962), 229–32.

JULIAN D. MASON, JR.
University of North Carolina
Charlotte, North Carolina

THOMAS HOLLEY CHIVERS (1809-1858)

S. Foster Damon's *Thomas Holley Chivers: Friend of Poe* (1930) remains the standard biographical and critical work. Charles H. Watts added a significant critical study in 1956. Much of what has been written about Chivers centers around his relations with Poe, and valuable material on Chivers can be found in the biographies and critical studies of Poe. Richard Beale Davis' edition of *Chivers' Life of Poe* is of particular importance. A *Complete Works* of Chivers is now being prepared. Volume I, *The Correspondence*, including letters both to and from Chivers, appeared in 1957. Three more volumes are to follow.

DAB, IV, pp. 81–83; *Hubbell* pp. 550–59, *924; LSL*, II, pp. 845–49; *LHUS*, II, pp. 440–41, *Supp*, p. 93.
Bell, Landon C., *Poe and Chivers* (Columbus, Ohio, 1931).
Benton, Joel, *In the Poe Circle* (New York, 1899).
*Blanck, *Bibliography of American Literature*, II, pp. 157–59.
Chase, Emma Lester, and Lois Ferry Parks, eds., *The Correspondence of Thomas Holley Chivers*, I, *Complete Works* (Providence, 1957).
*Damon, S. Foster, *Thomas Holley Chivers: Friend of Poe* (New York, 1930).
Davis, Richard Beale, intro to *Chivers' Life of Poe* (New York, 1952), pp. 9–20.
———, "Thomas Holley Chivers and the Kentucky Tragedy," *TSLL*, I (1959), 281–88.
Eidson, John O., "The Letters of Thomas Holley Chivers," *GaR*, XVIII (1964), 143–49.
Harrison, James A., "Poe and Chivers," in *Complete Works of Edgar Allan Poe* (New York, 1902), VII, pp. 266–88.
Newcomer, A. G., "The Poe-Chivers Tradition Reexamined," *SeR*, XII (1904), 20–35.
Parks, Edd Winfield, "Thomas Holley Chivers: Mystic," *Ante-Bellum Southern Literary Critics* (Athens, Ga., 1962), pp. 158–84.

Pitfield, R. L., "Thomas Holley Chivers: 'The Wild Mazeppa of Letters,'" *Gen Mag and Hist Chron*, XXXVII (1934), 73–92.

Scott, W. S., "The Astonishing Chivers: Poet for Plagiarists," *Princeton U Lib Chron*, V (1944), 150–53.

*Watts, Charles Henry, II, *Thomas Holley Chivers: His Literary Career and His Poetry* (Athens, Ga., 1956).

Woodberry, George E., "The Poe-Chivers Papers," *Century*, LXV (1903), 435–48, 545–58.

JOHN O. EIDSON
Georgia Southern College
Statesboro, Georgia

KATE CHOPIN (1851-1904)

So far, only one book and some twenty-five articles, etc., of any importance have been devoted to Kate Chopin. Up to and including the *Literary History of the United States*, she was seen almost solely as an outstanding Louisiana local colorist; emphasizing her obvious involvement with her region, the critics neglected her even stronger urge to apply a French realism to the description of emancipated women. In fact, her boldness remained largely unappreciated until Cyrille Arnavon in 1953 discussed it in an introduction to his French translation of her last novel.

Since then, others have joined him in treating Mrs. Chopin's realism, and it will be dealt with at length in a forthcoming book on her to be published in 1969. (The author of this book—and of the present entry— will also bring out the *Complete Works of Kate Chopin*, due for publication in 1969, which is to include much previously unpublished material.) During the last fifteen years, Kate Chopin scholarship has come to see her not primarily as a Southern local colorist, but as an important American realist of the 1890s.

Arms, George, "Kate Chopin's *The Awakening* in the Perspective of Her Literary Career," in *Essays in American Literature in Honor of J. B. Hubbell*, ed. Clarence Gohdes (Durham, 1967), pp. 215–28.

Arnavon, Cyrille, intro to Kate Chopin, *Edna* (Paris, 1953), pp. 1–22.

Berthoff, Warner, *The Ferment of Realism: American Literature 1884–1919* (New York, 1965), pp. 88–90.

Bush, Robert Burton, "The Fiction of Kate Chopin," "Louisiana Prose Fiction, 1870–1900," Iowa, 1957, pp. 232–76. [diss]

Eble, Kenneth, "A Forgotten Novel: Kate Chopin's *The Awakening*," *WHumR*, X (1956), 261–69.

Jordan, Merle Mae T., "Kate Chopin: Social Critic," Texas, 1959. [MA thesis]

Pattee, Fred Lewis, *The Development of the American Short Story* (New York, 1923), pp. 324–27.

Quinn, *American Fiction*, pp. 354–57.

*Rankin, Daniel S., *Kate Chopin and Her Creole Stories* (Philadelphia, 1932).

Reilly, Joseph J., "Stories by Kate Chopin," *Commonweal*, XXV (March 26, 1937), 606–607.

Seyersted, Per, "Kate Chopin: An Important St. Louis Writer Reconsidered," Mo Hist Soc *Bull*, XIX (1963), 89–114.

Wilson, Edmund, *Patriotic Gore* (New York, 1962), pp. 587–93.

Ziff, Larzer, *The American 1890s: Life and Times of a Lost Generation* (New York, 1966), pp. 296–305.

PER SEYERSTED
*American Institute,
University of Oslo
Oslo, Norway*

SAMUEL LANGHORNE CLEMENS (1835-1910)

Surprisingly little of consequence has been written on Samuel Langhorne Clemens—or his persona Mark Twain—as a Southerner, an oversight bound to be corrected and soon. Otherwise—one says almost wearily—Mark Twain has elicited comment from a myriad of perspectives. Since he tends to transcend or at least burst out of the domain of belles lettres, just about every attempt to survey nineteenth-century culture feels obliged to take him up as an epitome of American character. In literary history he now rates, of course, as a major figure, who always demands his share of the honors. Most books on a highly selective theme, such as the search for an ideal community or the hunger for a self-contained esthetic, also include him, often at the cost of cogency. As one result, few critics have absorbed everything written about him, even when further publication is the name of the game. Not quite inevitably, some of the latest commentary is repetitious.

Yet, overall, scholarship and criticism add up still to a sensible process. To winnow the mountain of words about Mark Twain is to discover that there has been cumulative gain. Certainly the work of the last .ten years has often absorbed or refined and therefore superseded what came earlier. This checklist is consequently weighted toward the more recent, though a heartening degree of the less recent continues to hold unique or worthwhile material. As for *Adventures of Huckleberry Finn*, one is tempted to predict that thirty-five years of heightening debate have underlined and systematized most of what our generation will find in it. A less risky way of making this point is to observe that we have reached a loose consensus about *Huckleberry Finn*; the four or five most widely used collections reprint many of the same essays, elected from several hundred plausible candidates. Though more candidates join the field monthly or quarterly, a rewarding shift toward explicating Mark Twain's other books and even some of the lesser-known sketches seems sure to accelerate. Furthermore, his writings, published and unpublished, are naturally included in the wave of meticulous editing, which is already stirring up side effects; the American Studies movement, again waxing, will always draw on him as an especially varied resource; thanks to his unreliability and his conglomerate career, neither plain fact-finding nor sophisticated literary history has begun to exhaust the challenges posed. While perhaps never "prestige" stocks, Mark Twain scholarship and criticism keep looking like growth industries.

DAB, IV, pp. 192–98; *Hubbell*, pp. 822–36, *924–25; *LHUS*, I, pp. 917–34, *II, pp. 442–50. *Supp*, pp. 94–99.

Adams, Richard P., "The Unity and Coherence of *Huckleberry Finn*," *Tulane Stud in Eng*, VI (1956), 87–103.

Andrews, Kenneth R., *Nook Farm: Mark Twain's Hartford Circle* (Cambridge, Mass., 1950).

*Asselineau, Roger, *The Literary Reputation of Mark Twain from 1910–1950: A Critical Essay and a Bibliography* (Paris, 1954).

Baender, Paul, "The 'Jumping Frog' as a Comedian's First Virtue," *Mod Phil*, LX (1963), 192–200.

Baetzhold, Howard G., "The Course of Composition of *A Connecticut Yankee*: A Reinterpretation," *AL*, XXXIII (1961), 195–214.

*Baldanza, Frank, *Mark Twain: An Introduction and Interpretation* (New York, 1961).

Barchilon, Jose, and Joel S. Kovel, "Huckleberry Finn: A Psychoanalytic Study," *Jour of the Amer Psychoanalytic Assn*, XIV (1966), 775–814.

Bellamy, Gladys C., *Mark Twain as a Literary Artist* (Norman, Okla., 1950).

*Benson, Ivan. *Mark Twain's Western Years* (Stanford, Calif., 1938).

Berthoff, Warner, "Mark Twain," in *The Ferment of Realism: American Literature 1884–1914* (New York, 1965), pp. 61–76.

Blair, Walter, "Mark Twain," in *Native American Humor (1800–1900)* (New York, 1937), pp. 147–62.

*———, *Mark Twain & Huck Finn* (Berkeley and Los Angeles, 1960).

———, "On the Structure of *Tom Sawyer*," *Mod Phil*, XXXVII (Aug 1939), 75–88.

Branch, Edgar M., *The Literary Apprenticeship of Mark Twain* (Urbana, Ill., 1950).

———, "Mark Twain and J. D. Salinger: A Study in Literary Continuity," *AQ*, IX (1957), 144–58.

———, " 'My Voice Is Still for Setchell': A Background Study of 'Jim Smiley and His Jumping Frog'," *PMLA*, LXXXII (1967), 591–601.

*Brashear, Minnie M., *Mark Twain, Son of Missouri* (Chapel Hill, 1934).

Bridgman, Richard, "Henry James and Mark Twain," *The Colloquial Style in America* (New York, 1966), pp. 106–30.

Brooks, Van Wyck, *The Ordeal of Mark Twain* (New York, rev ed, 1933).

Budd, Louis J., "Mark Twain and the Upward Mobility of Taste," in *New Voices in Amer Stud*, ed. Ray B. Browne et al (West Lafayette, Ind., 1966), pp. 21–34. [on attitudes toward painting]

_____, *Mark Twain: Social Philosopher* (Bloomington, Ind., 1962).

Canby, Henry Seidel, *Turn West, Turn East: Mark Twain and Henry James* (Boston, 1951).

Cardwell, Guy A., *Twins of Genius* (East Lansing, Mich., 1953). [relations between Clemens and G. W. Cable]

Chase, Richard, "Mark Twain and the Novel," *The American Novel and Its Tradition* (Garden City, N.Y., 1957), pp. 139–56.

*Clark, Harry Hayden, "Mark Twain," in *Eight American Authors: A Review of Research and Criticism*, ed. Floyd Stovall (New York, 1956), pp. 319–63. Supp by J. Chesley Matthews (New York, 1963 ed), pp. 451–58.

Covici, Pascal, Jr., *Mark Twain's Humor: The Image of a World* (Dallas, 1962).

Cowie, "Mark Twain," *The Rise of the American Novel*, pp. 599–652.

Cox, James M., *Mark Twain: The Fate of Humor* (Princeton, 1966).

_____, "Remarks on the Sad Initiation of Huckleberry Finn," *SeR*, LXII (1954), 389–405.

Cummings, Sherwood, "Mark Twain's Acceptance of Science," *Centennial R*, VI (Spring 1962), 245–61.

DeVoto, Bernard, *Mark Twain at Work* (Cambridge, Mass., 1942).

_____, *Mark Twain's America* (Boston, 1932).

Dreiser, Theodore, "Mark the Double Twain," *Eng Jour*, XXIV (1935), 615–27.

*Duckett, Margaret, *Mark Twin and Bret Harte* (Norman, Okla., 1964).

Dyson, A. E., "Huckleberry Finn and the Whole Truth," *CritQ*, III (Spring 1961), 29–40.

Eliot, T. S., intro to *The Adventures of Huckleberry Finn* (New York, 1950), pp. vii–xvi.

Elliott, George P., "Wonder for *Huckleberry Finn*," in *Twelve Original Essays on Great American Novels*, ed. Charles Shapiro (Detroit, 1958), pp. 69–95.

Falk, Robert, "Mark Twain and the Earlier Realism," *The Victorian Mode in American Fiction, 1865–1885* (East Lansing, Mich., 1965), pp. 159–66.

Fatout, Paul, *Mark Twain in Virginia City* (Bloomington, Ind., 1964).

_____, *Mark Twain on the Lecture Circuit* (Bloomington, Ind., 1960).

Ferguson, DeLancey, *Mark Twain: Man and Legend* (Indianapolis, 1943).

Fiedler, Leslie A., "*Huckleberry Finn*: Faust in the Eden of Childhood," *Love and Death in the American Novel* (Cleveland, 1960), pp. 553–91.

*Foner, Philip S., *Mark Twain: Social Critic* (New York, 1958).

Frantz, Ray W., Jr., "The Role of Folklore in *Huckleberry Finn*," *AL*, XXVIII (1956), 314–27.

French, Bryant Morey, *Mark Twain and "The Gilded Age": The Book That Named an Era* (Dallas, 1965).

*Gerber, John C., "Mark Twain," in *American Literary Scholarship: An Annual*, ed James Woodress (Durham, 1965——); pp. 53–63 (for 1963); pp. 50–61 (for 1964); pp. 57–68 (for 1965).

_____, "The Relation between Point of View and Style in the Works of Mark Twain," in *Style in Prose Fiction: English Institute Essays, 1958*, ed. Harold C. Martin (New York, 1959), pp. 142–71.

Gohdes, Clarence, "Mirth for the Million," in *The Literature of the American People*, ed. Arthur H. Quinn (New York, 1951), pp. 708–20.

Grant, Douglas, *Mark Twain* (Edinburgh and New York, 1962).

Hansen, Chadwick, "The Character of Jim and the Ending of *Huckleberry Finn*," *MassR*, V (Autumn 1963), 45–66.

Hemminghaus, Edgar H., *Mark Twain in Germany* (New York, 1939).

Hicks, Granville, "A Banjo on My Knee," *The Great Tradition* (New York, rev ed, 1935), pp. 38–49.

Hill, Hamlin, *Mark Twain and Elisha Bliss* (Columbia, Mo., 1964).

Hoffman, Daniel G., "Mark Twain," *Form and Fable in American Fiction* (New York, 1961), pp. 317–50.

Howells, William Dean, *My Mark Twain: Reminiscences and Criticisms* (New York, 1910; Baton Rouge, 1967).

*Johnson, Merle, *A Bibliography of the Works of Mark Twain* (New York, rev ed, 1935).

Kaplan, Justin, *Mr. Clemens and Mark Twain, A Biography* (New York, 1966).

Kaul, A. N., "*Huckleberry Finn:* A Southwestern Statement," in *The American Vision: Actual and Ideal Society in Nineteenth-Century Fiction* (New Haven, 1963), pp. 280–304.

*Krause, Sydney J., *Mark Twain as Critic* (Baltimore, 1967).

———, "Twain's Method and Theory of Composition," *Mod Phil*, LVI (1959), 167–77.

*Leary, Lewis, "Clemens, Samuel Langhorne," in *Articles on American Literature, 1900–1950* (Durham, 1954), pp. 43–55.

*———, *Mark Twain* (Minneapolis, 1960). [Minn pamph]

———, "Tom and Huck: Innocence on Trial," *VQR*, XXX (1954), 417–30.

Leavis, F. R., "Mark Twain's Neglected Classic: The Moral Astringency of *Pudd'nhead Wilson*," *Commentary*, XXI (Feb 1956), 128–36.

Liljegren, S. B., *The Revolt Against Romanticism in American Literature as Evidenced in the Works of S. L. Clemens* (Uppsala, Sweden, 1945).

*Long, E. Hudson, *Mark Twain Handbook* (New York, 1958).

Lynn, Kenneth S., *Mark Twain and Southwestern Humor* (Boston, 1959).

Macdonald, Dwight, "Mark Twain: An Unsentimental Journey," *New Yorker*, XXXVI (Apr 9, 1960), 160–96. [r essay; non-specialist's overview of Clemens]

Martin, Jay, "Mark Twain: The Dream of Drift and the Dream of Delight," *Harvests of Change: American Literature 1865–1914* (Englewood Cliffs, N.J., 1967), pp. 165–201.

Marx, Leo, "Mr. Eliot, Mr. Trilling, and *Huckleberry Finn*," *Amer Schol*, XXII (1953), 423–40.

———, "Two Kingdoms of Force," in *The Machine in the Garden: Technology and the Pastoral Ideal in America* (New York, 1964), pp. 319–40. [on *Huckleberry Finn*]

Morgan, H. Wayne, "Mark Twain: The Optimist as Pessimist," in *American Writers in Rebellion: From Mark Twain to Dreiser* (New York, 1965), pp. 1–36.

Paine, Albert Bigelow, *Mark Twain: A Biography* (New York, 1912).

Parks, Edd W., "Mark Twain as Southerner," in *Segments of Southern Thought* (Athens, Ga., 1938), pp. 245–49. [r essay]

Parrington, Vernon L., "The Backwash of the Frontier—Mark Twain," in *Main Currents in American Thought* (New York, 1927–30), III, 86–101.

Ramsay, Robert L., and Frances G. Emberson, "A Mark Twain Lexicon," *U of Mo Stud*, XIII (Jan 1938), i–cxix, 1–278.

Regan, Robert, *Unpromising Heroes: Mark Twain and His Characters* (Berkeley and Los Angeles, 1966).

Rogers, Franklin R., intro to *Mark Twain's Satires and Burlesques* (Berkeley and Los Angeles, 1967), pp. 1–16.

_____, *Mark Twain's Burlesque Patterns: As Seen in the Novels and Narratives, 1855–1885* (Dallas, 1960).

Rubin, Louis D., Jr., "Mark Twain Tonight," *The Teller in the Tale* (Seattle, 1967), pp. 52–82.

_____, "Tom Sawyer and the Use of Novels," *AQ*, IX (Summer 1957), 209–16. Repr in Rubin, *The Curious Death of the Novel*, 88–99.

Salomon, Roger B., "Realism as Disinheritance: Twain, Howells, and James," *AQ*, XVI (Winter 1964), 531–44.

_____, *Twain and the Image of History* (New Haven, 1961).

Scott, Arthur L., *On the Poetry of Mark Twain with Selections from His Verse* (Urbana, Ill., 1966).

Smith, Henry Nash, and William M. Gibson, eds., *Mark Twain—Howells Letters: The Correspondence of Samuel L. Clemens and William D. Howells, 1872–1910*, 2 vols (Cambridge, Mass., 1960).

Smith, Henry Nash, *Mark Twain's Fable of Progress: Political and Economic Ideas in "A Connecticut Yankee"* (New Brunswick, N.J., 1964).

_____, *Mark Twain: The Development of a Writer* (Cambridge, Mass., 1962).

Spengemann, William C., *Mark Twain and The Backwoods Angel: The Matter of Innocence in the Works of Samuel L. Clemens* (Kent, Ohio, 1966).

Stone, Albert E., Jr., *The Innocent Eye: Childhood in Mark Twain's Imagination* (New Haven, 1961).

Tanner, Tony, "Mark Twain," *The Reign of Wonder: Naivety and Reality in American Literature* (Cambridge, Eng., 1965), pp. 97–183.

Tracy, Robert, "Myth and Reality in *The Adventures of Tom Sawyer*." *SoR*, n.s., IV (1968), 530–41.

Trilling, Lionel, "Huckleberry Finn," *The Liberal Imagination* (New York, 1950), pp. 104–17.

Tuckey, John S., intro to *Mark Twain's "Which Was the Dream?" and Other Symbolic Writings of the Later Years* (Berkeley and Los Angeles, 1967), pp. 1–29.

_____, *Mark Twain and Little Satan: The Writing of "The Mysterious Stranger"* (West Lafayette, Ind., 1963).

Turner, Arlin, *Mark Twain and G. W. Cable: The Record of a Literary Friendship* (East Lansing, Mich, 1960).

_____, "Mark Twain and the South: An Affair of Love and Anger," *SoR*, n.s., IV (1968), 493–519.

*Wagenknecht, Edward, *Mark Twain: The Man and His Work* (Norman, Okla., rev ed, 1967).

Webster, Samuel C., ed., *Mark Twain, Business Man* (Boston, 1946).

Wecter, Dixon, *Sam Clemens of Hannibal* (Boston, 1952).

Wiggins, Robert A., *Mark Twain: Jackleg Novelist* (Seattle, 1964).

Young, Philip, "Adventures of Huckleberry Finn," *Ernest Hemingway* (New York, 1952), pp. 181–212.

LOUIS J. BUDD
Duke University
Durham, North Carolina

JOHN ESTEN COOKE (1830-1886)

The first and only full-length study of John Esten Cooke that has been published is John O. Beaty's critical biography, *John Esten Cooke, Virginian* (New York, 1922). Beaty's treatment of Cooke's life and work is based on "first-hand material of family and friends," and his estimate of Cooke's importance as a literary figure is fundamentally that of subsequent scholars: "On the whole. . . Cooke was not so much the advocate, as the social historian, of Virginia," a writer who "will be remembered chiefly for the *Virginia Comedians, Surry of Eagle's-Nest,* and *Mohun.*"

Brief appraisals, which appear in histories of American fiction, supplement Beaty's biography. Three of the more important essays are to be found in Arthur Hobson Quinn's *American Fiction,* pp. 126–31; Alexander Cowie's *The Rise of the American Novel,* pp. 463–72; and Jay B. Hubbell's *The South in American Literature,* pp. 511–21, pp. 926–27. Professor Hubbell's comprehensive essay and selected bibliography provide an especially sound introduction to Cooke's fiction as it relates to the historical and social setting of the South.

Since the publication of *The South in American Literature,* an exhaustive dissertation—William Edward Walker's *John Esten Cooke: A Critical Biography*—has been written. Mr. Walker has drawn material from Cooke's "notebooks, letters, and published works to re-create his life and milieu"; and in addition to a 735-page treatment of Cooke's life and work, he includes a 24-page bibliography that contains a full list of manuscript material, Cooke's books, and his publications in journals. Walker's critical conclusions are essentially those of John O. Beaty: Cooke "did not blindly write to 'glorify' the Old South," but "was more the social historian than the advocate." The chief value of this dissertation is its complete account of Cooke's life and work and its useful bibliography.

Although Mr. Walker's dissertation will provide most information needed in regard to John Esten Cooke, two bibliographies are worth consulting as cross-references: Doris M. Call's "John Esten Cooke: Civil War Novelist, 1830-1886. A Bibliography," and Oscar Wegelin's "A Bibliography of the Separate Writings of John Esten Cooke of Virginia, 1830–1886."

DAB, IV, pp. 385–87; *Duyckinck,* II, p. 636; *Hubbell,* pp. 511–21, *926–27; *LSL,* III, pp. 103–37.

Beaty, John O., *John Esten Cooke, Virginian* (New York, 1922).

*Call, Doris, "John Esten Cooke; Civil War Novelist, 1830–1886. A Bibliography," Library School, Wisconsin, 1938. [unpubl paper]

Cauthen, J. B., "John Esten Cooke in Publishing, 1865," *SB*, VIII (1956), 239–41. [note]

Collins, Carvel, "John Esten Cooke and Local Color," *SLM*, n.s., VI (1944), 82–84.

Cowie, *The Rise of the American Novel*, pp. 463–72.

Derby, J. C., *Fifty Years Among Authors, Books and Publishers* (New York, 1884), pp. 400–406.

Gaines, Francis Pendleton, *The Southern Plantation, A Study in the Development and the Accuracy of a Tradition* (New York, 1924), pp. 54–56.

Goolrich, Chester R., Jr., "The Scrapbook of John Esten Cooke," *VMHB*, LVIII (1950), 516–18.

Griswold, Rufus W., *Prose Writers of America*, 4th ed (Philadelphia, 1851).

*Harwell, Richard B., *Confederate Belles-Lettres* (Hattiesburg, Miss., 1941), p. 70.

———., "A Confederate View of the Southern Poets," *AL*, XXIV (1952), 51–61.

———, "John Esten Cooke, Civil War Correspondent," *JSH*, XIX (1953), 501–16.

Holliday, Carl, "John Esten Cooke as a Novelist," *SeR*, XIII (1905), 216–20.

Hubbell, Jay B., *Virginia Life in Fiction* (Dallas, 1922), pp. 26–27.

———., "The War Diary of John Esten Cooke," *JSH*, VII (1941), 526–40.

Johnson, Emma Bain, "John Esten Cooke and the Civil War," Duke, 1943. [MA thesis]

Link, S. A., *Pioneers of Southern Literature*, I (Nashville, 1899), pp. 248–70.

Paine, Gregory, *Southern Prose Writers* (New York, 1947), pp. 171–81.

Quinn, "The Development of Idealistic Romance," *American Fiction*, pp. 126–31.

Van Doren, Carl, *The American Novel* (New York, 1921), pp. 104–105.

Walker, William Edward, "John Esten Cooke: A Critical Biography," *DA*, 22,028 (Vanderbilt).

*Wegelin, Oscar, *A Bibliography of the Separate Writings of John Esten Cooke of Virginia, 1820–1886*, 2nd rev ed (Hattiesburg, Miss., 1941).

THEODORE L. GROSS
City College of New York
New York, New York

PHILIP PENDLETON COOKE (1816-1850)

DAB, IV, pp. 338–89; *Duyckinck*, II, 635; *Hubbell*, II, pp. 502–11, *927; *LSL*, III, pp. 1063–68.

*Allen, John D., "Philip Pendleton Cooke: A Critical and Biographical Study," Vanderbilt, 1939. [diss; bibl includes 38 poems, eight essays, nine sketches and prose tales, and 69 letters by Cooke; 46 letters to or related to him, 16 unpubl mss, 91 books and periodical references]

———, *Philip Pendleton Cooke* (Chapel Hill, 1942). [consensed version of diss; retains bibl]

———, Philip Pendleton Cooke: Poet, Critic, Novelist. Selections ed. with an intro. [to be published: 20 poems, five tales, five essays, 16 letters]

Cooke, John Esten, "Recollections of Philip Pendleton Cooke," *SLM*, XXVI (1858), 419–32.

Griswold, Rufus W., "Philip Pendleton Cooke," in *The Intern Mag*, IV (1851), 300–303. Repr in *SLM*, XVII (1851), 669–73.

*Jackson, David K., *The Contributors and Contributions to The Southern Literary Messenger (1834–1864)* (Charlottesville, 1936).

———, "Philip Pendleton Cooke: Virginia Gentleman, Lawyer, Hunter, and Poet," in *American Studies in Honor of William Kenneth Boyd*, pp. 282–326.

Parks, Edd Winfield, ed., *Southern Poets* (New York, 1936), pp. 83–88.

*Thompson, May Alcott, "Philip Pendleton Cooke," Columbia, 1923. [MA thesis; the first scholarly study of Cooke]

Whiting, W. H. Jr., "Philip Pendleton Cooke," *Hampden-Sydney Mag* (Apr 1928), 9–14.

JOHN D. ALLEN
East Tennessee State University
Johnson City, Tennessee

WILLIAM CRAFTS (1787-1826)

Little has been written about William Crafts. George H. Genzmer's article in *Dictionary of American Biography* and Jay B. Hubbell's treatment in *The Literature of the South* are the two best readily available sources, although Hugh Swinton Legaré's unfriendly criticism in the *Southern Review* (1828) should be noted, as should the sketch and brief selections in the Duyckinck's *Cyclopedia of American Literature.*

DAB, IV, pp. 493–94; *Duyckinck*, II, p. 86; *Hubbell*, pp. 259–63, *929.

Crafts, J. M. and W. F., *The Crafts Family* (Charleston, S.C., 1893). ["family" sketch]

Fraser, Charles, *Reminiscences of Charleston* (Charleston, S.C., 1854), pp. 82–84.

Gilman, Samuel, "Memoir," in *A Selection, in Prose and Poetry, from the Miscellaneous Writings of the Late William Crafts* (Charleston, S.C., 1828). [detailed biog information]

Legaré, Hugh Swinton, "Crafts's Fugitive Writings," *SoR*, I (1828), 503–29. Repr in *Writings of Hugh Swinton Legaré*(Charleston, S.C., 1845), II, pp. 142–65.

Lewisonn, Ludwig, "The Books We Have Made," *Charleston* (S.C.) *News and Courier*, July 12, 1903.

O'Neall, John B., *Biographical Sketches of the Bench and Bar of South Carolina* (Charleston, S.C., 1859), II, pp. 345–67.

Parrington, Vernon Louis, *Main Currents in American Thought*, II, *The Romantic Revolution in America, 1800–1860* (New York, 1927), pp. 112–14.

C. HUGH HOLMAN
University of North Carolina
Chapel Hill, North Carolina

RICHARD DABNEY (1787-1825)

Relatively little scholarly interest has been shown in Richard Dabney, whose *Poems, Original and Translated* (1815) received scant attention even in his own day. Jay B. Hubbell in *The South in American Literature* states that Dabney was perhaps a better scholar than a poet, and notes the literary influences on his poetry and the possible sources for his poetic theory. Two reviews of Dabney's poems appear in [George Tucker], *Letters from Virginia, Translated from the French* (1816) and the *Port Folio* (July 1815); in both essays the writers praise the sentiment of the poems but criticize the metrics. The article contributed by Lucian Minor to the Duyckincks' *Cyclopaedia of American Literature* is prejudicial: Minor's obvious disgust with Dabney's personal habits (drug addiction and excessive drinking) colors his estimate of the poet.

What seems to be a complete bibliography of pertinent literary references to Dabney appears in the checklist.

DAB, V, p. 20; *Duyckinck*, II, p. 98; *Hubbell*, pp. 296–98, *930.
[Allen, Paul], "Poems, Original and Translated—by Richard Dabney," *Port Folio*, VI (July 1815), 56–58. [r essay]
Bradsher, Earl L., "Richard Dabney," *SeR*, XXIII (1915), 326–36.
Dabney, William H., *Sketch of the Dabneys of Virginia* (Chicago, 1888), pp. 124–25. [biog]
"Richard Dabney" in *Appletons' Cyclopaedia of American Biography*, ed. James Grant Wilson and John Fiske (New York, 1896), II, p. 51. [biog]
[Tucker, George], *Letters from Virginia, Translated from the French* (Baltimore, 1816), pp. 62–72. [r essay]

WILLIAM S. OSBORNE
Southern Connecticut State College
New Haven, Connecticut

OLIVE TILFORD DARGAN (1869-1968)

Mrs. Dargan's role as a proletarian novelist of the 1930s, when she wrote under the pseudonym of Fielding Burke, has not been adequately assessed. There is no bibliography of her poetry appearing in periodicals.

LSL, III, pp. 1195–1200.
Adams, J. Donald, "Two Novels about Industrial Unrest," *N.Y. Times Bk R*, Dec 15, 1935, p. 7. [r of *A Stone Came Rolling*]
Golden, Harry, Sr., "Olive Tilford Dargan Hailed as Trail-Breaking N.C. Writer," *Charlotte* (N.C.) *Observer*, July 31, 1955, p. 8–D. [newsp art]

Lathrop, Virginia Terrell, "Olive Tilford Dargan," *North Carolina Librarian*, XVIII (Spring 1960), 68–76. [biog]

Polsky, Jane and Thomas, "The Two Lives of Olive Tilford Dargan," *So Packet* [Asheville, N.C.], IV (June 1948), 1–5.

*[Polsky, Thomas], "Olive Tilford Dargan," *North Carolina Authors: A Selective Handbook* (Chapel Hill, 1952), pp. 29–31, U of N.C. Lib Ext Pub, XVIII, No. 1.

Walser, Richard, ed., "Olive Tilford Dargan," *Poets of North Carolina* (Richmond, 1962), pp. 9–21.

Young, Charlotte, "Carolina Woman Writes Literature for All Time," *Charlotte* (N.C.) *Observer*, July 24, 1932, Sec. 3, p. 4. [newsp art]

RICHARD WALSER
North Carolina State University
Raleigh, North Carolina

DONALD DAVIDSON (1893-1968)

Because his performance has been so much across the grain of our times, because the body of his work is so vast and touches upon so many interests and disciplines, and most of all because he continued (through his eighth decade) to be both productive and—in all his obdurate and principled anachronism—himself, serious study of the career of the late Donald Davidson has just begun. Of careful and detailed examination of Davidson's poetry, there has been very little; and that comment which has appeared is, for the most part, too general or occasional to clear away the difficulties that for the modern reader follow from Davidson's poetics; or else it is too much informed by hostility to his traditionalism to illuminate the connection of his doctrine with his verse. There are very few printed sources for study of his distinguished criticism and his artistic practice. The public man—the historian, the political and social essayist—has not been received with silence: praise and blame, concurrence and reproach, here exist in great plenty; but of explanation and exposition, there is nothing substantial.

Hereafter, the major problem facing the student of Davidson will be the exceptionally difficult one of cutting his way through the handiwork of certain of his predecessors: John M. Bradbury, John Lincoln Stewart, Alexander Karanikas—to mention only three principal malefactors.

The study will be clarified with the appearance of Virginia Rock's volume on the Agrarian movement, soon to be published by the Louisiana State University Press, and a study of Davidson by Thomas Daniel Young and M. Thomas Inge, scheduled in the *Twayne United States*

Authors Series. These along with Young and Inge's 1965 volume, *Donald Davidson: An Essay and a Bibliography,* will be as indispensable as Louise Cowan's *The Fugitive Group* and her essays.

Other new essays due shortly and a chapter in this volume, "Agrarian Themes and Ideas in Southern Writing," by Virginia Rock will assist the student. The papers of Randall Stewart, Louis Rubin, and Lawrence Bowling will also retain their value, as will the review essays of John R. Doyle, Allen Tate, and John Crowe Ransom, and the Introduction to *The Spyglass, Views and Reviews, 1924–1930* by John Tyree Fain—plus critical reviews of the aforementioned hostile critics.

The immediate business of Davidson scholarship should be to read the individual poems as thoroughly as possible, to read them in context—and therefore to read them as reflections of only one of many interacting facets of a unified sensibility. A similar procedure is required by his essays. For these reasons, the literary historian has work to do. It will be necessary to determine Davidson's literary antecedents; and *his* understanding of Western, American, and Southern history must be explained—learned from the inside. Above and beyond published evidence, there is a wealth of manuscript material, much of it already on deposit at Vanderbilt University. It supplements the Tennessean's already available reminiscences in *Southern Writers in the Modern World* (Athens, Georgia, 1958) and elsewhere. Even if Davidson's craftsmanship were far less impressive than it is, the scope of his influence on readers, friends, and students calls for a full-scale literary biography. For he is indisputably one of the central figures in the Southern Renaissance.

Beatty, Richmond Croom, "Donald Davidson as Fugitive-Agrarian," in Rubin and Jacobs, *Southern Renascence*, pp. 392–412.

Bowling, Lawrence E., "An Analysis of Davidson's 'Lee in the Mountains,'" *GaR*, VI, (1952), pp. 69–88.

Bradbury, John M., *The Fugitives, A Critical Account* (Chapel Hill, 1958), pp. 24–26, 68–74, 263–65, *passim*.

Bradford, M. E., "A Comment on the Poetry of Davidson," *MissQ*, XIX (1966), 41–43. [on Davidson's "monument" poems, "On a Replica of the Parthenon" and "Twilight on Union Street"]

———, "A Durable Fire: Donald Davidson and the Profession of Letters," *SoR*, n.s., III (1967), 721–41. [r essay]

———, "Meaning and Metaphor in Donald Davidson's 'A Touch of Snow,'" *SoR*, n.s., II (Summer 1966), 516–23.

Cowan, Louise, "Donald Davidson: The 'Long Street,'" in *Reality and Myth*, pp. 98–116. [emphasis on later poetry]

———, "The Communal World of Southern Literature," *GaR*, XIV (1960), 248–57. [esp 255–56]

———, *The Fugitive Group: A Literary History* (Baton Rouge, 1959). [throughout]

―――, "The *Pietas* of Southern Poetry," in Rubin and Jacobs, *South*, pp. 95–114. [esp 95–98]

Doyle, John R., "Pacing the Long Street with Donald Davidson," *SeR*, LXXIV (1966), 946–50. [r essay]

Eaton, Charles Edward, "Donald Davidson and the Dynamics of Nostalgia," *GaR*, XX (1966), 261–69. [r essay]

Fain, John Tyree, intro to Donald Davidson, *The Spyglass, Views and Reviews, 1924-1930* (Nashville, 1963), pp. v–xviii.

Fletcher, John Gould, "The Modern Southern Poets," *Westminster Mag*, XXIII (1935). 229–51. [esp 233–36]

Karanikas, Alexander, *Tillers of a Myth: Southern Agrarians as Social and Literary Critics* (Madison, Wis., 1966), pp. 13–14, *passim*.

Kirk, Russell, "The Poet as Guardian: Donald Davidson," *NatR*, XIII (July 17, 1962), 25. Repr in Kirk, *Confessions of a Bohemian Tory* (New York, 1963), pp. 152–55. [r essay]

Montgomery, Marion, "Bells for John Stewart's Burden: A Sermon upon the Desirable Death of the 'New Provincialism' Here Typified," *GaR*, XX (1966), 145–81. [148–53 et seq]

*Pratt, William, "In Pursuit of the Fugitives," Pratt ed., *The Fugitive Poets* (New York, 1965), pp. 13–46. [pp. 42–43 *passim*]

Ransom, John Crowe, "The Most Southern Poet," *SeR*, LXX (1962), 202–207. [r essay]

*Rock, Virginia, "The Making and Meaning of *I'll Take My Stand*: A Study in Utopian Conservatism, 1925–1939," Minnesota, 1961, 474–84 *et passim*. [diss; several essays drawn from her more recent work are listed above under "Agrarian Themes and Ideas in Southern Writing"]

Rubin, Louis D., Jr., "The Concept of Nature in Modern Southern Poetry," *AQ*, IX (Spring 1957), 63–71. [esp 65–67]

*―――, "Four Southerners," in *American Poetry*, ed. John R. Brown, Bernard Harris, and Irwin Ehrenpreis (London, 1965; New York, 1966), pp. 11–43. [Stratford-upon-Avon Studies No. 7; see esp pp. 21–24]

―――, "The Poetry of Agrarianism," in *The Faraway Country*, pp. 155–84. [esp. pp. 161–65; this and the other overlapping Rubin papers listed above are concerned with Davidson's pre-1945 poetry]

Stewart, John Lincoln, *The Burden of Time: The Fugitives and Agrarians* (Princeton, 1965), pp. 15–17, 46–47, 52–55, 58–59, 118–24, *et passim*. Rev of "The Fugitive-Agrarian Writers: A History and a Criticism," Ohio State, 1947. [diss]

Stewart, Randall, "Donald Davidson," in Rubin and Jacobs, *South*, pp. 248–59. Repr in George Core, ed., *Regionalism and Beyond: Essays of Randall Stewart* (Nashville, 1968), pp. 241–54. [on the total career]

Tate, Allen, "The Gaze Past, The Glance Present," *SeR*, LXX (1962), 671–73. [r essay]

*Young, Thomas Daniel, and M. Thomas Inge, *Donald Davidson: An Essay and a Bibliography* (Nashville, 1965). [indispensable lists of Davidson's pub, of r of his work, and of other crit through 1964; essay is a reading and a study of the composition, from ms evidence, of "Lee in the Mountains"]

M. E. BRADFORD
University of Dallas
Irving, Texas

SAMUEL DAVIES (1723-1761)

See in addition to the checklist below, W. W. Sweet, *Religion in Colonial America;* W. B. Sprague, *Annals of the American Pulpit;* W. M. Gewhr, *The Great Awakening in Virginia;* the fourteen editions of Davies' sermons in London, New York, and Philadelphia from 1766–1771 to 1864. In my opinion Davies will emerge in the next decade as the great literary figure of the South of the generation before the Revolution. All authorities proclaim him the greatest pulpit orator of the eighteenth century in this country, not excluding Jonathan Edwards. The new complete edition of his diary will give him new significance as an introspective Calvinist thinker. The edition of his poems includes his one published volume of fifty (in 1752) plus some forty-odd now first collected.

DAB, V, pp. 102–103; *Duyckinck,* p. 271; *Hubbell,* pp. 51–55, *930.

Benson, Louis F., "President Davies as Hymn Writer," *Jour Presby Hist,* II (1904), 277–86, 343–73.

Bost, George H., "Samuel Davies, Preacher of the Great Awakening," *Jour Presby Hist,* XXVI (1948), 65–86.

———, "Samuel Davies as President of Princeton," *Jour Presby Hist,* XXVI (1948), 165–81.

———, "Samuel Davies, the South's Great Awakener," *Jour Presby Hist,* XXXIII (1955), 135–55.

Davis, Richard Beale, intro to *Collected Poems of Samuel Davies* (Gainesville, 1968).

Gilborn, Craig, "Samuel Davies' Sacred Muse," *Jour Presby Hist,* XLI (1963), 63–79.

Gummere, Richard M., "Samuel Davies: Classical Champion of Religious Freedom," *Jour Presby Hist,* XL (1962), 67–74.

Heimert, Alan, *Religion and the American Mind: From the Great Awakening to the Revolution* (Cambridge, Mass., 1966), *passim.*

Pilcher, George W., intro to *The Reverend Samuel Davies Abroad: The Diary of a Journey to England and Scotland 1753–1755* (Urbana, Ill., 1967), pp. ix–xiii.

RICHARD BEALE DAVIS
University of Tennessee
Knoxville, Tennessee

JAMES DICKEY (1923–)

James Dickey is the best known poet to emerge in the South since World War II. His individual collections have received increasing critical attention since *Drowning With Others* (1962), his second volume. Many of the best reviews appear in little magazines, which are ignored in Mary Lillis Latimer's incomplete bibliography. Dickey has been violently anti-academic in his reviews of contemporary poets; therefore, when the academic poets review his books, they are something less than objective. (The student of his poetry must read *The Suspect in Poetry*, a paperback collection of his almost lethal reviews and essays on the nature of poetry.)

Recently Dickey has become good copy. Journalists and *Life* writers have discovered him and helped turn him into the Hemingway of the poets: the giant, hairy-chested war hero who is a guitar-playing hunter and fisherman who writes man-sized poems about copulation and bombing the Japs. As is the case with Hemingway, the public image has a way of getting between the reader and the poems.

Now that *Buckdancer's Choice* has won the National Book Award, and Dickey has been writing steadily for a decade, scholars are beginning to assess his poetry, but there is a need for more objective appraisals and analyses of his more ambitious later poems. Richard J. Calhoun's study of his poetic development will appear in *Modern American Poetry: Essays in Criticism* (Everett Edwards Press, DeLand, Florida) in the spring of 1969.

Berry, Wendell, "James Dickey's New Book," *Poetry*, CV (Nov, 1964), 130–31. [r essay]

Bly, Robert, "*Buckdancer's Choice*," *The Sixties*, IX (Spring 1957), 70–79.

[———] "Crunk," "The Work of James Dickey," *The Sixties*, VII (Winter 1964), 41–57.

Davidson, Peter, "The Difficulties of Being Major: The Poetry of Robert Lowell and James Dickey," *Atlantic*, CCXX (Oct 1963), 116–21.

Corrington, John William, "James Dickey's Poems, 1957–1967: A Personal Appraisal," *GaR*, XXII (1968), 12–23.

Dickey, James, *The Suspect in Poetry* (Madison, Minn, 1964). [collection of Dickey's crit]

Goldman, Michael, "Inventing the American Heart," *Nation*, CCIV (Apr 17, 1967), 529–30. [r essay]

Howard, Richard, "On James Dickey," *PartisanR*, XXXIII (1966), 414–28, 479–86.

Kizer, Carolyn, and James Boatwright, "A Conversation with James Dickey," *Shen*, XVIII (Autumn 1966), 3–28. [interv devoted more to discussion of sex than to Dickey's poems]

*Latimer, Mary Lillis, "James Dickey: A Bibliography," Bibl and Reference Correspondence Section, Reference Dept, Lib of Congress (Sept 1966). [incomplete mimeographed bibl]

Nemerov, Howard, "Poems of Darkness and a Specialized Light," *SeR*, LXXI (1963), 99–104. [r essay]

O'Neil, Paul, "The Unlikeliest Poet," *Life*, LXI (July 22, 1966), 68–70, 72–79.

Roberts, Carey, "How James Dickey Views Poetry," *Atlanta Jour and Constitution Mag*, Apr 17, 1966. [newsp art]

Taylor, William E., "The Champ," *Florida Poetry And . . .,* I (Fall 1967). [r essay]

Weatherly, H. L., "The Way of Exchange in James Dickey's Poetry," *SeR*, LXXIV (1966), 669–80.

Wheelock, John Hall, "Introductory Essay: Some Thoughts on Poetry," *Poets of Today*, VII (New York, 1960), pp. 13–32. [discussion of Dickey's *Into the Stone* and work of two other poets]

GUY OWEN
North Carolina State University
Raleigh, North Carolina

THOMAS DIXON, JR. (1864-1946)

The study of Dixon's racial novels during recent years is due largely to his stand as a violent white supremacist in sharp contrast to the position of pro-Negro writers of fiction. This revival of interest has brought about the reprinting of two volumes of his once enormously popular Reconstruction Trilogy.

LSL, IV, pp. 1405–408.

Baldwin, Charles C., *The Men Who Make Our Novels* (New York, 1928), pp. 134–37.

Bloomfield, Maxwell, "Dixon's *The Leopard's Spots*: A Study in Popular Racism," *AQ*, XVI (1964), 387–401.

Carter, Everett, "Cultural History Written with Lightning: The Significance of *The Birth of a Nation*," *AQ*, XII (1960), 347–57.

*Cook, Raymond Allen, *Fire from the Flint: The Amazing Careers of Thomas Dixon* (Winston-Salem, 1968).

_____, "The Literary Principles of Thomas Dixon," *GaR*, XIII (1959), 97–102.

_____, "The Man behind *The Birth of a Nation*," *N.C. Hist R*, XXXIX (1962), 519–40.

_____, "Thomas Dixon: His Books and His Career," *DA*, XIX (1959), 2949–50 (Emory).

Crowther, Bosley, "The Birth of *The Birth of a Nation*," *New York Times Mag*, Feb. 7, 1965, pp. 24–25, 83–85.

Dedmond, F. B., "The Tar Heel Who Wrote *Birth of a Nation*," *Winston-Salem Journal and Sentinel*, Oct. 31, 1954, Sec. C, p. 4 [newsp art about unpub autobiog]

Dickey, Charles H., "Tom Dixon under 21 When Elected to Legislature," *Charlotte Observer*, Apr 19, 1934, Sec. 3, p. 4 [newsp art]

Dixon, Thomas, Jr., *The Life Worth Living: A Personal Experience* (New York, 1905).

Hamrick, Forrest, "Thomas Dixon, Jr.," *The Carolina Magazine* [Chapel Hill], LII (Feb 1922), 27–28.

McNeill, John Charles, "Thomas Dixon, Jr.," in *Biographical History of North Carolina*, ed. Samuel A. Ashe and Stephen B. Weeks (Greensboro, N.C., 1908), VII, 88–93.

Oakes, Frances, "Whitman and Dixon: A Strange Case of Borrowing," *GaR*, XI (1957), 333–40.

*Wright, J. Zeb, "Thomas Dixon: The Mind of a Southern Apologist," Peabody, 1966. [diss]

RICHARD WALSER
North Carolina State University
Raleigh, North Carolina

HARRY STILLWELL EDWARDS (1855-1938)

Very little has been published on Edwards. There is a collection of newspaper clippings and mss, including two M.A. theses, in the University of Georgia Library.

LSL, IV, pp. 1497–1501.

Garrett, George Palmer, "Old Books: *Aeneas Africanus*, by Harry Stillwell Edwards," *GaR*, XI (1957), 219–23.

Lovett, Howard Meriwether, "Harry Stillwell Edwards: An Appreciation," *So Lit Mag*, I (Sept 1923), 20, 35. Publ as pamph with same title and additional material (Macon, Ga., 1926).

Rutherford, Mildred L., "Harry Stillwell Edwards," *The South in History and Literature* (Atlanta, 1907), pp. 529–31.

JOHN O. EIDSON
Georgia Southern College
Statesboro, Georgia

WILLIAM ELLIOTT (1788-1863)

William Elliott's only well known work is *Carolina Sports by Land and Water*, which was reprinted in New York and London after the original Charleston edition of 1846. His essays and reviews, mostly on political and economic topics, are intelligent and well written but lack the charm and gusto of *Carolina Sports* and of his personal letters (many of which are in the Elliott-Gonzales Collection of the Southern

Historical Collection at the University of North Carolina). Ambrose Elliott Gonzales (1857-1926), author of Gullah dialect tales, is Elliott's grandson. There has been no critical work on Elliott since Hubbell, *The South in American Literature.*

DAB, VI, p. 101; *Duyckinck*, II, p. 100; *Hubbell*, pp. 564–68, *931–32; *LSL*, IV, pp. 1569–71.

*Jones, Lewis Pinckney, "Carolinians and Cubans: The Elliots and Gonzales, Their Work and Their Writings," North Carolina, 1952. [diss]

———, "William Elliott, South Carolina Nonconformist," *JSH* (1951), 361–81. [condensed portion of Jones's diss]

FRANK ALBRECHT
Hollins College
Hollins College, Virginia

RALPH ELLISON (1914–)

The best criticism of Ellison is his own perceptive critical work, collected in *Shadow and Act.* The interviews and comments other than this are largely critiques of *Invisible Man*, usually efforts to interpret the allegory and the historical backgrounds for his fable, or to place him in the pattern of the modern novel.

Baumbach, Jonathan, "Nightmare of a Native Son," in *The Landscape of Nightmare* (New York, 1965), pp. 68–86.

Bone, Robert A., *The Negro Novel in America* (New Haven, 1958), pp. 196–212.

Ellison, Ralph, *Shadow and Act* (New York, 1966). [collection of Ellison's best crit essay]

———, "Society, Morality, and the Novel," in *The Living Novel: A Symposium*, ed. Granville Hicks (New York, 1957), pp. 58–91.

Glicksberg, Charles I., "The Symbolism of Vision," *SWR* (1954), 259–65.

Hassan, Ihab, "The Qualified Encounter," in *Radical Innocence: Studies in the Contemporary American Novel* (Princeton, 1961), pp. 168–179.

Horowitz, Ellin, "The Rebirth of the Artist," in *On Contemporary Literature*, ed. Richard Kostelanetz (New York, 1964), pp. 330–46.

Horowitz, Floyd R., "Ralph Ellison's Modern Version of Brer Bear and Brer Rabbit in *Invisible Man*," *Midcontinent Amer Stud Jour*, IV (1963), 21–27.

Howe, Irving, "Black Boys and Native Sons," *Dissent* (1963), 353–68. [crit of *Invisible Man* evoked Ellison's reply "The World and the Jug," included in *Shadow and Act*. Howe answered Ellison in *The New Leader* Feb. 3, 1964]

Hyman, Stanley Edgar, "The Negro Writer in America: An Exchange," *PartisanR*, XXV (1958), 197–211. [Discussion of the folk tradition provoked a reply from Ellison: "Change the Joke and Slip the Yoke," in *PartisanR*, repr in *Shadow and Act*]

————, "Ralph Ellison in Our Time," *Standards: A Chronicle of Books for Our Time* (New York, 1966), pp. 249–53.

Isaacs, Harold R., "Five Writers and Their African Ancestors," *Phylon*, XXI (1960), 317–22.

Klein, Marcus, "Ralph Ellison's *Invisible Man*," *After Alienation* (Cleveland, 1964), pp. 71–146. Repr in *Images of the Negro in American Literature*, ed. Seymour L. Gross and John Edward Hardy (Chicago, 1966), pp. 249–64.

Rovit, Earl H., "Ralph Ellison and the American Comic Tradition," in *Recent American Fiction: Some Critical Views*, ed. Joseph J. Waldmeir (Boston, 1963), pp. 34–42. Repr from *WSCS* (Fall 1960), 34–42.

Warren, Robert Penn, "The Unity of Experience," *Commentary*, XXXIX (1965), 91–96.

Nancy M. Tischler
Pennsylvania State University
Capitol Campus
Middletown, Pennsylvania

WILLIAM FAULKNER (1897-1962)

Michael Millgate, *The Achievement of William Faulkner* (New York, 1966) is in most ways the place to begin in Faulkner studies. The introductory essay on Faulkner's life and career is by far the best and most reliable biographical study, despite its brevity. Subsequent chapters deal chronologically with all the novels. Professor Millgate's analyses of the novels are models of clarity and compression, and he makes use of a great deal of previously unused or unavailable material, including the collections of Faulkner manuscripts at the University of Virginia and the University of Texas. Much more full and detailed critical examinations of the thirteen Yoknapatawpha novels are contained in Cleanth Brooks, *William Faulkner: The Yoknapatawpha Country* (New Haven, 1963). One of the most distinguished works of literary criticism about an American writer ever published, this study is also of particular value for its comments on the Southern background of Faulkner and his fiction.

Although there is too much overlapping between the two books, two very useful collections of essays on Faulkner are *William Faulkner: Three Decades of Criticism*, ed. Frederick J. Hoffman and Olga W. Vickery (East Lansing, Michigan, 1960), and *Faulkner: A Collection of Critical Essays*, ed. Robert Penn Warren (Englewood Cliffs, New Jersey, 1967). In the latter, see particularly Warren's own writings on Faulkner. I have also listed several essays from *Three Decades* below as meriting special attention. Still useful for its comprehensive scope and careful critical analyses is Olga W. Vickery, *The Novels of William Faulkner* (rev ed, Baton Rouge, 1964). Warren Beck, *Man in Motion* (Madison, Wisconsin, 1963) is a brilliant study of the Snopes trilogy. Among other special critical studies, three of particular value are John W. Hunt, *William Faulkner: Art in Theological Tension* (Syracuse, 1965); John L. Longley, Jr., *The Tragic Mask: A Study of Faulkner's Heroes* (Chapel Hill, 1963); and Charles H. Nilon, *Faulkner and the Negro* (New York, 1965).

A valuable picture of Faulkner's family background and early years appears in the books by his brothers, Murry Falkner's *The Falkners of Mississippi* (Baton Rouge, 1967), and John Faulkner's *My Brother Bill* (New York, 1963), which is more comprehensive but less good. Other biographical material is provided in *William Faulkner of Oxford,* ed. James W. Webb and A. Wigfall Green (Baton Rouge, 1965); and Carvel Collins' introductions to the two collections of Faulkner's early writings he compiled are of especial biographical value: *William Faulkner: New Orleans Sketches* (New Brunswick, New Jersey, 1958), and *William Faulkner: Early Prose and Poetry* (Boston, 1962). But we still need badly a scholarly, comprehensive biography.

Though a good many of Faulkner's remarks to interviewers need to be treated with caution, the three collections of his published interviews also include some of the most interesting of all critical comments of Faulkner's fiction: *Faulkner in the University*, ed. Frederick L. Gwynn and Joseph L. Blotner (Charlottesville, 1959); *Faulkner at West Point,* ed, Joseph L. Fant and Robert Ashley (New York, 1964); and *Lion in the Garden*, ed. James B. Meriwether and Michael Millgate (New York, 1968). Faulkner's important correspondence with Malcolm Cowley is contained in *The Faulkner-Cowley File*, Cowley ed. (New York, 1966).

Bibliographical data about Faulkner's own writings appear in James B. Meriwether's *William Faulkner: A Check List* (Princeton, 1957), *The Literary Career of William Faulkner* (Princeton, 1961), and "The Text of Faulkner's Books: An Introduction and Some Notes," *MFS*, IX (1963), 159–70. For work about Faulkner, the most comprehensive listing is Maurice Beebe's "Criticism of William Faulkner: A Selected Checklist," *MFS*, XIII (1967), 115–61.

In addition, the following highly selective list of other individual critical essays and studies should prove of particular use to the Faulkner student. In choosing them from among the many hundreds that have been published on Faulkner, here and abroad, during the past forty years, I have obviously omitted a good many of real merit. But I have tried to omit those which do not add significantly to what is said in the recent books (particularly those by Brooks and Millgate) already cited, and though generally I have preferred here to call attention to recent work, I have also included a few examples of less well-known but still important older contributions to the field—a category that is not as small as it might seem.

LHUS, I, pp. 1304–306, *II, 502–503, *Supp,* 119–21.

Adams, Percy G., "Humor as Structure and Theme in Faulkner's Trilogy," *WSCL,* V (1964), 205–12.

Adams, Richard P., "The Franco-American Faulkner," *Tenn Stud in Lit,* V (1960), 1–13.

———, "The Apprenticeship of William Faulkner," *Tulane Stud in Eng,* XII (1962), 113–56.

Antrim, Harry T., "Faulkner's Suspended Style," *UR (Kansas City, Mo.), XXXII* (1965), 122–28.

Baum, Catherine B., " 'The Beautiful One': Caddy Compson as Heroine of *The Sound and the Fury,*" *MFS,* XIII (1967), 33–34.

Beck, Warren, "Faulkner: A Preface and a Letter," *YaleR,* LII (1962), 157–60.

———, "Faulkner's Point of View," *Coll Eng,* II (1941), 736–49.

———, "William Faulkner's Style," *Amer Prefaces,* VI (Spring 1941), 195–211. [repr in *Three Decades*]

Bjork, Lennart, "Ancient Myths and the Moral Framework of Faulkner's *Absalom, Absalom!*," *AL,* XXXV (1963), 196–204.

Blotner, Joseph, "William Faulkner, Roving Ambassador," *International Educational and Cultural Exchange* (U.S. Advisory Commission on International Educational and Cultural Affairs), 1966, pp. 1–22.

Bowling, Lawrence, "Faulkner: The Theme of Pride in *The Sound and the Fury,*" *MFS,* XI (1965), 129–39.

Bradford, Melvin E., "Faulkner's 'Tall Men,' " *SAQ,* LXI (1962), 29–39.

———, " 'Spotted Horses' and the Short Cut to Paradise: A Note on the Endurance Theme in Faulkner," *La Stud* (Northw St Coll of La), IV (1965), 324–31.

———, "The Winding Horn: Hunting and the Making of Men in Faulkner's 'Race at Morning,' " *Papers on Eng Lang and Lit,* I (1965), 272–78.

Brown, Calvin S., "Faulkner's Geography and Topography," *PMLA,* LXXVII (1962), 652–59.

Buckley, G. T., "Is Oxford the Original of Jefferson in William Faulkner's Novels?," *PMLA,* LXXVI (1961), 447–54.

Butor, Michel, "Les Relations de parenté dans *l'Ours* de W. Faulkner," *Lettres Nouvelles,* IV (1956), 734–45.

Coanda, Richard, "*Absalom, Absalom!*: The Edge of Infinity," *Renascence,* XI (1958), 3–9.

Coindreau, Maurice Edgar, "The Faulkner I Knew," *Shen,* XVI (1965), 27–35. Transl by James S. Patty from "Faulkner tel que je l'ae connu," *Preuves,* No. 144 (1963), 9–14.

Collins, Carvel, foreword to *The Unvanquished* (New York: Signet paperback, 1959), pp. vii–xii.

———, "The Interior Monologues of *The Sound and the Fury,*" *Eng Inst Essays, 1952,* ed. Alan Downer (New York, 1954), pp. 29–55.

———, "Miss Quentin's Paternity Again," *TSLL,* II (1960), 253–60.

———, "The Pairing of *The Sound and the Fury* and *As I Lay Dying,*" *Princeton U Lib Chron,* XVIII (1957), 114–23.

Couch, John Philip, "Camus and Faulkner: The Search for the Language of Modern Tragedy," *Yale French Stud*, No. 25 (1960), 120–25.

Daniel, Bradford, "William Faulkner and the Southern Quest for Freedom," *Black, White and Gray: Twenty-one Points of View on the Race Question*, ed. Bradford Daniel (New York, 1964), pp. 291–308.

Dickerson, Mary Jane, "Some Sources of Faulkner's Myth in *As I Lay Dying*," *MissQ*, XIX (1966), 132–42.

Douglas, Harold J., and Robert Daniel, "Faulkner and the Puritanism of the South," *Tenn Stud in Lit*, II (1957), 1–13.

Emerson, O. B., "Prophet Next Door," in *Reality and Myth*, pp. 237–74.

Farnharm, James F., "Faulkner's Unsung Hero: Gavin Stevens," *ArizQ*, XXI (1965), 115–32.

Flint, R. W., "Faulkner as Elegist," *HudR*, VII (1954), 246–57.

Garrett, George, "Faulkner's Early Literary Criticism," *TSLL*, I (1959), 3–10.

———, "An Examination of the Poetry of William Faulkner," *Princeton U Lib Chron*, XVIII (1957), 124–35.

———, "The Influence of William Faulkner," *GaR*, XVIII (1964), 419–27.

Gibbons, Kathryn Gibbs, "Quentin's Shadow," *Lit and Psychology*, XII (1962), 16–24.

Gilley, Leonard, "The Wilderness Theme in Faulkner's 'The Bear'," *MidwQ* (Pittsburg, Kansas), VI (1965), 379–85.

Gold, Joseph, "The 'Normality' of Snopesism: Universal Themes in Faulkner's *The Hamlet*," *WSCL*, III (1962), 25–34.

Greene, Theodore M., "The Philosophy of Life Implicit in Faulkner's *The Mansion*," *TSLL*, II (1961), 401–18.

Gresset, Michel, "Psychological Aspects of Evil in *The Sound and the Fury*," *MissQ*, XIX (1966), 143–53.

Hafley, James, "Faulkner's *Fable*: Dream and Transfiguration," *Accent*, XVI (1956), 3–14.

Hardy, John Edward, *Man in the Modern Novel* (Seattle, 1964), pp. 137–58.

Howell, Elmo, "William Faulkner and the Plain People of Yoknapatawpha County," *Jour of Miss Hist*, XXIV (1962), 73–87.

Inge, M. Thomas, "William Faulkner and George Washington Harris: In the Tradition of Southwestern Humor," *Tenn Stud in Lit*, VII (1962), 47–59.

Kaluza, Irena, "William Faulkner's Subjective Style," *Kwartalnik Neofilologiczny*, XI (1964), 13–29.

Knoll, Robert E., "*The Unvanquished* for a Start," *Coll Eng*, XIX (1958), 338–43.

Langston, Beach, "The Meaning of Lena Grove and Gail Hightower in *Light in August*," *Boston U Stud in Eng*, V (1961), 46–63.

Larsen, Eric, "The Barrier of Language: The Irony of Language in Faulkner," *MFS*, XIII (1967), 19–31.

Leibowitz, Herbert A., "The Snopes Dilemma and the South," *U of Kan Cy R*, XXVIII (1962), 273–84.

Lytle, Andrew, "The Son of Man: He Will Prevail," pp. 103–28, and "*The Town*: Helen's Last Stand," pp. 137–47, in *The Hero with the Private Parts* (Baton Rouge, 1966).

McHaney, Thomas L., "Faulkner Borrows from the Mississippi Guide," *MissQ*, XIX (1966), 116–20.

MacLure, Millar, "Snopes: A Faulkner Myth," *Canadian Forum*, XXXIX (1960), 245–50.

Meriwether, James B., "Notes on the Textual History of *The Sound and the Fury*," *Pub of Bibl Soc of Amer*, LVI (1962), 285–316.

Moldenhauer, Joseph L., "Unity of Theme and Structure in *The Wild Palms*," in Hoffman and Vickery, eds., *William Faulkner: Three Decades of Criticism*, pp. 305–22.

Monteiro, George, "Bankruptcy in Time: A Reading of William Faulkner's *Pylon*," *Twentieth Cent Lit*, IV (1958), 9–20.

Price-Stephens, Gordon, "The British Reception of William Faulkner, 1929–1962," *MissQ*, XVIII (1965), 119–200.

Pusey, William Webb, III, "William Faulkner's Works in Germany to 1940: Translations and Criticism," *GermanicR*, XXX (1955), 211–26.

Reeves, Carolyn H., "*The Wild Palms*: Faulkner's Chaotic Cosmos," *MissQ*, XX (1967), 148–57.

Riedel, F. C., "Faulkner as Stylist," *SAQ*, LVI (1957), 462–79.

Rossky, William, "*The Reivers*: Faulkner's *Tempest*," *MissQ*, XVIII (1965), 82–93.

Sandeen, Ernest, "William Faulkner: His Legend and His Fable," *R of Politics* (Notre Dame), XVIII (1956), 47–68.

Scholes, Robert, "Myth and Manners in *Sartoris*," *GaR*, XVI (1962), 195–201.

Schwartz, Delmore, "William Faulkner's 'A Fable,'" *Perspectives U.S.A.*, No. 10 (1955), 126–36.

Simon, John K., "The Scene and the Imagery of Metamorphosis in *As I Lay Dying*," *Criticism*, VII (1965), 1–22.

Simpson, Lewis P., "Isaac McCaslin and Temple Drake: The Fall of New World Man," *Nine Essays in Modern Literature (La State U Stud, Hum Ser*, No. 15), ed. Donald E. Stanford (Baton Rouge, 1965), pp. 88–106.

[Sister Kristin] Morrison, "Faulkner's Joe Christmas: Character Through Voice," *TSLL*, II (1961), 419–43.

Slabey, Robert M., "Joe Christmas: Faulkner's Marginal Man," *Phylon*, XXI (1960), 266–77.

Straumann, Heinrich, "An American Interpretation of Existence: Faulkner's *A Fable*," in Hoffman and Vickery eds., *William Faulkner: Three Decades of Criticism*, pp. 349–72.

Sultan, Stanley, "Call Me Ishmael: The Hagiography of Isaac McCaslin," *TSLL*, III (1961), 50–66.

Sutherland, Ronald, "*As I Lay Dying*: A Faulkner Microcosm," *Queen's Q*, LXXIII (1966), 541–49.

Taylor, Nancy Dew, "The Dramatic Productions of *Requiem for a Nun*," *MissQ*, XX (1967), 123–34.

Torchiana, Donald T., "Faulkner's *Pylon* and the Structure of Modernity," *MFS*, III (1957), 291–308.

Turner, Arlin, "William Faulkner, Southern Novelist," *MissQ*, XIV (1961), 117–30.

Walker, William E., "*The Unvanquished*: The Restoration of Tradition," in *Reality and Myth*, ed. Walker and Welker, pp. 275–97.

Warren, Joyce W., "Faulkner's 'Portrait of the Artist,'" *MissQ*, XIX (1966), 121–31.

Watkins, Floyd C., "William Faulkner, the Individual, and the World," *GaR*, XIV (1960), 238–47.

Webb, James W., "Faulkner Writes *A Fable*," *U of Miss Stud in Eng*, VII (1966), 1–13.

Whicher, Stephen E., "The Compsons' Nancies: A Note on *The Sound and the Fury* and 'That Evening Sun,'" *AL*, XXVI (1954), 253–55.

Zink, Karl E., "William Faulkner: Form as Experience," *SAQ*, LIII (1954), 384–403.

JAMES B. MERIWETHER
University of South Carolina
Columbia, South Carolina

JOHN GOULD FLETCHER (1886-1950)

John Gould Fletcher was a Southerner who managed to be both expatriate and regionalist and a nominal member of two major modern poetic schools: the Imagists and the Fugitives. The volume and range of his writing are impressive enough in themselves, but so far only doctoral dissertations have been devoted to his work as a whole; only one biographical and critical study has as yet been published (by Edna B. Stephens in the Twayne series). The best short critique to date is probably to be found in Donald Davidson's memoir written at the time of Fletcher's death.

LHUS, II, pp. 506–507, *Supp*, p. 133.

Behrens, R., "John Gould Fletcher and Rimbaud's *Alchimie du Verbe*," *Comp Lit*, VIII (1956), 46–62.

Blackmur, R. P., "Versions of Fletcher," *Poetry*, XLVII (1936), 344–47. [r essay]

Coffman, Stanley, *Imagism: A Chapter for the History of Modern Poetry* (Norman, Okla., 1951), 175–80.

Crowder, Richard, "John Gould Fletcher as Cassandra," *SAQ*, LII (1953), 88–92.

Davidson, Donald, "In Memory of John Gould Fletcher," *Poetry*, LXXVII (1950), 154–61.

Fletcher, John Gould, *Life is My Song: The Autobiography of . . .* (New York, 1937).

Fulkerson, B., "John Gould Fletcher," *SeR*, XLVI (1938), 275–87.

Grudin, Louis, "A Naive Mystic," *Poetry*, XXI (1923), 270–75. [r essay]

Hughes, Glenn, *Imagism and the Imagists: A Study in Modern Poetry* (Stanford, 1931). ("John Gould Fletcher: Pictorialist and Mystic," 125–52.)

Kimpel, Ben, "John Gould Fletcher in Retrospect," *Poetry*, LXXXIV (1954), 284–96. [r essay]

Lowell, Amy, *Tendencies in Modern American Poetry* (Cambridge, Mass., 1917), pp. 280–343.

———, *Poetry and Poets* (Boston, 1930), pp. 137–47.

Lund, Mary Graham, "John Gould Fletcher; Geographer of the Uncharted Province of Beauty," *SeR*, LXXVI (1968), 76–89.

———, "The Love Songs of John Gould Fletcher," *MidwQ*, VII (1965), 83–91. [r essay]

Monroe, Harriet, "John Gould Fletcher," *Poetry*, XXVII (1926), 206–10.

Osborne, William R., "The Poetry of John Gould Fletcher, A Critical Analysis," Peabody, 1956. [diss]

Pound, Ezra, "Peals of Iron," *Poetry*, III (1913), 111–13. [r essay]

Pratt, William, "In Pursuit of the Fugitives," intro to *The Fugitive Poets: Modern Southern Poetry in Perspective* (New York, 1965), pp. 14–15.

Quinn, Kerker, "Story of an Arkansas Poet," *Poetry*, LVIII (1941), 334–36. [r essay]

Simon, Charlie May, *Johnswood* (New York, 1954). [memoir by Fletcher's second wife]

Stephens, Edna Buell, *John Gould Fletcher* (New York, 1967). [TUSAS]

―――, "The Oriental Influence in John Gould Fletcher's Poetry," *DA*, XXII, 264–65 (Arkansas).

Van Doren, Mark, "Poetic Space and Time," *Nation*, CXII (Apr 13, 1921), 252. [r essay]

Warren, Robert Penn, "A Note on Three Southern Poets," *Poetry*, XL (1932), 103–13. [r essay]

Webster, Harvey Curtis, "Music vs. Eloquence," *Poetry*, LXIX (1947), 353–56. [r essay]

Zabel, M. D., "Dust Discrowned," *Poetry*, XXXIII (1929), 222–24. [r essay]

Zur, Bernard Philip, "John Gould Fletcher, Poet: Theory and Practice," *DA*, XIX, 2605–606 (Northwestern).

WILLIAM C. PRATT
Miami University
Oxford, Ohio

SHELBY FOOTE (1916–)

The student looking for good criticism of Shelby Foote's novels is likely to be disappointed, because most critics have neglected them. But fortunately there are several revealing interviews which are helpful in a general way: they show something of Foote's theory of art, the writers who influenced him, and his problems as an artist. In addition, they are useful because they include some of Foote's own comments about his novels. He has also written three essays dealing with his life and work. These and the interviews are the places for the new student to begin.

Very few reviews of the novels offer any help at all. There are over fifty of them, but most are only summaries or paragraph notices and are of no value whatsoever to the student. Those reviews cited, however, offer worthwhile critical insights and must act in the place of scholarship until Foote receives the critical attention he deserves. Often novelists themselves are the most perceptive critics of other writers' works; and Miss Elizabeth Spencer, with her exceptional review of *Follow Me Down*, again proves this generalization to be true.

As for articles and essays included in books and journals, they are virtually nonexistent. The only book reference over a page long is in *South: Modern Southern Literature in Its Cultural Setting* ed. Louis D. Rubin, Jr., and Robert D. Jacobs. However, a forthcoming issue of *The Mississippi Quarterly* will be devoted entirely to Foote and will offer criticism and a bibliographical checklist of his stories, essays, and novels, as well as a more complete listing of reviews and interviews.

Breit, Harvey, "Talk with Shelby Foote," *N.Y. Times Bk R*, Apr 27, 1952, p. 16. [interv, also autobiog]

Covington, Jimmie, "Writer's Home Has Windows on Past, Present" (Memphis) *Commercial Appeal*, Aug 21, 1966, Sec. I, p. 15. [interv]

Edmundson, Charles, "Shelby Foote Continues [Civil War] Trilogy, Writing Another Novel," (Memphis) *Commercial Appeal*, Nov 27, 1961, p. 17. [inter, also autobiog]

Flint, F. Cudworth, "Nine First Novels," *SeR*, LIX (1951), 137–51. [r of *Tournament*, pp. 142–43]

Flowers, Paul, "The Greenville Tradition," (Memphis) *Commercial Appeal*, June 21, 1953, Sec V, p. 12. [interv, also shows one page of ms from *Shiloh*]

Foote, Shelby, intro to *The Night before Chancellorsville and Other Civil War Stories* (New York, 1957), pp. vii–ix. [essay]

———, "About the Authors," in *New Short Novels*, ed. Mary Louise Aswell (New York, 1954), p. 189. [autobiog essay, also views on writing]

———, "The Novelist's View of History," *MissQ*, XVII (1964), 219–25. [essay]

Maloney, John J., "Eight Ways of Looking at a Murder in Mississippi," *N.Y. Her Trib Bk R*, July 16, 1950, p. 6. [r of *Follow Me Down*]

*Meriwether, James B., List of Foote's books, in Rubin and Jacobs, *South* p. 408. [also, see pp. 377–79.]

Mudrick, Marvin, r of *Jordan County*, *Shen*, VI (Winter 1954), 73–78.

Spencer, Elizabeth, "Author & Critic Predicts Second Foote Book May Mark Emergence of New Leading Novelist" (Greenville, Miss.) *Delta Democrat-Times*, June 25, 1950, p. 17. [r of *Follow Me Down*]

———, "Foot's [sic] Third Novel Scores with Theme Centered on Money" (Greenville, Miss.) *Delta Democrat-Times*, Sept 23, 1951, p. 18. [r of *Love in a Dry Season*]

Vincent, Edwin, "Shelby Foote, Greenville Author Says Writing Is His Hardest Job" (Greenville, Miss.) *Delta Democrat-Times*, June 25, 1950, pp. 1–2. [interv, also autobiog, and material on *Jordan County*]

JAMES E. KIBLER, JR.
University of South Carolina
Columbia, South Carolina

JOHN FOX, JR. (1863-1919)

John Fox, Jr., is the abiding symbol of the Bluegrass region of Kentucky and of the Southern Appalachians, but there is virtually no critical literature on Fox. His family, enthusiasts for Kentuckiana, and graduate students in search of thesis topics are the main contributors to his bibliography and all are infatuated with the local-color aspects of his work.

Factual resumés of Fox's full-length fiction may be found in *The Kentucky Novel* (1953) by Lawrence S. and Algernon D. Thompson. The two biographies are uneven. Lieutenant Harold Everett Green's *Towering Pines* (1943) is cited only as what a biography should not be. It is full of error. Mrs. Cabell Moore's *John Fox, Jr. : Personal and Family Letters and Papers* (1955) should be a point of departure for the much-needed definitive study of Fox as a prototype of the American local-color author of the turn of the century. Manuscript collections at the University of Virginia and the University of Kentucky will also be basic sources. The "Kentucky Authors Scrapbook" in the Louisville Free Public Library contains other source material. Mrs. Moore, now residing at the Fox home in Big Stone Gap, Virginia, and other residents of the area should be interviewed for their memoirs of Fox before it is too late.

DAB, VI, p. 570; *LSL*, IV, pp. 1683–88.

Blanck, "John William Fox, Jr.," in *Bibliography of American Literature*, III, pp. 212–16.

*Brame, Walter H., "The Life and Longer Stories of John Fox, Jr.," Peabody, 1933. [MA thesis]

Creason, Joe, "The Lonesome Pine's Gone from the Trail," *Louisville* (Ky.) *Courier-Jour Mag*, February 22, 1961, p. 16. [other articles by Mr. Creason on Fox and locale of his work in *Courier-Jour* on Feb 22, 1948, June 12, 1949, Nov 12, 1950, and Jul 9, 1957, all except last in *Mag*]

Green, Harold Everett, *Towering Pines: The Life of John Fox, Jr.* (Boston, 1943). [unreliable]

"John Fox, Jr., and His Kentucky," *Nation*, CIX (1919), 72–73.

*Kruger, Arthur Newman, "The Life and Works of John Fox, Jr.," Louisiana, 1941. [diss]

Lawson, Morgan, "In the Spirit of Christmas," *Louisville* (Ky.) *Courier-Jour Mag*, Dec 10, 1961, pp. 58, 60. [includes repr of "Christmas Eve on Lonesome"]

Moore, Elizabeth Fox (Mrs. William Cabell Moore), *John Fox, Jr.: Personal and Family Letters and Papers* (Lexington, Ky., 1955).

Moore, William Cabell, *John Fox, Jr.* (n.p., 1957.) [caption title: "An address delivered Oct. 21, 1957, at the Club of Colonial Dames, Washington, D.C."]

*Osborn, Scott Compton, "A Study and Contrast of the Kentucky Mountaineer and the Blue Grass Aristocrat in the Works of John Fox, Jr.," Kentucky, 1939. [MA thesis]

*Page, Ruth Eubank, "John Fox, Jr., and His Mountain Folk," Texas, 1938. [MA thesis]

*Sheeran, Joseph A., "John Fox, Jr., a Critical Appreciation," Catholic University, 1939. [MA thesis]

Thompson, Lawrence S., and Algernon D., *The Kentucky Novel* (Lexington, Ky., [1953]) [short commentary on Fox in intro; resumés of all of Fox's full-length novels, pp. 54–61]

*Titus, Warren I., "John Fox, Jr.," *Amer Lit Realism*, No. III (1968), 5–8.

*Townsend, John Wilson, *Kentucky in American Letters 1784–1912.* intro by James Lane Allen (Cedar Rapids, Iowa, 1913), 2 vols. [biog and crit comment, short bibl, II, pp. 172–184]

U.S. Works Projects Administration, "John Fox, Jr.," *Kentucky Biography, Biographical and Critical Materials Pertaining to Kentucky Authors* (Louisville, 1941), II, pp. 69–75. [Louisville Lib Coll, Biog Ser, No. 2]

Wagenknecht, Edward, *Cavalcade of The American Novel* (New York, 1952), pp. 196–97.

LAWRENCE S. THOMPSON
University of Kentucky
Lexington, Kentucky

GEORGE GARRETT (1929–)

George Garrett's work (at this writing: three novels, four books of poems, three books of stories, and several plays and screenplays) has yet to receive the serious critical attention it deserves. James Meriwether's essay and checklist is certainly the most useful item for future Garrett scholarship which has yet appeared. What articles there are in scattered and often unlikely places are good ones, but his work is of a high quality deserving intelligent and detailed consideration. Hopefully, such attention will be forthcoming.

Alexander, Bevin, "The Kandy-Kolored Playboy-Flake Streamline Faerie Queene, or a Portrait of a Writer as a University Student," *U of Va Alumni News*, LIV (Dec 1965), 4–6. [mag article]

Deutsch, Babette, r of *The Sleeping Gypsy*, N.Y. Her Trib Bk R, Aug 3, 1958, p. 4.

———, r of *Abraham's Knife*, N.Y. Her Trib Bk R, July 30, 1961, pp. 6–7.

Dillard, R. H. W., "Cold Ground Was My Bed Last Night," in *Masterplots 1965 Annual*, ed. Frank N. Magill and Dayton Kohler (New York, 1965), pp. 47–50. [essay r]

———, "Do, Lord, Remember Me," in *Masterplots 1966 Annual*, ed. Frank N. Magill and Dayton Kohler (New York, 1967), pp. 74–77. [essay r]

Garrett, George, "The Triumph of Shinola," *The Hanging Dog News*, II (Apr 1966),

3–4, 10. [essay on fict with autobiog anecdote]

———, "Don't Make Waves," in *Man and the Movies,* ed. W. R. Robinson (Baton Rouge, 1967), pp. 227–60. [autobiog essay about writing for movies]

*Meriwether, James B., "George Palmer Garrett, Jr.," *Princeton U Lib Chron,* XXV (Autumn 1963). 26–39. This issue was also released as a book, *Seven Princeton Poets,* ed. Sherman Hawkins (Princeton, 1963). [essay and checklist]

Robinson, William, "The Fiction of George Garrett," in *Red Clay Reader II* (Charlotte, 1965), pp. 15–16.

Soellner, Hedda, afterword to *Die Rivallen* (Munich, 1960), pp. 155–57. [intro to collection of Garrett's stories in transl]

Wheelock, John Hall, "To Recapture Delight," intro to *Poets of Today IV* (New York, 1957), pp. 3–17. [intro to Garrett's first bk of poems, *The Reverend Ghost*]

R. H. W. DILLARD
Hollins College
Hollins College, Virginia

CHARLES GAYARRÉ (1805-1895)

DAB, VII, pp. 196–97; *Duyckinck,* II, p. 401; *Hubbell,* pp. 650–57, *932–33; *LHUS* II, pp. 529–30, *Supp,* 130; *LSL,* IV, pp. 1773–75.

Anderson, Charles R., "Charles Gayarré and Paul Hayne: The Last Literary Cavaliers," in Jackson, ed., *American Studies in Honor of William Kenneth Boyd,* pp. 221–81.

*Dart, Henry Plauche, ed., "Autobiography of Charles Gayarré," *La Hist Q,* XII (1929), 5–27.

Davidson, James W., *The Living Writers of the South* (New York, 1869), pp. 216–23.

Fortier, Alcée, *Louisiana Studies: Literature, Customs and Dialects, History and Education* (New Orleans, 1894), pp. 24–25, 92–93, 102, 113–14.

Hayne, Paul Hamilton, "Charles Gayarré: The Statesman," *So Bivouac,* n.s., II (1886), 28–37.

———, "Charles Gayarré: The Author," *So Bivouac,* n.s., II (1886), 108–13, 172–76.

Kendall, John Smith, "The Last Days of Charles Gayarré," *La Hist Q,* XV (1932), 359–75.

King Grace, "Charles Gayarré," *Creole Families of New Orleans* (New York, 1921), pp. 269–90.

———, "Charles Gayarré: A Biographical Sketch," *La Hist Q,* XXXIII (1950), 159–88.

———, *Memories of a Southern Woman of Letters* (New York, 1932), pp. 30–45.

La Hist Q, "Some Letters of Charles Etienne Gayarré on Literature and Politics," XXXIII, (1950), 223–54.

Matas, Rudolph, M.D., "An Evening with Gayarré," *La Hist Q,* XXXIII (1950), 269–93. [includes Gayarré's address to the New Orleans Med and Surg Assn, Dec 3, 1887]

Nelson, John Herbert, "Charles Gayarré, Historian and Romancer," *SeR*, XXXIII (1925), 427–38.

Parsons, Edward Alexander, "Some Inedited Gayarré Manuscripts," *La Hist Q*, XXXIII (1950), 189–204.

Richardson, Frank D., "A Last Evening with Judge Gayarré," *La Hist Q*, XIV (1931), 81–85.

*Saucier, Earl N., "Charles Gayarré, the Creole Historian," Peabody, 1934. [diss]

*Socola, Edward, "Charles E. A. Gayarré: A Biography," Pennsylvania, 1954. [diss]

*Tinker, Edward L., "Charles Gayarré, 1805–95," *Papers of the Bibl Soc of Amer*, XXVII, part 1 (1933), 24–64.

Yearns, Wilford B., Jr., "Charles Gayarré, Louisiana's Literary Historian," *La Hist Q*, XXXIII (1950), 255–68.

ARLIN TURNER
Duke University
Durham, North Carolina

FRANCES WALKER GILMER (1790-1826)

Unpublished letters in the University of Virginia, the Virginia Historical Society, and other repositories reveal more about Gilmer as a major critical mind of the First National period than has material already published. His social, economic, scientific, and artistic theories deserve further study. Though he seems to have written verse, none is known to survive.

DAB, VII, p. 306; *Hubbell*, pp. 242–43, *933.

Davis, John H., "Francis Walker Gilmer, Prodigy and Prophet," *SwU Bull*, XXI, n.s., No. 3 (1934).

Davis, Richard Beale, "The Early American Lawyer and the Profession of Letters," *Huntington Lib Q*, XII (1949), 191–205.

———, "Forgotten Scientists in Georgia and South Carolina," *Ga Hist Q*, XXVII (1943), 271–84.

———, "Forgotten Scientists in Old Virginia," *VMHB*, XLVI (1938), 97–111.

———, *Francis Walker Gilmer: Life and Learning in Jefferson's Virginia* (Richmond, 1939).

*———, *Intellectual Life in Jefferson's Virginia, 1790–1830* (Chapel Hill, 1964), *passim*.

———, "Literary Tastes in Virginia before Poe," *WMQ*, 2nd ser, XIX (1939), 55–68.

Trent, William Peterfield, *English Culture in Virginia* (Baltimore, 1889).

RICHARD BEALE DAVIS
University of Tennessee
Knoxville, Tennessee

ELLEN GLASGOW (1874-1945)

Ellen Glasgow's significance is still overestimated or understated. At this moment her importance is mostly underrated; she appears in anthologies and histories of American literature far less frequently and extensively than writers of lesser stature such as Mary Wilkins Freeman, Sarah Orne Jewett, Mary Noailles Murfree, and Joel Chandler Harris. Present critical neglect mostly springs from the unavailability of her work, the result apparently of a change of publisher late in her career. Major novels such as *The Deliverance, The Miller of Old Church, Virginia, The Romantic Comedians, They Stooped to Folly*, and *The Sheltered Life* are out of print. Of first importance, then, is the reprinting of her major books. Critical editions of those novels which she revised most radically (*The Voice of the People, The Deliverance, The Miller of Old Church*, and *Virginia*) would be helpful. Her last novel, *Beyond Defeat*, has been edited by Luther Gore (Charlottesville, 1966). Richard K. Meeker has edited *The Collected Stories of Ellen Glasgow* (Baton Rouge, 1963), including four uncollected stories and one manuscript story. Ellen Glasgow's essays are informative and should be brought together—one or two important unpublished essays remain—to supplement "Literary Realism or Nominalism," edited by Gore, *American Literature*, XXXIV (March, 1962), 72–79. William W. Kelley's *Ellen Glasgow: A Bibliography* (Charlottesville, 1964) is standard and not likely soon to be superseded; the preface contains a useful summary of her career. The *Letters of Ellen Glasgow*, edited by Blair Rouse (New York, 1958) are incomplete, especially for the crucial years 1900–1920; many new letters are already available, including the series to Maxwell Perkins from the 1930s. When letters to her family and to James Branch Cabell can be made public, a complete edition of the correspondence will be essential. A critical biography is needed, although the obstacles to its completion are formidable. Ellen Glasgow remains a controversial figure in Richmond; and the difficulties alone in documenting and interpreting her autobiography, *The Woman Within* (New York, 1954), are great. Her artistry, her relation to Southern social history, and her relationships to the European, American, and Southern literary traditions require fuller study than Louis D. Rubin, Jr., Frederick P. W. McDowell, and Louis Auchincloss have accorded them. The complex of social, ethical, philosophical, and religious values out of which Ellen Glasgow wrote require sharper definition than they have received from Monique Parent and from

Joan Santas in *Ellen Glasgow's American Dream* (Charlottesville, 1965).

In this listing I have not included materials mentioned by title in the above paragraph.

Hubbell, 842–45; *LSL*, IV, pp. 1847–49; *LHUS*, I, pp. 1216–19, *II, 532–33, *Supp*, 130–31.

*Auchincloss, Louis, *Ellen Glasgow* (Minneapolis, 1964) [Minn pamph]; Repr in Auchincloss, *Pioneers and Caretakers* (Minneapolis, 1965).

Bradbury, *Renaissance in the South*, pp. 43–44.

Cabell, James Branch, "Miss Glasgow of Virginia," in *Let Me Lie* (New York, 1947), pp. 229–67. [rev Cabell's earlier articles]

———, "Speaks with Candor of a Great Lady," *As I Remember It* (New York, 1955), pp. 217–33.

Clark, Emily, "Ellen Glasgow," in *Innocence Abroad* (New York, 1931), pp. 55–69.

Commager, Henry Steele, *The American Mind: An Interpretation of American Thought and Character since the 1880's* (New Haven, 1950), pp. 56, 65–66, 145–47.

Fishwick, Marshall W., *Virginia: A New Look at the Old Dominion* (New York, 1959), pp. 185–95, *passim*.

Geismar, Maxwell, "The Armor of the Legend," in *Rebels and Ancestors: The American Novel, 1890–1915* (Boston, 1953), pp. 219–86, *passim*.

*Glasgow, Ellen, *A Certain Measure: An Interpretation of Prose Fiction* (New York, 1943). [repr rev prefaces from Virginia ed and preface for *In This Our Life*]

———, "Ellen Glasgow," in *I Believe: The Personal Philosophies of Certain Eminent Men and Women of Our Time*, ed. Clifton Fadiman (New York, 1939), pp. 93–110.

Hardy, John Edward, "Ellen Glasgow," in Rubin and Jacobs, *Southern Renascence*, pp. 236–50.

Hoffman, Frederick J., *The Modern Novel in America, 1900–1950* (Chicago, 1951), pp. 65–75, *passim*. [rev ed, 1965]

Holman, C. Hugh, "Ellen Glasgow and the Southern Literary Tradition," in *Virginia in History and Tradition*, ed. R. C. Simonini, Jr. (Farmville, Va., 1958), pp. 85–105. Repr in Simonini, ed., *Southern Writers*, pp. 103–23.

———, "Ellen Glasgow: The Novelist of Manners as Social Critic," in *Three Modes of Modern Southern Fiction: Ellen Glasgow, William Faulkner, Thomas Wolfe* (Athens, Ga., 1966), pp. 11–25, *passim*.

Jones, Howard Mumford, "Ellen Glasgow, Witty, Wise and Civilized," *N.Y. Her Trib Bks*, XIV (Jul 24, 1938), pp. 1–2. [r essay, Va. edition]

Kazin, Alfred, *On Native Grounds* (New York, 1942), pp. 247–49, 257–64.

Kilmer, Joyce, "Evasive Idealism in Literature," in *Literature in the Making*, ed. Joyce Kilmer (New York, 1917), pp. 229–38. [interv]

*McDowell, Frederick P. W., *Ellen Glasgow and the Ironic Art of Fiction* (Madison, Wis., 1960).

Monroe, N. Elizabeth, "Contemplation of Manners in Ellen Glasgow," in *The Novel and Society* (Chapel Hill, 1941), pp. 139–87, *passim*.

*Parent, Monique, *Ellen Glasgow, Romancière* (Paris, 1962).

*Quinn, "Ellen Glasgow and the New South," *American Fiction*, pp. 670–82.

*Rouse, Blair, *Ellen Glasgow* (New York, 1962). [TUSAS]

Rubin, Louis D., Jr., *No Place on Earth: Ellen Glasgow, James Branch Cabell and Richmond-in-Virginia* (Austin, Tex., 1959). [Supp *TQ*, II (Autumn 1959)]

———, "Two in Richmond: Ellen Glasgow and James Branch Cabell," Rubin and

Jacobs, in *South*, pp. 115–41. [rev of *No Place On Earth*, above]

*Wagenknecht, Edward, "Ellen Glasgow: Triumph and Despair," in *The Cavalcade of the American Novel* (New York, 1952), pp. 267–80.

FREDERICK P. W. McDOWELL
University of Iowa
Iowa City, Iowa

CAROLINE GORDON (1895–)

There is no full-length study of Caroline Gordon's novels and stories, but there have been several general essays beginning with Robert Penn Warren's as well as Frederick P. W. McDowell's recent pamphlet. Joan Griscom's bibliography lists a few perceptive reviews by Katherine Anne Porter and others.

LHUS, II, *Supp*, pp. 222–23.

Brown, Ashley, "The Novel as Christian Comedy," in Walker and Welker, *Reality and Myth*, pp. 161–78. [on *The Malefactors* and Dante's *Purgatorio*]

Cheney, Brainard, "Caroline Gordon's Ontological Quest," *Renascence*, XVI (Fall 1963), 3–12.

Cowan, Louise, "Nature and Grace in Caroline Gordon," *Crit*, I (Winter 1956), 11–27.

Fletcher, Marie, "The Fate of Woman in the Changing South: A Persistent Theme in the Fiction of Caroline Gordon," *MissQ*, XXI (1967–68), 17–28.

Ford, Ford Madox, "A Stage in American Literature," *Bookman*, LXXIV (1931), 371–76. [on *Penhally*]

*Griscom, Joan, "Bibliography of Caroline Gordon," *Crit*, I (Winter 1956), 74–78.

Heilman, Robert B., "School for Girls," *SeR*, LX (1952) 293–302. [on *The Strange Children*]

Hoffman, Frederick J., "Caroline Gordon: The Special Yield," *Crit*, I (Winter 1956), 29–35.

Koch, Vivienne, *The Conservatism of Caroline Gordon*, in Rubin and Jacobs, *Southern Renascence*, pp. 325–37.

Lytle, Andrew, "Caroline Gordon and the Historic Image," *SeR*, LVII (1949), 560–86.

———, "The Forest of the South," *Crit*, I (Winter 1956), 3–9.

McDowell, Frederick P. W., *Caroline Gordon* (Minneapolis, 1966). [Minn pamph]

O'Connor, William Van, "The Novel of Experience," *Crit*, I (Winter 1956), 37–44.

Rocks, James E., "The Mind and Art of Caroline Gordon," *Miss Q*, XXI (1967–68), 1–16.

Thorp, Willard, "The Way Back and the Way Up: The Novels of Caroline Gordon," *Bucknell R*, VI (Dec 1956), 1–15. See also Thorp, *American Writing in the Twentieth Century* (Cambridge, Mass., 1960), pp. 249–52.

Warren, Robert Penn, "The Fiction of Caroline Gordon," *SWR*, XX (1934), 5–10.

ASHLEY BROWN
University of South Carolina
Columbia, South Carolina

SHIRLEY ANN GRAU (1929–)

At present, criticism of Miss Grau's fiction is to be found chiefly in reviews, only a few of which are included in this checklist.

Berland, Alwyn, "The Fiction of Shirley Ann Grau," *Crit*, VI (Spring-Summer 1963), 78–84.

Coles, Robert, "Mood and Revelation in the South," *New Rep*, CL (Apr 18, 1964), 17–19. [r of *Keeper of the Keys*]

Going, William T., "Alabama's Geography in Shirley Ann Grau's *The Keeper of the Keys*," *AlaR*, XX (Jan 1967), 62–68.

Gossett, "Primitives and Violence: Shirley Ann Grau," in *Violence in Recent Southern Fiction*, pp. 177–95.

Hoffman, "The Mark of Time," in *The Art of Southern Fiction*, pp. 106–109.

Hicks, Granville, "Filled with Sawdust and Sadness," *SatR*, XL (June 16, 1961), 20. [r of *House on Coliseum Street*]

———, "A Shining Young Talent," *SatR*, XLI (June 5, 1958), 12. [r of *Hard Blue Sky*]

Peden, William, "Vibrant World," *SeR*, XXXVIII (Jan 29, 1955), 16. [r of *The Black Prince*]

RUTH M. VANDE KIEFT
Queens College of the
City University of New York
New York, New York

WILLIAM JOHN GRAYSON (1788-1863)

Grayson is chiefly known for his didactic poem, *The Hireling and the Slave* (Charleston, 1854), in defense of slavery. His other long poems are, however, of somewhat greater literary merit. The prose of his political and historical essays is at times distinguished; it displays a rigor of mind and a disciplined wit not often associated with Ante-bellum South Carolina. Frank Albrecht is preparing an edition of *The Hireling and the Slave* which will include some of Grayson's other writings as well as a critical and historical introduction. The best published sketch of Grayson may be found in Jay B. Hubbell, *The South in American Literature*.

DAB, VII, pp. 525–26; *Duyckinck*, II, p. 103; *Hubbell*, pp. 438–46, *933–34; *LSL*, V, pp. 2011–13.

*Bass, Robert D., "The Autobiography of William J. Grayson," South Carolina, 1933. [diss]

Hayne, Paul Hamilton, "Ante-Bellum Charleston," *The Southern Bivouac*, I (1884–85), pp. 330–35. [Hayne's reminiscences of Grayson and of his contributions to *Russell's Mag*]

*Jarrett, Thomas Dunbar, "William Grayson's *The Hireling and the Slave*: A Study of Ideas, Form, Reception, and Editions," Chicago, 1947. [diss]

———, "The Literary Significance of William J. Grayson's *The Hireling and the Slave*," *GaR* V (1951), 487–94. [portion of Jarrett's diss]

Parks, Edd Winfield, *Ante-Bellum Southern Literary Critics* (Athens, Ga., 1962), pp. 185–91.

Parrington, Vernon Louis, *Main Currents of American Thought* (New York, 1927), II, pp. 103–108.

Taylor, William R., *Cavalier and Yankee* (New York, 1961), pp. 55–65. [considers Grayson as example of important ante-bellum intellectual type]

Wilson, Edmund, *Patriotic Gore: Studies in the Literature of the American Civil War* (New York, 1966) pp. 336–74. [comparison of Grayson, Fitzhugh and Helper]

FRANK ALBRECHT
Hollins College
Hollins College, Virginia

PAUL GREEN (1894–)

Though considerable attention has been devoted to Green as a writer of folk plays and as the man who originated the "symphonic drama" (a term he created), his short stories, novels, and essays have been generally overlooked. As well as an inclusive bibliography, studies of Green as humanist and aesthetician are needed.

Adams, Agatha Boyd, *Paul Green of Chapel Hill* (Chapel Hill, 1951), U of N.C. Lib Ext Pub, XVI, No. 2.

Carmer, Carl, "Paul Green: The Making of an American Dramatist," *Theatre Arts*, XVI (1932), 995–1006.

Clark, Barrett H., "Paul Green," *An Hour of American Drama* (Philadelphia, 1930). pp. 122–42.

Clark, Emily, "Paul Green and Gerald Johnson," *Innocence Abroad* (New York, 1931), pp. 253–70.

Free, William, and Charles Lower, eds., *History into Drama: A Source Book on Symphonic Drama* (New York, 1963), pp. 117–71. [26 articles and excerpts by 18 authors]

*Groff, Edward B., "Paul Green: A Critical Study of America's Leading Folk Dramatist," Kansas, 1957. [diss]

Hewes, Henry, "The Playwright as Believer," *SatR*, XXXVII (July 10, 1945), 24. [r essay]

Hoyle, Bernadette, "Paul Green," *Tar Heel Writers I Know* (Winston-Salem, 1956), pp. 72–79.

"Interview with Paul Green," in *The North Carolina Miscellany*, ed Richard Walser (Chapel Hill, 1962), pp. 191–208.

Isaacs, Edith J., "Paul Green: A Case in Point," *Theatre Arts*, XXV (1941), 489–98.

Jones, Howard Mumford, "Paul Green," *SWR*, XIV (Autumn, 1928), 1–8.

*Owen, Henry Grady, "The Social Thought and Criticism of Paul Green," New York, 1945. [diss]

Sievers, W. David, *Freud on Broadway* (New York, 1955), pp. 311–21.

Stem, Thad, Jr., "Paul Green and the Symphonic Drama" (Raleigh, N.C.) *News and Observer,* Sept 12, 1965, Sec. 3, p. 1. [newsp art]

Treat, Donald Robert, "Paul Green's Concept of Symphonic Drama and Its Application to His Outdoor Plays," *DA*, XXV (1964), 1415–16 (Denver).

RICHARD WALSER
North Carolina State University
Raleigh, North Carolina

CHARLES HANSFORD (*ca.* 1685-1761)

There has as yet been no scholarly or critical attention paid to the recently-discovered verses of this self-taught blacksmith-poet of eighteenth-century York County, Virginia, other than the introductory comments in the edition of Hansford's poems listed below. The manuscript of this work, containing four long poems in heroic couplets together with appreciative verses by the poet's friends, is in the Blow Collection of the Earl G. Swem Library at the College of William and Mary.

Servies, James A. and Carl R. Dolmetsch, eds., *The Poems of Charles Hansford* (Chapel Hill, 1961). [Hansford's biog is in the preface, pp. ix–xix, by Servies; intro pp. xxi–xlii, by Dolmetsch, gives crit estimates, including sources and influences]

CARL R. DOLMETSCH
College of William and Mary
Williamsburg, Virginia

WILL N. HARBEN (1858-1919)

The earliest important critical essay championing Harben's work is William Dean Howells, "Mr. Harben's Georgia Fiction" (1910). Although no biography or dissertation has appeared on him, his work is discussed by Isabella D. Harris in her dissertation, "The Southern Mountaineer in American Fiction 1824–1910" (1948). Robert Bush, "Will N. Harben's Northern Georgia Fiction" (1967) is a critical survey of the more important novels and stories. It includes a checklist of works by and about Harben.

DAB, VIII, p. 238; *LSL*, V, pp. 2073–75.

"Books and Bookmen," *Harper's Weekly*, XLVII (March 7, 1903), 394.

*Bush, Robert, "Will N. Harben's Northern Georgia Fiction," *MissQ*, XX (1967), 103–117.

Harben, Will N., "American Backgrounds for Fiction; Georgia," *Bookman*, XXXVIII (1913), 186–92.

Harris, Isabella D., "The Southern Mountaineer in American Fiction, 1824–1910," Duke, 1948, pp. 181 *ff*. [diss]

Hart, Bertha Sheppard, *Introduction to Georgia Writers* (Macon, Ga., 1929), 64–66.

Howells, William Dean, "Mr. Harben's Georgia Fiction," *NoAmerR*, CXCI (1910), 356–63. Repr as intro to Harben's novel *The Triumph* (New York, 1917).

Kilmer, Joyce, ed., "The Novel Must Go," in *Literature in the Making by Some of Its Makers* (New York, 1917), pp. 189–96. [interv]

New York Times, August 8, 1919. [obit]

Rutherford, Mildred L., *The South in History and Literature* (Athens, Ga., 1907), 730–31.

ROBERT BUSH
Hunter College
New York, New York

GEORGE WASHINGTON HARRIS (1814-1869)

George Washington Harris is at present the most intensively studied of all the humorists of the Old Southwest, partly because Mark Twain, William Faulkner, and other artists admired him, and partly because his art and his meanings illuminate many strange and disturbing facets of the American and Southern vision and experience. His one book, *Sut Lovingood* (New York, 1867), remained in print into the 1950s. The volume included roughly one-third of his work, and the remaining two-thirds, widely scattered in nineteenth century newspapers, has been largely discovered and reprinted since the 1930s. Franklin J. Meine's *Tall Tales of the Southwest* (1930) included two sketches from the old sporting journal, the New York *Spirit of the Times*. Edd W. Parks edited the three Lincoln satires in 1937 under the title *Sut Lovingood Travels with Old Abe Lincoln*. In 1954 Grove Press published Brom Weber's edition, which opened with a brilliant introduction and included eighteen of the twenty-four stories from the *Yarns*, plus the three Lincoln satires, printed in a modernized text in order to make them more penetrable to the general reader. This edition was widely reviewed in newspapers.

Early in the 1960s, Ben Harris McClary organized the Sut Society and edited four annual issues of *The Lovingood Papers* between 1962 and 1965. Each issue reprinted several uncollected sketches with introductions by various scholars, and each also published notes, essays, and editorial comments—criticism which Richard Dorson has praised for its "remarkable variety and originality." Next, M. Thomas Inge edited all the stories from the 1867 edition, plus twenty-two uncollected sketches, in corrected texts as *Sut Lovingood's Yarns* (New Haven, 1966). Finally the indefatigable Inge crowned his years of devotion to Harris' work by editing *High Times and Hard Times: Sketches and Tales by George Washington Harris* (Nashville, 1967), in which he makes available all of Harris's uncollected writings now known. This edition, handsomely published by the Vanderbilt University Press, includes authoritative introductions to its several sections, a slightly revised text, useful notes, and an extensive bibliography.

Still to be discovered in nineteenth-century newspapers are stories mentioned by Harris about Sut's outrunning Old Burns's fox hounds, some "highly seasoned" incidents, "Sister Sall's onlawful baby," Sut's funeral, and others.

DAB, VIII, pp. 309–10; *Hubbell*, pp. 678–79, *934; *LSL*, V, pp. 2099–102.

*Blair, Walter, *Native American Humor* (San Francisco, 1960), pp. 96–101.

———, "Sut Lovingood," *SatR*, XV (Nov 7, 1936), 3–4, 16.

*Blanck, *Bibliography of American Literature*, III, pp. 384–86.

Covici, Pascal, Jr., *Mark Twain's Humor* (Dallas, 1962), pp. 11–12, 73–77.

Day, Donald, "The Humorous Works of George W. Harris," *AL*, XIV (1943), 391–406.

———, "The Life of George Washington Harris," *Tenn Hist Q*, VI (1947), 3–38.

———, "The Political Satires of George W. Harris," *Tenn Hist Q*, IV (1945), 320–38.

Inge, M. Thomas, "George Washington Harris and Southern Poetry and Music," *MissQ*, XVII (1963–64), 36–44.

———, "The Satiric Artistry of George W. Harris," *Satire Newsletter*, IV (1967), 63–72.

*———, intro to *High Times and Hard Times: Sketches and Tales by George Washington Harris* (Nashville, 1967), pp. 3–8, 10–14, 34–43, 106–18, 222–31. [Harris's newsp writings]

McClary, Ben Harris, ed., *The Lovingood Papers* (Athens, Tennessee, 1962; Knoxville,

1963, 1964, 1965). [jour publ by the Sut Society; four issues printed]

————, "The Real Sut," *AL*, XXVII (1955), 105–106.

Matthiessen, F. O., *American Renaissance: Art and Expression in the Age of Emerson and Whitman* (New York, 1941), pp. 603, 637, 641–45.

Meine, Franklin J., ed., *Tall Tales of the Southwest* (New York, 1930), pp. xxiii–xxiv.

Penrod, James H., "Folk Humor in Sut Lovingood's Yarns," *Tenn Folkl Soc Bull*, XVI (Dec 1950), 76–84.

*Rickels, Milton, *George Washington Harris* (New York, 1965). [TUSAS]

————, "The Imagery of George Washington Harris," *AL*, XXXI (1959), 173–87.

Weber, Brom, intro to *Sut Lovingood's Yarns by George Washington Harris* (New York, 1954), pp. ix–xxix.

Wilson, Edmund, "Poisoned!" *New Yorker*, XXXI (May 7, 1955), 150–54. repr with minor changes in Wilson, *Patriotic Gore* (New York, 1962), pp. 507–519.

MILTON RICKELS
University of Southwestern Louisiana
Lafayette, Louisiana

JOEL CHANDLER HARRIS (1848-1908)

Harris' activities as folklorist and journalist have been well studied. Considerable attention has also been given to the "realistic" and "romantic" aspects of his fiction. His treatment of dialect and his general handling of Negro character also form a considerable amount of the scholarly literature. And although some attention has been given to his so-called "Cracker" sketches, these have not received the attention which might well be given to them. His biographers have assiduously pointed out the books that were said to have been influential (one critic says his approach to literature is between Goldsmith's *Vicar of Wakefield* and E. W. Howe's *The Story of a Country Town*) in his background, but there is no systematic study of the precise forces that made him the shrewd critic of literature that some commentators say that he is.

There is no collected edition of Harris' works yet, although the separate volumes, with occasional reprints of the Uncle Remus series, are not hard to come by. With the advent of research by computers, students of linguistic science may well find in the Negro and "Cracker" dialect additional avenues for study aimed at preserving the language of Harris's time and place.

Whether a "minor master among the Southern genre writers," editorialist for the New South, humorist who enjoyed the high regard of Mark Twain, or writer of occasional sketches after the manner of his 18th century masters, Harris deserves more complete treatment as a man of letters than he has received to date. A thoroughgoing critical biography identifying him with the *Zeitgeist* should prove an important contribution to American letters.

DAB, VIII, pp. 312–14; *Hubbell*, pp. 782–95, *984–85; *LSL*, V, pp. 2111–20; *LHUS*, I, pp. 852–54, *II, pp. 540–42, *Supp*, 132–33.

Baskervill, W. M., "Joel Chandler Harris," in *Southern Writers: Biographical and Critical Studies*, I (Nashville, 1897) pp. 41–85. [estimate by a contemporary friend]

Brown, Sterling, *The Negro in American Fiction* (Washington, 1937) pp. 57–58. [Harris's Negro portrayals above Thomas Nelson Page's, but below those of Twain and Cable]

*Brookes, Stella Brewer, *Joel Chandler Harris: Folklorist* (Athens, Ga., 1950). [an "account of Harris' ideas of folklore and an analysis of his tales, proverbs, and songs by types"]

Buck, Paul, *The Road to Reunion* (Boston, Mass., 1937), p. 205. [Harris' role in sectional reconciliation]

Cousins, Paul M., "The Debt of Joel Chandler Harris to Joseph Addison Turner," *Chimes*, XLII (March 1930), 9–10.

*———, *Joel Chandler Harris* (Baton Rouge, 1968).

Dauner, Louise, "Myth and Humor in the Uncle Remus Fables," *AL*, XX (1948), 129–43. [significant in reinterpretation of tales]

Gaines, Francis P., *The Southern Plantation* (New York, 1924), pp. 76–216. [Harris' role in plantation tradition of Old So]

Garland, Hamlin, *Roadside Meetings* (New York, 1930), pp. 351–52. [Harris was "not bitter" but "bluntly critical about the old regime"]

Harlow, Alvin F., *Joel Chandler Harris: Plantation Story Teller* (New York, 1941). [popular biog; little new information]

*Harris, Julia Collier, *The Life and Letters of Joel Chandler Harris* (Boston, 1918). [biog ed. by Harris' daughter-in-law with bibl comp by Katherine Ann Wooten in 1907]

———, ed., *Joel Chandler Harris: Editor and Essayist*. (Chapel Hill, 1931). [Harris' daughter-in-law selects representative writings from newsp (mainly Atlanta *Constitution*) and contemporary periodicals]

———, "Joel Chandler Harris: Constructive Realist," in H. W. Odum, *Southern Pioneers in Social Interpretation* (Chapel Hill, 1925). [examines Harris' role as one of journalistic spokesmen for the New So]

*Herndon, Jerry A., "Social Comment in the Writings of Joel Chandler Harris," Duke, 1966. Bibl pp. 229–33. [diss]

Nelson, John H. *The Negro Character in American Literature* (Lawrence, Kansas, 1926), pp. 105–18. [this early estimate should be balanced with Brown's *The Negro in American Fiction* and the same author's "Negro Characters as Seen by White Authors," *Jour of Negro Educ*, II (Apr 1933), 180–89; also see entries under *LHUS* and *Hubbell*]

*Nixon, Raymond B., *Henry W. Grady: Spokesman of the New South* (New York, 1943), pp. 64, 128–29, 155, 166, 202. [biog of Harris' chief ed. on *Constitution* discusses Harris' editorial contributions]

*Ray, Charles A., "A Study of Realism in the Writings of Joel Chandler Harris," Southern California, 1952. [diss; examines Harris' writings for estimate of "realistic" qualities of his tales and fiction; bibl 235–43]

Stafford, John, "Patterns of Meaning in *Nights With Uncle Remus*," *AL*, XVIII (1946), 89–108. [significant reinterpretation of the familiar tales]
*Turner, Arlin, "Joel Chandler Harris," *Amer Lit Realism*, No. 3 (1968), 18–23.
Wade, John Donald, "Profits and Losses in the Life of Joel Chandler Harris," *AmerR, I.* (Apr 1933), 17–35. [notwithstanding Harris' talk of realism, Wade says he was a romanticist, "who must have worked consciously to make his Uncle Remus stories propagandist in nature"]
*Wiggins, Robert L. *The Life of Joel Chandler Harris* (Nashville, 1918). [this early biog also contains bibl of primary and secondary materials, pp. 429–44.]

CHARLES A. RAY
North Carolina College at Durham
Durham, North Carolina

HENRY SYDNOR HARRISON (1880-1930)

During his lifetime, and particularly during the years just prior to World War I, the novels of Henry Sydnor Harrison were best-sellers, and both author and works received much notice in periodicals. This great popularity was triggered by the appearance of his *Queed* (1911), *V.V.'s Eyes* (1913), and *Angela's Business* (1915). Some interest remained during the 1920s, and since then, larger studies have included discussions of his works in broader contexts. But his reputation, popularity, and critical acclaim are now eclipsed. No detailed critical study has been made of Harrison's fiction.

DAB, VIII, pp. 342–43; *LSL*, XVII, pp. 285–89.
Bookman, XLI (Oct 1911), 60. [r of *Queed*]
Bookman, XLIV (Jul 1913), 182. [r of *V.V.'s Eyes*]
Columbia UQ, XV (1913), 341. [portrait]
Current Lit, LI (1911), 221–22. [r of *Queed*]
Du Breuil, Alice Jouveau, "The Novel of Democracy in America: A Contribution to the Study of the Progress of Democratic Ideas in the American Novel," Johns Hopkins, 1922. [diss; Harrison and eight other novelists]
"Harrison's *V.V.'s Eyes*," *Lit Digest*, XLVII, (Aug 16, 1913).
Herrick, R., "Novels of Harrison," *New Rep*, II (March 27, 1915), 199–201.
Hockey, Dorothy C., "The Good and the Beautiful, a Study of Best-Selling Novels in America, 1895–1920," Western Reserve, 1947. [diss]
Marmur, Justine, "The Anti-War Novel in America (1918–1928)," Columbia, 1948. [diss; Faulkner, Harrison, and Elizabeth Robins]

Wynn, William T., *Southern Literature: Selections and Biographies* (New York, 1932), p. 467.

WILLIAM K. BOTTORFF
University of Toledo
Toledo, Ohio

PAUL HAMILTON HAYNE (1830-1886)

Scholarship on Hayne may be checked chiefly in the two bibliographical volumes of *Literary History of the United States* and in Jay B. Hubbell's *The South in American Literature*. Items published since the late 1950s may be readily found in the quarterly checklist in *American Literature* and in the annual bibliography in *PMLA*.

The present state of scholarly work on Hayne is soon described. Articles and notes abound; studies of a more substantial length and quality, though not so plentiful, may be readily ascertained. The poet's career as a man of letters (to some the most vital aspect of his present importance) has been discussed by Hubbell; his relations with Charles Gayarré and Sidney Lanier have been examined by Charles R. Anderson in separate essays; and his literary opinions have been dealt with by Edd Winfield Parks in *Ante-Bellum Southern Literary Critics* (1962). Moreover, many of Hayne's letters have been collected and edited by Daniel M. McKeithan and Charles Duffy; his relations with Northern literary men have been treated by Victor H. Hardendorff in a Master's thesis (Duke, 1942), and his contributions to Southern and Northern magazines have been set forth by Ray M. Atchison and Rayburn S. Moore in dissertations completed at Duke in 1956.

Still, much remains to be done. Despite the abundance of available primary materials, there is no scholarly biography, no critical edition of the poems, no full-scale critical assessment of the poetry, no edition of the hundreds of letters in the large collection of Hayne manuscripts in the Duke University Library.

Several of these needs may be partially met in Rayburn S. Moore's forthcoming book on Hayne in the Twayne series. Chiefly a descriptive and critical treatment of the poems, this study also offers a long chapter on the poet's life, a shorter version of which appeared in the *Georgia Review* for Spring, 1968. Furthermore, James S. Purcell plans to edit Hayne's last poems, those which appeared after the so-called Complete Edition came out in the fall of 1882. For other hands, then, this leaves three projects in particular: a full-dress biography, a critical and selected edition of the poems, and a scholarly edition of the letters in the Duke Library.

DAB, VIII, pp. 455–56; *Duyckinck*, II, p. 722; *Hubbell*, pp. 743–57, 773–77, *935–37; *LSL*, V, pp. 2265–71; *LHUS, II, pp. 554–56, *Supp*, 136.

Anderson, Charles R., "Charles Gayarré and Paul Hayne: The Last Literary Cavaliers," in David K. Jackson, ed., *American Studies in Honor of William Kenneth Boyd*, pp. 221–81.

———, "Poet of the Pine Barrens," *GaR*, I (1947), 280–93. [relations between Hayne and Lanier]

Atchison, Ray M., "Southern Literary Magazines, 1865–1887," Duke, 1956. [diss; describes Hayne's contributions to many periodicals]

Becker, Kate H., *Paul Hamilton Hayne: Life and Letters* (Belmont, N.C. 1951). ["compiled" from secondary sources only]

Carter, John A., "Paul Hayne's Sonnet 'To the New South,'" *Ga Hist Q*, XLVIII (1964), 193–95. [reply (in part) to Flory; see below]

Davis, Richard Beale, ed., "Paul Hamilton Hayne to Dr. Francis Peyre Porcher," *SP*, XLIV (1947), 529–48.

Duffy, Charles, ed., *The Correspondence of Bayard Taylor and Paul Hamilton Hayne* (Baton Rouge, 1945).

———, "A Southern Genteelist: Letters of Paul Hamilton Hayne to Julia C. R. Dorr," *S.C. Hist & Geneal Mag*, LII (Apr 1951), 65–73, to LIII (Jan 1952), 19–30.

Flory, Claude R., "Paul Hamilton Hayne and the New South," *Ga Hist Q*, XLVI (1962), 388–94.

Griffin, Max L., "Whittier and Hayne: A Record of Friendship," *AL*, XIX (1947), 41–58.

Hardendorff, Victor H., "Paul Hamilton Hayne and the North," Duke, 1942. [MA thesis]

Harwell, Richard B., "A Confederate View of the Southern Poets," *AL*, XXIV (1952), 51–61. [includes text of Hayne, "The Southern Lyre"]

Hayne, William H., "Paul H. Hayne's Methods of Composition," *Lippincott's Mag* L (1892), 793–96.

———, ed., "Some Unpublished Letters of Wilkie Collins [to Hayne]," *Bookman*. XXXVII (1913), 66–71.

Hubbell, Jay B.. ed., *The Last Years of Henry Timrod* (Durham, 1941).

———, ed., "Some New Letters of Constance Fenimore Woolson [to Hayne]," *New Eng Q*, XIV (1941), 715–35.

Lang, Cecil, "Swinburne and American Literature: With Six Hitherto Unpublished Letters," *AL*, XIX (1948), 336–50. [five letters to Hayne]

Lanier, Sidney, *Works*, ed. Charles R. Anderson et al, Centennial ed (Baltimore, 1945), 10 vols. [contains Lanier's letters to Hayne and excerpts from Hayne's; repr Lanier's r of *Legends and Lyrics*]

Lewisohn, Ludwig, "The Books We Have Made. A History of Literature in South Carolina . . ., XIV—Paul Hamilton Hayne," *Charleston* (S.C.) *Sunday News*, Sept 20, 1903, p. 20. [last of a series of articles; Lewisohn later tempered his views in *Expression in America* (New York, 1932), pp. 82–83]

McKeithan, Daniel M., ed., *A Collection of Hayne Letters* (Austin, Tex. 1944). [contains letters from every major collection except Duke Lib]

———, "A Correspondence Journal of Paul Hamilton Hayne," *Ga Hist Q*, XXVI

(1942), 249–72. [covers late 1870s and early 1880s]

———, "Paul Hamilton Hayne and *The Southern Bivouac*." *U Tex Stud Eng*, XVII (1937), 112–23.

———, ed., *Selected Letters: John Garland James to Paul Hamilton Hayne and Mary Middleton Michel Hayne* (Austin, Tex., 1946).

Moore, Rayburn S., "Paul Hamilton Hayne," *GaR*, XXII (1968), 106–24. [sketches Hayne's life and lit career]

———, "Southern Writers and Northern Literary Magazines, 1865–1890," Duke, 1956. [diss; discusses Hayne's contributions to five great No monthlies]

Parks, Edd Winfield, "Paul Hamilton Hayne: Eclecticist," in *Ante-Bellum Southern Literary Critics* (Athens, 1962), pp. 227–59, 329–44.

———, *Henry Timrod* (New York, 1964). [TUSAS—contains much information on Hayne]

———, ed., *Southern Poets* (New York, 1936). [see esp intro]

Preston, Margaret J., "Paul Hamilton Hayne," *Southern Bivouac*, n.s., II (1886), 222–29. [appreciative tribute by old friend]

———, intro to *Poems of Paul Hamilton Hayne*. Complete ed (Boston, 1882), v–viii. [chiefly biog]

Simms, William G., *The Letters*, ed. Mary C. Simms Oliphant et al (Columbia, S.C., 1952–56), 5 vols. See esp IV–V.

Trent, William P., *William Gilmore Simms* (Boston, 1892). [Hayne appears frequently and prominently; contains some information not available elsewhere]

RAYBURN S. MOORE
University of Georgia
Athens, Georgia

LAFCADIO HEARN (1850-1904)

The best biography of Lafcadio Hearn is Elizabeth Stevenson's *Lafcadio Hearn*; the best critical study is Beongcheon Yu's *An Ape of Gods*. Beongcheon Yu also has provided an authoritative comment on the status of Hearn studies in *American Literary Realism, 1870–1910*, No. 1 (Fall 1967), 52–55. All students of Hearn must refer to this essay for bibliographical and critical orientation. Beongcheon Yu may be overly pessimistic when he says that the subject of Hearn is "hopelessly complicated." His own suggestions for further research—calling for a complete bibliography of Hearn's writings, including his contributions to newspapers, and better critical evaluations of such problems as Hearn's relationship to American journalism and of Japanese attitudes toward Hearn—indicate the likelihood that the complexities which defy the student of his life and works will in time be reduced.

The student of Southern American letters should not rest easy in the assumption that Hearn is properly a "Southern" writer. By calling this into question, he brings up the larger issue of whether or not Hearn was an American writer. This leads to the central problem of Hearn: the definition of his literary and spiritual identity. A study of Hearn in the direction of a broad effort to define his relationship to an "American cosmopolitanism" may well be one of the most fruitful approaches that can now be taken in Hearn studies. Paradoxically, literary cosmopolitanism has always been subject to regional and national attitudes. Thus, for example, a French cosmopolitan writer is we all know not the same as a German cosmopolite. Like Ezra Pound and T. S. Eliot, even though his early background was not American, Hearn may present to us the paradox of a study in American cosmopolitanism.

DAB, VIII, pp. 484–87; *LSL*, VI, pp. 2341–46; *LHUS*, I, pp. 1070–72, *II, 556–59, **Supp*, 137.

Amenomori, Nobushige, "Lafcadio Hearn, the Man," *Atlantic*, XCVI (1905), 510–25.

Bisland, Elizabeth, *The Life and Letters of Lafcadio Hearn* (Boston and New York, 1906), 2 vols.

Cohn, Isidore (with Hermann B. Deutsch), *Rudolph Matas: A Biography of One of the Great Pioneers in Surgery* (New York, 1960). [varied information about Hearn's life in New Orleans]

Cowley, Malcolm, "Lafcadio Hearnun-san," *New Rep*, CXX (Apr 18, 1949), 22–24.

———, "Lafcadio Hearn," intro to *The Selected Writings of Lafcadio Hearn*, ed. Henry Goodman (New York, 1949), pp. 1–15.

Espey, John J., "The Two Japans of Lafcadio Hearn," *Pacific Spectator*, IV (1950), 342–51.

Frost, Orcutt W., *Young Hearn* (Tokyo, 1958).

*Gould, George M., *Concerning Lafcadio Hearn* (Philadelphia, 1908), bibl by Laura Stedman.

Josephson, Matthew, "An Enemy of the West: Lafcadio Hearn," *Portrait of the Artist as American* (New York, 1930), pp. 199–231.

Kennard, Nina H., *Lafcadio Hearn* (New York, 1912).

Lawless, Ray McKinley, "Lafcadio Hearn: Critic of American Life and Letters," Chicago, 1940. [diss]

Lewis, Oscar, *Hearn and His Biographers* (San Francisco, 1930). [appraisal of biog controversies; also contains letters from Hearn to Joseph Tunison]

*McWilliams, Vera, *Lafcadio Hearn* (Boston, 1946).

Miner, Earl, *The Japanese Tradition in British and American Literature* (Princeton, 1958).

More, Paul Elmer, "Lafcadio Hearn," in *Shelburne Essays*, 2nd ser (New York, 1905), pp. 46–72.

Morrison, Robert Felix, "The Growth of the Mind and Art of Lafcadio Hearn," Wisconsin, 1941. [diss]

Noguchi, Yone, *Lafcadio Hearn in Japan* (Yokohama, 1910).

Robert, Marcel, *Lafcadio Hearn* (Tokyo, 1950–51), 2 vols.

*Perkins, P. D., and Iona, *Lafcadio Hearn: A Bibliography of His Writings* (Boston. 1934). [standard though incomplete]

Porter, Katherine Anne, "A Disinherited Cosmopolitan," *N.Y. Her Trib Bks,* Feb. 16, 1930, p. 22.

Salvan, Albert J., "Lafcadio Hearn's Views on the Realism of Zola," *PMLA,* LXVII (1952), 1163–67.

Stempel, Daniel, "Lafcadio Hearn: Interpreter of Japan," *AL,* XX (1948), 1–19.

Stevenson, Elizabeth, *Lafcadio Hearn* (New York, 1961).

Temple, Jean, *Blue Ghost: A Study of Lafcadio Hearn* (New York, 1931).

Tinker, Edward Larocque, *Lafcadio Hearn's American Days* (New York, 1924).

Tuttle, Allen E., "Lafcadio Hearn and Herbert Spencer," Northwestern, 1950. [diss]

———,."The Achievement of Lafcadio Hearn," *Dublin Mag,* XXXI (Apr–June, 1956), 6–13.

Yu, Beongcheon, "Lafcadio Hearn's Aesthetics of Organic Memory," *Stud in Eng Lit,* (Tokyo), XXXVIII (Nov 1961), 1–28.

———, "Lafcadio Hearn's Twice-Told Legends Reconsidered," *AL,* XXXIV (1962), 56–71.

———, *An Ape of Gods: The Art and Thought of Lafcadio Hearn* (Detroit, 1964).

*———, "Lafcadio Hearn," in *American Literary Realism, 1870–1910,* No. 1 (1967), pp. 52–55. [bibl essay on status of Hearn stud]

Lewis P. Simpson
Louisiana State University
Baton Rouge, Louisiana

LILLIAN HELLMAN (1905–)

There has been no full-length study of Lillian Hellman in English. Almost all briefer studies have been concerned either with a single one of her plays, or with her relationship to intellectual or political movements, or they have been part of critical histories of modern drama.

Adler, Jacob H., "Miss Hellman's Two Sisters," *Educ Theatre Jour,* XV (1963), 112–17. [study of *Toys in the Attic*]

———, "The Rose and the Fox: Notes on the Southern Drama," in Rubin and Jacobs, *South,* pp. 349–75.

Clark, Barrett H., "Lillian Hellman," *Coll Eng,* VI (1944), 127–33.

Downer, Alan S., *Fifty Years of American Drama, 1900–1950* (Chicago, 1951), pp. 60–61, 139–41.

Dusenbury, Winifred L., *The Theme of Loneliness in Modern American Drama* (Gainesville, 1960), pp. 143–49.

Felheim, Marvin, "*The Autumn Garden*: Mechanics and Dialectics," *Mod Drama,* III (1960), 191–95.

Harriman, Margaret C., "Miss Lily of New Orleans: Lillian Hellman," in *Take Them Up Tenderly* (New York, 1945), pp. 94–109. ["profile" from *New Yorker*]

Hellman, Lillian, intro to *Four Plays* (New York, 1942), pp. vii–xiv.

Krutch, Joseph W., *The American Drama Since 1918* (New York, 1957), pp. 130–33.

Meehan, Thomas, "Q: Miss Hellman, What's Wrong with Broadway? A: It's a Bore," *Esq*, LVIII (Dec 1962), 140, 142, 235–36. [interv]

Phillips, John, and Ann Hollander, "The Art of the Theater I," *ParisR*, IX (Winter-Spring 1965), 64–95. [interv]

Sievers, W. David, *Freud on Broadway: A History of Psychoanalysis and the American Drama* (New York, 1955), pp. 279–89.

Stern, Richard G., "Lillian Hellman on Her Plays," *Contact*, III (1959), 113–19. [interv]

*Triesch, Manfred, "Lillian Hellman: A Selective Bibliography," *Amer Bk Collector*, XIV (June 1964), 57.

*Triesch, Manfred, *Lillian Hellman: Eine Analyse and Würdigung ihrer Dramen* (Frankfurt-am-Main, 1961).

JACOB H. ADLER
University of Kentucky
Lexington, Kentucky

CAROLINE LEE HENTZ (1800-1856)

Mrs. Hentz's sentimental novels were reprinted as late as 1889, but there has been little interest in her writings since then, except for a rash of graduate theses in the late 1930s and the 1940s. In standard histories of regional literature she is fortunate to be merely mentioned. Jay B. Hubbell in *The South in American Literature*, page 604, named her as one of the best Southern women writers of her period but did not discuss her work. Ralph L. Rusk in *The Literature of the Middle Western Frontier* wrote briefly of the three forgotten plays she composed in Covington, Kentucky, which are mentioned also by Arthur Hobson Quinn in *A History of the American Drama from the Beginning to the Civil War* (New York, 1923), pages 264–65. Only Fred Lewis Pattee in *The Feminine Fifties* devoted as much as two pages to her novels. She has suffered the fate of the best-selling novelist whose works survive only as curiosities after tastes have changed. Interest in her, today, is largely historical, as the titles of many of the theses listed below reveal. No complete bibliography has been published.

DAB, VIII, pp. 565–66; *Duyckinck*, II, p. 486; *LSL*, IV, pp. 2375–79.

Berdan, Alan, "Caroline Lee Hentz: Northern Defender of Southern Tradition," St. John's, 1948. [MA thesis]

Browne, Margaret, "Southern Reactions to Uncle Tom's Cabin," Duke, 1946. [MA thesis]

Carter, Maude, "A Study of Caroline Lee Hentz, Sentimentalist of the Fifties," Duke, 1942. [MA thesis]

Ellison, Rhoda Coleman, *Early Alabama Publications: A Study in Literary Interests* (University, Ala., 1947). [numerous references to Mrs. Hentz's works, esp Chap 4, pp. 139–40, 163–64, 170–75, 187–88]

————, "Mrs. Hentz and the Green-Eyed Monster," *AL*, XX (1950), 345–50.

————, "Propaganda in Early Alabama Fiction," *Alabama Hist Q*, VII (1945), 425–33. [Mrs. Hentz is one of seven ante-bellum novelists discussed]

Enloe, Mildred, "A Criticism of Mrs. Caroline Lee Hentz," Auburn, 1936. [MA thesis]

Hardy, Evelyn, "Mrs. Caroline Lee Hentz, a Woman of Her Time," Auburn, 1935. [MA thesis]

Julian, Grace L., "Southern Novels, 1850–1855: A Study in Culture," Tulane, 1942. [MA thesis; emphasis on Mrs. Hentz and Mrs. Southworth]

Moran, Neva R., "Caroline Lee Hentz, an Early Southern Novelist: A Study of the Life and Works of Mrs. Caroline Lee Hentz," Birmingham-Southern, 1937. [MA thesis]

Pattee, Fred Lewis, *The Feminine Fifties* (New York, 1940), pp. 120–22.

Rusk, Ralph L., *The Literature of the Middle Western Frontier* (New York, 1925), I, pp. 300–301; II, pp. 422–23.

Woolridge, Nancy B., "The Negro Preacher in American Fiction before 1900," Chicago, 1942. [diss; Mrs. Hentz is one of twelve So writers included]

RHODA COLEMAN ELLISON
Huntingdon College
Montgomery, Alabama

DUBOSE HEYWARD (1885-1940)

In the 1920s and early 1930s DuBose Heyward of Charleston, South Carolina, was generally recognized as one of the prime movers in the so-called Southern Literary Renascence, as a poet, as a novelist, as a playwright, and as the librettist and co-lyricist of perhaps the best folk opera done in America. But starting in the late 1930s, with the dominance of what George Tindall calls the Fugitive-Agrarian-New Criticism axis, Heyward suffered the critical fate of so many Southern writers whose works did not lend themselves readily to the rules of thumb emanating from Nashville and the Nashville-dominated quarterlies. He was dismissed contemptuously as a belated "local colorist," as one whose portrayal of the Negro was vivid, but romanticized and "paternalistic," as—God save the mark!—one outside the "tradition." And sometimes in these curt dismissals insult was added to injury: he was misspelled—"Dubose" or "Dubois Haywood." But more often he was ignored.

In the 1950s and 1960s there was no striking rediscovery of the neglected genius of Heyward, but there has been an increasing cognizance
of his being the trustee of a modest but admirable talent, one worthy
of consideration in any study of Southern and American literature. His
papers have been deposited at the South Carolina Historical Society in
Charleston. A critical biography and several articles, doctoral dissertations and masters' theses at universities both in and outside the South,
a new hardback edition of the novel *Porgy*, the inclusion of the play
Porgy in anthologies of modern drama—all these attest to the renewed
interest in DuBose Heyward. Again his name appears—sometimes favorably—in studies of twentieth-century American literature, and a new
book-length study of him is being prepared for Twayne's United States
Authors Series.

Allen, Hervey, *DuBose Heyward, A Critical and Biographical Sketch, Including
   Contemporary Estimates of His Work* (New York, n.d. [1926]). [pamph]
*Bailey, Rosalie Vincent, "DuBose Heyward: Poet, Novelist, Playwright," Duke, 1941.
   [MA thesis]
Bradbury, *Renaissance in the South*, pp. 10 ff, 28, 97. [consistently spells the name
   "Dubose"]
Clark, Emily, "DuBose Heyward," *VQR*, VI (1930). 546–56.
Cooper, Anice Page, *DuBose Heyward: An Appreciation* (New York, 1930). Repr with
   slight changes from *Boston Evening Transcript*, Bk Sec, Feb 23, 1929, p. 2.
*Cooper, John Webb, "A Comparative Study of *Porgy*, the Novel, *Porgy*, the Play,
   and *Porgy and Bess*, the Folk Opera," Columbia, 1950. [MA thesis]
*Cox, H. Morris, Jr., "The Charleston Poetic Renascence, 1920–1930," Pennsylvania,
   1959. [diss]
*Creighton, Nannie Elizabeth, "DuBose Heyward and His Contribution to Litera-
   ture," South Carolina, 1933. [MA thesis]
*Durham, Francis Marion, "DuBose Heyward: The Southerner as Artist, A Critical
   and Biographical Study," Columbia, 1953. [diss]
Durham, Frank, [same as Francis Marion], "South Carolina's Poetry Society,"
   SAQ, LII (1953), 277–85.
———, *DuBose Heyward: The Man Who Wrote Porgy* (Columbia, S.C., 1954), 2nd ed
   with new Foreword (Port Washington, N.Y., 1965). [much abr version of diss
   above]
———, "The Opera That Didn't Get to the Metropolitan," *SAQ*, LIII (1954), 497–507.
   [on *Porgy and Bess*] Repr in *Essays Today*, ed. Richard M. Ludwig (New York,
   1955), pp. 56–64.
———, *DuBose Heyward's Use of Folklore in His Negro Fiction* (Charleston, S.C.,
   1961). The Citadel Monograph Series, No. II.
———, "DuBose Heyward's 'Lost' Short Stories," *Stud in Short Fict*, II (1965) 157–63.
———, "The Rise of DuBose Heyward and the Rise and Fall of the Poetry Society of
   South Carolina," *MissQ*, XIX (1966), 67–78.
Ewen, David, "*Porgy and Bess*," *A Journey to Greatness, The Life and Music of George
   Gershwin* (New York, 1956), pp. 251–86. [writing and stage list of opera]
Harrigan, Anthony, "DuBose Heyward: Memorialist and Realist," *GaR*, V (1951),
   335–44.

Jablonski, Edward, and Lawrence D. Stewart, "1933–1935," *The Gershwin Years* (Garden City, N.Y., 1958), pp. 177–81, 190–220. [illus writing and stage history of *Porgy and Bess*]

Parks, Edd Winfield, intro to *Southern Poets* (New York, 1936), pp. xvii-cxxix.

Pinckney, Josephine, "Charleston's Poetry Society," *SeR*, XXXVIII (1930), 50–56.

Thomson, Keith, and Frank Durham, "The Impact of *Porgy and Bess* in New Zealand," *MissQ*, XX (1967), pp. 207–16.

Tindall, George B., *The Emergence of the New South, 1913–1945* (Baton Rouge, 1967), pp. 160, 292, 308–309, 312.

FRANK DURHAM

University of South Carolina

Columbia, South Carolina

JOHNSON JONES HOOPER (1815-1862)

Scholarship on Hooper may be conveniently divided into two categories, Before Hoole (so to speak), and After Hoole. Biographically if not critically, Hoole is so thorough that, until recently, subsequent commentators have done little more than supply extended footnotes to his book.

However, Hooper's writings, including several unreprinted pieces in periodicals, should be brought together in an available, annotated edition. The doctoral dissertation by Howard Winston Smith, "An Annotated Edition of Hooper's *Some Adventures of Captain Simon Suggs*" (Vanderbilt, 1966), though unpublished, could serve as the starting point for such a project. In another study (see below), Dr. Smith has also given Hooper's style and its relationship to his political views some of the attention these aspects of Hooper's work have long deserved.

DAB, IX, p. 202; *Hubbell*, pp. 672–75, *938; *LSL*, VI, pp. 2489–91.

Blair, Walter, *Horse Sense in American Humor* (Chicago, 1942), pp. 102–107.

*———, *Native American Humor* (San Francisco, 1960), pp. 86–89. See also pp. 63, 74, 108–109, 308.

*Cohen and Dillingham, "Johnson Jones Hooper," *Humor of the Old Southwest,* pp. 203–204. See also p. 417.

*Hoole, W. Stanley, *Alias Simon Suggs: The Life and Times of Johnson Jones Hooper* (University, Ala. 1952).

Hopkins, Robert, "Simon Suggs: A Burlesque Campaign Biography," *AQ*, XV (1963), 459–63. [*Suggs* a burlesque of political biog of Andrew Jackson]

Kitch, John C., "Dark Laughter: A Study of the Pessimistic Tradition in American Humor," Northwestern, 1964, pp. 48–50. [diss]

*Kunitz and Haycraft, "Johnson Jones Hooper," *A Biographical Dictionary of American Literature, 1600–1900*, pp. 48–49.

Lynn, Kenneth S., "Johnson J. Hooper," *The Comic Tradition in America* (Garden City, N.Y., 1958), pp. 94–97.

―――, "The Confidence Man," *Mark Twain and Southwestern Humor* (Boston and Toronto, 1959), pp. 77–86. See also pp. 86–88.

McIlwaine, Shields, *The Southern Poor-White* (Norman, Okla, 1939), pp. 49–51, 57–59.

*Meine, Franklin J., intro to *Tall Tales of the Southwest 1830–1860* (New York, 1930), pp. xxii–xxiii. See also pp. 29, 173, 239, 297, 323, 423, 452.

*Smith, Howard Winston, *Johnson Jones Hooper: A Critical Study* (Nashville, 1962). Microcards, ser A, mod lang ser. Sponsored by So Atl Mod Lang Assoc, No. 130. [monograph on microcard]

Tandy, Jennette, *Crackerbox Philosophers in American Humor and Satire* (New York, 1925), pp. 83–89.

Thorp, Willard, "Suggs and Sut in Modern Dress: The Latest Chapter in Southern Humor," *MissQ*, XIII (1960), 169–75. [analogues in mod fict]

NORRIS W. YATES
Iowa State University
Ames, Iowa

WILLIAM HUMPHREY (1924–)

As the reviews show (no extended studies have come to my attention other than that of Frederick J. Hoffman), the almost corporeal specter that hangs over Humphrey's two novels is the familiar ghost of Faulkner. D. L. Stevenson, Walter Sullivan and Hoffman offer the most serious negative responses to Humphrey's work; J. R. Frakes and Elizabeth Janeway are perhaps most persuasive in their admiration for *The Ordways*.

Allen, Walter, *New Statesman*, LV (Apr 12, 1958), 480. [r of *Home from the Hill*]

Boatwright, Taliaferro, *N.Y. Her Trib Bk R*, Jan. 12, 1958, p. 1. [r of *Home from the Hill*]

Dienstag, Eleanor, *New Rep*, CLII (Feb 27, 1965), 24–25. [r of *The Ordways*]

Frakes, J. R., *Bk Week* (Jan 31, 1965), 5. [r of *The Ordways*]

Goyen, William, *N.Y. Times Bk R*, Jan 12, 1958, p. 4. [r of *Home from the Hill*]

Havighurst, Walter, *SatR*, XLI (Jan 11, 1958), 15. [r of *Home from the Hill*]

Hicks, Granville, *SatR*, XLVIII (Feb 6, 1965), 25. [r of *The Ordways*]

Hoffman, *The Art of Southern Fiction*, pp. 103–6.

Holzhauer, Jean, *Commonweal*, LXVII (Feb 28, 1958), 517. [r of *Home from the Hill*]

Janeway, Elizabeth, *New York Times Bk R*, Jan. 31, 1965, p. 1. [r of *The Ordways*]

Popkin, Henry, *Commonweal*, LXXXII (March 26, 1965), 26. [r of *The Ordways*]

Rubin, *The Curious Death of the Novel*, pp. 263–65, 268, 280, 283–84.

Stevenson, D. L., *Nation*, CLXXXVI (Feb 22, 1958), 172. [r of *Home from the Hill*]

Sullivan, Walter, *SeR*, LXXIII (1965), 783–84. [r of *The Ordways*]
TLS, June 17, 1965, p. 489. [r of *The Ordways*]

JAMES BOATWRIGHT
Washington and Lee University
Lexington, Virginia

JOSEPH HOLT INGRAHAM (1809-1860)

We still possess remarkably little accurate information about Ingraham, who was one of our earliest prolific, popular authors. Even the accounts listed below are fragmentary and cannot be wholly trusted. The best short biographical sketch is in Albert Johannsen's book. As Jacob Blanck's bibliography makes clear, even the canon of Ingraham's work is far from established.

Hubbell, pp. 623–24, *938; *LSL*, VI, pp. 2591–96.

*Blanck, *Bibliography of American Literature,* IV, pp. 459–91 [most complete listing of Ingraham's many works]

Cowie, *Rise of the American Novel,* pp. 288–92. [detailed analysis of Ingraham's *Lafitte*]

Derby, Frank, *Fifty Years among Books, Authors and Publishers* (New York, 1884). [unique source of first-hand information]

French, Warren, "One Hundred Years of a Religious Best-Seller," *WHumR*, X (Winter 1955–56), 45–54. [history of *The Prince of the House of David*]

————, "A Sketch of the Life of Joseph Holt Ingraham," *Jour of Miss Hist,* XI (1949), 155–71.

————, "The Twice-Told Travels of Joseph Holt Ingraham," *Amer Notes and Queries,* I (Dec 1962), 51–52.

*Johannsen, Albert, *The House of Beadle and Adams* (Norman, Okla., 1950), II, 151–55. [biog sketch and example of author's style]

Pennington, Edgar Legare, "The Ministry of Joseph Holt Ingraham in Mobile, Alabama," *Hist Mag of the Prot Epis Church,* XXVI (1958), 344–60.

Stietenroth, Charles W., *One Hundred Years of "Old Trinity" Church, Natchez* (Natchez, Miss, 1922).

Sykes, James Lundy, *A History of Saint John's Parish, Aberdeen, Mississippi* (n.p., n.d.).

Tryon, Warren S., ed., *A Mirror for Americans* (Chicago, 1952), II, pp. 293–347. Repr in *My Native Land: Life in America, 1790–1870* (Chicago, 1961), pp. 155–205. [contains brief, unreliable biog sketch and extensive autobiog quotations from Ingraham's first bk, *The South-West, by a Yankee* (1835)]

WARREN FRENCH
University of Missouri
Kansas City, Missouri

RANDALL JARRELL (1914-1965)

Except for two excellent descriptive bibliographies covering Jarrell's own work up to 1961, the major work on Jarrell is yet to be done. Three years after his death there are still no book-length critical and biographical studies. The volume edited by Robert Lowell, Peter Taylor, and Robert Penn Warren is basically a memorial volume, with important reminiscences by his friends and by Mrs. Jarrell plus a few important essays. Other essays on Jarrell are printed in a volume of the University of North Carolina at Greensboro literary magazine, *Analects* (1961), dedicated to Jarrell.

The *Alumni News* of the University of North Carolina at Greensboro for Spring 1966 (LIV) contains tributes to him from friends and former students.

In order to assess the decline in Jarrell's reputation in the 1960s, one might also examine additional reviews of his last volume, *The Lost World*. A critical evaluation avoiding the extremes of the unfavorable reviews of that volume and the praise by some of his friends in the Lowell-Taylor-Warren volume is needed.

*Adams, Charles M., *Randall Jarrell: A Bibliography* (Chapel Hill, 1958). [descriptive bibl of work by Jarrell to 1958]

*_____, "A Supplement to Randall Jarrell: A Bibliography," *Analects* (Women's Coll, U of N.C.), I (Spring 1961), 49–56.

Calhoun, Richard J., "Randall Jarrell: Towards a Reassessment," *So Atl Bull*, XXXII (Nov 1967) 1–4.

Cambon, Glauco, "Jarrell's War Poems and the Syntax of Eloquence," *Analects*, I (Spring 1961), 11–13.

Dickey, James L., "Some of All of It," *SeR*, LXIV (1956), 324–48. Repr in Dickey, *The Suspect in Poetry* (Madison, Minn., 1964), pp. 73–84. [r essay]

Donoghue, Denis, "The Lost World," in *Randall Jarrell 1914–1965*, ed. Robert Lowell, Peter Taylor, and Robert Penn Warren (New York, 1967), pp. 49–62. [r essay]

Fein, Richard, "Randall Jarrell's World of War," *Analects*, I (Spring 1961), 14–23.

Flint, R. W., "On Randall Jarrell," *Commentary*, XLI (Feb 1966), 78–81. Repr in *Randall Jarrell 1914–1965*, pp. 76–85. [crit evaluation of poetry]

Glick, Nathan, "About American Poetry: An Interview with Randall Jarrell," *Analects*, I (Spring 1961), 5–10.

Jarrell, Randall, "Answer to Questions (1) Comments on Poetry," in *Mid-Century Poets*, ed. John Ciardi (New York, 1950), pp. 182–85. [crit comments on his own poetry]

_____, "The Woman at the Washington Zoo," in *A Sad Heart at the Supermarket: Essays and Fables* (New York, 1962), pp. 160–73. [autobiog comments on composition of poem]

Jarrell, Mrs. Randall, "The Group of Two: A Memoir of a Marriage," *Harper's*, CCXXXIV (Apr 1967), 73–79. Repr in *Randall Jarrell 1914–1965*, pp. 274–98.

Kazin, Alfred, "Prince of Reviewers," *Reporter*, XXXV (Sept 8, 1966), 45–58. Repr in *Randall Jarrell 1914–1965*, pp. 86–100. [Jarrell as lit crit]

*Kisslinger, Margaret V., "Randall Jarrell: A Bibliography," *BB*, XXIV (1966), 243–47.

Lowell, Robert, "On *The Seven League Crutches*," in *Randall Jarrell 1914–1965*, pp. 113–17. [r essay, first publ in *N.Y. Times Bk R*, Oct 7, 1951]

———, "Randall Jarrell," in *Randall Jarrell 1914–1965*, pp. 101–12 [biog]

Maguire, C. E., "Shape of the Lightning: Randall Jarrell," *Renascence*, VII (1955), 115–20, 181–86, 195.

*Quinn, Sister M. Bernetta, "Randall Jarrell: His Metamorphosis," *The Metamorphic Tradition in Modern Poetry* (New Brunswick, N.J., 1955), pp. 168–206. [metamorphosis as major theme and poetic device in Jarrell's poetry]

———, "Jarrell and the Art of Translation," *Analects*, I (Spring 1961), 37–48.

———, "Metamorphoses in Randall Jarrell," in *Randall Jarrell 1914–1965*, pp. 139–54.

Ransom, John Crowe, "The Rugged Way of Genius—A Tribute to Randall Jarrell," *SoR*, III n.s. (1967), 263–81. Repr in *Randall Jarrell 1914–1965*, pp. 155–81. [biog and crit]

Ray, David, "The Lighting of Randall Jarrell," *Prairie Schooner*, XXXV (Spring 1961), 45–52.

Rideout, Walter B., "'To Change, To Change!': The Poetry of Randall Jarrell," in *Poets in Progress: Critical Prefaces to Ten Contemporary Americans*, ed. Edward B. Hungerford (Evanston, Ill., 1962), pp. 156–78. [detailed crit evaluation]

Shapiro, Karl, "The Death of Randall Jarrell," in *Randall Jarrell 1914–1965*, pp. 195–229. [Jarrell's relation to his own generation of poets]

Stepanchev, Stephen, *American Poetry Since 1945* (New York, 1965), pp. 37–53. [crit assessment]

Taylor, Peter, "Randall Jarrell," in *Randall Jarrell 1914–1965*, pp. 241–52. [biog]

Tyler, Parker, "The Dramatic Lyricism of Randall Jarrell," *Poetry*, LXXIX (1952), 335–46. [r essay]

Watson, Robert, "Randall Jarrell: The Last Years," in *Randall Jarrell 1914–1965*, pp. 257–73. [biog and crit]

RICHARD JAMES CALHOUN
Clemson University
Clemson, South Carolina

THOMAS JEFFERSON (1743-1826)

Very little direct criticism of Jefferson as writer or even as philosophical thinker has appeared. There is, however, a considerable body of commentary on his methods of composing, and analyses of some of his theories in biographies and other studies of his general and specific interests. The books by Adrienne Koch, Stuart G. Brown, and Merrill D. Peterson are especially useful.

DAB, X, pp. 17–35; *Duyckinck*, I, p. 239; *Hubbell*, pp. 122–34, *939–40; *LSL*, VI, pp. 2677–85; *LHUS*, I, pp. 147–54, *II, pp. 595–602, *Supp*, 148.

Becker, Carl., *The Declaration of Independence; A Study in the History of Political Ideas* (New York, 1942).

Berman, Eleanor D., *Thomas Jefferson among the Arts* (New York, 1947).

———, and E. C. McClintock, "Thomas Jefferson and Rhetoric," *Q Jour Speech*, XXXIII (1947), 218–22.

Brown, Stuart G., *Thomas Jefferson* (New York, 1963).

Chinard, Gilbert, *Thomas Jefferson: The Apostle of Americanism* (Boston, 1929).

Colbourn, H. Trevor, "Thomas Jefferson's Use of the Past," *WMQ*, 3rd ser, XV (1958), 56–70.

*Davis, Richard Beale, *Intellectual Life in Jefferson's Virginia, 1790–1830* (Chapel Hill, 1964), *passim*.

———, "Jefferson as Collector of Virginiana," *SB*, XIV (1961), 117–44.

Gabriel, Ralph H. "Thomas Jefferson and Twentieth Century Rationalism," *VQR*, XXVI (1950), 321–35.

Hillbruner, Anthony, "Word and Deed: Jefferson's Addresses to the Indians," *Speech Monographs*, XXX (1963), 328–34.

Koch, Adrienne, *The Philosophy of Thomas Jefferson* (New York, 1943).

Lehmann, Karl, *Thomas Jefferson, American Humanist* (New York, 1947).

Malone, Dumas, *Jefferson and His Time*, 3 vols to date (Boston, 1948———).

Parks, Edd Winfield, "Jefferson as a Man of Letters," *GaR*, VI (1952), 450–59.

*Peterson, Merrill D., *The Jefferson Image in the American Mind* (New York, 1960).

Smith, William R., "The Rhetoric of the Declaration of Independence," *Coll Eng*, XXVI (1965), 306–309.

Sowerby, E. M., *Catalogue of the Library of Thomas Jefferson*, 5 vols (Washington, D.C., 1952–59).

Wright, Louis B., "Thomas Jefferson and the Classics," *Proceed Amer Philos Soc*, LXXXVII (1943), 223–33.

RICHARD BEALE DAVIS
University of Tennessee
Knoxville, Tennessee

JAMES WELDON JOHNSON (1871-1938)

Of the half dozen really significant American Negro writers in the years 1915–1935, only one was born and principally schooled in the South. Though W. E. B. DuBois lived and worked in the South on and off for a quarter of a century and his best work was generated by the South, he thought of himself as a French-derived black Yankee. Alain Locke was a native of Pennsylvania; Langston Hughes, of Missouri, which he referred to as mid-western; and though Countee Cullen was probably born in Kentucky, the only childhood home he remembered was in New York. But Johnson was a Southerner, and the life-style he eventually carried to New York and around the world was Southern. And the cadences of his poetry and the themes of his prose are Southern.

In the years before the Great Depression, he was accused of "radicalism"; but no longer. Indeed, his lovely hymn, "Lift Every Voice and Sing," which was adopted as a sort of Negro national anthem, has been scorned, even by some moderates, as "too soft and pleading" and "Uncle Tom-ish." It is no longer sung at Negro gatherings. Johnson's poetry, some of which broke new ground in the use of Negro dialect, has not suffered quite the same degree of repudiation, but much of it is now thought of as merely pretty and old-fashioned. Such criticism, of course, is relative. Johnson has not been the subject of scholarly enquiry. There is no definitive Johnson bibliography, and references to him are scattered and inconclusive. Of these latter, what follows are representative.

DAB, XXII, pp. 345–47.

Brawley, Benjamin, *Negro Builders and Heroes* (Chapel Hill, 1937), p. 237.

———, "The Negro Literary Renaissance," in *The Southern Workman*, LVI (Apr 1927), 177–80.

Brown, Sterling, Arthur P. Davis and Ulysses Lee, *The Negro Caravan* (New York, 1941), pp. 324–25.

Butcher, Margaret Just, *The Negro in American Culture* (New York, 1956), pp. 48–49, 122–23.

Davis, John P., *American Negro Reference Book* (Englewood Cliffs, N.J., 1966), p. 873.

DuBois, William E. B., *Dusk of Dawn* (New York, 1940), pp. 264–66, 292–93. [autobiog]

Ferguson, Blanche E., *Countee Cullen and the Negro Renaissance* (New York, 1966), pp. 46–47, 156–57. [biog]

Franklin, John Hope, *From Slavery to Freedom* (New York, 1947), pp. 493–94.

Furnas, J. C., *Goodbye to Uncle Tom* (New York, 1956), pp. 368–76.

Gloster, Hugh Morris, *Negro Voices in American Fiction* (Chapel Hill, 1948), pp. 79–83.

Johnson, James Weldon, *Along This Way* (New York, 1933). [autobiog]

Littlejohn, David, *Black on White: A Critical Survey of Writing by American Negroes* (New York, 1966), pp. 24–27.

Meier, August, *Negro Thought in America* (Ann Arbor, 1963), pp. 79, 254–55, 269–70.

Redding, Saunders, *To Make a Poet Black* (Chapel Hill, 1939), pp. 97, 120–22.

SAUNDERS REDDING
National Endowment for the Humanities
Washington, D.C.

MARY JOHNSTON (1870-1936)

Scholarly critical study of Mary Johnston and her work is notable mainly for its scarcity. Most of the histories of American literature give her work only passing, often unfavorable mention. Two exceptions to this are Edward Wagenknecht in his *Cavalcade of the American Novel* and Arthur Hobson Quinn in his *American Fiction*. No items for Mary Johnston appear in Lewis Leary's list of articles on American literature, 1900–1950, nor in Thomas F. Marshall's index to *American Literature, 1929–1959*. Richard Chase does not mention Mary Johnston in his *The American Novel and Its Tradition*, nor does Alfred Kazin in *On Native Grounds*, nor does Edmund Wilson in his *Patriotic Gore*, his study of Civil War writings; nor does she appear in Louis D. Rubin, Jr., and Robert Jacobs, *South: Modern Southern Literature in Its Cultural Setting*. The list which follows offers those works which present something more than brief review description of Johnston novels, the form of the usual mention of her work.

DAB, XXII, pp. 349–50; *LSL*, VI, pp. 2757–62.

Benét, Stephen Vincent, "Out of Focus," *SatR*, II (May 15, 1926), 786. [fair, mild, but largely unfavorable r essay of *The Great Valley*]

Boynton, H. W., "Shadow and Substance," *Independent*, CVIII (Apr 8, 1922), 354. [*Silver Cross* r with another novel; some comment on hist fict; unfavorable comment on Mary Johnston's bk]

*Coan, Otis W., and Richard G. Lillard, *America in Fiction* (Stanford, 1945), pp. 5, 51, 133, 139, 164.

Hubbell, Jay B., "Cavalier and Indentured Servant in Virginia Fiction," *SAQ*, XXVI (1927), 22–39.

*Johnson, Merle "American First Editions: Mary Johnston, 1870____," *PW*, CXVIII (Jul 19, 1930), 276–77.

Leisy, Ernest E., *The American Historical Novel* (Norman, Okla. 1950), pp. 17, 18, 22.

_____, "The Literary Spotlight, X: Mary Johnston," *Bookman*, LV (1922), 491–95.

Lively, Robert A., *Fiction Fights the Civil War: An Unfinished Chapter in the Literary History of the American People* (Chapel Hill, 1957), pp. 12, 17, 24, 59, 66, 70, 98, 102, 106.

M. H. V., "Mary Johnston's 'Audrey,' " *Critic*, XL (1902), 260. [r essay]

"Mary Johnston's Suffrage Speech," *Current Opinion*, LVI (Jan 1914), 49.

Mott, Frank Luther, *Golden Multitudes* (New York, 1947), pp. 213–214, 324, 329.

Nelson, Lawrence W., "Mary Johnston and the Historic Imagination," in *The Dilemma of the Southern Writer*, ed. Richard K. Meeker (Farmville, Va., 1961), pp. 61–94. Repr in *Southern Writers: Appraisals in Our Time*, ed. Simonini, pp. 71–102.

Parsons, Alice Beal, "The People of Youth," *The Nation* (June 30, 1926), 727–28. [r essay]

Quinn, *American Fiction*, pp. 501–504, 671. [in Chap 22, "The Romance of History and Politics"]

Robeson, John R., ed., "Two Virginia Novelists on Woman's Suffrage: An Exchange.

of Letters between Mary Johnston and Thomas Nelson Page," *VMHB*, LXIV (1956), 286–90.

*Sherman. Caroline B., "The Rediscovery of Mary Johnston," *SLM*, n.s., IV (1942), pp. 431–32.

Van Auken, Sheldon, "The Southern Historical Novel in the Early Twentieth Century," *JSH*, XIV (1948), 169–91.

Van Doren, Carl, *The American Novel*, rev ed (New York, 1940), pp. 216–17.

Wagenknecht, Edward, *Cavalcade of the American Novel* (New York, 1952), pp. 197–203, 436, and 528b.

———, "The World and Mary Johnston," *SeR*, XLIV (1936), 188–206. [rather excessive praise]

BLAIR ROUSE
University of Arkansas
Fayetteville, Arkansas

RICHARD MALCOLM JOHNSTON (1822-1898)

Richard Malcolm Johnston has attracted considerable attention from scholars, and the list of writings about him is extensive. As early as 1888 Sophie Bledsoe Herrick recognized the merits of his work and published a biographical-critical article in the *Century Magazine*. Ten years later, in the year of Johnston's death, the editor of *Dial* wrote a discerning editorial on Johnston's life and works. In the same year, Edmund Clarence Stedman published a "literary estimate" which appeared jointly with a bibliography of Johnston's writings compiled by Stephen B. Weeks.

Since then, numerous specialized and general studies have been published. Edd Winfield Parks has shown the most continued and active interest in him. Dr. Parks's efforts have been manifested in his own creative scholarship and also in the production of theses under his direction. His essay on Johnston in *Segments of Southern Thought* is outstanding. Johnston's Maryland years are admirably covered by Francis Taylor Long in the three-part article which was printed in the *Maryland Historical Magazine*.

Although Johnston has attracted wide interest and the works on him are numerous, they are not exhaustive.

DAB, X, pp. 148–49; *Hubbell*, pp. 777–82, *940–41; *LSL*, VI, pp. 2781–84.

Brinson, Mrs. Fred, "Richard Malcolm Johnston; Georgia Author," Georgia, 1927. [MA thesis]

Brinson, Lessie B., *A Study of the Life and Works of Richard Malcolm Johnston* (Nashville, 1937). [abstract of Peabody Coll diss]

Bush, Robert, "Richard Malcolm Johnston's Marriage Group," *GaR*, XVIII (1964), 429–36.

*Dyar, Pat McWhorter, "Schools and Teachers of Richard Malcolm Johnston," Georgia, 1940. [MA thesis]

Edwards, Corliss Hines, Jr., "Richard Malcolm Johnston's View of the Old Field School," *Ga Hist Q*, L (1966), 382–90.

Eyler, C. M., "Richard M. Johnston, And the Dukesborough Tales," Columbia, 1926. [MA thesis]

*Garner, Leona Clack, " 'Richard Malcolm Johnston,' A Study of Local Color with Emphasis on Selected Works of Three Georgia Authors," Georgia, 1965, pp. 23–57. [MA thesis]

Herrick, Sophie Bledsoe, "Richard Malcolm Johnston," *Century*, XIV (1888), 276–80.

Johnston, Richard Malcolm, *Autobiography of Col. Richard Malcolm Johnston* (Washington, 1901).

Long, Francis Taylor, "The Life of Richard Malcolm Johnston in Maryland, 1867–1898," *Md Hist Mag*, XXXIV (1939), 305–24; XXXV (1940), 270–86; and XXXVI (1941), 54–69.

Parks, Edd Winfield, "Professor Richard Malcolm Johnston," *Ga Hist Q*, XXV (1941), 1–15.

———, "Richard Malcolm Johnston," *Segments of Southern Thought* (Athens, Ga., 1938), pp. 223–44.

"Richard Malcolm Johnston," *Dial*, XXV (1898), 213–15.

*Stedman, Edmund Clarence, and Stephen B. Weeks, "Literary Estimate And Bibliography of Richard Malcolm Johnston," Southern Historical Association *Publications*, II (1898), 315–27.

W. PORTER KELLAM
University of Georgia
Athens, Georgia

MADISON JONES (1925—)

Madison Jones is Writer-in-Residence at Auburn University. In addition to short stories, he has published four novels: *The Innocent* (1957), *Forest of the Night* (1960), *A Buried Land* (1963), and *An Exile* (1967). His story "Dog Days" was published in *The Best American Short Stories* (1953). *The Sewanee Review* (Winter 1966) devoted an entire issue to the first publication of *An Exile*. There is very little scholarship on Jones. However, in the list below, the reviews represent the wide-spread attention his books have received.

Curley, Thomas, "The Tree of Knowledge of Good and Evil," *Commonweal*, LXV (March 22, 1957), 642. [r of *The Innocent*]

Ethridge, James M., and Barbara Kopala, ed., *Contemporary Authors*, XIII–XIV (Detroit, 1965), p. 237. [biog]

Jack, W. T., "Return to the Past," *N.Y. Times Bk R*, Sept 3, 1967, p. 22. [r of *An Exile*]

Long, Grady M., "Shattering Climax," *Chattanooga Times*, Sept 24, 1967, p. 24. [r of *An Exile*]

Meeker, Richard K., "The Youngest Generation of Southern Fiction Writers," in *Southern Writers: Appraisals in Our Time*, ed. Simonini, pp. 168–70.

Murray, Michele, "Southern Guilt," *Commonweal*, LXXVII (Aug 9, 1963), 486–87. [r of *A Buried Land*]

Parrill, William, "Jones Is Worth Keeping Up With," *Nashville Tennessean*, Aug 27, 1967, p. 12D. [r of *An Exile*]

Pearre, Howell, "Southern Novel Maintains Tradition" *Nashville Banner*, Aug 25, 1967, p. 28. [r of *An Exile*]

Rubin, Louis D., Jr., "The Difficulties of Being a Southern Writer Today: Or, Getting Out from Under William Faulkner," *JSH*, XXIX (1963), pp. 486–94. Repr in Rubin, *The Curious Death of the Novel*, pp. 282–93. [*A Buried Land* as example of movement away from Faulkner in So writing]

"South in Ferment," *Time*, LXIX, No. 8 (Feb 25, 1957), 102. [r of *The Innocent*]

Sullivan, Walter, "The Continuing Renascence: Southern Fiction in the Fifties," in Rubin and Jacobs, *South*, pp. 376–91. See esp pp. 380–81.

Warren, Robert Penn, "A First Novel," *SeR*, LXV (1957), 347–52. [r of *The Innocent*]

Wetzel, Donald, "Tale of a Dark Frontier" *N.Y. Her Trib Bk R*, March 13, 1960, p. 10. [r of *Forest of the Night*]

Wyllie, John Cook, "Guilt-Ridden Dixie," *SatR*, XL (Feb 23, 1957), 18. [r of *The Innocent*]

MARION C. MICHAEL
Auburn University
Auburn, Alabama

JOHN PENDLETON KENNEDY (1795-1870)

The student of Kennedy is now well equipped with modern biographical and critical works and with paperback editions of his three major works of fiction. However, much untouched material is available in the Kennedy Papers—the principal manuscript collection—which he deposited in the Peabody Institute Library, Baltimore; see the article by Griffin for a detailed description. For Kennedy's relationships with two other important Southern writers, consult also the biographies and editions of letters listed under Poe and Simms.

DAB, X, pp. 333–34; *Duyckinck*, II, p. 219; *Hubbell*, pp. 481–95, *941–42; *LSL*, VII, pp. 2897–901; *LHUS*, I, pp. 309–310, *II, 604; *Supp*, 153.

*Bohner, Charles H., *John Pendleton Kennedy: Gentleman from Baltimore* (Baltimore, 1961).

Cowie, *The Rise of the American Novel*, pp. 258–70.

Ellison, Rhoda Coleman, "An Interview with Horse-Shoe Robinson," *AL*, XXXI (1959), 329–32.

———, "Early Alabama Interest in Southern Writers," *AlaR*, I (Apr 1948), 101–10.

Griffin, Lloyd W., "The John Pendleton Kennedy Manuscripts," *Md Hist Mag*, XLVIII (1953), 327–36.

*Leisy, Ernest E., intro to John Pendleton Kennedy, *Horse-Shoe Robinson* (New York, 1962), pp. ix–xxxii. [repr; first publ 1937]

Moore, John Robert, "Kennedy's *Horse-Shoe Robinson*: Fact or Fiction?" *AL*, IV (1932), 160–66.

Osborne, William S., intro to John Pendleton Kennedy, *Rob of the Bowl* (New Haven, 1966), pp. 5–27.

———, intro to John Pendleton Kennedy, *Swallow Barn* (New York, 1962), pp. ·xiii–xlv.

———, "John Pendleton Kennedy's *Horse Shoe Robinson*: A Novel with 'the Utmost Historical Accuracy,' " *Md Hist Mag*, LIX (1964), 286–96.

———, " 'The Swiss Traveller' Essays: Earliest Literary Writings of John Pendleton Kennedy," *AL*, XXX (1958), 228–33.

Parrington, Vernon Louis, "John Pendleton Kennedy," *Main Currents in American Thought* (New York, 1927), II, 46–56.

Pretzer, Wallace Leonard. "Eighteenth-Century Literary Conventions in the Fictional Style of John Pendleton Kennedy," *DA*, XXIV, 731–32 (Michigan).

*Ridgely, J. V., *John Pendleton Kennedy* (New York, 1966). [TUSAS]

Roberts, Warren E., "Some Folksong References in Kennedy's *Swallow Barn*," *SFQ*, XVII (1953), 249–54.

Taylor, William R., "A Squire of Change Alley," *Cavalier and Yankee* (New York, 1963), pp. 156–81.

Tuckerman, Henry T., *The Life of John Pendleton Kennedy* (New York, 1871).

Uhler, John E., "Kennedy's Novels and His Posthumous Works," *AL*, III (1932), 471–79.

Walhout, Clarence Peter, "Religion in the Thought and Fiction of Three Ante-Bellum Southerners: Kennedy, Caruthers, and Simms," *DA*, XXV, 6604 (Northwestern).

Wermuth, Paul C., "*Swallow Barn*: A Virginia Idyll," *Virginia Cavalcade*, IX, i (Summer 1959), 30–34.

J. V. RIDGELY
Columbia University
New York, New York

GRACE ELIZABETH KING (1851-1932)

DAB, X, pp. 389–90; *LSL*, VII, pp. 2927–31.

*Beer, William, "List of Writings of Grace King," *La Hist Q*, VI (1923), 378–79.

Cocks, R. S., "The Fiction of Grace King," *La Hist Q*, VI (1923), 353–59.

Dart, Henry Plauche, "The Ideals of Grace King," *La Hist Q*, XV (1932), [339]–44.

———, "Miss King's Historical Works," *La Hist Q*, VI (1923) 347–53.

Guyol, Louise Hubert, "A Southern Author in Her New Orleans Home," *La Hist Q*, VI (1923), 365–74.

Kendall, John Smith, "A New Orleans Lady of Letters," *La Hist Q*, XIX (1936), 436–65.

King, Grace Elizabeth, *Memories of a Southern Woman of Letters* (New York, 1932).

Pattee, Fred Lewis, *The Development of the American Short Story* (New York, 1923), pp. 323–27.

*_____, *A History of American Literature Since 1870* (New York, 1915), pp. 362–64, 382.

Snyder, Henry N., "Miss Grace Elizabeth King," in W. M. Baskervill, *Southern Writers* (Nashville, 1903), II, pp. 272–91.

*Vaughn, Bess, "A Bio-Bibliography of Grace Elizabeth King," *La Hist Q*, XVII (1934), 752–70.

ARLIN TURNER
Duke University
Durham, North Carolina

MIRABEAU B. LAMAR (1798-1859)

Widely known in the South during his lifetime for his occasional poetry, Lamar collected and published only one volume of his poems, which had appeared mainly in newspapers. Philip Graham searched newspapers, scrapbooks, albums, and journals, and brought together eighty-seven poems (probably all that Lamar wrote) in *The Life and Poems of Mirabeau Buonaparte Lamar* (1938). This definitive biographical and critical study stresses Lamar's personal life as distinct from his public career and concludes that his early poems imitate eighteenth-century English poetry, though his verse after 1820 shows influence of the new romanticism, particularly that of Thomas Moore. "The Daughter of Mendoza," written in 1858, has been Lamar's most widely anthologized poem. Altogether, Lamar's poetry shows no influence of his public life as a hero of the Texas Revolution and as second president of the Republic of Texas.

Dab, X, pp. 553–54; *Hubbell*, pp. 629–34, *943; *LSL*, VI, pp. 2987—90.

Christian, Asa K., *Mirabeau Buonaparte Lamar* (Austin, Tex., 1922), repr from *SW Hist Q*, XXIII–XXIV (Jan 1920; Apr 1921). [biog, emphasis on public life]

Dixon, Sam H., *The Poets and Poetry of Texas* (Austin, Tex., 1885). [biog sketch, portrait, and five poems]

Eagleton, Davis F., *Writers of Texas* (New York, 1913). [biog note and four poems]

Gambrell, Herbert P., *Mirabeau Buonaparte Lamar, Troubadour and Crusader* (Dallas, 1934). [almost entirely biog]

*Graham, Philip, *The Life and Poems of Mirabeau Buonaparte Lamar* (Chapel Hill, 1938).

———, "Mirabeau Lamar's First Trip to Texas," *SWR*, XXI (1936), 369–89. [autobiog]

Greer, Hilton R., *Voices of the Southwest* (New York, 1923). [biog note, one poem, "The Daughter of Mendoza"]

Lamar, Mirabeau B., *The Papers of Mirabeau Buonaparte Lamar*, ed. Charles A. Gulick, Winnie Allen, and Harriet Smither (Austin, Tex., 1920–27), 6 vols. [state papers, correspondence, and mss Lamar collected on Texas and Mexican hist]

———, *Verse Memorials* (New York, 1857), privately printed.

Quintero, J. A., *"Verse Memorials"* (Austin, Tex. [1857?]), in *Lamar Papers*, VI, 356–61. [laudatory r]

Reese, Ruth Sara, "Mirabeau B. Lamar, Father of Texas Education," Texas, 1933. (MA thesis)

JOHN Q. ANDERSON
University of Houston
Houston, Texas

SIDNEY LANIER (1842-1881)

Scholarly writing about Sidney Lanier has tended to deal with his life record, character, and psychological traits, his compositions being treated less as independent works of art than as reflections of his own or of the South's experience after the Civil War. His lyrics and longer poems are better constructed than most critics have discovered, and his artistic innovations need further explanation.

DAB, X, pp. 601–605; *Hubbell*, pp. 758–77, *943; *LSL*, VII, pp. 3041–45; *LHUS*, I, pp. 901–907, *II, 605–608, *Supp*, 153–54.

Allen, Gay Wilson. *American Prosody* (New York, 1935), pp. 121–38.

*Anderson, Charles R., gen ed., *The Centennial Edition of the Works of Sidney Lanier*, 10 vols (Baltimore, 1945). [admirably ed. with schol intros; starting point of research; bibl VI, pp. 379–412]

———, "Two Letters from Lanier to Holmes," *AL*, XVIII (1947), 321–26.

———, "Poet of the Pine Barrens," *GaR*, I (1947), 280–93. [Hayne-Lanier correspondence]

Baskervill, William Malone, *Southern Writers* (Nashville, 1897), I, pp. 137–298.

Beaver, Joseph, "Lanier's Use of Science for Poetic Imagery," *AL*, XXIV (1953), 520–33.

Bradford, Gamaliel, "Sidney Lanier," in *American Portraits* (Boston, 1922), pp. 59–83.

Edwards, John S., "Sidney Lanier: His Life and Work in Music," Georgia, 1967. [MA thesis; most complete study extant of Lanier's musical compositions]

Fletcher, John G., "Sidney Lanier," *U Kan Cy R*, XVI (1949), 97–102.

Foerster, Norman, *Nature in American Literature* (New York, 1923), pp. 221–37.

Graham, Phillip, "A Note on Lanier's Music," *Stud in Eng*, XVII (1937), 107–111.

———, "Lanier's Reading," in *U of Tex Stud in Eng*, No. 11 (1931), 63–89.

Kent, Charles W., "A Study of Lanier's Poems," *PMLA*, VII (1892), 33–63. [first scholarly treatment]

Lanier, Clifford L., "Reminiscences of Sidney Lanier," *Chatauquan*, XXI (1895), 403–409.

Leary, Lewis, "The Forlorn Hope of Sidney Lanier," *SAQ*, XLVI (1947), 263–71.

Lorenz, Lincoln. *Sidney Lanier* (New York, 1935). [popularized biog]

Mims, Edwin, *Sidney Lanier* (Boston, 1905). [sympathetic and still useful biog]

Moore, Rayburn S., "Southern Writers and Northern Literary Magazines, 1865–1890," Duke, 1956, pp. 66–69, 136–40. [diss]

Parks, Edd Winfield, "Lanier as Poet," in *Essays on American Literature in Honor of Jay B. Hubbell*, ed. Clarence Gohdes (Durham, 1967), pp. 183–201.

————, *Sidney Lanier: The Man, The Poet, The Critic* [Forthcoming from University of Georgia Press; expansion of Lamar Lectures, Apr 1968, Wesleyan Coll, Macon, Ga.]

Pearce, Roy Harvey, *The Continuity of American Poetry* (Princeton, 1961), pp. 236–46. [Lanier's shortcomings]

Ransom, John Crowe. "Hearts and Heads," *AmerR*, II (1934), 554–71. [rebuttal to Starkes's attack on Warren's r art]

Ross, Robert H., " 'The Marshes of Glynn': A Study in Symbolic Obscurity," *AL*, XXXII (1961), 403–16. [somewhat strained interpretation]

*Starke, Aubrey H., *Sidney Lanier: A Biographical and Critical Study* (Chapel Hill, 1933). [fullest biog, with bibl pp. 455–73]

————, "The Agrarians Deny a Leader," *AmerR*, II (1934), 534–53. [attack on Warren's r article, and Allen Tate's r, *New Rep*, Aug 30, 1933]

Stedman, E. C., "The Late Sidney Lanier," *The Critic*, I (1881), 289. [set tone for 19th-cent evaluations]

Tankersley, Allen P., "College Life in Old Oglethorpe" (Athens, Ga., 1951). [Lanier's coll days]

Warfel, Harry R., "Mystic Vision in 'The Marshes of Glynn,' " *MissQ*, (1966), XIX, 34–40.

Warren, Robert Penn, "The Blind Poet: Sidney Lanier," *AmerR*, II (1933), 27–45. [scathing but prejudiced attack on Lanier, mainly on his poetry]

Webb, Richard, and Edwin R. Coulson, *Sidney Lanier: Poet and Prosodist* (Athens, Ga., 1941). [Webb's essay written at Yale in 1903]

HARRY R. WARFEL
University of Florida
Gainesville, Florida
and
EDD WINFIELD PARKS
University of Georgia
Athens, Georgia

HUGH SWINTON LEGARÉ (1797-1843)

There has never been a period of intense interest in Hugh Swinton Legaré, but over the years a considerable amount of work has in fact been done on him. Following in the wake of numerous sketches and reminiscences, the Rhea biography (1934) is more than adequate as the first full-length study of Legaré's life. The definitive biography which remains to be written will have to be preceded by an edition of the letters and bibliography; volume V of Jacob Blanck, comp., *Bibliography of American Literature* will presumably supply the latter. Legaré never devoted enough of his talent and energy to literature to become more than a minor figure, but a knowledge of his thought and writings provides a number of significant footnotes to a study of American letters.

DAB, XI, pp. 144–45; *Duyckinck*, II, pp. 24–26; *Hubbell*, 263–74, *945–46; *LSL*, VII, pp. 3169–71.

[Bullen, Mary Legaré, ed.], *Writings of Hugh Swinton Legaré* . . . (Charleston, 1846–45 [sic], 2 vols, "Biographical Notice" by E[dward] W. J[ohnston], I, v–lxxli. [includes some letters]

Carleton, William G., "The Celbrity Cult a Century Ago," *GaR*, XIV (1960), 133–42. [Legaré as orator]

Christophersen, Merrill Guerdon, "The Charleston Conversationalists," *So Speech Jour*, XX (1954), 99–108.

———, "A Rhetorical Study of Hugh Swinton Legaré: South Carolina Unionist," Florida State, 1954. [diss]

Davis, Richard Beale, "The Early American Lawyer and the Profession of Letters," *Huntington Lib Q*, XII (1949), 191–205.

Eby, E. H., "American Romantic Criticism, 1815–1860," Washington, 1927. [diss]

Hayne, Paul Hamilton, *Lives of Robert Young Hayne and Hugh Swinton Legaré* (Charleston, 1878).

"Hugh S. Legaré," *Whitaker's Mag: The Rights of the South*, II (1850), 194–201.

[Johnston, Edward W.], "Life and Labors, Literary, Professional and Public, of Legaré," *Amer Whig R*, II (1845), 417–30.

Krumpelmann, John T., "South Carolina—Hugh Swinton Legaré," in *Southern Scholars in Goethe's Germany* (Chapel Hill, [1965]), pp. 6–22.

Laurent, Henri, "Les débuts de la mission de Hugh Swinton Legaré, chargé d'affaires des Etats-Unis à Bruxelles (septembre-décembre 1832)," *Bulletin de la Commission Royale D'Histoire*, CII (1937). [prints various diplomatic letters]

"Life and Career of Hugh S. Legaré," *Scott's Month Mag*, II (1866), 496–505.

Parks, Edd Winfield, "Hugh Swinton Legaré: Humanist," *Ante-Bellum Southern Literary Critics* (Athens, Ga., 1962), pp. 23–50.

———, "Legaré and Grayson: Types of Classical Influence on Criticism in the Old South," *SWR*, XXII (1937), 354–65. Repr in *Segments of Southern Thought* (Athens, Ga., 1938), pp. 156–71.

Parrington, Vernon Louis, "Hugh Swinton Legaré: Charleston Intellectual," *Main Currents in American Thought* (New York, 1927), II, pp. 114–24.

Perry, Benjamin Franklin, "Hugh S. Legaré," *Reminiscences of Public Men* (Phila-delphia, 1883), pp. 251–55.

Preston, William Campbell, *Eulogy on Hugh Swinton Legaré; Delivered, at the Request of the City of Charleston . . . November 7, 1843* (Charleston, 1843).

Ramage, B. J., "Hugh Swinton Legaré," *SeR*, X (1902), 43–55 and 167–80. [see also r with correction, in the *S.C. Hist and Geneal Mag* for Apr and Jul, 1902]

*Rhea, Linda, *Hugh Swinton Legaré: A Charleston Intellectual* (Chapel Hill, 1934). [standard biog; Vanderbilt diss 1932]

Rives, W. C., "H. S. Legaré, Late Attorney General of the United States," *SLM*, IX (1843), 570–74.

"Sketch of the Character of the Hon. Hugh S. Legaré," *SoQR*, IV (1843), 347–62.

Ticknor, George, *Life, Letters, and Journals of George Ticknor* (Boston, 1876). [records important friendship]

Tyler, Lyon Gardiner, *The Letters and Times of the Tylers* (Richmond, 1885), II *passim*. [on Legaré's term as Attorney-General of the U.S. under President Tyler]

Willis, Larry Jordan, "The Character and Literary Style of Hugh Swinton Legaré," South Carolina, 1928. [MA thesis]

WILLIAM S. KABLE
University of South Carolina
Columbia, South Carolina

JAMES MATHEWES LEGARÉ (1823-1859)

Duyckinck, II, p. 720; *Hubbell*, pp. 559–64, *946–47; *LSL*, VII, pp. 3191–93.

Davis, Curtis Carroll, "Poet, Painter, and Inventor: Some Letters by James Mathewes Legaré, 1823–1859," *N.C. Hist R*, XXI (1944), 215–31.

———, "A Letter from the Muses: The Publication and Critical Reception of James M. Legaré's 'Orta-Undis, and Other Poems' (1848)," *N.C. Hist R*, XXVI (1949), 417–38.

———, "Fops, Frenchmen, Hidalgos, and Aztecs: Being a Survey of the Prose Fiction of J. M. Legaré of South Carolina (1823–1859)," *N.C. Hist R*, XXX (1953), 524–60. [illus]

———, "Mr. Legaré Inscribes Some Books: The Literary Tenets, and the Library, of a Carolina Writer." *Papers of Bibl Soc of Amer*, LVI (1962), 219–36.

*———, *The Ambitions of James Legaré: A Biography, And a Collected Edition of His Verse* (Columbia, S.C., 1969). [illus]

CURTIS CARROLL DAVIS
Baltimore, Maryland

HENRY CLAY LEWIS (1825-1850)

Walter Blair in *Native American Humor* (1937) ranked "Madison Tensas" among the ten most important humorists of the Old Southwest, although the identity of "the Louisiana Swamp Doctor" was then unknown. In 1955 John Q. Anderson identified "Madison Tensas" as Henry Clay Lewis, a young medical doctor who practiced in northeast Louisiana. Posing as an elderly country practitioner, Lewis published humorous accounts in the *Spirit of the Times* about his apprenticeship, student days, and subsequent practice. In 1849 he collected his published sketches, added new ones, and published them as *Odd Leaves from the Life of a Louisiana Swamp Doctor* in 1850, the year he was drowned in a flooded bayou at the age of twenty-five. Several of Lewis' sketches were reprinted in the United States and England, and his book was reissued many times.

Anderson, John Q., "Henry Clay Lewis, Alias 'The Louisiana Swamp Doctor,'" *Bull of the Medical Lib Assn,* XLIII (1955), 58–73. [biog]

———, "Mike Hooter—The Making of a Myth," *SFQ,* XIX (1955), 90–100. [crit]

———, "Folklore in the Writings of 'The Louisiana Swamp Doctor,'" *SFQ,* XIX (1955), 243–51. [crit]

———, "Henry Clay Lewis, Student at the Louisville Medical Institute, 1844–1846," *Filson Club Q,* XXXII (1958), 30–37. [biog, crit]

*———, *Louisiana Swamp Doctor: The Life and Writings of Henry Clay Lewis* (Baton Rouge, 1962). [repr of all Lewis' known sketches; biog and crit]

*Blair, Walter, *Native American Humor* (New York, 1937). ["Tensas" considered along with other SW humorists; gen biblio]

Chittick, V. L. O., *Ring-Tailed Roarers: Tall Tales of the American Frontier, 1830–1860* (Caldwell, Idaho, 1943). [repr four sketches with notes; erroneous dating of *Odd Leaves*]

Cohen and Dillingham, eds. *Humor of the Old Southwest.* [intro, biog and crit, repr three sketches]

Haliburton, T. C., *Traits of American Humor* (London, 1852). [repr one sketch; comtemp evaluation in intro]

Hudson, Arthur Palmer, *Humor of the Old Deep South* (New York, 1936). [crit, "Tensas" among other humorists]

"Madison Tensas," [pseud Henry Clay Lewis], *Odd Leaves from the Life of a Louisiana Swamp Doctor* (Philadelphia, 1850). [autobiog; first and only ed; subsequent printings variously dated, including a spurious 1846]

Meine, Franklin J., *Tall Tales of the Southwest* (New York, 1930). [crit; repr Lewis's first sketch]

*Rickels, Milton, "The Humor of the Old Southwest in London," *AL,* XXVII (1956), 557–60. [Lewis and other humorists repr in *Bentley's Miscellany*]

Turner, Arlin, "Seeds of Literary Revolt in the Humor of the Old Southwest," *La Hist Q,* XXXIX (1956), 143–51. [crit]

_____, ed., *Southern Stories* (New York, 1960). [crit, intro; repr one story]

JOHN Q. ANDERSON
University of Houston
Houston, Texas

RICHARD LEWIS (*ca.* 1699 - *ca.* 1733)

The Maryland schoolmaster-poet, Richard Lewis, is only now being recognized as perhaps the most accomplished of the several Augustan lyricists who flourished in Colonial America. The first collected edition of his poems is in preparation by J. A. Leo Lemay and this, when completed, should bring Lewis at long last the critical and scholarly attention he deserves.

Hubbell, pp. 65–67, *947.
Carlson, C. Lennart, "Richard Lewis and the Reception of his Works in England," *AL*, IX (1937), 301–16.
*Lemay, J. A. Leo, "A Literary History of Colonial Maryland," University of Pennsylvania, 1964, pp. 133–88. [diss; see also *DA*, XXV, 7246]
_____, "Richard Lewis and Augustan American Poetry," *PMLA*, LXXXIII (1968), 80–101.

CARL R. DOLMETSCH
College of William and Mary
Williamsburg, Virginia

AUGUSTUS BALDWIN LONGSTREET
(1790-1870)

Since the extensive and intensive biography by John Donald Wade (1924), little of major importance has been added to available information or to critical interpretation concerning this writer. Commentators on humor of the Old Southwest continue, paradoxically, to stress the relative decorum (and by implication, the inferiority) of Longstreet in comparison with other humorous realists of his time and region, and yet to allott him the lion's share of space in their discussions.

Recently, three publishers—Sagamore Press, Hill and Wang, and
Peter Smith—have reprinted *Georgia Scenes*, and the slender Long-
street canon has been slightly augmented: see "An Unreprinted Georgia
Scene," *Emory University Quarterly*, II, 100–101 (June 1946). Kenneth
Silverman has reinterpreted "The Gander Pulling" symbolically, but
the rest of Longstreet's work needs fresh assessment.

DAB, pp. 390–91; *Duyckinck*, II, pp. 314; *Hubbell*, pp. 666–69, *947–48; *LSL*, VII,
pp. 3241–44.

*Cohen and Dillingham, "Augustus Baldwin Longstreet," *Humor of the Old South-
west*, pp. 28–29. See also pp. x, xxiv, 418.

Ford, Thomas W., "Ned Brace of *Georgia Scenes*," *SFQ*, XXIX (1965), 220–27.
[original of Brace is Edmund Burke Brown, a lawyer]

Lynn, Kenneth S., *Mark Twain and Southwestern Humor* (Boston, Toronto, 1959)
pp. 61–72.

McElderry, Jr., B. R., intro to A. B. Longstreet, *Georgia Scenes* (New York, 1957),
pp. v–x. [Sagamore Press ed cited in headnote]

McIlwaine, Shields, *The Southern Poor-White* (Norman, Okla. 1939), pp. 49–51,
57–59. See also pp. 60, 62–63.

*Meine, Franklin J., intro to *Tall Tales of the Southwest 1830–1860* (New York,
1930), pp. xvii–xix. See also pp. 103, 137, 257, 303, 335, 397, 453, 455–56.

*Paine, Gregory, "Augustus Baldwin Longstreet," *Southern Prose Writers* (New York,
1947), pp. 121–22. See also pp. cxxxvii–cxxxviii [bibl], lxxv, and 125–33. [selections
from out-of-print novel *Master William Mitten*]

Parrington, Vernon Louis, "Augustus Longstreet," *Main Currents of American Thought*
(New York, 1927), II, pp. 166–72.

Poe, Edgar Allan, "Georgia Scenes," *SLM*, II (1836), 287–92. [r essay]

Silverman, Kenneth, "Longstreet's 'The Gander Pulling,'" *AQ*, XVIII (1966), 548–49.
[symbolic of No-So tensions]

Tandy, Jennette, *Crackerbox Philosophers in American Humor and Satire* (New York,
1925), pp. 74–77.

*Wade, John Donald, *Augustus Baldwin Longstreet: A Study of the Development of
Culture in the South* (New York, 1924).

———, "Augustus Baldwin Longstreet, a Southern Cultural Type," in *Southern
Pioneers in Social Interpretation*, ed. Howard W. Odum (Chapel Hill, 1925), pp.
119–40.

———, "Old Books: Georgia Scenes," *GaR*, XIV (1960), 444–47.

NORRIS W. YATES
Iowa State University
Ames, Iowa

ANDREW NELSON LYTLE (1902—)

Andrew Nelson Lytle has not yet had a full-length critical presentation. So far there have been one general essay (by Thomas H. Carter), several pages in the books by John M. Bradbury, Chester Eisinger, and Frederick J. Hoffman, and a few perceptive reviews. The essays by Jack De Bellis (on *A Name for Evil*) and Lytle himself (on *The Velvet Horn*) are the most thorough studies of two of the novels.

Bradbury, John M., *The Fugitives, A Critical Account* (Chapel Hill, 1958), pp. 193–96.

*Carter, Thomas H., "Andrew Lytle," in Rubin and Jacobs, *South*, pp. 287–300.

*De Bellis, Jack, *An Andrew Nelson Lytle Check List* (Charlottesville. Bibl Soc of the U of Va., 1960).

———, "Andrew Lytle's *A Name for Evil*: A Transformation of *The Turn of the Screw*," *Crit*, VIII (Spring-Summer 1966), 26–40.

Eisinger, Chester, *Fiction of the Forties* (Chicago, 1963), pp. 193–96. [on *At the Moon's End* and *A Name for Evil*]

Ghiselin, Brewster, "Trial of Light," *SeR*, LXV (1957), 657–65. [on *The Velvet Horn*]

Hoffman, *The Art of Southern Fiction*, pp. 99–102. [on *The Long Night* and *The Velvet Horn*]

Lytle, Andrew Nelson, "The Working Novelist and the Mythmaking Process," *The Hero with the Private Parts* (Baton Rouge, 1966), pp. 178–92.

Phelps, Robert, "Dust for an Adam," *Nat R*, IV (Aug 24, 1957), 162–63. [on *The Velvet Horn*]

Ransom, John Crowe, "Fiction Harvest," *SoR*, o.s. II (1936), 399–418. [on *The Long Night*, 403–405]

Tate, Allen, "A Prodigal Novel of Pioneer Alabama," *N.Y. Her Trib Bks*, Sept 6, 1936, p. 3. [on *The Long Night*]

ASHLEY BROWN
University of South Carolina
Columbia, South Carolina

CARSON McCULLERS (1917-1967)

Baldanza, Frank, "Plato in Dixie," *GaR*, XII (1958), 151–67.

Dodd, Wayne D., "The Development of Theme through Symbol in the Novels of Carson McCullers," *GaR*, XVII (1963), 206–13.

Durham, Frank, "God and No God in *The Heart Is a Lonely Hunter*," *SAW*, LVI (1957), 494–99.

Dusenbury, Winifred L., *The Theme of Loneliness in Modern American Drama* (Gainesville, 1960), pp. 58–67.

Eisinger, Chester E., "Carson McCullers and the Failure of Dialogue," *Fiction of the Forties* (Chicago, 1963), pp. 243–58.

Emerson, Donald, "The Ambiguities of *Clock Without Hands,*" *WSCL,* III (Fall 1962), 15–28.

Evans, Oliver Wendell, *The Ballad of Carson McCullers: A Biography* (New York, 1966). Publ originally as *Carson McCullers: Her Life and Work* (London, 1965).

Felheim, Marvin, "Eudora Welty and Carson McCullers," in *Contemporary American Novelists,* ed. Harry T. Moore (Carbondale, Ill., 1964), pp. 41–53.

Folk, Barbara Nauer, "The Sad Sweet Music of Carson McCullers," *GaR,* XVI (1962), 202–209.

Gossett, "Dispossessed Love: Carson McCullers," *Violence in Recent Southern Fiction,* pp. 159–77.

Hart, Jane, "Carson McCullers, Pilgrim of Loneliness," *GaR,* XI (1957), 53–58.

Hassan, Ihab, "Carson McCullers: The Alchemy of Love and Aesthetics of Pain," *MFS,* V (1959–60), 311–26. Rev as "Carson McCullers: The Aesthetics of Love and Pain," *Radical Innocence: Studies in the Contemporary American Novel* (Princeton, 1961), pp. 205–29.

Hoffman, *The Art of Southern Fiction,* pp. 65–73.

Kohler, Dayton, "Carson McCullers: Variations on a Theme," *Coll Eng,* XIII (Oct 1951), 1–8. Also in *Eng Jour,* XL (1951), 415–22.

Madden, David, "The Paradox of the Need for Privacy and the Need for Understanding in Carson McCullers' *The Heart is a Lonely Hunter,*" *Lit and Psychology,* XVII, No. 2–3 (1968), 128–40.

Malin, Irving, *New American Gothic* (Carbondale, Ill., 1962).

Moore, Jack B., "Carson McCullers: The Heart Is a Timeless Hunter," *Twentieth Cent Lit,* XI (1965), 76–81.

*Phillips, Robert S., "Carson McCullers: 1956–1964; A Selected Checklist," *BB,* XXIV (1964), 113–16.

———, "Dinesen's 'Monkey' and McCullers' 'Ballad': A Study in Literary Affinity," *Stud in Short Fict,* I (1964), 184–90.

———, "The Gothic Architecture of *The Member of the Wedding,*" *Renascence,* XVI (1964), 59–72.

———, "Painful Love: Carson McCullers' Parable," *SWR,* LI (1966), 80–86.

Schorer, Mark, "McCullers and Capote: Basic Patterns," in *The Creative Present,* ed. Nona Balakian and Charles Simmons (Garden City, N.Y., 1963), pp. 83–107.

Sherrill, Rowland A., "McCullers' *The Heart Is a Lonely Hunter:* The Missing Ego and the Problem of the Norm," *KyR,* II, No. 1 (1968), 5–17.

*Stewart, Stanley, "Carson McCullers, 1940–1956: A Selected Checklist," *BB,* XXII (1959), 182–85.

Taylor, Horace, "*The Heart Is a Lonely Hunter*: A Southern Wasteland," in *Studies in American Literature,* ed. Waldo McNeir and Leo B. Levy (Baton Rouge, 1960), La State U Stud, Hum Ser No. 8, pp. 154–60.

Vickery, John B. "Carson McCullers: A Map of Love," *WSCL,* I (Winter 1960), 13–24.

Williams, Tennessee, intro to *Reflections in a Golden Eye* (New York, 1950), pp. i–xxi.

Tinkham, Charles B., "The Members of the Side Show," *Phylon,* XVIII (1957), 383–90.

FLOYD C. WATKINS
Emory University
Atlanta, Georgia

ALEXANDER BEAUFORT MEEK (1814-1865)

The only recent, noteworthy treatment of Meek appears in Jay B. Hubbell, *The South in American Literature*, though Meek figures prominently in William Gilmore Simms's "Americanism in Literature," the first essay in *Views and Reviews* (1845), a new edition of which has been edited by C. Hugh Holman (1962). Excerpts from Meek's letters to Simms and extant Simms letters to Meek are printed in the five volumes of *The Letters of William Gilmore Simms*, edited by Mary C. Simms Oliphant et al (Columbia, South Carolina, 1952–56). The fullest account of Meek's life and work is still to be found in Herman C. Nixon's *Alexander Beaufort Meek* (Auburn, Alabama, 1910), long out of print. A new biography is needed, and a collection of the letters and a critical edition of the poems are greatly to be desired.

DAB, XII, p. 493; *Hubbell*, pp. 624–28, *950; *LSL*, VIII, pp. 3599–605.

Canby, Henry Seidel, "Mr. Meek on America," *SatR*, VII (Apr 16, 1932), 661, 664.

Ellison, Rhoda C., *Early Alabama Publications* (University, Ala., 1947). [Meek mentioned often but never fully discussed in one place]

Figh, M. G., "Alexander Beaufort Meek: Pioneer Man of Letters," *Ala Hist R*, II (1940), 127–51.

Garrett, William, *Reminiscences of Public Men in Alabama, for Thirty Years* (Atlanta, 1872). [see esp pp. 711–13]

Moses, Montrose J., *The Literature of the South* (New York, 1910). [Meek figures importantly in discussions on pp. 167–83 and 265–70]

Nixon, Herman C., *Alexander Beaufort Meek: Poet, Orator, Journalist, Historian, Statesman* (Auburn, Ala., 1910). [contains some uncollected poems on pp. 30–53; still the fullest account]

Ross, Charles H., "Alexander Beaufort Meek," *SeR*, IV (1896), 411–27. [contains a few of Meek's letters to Simms]

Simms, William G., *The Letters*, ed., Mary C. Simms Oliphant et al (Columbia, S.C., 1952–56), 5 vols. [references and letters scattered throughout]

———, "Americanism in Literature," *So and W Mag*, I (Jan 1845), 1–14. Repr in *Views and Reviews in American Literature, History and Fiction*, 1st ser, 1845. [new ed. by C. Hugh Holman (Cambridge, Mass., 1962) available; r of Meek's oration of same title delivered at U of Ga., 1844 and printed later that year as 39-page pamph; Simms's essay contains copious extracts from Meek's long speech]

Smith, William R., *Reminiscences of a Long Life: Historical, Political, Personal, and Literary* (Washington, D.C., 1889). [see esp. I, pp. 315–44]

RAYBURN S. MOORE
University of Georgia
Athens, Georgia

MARGARET MITCHELL (1900-1949)

Margaret Mitchell has been and will continue to be a difficult subject for biographers because of the lack of source materials. John Marsh, her husband, acquiesced to her wishes and burned all save a few pages of the manuscript of *Gone With the Wind*, and all of her unpublished writings and almost all of her personal correspondence. This idea of self-effacement was carried even to the point of razing the family home. Apparently, Miss Mitchell gave the information she wished the public to know to her close friend, Medora Field Perkerson, who published it in a series of articles, most of which appeared in the magazine section of the *Atlanta Journal*. These are written in a journalistic rather than a critical style but have considerable value and are included in the bibliography.

The best information about Miss Mitchell is contained in relatively few sources. The December 18, 1949, issue of *The Atlanta Journal Magazine* was published as a memorial to her. The several articles in it provide a detailed account of her life—childhood, education, newspaper career, all stages of *Gone With the Wind*, and her death. This was followed by a special number of *The Historical Society Bulletin* (May 1950) in which her brother Stephens Mitchell and a group of writers presented another record of her life. In 1964, Mr. Mitchell authorized Finis Farr to write a biography of Miss Mitchell. Mr. Farr was the first to be given access to the papers of the Margaret Mitchell Estate and to an unpublished memoir of Mr. Mitchell. Most of the estate's materials relate to *Gone With the Wind*. The resulting biography, although quite readable, is not over-popularized. It, however, cannot be considered as definitive. In fact, owing to the destruction of her papers, a definitive biography probably cannot be written.

Atlanta Historical Bulletin: Margaret Mitchell Memorial Issue, IX, (May 1950). [six papers: Stephens Mitchell, "Margaret Mitchell and Her People in the Atlanta Area," 5–26; Hughes Spalding, "Margaret Mitchell in Public Affairs," 29–30; John R. Marsh, "Margaret Mitchell and the Wide, Wide World," 33–44; William S. Howland, "Peggy Mitchell, Newspaperman," 47–66; Blythe McKay, "Margaret Mitchell in Person, and Her Warmth of Friendship," 100–107; William Key, "Margaret Mitchell and Her Last Days on Earth," 108–28]

Atlanta Jour Mag: Margaret Mitchell Memorial Issue, Dec 18, 1949. [seven papers: Harold S. Latham, "The Publisher's Story—How I Found *Gone With the Wind*," 20, 22; "Margaret Mitchell Told in Her Only Radio Broadcast How *GWTW* Was Written," 24–26, "Margaret Mitchell's Journal Magazine Stories," 15–19; Stephens Mitchell, "Her Brother Remembers—Margaret Mitchell's Childhood," 12; Medora Field Perkerson, "Was Margaret Mitchell Writing Another Book?" 4–7; Wylly Folk St. John, "Atlanta's Biggest Week, *Gone With the Wind* Premiere," 8–10; Marguerite

Steedman, "Margaret Mitchell's Last Hours," 26]

Brickell, Herschel, "A Talk with Margaret Mitchell about Her Novel and the Reasons for Its Popularity," *N.Y. Eve Post*, Aug 27, 1936, p. 13.

Daniel, Frank, "Margaret Mitchell Files Opened for Biographer," *Altanta Jour*, June 10, 1964, p. 7.

*Darwin, Patsy Evans, "Margaret Mitchell And Her Book, *Gone With the Wind*," in "The Theory of the Creative Personality And Its Application to Three Georgia Women Journalists—Lollie Belle Wylie, Emily Woodward, And Margaret Mitchell," Georgia, 1965, pp. 95–129. [MA thesis]

Drake, Robert Y. Jr., "Tara Twenty Years After," *GaR*, XII (1958), 142–50. [crit of *Gone With the Wind*]

Farr, Finis, *Margaret Mitchell of Atlanta: The Author of "Gone With the Wind"* (New York, 1965).

Granberry, Edwin, "Private Life of Margaret Mitchell," *Colliers*, XCIX (March 13, 1937), 22, 24, 25.

Grover, Robert L., "Margaret Mitchell, The Lady from Atlanta," *Ga Hist Q*, LII (1968), 53–69.

Howland, William S., "Margaret Mitchell—Romantic Realist," in *Margaret Mitchell Memorial of the Atlanta Public Library* (Atlanta, 1954), pp. 1–16.

Perkerson, Medora Field, "Double Life of Margaret Mitchell," *Atlanta Jour Mag*, May 16, 1937, pp. 1–2.

_____, "The Mystery of Margaret Mitchell," *Look*, XIX (Nov 15, 1955), 113–18.

_____, "When Margaret Mitchell Was a Girl Reporter," *Atlanta Jour Mag*, Jan 7, 1945, pp. 5–7.

_____, "Why Margaret Mitchell Hasn't Written Another Book," *Atlanta Jour Mag*, Dec 14, 1947, pp. 5–7.

Sparks, Andrew, "Why Were Margaret Mitchell's Letters Burned?," *Atlanta Jour and Constitution Mag*, Oct 5, 1952, pp. 7–9, 52.

W. PORTER KELLAM
University of Georgia
Athens, Georgia

MERRILL MOORE (1903-1957)

Merrill Moore's reputation as a poet has depended chiefly on his having been the most prolific member of the Fugitive group, although at least one book (by Henry W. Wells) has been devoted to his dual talents as poet and psychiatrist. Few have taken him seriously as an experimenter with the sonnet form, but in sheer number he stands as probably the most productive sonneteer in literary history, and since his individual fame rests on that fact, his sonnets surely deserve further and more serious study than they have had so far.

Basler, Roy P., "Proteus as Apollo: The Poetry of Merrill Moore," *LitR*, I (1958), 233–47.

Bradbury, John W., *The Fugitives: A Critical Account* (Chapel Hill, 1958).

Breit, Harvey, "Talk with Merrill Moore," *N.Y. Times Bk R* (Jul 15, 1951), 17. [interv]

Burden, Jean, The Prolific Dr. Moore," *Poetry*, LXXXIV (Apr 1954), 32–37. [r essay]

Ciardi, John, "Merrill Moore: A Goodbye," *SatR*, XL (Oct 12, 1957), 27.

Cowan, Louise, *The Fugitive Group: A Literary History* (Baton Rouge, 1959), pp. 55–8, *et passim*.

Eberhart, Richard, "Warmth and Ease and Charm and Aptitude," *Poetry*, LIV (June 1939), 160–63. [r essay]

Fitts, Dudley, The Sonnets of Merrill Moore," *SeR*, XLVII (1939), 268–93.

Holden, Raymond, "Activities of an Amateur," *Poetry*, XLVII (Oct 1935), 49–52.

Honig, Edwin, "The Psychiatrist as Poet," *Poetry*, LXXX (Apr 1952), 58–59.

Nemerov, Howard, r of *More Clinical Sonnets, SeR*, LXII (1954), 305–19.

Pratt, William, "In Pursuit of the Fugitives," intro to *The Fufitive Poets: Modern Southern Poetry in Perspective* (New York, 1965), pp. 45–46, *et passim*.

Ransom, John Crowe, "Postscript" to *The Fugitive: Clippings and Comment Collected by Merrill Moore* (Boston, 1939).

Salomon, I. L., "Astonishing Begetter of Sonnets," *SatR*, XXXIX (Jul 28, 1956), 12. [r essay]

Scott, W. T., "Sex and a Leering Poet," *SatR*, XL (Nov 9, 1957), 42. [r essay]

Untermeyer, Louis, "Merrill Moore," *SeR*, XLIII (1935), 58–69.

———, "Merrill Moore: 1903–1957," intro to Moore's *Poems of American Life* (New York, 1958).

———, "More Moore," *SatR*, XXXVII (Jan 16, 1954), 20.

Wells, Henry W., "Poet and Psychiatrist: Merrill Moore," in Rubin and Jacobs, *Southern Renascence*, pp. 427–35.

———, *Poet and Psychiatrist: Merrill Moore, M.D.: A Critical Portrait with an Appraisal of Two Hundred of his Poems* (New York, 1955).

Winters, Yvor, "Merrill Moore's Poems," *Poetry*, XXXVI (May 1930), 104–106. [r essay]

WILLIAM C. PRATT
Miami University
Oxford, Ohio

ROBERT MUNFORD (*ca.* 1737-1783)

Information about Robert Munford of "Richland" in Mecklenburg County, Virginia, had been sparse and uncertain until the publication of Rodney M. Baine's *Robert Munford: America's First Comic Dramatist* (Athens, Georgia, 1967). Baine's critical biography, with extensive notes and bibliography, establishes with reasonable certainty the dates of Munford's birth and death, recounts his careers as soldier and politician, traces the confusion about the authorship of his plays, and discusses in detail the literary merits of the two published dramas—*The Candidates; or, the Humours of a Virginia Election* and *The Patriots*. Students should check all earlier accounts against Baine's biography, for many of the earlier accounts contain inaccuracies.

Another helpful account is Jay B. Hubbell's "Robert Munford" in *The South in American Literature*. Both of Munford's plays have been reprinted (see below).

Students should be cautioned not to confuse Robert Munford with his son, William Munford (1775–1825), who was a poet and the editor of his father's posthumously published work in 1798.

DAB, XIII, pp. 325–26; *Hubbell*, pp. 142–48, *950–51.

*Baine, Rodney M., *Robert Munford: America's First Comic Dramatist* (Athens, Ga., 1967).

Canby, Courtlandt, ed., "*The Patriots*," in *WMQ*, 3rd ser, VI (1949), 437–503. [intro with crit comment]

Hubbell, Jay B., and Douglass Adair, eds., *The Candidates; or, the Humours of a Virginia Election* (Williamsburg, 1948). Also in *WMQ*, 3rd ser, V (1948), 217–57. [intro, crit comment]

Munford, Robert, *A Collection of Plays and Poems, by the Late Col. Robert Munford, of Mecklenburg, in the State of Virginia* (Petersburg, Va., 1798). [rare; brief preface by William Munford; besides *The Candidates* and *The Patriots*, includes some verse and Munford's translation of first book of Ovid's *Metamorphoses*]

Quinn, Arthur Hobson, *A History of the American Drama from the Beginnings to the Civil War* (New York, 1923), pp. 54–56. Also 2nd ed (New York, 1943), pp. 54–56. [brief crit comments]

ROBERT BAIN
University of North Carolina
Chapel Hill, North Carolina

MARY NOAILLES MURFREE ("CHARLES EGBERT CRADDOCK") (1850-1922)

DAB, XIII, pp. 344–45; *LSL*, VIII, pp. 3721–26; *LHUS*, II, pp. 667–68.

Adkins, Milton T., "The Mountains and Mountaineers of Craddock's Fiction," *Mag of Amer Hist*, XXIV (1890), 305–309.

Baskervill, William Malone, *Southern Writers: Biographical and Critical Studies* (Nashville, 1897), I, pp. 357–404.

*Cary, Richard, *Mary N. Murfree (Charles Egbert Craddock)* (New York, ———). [TUSAS; forthcoming]

Collins, Carvel E., "The Literary Tradition of the Southern Mountaineer, 1824–1900," Chicago, 1944. [diss]

Harris, Isabella D., "The Southern Mountaineer in American Fiction, 1824–1910," Duke, 1948. [diss]

Kephart, Horace, *Our Southern Highlanders* (New York, 1916).

Moore, Rayburn S., "Southern Writers and Northern Literary Magazines, 1865–1890," Duke, 1956. [diss; discusses esp Miss Murfree's contributions to *Lippincott's*, pp. 63–64, and to *Atlantic*, pp. 331–33, 341–42, 345–47]

*Parks, Edd Winfield, *Charles Egbert Craddock (Mary Noailles Murfree)* (Chapel Hill, 1941). [rev of diss, Vanderbilt, 1933]

Pattee, Fred L., *The Development of the American Short Story* (New York, 1923), pp. 271–75.

Reichert, Alfred, *Charles Egbert Craddock und die Amerikanische Short Story* (Leipzig, 1912).

EDD WINFIELD PARKS
University of Georgia
Athens, Georgia

FLANNERY O'CONNOR (1925-1964)

Any discussion of Flannery O'Connor criticism should probably begin with the Fall, 1958, number of *Critique.* The editors had the inspired notion of dividing their special issue between the two most talented American Roman Catholic writers of their generation, Flannery O'Connor and J. F. Powers; on the O'Connor side we have three essays on her fiction and a bibliography of works by and about her skillfully arranged. *The Sewanee Review* devoted part of its Summer, 1962, number to her by publishing her novella "The Lame Shall Enter First" and following it with discussions of her work by the novelist John Hawkes and the poet and translator Robert Fitzgerald (now her literary executor); in 1968, its pages contained a four-part symposium on her fiction. *Esprit,* published at the Roman Catholic-affiliated University of Scranton, devoted its Winter, 1964, number to the memory of the then recently deceased Flannery O'Connor by offering brief testimonials by an impressive group of poets, novelists, critics, and theologians; by printing some appreciate studies; and by reprinting a variety of literary obituaries from such periodicals as *The New York Review of Books, The Christian Century,* and *Commonweal.* Two essays about her appeared in a special issue of *Comparative Literature Studies* (volume III, number 2, 1966) devoted to "Literature and Religion." Quarterlies as different as

Renascence, The Georgia Review, and *Studies in Short Fiction* have proved uncommonly receptive to articles on her work, although none has as yet devoted a special issue to her. (The emphases of these last three journals illustrate three basic assumptions about her fiction: that it is rooted metaphorically in Roman Catholicism; that it is a part of a tradition in Southern literature which includes William Faulkner, Eudora Welty, Carson McCullers, Truman Capote, and the Fugitives; and that, as Robert Drake has said in his *Flannery O'Connor: A Critical Essay,* "her real *forte* is the short story.")

Flannery O'Connor criticism has matured considerably in the decade since William Esty used the much disputed expression "Gratuitous Grotesque" to describe her work (*Commonweal,* March 7, 1958). Words like "grotesque," "violence," "redemption," and "gothic" are found frequently in the early essays and reviews; they are used more sparingly and with more precision in the more recent criticism. There has been a gradual increase yearly in the number of O'Connor studies—certainly nothing to alarm the bibliographer—to the point where there were fifteen items listed in the 1967 *PMLA* bibliography, the high up to now. (One might compare this with the off-year Faulkner had in the same bibliography which listed sixty-eight items under his name.)

Some of the most valuable critical writing on Flannery O'Connor has appeared in books devoted to recent Southern fiction (such as Louise Y. Gossett's *Violence in Recent Southern Fiction* and Frederick J. Hoffman's *The Art of Southern Fiction*), to the post-World War II American novel (such as Jonathan Baumbach's *The Landscape of Nightmare*), and to certain generic and thematic questions associated with the novel (such as Louis D. Rubin, Jr.'s *The Curious Death of the Novel* and Irving Malin's *New American Gothic*). As yet there has been no book-length study by a single author devoted to Flannery O'Connor, but Stanley Edgar Hyman has done a pamphlet for the Minnesota series and Robert Drake one for the "Contemporary Writers in Christian Perspective" series. Hyman brilliantly classifies her as "the most radical Christian dualist since Dostoevski" and throws out the useful warning to critics "that any discussion of her theology can only be preliminary to, not a substitute for, aesthetic analysis and evaluation." Drake also offers valuable advice in the same direction: "She has never lacked commentators; she has needed—and still needs—more disinterested ones who will approach her work with a genuine spirit of good will, willing, as far as lies within their power, to grant her as an artist her *donnée,* even when they cannot share all her fundamental assumptions about man and God." I might add to Hyman and Drake another need for future O'Connor commentators. They should concentrate more on the use of

narrative technique in her novels and stories. The hope is that future
authors of books like Wayne Booth's *The Rhetoric of Fiction*, Robert
Scholes's and Robert Kellogg's *The Nature of Narrative*, and Louis D.
Rubin, Jr.'s *The Teller in the Tale* will devote chapters to Flannery
O'Connor's handling of point of view and the relationship she sets up
between author and reader and between author and narrator.

We might hope also for a collection of Flannery O'Connor's letters;
we already have the letters released by Richard Stern (*Shenandoah*,
Winter 1965), Sister Mary-Alice, O.P. (*Saturday Review*, May 29, 1965),
and William Sessions (*The Added Dimension*), to build upon. A biography and a collection of her scattered essays and interviews would
also be welcome.

Baumbach, Jonathan, "The Acid of God's Grace: *Wise Blood* by Flannery O'Connor,"
    The Landscape of Nightmare: Studies in the Contemporary American Novel (New
    York, 1965), pp. 87–100. [earlier form of essay appeared as "The Acid of God's
    Grace: The Fiction of Flannery O'Connor," *GaR*, XVII (1963), 334–46]
*Brittain, Joan T., "Flannery O'Connor: A Bibliography—Part One," *BB*, XXV (1967).
    98–100; "Part II," *BB*, XXV (1968), 123–24; "Addenda," *BB* (1968), 142.
Burns, Stuart L., Flannery O'Connor's "*The Violent Bear It Away*: Apotheosis in
    Failure," *SeR*, LXXVI (1968), 319–36.
Cheney, Brainard, "Miss O'Connor Creates Unusual Humor Out of Ordinary Sin,"
    SeR, LXXI (1963), 644–52. [reply to Hawkes's "Flannery O'Connor's Devil"]
Coffey, Warren, "Flannery O'Connor," *Commentary*, XL (Nov 1965). 93–99. [r essay
    on *Everything That Rises Must Converge*]
Detweiler, Robert, "The Curse of Christ in Flannery O'Connor's Fiction," *Comp Lit
    Stud*, III (1966), 235–45. [repr in *Mansions of the Spirit: Essays in Religion and
    Literature*, ed. George A. Panichas (New York, 1967), pp. 358–71.]
*Drake, Robert, *Flannery O'Connor: A Critical Essay* (Grand Rapids, 1966). ["Con-
    temporary Writers in Christian Perspective," pamph]
Driskell, Leon, "'Parker's Back' vs. 'The Partridge Festival': Flannery O'Connor's
    Critical Choice," *GaR*, XXI (1967), 476–90. [explains why author used "Parker's
    Back" instead of "The Partridge Festival" in *Everything That Rises*]
Fitzgerald, Robert, "The Countryside and the True Country," *SeR*, LXX (1962),
    380–94. [analysis of "The Displaced Person"]
———, intro to Flannery O'Connor, *Everything That Rises Must Converge* (New
    York, 1965), pp. vii–xxxiv.
*Friedman, Melvin J., and Lewis A. Lawson, eds., *The Added Dimension: The Art and
    Mind of Flannery O'Connor* (New York, 1966). [intro by Melvin J. Friedman;
    ten essays: Frederick J. Hoffman, "The Search for Redemption: Flannery O'Connor's
    Fiction"; Louis D. Rubin, Jr., "Flannery O'Connor and the Bible Belt"; C. Hugh
    Holman, "Her Rue with a Difference: Flannery O'Connor and the Southern Literary
    Tradition"; P. Albert Duhamel, "The Novelist as Prophet"; Irving Malin, "Flan-
    nery O'Connor and the Grotesque"; Caroline Gordon, "An American Girl"; Nathan
    A. Scott, Jr., "Flannery O'Connor's Testimony: The Pressure of Glory"; Sister M.
    Bernetta Quinn, O.S.F., "Flannery O'Connor, a Realist of Distances"; Harold C.
    Gardiner, S.J., "Flannery O'Connor's Clarity of Vision"; Melvin J. Friedman,

"Flannery O'Connor's Sacred Objects."; "A Correspondence" by William Sessions; bibl by Lewis A. Lawson]

Gordon, Caroline, "Flannery O'Connor's *Wise Blood*," *Crit*, II (Fall 1958), 3–10.

———, "Heresy in Dixie," *SeR*, LXXVI (1968), 263–97.

Gossett, *Violence in Recent Southern Fiction*, pp. 75–97.

Hart, Jane, "Strange Earth, the Stories of Flannery O'Connor," *GaR*, XII (1958), 215–22.

Hawkes, John, "Flannery O'Connor's Devil," *SeR*, LXX (1962), 395–407.

Hoffman, *The Art of Southern Fiction*, pp. 74–95. [enlargement of essay in *The Added Dimension*]

*Hyman, Stanley Edgar, *Flannery O'Connor* (Minneapolis, 1966). [Minn pamph]

Jacobsen, Josephine, "A Catholic Quartet," *Christian Schol*, XLVII (1964), 139–54. [O'Connor, Spark, Greene, and Powers]

Lawson, Lewis A., "Flannery O'Connor and the Grotesque: *Wise Blood*," *Renascence*, XVII (1965), 137–47, 156.

Malin, Irving, *New American Gothic* (Carbondale, Ill., 1962), *passim*. [treats O'Connor along with Capote, Hawkes, McCullers, Purdy, and Salinger under following categories: self-love, the family, imagery of haunted castle, voyage into the forest, and reflection in the mirror]

Rechnitz, Robert M., "Passionate Pilgrim: Flannery O'Connor's *Wise Blood*," *GaR*, XIX (1965), 310–16.

Rubin, *The Curious Death of the Novel*, pp. 239–61, 265–68. [repr of essay from *The Added Dimension* (without final paragraph and notes), and pages on *Everything that Rises*]

———, "Flannery O'Connor: A Note on Literary Fashion," *Crit*, II (Fall 1958), 11–18.

Shear, Walter, "Flannery O'Connor: Character and Characterization," *Renascence*, XX (1968), 140–46.

Shinn, Thelma J., "Flannery O'Connor and the Violence of Grace," [WS] *CL*, IX (Winter 1968), 58–73.

Snow, Ollye Tine, "The Functional Gothic of Flannery O'Connor," *SWR*, L (1965), 286–99.

Spivey, Ted R., "Flannery O'Connor's View of God and Man," *Stud in Short Fict*, I (1964), 200–206.

Stern, Richard, "Flannery O'Connor: A Remembrance and Some Letters," *Shen*, XVI (Winter 1965), 5–10.

Sullivan, Walter, "Flannery O'Connor, Sin, and Grace: *Everything That Rises Must Converge*," *Hollins Crit*, II, No. 4 (Sept [sic] 1965), 1–8, 10.

Trowbridge, Clinton, "The Symbolic Vision of Flannery O'Connor: Patterns of Imagery in *The Violent Bear It Away*," *SeR*, LXXVI (1968), 298–318.

Vande Kieft, Ruth, "Judgment in the Fiction of Flannery O'Connor," *SeR*, LXXVI (1968), 337–56.

MELVIN J. FRIEDMAN
University of Wisconsin
Milwaukee, Wisconsin

THOMAS NELSON PAGE (1853-1922)

Page was the chief spokesman for the plantation literary tradition, and most of his stories, poems, novels, and essays commemorate the chivalric behavior of Ante-bellum Virginians and lament the passing of the Old Order. He was especially famous as a local color writer of the New South, depicting the glamor of the Tidewater region and frequently employing the romantic devices of the popular novel—such as the marriage of a Northerner and a Southerner during the Reconstruction era. The Plantation edition of his works in eighteen volumes was published by Charles Scribner's Sons in 1906–1912.

Duke University possesses the largest collection of Page's manuscripts and letters, about 9,000 items in all. The College of William and Mary also has a sizeable collection of the author's materials, as does the Library of Congress. His diplomatic correspondence, which has received very little attention from historians, is impressive and can be found with the personal correspondence in the Duke Collection.

DAB, XIV, pp. 141–42; *Hubbell*, pp. 795–804, *952; *LSL*, IX, pp. 3849–53; **LHUS*, II, pp. 613–44, *Supp*, 174.

Gross, Theodore L., *Thomas Nelson Page* (New York, 1967). [TUSAS]

―――, "Thomas Nelson Page: Creator of a Virginia Classic," *GaR*, XX (1966), 338–51.

Harris, L. H. (Corra), "The Waning Influence of Thomas Nelson Page," *Current Opinions*, XLIII (1907), 171–72. [even during his lifetime Page's views seemed anachronistic to many]

Holman, Harriet R., "The Literary Career of Thomas Nelson Page: 1884–1910," Duke, 1947. [diss; available on micro-cards]

Johnson, Gerald W., "To Live and Die in Dixie," *Atlantic*, CCVI (July 1960), 29–34. [Page, along with Stephen Foster, propagated harmful myths about Old So]

Kent, Charles W., "Thomas Nelson Page," *SAQ*, VI (1907), 263–71.

King, Kimball, "George Washington Cable and Thomas Nelson Page: Two Literary Approaches to the New South," Wisconsin, 1964. [diss; contrasts lib and conserv attitudes toward So problems as reflected in lit]

―――, "Satirical Portraits by Thomas Nelson Page," *MissQ*, XVIII (1965), 74–81. [discusses Page's satires of N.Y. and Chicago socialites]

Mims, Edwin, "Thomas Nelson Page." *Atlantic*, C (1907), 109–15.

Page, Rosewell, *Thomas Nelson Page: A Memoir of a Virginia Gentleman* (New York, 1923). [appreciative memoir by brother, with sketchy biog details, but interesting for picture of Page family life]

Pattee, Frederick L., *A History of American Literature Since 1870* (New York, 1915), pp. 265–69.

Quinn, *American Fiction*, pp. 257–362.

Sowder, William J., "Gerald W. Johnson, Thomas Nelson Page, and the South," *MissQ*, XIV (1961), 197–203. [reply to Johnson, above]

Tree, Ronald, "Thomas Nelson Page," *Forum*, LXIX (1923), 1137–42. [Page's diplomatic career]

KIMBALL KING
*University of North Carolina
Chapel Hill, North Carolina*

WALTER HINES PAGE (1855-1918)

Walter Hines Page is noted for his contribution to Southern educational reforms, for his role as Ambassador to the Court of St. James, for
his position as editor of *The Forum, World's Work*, and the *Atlantic
Monthly*, and for his founding of the publishing house of Doubleday,
Page and Company. However, of primary interest to the student of
Southern literature is his single novel *The Southerner*, which he published in 1909 under the pseudonym Nicholas Worth.

The historical scholarship done concerning Page discusses his importance as Ambassador or outlines his intellectual position with regard to
"the New South." The three-volume biography by Burton O. Hendrick,
with its supplementary volume *The Training of an American*, is concerned with the events in Page's life which culminated in his appoint-
ment as Ambassador. Although he includes extensive and valuable
quotations from Page's letters, Hendrick spends little time on Page's
novel. He subordinates the literary importance of Page's editorial posi-
tions, stressing Page's relationship with Woodrow Wilson, his appoint-
ment and tenure as Ambassador, and his influence on United States-
British relations. *The Training of an American* is the most useful
volume, both because it includes events which parallel those presented
in *The Southerner,* which is partially autobiographical, and also
because it is the volume primarily concerned with Page's work as editor.

The items listed below are the most relevant works available with
regard to Page as a literary figure. Mrs. L. H. Harris' article is an
interesting indictment of *The Southerner* and its author, while the
article by H. M. Stanley is a brief, favorable review of the novel. Two
central articles concerning Page's beliefs and their reflection in his call
for political and social reform are those by Robert W. D. Connor and
Edwin Mims. Although biographical material concerning Page is plentiful, critical commentary on his speeches, his novel, his influence as

editor is not. Page is presented as "a Southern nationalist," a represensative of "the New South," and "a sentinel on guard," but rarely as
a writer.

DAB, XIV, pp. 142–44; *LSL*, XVII, pp. 425–31.

Boswell, George Worley, "Walter Hines Page as a Southerner," Vanderbilt, 1940.
[MA thesis]

Connor, Robert D. W., "Walter Hines Page, A Southern Nationalist," in *Southern
Pioneers in Social Interpretation*, ed. Howard W. Odum (Chapel Hill, 1925), pp.
53–67. Also appears in *Jour of Soc Forces*, II (1924), 164–68. [biog]

Cox, Mary Josephine, "Walter Hines Page: Journalist, Reformer, Statesman," Southern
Methodist, 1925. [MA thesis]

Davidson, Donald, "The Dilemma of Southern Liberals," in *The Attack on Leviathan*
(Chapel Hill, 1938), pp. 261–284; note esp pp. 261–62, 274–78. [Page's intellectual,
political beliefs; brief comment on *The Southerner* as "propaganda novel"]

Gregory, Ross, "The Ambassadorship of Walter Page," *DA*, XXV, 5237 (Indiana).

Gibson, J. M., "Walter Hines Page Has Been Forgiven," *SAQ*, XXXII (1933), 283–93.
[attitude of No Carolinians toward Page]

Harris, Mrs. L. H., "A Southerner's View of *The Southerner*," *Independent*, CXVII
(1909), 1090–91.

Hendrick, Burton J., *The Life and Letters of W. H. Page*, 3 vols (Garden City and New
York, 1922–25). [comments on *The Southerner*, I, 90–94]

———, *The Training of an American: The Earlier Life and Letters of Walter H.
Page, 1855–1913* (Cambridge, Mass., 1928).

Mims, Edwin, "Walter Hines Page," in *Biographical History of North Carolina*, ed.
Samuel A. Ashe III (Greensboro, 1905), 315–19.

———, "Walter Hines Page: Friend of the South," *SAQ*, XVIII (1919), 97–115.

———, "Walter Hines Page: Friendly Critic of the South," *The Advancing South:
Stories of Progress and Reaction* (New York, 1926), pp. 23–49. [biog; contrast of
W. H. Page and Thomas N. Page; brief remarks on *The Southerner*]

Minor, Olive, "Walter Hines Page's Reconstruction Policy with the *Atlantic Monthly*,"
Columbia, 1934. [MA thesis]

Sellers, Charles Grier, "Walter Hines Page and the Spirit of the New South," *N.C.
Hist R*, XXIX (1952), 481–99. [Page's involvement in educ reforms]

Stanley, H. M., r of Walter H. Page, *The Southerner*, *The Nation*, LXXXIX (1909),
511–12.

PAMELA GLENN MENKE
*Guilford Technical Institute
Jamestown, North Carolina*

WALKER PERCY (1917—)

Very little has been written thus far about Walker Percy. He has written only two novels, *The Moviegoer*, which won the 1962 National Book Award, and *The Last Gentleman*. Still, he is intellectually and artistically the most provocative Southern writer today. To compensate for the timidity of the critics he has contributed profusely to magazines such as *Commonweal, America, Partisan Review* and several psychological journals. Some of the more interesting pieces are listed below.

Brown, Ashley, "An Interview with Walker Percy," *Shen,* XVIII (Spring 1967), 3–10. [important interv]

Buitenhuis, Peter, *N.Y. Times Bk R,* June 26, 1966, p. 5. [r of *The Last Gentleman*]

Byrd, Scott, "The Dreams of Walker Percy," *Red Clay Reader,* No. 3 (1966), 70–73. [mag essay; best to date, though short and sketchy]

Cheney, Brainerd, "Secular Society as Deadly Farce," *SeR,* LXXV (1967), 345–50. [mag art on Percy's satiric treatment of 'orgasm only' worship in contemporary soc]

———, "To Restore a Fragmented Image," *SeR,* LXIX (1961), 691–70. [r based on *The Moviegoer*]

Cremeens, Carlton, "Walker Percy: The Man and the Novelist, An Interview," *SoR,* n.s., IV (1968), 271–90. [interv]

Goodman, W., "Elegant Quest for Ordinariness," *Life,* LX (June 24, 1966), 20.

Hoffman, *The Art of Southern Fiction,* pp. 129–37.

Hoggard, James, "Death of the Vicarious," *SWR,* XLIX (1964), pp. 366–74. [mag article on *The Moviegoer*]

Kennebeck, Edwin, "*The Moviegoer* by Walker Percy," *Commonweal,* LXXIV (June 2, 1961), 260. [r of *The Moviegoer*]

Knickerbocker, Paine, *San Francisco Chron,* June 14, 1961, p. 30. [r of *The Moviegoer*]

Lehan, Richard, "The Way Back: Redemption in the Novels of Walker Percy," *SR,* n.s., IV (1968), 306–19.

Massie, Robert, *N.Y. Times Bk R,* May 28, 1961, p. 30. [very perceptive r of *The Moviegoer*]

Percy, Walker, "Culture Critics," *Commonweal,* LXX (June 5, 1959), 247–50.

———, "Decline of the Western," *Commonweal,* LXVIII (May 16, 1958), 181–83.

———, "Metaphor as Mistake," *SeR,* LVII (1958), 79–99.

———, "Modern Man on the Threshold," *America,* CV (Aug 12, 1961), 612.

———, "Southern View," *America,* XCVII (July 20, 1957), 428–29.

———, "The Man on the Train," *PartisanR,* XXIII (1956), 478–94. [most important aid to Percy's aesthetic position]

———, "Truth or Pavlov's Dogs," *Amer,* XCVII (June 8, 1957), 306–307.

———, "Virtues and Vices in Southern Literary Renascence," *Commonweal,* LXXVI (May 11, 1962), 181–82.

Sheed, Wilfred, *Critic,* XXV (Oct 1966), 92. [r, very perceptive]

Tanner, Tony, *The Reign of Wonder: Naivete and Reality in American Literature* (New York, 1965). [afterword centers on Percy and Salinger]

Time, LXXXI (Feb 1, 1963), 82. [*Time* portrait]

NEWTON SMITH
Western Carolina University
Cullowhee, North Carolina

WILLIAM ALEXANDER PERCY (1885-1942)

Bradford, Roark, foreword to *Collected Poems of William Alexander Percy* (New Haven, 1943), pp. 3–7.

Carter, Hodding, "The Most Unforgettable Character I've Met," *Reader's Digest,* LXI (Aug 1952), 21–25.

———, *Where Main Street Meets the River* (New York, 1953), pp. 67–78.

Cash, Wilbur J., r of *Lanterns on the Levee,* in *Charlotte News,* May 10, 1941. Repr in Joseph L. Morrison, *W. J. Cash: A Biography and a Reader* (New York, 1967), pp. 290–94.

Cohn, David L., "Eighteenth Century Chevalier," *VQR,* XXXI (1955), 561–75.

Dabbs, James McBride, *Who Speaks for the South?* (New York, 1964), pp. 121–22.

Daniels, Jonathan, *A Southerner Discovers the South* (New York, 1938), pp. 172–80.

Percy, William Alexander, *Lanterns on the Levee: Recollections of a Planter's Son* (New York, 1941). [autobiog, but best source of information on Percy's life]

Spalding, Phinizy, "A Stoic Trend in William Alexander Percy's Thought," *GaR,* XII (1948), 241–51.

EUGENE NOLTE
State College of Arkansas
Conway, Arkansas

JULIA PETERKIN (1880-1961)

A protegée of Mencken, Mrs. Peterkin made her debut in the *Smart Set* with, for the times, a somewhat grim and shocking story about Southern Negroes. Other sketches and stories followed, mainly in the "little" magazine *The Reviewer,* as they were "too strong" for even the editor who was to dare with "Hatrack." When in 1924 she published a volume of loosely-linked stories about Gullah Negroes on a remote plantation—*Green Thursday,* her work was generally praised as a new, objective, and perceptive fictional treatment of the Negro, avoiding the traditional paternalism and sentimentality. Local critics, however, were less pleased, for she wrote in a way and about things no "South Carolina lady" was supposed to. Novels—*Black April* (1927), *Scarlet Sister Mary* (1928 Pulitzer Prize winner), and *Bright Skin* (1932)—followed, with *Black April* usually recognized as her best. In later years, the tone of the critical response to her work altered; no longer praised for her pioneering in the realistic portrayal of the Negro, she was more and more relegated to the apparently despised local colorists who presented exotic, strange, and eccentric characters and settings for their own sakes. She had never had a racial axe to grind, only a human and a humane one; she had presented with unflagging accuracy a segment of Southern life admittedly restricted and now, unaccountably, unfashionable. Her critical reputation sank because she was charged with committing the very literary sins of which earlier critics had proclaimed her guiltless.

During her lifetime, only fugitive articles and reviews of her works appeared, and she received brief but generally favorable attention in books on American and Southern fiction. Recently, after a fairly long period of neglect, her books are arousing a renewed interest. Both a paperback and a facsimile of the first edition of *Scarlet Sister Mary* have been issued. At least two full-length studies of Mrs. Peterkin are now in preparation. Perhaps ultimately her reputation will achieve a fair balance between her early high praise and her later oblivion.

Beach, Joseph Warren, *The Twentieth Century Novel* (New York, 1932), pp. 232–33. [on fict treatment of Negro]

Bennett, Isadora, " 'Lang Syne's Miss,' The Background of Julia Peterkin, Novelist of the Old South," *Bookman*, LXIX (1929). 357–66.

Brickell, Herschel, "Plantation Folk," *SatR*, VIII (Apr 9, 1932), 648. [r of *Bright Skin*]

Chamberlain, John, "Julia Peterkin Writes Again of the Gullah Negroes," *N.Y. Times*, Oct 2, 1928, sec IV, p. 4. [illus r of *Scarlet Sister Mary*]

_____, "Books of the Times," *N.Y. Times*, Dec 15, 1933, p. 21. [r of *Roll, Jordan, Roll*]

Clark, Edwin, "Six Months in the Field of Fiction—Among New American Novelists Brought Forward This Season Julia Peterkin and Nathalie Colby Are Noteworthy," *N.Y. Times*, June 26, 1927, sec III, p. 5. [r of *Black April*]

Clark, Emily, "Julia Peterkin," *Innocence Abroad* (New York, 1931), pp. 213–31. [account of early career]

Crawford, John W., "Hound-Dogs and Bible Shouting: Julia Peterkin's Fine Novel of 'Blue-Gum' Negroes Is Suffused With Life," *N.Y. Times*, March 6, 1927, sec III, p. 5. [r of *Black April*]

Davidson, Donald, "Julia Peterkin," *The Spyglass: Views and Reviews, 1924–1930*, selected and ed. J. T. Fain (Nashville, 1963), pp. 20–23. [r essay]

Durham, Frank, "The Art of Writing" (Columbia, S.C.) *Carolinian*, XLV (May 1932), 6, 18. [interv]

Hatcher, Harlan, *Creating the Modern American Novel* (New York, 1935), pp. 146–47. [crit evaluation]

Law, Robert Adger, "Mrs. Peterkin's Negroes," *SWR*, XIV (1929), 455–61. [moderate So reaction]

Loggins, Vernon, "Julia Peterkin," in *I Hear America: Literature in the United States Since 1900* (New York, 1937), pp. 216–19.

*Maddox, Marilyn Price, "The Life and Works of Julia Peterkin," Georgia, 1956. [MA thesis]

New York Times, "Again a Serious Study of Negroes in Fiction: *Green Thursday*," Sept 28, 1924, sec III, p. 8. [r]

————, "1928 Pulitzer Prize for Peterkin Novel," May 13, 1929, pp. 1, 14. [newsp article]

Overton, Grant, "Julia Peterkin," in *The Women Who Make Our Novels* (New York, 1928), pp. 257–61.

Perkerson, Medora Field, "Julia Peterkin—Author and Farmer," *Atlanta Jour Mag* Apr 28, 1940, pp. 1–2. [illus]

Peterkin, Julia, "Seeing Things," *Amer Mag*, CV (Jan 1928), 26–27, 115–16. [illus autobiog essay]

Puckette, Charles McD., "On a Carolina Plantation," *SatR*, III (March 19, 1927), 660. [r of *Black April*]

Richardson, Eudora Ramsay, "The South Grows Up," *Bookman*, LXX (1931), 548–49.

FRANK DURHAM
University of South Carolina
Columbia, South Carolina

ALBERT PIKE (1809-1891)

The most detailed available account of Albert Pike's life and his wide range of activities is in Frederick Allsopp's *Albert Pike: A Biography* (Little Rock, 1928). His significance in American letters is the subject of Susan B. Riley's "The Life and Works of Albert Pike to 1860" (Peabody, 1934). William Boyden's *Bibliography of the Writings of Albert Pike* (Washington, 1921) provides good evidence of the volume and range of Pike's writings; however, Susan Riley notes that many of Pike's newspaper essays and sketches are not included in Boyden's *Bibliography*.

DAB, XIV, pp. 593–95; *Duyckinck*, II, p. 520; *Hubbell*, pp. 640–50, *953–54; *LSL*, IX, pp. 4037–41.

*Allsopp, Frederick William, *Albert Pike: A Biography* (Little Rock, 1928).

*Boyden, William Llewellyn, *Bibliography of the Writings of Albert Pike: Prose, Poetry, Manuscript* (Washington, 1921).

Donoghue, David, "Explorations of Albert Pike in Texas," *SW Hist Q*, XXXIX (1935), 135–38.

Hallum, John, *Biographical and Pictorial History of Arkansas*, I (Albany, 1887), pp. 215–36. [includes autobiog sketch]

"Obituary—Albert Pike," *N.Y. Times*, Apr 13, 1891, p. 5. [newsp article]

Riley, Susan B., "The Life and Works of Albert Pike to 1860," Peabody, 1934. [diss]

[Roome, Lillian Pike] "Biographical Sketch of Albert Pike," in *General Albert Pike's Poems* (Little Rock, 1900), pp. 9–29. [intro chap]

DARWIN H. SHRELL
Louisiana State University
Baton Rouge, Louisiana

EDWARD COOTE PINKNEY (1802-1828)

Little of value has been published about this Maryland poet of the 1820s. The Mabbott and Pleadwell volume listed below is indispensable, and the best essay is that of Jay B. Hubbell in *The South in American Literature*. W. F. Melton was the first twentieth-century scholar to devote some attention to Pinkney.

DAB, VII, pp. 625; *Duyckinck*, II, p. 338; *Hubbell*, pp. 301–304, *953–54; *LSL*, IX, pp. 4063–67.

Greenwood, F. W. P., "Pinkney's Poems," *NoAmerR*, XXI (1825), 360–76. [contemporary r]

*Mabbott, T. O., and Frank Lester Pleadwell, *The Life and Works of Edward Coote Pinkney* (New York, 1926).

Melton, W. F., "Edward Coote Pinkney," *SAQ*, XI (1912), 328–36.

————, "The Influence of Petrarch upon Edward Coote Pinkney," *Mod Lang Notes*, XXVIII (1913), 199–200.

*Parks, Edd Winfield, ed., *Southern Poets: Representative Selections* (New York, 1936), p. 18.

Ross, C. H., "Edward Coate [sic] Pinkney," *SeR*, IV (1896), 287–98.

Simmons, J. P., "Edward Coote Pinkney—American Cavalier Poet," *SAQ*, XXVIII (1929), 406–18.

ROBERT D. JACOBS
University of Kentucky
Lexington, Kentucky

EDGAR ALLAN POE (1809-1849)

One of the most controversial figures in American literature, Edgar Poe has never lacked attention, but until the past twenty years this attention has been chiefly biographical and bibliographical. The first task of Poe scholarship was to clear away the legends, some of them fostered by Poe himself, others by both his friends and his enemies, that accumulated about his life and character. The first balanced appraisal of Poe's life and work by a competent scholar was that of George E. Woodberry, whose American Men of Letters biography (q.v.) appeared in 1885, to be revised and expanded in 1909. Other biographies appeared, but the next of more than usual significance was that by Hervey Allen, whose Israfel: The Life and Times of Edgar Allan Poe (New York, 1926), became a best seller among biographies and is still perhaps the most widely known. Allen, a novelist, tended to sentimentalize his subject, however, and lacked the proper caution in evaluating his sources. The best biography to date is that of Arthur Hobson Quinn (q.v.), published in 1941. Labelled a critical biography, this work has been superseded as far as its literary criticism is concerned, but it does present the facts of Poe's life with scholarly precision. The most recent biography is Edward Wagenknecht's Edgar Allan Poe: The Man Behind the Legend (q.v.). Wagenknecht, a veteran biographer, has been indefatigable in consulting all previous material on Poe, but his special approach, which consists of examining the Poe legends and then dismissing them, either by presenting facts or informed opinions, impairs the usefulness of his work to those who wish a detailed account of Poe's life. Another recent biography is Frances Winwar's The Haunted Palace (New York, 1959), readable but a "popular" rather than a scholarly biography.

Biographies with a specialized point of view, such as those that employ depth psychology (usually Freud's) to analyze Poe's character, have been fairly plentiful. Of these the best known have been Joseph Wood Krutch's Edgar Allan Poe, A Study in Genius (New York, 1926), John W. Robertson's Edgar A. Poe, a Psychopathic Study (New York, 1923), and Marie Bonaparte's Edgar Poe, Etude Psychanalytique (q.v.). Madame Bonaparte's study has been the most influential of these and still has its admirers, although in recent years the tendency has been away from the Freudian approach. David M. Rein's Edgar A. Poe: The Inner Pattern (New York, 1960), the latest book to employ depth psychology in the interpretation of Poe's works in relation to his neurotic tendencies, has not found favor among the more qualified reviewers.

Editions of Poe's works have been plentiful, but unfortunately no definitive and accurate scholarly edition has yet appeared. The nearest to a complete edition is that of James A. Harrison, *The Complete Works of Edgar Allan Poe,* 17 volumes (New York, 1902), but even this edition omits some of Poe's journalistic criticism and includes some reviews which he did not write. Professor T. O. Mabbott has for some years been preparing a definitive edition of Poe, but it has not yet been published. There are, however, two excellent editions of Poe's poems, the first edited by Killis Campbell (Boston, 1917), and the second by Floyd Stovall (Charlottesville, 1965). Another carefully edited publication of some of Poe's works is *The Complete Poems and Stories of Edgar Allan Poe, with Selections from his Critical Writings,* ed. Arthur Hobson Quinn and Edward H. O'Neill, 2 volumes (New York, 1946). Because a definitive edition of Poe's works has not yet been published, the student should familiarize himself with the bibliographies that have been published in an attempt to establish the Poe canon. Three of these are listed in the following bibliography, and they may prevent the beginning student from making the error, still sometimes committed, of establishing a point on the basis of an item not secure within the Poe canon.

Fortunately there is an excellent edition of Poe's letters. *The Letters of Edgar Allan Poe,* edited by John Ward Ostrom, 2 volumes (Cambridge, Mass, 1948), together with two supplements published in *American Literature,* XXIV (1952), pp. 358–66, and *American Literature,* (1957), pp. 79–86, contain nearly all the Poe letters that have been discovered, though occasionally another still comes to light.

Because of the extensive amount of biographical and bibliographical work that has been done on Poe, the student today is in an unusually good position to devote himself to the as yet incomplete task of evaluation and interpretation. With the exception of a few notable early essays, some of which are included in the following list, there was comparatively little criticism of Poe in English until the last two decades. The French had long found Poe an exciting writer, but relatively few of the French studies of Poe have been translated into English. T. S. Eliot's lecture, "From Poe to Valery" (q.v.), delivered in 1948 and subsequently published in a number of places, signalled the recognition of Poe by the dominant literary figure then writing in English. Shortly thereafter, Patrick F. Quinn began his investigation of the French criticism of Poe which resulted in a valuable study, *The French Face of Edgar*

Poe (q.v.). Quinn's book not only reveals the insights of a number of French critics little known in America but also provides a symbolistic interpretation of Poe's tales which has set the pattern for much subsequent work. Published in the same year as Quinn's book was Edward Davidson's *Poe: A Critical Study* (q.v.), which sets Poe against the general background of romanticism and convincingly develops an interpretation of Poe as a symbolic artist.

In recent years critics have found Poe's tales of more interest than his poems, but only very recently has he been taken seriously as a critic— again we must except the French and a few distinguished early essays in English. Norman Foerster's essay in his *American Criticism: A Study of Literary Theory from Poe to the Present* (q.v.) is one notable exception, as is Margaret Alterton's 1926 study, *Origins of Poe's Critical Theory* (q.v.). There have been two recent books on Poe as a literary critic, however, Sidney Moss's *Poe's Literary Battles* (q.v.) and Edd Winfield Parks's *Edgar Allen Poe as Literary Critic* (q.v.). Moss concentrates upon the controversies Poe engaged in with other journalists of his time, and Parks gives a brief but valuable survey of Poe's literary opinions. The present writer's study of Poe as critic will appear this year.

The following bibliography of works about Poe is highly selective. The guiding principle, all things considered, has been to list the more recent essays and books, particularly those that touch upon Poe as a Southern writer. To the Poe scholar there will appear to be some unaccountable omissions. No one who has worked with Poe can fail to acknowledge the accomplishments of T. O. Mabbott, whose many years of Poe scholarship have resulted in a host of articles. Yet, while cumulatively valuable, these articles individually are too brief for a listing of this sort. A similar type of omission has been made of hundreds of explications of single tales and poems by Poe. Only when the explications are broad enough in scope or when they open up avenues for a significantly new interpretation of Poe have they been listed. This bibliography, then, is for the beginning student of Poe and Southern literature. Other and more detailed bibliographies are available for the advanced student.

DAB, XV, pp. 19–28; *Duyckinck*, II, p. 536; *Hubbell*, pp. 528–50, *955–56; *LSL*, IX, pp. 4078–84; *LHUS*, I, pp. 321–42, *II, 689–96, *Supp, 178–80.

I.   Biographies

Allen, Hervey, *Israfel. The Life and Times of Edgar Allan Poe*, 2 vols (New York, 1926; [rev ed 1934; 1956]).

Bonaparte, Marie P., *The Life and Works of Edgar Allan Poe: A Psychoanalytical Interpretation*, translation John Rodker (London, 1949).
*Fagin, N. Bryllion, *The Histrionic Mr. Poe* (Baltimore, 1949). [interpretation rather than detailed biog]
Lauvrière, Emile, *The Strange Life and the Strange Loves of Edgar Allan Poe*, translation Edwin G. Rich (Philadelphia, 1935).
Phillips, Mary E., *Edgar Allan Poe, The Man*, 2 vols (Philadelphia, 1926).
*Quinn, Arthur Hobson, *Edgar Allan Poe: A Critical Biography* New York, 1941). [most reliable biog to date]
*Wagenknecht, Edward, *Edgar Allan Poe: The Man Behind the Legend* (New York, 1963).
Woodberry, George E., *The Life of Edgar Allan Poe, Personal and Literary, with his Chief Correspondence with Men of Letters*, 2 vols (Boston, 1909).

II. *Bibliographies

Dameron, J. Lasley, *Edgar Allan Poe: A Checklist of Criticism 1942–1960* (Charlottesville, 1966).
Heartman, Charles F., and Kenneth Rede, *A Census of First Editions and Source Materials by Edgar Allan Poe in American Collections* (Metuchen, N.J., 1932).
Heartman, Charles F., and J. R. Canny, *A Bibliography of First Printings of the Writings of Edgar Allan Poe* (Hattiesburg, Miss., 1940). [contains some errors; rev ed 1943]
Hubbell, Jay B., "Poe," in *Eight American Authors*, ed. Floyd Stovall (New York, 1956), pp. 1–46. Rev ed with supp. ed. J. Chesley Matthews (New York, 1963), pp. 421–24.
Hull, William Doyle, "A Canon of the Critical Works of Edgar Allan Poe with a Study of Poe the Magazinist," Virginia, 1941. [diss]
Robertson, John W., *A Bibliography of the Writings of Edgar A. Poe*, 2 vols (San Francisco, 1934).

III. Critical and Historical Studies

Abel, Darrel, "A Key to the House of Usher," *U Toronto Q*, XVIII (1949), 176–85.
————, "Edgar Poe: A Centennial Estimate," *U Kan Cy R*, XVI (Winter 1949), 77–96.
Allen, Gay Wilson, "Edgar Allan Poe," *American Prosody* (New York, 1935), pp. 56–85.
Alterton, Margaret, *Origins of Poe's Critical Theory* (Iowa City, Iowa, 1925).
Auden, W. H., intro to *Edgar Allan Poe: Selected Prose and Poetry* (New York, 1950), pp. v–xvii.
Bailey, James O., "The Geography of Poe's 'Dream-Land' and 'Ulalume'," *SP*, XLV (1948), 512–23.
Basler, Roy P., "Poe's Dream Imagery," *Sex, Symbolism, and Psychology in Literature* (New Brunswick, N.J., 1948), pp. 177–201.
Beebe, Maurice, "The Universe of Roderick Usher," *Personalist*, XXXVII (Spring 1956), 147–60.
Belgion, Montgomery, "The Mystery of Poe's Poetry," *Essays in Crit* I (1951), 51–66.
Bezanson, Walter E., "The Troubled Sleep of Arthur Gordon Pym," in *Essays in Literary History Presented to J. Milton French*, ed. Rudolph Kirk and C. F. Main (New Brunswick, N.J., 1960), pp. 149–75.

Blackmur, Richard P., ed., *The Fall of the House of Usher and Other Tales*, afterword by Blackmur (New York, 1960), pp. 375–83.

Blair, Walter, "Poe's Conception of Incident and Tone in the Tale," *Mod Phil*, XLI (1944), 228–40.

Bowra, Sir Cecil M., "Edgar Allan Poe," *The Romantic Imagination* (Cambridge, Mass., 1949), pp. 174–96.

Braddy, Haldeen, *Glorious Incense: The Fullfillment of Edgar Allan Poe* (Washington, D.C., 1953).

Brooks, Van Wyck, "Poe in the South" and "Poe in the North," in *The World of Washington Irving* (Cleveland, 1944), pp. 337–61, 443–56.

*Buranelli, Vincent, *Edgar Allan Poe* (New Haven, 1961). [TUSAS]

Burke, Kenneth, "The Principle of Composition," *Poetry*, XCIX (1961), 46–53.

Cambiaire, Celéstin P., *The Influence of Edgar Allan Poe in France* (New York, 1927).

Campbell, Killis, *The Mind of Poe, and Other Studies* (Cambridge, Mass., 1932).

Caputi, Anthony, "The Refrain in Poe's Poetry," *AL*, XXV (1963), 22–37.

Carlson, Eric W., "Symbol and Sense in Poe's 'Ulalume,'" *AL*, XXXV (1963), 22–37.

Charvat, William, "Poe: Journalism and the Theory of Poetry," in *Aspects of American Poetry*, ed. Richard M. Ludwig (Columbus, Ohio, 1962), pp. 61–78.

Cooke, John Esten, *Poe as a Literary Critic*, ed. N. Bryllion Fagin (Baltimore, 1946). [estimate of Poe by 19th cent Va novelist]

Cox, James W., "Edgar Poe: *Style or Pose*," *VQR*, XLIV (1968), 67–89.

Chinol, Elio, "Poe's Essays on Poetry," translation B. M. Arnett, *SeR*, LXVIII (1960), 390–97.

Dameron, J. Lasley, "Poe's Reading of the British Periodicals," *MissQ*, XVIII (1964–65), 19–25.

Davidson, Edward H., *Poe: A Critical Study* (Cambridge, Mass., 1957).

Davis, Richard Beale, intro to *Chivers' Life of Poe* (New York, 1952), pp. 9–21.

———, "Poe and William Wirt," *AL*, XVI (1944), 212–20.

Durick, Jeremiah K., "The Incorporate Silence and the Heart Divine," in *American Classics Reconsidered*, ed. H. C. Gardiner (New York, 1958), pp. 176–92.

Eliot, T. S., "From Poe to Valery," *HudR*, II (1949), 327–43. Repr in *To Criticize the Critic* (London, 1965), pp. 27–42; also printed in *Literary Opinion in America*, ed. M. D. Zabel (New York, 1951), pp. 626–38.

Feidelson, Charles, Jr., *Symbolism and American Literature* (Chicago, 1953), pp. 35–42.

Fiedler, Leslie A., "Blackness of Darkness: E. A. Poe and the Development of the Gothic," *Love and Death in the American Novel* (New York, 1960), pp. 370–414.

Foerster, Norman, "Poe," in *American Criticism: A Study in Literary Theory from Poe to the Present* (New York, 1928; 1962), pp. 1–51.

———, "Quantity and Quality in Poe's Aesthetic," *SP*, XX (1923), 310–35.

Forrest, William M., *Biblical Allusions in Poe* (New York, 1928).

Gargano, James W., "'The Black Cat': Perverseness Reconsidered," *TSLL*, II (1960), 172–78.

Gregory, Horace, "Within the Private View," *PartisanR* (1943), 263–74.

Halline, Allan G., "Moral and Religious Concepts in Poe," *Bucknell U Stud*, II (1951), 126–50.

Hubbell, Jay B., "Poe and the Southern Literary Tradition," *TSLL*, II (Summer 1960), 151–71.

———, "Poe and the Southern Literary Tradition," *TSLL*, II (Summer 1960), 151–71.

Jackson, David K., *Poe and the Southern Literary Messenger* (Richmond, 1934).

Jacobs, Robert D., "Poe's Earthly Paradise," *AQ*, XII (1960), 404–13.

———, "Poe in Richmond: The Double Image," in *Southern Writers: Appraisals in*

Our Time, ed. Simonini, pp. 19–49.

Kelly, George E., "Poe's Theory of Beauty," *AL*, XXVII (1956), 521–36.

———, "Poe's Theory of Unity," *PhilQ*, XXXVII (1958), 34–44.

Laser, Marvin, "The Growth and Structure of Poe's Concept of Beauty," *Eng Lit Hist*, XV (1948), 69–84.

Lawrence, D. H., "Edgar Allan Poe," *Studies in Classical American Literature* (New York, 1923), pp. 93–120. Repr in *The Portable D. H. Lawrence*, ed. Diana Trilling (New York, 1947), pp. 671–92.

Lemonnier, Léon, *Edgar Poe et la critique française de 1845 á 1875* (Paris, 1928).

———, *Edgar Poe et les poètes français* (Paris, 1932).

Levin, Harry, *The Power of Blackness: Hawthorne, Poe, Melville* (New York, 1958).

McLuhan, Herbert M., "Edgar Poe's Tradition," *SeR*, LII (1944), 24–33.

Maddison, Carol H., "Poe's *Eureka*," *TSLL*, II (1960), 350–67.

Marchand, Ernest, "Poe as a Social Critic," *AL*, VI (1934), 28–43.

Marks, E. R., "Poe as Literary Theorist: A Reappraisal," *AL*, XXXIII (1961), 296–306.

Martin, Terence, "The Imagination at Play: Edgar Allan Poe," *KR*, XXVIII (1966), 194–209.

Mauclair, Camille, *Le Génie d'Edgar Poe; la légende et la vérité—la méthode—la pensée—l'influence en France* (Paris, 1925).

Miller, Perry, *The Raven and the Whale* (New York, 1956), pp. 112–49, *passim.*

Mooney, S. L., "The Comic in Poe's Fiction," *AL*, XXXIII (1962), 433–41.

———, "Poe's Gothic Waste Land," *SeR*, LXX (1962), 261–83.

Moss, Sidney P., *Poe's Literary Battles* (Durham, 1963).

Parks, Edd Winfield, *Edgar Allan Poe as Literary Critic* (Athens, Ga., 1964). [Lamar Lectures]

Pochmann, Henry A., "Germanic Materials and Motifs in the Short Story: Edgar Allan Poe," in *German Culture in America* (Madison, Wis., 1957), pp. 388–408.

Praz, Mario, "Poe and Psychoanalysis," translated by B. M. Arnett, *SeR*, LXVIII (1960), 375–89.

Pritchard, John P., "Edgar Allan Poe," in *Criticism in America* (Norman, Okla., 1956), 70–86.

*Quinn, Patrick F., *The French Face of Edgar Poe* (Carbondale, Ill., 1957).

*Rans, Geoffrey, *Edgar Allan Poe* (London, 1965).

Ridgely, Joseph V., and Iola S. Haverstick, "Chartless Voyage: The Many Narratives of Arthur Gordon Pym," *TSLL*, VIII (1966), 63–80.

Robinson, E. Arthur, "Order and Sentience in 'The Fall of the House of Usher,'" *PMLA*, LXXVI (1961), 68–81.

———, "Poe's 'The Tell Tale Heart,'" *Nineteenth-Cent Fiction*, XIX (1965), 369–78.

Simpson, Lewis P., "Touching 'The Stylus': Notes on Poe's Vision of Literary Order," in *Studies in American Literature*, ed. Waldo McNeir and Leo B. Levy (Baton Rouge, 1960), pp. 33–48. [L.S.U. Stud No. 8]

Snell, George D., "First of the New Critics," *QR of Lit*, II (1945), 333–40.

Spitzer, Leo, "A Reinterpretation of 'The Fall of the House of Usher,'" *Comp Lit*, IV (1952), 351–63.

Stauffer, Donald B., "Style and Meaning in 'Ligeia' and 'William Wilson,'" *Stud in Short Fict*, II (1965), 316–30.

Stern, Madeline B., "Poe: The Mental Temperament for Phrenologists," *AL*, XL (1968), 155–63.

Stovall, Floyd, "An Interpretation of Poe's 'Al Aaraaf,'" *U of Tex Stud in Eng*, IX (1929), 106–33.

————, "Poe's Debt to Coleridge," *U Tex Stud in Eng*, X (1930), 70–127.

Tate, Allen, "The Angelic Imagination: Poe and the Power of Words," *KR*, XIV (1952), 455–75. Repr in Tate, *The Forlorn Demon* (Chicago, 1953), and in Tate, *The Man of Letters in the Modern World* (New York, 1955).

————, "Our Cousin, Mr. Poe," *PartisanR*, XVI (1949), 1207–19. Repr in Tate, *The Forlorn Demon*, and Tate, *The Man of Letters in the Modern World*.

————, "The Poetry of Edgar Allan Poe," *SeR*, LXXVI (1968), 214–25.

Wilbur, Richard, "The House of Poe," *Anniversary Lectures 1959* (Washington, D.C., 1959), pp. 21–38. [Lib of Cong Whittall Lectures]

————, intro to *Poe*, ed. Wilbur (New York, 1959), pp. 7–39. [Poe's complete poems]

Williams, William Carlos, "Edgar Allan Poe," *In the American Grain* (New York, 1956), pp. 216–33. [repr of 1925 pub]

Wilson, Edmund, "Poe as a Literary Critic," *Nation*, CLV (Oct 31, 1942), 452–53.

————, "Poe at Home and Abroad," *New Rep*, XLIX (Dec 8, 1926), 77–80. Repr in Wilson, *The Shores of Light* (New York, 1952).

Wimsatt, W. K., "What Poe Knew About Cryptography," *PMLA*, LVIII (1943), 754–79.

Winters, Yvor, "Edgar Allan Poe: A Crisis in the History of American Obscurantism," *AL*, VIII (1937), 379–401. Repr in Winters, *In Defense of Reason* (New York, 1947).

Young, Philip, "The Early Psychologists and Poe," *AL*, XXII (1951), 442–54.

Robert D. Jacobs
University of Kentucky
Lexington, Kentucky

KATHERINE ANNE PORTER (1894–)

Katherine Anne Porter has never lacked percipient readers, even though it has taken over three decades for her work to reach a large audience. When *Flowering Judas* appeared in 1930, Allen Tate praised Miss Porter as "a new star" in the *Nation* for October, and at the same time Louise Bogan said of the book in the *New Republic*: "There is nothing quite like it, and very little that approaches its strength in contemporary writing." Miss Porter has always been recognized as a fine stylist (often to the detriment of her other virtues as a fictionist), but opinion has varied about the breadth and vitality of her subject matter as well as the range and significance of her themes. The most serious attacks have involved these alleged limitations, and William Nance's *Katherine Anne Porter and the Art of Rejection* (1964) may be seen as a culmination of this kind of critical approach to her fiction. More recently John W. Aldridge has argued that the art and passion are separated in all of Miss Porter's stories which are laid outside the South. Other critics, notably Glenway Wescott, Lodwick Hartley, Robert Penn Warren, and Edward Schwartz, have seen the restrictions in Miss Porter's art as consciously imposed; and they find her deliberate "self-limitation" to be an integral aspect of her craft.

Thus far, there is no thorough and sound book or monograph which can be considered a standard work; however, there have been a number of excellent articles, beginning with those of Hartley and Warren in the early forties. (It is interesting that the best critics of Katherine Anne Porter's work have often written more than one article about her.) On the whole, the essays which are general treatments of Miss Porter's short fiction are considerably better than the studies which concern individual stories, and accordingly a good many pieces of the latter kind have been omitted. The great need at present is for a solid, book-length study which would contain definitely established biographical particulars and a sympathetic critical (and scholarly) reading of the fiction, with some attention being given to the criticism and miscellaneous pieces. One may hope that Paul R. Baumgartner's *Katherine Anne Porter* (forthcoming in the American Authors and Critics Series in 1969) will be written in these terms. In the meantime George Hendrick's book is the most useful full-length account, while Miss Porter's many interviews provide much of the best biographical information and many arresting critical remarks.

Aldridge, John W., "Art and Passion in Katherine Anne Porter," *Time to Murder and Create: The Contemporary Novel in Crisis* (New York, 1966), pp. 178–84. [Miss Porter as essentially So storyteller and memoirist]

Alexander, Jean, "Katherine Anne Porter's Ship in the Jungle," *Twentieth Cent Lit* XI (1966), 179–88.

Allen, Charles A., "Katherine Anne Porter: Psychology as Art," *SWR*, LI (1956), 223–30. [contains good reading of "The Downward Path to Wisdom"]

————, "The Nouvelles of Katherine Anne Porter," *UnivR*, XIX (1962), 87–93.

————, "Southwestern Chronicle: Katherine Anne Porter," *Arizona Q*, II (1946), 90–95. [on Miss Porter's characters and her belief]

Auchincloss, Louis, "Katherine Anne Porter," *Pioneers & Caretakers: A Study of 9 Novelists* (Minneapolis, 1965), pp. 136–51. [emphasis on "Noon Wine" and *Ship of Fools*]

Baker, Howard, "The Upward Path: Notes on the Work of Katherine Anne Porter," *SoR*, n.s., IV (1968), 1–19. [r essay]

Bates, H. E., *The Modern Short Story* (London and Boston, 1941), pp. 185–87.

Becker, Laurence A., " 'The Jilting of Granny Weatherall': The Discovery of Pattern," *Eng Jour*, LV (1966), 1164–169.

Bell, Vereen M., " 'The Grave' Revisited," *Stud in Short Fict*, II (1965), 39–45. [rebuttal to earlier interpretations, esp Curley's]

Bride, Sister Mary, "Laura and the Unlit Lamp," *Stud in Short Fict*, I (1963), 61–63. [on Laura's "accedia" in "Flowering Judas"]

Core, George, " 'The Best Residuum of Truth,' " *GaR*, XX (1966), 278–91. [r essay;

includes a reading of "Holiday"]

Curley, Daniel, "Katherine Anne Porter: The Larger Plan," *KR*, XXV (1963), 671–95. [argues that Miranda is key to Miss Porter's fict]

———, "Treasure in 'The Grave,' " *MFS*, IX (1964), 377–84.

Hartley, Lodwick, "Dark Voyagers: A Study of Katherine Anne Porter's *Ship of Fools*," *UnivR*, XXX (1963), 83–94. [the best reading of the novel]

———, "Katherine Anne Porter," *SeR*, XLVIII (1940), 206–216.

———, "The Lady and the Temple: "The Critical Theories of Katherine Anne Porter," *Coll Eng*, XIV (1953), 386–91.

*Hendrick, George, *Katherine Anne Porter* (New York, 1965). [TUSAS]

Hertz, Robert, "Sebastian Brant and Porter's *Ship of Fools*," *MidwQ*, VI (1965), 389–401.

Johnson, James William, "Another Look at Katherine Anne Porter," *VQR*, XXXVI (1960), 598–613. [fine ordering of fiction according to recurrent themes, with emphasis on short novels]

Joselyn, Sister Mary, O.S.B., "Animal Imagery in Katherine Anne Porter's Fiction," in *Myth and Symbol: Critical Approaches and Applications*, ed. Bernice Slote (Lincoln, Neb., 1963), pp. 101–15.

———, "On the Making of *Ship of Fools*," *So Dakota R*, I, No. 2 (1964), 46–52.

Kaplan, Charles, "True Witness: Katherine Anne Porter," *ColoQ*, VII (1959), 319–27. [on Miranda stories, esp "The Circus"]

"Katherine Anne Porter: A Birthday Tribute," *YaleR*, LV (1966), 265–90. [contains three excellent essays: Cleanth Brooks, "On 'The Grave' "; Robert Penn Warren, "Uncorrupted Consciousness: The Stories of Katherine Anne Porter"; Eudora Welty, "The Eye of the Story"]

Katherine Anne Porter Number, *Four Quarters*, XII (1962), [important document; best pieces are: John Hagopian, "Katherine Anne Porter: Feeling, Form, and Truth"; Robert B. Heilman, "*Ship of Fools*: Notes on Style"; J. F. Powers, "She Stands Alone"]

Kirkpatrick, Smith, "The *Ship of Fools*," *SeR*, LXXI (1963), 94–98. [r essay]

Liberman, M. M., "Responsibility of the Novelist: The Critical Reception of *Ship of Fools*," *Crit*, VIII (1966), 377–88. [argues persuasively that novel is "a kind of modern apologue"]

Mathiessen, F. O., r of "*The Leaning Tower and Other Stories*," in *Accent*, V (1945), 121–23. Repr as "That True and Human World," in *Accent Anthology*, ed. Kerker Quinn and Charles Shattuck (New York, 1946), pp. 619–23. [r essay, with comparison of Miss Porter and "narrow regionalists"]

Mooney, Harry John, Jr., *The Fiction and Criticism of Katherine Anne Porter*, rev ed (Pittsburgh, 1962). [No. 2 in U of Pittsburgh *Critical Essays in English and American Literature*]

Nance, William L., S. M., *Katherine Anne Porter and the Art of Rejection* (Chapel Hill, 1964).

Perry, Robert L., "Porter's 'Hacienda' and the Theme of Change," *MidwQ*, VI (1965), 403–15.

Pierce, Marvin, "Point of View: Katherine Anne Porter's 'Noon Wine,' " *Ohio U R*, III (1961), 95–113.

Porter, Katherine Anne, *The Days Before* (New York, 1952). [many essays contain comments which can be applied to Miss Porter's fiction: for example, "No Plot, My Dear, No Story," "Portrait: Old South," and "The Art of Katherine Mansfield"]

———, " 'Noon Wine': The Sources," *YaleR*, XLVI (1956), 22–39. Repr in *Under-*

standing Fiction, ed. Robert Penn Warren and Cleanth Brooks, 2nd ed (New York, 1959), 610–20.

———, "From the Notebooks of Katherine Anne Porter—Yeats, Joyce, Eliot, Pound—" *SoR*, n.s., I (1965), 570–73.

———, "Ole Woman River: A Correspondence with Katherine Anne Porter," *SeR*, LXXIV (1966), 754–67. [letters to and from Donald Sutherland—mainly about Miss Porter and Gertrude Stein]

———, "A Country and Some People I Love: An Interview by Hank Lopez with Katherine Anne Porter," *Harper's*, CCXXI (Sept 1965), 58–62, 65–68.

———, "An Interview with Katherine Anne Porter," *McCall's*, XCII (Aug 1965), 88–89, 137–43.

———, "Symposium: The Situation in American Writing," *PartisanR*, VI (1939), 36–39. [Miss Porter on her "usable past"]

Pritchett, V. S., "Stories and Stories," *New Statesman*, LXIII (1964), 47–48. [r of Collected Stories]

Ryan, Majorie, "*Dubliners* and the Stories of Katherine Anne Porter," *AL*, XXXI (1960), 464–73.

———, "Katherine Anne Porter: *Ship of Fools* and the Short Stories," *Bucknell R*, XII (1964), 51–63.

Schwartz, Edward G., "The Fictions of Memory," *SWR*, XLV (1960), 204–15. [on Miranda and "Miranda stories"]

*———, "Katherine Anne Porter: A Critical Bibliography," intro by Robert Penn Warren. *Bull of N.Y. Public Lib*, LVII (1953), 211–47. [comprehensive through 1952—and invaluable]

———, "The Way of Dissent: Katherine Anne Porter's Critical Position," *WHumR*, VIII (1954), 119–30.

Smith, J. Oates, "Porter's 'Noon Wine': A Stifled Tragedy," *Renascence*, XVII (1965), 157–62.

Stein, William Bysshe, " 'Theft': Porter's Politics of Modern Love," *Perspective*, XI (1960), 223–28.

Thompson, Barbara, "The Art of Fiction XXIX—Katherine Anne Porter: An Interview," *ParisR*, No. 29 (1963), 87–114. Repr in *Writers at Work: The Paris Review Interviews, Second Series* (New York, 1963), pp. 137–63.

Warren, Robert Penn, "Irony with a Center: Katherine Anne Porter," *Selected Essays* (New York, 1958), pp. 136–56. [best single study of fict]

Welker, Robert L., and Herschel Gower, " 'The Grave': Investigation and Comment," in *The Sense of Fiction* (Englewood Cliffs, N.J., 1966), pp. 150–54.

Wescott, Glenway, "Praise," *SoR*, o.s., V (1939), 161–73. [r essay about *Pale Horse, Pale Rider*]

———, "Katherine Anne Porter Personally," *Images of Truth: Remembrances and Criticism* (New York, 1962), pp. 25–58.

West, Ray B., Jr., *Katherine Anne Porter* (Minneapolis, 1963). [Minn pamph]

———, "Katherine Anne Porter: Symbol and Theme in 'Flowering Judas,' " *Accent*, VII (1947), 182–87. Repr in *The Art of Modern Fiction*, ed. West and Robert W. Stallman (New York, 1949), pp. 287–92.

Wilson, Edmund, "Katherine Anne Porter," *New Yorker*, XX (Sept. 30, 1944), 72–75. Repr in Wilson, *Classics and Commercials* (New York, 1950), pp. 219–23.

Young, Vernon A., "The Art of Katherine Anne Porter," *NMexQ*, XV (1945), 326–41. Repr in Young, *American Thought* (New York, 1947), pp. 223–38. [on Miss Porter's themes, style, and realism]

Youngblood, Sarah, "Structure and Imagery in Katherine Anne Porter's *Pale Horse, Pale Rider*," *MFS*, V (1959–60), 344–52.

GEORGE CORE
University of Georgia
Athens, Georgia

WILLIAM SYDNEY PORTER ("O. HENRY")
(1862-1910)

Recent publication in the *Kenyon Review* of an amusing piece on O. Henry by William Saroyan ("O What a Man Was O. Henry") points up anew the paradox of William Sydney Porter, a writer whose short stories have won him millions of devoted readers the world over, yet stimulated relatively little interest among contemporary scholars and critics. By means of a tiny creature reminiscent of Frost's "Considerable Speck," Saroyan's story captures emblematically the vital essence in O. Henry's writing and thereby clarifies the mystery of his enduring popular appeal as well as the essence of his artistry. But the paradox remains unsolved, for despite the fact that O. Henry's techniques revamped the form of short fiction and influenced a generation of younger writers, serious students of modern literature during the last quarter century have either brushed him aside with an epithet or ignored him altogether.

During the decade after his death O. Henry's popularity soared, and many laudatory essays paid tribute to his achievement, most of them placing it on a par with that of Poe, Hawthorne, Maupassant, and Chekhov. By 1919, when the annual volume of selections called the *O. Henry Memorial Award Prize Stories* was inaugurated, his name was the inevitable choice with which to symbolize pre-eminence in this art form, because his work was then regarded as the highest standard of literary excellence in the short story. But beginning in the 1920s his reputation among the critics declined almost as swiftly as it had risen, and by the 1930s his style of writing no longer seemed important enough to notice, even favorably. Throughout the nation during this decade scarcely more than ten or twelve masters' theses on O. Henry were written, one of which was later published; while only three or four important articles, appearing in respectable journals like the *Southwest Review* and *American Literature*, and two or three books (notably, Clarkson's *Bibliography*) served to keep up interest in his work. Slight as this notice seems for a writer who had dominated the scene just twenty years before, it far exceeded the attention O. Henry's writing received during the 1940s and most of the 1950s, when only a few more masters' theses were completed, along with a single published dissertation and one scholarly article that re-examined the facts in Porter's embezzlement trial. The general critical indifference toward his literary achievement at this point was summed up in the brusque words of a leading literary historian, who dismissed him from further academic consideration by saying that "the world of O. Henry is an intellectual Sahara." And to prove the point, in 1961, the author of an elaborate treatise on the American short story, bluntly asserting that O. Henry's reputation had died, ignored his work entirely.

Meanwhile, however, O. Henry's popular appeal has flourished for sixty years wherever fiction is read, ironically defying the critics' contumely as sales of his stories have mounted to tens of millions of volumes. Translated into more than fifty languages, they are still among the top favorites in Russia, Latin America, and the Far East, as well as in all English-speaking countries; and they seem likely to have established for him a permanent, if minor niche in the world's literary hall of fame. Because they embody a special, unique bouquet which Saroyan fittingly calls "a quality of something lonely and denied that people could make their own," their lasting appeal to the masses may well inspire among future scholars a renewed interest in their author.

DAB, XV, pp. 105–107; *Hubbell*, pp. 840–42; *LSL*, VI, pp. 2354A–2354N; **LHUS*, II, pp. 696–98, *Supp*, 180.

*Clarkson, Paul S., *A Bibliography of William Sydney Porter* (Caldwell, Idaho, 1938).
———, "A Decomposition of Cabbages and Kings," *AL*, VII (1935), 195–202.
Courtney, L. W., "O. Henry's Case Reconsidered," *AL*, XIV (1943), 361–71.
*Current-Garcia, Eugene, *O. Henry* (New York, 1965). [TUSAS]
Echols, Edward C., "O. Henry's Shaker of Attic Salt,'" *Classical Jour*, XLIII (1947–48), 488–89; XLIV (1948–49), 209–10.
Gallegly, J. S., "Backgrounds and Patterns of O. Henry's Texas Badman Stories," *Rice Inst Pamph*, No. 42 (Houston, Oct 1955), 1–32.
*Harrell, Mary S., intro to *O. Henry Encore* (New York, 1939), pp. vii–xvii. [important discussion of stories and sketches by Porter originally publ in Houston *Post*]
Kercheville, F. M., "O. Henry and Don Alfonso," *NMexQR*, I (1931), 367–88. [useful discussion of Porter's fluency in vernacular Spanish]
*Langford, Gerald, *Alias O. Henry: A Biography of William Sidney Porter* (New York, 1957). [most carefully documented and evenly balanced treatment of Porter's life now available]
Lomax, J. A., "Henry Steger and O. Henry," *SWR*, XXIV (1939), 299–316.
*Long, E. Hudson, *O. Henry, The Man and His Work* (Philadelphia, 1949). [first competent, scholarly book, now superseded by Langford's study]
———, "O. Henry as a Regional Artist," in *Essays on American Literature in Honor of Jay B. Hubbell*, ed. Clarence Gohdes (Durham, 1967), pp. 229–40.

McLean, Malcolm D., "O. Henry in Honduras," *Amer Lit Realism*, No. 3 (1968), 39–46.

O'Quinn, Trueman, "O. Henry in Austin," *SW Hist Q*, XLVIII (1939), 143–57.

*Pattee, Fred Lewis, "O. Henry and the Handbooks," *The Development of The American Short Story* (New York, 1923), pp. 357–79.

Payne, L. W., Jr., "The Humor of O. Henry," *TexR*, IV (1918), 18–37. [excellent crit analysis of sources and humor devices]

Peel, Donald F., "A Critical Study of The Short Stories of O. Henry," [*NW Mo St Coll Stud*] XXV (1961), iv, 3–24.

Rollins, Hyder E., "O. Henry," *SeR*, XXII (1914), 213–32.

———, "O. Henry's Texas," *TexR*, IV (1919), 295–307.

Saroyan, William, "O What a Man was O. Henry," *KR*, XXIV (1967), 671–75.

*Smith, C. Alphonso, *O. Henry Biography* (New York, 1916). [first full-length authorized biog; outdated but still authoritative source]

Travis, Edmunds, "O. Henry's Austin Years," and "O. Henry Enters the Shadows," *Bunker's Month*, I (1928), 493–508, 669–84.

Van Doren, Carl, "O. Henry," *TexR*, II (1917), 248–59. [excellent crit analysis of O. Henry's artistic strengths and weaknesses]

*Watson, Grace Miller, "O. Henry on the Houston *Post*," Texas, 1934. [MA thesis; important discussion and facsimile repro of all sketches and stories by Porter originally publ in Houston *Post*]

EUGENE CURRENT-GARCIA
Auburn University
Auburn, Alabama

REYNOLDS PRICE (1933–)

Reynolds Price himself offers much helpful comment on his work, both in interviews and essays. There is one article on the short stories in the following list; the other entries are representative reviews of the three books.

Boatwright, James, *Masterplots 1964 Annual*, ed. Frank Magill (New York, 1964), pp. 185–87. [r]

Flatto, Elie, *Village Voice*, Apr 5, 1962.

Hicks, Granville, *Sat R*, XLV (March 10, 1962) 17–18. [r, biog sketch]

Hoffman, *The Art of Southern Fiction*, pp. 137–43.

Janeway, Elizabeth, *N.Y. Times Bk R*, March 27, 1966, p. 6. [r, inter, p. 44]

Kaufman, Wallace, "A Conversation with Reynolds Price," *Shen*, XVII (Summer, 1966), 3–25. [interv]

Knickerbocker, Conrad, *N.Y. Times*, March 26, 1966, p. 27. [r]

McPherson, William, *Life*, Apr 8, 1966, p. 10. [r]

Moore, Eugene, "On Writing, Readers, and Critics," *Red Clay Reader*, III (1966), 18–26. [interv]

Price, Reynolds, *"A Long and Happy Life*: Fragments of Groundwork," *VQR*, XLI
(1965), 236–47.

———, "A Question of Influence," *N.Y. Times Bk R*, May 29, 1966, pp. 2, 12–13.

Sloss, Henry E., Jr., "Sir Milo the Generous," *Shen*, XVIII (Autumn 1966), 93–96. [r]

Stevenson, John W., "The Faces of Reynolds Price's Short Fiction," *Stud in Short Fict*,
III (1966), 300–306.

Tracy, Honor, *New Leader*, XLV (Aug 6, 1962), 21–22. [r]

Wain, John, *New Republic*, CLIV (May 14, 1966), 31–33. [r]

JAMES BOATWRIGHT
Washington and Lee University
Lexington, Virginia

JOHN CROWE RANSOM (1888–)

This checklist does not attempt to cite the many biographical sketches
or brief critical notes that have appeared as introductions to Ransom's
writings included in textbooks or anthologies. Neither does it include
the general works on the Fugitives, the Agrarians, or the New Critics,
except when the comment on Ransom is thought to be particularly
significant. For an almost exhaustive list of writings by or about Ransom, one should consult the "Bibliography" of Mildred Brooks Peters
included in *John Crowe Ransom: Critical Essays and a Bibliography*,
edited by Thomas Daniel Young (Baton Rouge, 1968).

LHUS, II, *Supp*, pp. 225–27.

Beatty, Richmond Croom, "John Crowe Ransom as Poet," *SeR*, LII (1944), 344–66.

Bergonzi, Bernard, "A Poem about the History of Love: 'The Equilibrists' by John
Crowe Ransom," *CritQ*, IV (1962), 127–37.

Blum, Morgan, "The Fugitive Particular: John Crowe Ransom, Critic," *WR*, XIV
(1950), 85–102. [in Young]

Bradbury, John M., *The Fugitives: A Critical Account* (Chapel Hill, 1958).

*———, "Ransom as Poet," *Accent*, XI (1951), 45–57.

Brooks, Cleanth, "The Doric Delicacy," *SeR*, LVI (1948), 402–15. [in Young]

———, *Modern Poetry and the Tradition* (Chapel Hill, 1939), pp. 85–95.

*Buffington, Robert, *The Equilibrist: A Study of John Crowe Ransom's Poems,
1916–63* (Nashville, 1967).

Burgum, Edwin Berry, "An Examination of Modern Critics: John Crowe Ransom,"
Rocky Mt R, VII (Spring 1944), 87–93.

Campbell, Harry M., "John Crowe Ransom," *SWR*, XXIV (1939), 476–89.

Cowan, Louise, *The Fugitive Group: A Literary History* (Baton Rouge, 1959).

Daniel, Robert, "The Critics of Nashville," *Tenn Stud in Lit*, I (1956), 19–26.

Davidson, Donald, *Southern Writers in the Modern World*, Lamar Lectures, 1957
(Athens, Ga., 1958).

Foster, Richard, *The New Romantics: A Reappraisal of the New Criticism* (Bloomington, Ind., 1962), pp. 138–44, 199–200, *et passim*.

Handy, William J., "The Ontological Theory of the Ransom Critics," *U Tex Stud in Eng*, XXXV (1956), 32–50.

Harder, Kelsie B., "John Crowe Ransom as Economist," *Mod Age*, II (1958), 389–93. [in Young]

Hough, Graham, "John Crowe Ransom: The Poet and the Critic," *SoR*, n.s., I (1965), 1–21. [in Young]

Jarvis, F. P., "F. H. Bradley's *Appearance and Reality* and the Critical Theory of John Crowe Ransom," *Papers on Eng Lang and Lit*, I (1965), 187–91. [in Young]

Karanikas, Alexander, *Tillers of a Myth: Southern Agrarians as Social and Literary Critics* (Madison, Wis., 1966).

Knight, Karl F., "Love as Symbol in the Poetry of Ransom," *MissQ*, XIII (1960), 132–40. [in Young]

*———, *The Poetry of John Crowe Ransom*, Stud in Amer Lit, II (The Hague, 1964).

Koch, Vivienne, "The Achievement of John Crowe Ransom," *SeR*, LVIII (1950), 227–61. [in Young]

Krieger, Murray, *The New Apologists for Poetry* (Minneapolis, 1956), pp. 82–87, 143–47, *et passim*.

Lynskey, Winifred, "A Critic in Action: Mr. Ransom," *Coll Eng*, V (1944), 239–49.

Mann, David, and Samuel H. Woods, Jr., "John Crowe Ransom's Poetic Revisions," *PMLA*, LXXXIII (1968), 15–21.

Matthiessen, F. O., "Primarily Language," *SeR*, LVI (1948), 391–401. [in Young]

Mills, Gordon H., "Myth and Ontology in the Thought of John Crowe Ransom," Iowa, 1942. [diss]

Nemerov, Howard, "Summer's Flare and Winter's Flaw," *SeR*, LVI (1948), 416–25.

Pratt, William, "In Pursuit of the Fugitives," in *The Fugitive Poets: Modern Southern Poetry in Perspective* (New York, 1965), pp. 13–46.

Purdy, Rob Roy, ed., *Fugitives' Reunion: Conversations at Vanderbilt, May 3–5, 1956* (Nashville, 1959).

Rock, Virginia, "The Making and Meaning of *I'll Take My Stand*: A Study in Utopian Conservatism, 1925–1939," Minnesota, 1961. [diss]

Rubin, "The Poetry of Agrarianism," *The Faraway Country*, pp. 155–84.

———, "Ransom's Cruell Battle," *Shen*, IX (Winter 1958), 23–35. [in Young]

Schwartz, Delmore, "Instructed of Much Mortality: A Note on the Poetry of John Crowe Ransom," *SeR*, LIV (1946), 439–48. [in Young]

*Stallman, Robert Wooster, "John Crowe Ransom: A Checklist," *SeR*, LVI (1948), 442–76.

Stauffer, Donald A., "Portrait of the Critic-Poet as Equilibrist," *SeR*, LVI (1948), 426–34. [in Young]

Stewart, John L., *The Burden of Time: The Fugitives and Agrarians* (Princeton, 1965).

———, *John Crowe Ransom* (Minneapolis, 1962). [Minn pamph]

———, "The Poetry of John Crowe Ransom," *Shen*, XIV (Spring 1967), 33–48.

Stocking, Fred H., "Poetry as Knowledge: The Critical Theory of John Crowe Ransom and Allen Tate," Michigan, 1946. [diss]

Sutton, Walter, *Modern American Criticism* (Englewood Cliffs, N.J., 1963), pp. 107–116, *et passim*.

Unger, Leonard, *The Man in the Name: Essays on the Experience of Poetry* (Minneapolis, 1956), pp. 35–40, 111–19, *et passim*.

Warren, Robert Penn, "John Crowe Ransom: A Study in Irony," *VQR*, XI (1935), 93–112. [in Young]

Wassermann, G. R., "The Irony of John Crowe Ransom," *U of Kan Cy R*, XXIII (1956), 151–60. [in Young]

Winters, Yvor, "John Crowe Ramsom: or Thunder Without God," *In Defense of Reason* (New York, 1947), pp. 502–55.

Woodward, Barbara, "Theories of Meaning in Poetry: A Critical History," Michigan, 1946. [diss]

*Young, Thomas Daniel, ed., *John Crowe Ransom: Critical Essays and a Bibliography* (Baton Rouge, 1968).

THOMAS DANIEL YOUNG
Vanderbilt University
Nashville, Tennessee

MARJORIE KINNAN RAWLINGS (1896-1953)

Listing the writings about Marjorie Kinnan Rawlings presents a problem because there is so much journalistic writing about her and so little critical or scholarly writing. Her books sold so well in the late 1930s and early 1940s that she became something of a national celebrity, with the result that there are literally hundreds of reviews of the books and numerous human interest feature articles and interviews. But until recent years she has suffered an almost total neglect by serious scholars. I have included in this list only a sampling of the more substantial reviews from the larger metropolitan newspapers or other serials generally available in research libraries, and a similar sampling of the more significant articles which have biographical interest. Anyone wishing to look further into materials of this sort should consult the six large notebooks of clippings in the Rawlings Collection at the University of Florida Library, Gainesville, Florida. The more serious critical writings I have listed in full.

Benet, Stephen Vincent and Rosemary, "Marjorie Kinnan Rawlings," *N.Y. Her Trib Bks*, Feb 9, 1941. [interv]

Bernard, Harry, *Le Roman Régionaliste aux Etats-Unis, 1913–1940* (Montreal, 1949), pp. 138–41.

*Bigelow, Gordon E., *Frontier Eden: The Literary Career of Marjorie Kinnan Rawlings* (Gainesville, 1966).

———, "Marjorie Kinnan Rawlings' Wilderness," *SeR*, LXXIII (1965), 299–310.

Canby, Henry Seidel, *Book-of-the-Month Club News*, March, 1938. [r essay]

Figh, M. G., "Folklore and Folk Speech in the Works of Marjorie Kinnan Rawlings," *SFQ*, XI (1947), 201–209.

Furlow, Carl Tim, "Folklore Elements in the Florida Writings of Marjorie Kinnan Rawlings," Florida, 1953. [MA thesis]

Gannett, Lewis, "Books and Things," *N.Y. Her Trib*, Apr 1, 1938.

Gray, James, "Local Habitation," in *On Second Thought* (Minneapolis, 1946), pp. 116–140.

McGuire, William J. "A Study of Florida Cracker Dialect Based Chiefly on the Prose Works of Marjorie Kinnan Rawlings," Florida, 1939. [MA thesis]

Morris, L., "New Classicist," *NoAmerR*, CCXXXXVI (1938), 179–84. [r essay]

Peck, Joseph R. "The Fiction-Writing Art of Marjorie Kinnan Rawlings," Florida, 1954. [MA thesis]

Rawlings, Marjorie Kinnan, autobiog articles, *Los Angeles Times*, Apr 26, May 3, May 10, May 17, May 24, 1953.

Robillard, Ambolena H., "Maxwell Evarts Perkins: The Author's Editor," Florida, 1954. [diss]

Sergeant, Elizabeth Shepley, "Literary Profile: Marjorie Kinnan Rawlings," *N.Y. Her Trib Bks*, June 18, 1933. [interv]

Slagle, Mary Louise, "The Artistic Uses of Nature in the Fiction of Marjorie Kinnan Rawlings," Florida, 1953. [MA thesis]

Gordon E. Bigelow
University of Florida
Gainesville, Florida

LIZETTE WOODWORTH REESE (1856-1935)

Significant writings about the life and craft of this tiny, withdrawn, yet not too sequestered Maryland singer may surprise by their relative abundance. To this day the Lizette Woodworth Reese Memorial Association, inaugurated in the year of her death, convenes annually to honor her name. The bulk of her literary remains went to the C. Waller Barrett Collection of American Literature in the University of Virginia Library. Other important holdings of Reese material—all by Baltimoreans—are those of Mrs. John D. Dietrich, Mrs. L. Ketchum Dietrich, Albert W. Dowling, and R. P. Harriss.

The moderately numerous list of repositories for other Reese items may be consulted in *American Literary Manuscripts . . .*, compiler, Committee on Manuscript Holdings, American Literature Group, Modern Language Association (Austin [Tex., 1960]), p. 310.

DAB, XXI, pp. 623–24; *LSL*, X, pp. 4379–81.

Brooke, Bissell, "Lizette Woodworth Reese: 1856–1956," *Baltimore Sunday Sun*, Jan 8,

1956, Sec. A, p. 1. [biog, plus six hitherto unpubl poems; illus]

Hunley, Effie S., "Lizette Woodworth Reese: A Normal Genius" [Baltimore, Md.] *Gardens, Houses, and People,* XXII (June-July 1947), 12–13, 22 et seq. [biog and crit by Reese's private secretary]

Kindilien, Carlin T., "The Village World of Lizette Woodworth Reese," *SAQ,* LVI (1957), 91–104. [crit]

Klein, L[aura] Ruth Murray, "Lizette Woodworth Reese . . ." Pennsylvania, 1943. [diss; crit biog, no formal bibl, but footnote annot]

*Malin, Vincent D., "Lizette Reese Stimulates Effective Writing," *Baltimore Bull of Educ,* XLIII (1965–66), 36–44. [biog and crit]

Mencken, Henry Louis, "In Praise of a Poet," *Smart Set,* XXXI (May 1910), 153–55. [crit of *A Wayside Lute*]

"Miss Reese, Poet, Dies in Hospital," *Baltimore Eve Sun,* Dec 17, 1935, pp. 44, et seq. [biog data; illus]

Paterson, Robert Hunter, "Recollections of Lizette Woodworth Reese" (typescr 7 pp., Hum Dept, Enoch Pratt Free Lib, Baltimore, Md. [*ca* 1947]).

Reese, Lizette Woodworth, "Teaching Days" (Chaps from Unwritten Autobiographies, VII), *Bookman,* LX (Sept 1924), 5–8.

_____, *A Victorian Village: Reminiscences of Other Days* (New York, 1929).

_____, *The York Road* (New York, [1931]). [autobiog]

Robinson, David M., "Lizette Woodworth Reese, the Poet," in *Lizette Woodworth Reese, 1856–1935: A Tribute Commemmorating the Unveiling of the Reese Memorial Tablet at the Enoch Pratt Free Library, May Second, Nineteen Hundred and Forty-Three* (Baltimore, 1944), pp. 11–30. [biog, crit; illus]

Tunstall, Virginia L., "Lizette Woodworth Reese: An Appreciation" (typscr 15 pp., Hum Dept, Enoch Pratt Free Lib, Baltimore, n.d.). [speech delivered at Johns Hopkins U Lib, Feb 6, 1938, biog]

Turnbull, Grace H., "The Reese Memorial," *Chips from My Chisel: An Autobiography* (Rindge, N.H., 1953), pp. 5–7, 231–36. [biog; illus]

Untermeyer, Louis, *From Another World: The Autobiography of . . .* (New York, [1939]), pp. 159–61.

CURTIS CARROLL DAVIS
Baltimore, Maryland

AMÉLIE RIVES (1863-1945)

After the publication of her short novel *The Quick or the Dead* in 1888, Miss Rives was considered a gifted, if misguided, novelist. The impact of a sensual novel produced by a "Southern lady" may be gauged by the comments of Edgar Fawcett, who forgives Miss Rives for creating "a love-story steeped in realism," and by Mildred Lewis Rutherford, who admires Miss Rives but who rejects the novel as "immoral" and "impure." The attention given to *The Quick or the Dead* and its sequel,

Barbara Dering, is the only critical attention, with the exception of brief book reviews, given to the work of Miss Rives, who wrote a number of other works, including *The Queerness of Celia, Shadows of Flames, The Ghost Garden, Hidden House, Witness the Sun,* and *The Golden Rose.* The range of interest and subject demonstrated in the fiction of Miss Rives is indicated by one reviewer who characterized her novels as "morbid psychological studies," and by another who included *The Golden Rose* as one of the "romances of the heart."

Interest in the exotic life of Miss Rives overshadowed concern with her novels, as is evident in the biographical accounts provided by Mrs. Rutherford, R. T. W. Duke, and J. D. Hurrell. Indeed, the story behind the loves of Miss Rives, who divorced John Armstrong Chanler and who later married Prince Troubetskoy of Russia, is intriguing. Welford D. Taylor, the author of the only recent article about Miss Rives, indicates the fascinating backdrop against which Miss Rives is seen by entitling his article: "Amélie Rives: A Virginia Princess."

Although there is little valuable critical material available at the present time, Welford D. Taylor is preparing a study of Miss Rives for the Twayne's United States Authors Series. The interested student of Southern literature will then be given the opportunity to judge the importance of Miss Rives as author and to complete the picture of Miss Rives, whom J. D. Hurrell presents as an author of "scurrilous paragraphs," yet a religious person; a fine horsewoman and lady, yet a vigorous young woman who appears in "mud-stained corduroy skirt, tan gaiters, . . . sturdy porpoise-hide boots . . . her face swept with color from brow to chin, the dark blue of her Tam o' Shanter crushing the short brown-gold curls against her forehead!"

LSL, X, pp. 4453–57.

Amer Review of Reviews, r of *The Golden Rose,* XXXVII (1908), 761.

Bancroft, Burton, r of *Hidden House* in *The Bookman,* XXXV (1912), 431.

Cosmopolitan, r of *Witness the Sun,* VII (May 1889), 103–104.

Fawcett, Edgar, "A Few More Words about Miss Rives," *Lippincott's Mag.,* XLII (1888), 390–94. [comments on Amélie Rives' "realism," specifically in *The Quick or the Dead*]

*Fullerton, B. M., "(Troubetskoy), Amélie Rives (Chanler)," *Selective Bibliography of American Literature 1775–1900* (New York, 1936), pp. 276–77.

Gallup, Donald, "More Letters of American Writers," *Yale U Lib Gaz,* XXXVII (Jul 1962), 30–25. [includes quotations from letters of Amélie Rives]

Hurrell, J. D., "Some Days with Amélie Rives," *Lippincott's Mag,* XLI (1888), 531–36.

Purcell, James Slicer, "The Southern Poor White in Fiction," Duke, 1938. [MA thesis]

Rutherford, Mildred Lewis, *The South in History and Literature: A Hand-Book of Southern Authors* (Athens, Ga., 1907), pp. 598–600.

SatR of Pol, Lit, Sci and Art, "Miss Amelie Rives's Novels," LXVII (1889), 765–66. [r of *Virginia of Virginia, The Witness of the Sun, A Brother to Dragons*]

Taylor, Welford Dunaway, "Amélie Rives: A Virginia Princess," *Va Calvalcade*, XII (Spring 1963), 11–17.

PAMELA GLENN MENKE
Guilford Technical Institute
Jamestown, North Carolina

ELIZABETH MADOX ROBERTS (1886-1941)

Adams, J. Donald, "Elizabeth Madox Roberts," *VQR*, XII (1936), 80–90.

———, *Elizabeth Madox Roberts: An Appraisal* (New York, 1938). [contributions by Rosamond Milner, Robert Morss Lovett, Edward Garnett, Harry Hansen, Allan Nevins, Carl Van Doren, Harry Emerson Wildes, Mary Ross, Joseph Henry Jackson, Louis Untermeyer]

Buchan, Alexander M., "Elizabeth Madox Roberts," *SWR*, XXV (1940), 463–81.

Campbell, Harry Modean, and Ruel E. Foster, *Elizabeth Madox Roberts: American Novelist* (Norman, Okla., 1956).

Davidson, Donald, "Analysis of Elizabeth Madox Roberts' *A Buried Treasure*," *Creat Reading*, VI (1931), 1235–49.

Elizabeth Madox Roberts Papers, Bureau of Manuscripts, Library of Congress.

Foster, Ruel E., "An Undiscovered Source for Elizabeth Madox Roberts' 'On the Mountainside,'" *W Va U Phil Papers*, XV (1965), pp. 57–61.

Janney, F. Lamar, "Elizabeth Madox Roberts," *SeR*, XLV (1937), 388–410.

Knight, Grant C., "Bluegrass and Laurel: The Varieties of Kentucky Fiction," *SatR*, L (Jan 6, 1945), 12–13.

*McDowell, Frederick P. W., *Elizabeth Madox Roberts* (New York, 1963). [TUSAS]

Niles, Rena, "Kentucky Profiles: She Writes the Way She Weaves," *Louisville Courier-Journal*, Jan 8, 1939.

Roberts, Elizabeth Madox, "Over the Trace to 'The Great Meadow,'" *Wings*, IV (March 1930), 6–9.

Rouse, H. Blair, "Time and Place in Southern Fiction," in Rubin and Jacobs, *Southern Renascence*, pp. 126–50.

*Rovit, Earl H., *Herald to Chaos: The Novels of Elizabeth Madox Roberts* (Lexington, Ky., 1960).

———, "Recurrent Symbols in the Novels of Elizabeth Madox Roberts," *Bost U Stud in Eng*, II (Spring 1956), 36–54.

*Spears, Woodridge, "Elizabeth Madox Roberts: A Biographical and Critical Study," Kentucky, 1953. [diss]

Thorp, Willard, *American Writing in the Twentieth Century* (Cambridge, Mass., 1960), pp. 239–41.

Van Doren, Mark, "Elizabeth Madox Roberts," *Eng Jour*, XXI (1932), 521–28.

*Wagenknecht, Edward, *Cavalcade of the American Novel* (New York, 1952), pp. 389–96.

Wescott, Glenway, "Elizabeth Madox Roberts: A Personal Note," *Bookman*, LXXI (1930), 12–15.

EARL ROVIT
City College of New York
New York, New York

IRWIN RUSSELL (1853-1879)

DAB, XVI, pp. 242–43; *Hubbell*, pp. 795–800, *952; *LSL*, X, pp. 4601–608.

Baskervill, William M., *Southern Writers: Biographical and Critical Studies* (Nashville, 1897), I, pp. 1–40.

Fulton, Maurice Garland, "Irwin Russell," in Irwin Russell, *Christmas Night in the Quarters* (New York, 1917), pp. vii–xxxiv. [hist sketch]

*Harrell, Laura D.S., "A Bibliography of Irwin Russell, with a Biographical Sketch," *Jour of Miss Hist*, VIII (1946), [3]–23.

Harris, Joel Chandler, intro to *Poems by Irwin Russell* (New York, [1888]), pp. ix–xi, and in *Christmas Night in the Quarters* (Richmond, [?1949]), pp. xv–xvi. [crit]

Kendall, John S., "Irwin Russell in New Orleans," *La Hist Q*, XIX (1931), 321–45. [biog and account of his lost play]

Kern, A.A., "Biographical Notes on Irwin Russell," *TexR*, II (Oct 1916), 140–49.

Marble, C. C., "Irwin Russell's Poems," *The Critic*, XII (Oct 27; Nov 3, 1888), 193 *ff*. and 213 *ff*.

Moses, Montrose J., *The Literature of the South* (New York, 1910), p. 472.

Musgrave, Maggie Williams, "Memories of Irwin Russell and His Home in Port Gibson," *New Orleans Daily Picayune*, June 2, 1907, p. 11.

Nott, G. William, "Irwin Russell, First Dialect Author," in *Christmas Night in the Quarters*, (Richmond, [?1949]), v–xiii, [biog and crit]

Schuman, R. Baird, "Irwin Russell's Christmas," *MissQ*, XV (1962), 81–84.

Trent, W.P., *Southern Writers—Selections in Prose and Verse* (New York, 1905), p. 457.

Untermeyer, Louis, ed., *Modern American Poetry* (New York, 1930), p. 108.

Young, Stark, *Southern Treasury of Life and Literature* (New York, 1937), pp. 90, 98–99.

HARRIET R. HOLMAN
Clemson University
Clemson, South Carolina

ABRAM JOSEPH RYAN (1838-1886)

DAB, XVI, pp. 260–61; *Hubbell*, pp. 477–79, *958; *LSL*, X, pp. 4623–26.

"Abram Ryan," *Irish Monthly*, XIX (1891), 629.

Allison, Y. E., "Father Abram Ryan," *So Bivouac*, V (1886), 167.|

Heagney, H. J., "Recollections of Father Ryan," *Cath World*, CXXVI (1928), 497–504.

Hewlett, J. H., "Unknown Poem by Father Ryan," *Mod Lang Notes*, XLIV (1929), 259–61.

Lovett, Howard Meriwether, "Father Ryan of the South," *Commonweal*, X (Sept 18, 1929), 503–504.

White, Kate, "Father Ryan, the Poet-Priest of the South," *SAQ*, XVIII (1919), 69–74.

EUGENE NOLTE
State College of Arkansas
Conway, Arkansas

GEORGE SANDYS (1568-1644)

Sandys as poet is discussed most fully in Miss Wallerstein's essay and in Davis' book. His connections with America are considered in two places by Davis, in the biography and in the *William and Mary Quarterly* essay.

DAB, XVI, pp. 344–46; *Duyckinck*, I, p. 1.

Barker, Russell H., "George Sandys' *Relation*," *Trans Wisconsin Acad Sciences, Arts and Letters*, XXX (1937), 253–73.

*Bowers, Fredson, and Richard Beale Davis, *George Sandys: A Bibliographical Catalogue of Printetl Editions in England to 1700* (New York, 1950).

*Bush, Douglas, "George Sandys," *English Literature in the Earlier Seventeenth Century, 1600–1660* (Oxford, Eng., 1962), pp. 639–40. [annot bibl]

Davis, Richard Beale, "America in George Sandys' 'Ovid,' " *WMQ*, 3rd ser, IV (1947), 297–304.

――――, "Early Editions of George Sandys' 'Ovid': the Circumstances of Production," *Papers Bibl Soc Amer*, XXXV (1941), 255–76.

――――, "George Sandys," in *Encycl Brit* (1966 ed), XIX, p. 1004.

*――――, *George Sandys, Poet-Adventurer* (New York and London, 1955).

Wallerstein, Ruth, "The Development of the Rhetoric and Metre of the Heroic Couplet, Especially in 1625–1645," *PMLA*, L (1935), 166–209.

RICHARD BEALE DAVIS
University of Tennessee
Knoxville, Tennessee

WILLIAM GILMORE SIMMS (1806-1870)

A very great amount of the biographical and critical work needed on Simms is still to be done. There is no adequate biography; William P. Trent's 1892 study in the old American Men of Letters Series, although inaccurate in places and dated in judgments, is still the most reliable and complete treatment. Joseph V. Ridgely's *William Gilmore Simms* is a critical study of only the works in the Redfield edition and suffers from being written to a thesis. Only as a literary critic, one of Simms's constant but minor vocations, has he received reasonably thorough treatment, in the work of Edd Winfield Parks, particularly *William Gilmore Simms as Literary Critic*, and in C. Hugh Holman's edition of Simms's *Views and Reviews*.

The indispensable work for the study of Simms is *The Letters of William Gilmore Simms*, in whose five volumes is a wealth of information in the introductory matter, in the letters themselves, and particularly in the very thorough notes. A supplementary volume is planned.

Of the shorter-than-book-length general treatments, the most inclusive and in many respects the best is that of Alexander Cowie, in *The Rise of the American Novel*, although Jay B. Hubbell's chapter in *The South in American Literature* is detailed and excellent. Clement Eaton's "The Romantic Mind: William Gilmore Simms," in his *The Mind of the Old South*, and William R. Taylor's "Revolution in South Carolina," in his *Cavalier and Yankee*, are thoughtful studies of Simms's place in Southern culture and history. Vernon L. Parrington's treatment of Simms in *Main Currents in American Thought* is a provocative appreciation, the most significant single statement about Simms of this century, although its central thesis that he was the victim of Charleston's patrician snobbishness has been seriously questioned. Van Wyck Brooks, in *The World of Washington Irving*, writes charmingly and sympathetically of Simms. Donald Davidson's appreciation of Simms's work, in the introduction to *The Letters*, will appear to most readers seriously to overpraise Simms.

Simms's participation in the literary life of the North, particularly in the 1840s and early 1850s, has been examined in the context of the literary wars between the "Young America" critics and the *Knickerbocker Magazine* in Perry Miller's lively study, *The Raven and the Whale*.

Much work is currently in progress on Simms. The University of South Carolina is bringing out a carefully edited edition of selected works by Simms. The first volume will be *Voltmeier*, a post-war serial never before published in book form; Donald Davidson is the editor. John C. Guilds will edit a volume of Simms's short stories. John R. Welsh is editing Simms's non-literary essays. Other plans call for a collection of his poetry. The bibliography, promised in 1961 by James B. Meriwether, will probably appear in a greatly augmented form as a part of this edition. It is badly needed, for the only detailed and reliable bibliography is the Catalogue of the A.S. Salley Collection, now in the South Caroliniana Library of the University of South Carolina. This catalogue is understandably incomplete. C. Hugh Holman is working on a biographical study.

DAB, XVII, pp. 171–74; *Duyckinck*, II, p. 427; *Hubbell*, pp. 572–602, *958–61; *LSL*, XI, pp. 2793–98; *LHUS*, I, pp. 311–14, *II, pp. 720–23, *Supp*, 189–90.

Barbour, Frances M., "William Gilmore Simms and the Brutus Legend," *Midw Folkl*, VII (1957), 159–162. [on dramatic sources for *The Yemassee*)]

Beatty, Richmond Croom, intro to *Woodcraft; or, Hawks About the Dovecote* (New York, 1961).

Brooks, Van Wyck, "Charleston and the Southwest: Simms," *The World of Washington Irving* (New York, 1944), pp. 228–48.

[Bryant, William Cullen], "Simms," in *Homes of American Authors* (New York, 1853), pp. 257–62. [picturing life at Woodlands, Simms's home]

Cecil, L. Moffitt, "Symbolic Pattern in *The Yemassee*," *AL*, XXXV (1964), 510–14.

Cowie, *The Rise of the American Novel*, pp. 228–46.

*_____, intro, chronology, and bibl to Cowie, ed., *The Yemassee* (New York, 1937).

Cullen, Maurice R., Jr., "William Gilmore Simms, Southern Journalist," *Journalism Q*, XXXVIII (1961), 298–302, 412.

Davidson, Donald, intro to *The Letters of William Gilmore Simms* (see Oliphant below), I, xxxi–lviii. [a crit appreciation]

Deen, Floyd H., "A Comparison of Simms's *Richard Hurdis* with Its Sources," *Mod Lang Notes*, LX (1945), 406–408.

_____, "The Genesis of *Martin Faber* in *Caleb Williams*," *Mod Lang Notes*, LIX (1944), 315–17.

Duvall, S.P.C., "W.G. Simms's Review of Mrs. Stowe," *AL*, XXX (1958), 107–17. [in the *SoQR*; attribution to Simms is questionable]

Eaton, Clement, "The Romantic Mind: William Gilmore Simms," *The Mind of the Old South* (Baton Rouge, 1964), pp. 181-201.

Erskine, John, "William Gilmore Simms," *Leading American Novelists* (New York, 1910), pp. 131–77. [early, detailed, but rather tepid crit of his novels]

Gates, W.B., "William Gilmore Simms and the Kentucky Tragedy," *AL*, XXXII (1960), 158–66. [on Simms's use of the Beauchamp-Sharp murder case in *Charlemont* and *Beauchamp*]

Griffin, Max L., "Bryant and the South," *Tulane Stud in Eng*, I (1949), 53–80. [much on Simms, who was a friend of Bryant]

Guilds, John C., "Simms's First Magazine: *The Album*," in *SB*, VIII (1956), 169–85.

_____, "Simms's Views on National and Sectional Literature, 1825–1845," *N.C. Hist R*, XXXIV (1957), 393–405.

_____, "William Gilmore Simms and the Cosmopolitan," *Ga Hist Q*, XLI (March, 1957), 31–41.

Hayne, Paul H., "Ante-Bellum Charleston," *So Bivouac*, n.s., I (1885), 257–68. [personal reminiscences of Simms]

Hayward, Edward F., "Some Romances of the Revolution," *Atlantic*, LXIV (1889), 627–36. [detailed crit of Simms's Revolutionary romances]

Heyward, DuBose, *Peter Ashley* (New York, 1932), pp. 30, 36, 61, 191–206. [although fiction, work portrays convincing picture of Simms as person in the circle of Charleston literati of late 1850s]

Higham, John W., "The Changing Loyalties of William Gilmore Simms," *JSH*, IX (1943), 210–23. [overstates extent and causes of the changes]

Holman, C. Hugh, "The *Hiawatha* Meter in *The Yemassee*," *Mod Lang Notes*, LXVII (1952), 418–19. [on Indian chants]

————, "The Influence of Scott and Cooper on Simms," *AL*, XXIII (1951), 203–18.

————, "Simms and the British Dramatists," *PMLA*, LXV (1950), 346–59. [theory of "humours" on characterization in novels]

————, "The Status of Simms," *AQ*, X (1958), 181–85.

————, intro and "Chronology of the Life of William Gilmore Simms," in Holman, ed., Simms's *Views and Reviews in American Literature, History and Fiction*, 1st ser (Cambridge, Mass., 1962), pp. vii–xliii. [on Simms and the "Young America" lit wars, with the most detailed chronology of his life]

————, "William Gilmore Simms and the American Renaissance," *MissQ*, XV (1962), 126–37.

————, "William Gilmore Simms's Picture of the Revolution as a Civil Conflict," *JSH*, XV (1949), 441–62. [on the historicity of the Revolutionary romances]

*————, intro and bibl note to Holman, ed., *The Yemassee: A Romance of Carolina* (Boston, 1961).

Hoole, William Stanley, "Alabama and W. Gilmore Simms," *AlaR*, XVI (1963), 83–107, 185–199.

————, "A Note on Simms's Visits to the Southwest," *AL*, VI (1934), 334–36.

————, "Simms's *Michael Bonham*, a 'Forgotten' Drama of the Texas Revolution," *SW Hist Q*, XLVI (1942), 255–61.

————, "William Gilmore Simms's Career as Editor," *Ga Hist Q*, XIX (1935), 47–54.

Hubbell, Jay B., "Five Letters from George Henry Boker to William Gilmore Simms," *Penn Mag of Hist and Biog*, LXIII (1939), 66–71.

————, *The Last Years of Henry Timrod* (Durham, 1941). [contains much information on Simms and the Charleston writers]

Jones, Alexander, "A Source for William Gilmore Simms," *Jour of Amer Folkl*, LXX (1957), 66–69. [the source is Baron Münchausen]

Jarrell, Hampton M., "Falstaff and Simms's Porgy," *AL*, III (1931), 204–12.

————, "Simms's Visits to the Southwest," *AL*, V (1933), 29–35.

Jillson, Willard, "The Beauchamp-Sharp Tragedy in American Literature," *Register Ky State Hist Soc*, XXXVI (1938), 54–60. [discusses, among other works, Simms's *Charlemont* and *Beauchamp*]

Keiser, Albert, "Simms's Romantic Naturalism," *The Indian in American Literature* (New York, 1933), pp. 154–74.

Link, Samuel A., "William Gilmore Simms," *Pioneers of Southern Literature*, 2 vols (Nashville, 1903–11), I, 149–221.

McDavid, Raven I., Jr., "*Ivanhoe* and Simms's *Vasconselos*," *Mod Lang Notes*, LVI (1941), 294–97.

Meriwether, James B., "The Proposed Edition of William Gilmore Simms," *MissQ*, XV (1962), 100–12. [describes the work in progress on the Selected Ed at U of S.C.]

Miller, Perry, *The Raven and the Whale: The War of Words and Wits in the Era of Poe and Melville* (New York, 1956). [contains much in passing on Simms's No lit relationships]

Morris, J. Allen, "Gullah in the Stories and Novels of William Gilmore Simms," *AS*, XXII (1947), 46–53.

*_____, "The Stories of William Gilmore Simms," *AL*, XIV (1942), 20–35. [bibl list and discussion of 58 stories]

Oliphant, Mary C. Simms, A. T. Odell, and T. C. Duncan Eaves, eds., *The Letters of William Gilmore Simms*, 5 vols (Columbia, S.C., 1952–56). [the one indispensable work on Simms]

Parks, Edd Winfield, *William Gilmore Simms as a Literary Critic* (Athens, Ga., 1961).

_____, "Simms's Edition of the Shakespeare Apocrypha," in *Studies in Shakespeare*, ed. Arthur D. Matthews and Clark M. Emery (U of Miami Pub in Eng and Amer Lit, Vol I, Coral Gables, 1953), pp. 30–39.

_____, "Simms: a Candid Self-portrait," *GaR*, XII (1958), 94–103.

_____, "William Gilmore Simms: Realistic Romanticist," *Ante-Bellum Southern Literary Critics* (Athens, Ga., 1962), pp. 83–135. [essentially the same material as that given in a little more detail in Parks's *William Gilmore Simms as a Literary Critic*]

Parrington, Vernon Louis, "Adventures in *Belles-Lettres*: William Gilmore Simms," *Main Currents in American Thought*, II, *The Romantic Revolution in America, 1800–1860* (New York, 1927), pp. 125–36. [Parrington's view must be examined in any serious analysis of Simms]

Ridgely, Joseph V., "*Woodcraft*: Simms's First Answer to *Uncle Tom's Cabin*," *AL*, XXXI (Jan 1960), 421–33.

*_____, *William Gilmore Simms* (New York, 1962). [primarily a reading of Border and Revolutionary romances; TUSAS]

_____, intro to *The Yemassee* (New York, 1962).

*Quinn, *American Fiction: An Historical and Critical Survey*, pp. 114–23, 743.

*Salley, Alexander S., Jr., "A Bibliography of William Gilmore Simms," *Pub So Hist Assn*, XI (1907), 343–44.

*_____, *Catalogue of the Salley Collection of the Works of Wm. Gilmore Simms* (Columbia, S.C., 1943). [most useful and fullest bibl tool for Simms]

_____, "[Biographical Sketch of] William Gilmore Simms," in *The Letters* (see Oliphant above), I, lix–lxxxix. [much information on Simms to age thirty, but not always accurate]

Shelton, Austin J., "African Realistic Commentary on Culture Hierarchy and Racistic Sentimentalism in *The Yemassee*," *Phylon*, XXV (1964), 72–78.

Stafford, John, *The Literary Criticism of Young America* (Berkeley, 1952). [useful on Simms's political ties with Loco-Foco Democrats of N.Y.]

Stone, Edward, " 'Caleb Williams' and 'Martin Faber': A Contrast," *Mod Lang Notes*, LXII (1947), 480–83. [reply to Deen's article (*Mod Lang Notes*, 1944) on the two novels]

Taylor, William R., "Revolution in South Carolina," *Cavalier and Yankee: The Old South and American National Character* (New York, 1961), pp. 261–297. [important]

Thomas, J. Wesley, "The German Sources of William Gilmore Simms," in *Anglo-German and American-German Crosscurrents*, I, ed. P. A. Shelley, A. O. Lewis, Jr., and W. W. Betts, Jr. (Chapel Hill, 1957), pp. 127–53. [important indication of some of Simms's lit and intellectual sources]

Trent, William Peterfield, *William Gilmore Simms* (Boston, 1892). [still the best biog stud; its statements of fact should be argued with only when one has really firm evidence]

Turner, Arlin, "William Gilmore Simms in His Letters," *SAQ*, LIII (1954), 404–15.

Van Diver, Edward P., Jr., "Simms's Border Romances and Shakespeare," *Shakespeare Q*, V (1954), 129–39.

*Wagenknecht, Edward, *Cavalcade of the American Novel* (New York, 1952), pp. 32–37, 506–507. [bibl very useful]

*Wegelin, Oscar, *A Bibliography of the Separate Writings of William Gilmore Simms, 1806–1870* (Hattiesburg, Miss., 1941). [3rd ed of useful but not always accurate or complete listing]

Welsh, John R., "William Gilmore Simms: Critic of the South," *JSH*, XXVI (1960), 201–14.

————, "The Charles Carroll Simms Collection," *So Atl Bull*, XXXI (Nov 1966), 1–3. [description of the collection of ms materials in the S.C. Lib, U. of S.C.]

Whaley, Grace Wine, "A Note on Simms's Novels," *AL*, II (1930), 173–74. [cites sources for headnotes in the novels]

Williams, Stanley T., "Spanish Influences on the Fiction of William Gilmore Simms," *Hispanic R*, XXI (1953), 221–28. [much more detailed than Williams' brief treatment in his *Spanish Backgrounds of American Literature*, I, 220–23.]

Wimsatt, Mary Ann, "Simms and Irving," *MissQ*, XX (1967), 25–37.

C. Hugh Holman
University of North Carolina
Chapel Hill, North Carolina

CHARLES HENRY SMITH ("BILL ARP")
(1826-1903)

Charles Henry Smith was an exceedingly popular and influential Southern humorist in the post-Civil War period. Yet he has not attracted the interest of many scholars. The bibliography regarding him is quite meager. Only four scholarly articles, three specialized ones by Mrs. Margaret Gillis Figh and one by James E. Ginther, have appeared about him. Of the general studies, the one by Jay B. Hubbell is the most significant. Insofar as could be found, no dissertation and only two Masters' theses have been written about him. His writings merit additional study, for they provide an insight into the cultural and social conditions existing in the South during the last three decades of the nineteenth century.

DAB, XVII, pp. 248–49; *Hubbell*, pp. 683–86, *961; *LSL*, XI, pp. 4885–87.

Aubrey, George H., "Charles Henry Smith (Bill Arp)," in *Men of Mark in Georgia,* ed. William J. Northern (Atlanta, 1912), III, pp. 393–96.

"Bill Arp." *Atlanta Constitution,* Aug 26, 1903, p. 6. [editorial]

Dutcher, Salem, "Bill Arp and Artemus Ward," *Scott's Month Mag,* II (June 1866), 472–78.

Figh, Margaret Gillis, "Folklore in Bill Arp's Works," *SFQ,* XII (1948), 169–75.

————, "Life in Nineteenth Century Georgia as Reflected in Bill Arp's Works," *Ga Hist Q,* XXXV (1951), 16–22.

————, "Tall Talk and Folk Sayings in Bill Arp's Works," *SFQ,* XIII (1949), 206–12.

Ginther, James E., "Charles Henry Smith, Alias 'Bill Arp,'" *GaR,* IV (1950), 313–22.

*Landrum, Louella, "Charles Henry Smith (Bill Arp): Georgia Humorist," Duke, 1938. [MA thesis]

"Maj. C. H. Smith Gone to Rest," Cartersville (Ga.) *News and Courant,* Aug 27, 1903, p. 1. [newsp obit]

Miller, Verdie Frances, "Bill Arp (Charles Henry Smith), Georgia Author. . .," Georgia, 1927. [MA thesis]

Moran, P. J., "The Fifty Golden Years of Major and Mrs. Smith," *Atlanta Constitution,* March 5, 1899, p. 23.

Smith, Charles Henry, *Bill Arp: from the Uncivil War to Date, 1861–1903,* Memorial ed (Atlanta, 1903). [autobiog]

Tandy, Jeannette, "Civil War and Reconstruction: Bill Arp and P. V. Nasby," *Crackerbox Philosophers in American Humor and Satire* (New York, 1925), pp. 103–18.

W. PORTER KELLAM
University of Georgia
Athens, Georgia

F. HOPKINSON SMITH (1838-1915)

Around the turn of the present century the fiction of F. Hopkinson Smith received much popular notice. The author himself was also much celebrated during the 1890s and on to the time of his death. This great popularity was the result of the prolific production, from the 1890s onward, of a series of best sellers or near best sellers. His works were frequently mentioned within the context of larger studies throughout the 1930s and 1940s, and were given considerable attention by dissertation and thesis writers during the same period. Nonetheless, his reputation among literary critics has never again risen, and his name and works have fallen into obscurity.

DAB, XVII, pp. 265–67; *LSL,* XI, pp. 4909–13.

Adams, Robert J., "Some Types and Backgrounds in Contemporary American Literature," Temple, 1928. [MA thesis; Smith, O. Henry, Elizabeth Robins, Daniel Steele]

Deal, Louise S., "Thackeray's Influence on Francis Hopkinson Smith," Southern Methodist, 1946. [MA thesis]

Fiske, Horace Spencer, *Provincial Types in American Fiction* (New York, 1903), pp. 97–105.

Hornberger, Theodore, "The Effect of Painting on the Fiction of F. Hopkinson Smith (1838–1915)," *U of Tex Stud in Eng*, XXIII (1943), 162–92.

_____, "Painters and Painting in the Writings of F. Hopkinson Smith," *AL*, XVI (1944), 1–10.

Jones, Dorothy Wooten, "Indebtedness of the Southern Novel to the Waverly Novels," Southern Methodist, 1939. [MA thesis; Smith and seven other novelists]

Mabie, H. W., "Hopkinson Smith and His Work," *Book Buyer*, XXV (Aug 1902). 17–20.

Myers, Ralph Garber, "The Small Town in the American Novel, 1870–1920," Virginia, 1934. [MA thesis; Smith and four other novelists]

Page, Thomas Nelson, "Francis Hopkinson Smith," *Scribner's*, LVIII (1915), 305–13.

*Quinn, *American Fiction*, pp. 362–68.

Saucier, Velma Marie, "The Short Stories and the Novels of Francis Hopkinson Smith," Louisiana, 1943. [MA thesis]

*White, Courtland Y., III, "Francis Hopkinson Smith," Pennsylvania, 1932. [diss; biog crit]

Willets, G., "F. Hopkinson Smith in Three Professions," *Arena*, XXII (Jul 1899), 68–70.

WILLIAM K. BOTTORFF
University of Toledo
Toledo, Ohio

CAPTAIN JOHN SMITH (1580?-1631)

The career and writings of Captain John Smith continue to fascinate students of the Colonial period; since 1950 alone, scholars have written more than twenty-five articles and some ten books about the Captain's life. The bibliography of books, articles, and monographs in Philip Barbour's *The Three Worlds of Captain John Smith* (Boston, 1964) lists more than 120 items, many of them book-length studies.

Barbour's study and Bradford Smith's *Captain John Smith, His Life and Legend* (Philadelphia, 1953) are the most extensive recent accounts. Barbour's *Three Worlds* includes more than 190 pages of notes and commentaries, plus thirty-four pages of bibliography. Bradford Smith's biography, also with extensive notes and bibliography, includes an appendix in which Laura Polanyi Striker discusses in detail Captain John Smith's adventures in Hungary and Transylvania. In addition, Everett H. Emerson has completed the manuscript for a volume in

Twayne's United States Authors Series to be entitled "Captain John Smith" and scheduled for publication in 1969. Emerson's volume will include a selected bibliography.

Scholars continue to debate Smith's veracity as historian, a controversy begun in 1867, when Henry Adams challenged Smith's accuracy in an essay in the *North American Review*. But the recent biographers—Bradford Smith, Barbour, and Mrs. Striker—have illustrated that the basic outlines of Smith's adventures are accurate.

Howard Mumford Jones's *The Literature of Virginia in the Seventeenth Century* (Boston, 1946) and Everett H. Emerson's "Captain John Smith as Editor: *The Generall Historie*," *VMHB*, LXXV (Apr 1967), discuss Smith as a literary figure.

DAB, XVII, pp. 294–96; *Duyckinck*, I, p. 5; *Hubbell*, pp. 17–20, *961–62; *LSL*, XI pp. 4929–33; *LHUS*, I, pp. 32–33, *II, pp. 725–27, *Supp*, 191.

Adams, Henry, "Captain John Smith," *NoAmerR*, CIV (1867), 1–30.

*Barbour, Philip L., *The Three Worlds of Captain John Smith* (Boston, 1964). [see above; Barbour is also author of at least six periodical articles on Smith]

Chatterton, Edward K., *Captain John Smith* (New York, 1927).

Davis, Richard Beale, "The First American Edition of Captain John Smith's *True Travels* and *Generall Historie*," *VMHB*, XLVIII (1939), 97–108.

Emerson, Everett H., "Captain John Smith as Editor: *The Generall Historie*," *VMHB*, LXXV (1967), 143–56.

———, "Captain John Smith, Autobiographer," *Early Amer Lit Newsletter*, II (Spring 1967), 18–23.

Fishwick, Marshall, "Virginians on Olympus: I. The Last Great Knight Errant." *VMHB*, LVIII (1950), 40–57. Repr as "John Smith, the Virginian as Colonist," in *Virginians on Olympus: A Cultural Analysis of Four Great Men* (Richmond, 1951), pp. 1–24. [discusses Smith's life as part of Amer myth; summarizes Smith-Pocahontas controversy]

Fletcher, John G., *John Smith—Also Pocahontas* (New York, 1928).

*———, ed., *The True Travels* (New York, 1930). Intro by Fletcher; bibl and notes by Lawrence C. Wroth. [see esp pp. 76–79 for Wroth's bibl note]

Glenn, Keith, "Captain John Smith and the Indians," *VMHB*, LII (1944), 228–48.

Hubbell, Jay B., "The Smith-Pocahontas Story in Literature," *VMHB*, LXV (1957), 275–300. [summarizes controversy over Smith's accounts of Pocahontas rescue; discusses handling of Smith story in poetry, drama, fict]

Jones, Howard Mumford, *The Literature of Virginia in the Seventeenth Century* (Boston, 1946), pp. 16–23.

Kropf, Lewis L., "Note on John Fiske's *Old Virginia and Her Neighbors*," *Amer Hist R*, III (1898), 737–38. [questions veracity of Smith's *True Travels*]

Morison, Samuel E., *Builders of the Bay Colony* (Boston, 1930), pp. 3–20.

Morse, J. M., "John Smith and His Critics: A Chapter in Colonial Historiography," *JSH*, I (1935), 123–37. [summary of controversy over Smith's accuracy as hist]

Pichler, J. Franz, "Captain John Smith in the Light of Styrian Sources," *VMHB*, LXV (1957), 332–54. [on Smith's adventures in Hungary, etc]

Raup, George B., "Captain John Smith, Adventurer Extraordinary," *VMHB*, LXI (1953), 186–92.

Rozwenc, Edwin C., "Captain John Smith's Image of America," *WMQ*, 3rd ser, XVI
(1959), 27–36.
Simms, William Gilmore, *The Life of Captain John Smith* (New York, 1846).
*Smith, Bradford, *Captain John Smith, His Life and Legend* (Philadelphia, 1953).
Appendix by Laura Polanyi Striker. [see above]
Striker, Laura Polanyi, "The Hungarian Historian, Lewis L. Kropf, on Captain John
Smith's *True Travels:* A Reappraisal," *VMHB*, LXVI (1958), 22–43.
Striker, Laura Polanyi, and Bradford Smith, "The Rehabilitation of Captain John
Smith," *JSH*, XXVIII (1962), 474–81.
Wharton, Henry, *The Life of John Smith, English Soldier* (1685), translation from
Latin ms with intro essay by Laura Polanyi Striker (publ for the Va Hist Soc at
Chapel Hill, 1957). [Richard Beale Davis discusses "Early American Interest in
Wharton's Manuscript" in an appendix]

ROBERT BAIN
University of North Carolina
Chapel Hill, North Carolina

LILLIAN SMITH (1897-1966)

Since the publication of *Strange Fruit* in 1944, the writing of Lillian
Smith has elicited a wide range of comment, but most of the critical
response has been from a sociological rather than a literary point of
view. The nature of much of her subject matter and her identification
with the civil rights movement have caused most readers to consider her
work purely polemical and to react according to the readers' own established views of the race issue. Consequently, the great bulk of attention
given her fiction has been centered on *Strange Fruit*, and her second
novel, *One Hour* (which is not about race), has been largely ignored.
The calm, judicious, critical appraisal which her work merits has been
infrequent but apparently is growing slowly.

Most of the standard works on recent Southern literature include only
brief treatment of Miss Smith. The reviews of her books are numerous, but they vary widely in quality as well as viewpoint. In addition to
the sources listed below, the student of her work will be rewarded by
consulting the little magazine she edited and published with Paula
Snelling under the following titles: *Pseudopodia* (1936–37), *North
Georgia Review* (1937–41), and *South Today* (1942–45). Two book-
length studies of Lillian Smith are currently underway: a biography by
Joan Titus, and a critical biography by Margaret Sullivan.

Besal, Dorothy, "Lillian Smith, Prophet for Our Time," *Community*, XXIV (June
1965), 3. [interv]

*Blackwell, Louise, and Frances Clay, *Lillian Smith* (New York, forthcoming). [TUSAS]

Brockway, George P., "You Do It Because You Love Somebody," *SatR*, XLIX (Oct 22, 1966), 53–54. [appreciation by her publ]

[DeVoto, Bernard], "Regionalism or the Coterie Manifesto," *SatR*, XV (Nov 28, 1936), 8. [earliest nat notice]

DeVoto, Bernard, "The Decision in the *Strange Fruit* Case: The Obscenity Statute in Massachusetts," *New Eng Q*, XIX (1946), 147–83.

Grafton, Sam, "We're Mighty Fond of Our Miss Lil," *Collier's*, CXXV (Jan 28, 1950), 28–29 and 58–59. [illus mag art]

Griffin, John Howard, "Again, Lillian Smith's South," *SWR*, XLVII (1962), 97–98. [r of *Killers of the Dream*, rev ed]

Hutchens, John K., "On an Author: Lillian Smith," *N.Y. Her Trib Bk R* (Oct 30, 1949), p. 2. [newsp article]

Jack, Homer A., "Lillian Smith of Clayton, Georgia," *Christian Cent*, LXXIV (Oct 2, 1957), 1166–68. [interv]

Long, Margaret, "The Sense of Her Presence: A Memorial for Lillian Smith," *New So*, XXI (Fall 1966), 71–77.

Marcus, Fred H., "*Cry, the Beloved Country* and *Strange Fruit*: Exploring Man's Inhumanity to Man," *Eng Jour*, L (1962), 609–16.

Nathan, George Jean, *The Theatre Book of the Year 1945–16: A Record and an Interpretation* (New York, 1946); "Strange Fruit," pp. 212–15. [crit of Broadway play]

Smith, Lillian and Paula Snelling, "Yes, We Are Southern," *So Today*, VII (Spring 1943), 41–44. [autobiog essay]

Sullivan, Margaret, "Lillian Smith: Public Image and Personal Vision," *Mad River R*, II (Summer-Fall 1967), 3–21.

Wright, Louis B., "Myth-Makers and the South's Dilemma," *SeR*, LIII (1945), 544–58. Repr in *A Southern Vanguard*, ed. Allen Tate (New York, 1947), pp. 136–47. [*Strange Fruit* an "inverted pastoral romance"]

PASCHAL REEVES
University of Georgia
Athens, Georgia

MRS. E.D.E.N. SOUTHWORTH (1819-1899)

The once-popular novels of Mrs. Southworth are forgotten today, although her name continues as a synonym for the sensational. Except for Fred Lewis Pattee, no literary historian has discussed her in this century. Jay B. Hubbell dismissed her with one unfavorable mention in *The South in American Literature*. No one shows interest in her except graduate students desperate for a topic. *Southern Literary Culture: A Bibliography of Masters' and Doctors' Theses*, by Clyde Cantrell and

Walton R. Patrick (University, Alabama, 1955) names seven items that concern her, all listed below. No complete bibliography has been published.

DAB, XVII, pp. 414–15; *Duyckinck*, II, p. 624.

Boyle, Regis Louise, "Mrs. E.D.E.N. Southworth, Novelist," Catholic U, 1938. [diss]

B., H. C., "A Noted Novel-Writer," *Washington Post*, Dec 2, 1894.

Cronkite, George Farris, "Literature as a Livelihood: the Attitude of Certain American Writers toward Literature as a Profession from 1820 to the Civil War," Harvard, 1948. [diss; Mrs. S. is one of six So writers studied]

Gray, Virginia G., "The Southern Lady of the Forties," Wisconsin, 1925. [MA thesis; Mrs. S. is one of four So writers studied]

Julian, Grace L., "Southern Novels, 1850–1855; A Study in Culture," Tulane, 1942. [MA thesis; emphasis on Mrs. S. and Mrs. Hentz]

Kenton, Edna, "Best-Sellers of Yesterday, VII, Mrs. E.D.E.N. Southworth," *Bookman*, XLIV (Oct 1916), 128–37.

Mason, James H., "Mrs. E.D.E.N. Southworth," Peabody, 1935. [MA thesis]

Monsell, Helen Albee, "A Study in Girlhood in American Fiction from 1850–1860," Columbia, 1922. [MA thesis; Mrs. S. is one of four So novelists studied]

Pattee, Fred Lewis, *The Feminine Fifties* (New York, 1940), pp. 122–24.

Washington, (D.C.) Evening Star, Jul 1, 1899. [obit]

RHODA COLEMAN ELLISON
Huntingdon College
Montgomery, Alabama

ELIZABETH SPENCER (1921–)

Between 1948 and 1967, Mrs. John Rusher, who writes under her maiden name, Elizabeth Spencer, has written six novels and numerous short stories which have been included in leading anthologies of short fiction. Her work, much of which has dealt with Mississippi or with Italy, is characterized by an exquisite prose style and by careful craftsmanship. Although she is already recognized as a writer of first rank, her work richly deserves more scholarly attention than it has yet received. Particular attention is called to the extended prefaces or introductions to individual novels by Miss Spencer, Matthieu Galey, and Mario Monti. In addition, several of the review articles, listed below, deal with her total production up to the time they were written.

Baker, Carlos, "Two American Marriages," *N.Y. Times Bk R*, Oct 22, 1967, p. 8. [r of *No Place for an Angel*]

Barrett, William, "Haunted Ladies," *Atlantic*, CCXVI (Jul 1965), 140–41. [r of *Knights and Dragons*]

Burger, Nash K., "Elizabeth Spencer's Three Mississippi Novels," *SAQ*, LXIII (1965), 351–62.

Galey, Matthieu, preface to *Lumière sur la Piazza*, trans Janine Ragoet (Paris, 1962).

Gill, Brendan, "All Praise," *New Yorker*, XXXII (Dec 15, 1956), 180–82. [r article on *The Voice at the Back Door*]

Hackett, Francis, "Portents from the New South," *New Rep*, CXXXV (Nov 19, 1956), 30–31. [r article on *The Voice at the Back Door*]

Hedden, Worth Tuttle, "A Thirty-Year Family Story Set in the Mississippi Delta Country," *N.Y. Her Trib Bk R*, March 16, 1952, p.5. [r of *This Crooked Way*]

———, "With Passion, Suspense, Humor," *N.Y. Her Trib Bk R*, Sept 5, 1948, p. 3. [r of *Fire in the Morning*]

Hicks, Granville, "Lives Like Assorted Pastries," *SatR*, L (Oct 21, 1967), 29–30. [r article on *No Place for an Angel*]

Monti, Mario, preface to *La Luce nella Piazza*, trans Adriana Pellegrini (Milan, 1962).

Smith, Harrison, "New Faces, Old Story," *SatR*, XXXI (Nov 6, 1948), 30. [r of *Fire in the Morning*]

Spencer, Elizabeth, intro to *The Voice at the Back Door* (Time Reading Prog Special Ed; New York, 1965).

Spieckerman, Shirley, "The Light in the Piazza," *NMexQ*, XXX (1960–61), 413–14. [r]

Summer, Cid Ricketts, "Delta Characters," *SatR*, XXXV (March 8, 1952), 16–17. [r of *This Crooked Way*]

JOHN PILKINGTON
University of Mississippi
Oxford, Mississippi

JAMES STERLING (*ca.* 1701-1763)

Before emigrating in 1737 to become Colonial Maryland's most prolific poet, James Sterling had had a successful career as a poet and dramatist in England. Nevertheless, critics and scholars have largely neglected his works until quite recently.

DAB, XVII, pp. 586–87.

*Lemay, J. A. Leo, "A Literary History of Colonial Maryland," Pennsylvania, 1964, pp. 259–341. [diss; see also *DA*, XXV, 7246]

Wroth, Lawrence C., "James Sterling: Poet, Priest and Prophet of Empire," *Proceed Amer Antiq Soc*, n.s., XLI (1931), 24–76.

CARL R. DOLMETSCH
College of William and Mary
Williamsburg, Virginia

T. S. STRIBLING (1881-1966)

Recent scholarship on Southern literature has tended to treat T. S. Stribling as little more than a footnote. The reasons for such treatment are varied and cannot be discussed here; it is enough to say that because he wrote nothing of significance after *These Bars of Flesh* (1938), Stribling, like an old soldier, seemed to "fade away."

In the late 1920s and early 1930s Stribling was a widely discussed (and read) author, primarily because of his discovery and literary exploitation of several rich veins of material dealing with Southern life, but even then he did not attract much scholarly attention. The early articles on Stribling deal primarily with a particular novel (or novels), attempting no codifying treatment, and the books in which he is mentioned do not discuss his work in any depth. Charles Baldwin's *The Men Who Make Our Novels* gives him some space, but at the time Baldwin wrote, Stribling had published only one novel of consequence, *Birthright*. Perhaps the Agrarians noticed him most—Robert Penn Warren and Donald Davidson in particular. Warren, in his article in the *American Review*, was quite negative toward the novelist, indicting his work as a "strange compound of hick-baiting, snobbery, and humanitarianism: in other words, disordered liberalism," while Davidson in a review accused him of "a specious 'sort of satire" against Tennessee and Tennesseans. Others have not been so harsh with Stribling, but as yet no one has really defined his place in Southern letters.

Although at present there is an occasional indication that some students and teachers of American literature see the Tennessean's work as a promising field for mining, Stribling may, in the final analysis, remain no more than a footnote. Few, however, will deny that footnotes are often significant in an understanding of history, literary or otherwise.

Baldwin, Charles, *The Men Who Make Our Novels* (New York, 1924), pp. 464–73.

Bates, Ernest, "Thomas Sigismund Stribling," *Eng Jour*, XXVI (1935), 91–100.

Becker, George J., "T. S. Stribling: Pattern in Black and White," *AQ*, IV (1952), 203–13.

Bradbury, *Renaissance in the South*, pp. 82, 86, 102–103.

[Davidson, Donald,] "T. S. Stribling," *The Spyglass*, ed. J. T. Fain (Nashville, 1963), pp. 11–16.

Dickens, Byrom, "T. S. Stribling and the South," *SeR*, XLII (1934), 341–49.

*Eckley, Wilton, "The Novels of T. S. Stribling: A Socio-Literary Study," Western Reserve, 1965. [diss]

———, "T. S. Stribling: Pioneer in the Southern Renaissance," *Iowa Eng Yearbk*, XI (1966), 47–54.

Hatcher, Harlan, *Creating the Modern American Novel* (New York, 1935), pp. 141, 142–45, 147, 149.

Hoffman, Arthur S., *Fiction Writing and Fiction Writers* (Indianapolis, 1923), *passim*. [ser of questions to a number of authors, followed by their answers]

Luccock, Halferd, *American Mirror: Social, Ethical, and Religious Aspects of American Literature* (New York, 1940), pp. 64, 71, 78, 84.

Stribling, T. S., "The Author's *Store*," *Wings*, VI (Jul 1932), 15–17, 26.

Wade, John D., "Two Souths," *VQR*, X (1934), 616–19.

Walsh, Ulysses, "Read and Write and Burn," *Writer*, XLV (May 1932), 127–29. [interv]

Warren, Robert Penn, "T. S. Stribling: A Paragraph in the History of Realism," *AmerR*, II (1934), 484–86.

Wilson, James S., "Poor-White and Negro," *VQR*, VIII (1932), 621–24.

WILTON ECKLEY
Drake University
Des Moines, Iowa

DAVID HUNTER STROTHER
("PORTE CRAYON") (1816-1888)

Thanks to Cecil D. Eby, Jr., the writings of David H. Strother, who used the pen name of "Porte Crayon" for his numerous journalistic writings during the mid-nineteenth century, have again come into public attention. Professor Eby edited an attractive selection of Strother's writings about the South from the old *Harper's Magazine*, and then followed it up with an excellent critical biography.

Strother is important not only because his descriptive writings about Virginia and the South were an early harbinger of local color, but because of his friendship with John Pendleton Kennedy and his experiences in the Union Army and as an official in Reconstruction Virginia.

Professor Eby's biography includes an excellent appendix which lists Strother's published work. It describes and gives the present location of Strother manuscripts and papers, many of which are in the possession of D. H. Strother II, of Milwaukee, Wisconsin.

Strother figures as a character in John Peale Bishop's collection of short stories, *Many Thousands Gone* (New York, 1931).

DAB, XVIII, pp. 156–57; *LSL*, XI, pp. 5131–33.

Bowles, Ella Shannon, "'Porte Crayon,' Berkeley Springs's Able Publicist," *Iron Worker*, XXII (Summer 1958), 10–11.

Carpenter, Charles, "The Berkeley Springs Home of 'Porte Crayon,'" *WVaR*, XIV 1937, pp. 184–85.

Costello, Sister Joseph Miriam, "The Life and Works of David Strother—'Porte Crayon,' " St. John's, 1956. [MA thesis]

Davis, Elmer, "Constant Reader," *Harper's*, CCI (Oct 1950), pp. 161–72. [includes reminiscence of reading Strother]

*Eby, Cecil D., Jr., *The Life of David Hunter Strother, Writer of the Old South* (Chapel Hill, 1960). [crit biog]

———, intro to *The Old South Illustrated, by Porte Crayon*, ed. Eby (Chapel Hill, 1959).

Hart, John S., *A Manual of American Literature* (Philadelphia, 1873), pp. 457–59. [contains autobiog sketch]

McDonald, Cornelia, *A Diary with Reminiscences of the War and Refugee Life in the Shenandoah Valley, 1860–1865*, annot and supplemented by Hunter McDonald (Nashville, 1934). [hostile account of Strother as Union soldier]

Morse, Edward Lind, *Samuel F. B. Morse: His Life and Letters* (Boston, 1914). [Strother described as Morse's student]

Tuckerman, Henry, *The Life of John Pendleton Kennedy* (New York, 1871).

Louis D. Rubin, Jr.
University of North Carolina
Chapel Hill, North Carolina

JESSE STUART (1905–)

Jesse Stuart is a genuine, original, marvellously fecund writing man, yet a man almost completely neglected by serious literary critics up to the present time. Author of thirty-odd published books of poetry, short stories, novels and autobiography, he has thousands of other published but uncollected pieces (poems, stories, articles) adrift in magazines and newspapers. Technically he is a regionalist of the southern Appalachian Highlands and probably the leading "Appalachian" writer. The Appalachian region has been curiously neglected in regard to its writers so far. The freshening interest in this area, sociologically, economically, etc., coincides with an awakening interest in Stuart as a writer. Five books on Stuart were scheduled for publication in 1967–68. Others are in preparation.

Stuart's writings lie outside the current vogue for irony, paradox, skepticism and existentialism. In spite of this he has had a very large audience and obviously merits serious consideration. Although he often writes too hastily and too voluminously, he has great talents and has accomplished much. He is the elegist of a lost world, the lost world of the Appalachians.

Bird, John, "My Friend Jesse Stuart," *Sat Eve Post*, CCXXXII (Jul 25, 1959), 32–33, 79, 81–83.

Blair, Everett Love, *Jesse Stuart His Life and Works* (Columbia, S.C., 1967).

Brandenburg, David and Phyllis, eds., *W-Hollow Harvest* (Cincinnati). [mag for Stuart enthusiasts; news, r's, occasional illus]

Clarke, Mary Washington, "As Jesse Stuart Heard It in Kentucky," *Ky Folkl Rec*, IX (1963), 75–86.

———, "Jesse Stuart's Writings Preserve Passing Folk Idiom," *SFQ*, XXVIII (1964), 157–98.

*Foster, Ruel E., *Jesse Stuart* (New York, 1968). [TUSAS]

———, "Jesse Stuart, Short Story Writer," in Walker and Welker, eds., *Reality and Myth*, pp. 145–160.

Kohler, Dayton, "Jesse Stuart and James Still, Mountain Regionalists," *Coll Eng*, III (1942), 523–33.

Pennington, Lee, *The Dark Hills: A Study of Vision and Symbolism in the Novels of Jesse Stuart* (Cincinnati, 1967).

The Stuart Scrapbooks, in the Jesse Stuart Collection, Murray State College Library, Murray, Ky. [112 scrapbooks of news clippings, photos and mag clippings from 1930s to the present; assembled by Stuart, scrapbooks contain thousands of items; from time to time Stuart sends additional scrapbooks to the collection]

Washington, Mary, *The Folklore of the Cumberlands As Reflected in the Writings of Jesse Stuart*, Pennsylvania, 1960, 498 leaves. [diss; assimilated and popularized for trade book *Jesse Stuart's Kentucky*, to be published by McGraw-Hill, Fall 1968; author is now Mary Washington Clarke]

*Woodbridge, Hensley C., *Jesse Stuart: A Bibliography* (Harrogate, Tenn., 1960).

*———, *Jesse Stuart: A Bibliography for May, 1960-May, 1965* [pamph repr from *Register of the Ky Hist Soc*, LXIII (1965), pp. 349–70]

RUEL E. FOSTER
West Virginia University
Morgantown, West Virginia

RUTH McENERY STUART (1852-1917)

The most recent and complete study of Ruth Stuart is Mary Frances Fletcher's unpublished dissertation (Louisiana State University, 1955), "A Biographical and Critical Study of Ruth McEnery Stuart." This work has a valuable bibliography and contains some previously unpublished letters, interviews, and family records. In this study, as in others, more attention has been given to Stuart's career as a writer than to her literary methods.

DAB, XVIII, pp. 177–78; *LSL*, XI pp. 5145–51.

Beer, William, "Tribute to Mrs. Ruth McEnery Stuart," *Pub of La Hist Soc*, X (1917), 115–22.

[Chopin, Kate], in Daniel S. Rankin's *Kate Chopin and Her Creole Stories* (Philadelphia, 1932), pp. 55–58. [Chopin's memories of Stuart]

*Fletcher, Mary Frances, "A Biographical and Critical Study of Ruth McEnery Stuart," Louisiana, 1955. [diss]

McEnery, Sarah Stirling, "Scrapbook," in Howard-Tilton Lib, Tulane. [collection of Stuart's letters, programs of reading, bk clippings, and interv]

Rollins, Hyder E., "The Negro in the Southern Short Story," *SeR*, XXIV (1916), 58–59. [Stuart's contrib to this type of story]

"Ruth McEnery Stuart, Southern Author, Dies," *N.Y. Times*, May 8, 1917, p. 11. [obit]

DARWIN H. SHRELL
Louisiana State University
Baton Rouge, Louisiana

WILLIAM STYRON (1925—)

Thus far William Styron has published four novels: *Lie Down in Darkness* (1951), *The Long March* (1956), *Set This House on Fire* (1960), and *The Confessions of Nat Turner* (1967). *Lie Down in Darkness* was hailed by most reviewers, and critical opinion has been equally favorable. *The Long March* did not receive nearly so many reviews, but recently, critical articles have begun to compliment it. *Set This House on Fire* received mixed reviews, and the early critical articles were somewhat unfavorable, but the more recent articles tend to be more appreciative. It is too early yet to know what the critical reception of *The Confessions of Nat Turner* will be. Most of the early reviews were very enthusiastic, some of them for dubious reasons. More recently, there have been several articles condemning Styron for his lack of complete adherence to historical accuracy. There is reason to believe, however, that when the work is read, not as a social tract or as history, but as a novel, Styron will still command as much respect and admiration as any American novelist of his generation.

Aldridge, John W., "William Styron and the Derivative Imagination," *Time to Murder and Time to Create* (New York, 1966), pp. 30–51.

Aptheker, Herbert, and William Styron, "Truth and Nat Turner," *Nation*, CCVI (Apr 22, 1968), 543–47.

Baumbach, Jonathan, "Paradise Lost: The Novels of William Styron," *SAQ*, LXIII (1964), 207–17. Repr in Baumbach, *The Landscape of Nightmare* (New York, 1965).

Brandriff, Welles T., "The Role of Order and Disorder in *The Long March*," *Eng Jour.* LVI (1967), 54–59.

Bryant, Jerry H., "The Hopeful Stoicism of William Styron." *SAQ*, LXII (1963), 539–50.

Canzoneri, Robert, and Page Stegner, "An Interview with William Styron," *Per Se*, I (Summer 1966), 37–44.

Davis, Robert G., "The American Individualist Tradition: Bellow and Styron," in *The Creative Present*, ed. Nona Balakian and Charles Simmons (Garden City, N.Y., 1963), pp. 111–41.

Fenton, Charles A., "William Styron and the Age of the Slob," *SAQ*, LIX (1960), 469–76.

Foster, Richard, "An Orgy of Commerce: William Styron's *Set This House on Fire*," *Crit*, III (Summer 1960), 59–70.

Friedman, Melvin J., "William Styron: An Interim Appraisal," *Eng Jour*, L (1961), 149–58.

Galloway, David D., "The Absurd Man as a Tragic Hero: The Novels of William Styron," *TSLL*, VI (1965), 512–34. Repr in Galloway, *The Absurd Hero in American Fiction* (Austin, Tex., 1966).

Geismar, Maxwell, "William Styron: The End of Innocence," *American Moderns: From Rebellion to Conformity* (New York, 1958), pp. 239–50.

Gilman, Richard, "Nat Turner Revisited," *New Rep*, CLXIII (Apr 27, 1968), 23–26, 28, 32.

Gossett, "The Cost of Freedom: William Styron," *Violence in Recent Southern Literature*, pp. 117–34.

Hays, Peter L., "The Nature of Rebellion in *The Long March*," *Crit*, VIII (Winter, 1965–66), 70–74.

Hoffman, "William Styron: The Metaphysical Hurt," *The Art of Southern Fiction*, pp. 144–61.

Lawson, Lewis A., "Cass Kinsolving: Kierkegaardian Man of Despair," *WSCL*, III (Fall, 1962), 54–66.

McNamara, Eugene, "William Styron's *Long March*: Absurdity and Authority," *WHumR*, XV (1961), 267–72.

Mattiessen, Peter, and George Plimpton, "William Styron," in *Writers at Work: The "Paris Review" Interviews*, ed. Malcolm Cowley (New York, 1959), pp. 267–82.

Mudrick, Marvin, "Mailer and Styron: Guests of the Establishment," *HudR*, XVII (1964), 346–66.

Nigro, August, "*The Long March*: The Expansive Hero in a Closed World," *Crit*, IX (Winter 1967), 103–12.

O'Connell, Shaun, "Expense of Spirit: The Vision of William Styron," *Crit*, VIII (Winter, 1965–66), 20–33.

O'Connor, William Van, "John Updike and William Styron: The Burden of Talent," in *Contemporary American Novelists*, ed. Harry T. Moore (Carbondale, Ill., 1964), pp. 205–21.

Robb, Kenneth A., "William Styron's Don Juan," *Crit*, VIII (Winter 1965–66), 34–46.

Rubin, Louis D., Jr., "William Styron and Human Bondage: *The Confessions of Nat Turner*," *Hollins Crit*, IV, 2 (1967), pp. 1–11. [r essay]

——, "William Styron: Notes on a Southern Writer in Our Time," *The Faraway Country*, pp. 185–230.

Stevenson, David, "Styron and the Fiction of the Fifties," *Crit*, III (Summer 1960), 47–58. Repr in *Recent American Fiction: Some Critical Views*, ed. J. J. Waldmeir (New York, 1963).

Thezwell, Mike, "Mr. Styron and the Reverend Turner," *MassR*, IX (1968), 7–29.

Urang, Gunnar, "The Voices of Tragedy in the Novels of William Styron," in Nathan A.

Scott, Jr., ed., *Adversity and Grace: Studies in Recent American Literature* (Chicago, 1968), pp. 183–209.

LEWIS A. LAWSON
University of Maryland
College Park, Maryland

JOHN BANISTER TABB (1845-1909)

DAB, XVIII, 262–63; *LSL*, XII, pp. 5163–66.

Bregy, K., "Of Father Tabb," *Cath World*, CXIV (1921), 308–18.

Finn, Sister Mary Paulina, *John Banister Tabb: The Priest-Poet* (Washington, D.C., 1915).

Goodwin, E. B., "Poet for the Winter Evening," *Cath World*, LXXIII (1909), 208–16.

Humilita, Sister Mary, "Religion and Nature in Father Tabb's Poetry," *Cath World*, CLXV (1947), 330–36.

Kelly, J. B., "Poetry of a Priest," *Cath World*, CIII (1916), 228–33.

Kessler, E., "Tabb and Wordsworth," *Cath World*, CXLIII (1936), 572–76.

Litz, F. A., "Experiments in Poetry; Father Tabb," *Mod Lang Notes*, LXIX (1954), 23–7.

_____, intro to *The Poetry of Father Tabb* (New York, 1928).

_____, *Father Tabb: A Study of His Life and Works* (Baltimore, 1923).

_____, *Father Tabb: A Study of His Poetry* (Baltimore, 1924).

Mather, F. J., "Poetry of Father Tabb," *Nation*, LXXXIX, (Dec 2, 1909), 534–36.

Meynell, Alice, "Father Tabb as a Poet," *Cath World*, XC (1910), 577–82.

"Poet and Priest," *Outlook*, XCIII (Dec 11, 1909), 807–808.

Starke, A., "Tabbiana," *Colophon*, n.s., III, No. 3 (1938), 427–34.

Tabb, Jennie Masters, *Father Tabb, His Life and Work*; a Memorial by his niece; intro by Charles Alphonso Smith (Boston, 1921).

EUGENE NOLTE
State College of Arkansas
Conway, Arkansas

ALLEN TATE (1899–)

As R. K. Meiners says in his preface to the most comprehensive single book on the subject to date, *The Last Alternatives: A Study of the Works of Allen Tate*, "Even the best criticism of Tate has been very partial, and much of that which has been written has been superficial and even banal." To say that Tate has provoked such partiality, whether in attack or defense, is only to indicate how magnetic his force has been in the field of modern American letters. To those who have admired him, he has sometimes seemed the epitome of his own ideal, the Man of Letters in the Modern World; to those who have opposed him, he has sometimes seemed the caricature of the reactionary Southern aristocrat. Some have seen him as a Classical Traditionalist, others as a Romantic Modernist. His influence has been as pervasive as it has been polar; probably in the long view T. S. Eliot's judgment will be vindicated, that "Allen Tate's eminence, among his contemporaries, consists in his uncommon combination of excellences." Eliot's note, and the rest of the *Sewanee Review* "Homage to Allen Tate," constitute the fullest critical tribute to Tate's achievement up to the present, though certainly further evaluations of his astonishing versatility as a writer are to be expected, and indeed, desired, if Tate's perennial brilliance is to receive the full measure of understanding and respect it deserves.

LHUS, II, *Supp*, pp. 230–32.

Abel, D., "Intellectual Criticism," *Amer Schol*, XII (1943), 414–28. [r essay]

Amyx, Clifford, "The Aesthetics of Allen Tate," *WR*, XIII (1949), 135–44.

Arnold, Williard B., *The Social Ideas of Allen Tate* (Boston, 1955).

Beatty, Richmond Croom, "Allen Tate as Man of Letters," *SAQ*, XLVII (1948), 226–41.

Berland, Alwyn, "Violence in the Poetry of Allen Tate," *Accent*, VII (1951), 161–71.

*Bishop, Ferman, *Allen Tate* (New York, 1967). [TUSAS]

Bradbury, John M., *The Fugitives: A Critical Account* (Chapel Hill, 1958).

Brégy, K., "Allen Tate, Paradoxical Pilgrim," *Cath World*, CLXXXVIII (1954), 121–25.

Brooks, Cleanth, (untitled essay on cover), "Yale Series of Recorded Poets: Allen Tate," New Haven, 1960.

———, "Allen Tate," *Poetry*, LXVI (Sept 1945), 324–29. [r essay]

———, "The Modern Southern Poet and Tradition," *VQR*, XI (1935) 305–20.

———, *Modern Poetry and the Tradition* (Chapel Hill, 1939), pp. 46–50, 95–109.

Brown, Ashley, "Allen Tate as Satirist," *Shen*, XIX (Winter 1968), 44–54.

Burke, Kenneth, "Tentative Proposal," *Poetry*, L (May 1937), 96–100. [rev essay]

Carruth, Hayden, "A Debt to Allen Tate," *Poetry*, XCIX (Nov 1961), 123.

Chapin, K. D., "Courage of Irony: The Poetry of Allen Tate," *New Rep*, CLIII (Jul 24, 1965), 22–24. [r essay]

Colum, M. M., "Double Men of Criticism," *Amer Mercury*, LII (June 1941), 766–67. [r essay]

Cowan, Louise, *The Fugitive Group: A Literary History* (Baton Rouge, 1959), 35–40, *et passim*.

Davidson, Donald, "The Meaning of War: A Note on Allen Tate's 'To The Lacedemonians,' " *SoR*, n.s., I (1965), 720–30.

Donahoe, Wade, "Allen Tate and the Idea of Culture," *Southern Renascence*, ed. Rubin and Jacobs, 47–62.

Dupee, F. W., "Frost and Tate," *Nation*, CLX (Apr 21, 1945), 464.

Eder, Ursula Elizabeth, "The Poetry of Allen Tate," Wisconsin, 1956. [diss]

Feder, Lillian, "Allen Tate's Use of Classical Literature," *Centennial R*, IV (1960), 89–114.

Fitzell, L., "Sword and the Dragon," *SAQ*, L (1951), 227–28. [r essay]

Fitzgerald, Robert, "The Poetic Responsibility," *New Rep*, CXVIII (Apr 26, 1948), 21–3.

Fleming, Rudd, "Dramatic Involution: Tate, Husserl, and Joyce," *SeR*, LX (1952), 445–64.

Foster, Richard, "Narcissus as Pilgrim: Allen Tate," *Accent*, XVII (1957), 158–71.

Gerlach, Lee, "The Poetry and 'Strategies' of Allen Tate," Michigan, 1955. [diss]

Glicksberg, C. D., "Allen Tate and Mother Earth," *SeR*, XLV (1937), 284–95.

Greenhut, Morris, "Sources of Obscurity in Modern Poetry: The Examples of Eliot, Stevens, and Tate," *Centennial R*, VII (1963), 171–90.

*Hemphill, George, *Allen Tate* (Minneapolis, 1963). [Minn pamph]

"HOMAGE TO ALLEN TATE: Essays, Notes, and Verses in Honor of His Sixtieth Birthday, *SeR*, LXVII (1959). [Contents: "In Amicitia," by John Crowe Ransom, 528–39; "Lines Written for Allen Tate on His Sixtieth Anniversary," [poem] by Donald Davidson, 540–41; "Allen Tate: Upon the Occasion of His Sixtieth Birthday," by Andrew Lytle, 542–44; "A Sprig of Mint for Allen," by Katherine Anne Porter, 545–46; "Two Winters with Hart Crane," by Malcolm Cowley, 547–56; "Visiting the Tates," by Robert Lowell, 557–59; "Mi Ritrovai Per Una Selva Oscura," by Eliseo Vivas, 560–66; "A Note," by Mark Van Doren, 567; "A Few Green Leaves," by Anthony Hecht, 568–71; "Our Cousin, Mr. Tate," by Herbert Read, 572–75; "A Note," by T. S. Eliot, 576; "Allen Tate," by John Hall Wheelock, 577–78; "A Note on the Vitality of Allen Tate's Prose," by Francis Fergusson, 579–81; "Mr. Tate and Mr. Adams," by Reed Whittemore, 582–84; "The Current of the Frozen Stream," by Howard Nemerov (repr from *Furioso*, 1948), 585–97; "Ode Aux Morts Confédérés" (French translation of "Ode to the Confederate Dead") by Jacques and Raissa Maritain (reprinted from *Le Figaro Littéraire*, May 24, 1952), 599–603; "*The Fathers*," by Arthur Mizener (repr from *Accent*, 1947), 604–13; "San Giovanni in Venere: Allen Tate as Man of Letters," by R. P. Blackmur, 614–31]

Johnson, Carol, "The Heroism of the Rational: The Poetry of Allen Tate," *Renascence*, XVII (1965), 89–96.

Kermode, Frank, "Contemplation and Method," *SeR*, LXXII (1964), 124–31.

―――, "The Dissociation of Sensibility," *KR*, XIX (1957), 169–94.

Knickerbocker, W. S., "Friction of Powder Puffs: Tatian Esoterics," *SeR*, XLVIII (1940), 315–21.

―――, "Return of a Native," *SeR*, XXXVIII (1930), 479–83.

Koch, Vivienne, "Poetry of Allen Tate," *KR*, XI (1949), 355–78. Repr in *The Kenyon Critics*, ed. John Crowe Ransom (New York, 1951), 169–81.

*Meiners, R. K., *The Last Alternatives: A Study of the Works of Allen Tate* (Denver, 1963). [bibl, 207–14]

Millgate, Michael, "An Interview with Allen Tate," *Shen*, XII (Spring 1961), 27–34.

Morgan, Frederick, "Recent Verse," *HudR*, I (1948), 258–66.

Morse, S. T., "Second Reading," *Poetry*, LI (Feb 1938), 262–66.

Newitz, Martin, "Tradition, Time, and Allen Tate," *MissQ*, XXI (1967–68), 37–42.

O'Dea, Richard J., "The Poetry of Allen Tate," in *Nine Essays in Modern Literature*, ed. Donald E. Stanford (Baton Rouge, 1965), pp. 145–58.

―――, "To Make the Eye Serene: The Criticism, Fiction, and Poetry of Allen Tate," *DA*, XXV, 4705, 1965 (Louisiana).

―――, "*The Fathers*: A Revaluation," *Twentieth Cent Lit*, 12 (Jul 1966), 87–95.

Pratt, William, "In Pursuit of the Fugitives," intro to *The Fugitive Poets: Modern Southern Poetry in Perspective* (New York, 1965), 35–36, 43–44, *et passim*.

Roellinger, Francis X., "Two Theories of Poetry as Knowledge," *SoR*, o.s., VII (1942), 690–705.

Rubin, Louis D., Jr., "Four Southerners," in *American Poetry*, ed. J. R. Brown, B. Harris and I. Ehrenpreis (London, 1965; New York, 1966), pp. 11–43. [Stratford-upon-Avon Series No. 7]

———, "The Poetry of Agrarianism," *The Faraway Country*, 172–76.

———, "The Serpent in the Mulberry Bush," *Southern Renascence*, 352–67.

Rubin and Jacobs, "Allen Tate: The Arrogant Circumstance," *South*, 221–47.

Schoeck, R. J., "Ordered Insight Which is Earned," *Commonweal*, LVIII (May 29, 1953), 205. [r essay]

Schwartz, Delmore, "Poetry of Allen Tate," *SoR*, o.s., V (1940), 419–38.

Smith, J. A., "End of the Old Dominion," *New Statesman*, LIX (May 14, 1960), 718–19.

Spears, Monroe K., "The Criticism of Allen Tate," *SeR*, LVII (1949), 317–34.

Squires, Radcliffe, "Mr. Tate: Whose Wreath Should Be a Moral," in *Aspects of American Poetry*, ed. Richard M. Ludwig (Columbus, 1962), 257–72.

Stanford, Derek, "Tradition and Mr. Allen Tate," *Month*, XXII, 39–45.

Svengli, M., "Allen Tate on the Top of the Ladder," *Poetry*, LXXXIII (Jan 1954), 220–27. [r essay]

Thompson, John, "Allen Tate 1961," *Poetry*, XCLX (Nov 1961), 120–22. [r essay]

Viereck, Peter, "Five Good Poets in a Bad Year," *Atlantic*, CLXXXII (Nov 1948), 95–96. [r essay]

Vivas, Eliseo, "Allen Tate as Man of Letters," *SeR*, LXXII (1954), 131–43. Repr in Vivas, *Creation and Discovery* (New York, 1955).

Winters, Yvor, "Poets and Others," *Hound and Horn*, V (1932), 675–86. [r essay]

Zabel, M. D., "The Creed of Memory," *Poetry*, XI (Apr 1932), 34–39. [r essay]

———, "A Critic's Poetry," *Poetry*, XXXIII (Feb 1929), 281–84. [r essay]

WILLIAM C. PRATT
Miami University
Oxford, Ohio

PETER TAYLOR (1917–)

For the author of a relatively small number of books over the last twenty years, Peter Taylor has received considerable critical consideration, including at least one full-length study (a doctoral dissertation at Notre Dame). His critics have been serious, and their work is a useful aid to an understanding of his deceptively simplistic fiction. The recent issue of *Critique,* devoted in part to his work, is certainly an indication of a continuing and growing critical interest.

Baumbach, Jonathan, "*Miss Leonora When Last Seen*," in *Masterplots 1965 Annual*, ed. Frank N. Magill and Dayton Kohler (New York, 1965), pp. 202–204. [r essay]

Blum, Morgan, "Peter Taylor: Self-Limitation in Fiction," *SeR*, LXX (1962), 559–78.

Brown, Ashley, "The Early Fiction of Peter Taylor," *SeR*, LXX (1962), 588–602.

Cathey, Kenneth Clay, "Peter Taylor: An Evaluation," *WR*, XVIII (1953), 9–18.

Cheney, Brainard, "Peter Taylor's Plays," *SeR*, LXX (1962), 579–87.

Critique, IX, No. 3 (1967), Symposium on Taylor: Barbara Schuler, "The House of Peter Taylor," 8–18; James Penny Smith, "Narration and Theme in Taylor's *A Woman of Means*," 19–30; James Penny Smith, "A Peter Taylor Checklist," 31–36.

Eisinger, Chester, "Conservative Fiction in Tennessee," *Fiction of the Forties* (Chicago, 1963), pp. 193–98.

Schuler, Sister Cor Mariae, R.S.H.M., "The House of Peter Taylor: Vision and Structure," *DA*, XXV (1964), 2519–20 (Notre Dame).

R. H. W. DILLARD
Hollins College
Hollins College, Virginia

JOHN REUBEN THOMPSON (1823-1873)

The best accounts of Thompson's life are the biographical introduction to *Poems of John R. Thompson* (1920) and a University of Virginia dissertation by J. Rodney Miller, Jr. (1930). A large collection of mss, including photostatic copies of portions of Thompson's European and London diaries, is in the University of Virginia Library.

DAB, XVIII, pp. 464; *Duyckinck*, II, pp. 713; *Hubbell*, pp. 521–28, *964; *LSL*, XII, pp. 5227–33.

Harrison, Constance Cary, *Recollections Grave and Gay* (New York, 1911), pp. 119–24.

Holliday, Carl, *A History of Southern Literature* (New York, 1906), pp. 302–306

Jackson, David K., "Some Unpublished Letters of John R. Thompson and Augustin Louis Taveau," *WMQ*, 3rd ser, XVI (1936), 206–21.

Manierre, William R., "A Southern Response to Mrs. Stowe: Two Letters of John R. Thompson," *VMHB*, LXIX (1961), 83–92.

*Miller, J. Rodney, Jr., "John R. Thompson: His Place in Southern Life and Literature," Virginia, 1930. [diss]

Nevins, Allan, *The Evening Post* (New York, 1922), pp. 407–41.

Patton, John S., intro to *Poems of John R. Thompson* (New York, 1920), pp. xi–lxii.

JOHN O. EIDSON
Georgia Southern College
Statesboro, Georgia

MAURICE THOMPSON (1844-1901)

Although most of the items in this checklist suggest an Indiana background, Thompson was reared in Georgia, served in the Confederate army, and always thought of himself as Southern in temperament and interests. He visited and wintered in the South, and much of his poetry and fiction has Southern settings and reflects New South values.

DAB, XVIII, pp. 460–61; *LSL*, XII, pp. 5255–58.

Banta, Richard E., ed., *Indiana Authors and Their Books* (Crawfordsville, Ind., 1949).

Baskervill, William M., *Southern Writers: Biographical and Critical Studies*, 2 vols (Nashville, 1897–1903), I, pp. 89–136.

Fertig, Walter L., "Maurice Thompson as a Spokesman for the New South," *Indiana Mag of Hist*, LX (1964), 323–30.

Flanagan, John T., intro to Thompson's *Hoosier Mosaics* (Gainesville, 1956).

Howells, William D., "Maurice Thompson and His Poems," *Independent*, XXXV (1883), 1249.

Nicholson, Meredith, *The Hoosiers* (New York, 1916), pp. 199–212.

*Russo, Dorothy R., and Thelma L. Sullivan, *Seven Authors of Crawfordsville, Indiana* (Indianapolis, 1952), pp. 173–283.

Shumaker, Arthur W., *A History of Indiana Literature* (Indianapolis, 1962).

Tracy, Henry C., *American Naturist* (New York, 1930), pp. 130–37.

Wheeler, Otis B., *The Literary Career of Maurice Thompson* (Baton Rouge, 1965).

OTIS B. WHEELER
Louisiana State University
Baton Rouge, Louisiana

WILLIAM TAPPAN THOMPSON (1812-1882)

DAB, XVIII, pp. 479–80; *Hubbell*, pp. 669–72, *964; *LSL*, XII, pp. 5283–86.

Blair, Walter, *Horse Sense in American Humor* (Chicago, 1942), pp. 102–22.

*_____, *Native American Humor* (New York, 1937), pp. 62–101.

Cohen and Dillingham, *Humor of the Old Southwest*, pp. 121–22.

Flanders, Bertram H., *Early Georgia Magazines* (Athens, Ga., 1944). [Thompson as magazinist]

*Howe, Will D., "Early Humorists," in *Cambridge History of American Literature*, ed. William P. Trent et al (New York, 1921), II, pp. 148–59.

McKeithan, Daniel M., "Mark Twain's Letters of Thomas Jefferson Snodgrass," *PhilQ*, XXXII (1953), 353–65. [Twain's debt to Major Jones's travel sketches]

Miller, Henry P., "The Authorship of *The Slave-holder Abroad*," *JSH*, X (1944), 92–94.

——, "The Background and Significance of *Major Jones's Courtship*," *Ga Hist Q*, XXX (1946), 267–96.

*——, "The Life and Works of William Tappan Thompson," Chicago, 1942. [diss]

*Tandy, Jennette, *Crackerbox Philosophers* (New York, 1925).

Thompson, Maurice, "An Old Southern Humorist," *Independent*, L (1898), 1103–05.

OTIS B. WHEELER
Louisiana State University
Baton Rouge, Louisiana

THOMAS BANGS THORPE (1815-1878)

T. B. Thorpe's training as an artist under John Quidor, his education at Wesleyan University, his twenty years of life in Louisiana as a painter, newspaper editor, writer, and politician make him one of the most culturally complex of the humorists of the Old Southwest. His "Big Bear of Arkansas" is in form and content the model work of the tradition. Thorpe's enthusiasm for the frontier and his hope for a noble new world man, combined with glimpses of coming disaster were best expressed in the comic mode. Kenneth Lynn's brief introduction "T. B. Thorpe" in his anthology *The Comic Tradition in America* (Garden City, 1958), pp. 108–10, compactly suggests the variety of Thorpe's contacts with the broad culture of his age and the centrality of a few of his symbols.

Very few of Thorpe's paintings have been discovered for our age. His books have not been reprinted, as *The Hive of "The Bee-Hunter"* especially deserves. Finally, the large body of his writing has not attracted as much scholarly or critical attention as it merits.

DAB, XVIII, pp. 509; *Duyckinck*, II, p. 612.

Benjamin, S. G. W., *Art in America* (New York, 1880), pp. 85–86. [brief comment on Thorpe as animal painter and on his satire in painting]

*Blair, Walter, *Native American Humor* (San Francisco, 1960), pp. 92–95.

——, "Technique in 'The Big Bear of Arkansas,' " *SWR*, XXVIII (1943), 426–35.

*——, and Franklin J. Meine, *Half Horse Half Alligator: The Growth of the Mike Fink Legend* (Chicago, 1956), pp. 67–68.

Callow, James T., *Kindred Spirits: Knickerbocker Writers and American Artists* (Chapel Hill, 1967), pp. 9–10, 171, 235.

*Cohen and Dillingham, *Humor of the Old Southwest*, pp. 267–68.

Current-Garcia, Eugene, "Thomas Bangs Thorpe and the Literature of the Ante-Bellum Southwestern Frontier," *La Hist Q*, XXXIX (1956), 199–222.

*Groce, George C., and David H. Wallace, *The New-York Historical Society's Dictionary of Artists in America, 1564–1860* (New Haven, 1957), pp. 628–29, 754.

Hayne, Barrie, "Yankee in the Patriarchy: T. B. Thorpe's Reply to *Uncle Tom's Cabin*," *AQ*, XX (1968), 180–95.

McDermott, John Francis, "T. B. Thorpe's Burlesque of Far West Sporting Travel," *AQ*, X (1958), 175–80.

*Masterson, James R., *Tall Tales of Arkansaw* (Boston, 1942), pp. 56–61, 107–9, *et passim*.

*Rickels, Milton, *Thomas Bangs Thorpe: Humorist of the Old Southwest* (Baton Rouge, 1962).

_____, "Thomas Bangs Thorpe in the Felicianas, 1836–1842," *La Hist Q*, XXXIX (1956), 169–97.

Simoneaux, Katherine G., "Symbolism in Thorpe's 'The Big Bear of Arkansas,'" *Ark Hist Q*, XXV (1966), 240–47.

Weber, Brom, "American Humor and American Culture," *AQ*, XIV (1962), 503–507. [r essay]

*Yates, Norris W., *William T. Porter and the Spirit of The Times"* (Baton Rouge, 1957), pp. 166–70, *et passim*.

Milton Rickels

University of Southwestern Louisiana
Lafayette, Louisiana

HENRY TIMROD (1828-1867)

DAB, XVIII, pp. 588–90; *Duyckinck*, II, p. 110; *Hubbell*, pp. 466–74. *965–66; *LSL*, XII, pp. 5391–98; *LHUS*, II, pp. 747–48, *Supp*, 200.

Bruns, John Dickson, "A Lecture on Timrod," *Charleston* (S.C.) *Sunday News*, Apr 30, 1899. Delivered in Charleston Oct 27, 1870. [perceptive and sympathetic, by a close friend]

Bryan, J. P. K., intro to *The Poems of Henry Timrod*, arrangement of peoms probably by W. A. Courtenay. Memorial ed (Boston, 1899; Richmond, 1901).

Cardwell, Guy A., Jr., "The Date of Henry Timrod's Birth," *AL*, VII (1935), 207–208. [Timrod was born in 1828, not 1829 or 1830]

_____, intro to *The Uncollected Poems of Henry Timrod* (Athens, Ga., 1942). [valuable]

Clare, Virginia P., *Harp of the South* (Atlanta, 1936). [pleasant, uncrit biog, often inaccurate]

Fidler, William, ed., "Unpublished Letters of Henry Timrod," *SLM*, n.s., II (1940), 527–35, 605–11, 645–51; and in *AlaR*, II (Apr 1949), 139–49.

Hayne, Paul Hamilton, "Ante-Bellum Charleston," *So Bivouac*, IV (1885), 327–36.

_____, "Sketch of the Poet's Life," in *The Poems of Henry Timrod* (New York, 1873). [indispensable; fond memoir, sometimes inaccurate, by Timrod's closest friend]

Hubbell, Jay B., *The Last Years of Henry Timrod* (Durham, 1941). [letters to P. H. Hayne and others; Hubbell's commentaries are of great value]

———, "Literary Nationalism in the Old South," in *American Studies in Honor of William Kenneth Boyd*, 175–220. [best treatment of subject; esp good on Timrod]

Lewisohn, Ludwig, "Books We Have Made," Chap 7, *Charleston* (S.C.) *News and Courier*, Jul 5-Sept 20, 1903. [stresses Timrod's artistry]

Mabbott, T. O., "Some Letters of Henry Timrod," *Amer Collector*, III (1927), 191–95.

Page, Walter Hines, "Henry Timrod," *South-Atlantic* (Washington, D.C.), I (1878), 359–67.

Parks, Edd Winfield, ed., intro to *The Essays of Henry Timrod* (Athens, Ga., 1942). [Timrod as literary critic, including Timrod's newsp ed on lit]

———, "Henry Timrod: Traditionalist," *Ante-Bellum Southern Literary Critics* (Athens, Ga., 1962), pp. 193–226.

———, ed., "Henry Timrod," in *Southern Poets* (New York, 1936), pp. lxv–lxix, civ–cv, 99–123.

———, and Aileen Wells Parks, intro to *The Collected Poems of Henry Timrod*, A Variorum Edition (Athens, Ga., 1965). [Timrod as poet; textual notes and variants]

———, *Henry Timrod* (New York, 1964). [TUSAS]

Robillard, D. J., ed., "Two Timrod Letters," *N.C. Hist R*, XXXIX (1962), 549–53. [to the poet R. H. Stoddard, in 1865]

Rubin, Louis D., Jr., "Henry Timrod and the Dying of the Light," *MissQ*, XI (1958), 101–11. [analysis of Timrod's poem "Charleston"]

Siegler, Milledge B., "Henry Timrod and Sophie Sosnowski," *Ga Hist Q*, XXXI (1947), 172–80.

Simms, William Gilmore, "The Late Henry Timrod," *So Society*, I (Oct 12, 1867), 18–19. Repr in Hubbell, *Last Years*, pp. 152–65. [appreciative memorial essay]

Taylor, Rupert, "Henry Timrod's Ancestress, Hannah Caesar," *AL*, IX (1938), 419–30. [disproves gossip that Timrod had Negro blood]

Thompson, Henry T., *Henry Timrod: Laureate of the Confederacy* (Columbia, S.C., 1928). [by son of Timrod's close friend Hugh S. Thompson]

Trent, William P., *William Gilmore Simms* (Boston, 1892). [thesis-ridden; contains some material now apparently lost]

Voigt, G. P., "New Light on Timrod's 'Memorial Ode,'" *AL*, IV (1933), 395–96. [ode published in 1866, not 1867]

———, "Timrod's Essays and Literary Criticism," *AL*, VI (1934), 163–67. [valuable, but brief]

———, "Timrod in the Light of Newly Revealed Letters," *SAQ*, XXXVII (1938), 2637–69. [good, but incomplete]

Wauchope, George A., *Henry Timrod: Man and Poet* (Columbia, S.C., 1915). [perceptive, but regrettably brief]

EDD WINFIELD PARKS
University of Georgia
Athens, Georgia

JEAN TOOMER (1894-1967)

Until recent years, few scholars have written about Jean Toomer, who, with *Cane* (1923), earned a place as one of America's most talented Negro poets and short story writers. Of course, *Cane* elicited the usual spate of reviews, the most perceptive probably being Montgomery Gregory's for *Opportunity*, Robert Littell's in *The New Review*, and Edward J. O'Brien's in *The Boston Evening Transcript*. Few articles appeared, however. Paul Rosenfeld, a friend who had vacationed with Toomer in Maine, sketched his personality in *Men Seen*. Gorham Munson, also a friend and literary associate, wrote a brief tribute. Neither appraised *Cane* critically. In 1927 Alain Locke wrote an introductory note for Toomer's poems which he included in *Four Negro Poets*, an anthology. Later in the same year William Braithwaite mentioned Toomer briefly but rapturously in an essay on literature by American Negroes.

For the next thirty years almost nothing appeared about Toomer. He published no books. Most critics forgot him. Negro critics, when they remembered, treated him cautiously as one who, having ceased to write and having disappeared across the color line, wished to be expunged from all lists of Negro authors. In those thirty years, Toomer was named in histories of the Negro in America—such as John Hope Franklin's *From Slavery to Freedom* (1948) and Margaret Just Butcher's *The Negro in American Culture* (1956). Only three significant appraisals appeared, however. In *To Make a Poet Black* (1939), Saunders Redding briefly sang a paean of praise. In *Negro Voices in American Fiction* (1948), Hugh Gloster examined the social ideas of *Cane*. In *The Negro Novel in America*, Robert Bone, interpreting *Cane* impressionistically, evoked admiration for Toomer's genius and lamented the public's refusal to encourage Toomer by buying *Cane*.

The donation of Toomer's papers to the library of Fisk University in 1963 revived interest among scholars who hoped to find biographical information and unpublished masterpieces equalling *Cane*. Arna Bontemps, then librarian at Fisk, described Toomer's literary importance in the Harlem Renaissance in an essay published in *Anger, and Beyond*, a collection of papers presented at a conference on Negro writers. In the most complete biographical study in print, S.P. Fullinwider considered *Cane*'s significance in Toomer's intellectual development. Refuting Bone's contention that lack of financial reward discouraged Toomer from continuing to write, Fullinwider argued that Toomer failed to find a publisher because, instead of continuing modern man's search for identity, he assumed the role of religious prophet. After studying Toomer's unpublished manuscripts, Darwin T. Turner examined Toomer's failure as an avant-garde playwright during the 1920s and suggested that some of his plays might win more favorable reception in the 1960s. In an unpublished doctoral dissertation, Mabel Dillard analyzed *Cane*. With Turner, she is working on a biographical-critical study.

Bone, Robert, "The Harlem School," in *The Negro Novel in America*, rev ed (New Haven, 1965), pp. 80–89.

Bontemps, Arna, "The Negro Renaissance: Jean Toomer and the Harlem of the 1920s," in *Anger, and Beyond: The Negro Writer in the United States*, ed. Herbert Hill (New York, 1966), pp. 20–36. [Toomer's significance as a writer]

Dillard, Mabel, "Jean Toomer: Herald of the Negro Renaissance," Ohio University, 1967. [diss]

Fullinwider, S.P., "Jean Toomer: Lost Generation, or Negro Renaissance?" *Phylon*, XXVII (1966), 396–403. [biog]

Gloster, Hugh M., ["Toomer"], *Negro Voices in American Fiction* (Chapel Hill, 1948), pp. 111, 114, 117, 128–130, 171, 194, 222, 238.

Holmes, Eugene, "Jean Toomer, Apostle of Beauty," *Opportunity*, III (1925), 252–54, 260. [Toomer's poetry]

Locke, Alain, ed., *Four Negro Poets* (New York, 1927). [anthol of works by McKay, Cullen, Toomer, and Hughes, with crit commentaries by the ed]

———, "From *Native Son* to *Invisible Man*: A Review of the Literature for 1952," *Phylon*, XIV (1953), 34–44. [comparison with Toomer as earlier writer of significance]

Munson, Gorham, "The Significance of Jean Toomer," *Opportunity*, III (1925), 262–63.

O'Brien, Edward J., "The Best Short Stories of 1923," *Boston Evening Transcript*, Dec 1, 1923. [newsp r]

Redding, Saunders, ["Toomer"], *To Make a Poet Black* (Chapel Hill, 1939), pp. 103, 104–106.

Rosenfeld, Paul, "Jean Toomer," *Men Seen* (New York, 1925), pp. 227–33.

Turner, Darwin T., "The Failure of a Playwright," *CLA Jour*, X (1967), 308–18.

DARWIN T. TURNER
North Carolina Agricultural and Technical State University Greensboro, North Carolina

GEORGE TUCKER (1775-1861)

With the increase in ante-bellum Southern literary studies, George Tucker is assuming greater interest for students of American literature. This interest stems partly from his various roles as lawyer, legislator, man of letters, moral philosopher, and political economist, which relate him to many of the most important intellectual currents of his age. But the controversial nature of his writings also helps explain his significance. Leonard C. Helderman and Jay B. Hubbell, for example, see him as an heir of Jeffersonian liberalism, while Joseph Dorfman and Robert Colin McLean view him as a prophet of the "New South," a "Hamiltonian in Disguise."

The question most debated by readers of Tucker is his position on the institution of domestic slavery. Dorfman and McLean believe that he was neither interested in freeing the Negro nor convinced of slavery's extinction in the future. Rather, they argue, he was concerned with enhancing the economic welfare of the South, protecting property, and retaining for the wealthy classes the political control of Virginia. Others, especially Helderman and Tipton R. Snavely, believe that Tucker viewed slavery as a "positive evil" whose demise in a hundred years was both desirable and certain.

For students of the Old South, the origins of Tucker's ideas are as important as the ideas themselves. As McLean has demonstrated, Tucker closely followed the tenets of Scottish Common Sense philosophy and literary criticism. From them he framed a conservative idea of progress and formed an interesting interpretation of the cyclical development of the arts and a coherent theory of the nature and function of poetry. His belief in society's progress and the march of civilization is even reflected in his early novel, *The Valley of Shenandoah; or, Memoirs of the Graysons* (1824).

The most recent study of Tucker as a political economist by Snavely attempts to establish him as one of the foremost economists "of the pre-Civil War era." A less favorable assessment is made by Dorfman.

DAB, XIX, pp. 29–30; *Hubbell*, pp. 216–17, 243–55, *967–68; *LSL*, XII, pp. 5515–19.

"Autobiography of George Tucker, 1775–1861," *Bermuda Hist Q*, XVIII (1961), Nos. 3, 4.

Bernard, Jessie, "George Tucker: Liberal Southern Social Scientist," *Social Forces*, XXV (1946–47), 131–45, 406–16.

Cady, George J., "The Early American Reaction to the Theory of Malthus," *Jour of Pol Econ*, XXXIX (1931), 601–32.

Cardwell, Guy A., "The Duel in the Old South: Crux of a Concept," *SAQ*, LXVI (1967), 50–69. [Tucker's defense of dueling]

*Davis, Richard Beale, *Intellectual Life in Jefferson's Virginia, 1790–1830* (Chapel Hill, 1964), pp. 266–67, 278–79, 287–89, 305–09, 423–28, *et passim*.

Dorfman, Joseph, "George Tucker: Hamiltonian in Disguise," *The Economic Mind in American Civilization 1606–1865* (New York, 1946), II, pp. 539–51. See also "George Tucker: A Southern Anachronism," in II, pp. 881–89.

Helderman, Leonard C., "A Social Scientist of the Old South," *JSH*, II (1936), 481–97.

*Hubbell, Jay B., "William Wirt and the Familiar Essay in Virginia," *WMQ*, 2nd ser, XXIII (1943), 136–52. [Tucker's role as essayist in Richmond]

*McLean, Robert Colin, *George Tucker: Moral Philosopher and Man of Letters* (Chapel Hill, 1961).

*Parks, Edd Winfield, *Ante-Bellum Southern Literary Critics* (Athens, Ga., 1962), pp. 66–67, 264, 280–82.

Peterson, Merrill D., *The Jefferson Image in the American Mind* (New York, 1960), pp. 122–27, *et passim*. [evaluation of Tucker's biog of Jefferson]

Popkin, Richard H., "George Tucker, An Early American Critic of Hume," *Jour of the Hist of Ideas*, XIII (1952), 370–75.

Snavely, Tipton R., *George Tucker as Political Economist* (Charlottesville, 1964).

Spengler, Joseph J., "Population Theory in the Ante-Bellum South," *JSH*, II (1936), 360–89.

ROBERT C. McLEAN
Washington State University
Pullman, Washington

NATHANIEL BEVERLEY TUCKER (1784-1851)

There is as yet no published full-length biographical or critical study of Tucker; for the fullest treatment, see the Percy W. Turrentine dissertation. The son of St. George Tucker and the half brother of John Randolph of Roanoke, he is frequently mentioned in the biographies of these two men. For Tucker's relationships with William Gilmore Simms and with Poe—who had high praise for his novel *George Balcombe*—see the biographies and editions of letters listed under their names. Manuscript materials are available in the Duke University Library, the library of the College of William and Mary, and the Research Department, Colonial Williamsburg, Inc.

DAB, XIX, pp. 36–37; *Duyckinck*, I, p. 665; *Hubbell*, pp. 424–33, *966–67; *LSL*, XII, pp. 5501–504.

Bridenbaugh, Carl, intro to Nathaniel Beverley Tucker, *The Partisan Leader* (New York, 1933), pp. ix–xxxiv.

Coleman, Mary H., *St. George Tucker* (Richmond, 1938), *passim*.

————, ed., *Virginia Silhouettes* (Richmond, 1934). [quotes Tucker's letters on slavery]

*Goodwin, Noma Lee, "The Published Works of Nathaniel Beverley Tucker," Duke, 1947. [MA thesis]

McDermott, J. F., "Nathaniel Beverley Tucker in Missouri," *WMQ*, 2nd ser, XX (1940), 504–507.

Parrington, Vernon Louis, "Nathaniel Beverley Tucker," *Main Currents in American Thought* (New York, 1927), II, 35–40.

*Turrentine, Percy W., "Life and Works of Nathaniel Beverley Tucker," Harvard, 1952. [diss]

Woodfin, Maude H., "Nathaniel Beverley Tucker," *Richmond Coll Hist Pap*, II (June 1917), 9–42.

J. V. RIDGELY
Columbia University
New York, New York

ST. GEORGE TUCKER (1752-1827)

So much of the material written about St. George Tucker is concerned with his public career as a lawyer, not with his literary interests. Jay B. Hubbell in *The South in American Literature* more properly concentrates on Tucker's antislavery pamphlets and the anti-Federalist verses in *The Probationary Odes of Jonathan Pindar, Esq., A Cousin of Peter's, and Candidate for the Post of Poet Laureat to the C.U.S.* (1796). William S. Prince, in his dissertation "St. George Tucker as a Poet of the Early Republic," supplies the best analysis to date of Tucker's poetry, modeled largely after eighteenth-century English satiric verse. He also has collected Tucker's poems for his study. Prince's excellent discussion of the poetry and the collected poems provide proof for Hubbell's comment that Tucker and his circle of Williamsburg friends produced verse often equal to that of their contemporaries, the Connecticut Wits.

Only the significant literary references appear in the checklist; other items are listed in Hubbell and Prince.

DAB, XIX, pp. 38–39; *Duyckinck*, I, p. 236; *Hubbell*, pp. 150–53, *968–69.

Bruce, William Cabell, *The Life of John Randolph of Roanoke* (New York, 1922), I, pp. 66–69.

Coleman, Charles W., Jr., "St. Mémin Portraits: St. George Tucker," *Mag of Amer Hist*, VII (1881), 217–21. [biog essay]

Coleman, Mary Haldane, "Randolph and Tucker Letters," *VMHB*, XLII (1934),

129–31. [John Adams' letter praising Tucker's poem "Resignation" (1807)]

———, *St. George Tucker: Citizen of No Mean City* (Richmond, 1938).

———, *Virginia Silhouettes: Contemporary Letters Concerning Negro Slavery in the State of Virginia* (Richmond, 1934). [foreword only]

Gordon, Armistead C., *Virginian Writers of Fugitive Verse* (New York, 1923), pp. 59–61.

Griswold, Rufus W., *The Poets and Poetry of America* (Philadelphia, 1856), p. 40.

Kennedy, John Pendleton, *Memoirs of the Life of William Wirt* (Philadelphia, 1849), I, pp. 295–96. [comment on "The Old Bachelor" (1810–11) and its contributors]

*Prince, William S., "St. George Tucker as a Poet of the Early Republic," Yale, 1954. [diss and collected poems]

"St. George Tucker," in *Appletons' Cyclopaedia of American Biography*, ed. James Grant Wilson and John Fiske (New York, 1899), VI, pp. 174–75. [biog essay]

Tucker, Henry St. George, "Patrick Henry and St. George Tucker," *U of Penn Law R*, LXVII (1919), 69–74. [Tucker's recollections of Henry]

Tucker, John Randolph, "The Judges Tucker of the Court of Appeals of Virginia," *Va Law Register*, I (1896), 789–96. [biog essay]

WILLIAM S. OSBORNE
Southern Connecticut State College
New Haven, Connecticut

ROBERT PENN WARREN (1905–)

Having published eight novels, a short story collection, five books of poetry, and a shelf of textbooks and criticism, Robert Penn Warren has at length attracted a considerable body of criticism to his work, especially during the last decade. Indeed, enough commentary has come into print to make this editor's task both gratifying and painful: gratifying, to see Warren get well-earned recognition; painful, to have to cut items from my list (space being limited) that cause a wrestling with my conscience.

Warren's relationship to the Fugitive-Agrarian group is closely examined in the three books by Louise Cowan, John M. Bradbury, and John L. Stewart. Of these, Bradbury's provides, in my opinion, the most profitable blend of biography and analytical criticism; Stewart's work, however, benefits from additional sources of information such as the letters accumulated over two decades and deposited in the Princeton University Library by Allen Tate. Leonard Casper's book, the first full-length study of Warren by a single author, may seem a bit overwritten at times, but it contains many useful insights and conveys a special blessing to Warren scholars in its excellent bibliography of writings by and about Warren up to 1960. Charles Bohner's book written four years later is solid, perceptive, and easily readable—an attractive guide for the general reader while useful for specialists too. While both Bohner and Casper treat all of Warren's work, Victor H. Strandberg's book limits itself to Warren's poetry, tracing recurrent patterns of thought and imagery. John Longley's book presents two original essays and some fifteen reprints, including two important essays by Warren himself; essays reprinted in this book are noted below as "in Longley." The two other book-length studies of Warren, the Carnegie Institute's study of *All the King's Men* and the *Modern Fiction Studies* special number on Warren, are presented each with its separate table of contents for the convenience of our readers.

LHUS, II, *Supp*, pp. 234–36.

Anderson, Charles R., "Violence and Order in the Novels of Robert Penn Warren." in Rubin and Jacobs, *Southern Renascence*, pp. 207–24.

Baker, Joseph E., "Irony in Fiction: *All the King's Men*," *Coll Eng*, IX (1947), 122–30.

*Beebe, Maurice, and Leslie A. Field, eds., *All the King's Men: A Critical Handbook* (Belmont, Calif, 1966).

Bentley, Eric, "The Meaning of Robert Penn Warren's Novels," *KR*, X (1948), 407–24.

Blum, Morgan, "*Promises* as Fulfillment," *KR*, XXI (1959), 97–120.

*Bohner, Charles H., *Robert Penn Warren* (New York, 1964). [TUSAS]

*Bradbury, John M., *The Fugitives: A Critical Account* (Chapel Hill, 1958).

———, "Robert Penn Warren's Novels: The Symbolic and Textural Patterns," *Accent*, XIII (Spring 1953), 77–89. [in Longley]

Brooks, Cleanth, *The Hidden God: Studies in Hemingway, Faulkner, Yeats, Eliot, and Warren* (New Haven, 1963). pp. 98–127.

Byrne, Clifford M., "The Philosophical Development in Four of Robert Penn Warren's Novels," *McNeese R*, IX, (Winter 1957), 56–68. [*Night Rider, At Heaven's Gate, All the King's Men, World Enough and Time*]

Campbell, Harry M., "Warren as Philosopher in *World Enough and Time*," in Rubin and Jacobs, *Southern Renascence*, pp. 225–35.

Cargill, Oscar, "Anatomist of Monsters," *Coll Eng*, LX (1947), 1–8.

*Carter, et al, *Modern Fiction Studies:* Special Robert Penn Warren Number, VI (Spring 1960), Seven articles plus checklist: Carter, Everett, "The 'Little Myth' of Robert Penn Warren," 3–12; Longley, John L., Jr., "At Heaven's Gate: The Major Themes," 13–24. [in Longley]; Kerr, Elizabeth M., "Polarity of Themes in *All the King's Men*," 25–46; Rathbun, John W., "Philosophy, *World Enough and Time*, and the Art of the Novel," 47–54; Berner, Robert, "The Required Past: *World Enough and Time*," 55–64; Casper, Leonard, "Journey to the Interior: *The Cave*," 65–72; Davis, Joe, "Robert Penn Warren and the Journey to the West," 73–82; and Beebe, Maurice, and Erin Marcus, "The Criticism of Robert Penn Warren: A Selected Checklist," 83–88.

*Casper, Leonard, *Robert Penn Warren: The Dark and Bloody Ground* (Seattle, 1960).

———, "Trial by Wilderness: Warren's Exemplum," *WSCS*, III (Fall 1962), 45–53. [on *Wilderness*; in Longley]

———, "Warren and the Unsuspecting Ancestor," *WSCS*, II (Spring-Summer 1961), 43–49. [on *You, Emperors, and Others*]

Cheney, Brainard, "Is There a Voice Unheard in Warren's Book Who Is Speaking for the Negro?", *SeR*, LXXIV (1966), pp. 545–50. [r article on *Who Speaks for the Negro?*]

Clements, A. L., "Theme and Reality in *At Heaven's Gate* and *All the King's Men*," *Criticism*, V (Winter 1963), 27–44.

Cowan, Louise, *The Fugitive Group: A Literary History* (Baton Rouge, 1959).

Douglas, Wallace W., "Drugstore Gothic: The Style of Robert Penn Warren," *Coll Eng*, XV (1954), 265–72.

Ellison, Ralph, and Eugene Walter, "The Art of Fiction, XVIII: Robert Penn Warren," *ParisR*, IV (Spring-Summer 1957), 112–40. [interv] Repr in *Writers at Work: The Paris Review Interviews*, ed. Malcolm Cowley (New York, 1958), pp. 183–207. [in Longley]

Flint, F. Cudworth, "Mr. Warren and the Reviewers," *SeR*, LXIV (1956), 632–45. [r article on *Band of Angels*; in Longley]

Frank, Joseph, "Romanticism and Reality in Robert Penn Warren," *HudR*, IV (1951), 248–58.

Frohock, W. M., "Mr. Warren's Albatross," *SWR*, XXXVI (1951), 48–59.

Girault, N.R., "The Narrator's Mind as Symbol: An Analysis of *All the King's Men*," *Accent*, VII (1947), 220–34.

Gross, Seymour L., "Conrad and *All the King's Men*," *Twentieth Cent Lit*, III (1957), 27–32.

Hardy, John Edward, "Robert Penn Warren's Double-Hero," *VQR*, XXXVI (1960), 583–97.

Heilman, Robert B., "Melpomene as Wallflower; or, The Reading of Tragedy," *SeR*, LV (1947), 154–66. [in Longley]

———, "Tangled Web," *SeR*, LIX (1951), 107–19. [on *World Enough and Time*; in Longley]

Hendry, Irene, "The Regional Novel: the Example of Robert Penn Warren," *SeR*, LIII (1945), 84–102.

Hynes, Sam, "Robert Penn Warren: The Symbolic Journey," *U' of Kan Cy R*, XVII (1951), 279–85.

Jones, Madison, et al, Symposium on Robert Penn Warren, *SAQ*, LXII (1963), four papers: Jones, Madison, "The Novels of Robert Penn Warren," 488–98; Rosenthal, M.L., "Robert Penn Warren's Poetry," 499–507; Hicks, John, "Exploration of Value: Warren's Criticism," 508–15; and Havard, William C., "The Burden of the Literary Mind: Some Meditations on Robert Penn Warren as Historian," 516–31. [Havard essay in Longley]

Justus, James H., "The Mariner and Robert Penn Warren," *TSLL*, VIII (1966), 117–28.

———, "The Uses of Gesture in Warren's *The Cave*," *Mod Lang Q*, XXVI (1965), 448–61.

———, "Warren's *World Enough and Time* and Beauchamp's *Confession*," *AL*, XXXIII (1962), 500–11.

Kaplan, Charles, "Jack Burden: Modern Ishmael," *Coll Eng*, XXII (1960), 19–24.

Kazin, Alfred, "The Seriousness of Robert Penn Warren," *PartisanR*, XXVI (1959), 312–19. [r of *Selected Essays*]

King, Roma, Jr., "Time and Structure in the Early Novels of Robert Penn Warren," *SAQ*, LVI (1957), 486–93.

Longley, John Lewis, Jr., *Robert Penn Warren: A Collection of Critical Essays* (New

York 1965). [contains two original new essays, Longley, "When all Is Said and Done: Warren's *Flood*," and George P. Garrett, "The Recent Poetry of Robert Penn Warren," with other repr noted herein as "in Longley"]

McDowell, Frederick P. W., "Psychology and Theme in *Brother to Dragons*," *PMLA*, LXX (1955), 565–86. [in Longley]

———, "Robert Penn Warren's Criticism," *Accent*, XV (1955), 173–96.

———, "The Romantic Tragedy of Self in *World Enough and Time*," *Crit*, I, ii (1957), 34–48. [in Longley]

Mizener, Arthur, "The Uncorrupted Consciousness," *SeR*, LXXII (1964) 690–98. [r article on *Flood*]

Moore, L. Hugh, Jr., "Robert Penn Warren and the Terror of Answered Prayer," *MissQ*, XXI (1967–68), 29–36.

———, "Robert Penn Warren, William Styron, and the Use of Greek Myth," *Crit*, VIII, No. 2 (1966), 75–87.

Moore, John Rees, "Robert Penn Warren: You Must Go Home Again," *SoR*, n.s., IV (1968), 320–32. [r essay on Strandberg, Longley, Warren as poet]

Ray, Robert J. and Ann, "Time in *All the King's Men*: A Stylistic Analysis," *TSLL*, IV (1963), 452–57.

Rubin, Louis D., Jr., "All the King's Meanings," *GaR*, VIII (1954), 422–34.

———, "The Eye of Time: Religious Themes in Robert Penn Warren's Poetry," *Diliman R*, IV (1958), 215–37.

———, *The Faraway Country*, pp. 11 *ff.*, 105–30. [primarily on *All the King's Men*]

———, "'Theories of Human Nature': Kazin or Warren?" *SeR*, LXIX (1961), 500–506. [on *The Legacy of the Civil War*]

Ruoff, James, "Humpty Dumpty and *All the King's Men*: A Note on Robert Penn Warren's Teleology," *Twentieth Cent Lit*, III (1957), 128–34.

Ryan, Alvan S., "Robert Penn Warren's *Night Rider*: The Nihilism of the Isolated Temperament," *MFS*, VII (1961–62), 338–46. [in Longley]

Shepherd, Allen, "Character and Theme in R.P. Warren's *Flood*," *Crit*, IX, No. 3 (1967), 95–102.

Sillars, Malcolm O., "Warren's *All the King's Men*: A Study in Populism," *AQ*, IX (1957), 345–53.

Sochatoff, A. Fred, et al, *All The King's Men: A Symposium, Carnegie Tech Stud in Eng*, No. 3 (Pittsburgh, 1957), Seven essays: Sochatoff, A. Fred, "Some Treatments of the Huey Long Theme," pp. 3–15; Steinberg, Erwin R., "The Enigma of Willie Stark," pp. 17–28; Slack, Robert C., "The Telemachus Theme," 29–38; Cottrell, Beekman W., "Cass Mastern and the Awful Responsibility of Time," pp. 39–49; Woodruff, Neal, Jr., "The Technique of *All The King's Men*," pp. 51–62; Hart, John A., "Some Major Images in *All The King's Men*," pp. 63–74; Schutte, William., "The Dramatic Versions of the Willie Stark Story," pp. 75–90.

Stewart, John L., *The Burden of Time: The Fugitives and Agrarians* (Princeton, 1965).

———, "Robert Penn Warren and the Knot of History," *Eng Lit Hist*, XXVI (1959), 102–36.

Strandberg, Victor H., *A Colder Fire: The Poetry of Robert Penn Warren* (Lexington, Ky., 1965).

———, "Warren's Osmosis," *Criticism*, X (Winter 1968), 23–40.

Warren, Robert Penn, "*All the King's Men*: The Matrix of Experience," *YaleR*, LIII (1964), 161–67. [in Longley]

———, "Knowledge and the Image of Man," *SeR*, LXII (1955), 182–92. [in Longley]

Wasserstrom, William, "Robert Penn Warren: From Paleface to Redskin," *Prairie Schooner*, XXXI (1957), 323–33.

Watkins, Floyd C., "Billie Potts at the Fall of Time," *MissQ*, XI (1958), 19–28.

Weathers, Winston, " 'Blackberry Winter' and the Use of Archetypes," *Stud in Short Fict*, I (1964), 45–51.

Weissbuch, Ted. M., "Jack Burden: Call Me Carraway," *Coll Eng*, XXII (1961), 361.

West, Paul, *Robert Penn Warren* (Minneapolis, 1964). [Minn pamph]

Zabel, Morton D., "Problems of Knowledge," *Poetry*, XLVIII (Apr 1936), 37–41. [r of *Thirty-six Poems*]

VICTOR H. STRANDBERG
Duke University
Durham, North Carolina

EUDORA WELTY (1909–)

Although Eudora Welty has published virtually no new fiction since *The Bride of the Innisfallen* (1955), her reputation remains secure, and critical interest, though not widespread, remains firm. Unless critics do indeed write only for each other, the appearance of a bibliographical checklist should prompt a few remarks specifically addressed to the undergraduate student. Eudora Welty is a New Critic's writer *par excellence*. Not surprisingly, the intricacies and obliquities that make her fiction so fascinating have also shaped the special and often very specialized nature of the critical commentary on that fiction. Most of the pieces on her in recent years have not been "essays" as such, but rather brief explications of one problematic story or another (see the annual *PMLA* bibliographies). It is rare when Welty criticism goes beyond the microscopic to view a work in some context, or to offer critical evaluation along with textual exegesis, though the best Welty criticism—by Ruth Vande Kieft, Robert Penn Warren, and Granville Hicks—has also been able to take a longer view. This is not meant as a quarrel or complaint, for Miss Welty's elusive fictions by definition demand close readings. Rather, it is a caveat for the critically unsophisticated student who may be confused by articles that are exclusively, if not hermetically, exegetal—not because one interpretation is "right" or "wrong," but because the component parts of a dissected story may only coalesce again for the specialist.

Appel, Alfred, Jr., "Powerhouse's Blues," *Stud in Short Fict*, II (1965), 221–34.

*————, *A Season of Dreams: The Fiction of Eudora Welty* (Baton Rouge, 1965).

Bogan, Louise, "The Gothic South," *Nation*, CLIII (Dec 6, 1941), 572. [r of *A Curtain of Green*]

Boyle, Kay, "Full-Length Portrait," *New Rep*, CV (Nov. 24, 1941), 707. [r of *A Curtain of Green*]

Brooks, Cleanth, and Robert Penn Warren, "Interpretation," in *Understanding Fiction*, 2nd ed (New York, 1959). [on "A Piece of News"]

Carter, Thomas H., "Rhetoric and Southern Landscapes," *Accent*, XV (1955), 293–95. [r of *The Bride of the Innisfallen*]

*Cole, McKelva, "Book Reviews by Eudora Welty: A Check-list," *BB*, XXIII (1963), 240.

Daniel, Robert, "Eudora Welty: The Sense of Place," in Rubin and Jacobs, *South*, pp. 276–86.

Drake, Robert Y., Jr., "The Reasons of the Heart," *GaR*, XL (1957), 420–26. [on *The Ponder Heart*]

Eisinger, Chester E., *Fiction of the Forties* (Chicago, 1963), pp. 258–83.

Elder, Walter, "That Region," *KR*, XVII (1955), 661–70. [r of *The Bride*]

*Folsom, Gordon R., "Form and Substance in Eudora Welty," *DA*, XXI, 621 (Wisconsin).

Glenn, Eunice, "Fantasy in the Fiction of Eudora Welty," in *A Southern Vanguard*, ed. Allen Tate (New York, 1947), pp. 78–91. Repr in *Critiques and Essays on Modern Fiction, 1920–1951*, ed. John W. Aldridge (New York, 1952), pp. 506–17.

*Griffith, Albert J., Jr., "Eudora Welty's Fiction," *DA*, XX, 2289–90 (Texas).

*Gross, Seymour L., "Eudora Welty: A Bibliography of Criticism and Comment," *Sec.'s News Sheet*, Bibl Soc, U of Va, No. 45 (Apr 1960), 1–32.

Hardy, John E., "*Delta Wedding* as Region and Symbol," *SeR*, LX (1952), 397–417. Repr in Hardy, *Man in the Modern Novel* (Seattle, 1964), pp. 175–93.

Hartley, Lodwick, "Proserpina and the Old Ladies," *MFS*, III (1957–58), 350–54. [on "A Visit of Charity"]

Hicks, Granville, "Eudora Welty," *CE*, XIV (1952), 69–76.

Hoffman, "Eudora Welty and Carson McCullers," *The Art of Southern Fiction*, pp. 51–73.

Holland, Robert B., "Dialogue as a Reflection of Place in *The Ponder Heart*," *AL*, XXXV (1963), 352–58.

Isaacs, Neil D., "Life for Phoenix," *SeR*, LXXI (1963), 75–81. [on "A Worn Path"]

Jones, Alun R., "The World of Love: The Fiction of Eudora Welty," in *The Creative Present*, ed. Nona Balakian and Charles Simmons (New York, 1963), pp. 175–92.

Lief, Ruth Ann, "A Progression of Answers," *Stud in Short Fict*, II (1964), 343–50. [on "A Memory"]

*McDonald, W. U., Jr., "Eudora Welty Manuscripts: An Annotated Finding List," *BB*, XXIV (1963), 44–63.

Morris, H.C., "Eudora Welty's Use of Mythology," *Shen*, VI (Spring 1955), 34–40.

Opitz, Kurt, "Eudora Welty: The Order of a Captive Soul," *Crit*, VII (Winter, 1964–65), 79–91.

Porter, Katherine Anne, intro to *Selected Stories of Eudora Welty* (New York, 1954), pp. xi–xxiii. Repr in *The Days Before* (New York, 1952), pp. 101–108.

Ransom, John Crowe, "Delta Fiction," *KR*, VIII (1946), 503–507. [r of *Delta Wedding*]

Rosenfeld, Isaac, "Consolations of Poetry," *New Rep*, CIX (Oct 18, 1943), 525–26. [r of *The Wide Net*]

*Rouse, Sarah Allman, "Place and People in Eudora Welty's Fiction: A Portrait of the Deep South," *DA*, XXIII (1962), 3901 (Florida State).

Rubin, "The Golden Apples of the Sun," *The Faraway Country*, pp. 131–54.

_____, "Two Ladies of the South," *SeR*, XLIII (1955), 671–81. [r essay of *The Bride*]

Schorer, Mark, "Comment," *The Story: A Critical Anthology* (New York, 1950), pp. 354–57. [on "Death of a Traveling Salesman"]

*Thurston, Jarvis, *et al*, eds., *Short Fiction Criticism* (Denver, 1960), pp. 197–200.

Trilling, Diana, "Fiction in Review," *Nation*, CLVII (Oct 2, 1943), 386–87. [r of *The Wide Net*]

_____, "Fiction in Review," *Nation*, CLXII (May 11, 1946), 578. [r of *Delta Wedding*]

Van Gelder, Robert, "An Interview with Eudora Welty," *Writers and Writing* (New York, 1946), pp. 287–90.

*Vande Kieft, Ruth M., *Eudora Welty* (New York, 1962). [TUSAS]

_____, intro and ed., *Thirteen Stories by Eudora Welty* (New York, 1965), pp. 3–14.

Warren, Robert Penn, "The Love and Separateness in Miss Welty," *KR*, VI (1944), 246–59. Repr in *Selected Essays* (New York, 1958), pp. 156–69.

Welty, Eudora, "How I Write," *VQR*, XXXI (1955), 240–51. Repr in Brooks and Warren, *Understanding Fiction*, 2nd ed (New York, 1959), pp. 545–53. [on "No Place for You, My Love"]

_____, "Literature and the Lens," *Vogue*, CIV (Aug 1, 1944), 102–103.

_____, *Place in Fiction* (New York, 1957). Unpaged. An edition limited to 300 signed copies. Originally published in *SAQ*, LV (1956), 57–72.

_____, *Short Stories* (New York, 1950). Shorter version, "The Reading and Writing of Short Stories," publ in *Atlantic*, CLXXXII (Feb 1949), 54–58 (Mar 1949), 46–49. Repr in *Modern Prose: Form and Style*, ed. William Van O'Connor (New York, 1959). pp. 427–43.

West, Ray B., Jr., "Analysis: Form Through Theme," *The Art of Modern Fiction*, ed. West and R. W. Stallman (New York, 1949), pp. 403–408. [on "Powerhouse"]

ALFRED APPEL, JR.
Northwestern University
Evanston, Illinois

RICHARD HENRY WILDE (1789-1847)

Some of Wilde's literary works are readily available: 104 of his original poems and 107 of his translations are in Tucker, *Wilde: Life and Poems*. At least 78 poems remain uncollected; some of these are in Graber's dissertation. Wilde's *Hesperia* (1867) and his *Conjectures and Researches Concerning the Love, Madness, and Imprisonment of Torquato Tasso* (1842) have never been reprinted.

The checklist has 33 letters by Wilde. Uncollected are his other prose works: at least 630 letters, his speeches, one short story, his introductions to *The Italian Lyric Poets*, his life of Dante, and a few additional works.

Edd Winfield Parks has written about Wilde as a literary critic, and J. Chesley Mathews has written about his interest in Dante. Other than these, there have been almost no recent critical studies.

DAB, XX, pp. 206–207; *Hubbell*, pp. 304–13, *970–72; *LSL*, XIII, pp. 5789–94.

Barclay, Anthony, *Wilde's Summer Rose: or The Lament of the Captive. An Authentic Account of the Origin, Mystery, and Explanation of Hon. R. H. Wilde's Alleged Plagiarism* (Savannah, 1871).

Beall, Chandler B., "Un Tassista Americano di Cent'Anni Fa, R. H. Wilde," *Bergamum*, XVII (Jul 1939), 91–99.

Cumming, Joseph B., "The Cumming-McDuffie Duels," *Ga Hist Q*, XLIV (1960), 1–23.

Graber, Ralph S., "The Fugitive Poems of Richard Henry Wilde with an Introduction," Pennsylvania, 1959. [diss]

———, "New Light on the Dedication of Richard Henry Wilde's *Hesperia*," *Ga Hist Q*, XLIV (1960), 97–99.

Greer, Louise, "Richard Henry Wilde to Elizabeth Barrett Browning: An Unpublished Sonnet," in *English Studies in Honor of James Southall Wilson*, ed. Fredson Bowers (Charlottesville, 1951), pp. 73–79.

Koch, Theodore W., "Richard Henry Wilde," in *Dante in America* (Boston, 1896), pp. 23–36.

Mathews, J. Chesley, "Richard Henry Wilde's Knowledge of Dante," *Italica*, XLV (March, 1968), 28–46.

Parks, Edd Winfield, "Richard Henry Wilde: Expatriate," *Ante-Bellum Southern Literary Critics* (Athens, Ga., 1962), pp. 51–59, 276–79.

Starke, Aubrey H., "The Dedication of Richard Henry Wilde's *Hesperia*," *Amer Bk Coll*, VI (1935), 204–209.

———, "Richard Henry Wilde in New Orleans and the Establishment of the University of Louisiana," *La Hist Q*, XVII (1934), 605–24.

*———, "Richard Henry Wilde: Some Notes and a Check-List," *Am Bk Coll*, IV (1933), 226–32, 285–88; V (1934), 7–10.

Tucker, Edward L., "Charles Sumner and Richard Henry Wilde," *Ga Hist Q*, XLIX (1965), 320–23.

———, "The Cumming-McDuffie Duel and Richard Henry Wilde," *GaR*, XIII (1959), 409–17.

———, "John Walker Wilde," *Ga Hist Q*, XLV (1961), 120–27.

———, "A Poem by Dr. Milton Antony," *Ga Hist Q*, XLV (1961), 403–406.

*———, *Richard Henry Wilde: His Life and Selected Poems* (Athens, Ga., 1966).

———, "Richard Henry Wilde in New Orleans: Selected Letters, 1844–1847," *La Hist*, VII (1966), 333–56. [contains 10 letters]

Wright, Nathalia, "The Death of Richard Henry Wilde: A Letter," *Ga Hist Q*, XLI (1957), 431–34.

———, "The Italian Son of Richard Henry Wilde," *Ga Hist Q*, XLIII (1959), 419–27.

———, "The Letters of Richard Henry Wilde to Hiram Powers," *Ga Hist Q*, XLVI (1962), 296–316, 417–37. [contains 23 letters]

———, "Richard Henry Wilde on Greenough's Washington," *AL*, XXVII (1956), 556–57.

———, "Richard Henry Wilde's Italian Order of Nobility," *Ga Hist Q*, XLIII (1959), 211–13.

EDWARD L. TUCKER
Virginia Polytechnic Institute
Blacksburg, Virginia

TENNESSEE WILLIAMS (1911–)

No other writer of the Southern Renascence, with the exception of Faulkner, has aroused more misunderstanding and controversy about the nature of his art than Tennessee Williams. While most critics acknowledge his exceptional theatrical talent—his ability to write effective dialogue and to create powerful characters—there still exists much disagreement about Williams' position in American drama. His reputation is currently at low ebb, primarily because of the brief runs of his latest Broadway ventures, *The Milk Train Doesn't Stop Here Anymore* and *Slapstick Tragedy*. In an essay in the Spring 1966 issue of *Tulane Drama Review*, entitled "The Restless Intelligence of Tennessee Williams," Gordon Rogoff examines the playwright's present crisis and critical neglect.

In spite of the current lack of critical attention, the general state of Williams scholarship has slowly improved over the past seven or eight years. Along with O'Neill, Miller, and Albee, Williams has been one of the most frequently analyzed of our dramatists (as well as one of the most frequently condemned because of his surface preoccupation with sex and violence). Since an extensive list of Williams criticism up to 1959 has already been published in *Modern Drama*—Nadine Dony's "Tennessee Williams: A Selected Bibliography" (December 1958), and Charles A. Carpenter, Jr., and Elizabeth Cook's "Addenda to 'Tennessee Williams: A Selected Bibliography'" (December 1959)—this checklist concentrates chiefly but not exclusively on scholarship after that time. Beginning in 1961, four book-length assessments of Williams' achievement have appeared, the most recent being Esther M. Jackson's *The Broken World of Tennessee Williams*, 1965. All four books attempt to evaluate the development of his work, and all assign him a relatively high place in contemporary American drama.

Williams' forewords to his plays, usually written shortly before their Broadway premiéres, have provided scholars with revealing statements of his views of life, art, and society. He has discussed his desire both to shock and to enlighten his audiences, and he has mentioned other artists who have influenced his work, such as Chekhov and Lawrence. In his Introduction to Carson McCullers' *Reflections in a Golden Eye*, he placed himself with Miss McCullers and Faulkner in the "Gothic school of writers," all of whom share "a sense, an intuition, of an underlying dreadfulness in modern experience." Included in this checklist are a number of examples of Williams' candid forewords.

The most neglected areas of Williams' artistic accomplishments are his poems, stories, novel (*The Roman Spring of Mrs. Stone*), and one-act plays—especially his recent short plays, many of which have not been produced in New York. His latest full-length works have not yet been adequately appraised by critics. For the most part, scholars have tended to emphasize the dark, pessimistic aspects of what Williams has called his "cycle of violent plays," while overlooking the fact that throughout his career he has made frequent use of exuberant comedy and farce in the midst of tragedy.

Adler, J.H., "The Rose and the Fox: Notes on the Southern Drama," in Rubin and Jacobs, *South*, pp. 349–75.

"The Angel of the Odd," *Time*, LXXIX (March 9, 1962), 53–60. [cover story]

*Dony, Nadine, "Tennessee Williams: A Selected Bibliography," *Mod Drama*, I (1958), 181–91. See also Charles Carpenter, Jr., and Elizabeth Cook, "Addenda to 'Tennessee Williams: A Selected Bibliography,' " *Mod Drama*, II (1959), 220–23.

Downer, Alan S., *Recent American Drama*, No. 7 (Minneapolis, 1961), 28–33. [Minn pamph]

Dusenbury, Winifred L., *The Theme of Loneliness in Modern American Drama* (Gainesville, 1960), pp. 134–54.

*Falk, Signi Lenea, *Tennessee Williams* (New York, 1961). [TUSAS]

Funke, Lewis, and John E. Booth, "Williams on Williams," *Theatre Arts*, XLVI (Jan 1962), 16–19, 72–73. [interv]

Ganz, Arthur, "The Desperate Morality of the Plays of Tennessee Williams," *Amer Schol*, XXXI (1962), 278–94. Repr in Alan S. Downer, ed. *American Drama and its Critics* (Chicago, 1965), pp. 203–17.

Gassner, John, *Theatre at the Crossroads* (New York, 1960), pp. 77–91, 218–31.

Goodman, Randolph ed., *Drama on Stage* (New York, 1961), pp. 274–316. [production record of *A Streetcar Named Desire*, Elia Kazan's directing notes, and interv with the author, designer, and two actresses who have played Blanche]

Hurrell, John D., ed., *Two Modern American Tragedies: Reviews and Criticism of "Death of a Salesman" and "A Streetcar Named Desire"* (New York, 1961). [Scribner research anthol]

Hurt, James R., "*Suddenly Last Summer*: Williams and Melville," *Mod Drama*, III (1961), 396–400.

Jackson, Esther Merle, *The Broken World of Tennessee Williams* (Madison and Milwaukee, 1965).

Kazan, Elia, "Notebook for *A Streetcar Named Desire*," in Toby Cole and Helen Krich Chinoy eds., *Directing the Play* (Indianapolis, 1953), pp. 296–310.

Nelson, Benjamin, *Tennessee Williams: The Man and His Work* (New York, 1961).

Popkin, Henry, "The Plays of Tennessee Williams," *Tulane Drama R*, IV (Spring 1960), 45–64.

Rogoff, Gordon, "The Restless Intelligence of Tennessee Williams," *Tulane Drama R*, X (Spring 1966), 78–92.

Stein, Roger B., "*The Glass Menagerie* Revisited: Catastrophe Without Violence," *WHumR*, XVIII (Spring 1964), 141–53.

Tischler, Nancy M., *Tennessee Williams: Rebellious Puritan* (New York, 1961).

Tynan, Kenneth, "Valentine to Tennessee Williams," *Curtains* (New York, 1961), pp. 266–71. [crit and biog]

Vowles, Richard B., "Tennessee Williams and Strindberg," *Mod Drama*, I (Dec 1958), pp. 166–71.

Weales, Gerald, *Tennessee Williams* (Minneapolis, 1965). [Minn pamph]

Williams, Tennessee, "On a Streetcar Named Success," *N.Y. Times*, Nov 30, 1947. Repr in Horst Frenz ed., *American Playwrights on Drama* (New York, 1965), pp. 63–67.

————, intro to Carson McCullers, *Reflections in a Golden Eye* (Norfolk, Conn., 1950), pp. ix–xxi.

————, "The Timeless World of a Play," *The Rose Tattoo* (New York, 1951), pp. vi–xi.

————, "Foreword" and "Afterword," *Camino Real* (Norfolk, Conn., 1953), pp. viii–xiii.

————, "Person-to-Person," *Cat on a Hot Tin Roof* (New York, 1955), pp. vi–x.

————, "The Past, the Present, and the Perhaps," *Orpheus Descending* (with *Battle of Angels*) (New York, 1958), pp. ix–x.

————, "Foreword," *Sweet Bird of Youth* (New York, 1959), pp. vii–xi.

————, "Tennessee Williams Presents His POV," *N.Y. Times Mag*, June 12, 1960, pp. 19, 78.

THOMAS R. ATKINS
Hollins College
Hollins College, Virginia

AUGUSTA JANE EVANS WILSON (1835-1909)

The only biography is William Perry Fidler's *Augusta Evans Wilson* (1951). Much of Fidler's information comes from family papers, now located in the Department of Archives and History, Montgomery, Alabama. This biography is closely documented, but contains no bibliography; for bibliography, students should consult Fidler's University of Chicago dissertation, "The Life and Works of Augusta Evans Wilson" (1947). In addition to this dissertation, Clyde Cantrell and Walton R. Patrick, *Bibliography of Masters' and Doctors' Theses* (1955), lists seven masters' theses on Wilson. Both Alexander Cowie, in *The Rise of the American Novel* (1948), and Jay B. Hubbell, in *The South in American Literature*, provide good estimates of Wilson's importance in relation to other domestic sentimentalists. There have been no recent reprints of her novels. In October 1965, the Springer Opera House of Columbus, Georgia, presented an original musical version of *St. Elmo*, music and lyrics by Donald Tucker.

DAB, VI, pp. 195–96; *Hubbell*, pp. 610–16, *972; *LSL*, XIII, pp. 5841–46.

*Brown, Herbert Ross, *The Sentimental Novel in America, 1789–1860* (Durham, 1940), pp. 189, 190, *et passim* [bibl, pp. 373–80]

*Cantrell and Patrick, *Southern Literary Culture*, pp. 76, 325, 701, 864, 1618, 1655, 1664, 1811.

Cowie, "Augusta Jane Evans Wilson," *The Rise of the American Novel*, pp. 430–34.

Fidler, William Perry, *Augusta Evans Wilson, 1835–1909* (University, Alabama), 1951.

———, "Augusta Evans Wilson as Confederate Propagandist," *AlaR*, II (Jan 1949), 32–44.

File of Augusta Evans Wilson, Department of Archives and History, Montgomery, Alabama.

*Moses, Montrose J., *The Literature of the South* (New York, 1910), pp. 330–38, 475–99.

Thorpe, Day, "Fatherhood and Motherhood with Augusta Evans Wilson," *Washington* (D.C.) *Sunday Star*, Dec 24, 1967, p. D–7. [r of *Infelice*]

Marion C. Michael
Auburn University
Auburn, Alabama

WILLIAM WIRT (1772-1834)

Twentieth-century scholarship on William Wirt is extremely scanty. Although he was an essayist of great popularity in his day, an eminent orator, and the biographer of Patrick Henry who probably recreated the final form of the latter's most famous speech, Wirt's literary reputation today is limited to that of a little-known pioneer figure in Southern literature. Jay B. Hubbell, Richard Beale Davis, Richard Lillich and William R. Taylor have contributed excellent articles. Beyond their work, however, there is nothing very substantial, with the exception of a single dissertation by Frank P. Cauble in 1933 and one master's thesis on Wirt's forensic ability. The Library of Congress and the Library of the Peabody Institute in Baltimore both contain sizeable collections of Wirt's papers.

DAB, XX, pp. 418–21; *Duyckinck*, I, pp. 617; *Hubbell*, pp. 234–42, *972–74; *LSL*, XIII, pp. 5903–9.

*Cauble, Frank P., "William Wirt and his Friends: A Study in Southern Culture, 1772–1834," North Carolina, 1933. [diss]

Cruse, Peter Hoffman, "Biographical Sketch of William Wirt," in *The Letters of the British Spy*, 10th ed, rev (New York, 1859), pp. 9–91.

Davis, Richard Beale, "Poe and William Wirt," *AL*, XVI (1944), 212–20.

————, "The Influence of William Wirt," *Francis Walker Gilmer* (Richmond, 1939), pp. 41–119.

Diehl, George West, "The Rise and Development of Southern Oratory," Richmond, 1917. [MA thesis; Wirt is one of twelve principal orators treated]

Guy, Mr. and Mrs. John H., eds., "Letters from Old Trunks," *VMHB*, XLVII (1939), 147–52. [letter of Agnes Sarah Bell Cabell, Feb 28, 1819, telling of Wirt and his family]

Hart, John S., *A Manual of American Literature* (Philadelphia, 1878), pp. 113–14. [biog sketch, mentioning his part in trial of Aaron Burr and speech before Rutgers Coll]

Hubbell, Jay B., "William Wirt and the Familiar Essay in Virginia," *WMQ*, 2nd ser, XXIII (1943), 136–52.

Kennedy, John Pendleton, *Memoirs of the Life of William Wirt, Attorney General of the United States*, 2 vols (Philadelphia, 1849; rev ed, 1850). [authorized biog]

Lillich, Richard B., "William Wirt: The Literary Lawyer," *Speaker*, XL (May 1958), 30–41.

Mathews, William, "William Wirt," *Mag of Am Hist*, XIII (1885), 108.

Page, Thomas Nelson, *The Old South* (1892), pp. 67–68.

Paine, Gregory, *Southern Prose Writers* (New York, 1947), pp. cxliv–cxlv, 378–79.

Parks, Edd Winfield, *Ante-Bellum Literary Critics* (Athens, Ga., 1962) and *Segments of Southern Thought* (Athens, Ga., 1938). [see indices of these two bks for incidental entries on Wirt]

Parrington, Vernon Louis, "William Wirt," *Main Currents in American Thought*, II (New York, 1927), pp. 30–35.

Pattee, Fred Lewis, Ed., *Neal's "American Writers"* (Durham, 1937), pp. 183–84.

Semmes, John B., *John H. B. Latrobe and His Times*, 1803–1891 (Baltimore, 1917), pp. 201–202. [description of Wirt]

Taylor, William R., "William Wirt and the Legend of the Old South," *WMQ*, 3rd Ser, XIV (1957), 477–94. Repr in Taylor, *Cavalier and Yankee* (New York, 1961), pp. 67–94. [uses Wirt's romanticized life of Patrick Henry to illustrate the legend and sees Wirt's "Activities in behalf of the legend" as playing "an important part in his own social and political advancement]

Thomas, Frederick William, *John Randolph of Roanoke, and Other Sketches of Character, Including William Wirt* (Philadelphia, 1853).

[Tyler, Lyon G.] "William Wirt's Life of Patrick Henry," *WMQ*, 2nd ser, XXII (1914), 250–57. [see also pp. 220–28 for comment on this same work and on *The Letters of the British Spy*]

Whicher, George Frisbie, "William Wirt," in *Camb Hist of Amer Lit*, II (New York, 1917), 136–37.

RICHARD E. AMACHER
Auburn University
Auburn, Alabama

THOMAS WOLFE (1900-1938)

The resurgence of scholarly and critical interest in Thomas Wolfe, which is still in progress, began at the end of the 1950s. The postwar years had seen a barren period in Wolfe scholarship, which was largely the fault of two men. John Terry, the official biographer, sat on the Wolfe material for fifteen years without producing a single page. Edward Aswell, the administrator of the Wolfe estate, guarded the Wolfe papers from academic investigators with hostile suspicion. The breakthrough began when Aswell sponsored the publication of Elizabeth Nowell's edition of Wolfe's letters in 1956 and her official biography in 1960. After Aswell's death, a stream of important publications began: in 1962 Richard Kennedy's study of Wolfe's mind and art, *The Window of Memory*; in 1964 Bruce McElderry's critical introduction, *Thomas Wolfe*; in 1968 Andrew Turnbull's factual biography, *Thomas Wolfe*. An edition of Wolfe's notebooks edited by Richard Kennedy and Paschal Reeves will appear in 1969.

The postwar period likewise saw a decline in critical attention to Wolfe's work. Because the form of Wolfe's fiction defies expectations, the school of analytical criticism tended to ignore Wolfe or to dismiss him as an artistic failure. As a result, most critical studies have not been concerned with aesthetic values. Those of Joseph Beach, Edwin Burgum, Bella Kussy, Monroe Stearns, and C. Hugh Holman have emphasized Wolfe's ideas and attitudes; Herbert Muller and Holman have examined his place in a tradition; Carlos Baker, Louis Budd, Náthan Rothman, Margaret Church, and Karin Pfister have shown the impact of a specific literary influence. Although a few critics, Floyd Watkins, Louis D. Rubin, Jr., and Richard Kennedy, have been able to apply the techniques of analytical criticism to several elements of Wolfe's work, most critical analysis has been focused on one feature, Wolfe's style. However that may be, three collections of essays and selections attest to a continuing, though varied, interest in Wolfe since his first publication: *The Enigma of Thomas Wolfe*, edited by Richard Walser (Cambridge, Mass., 1953); *The World of Thomas Wolfe*, edited by C. Hugh Holman (New York, 1962); *Thomas Wolfe: Three Decades of Criticism*, edited by Leslie Field (New York, 1968). Many of the essays listed below appear in these collections.

If the present interest in Wolfe continues, one may hope to see further editorial work. There is need for an edition of the Wolfe-Bernstein correspondence and of the Wolfe-Nowell correspondence. The publication of "O Lost," the first version of *Look Homeward, Angel*, and the reassembly and publication of the rejected manuscript "K 19" would allow a fresh look at Wolfe's work and at the editorial problem that colored his relationship with Scribner's. A critical edition of Wolfe's last manuscript might also be possible for a reassessment of Wolfe's posthumous fiction. The Wisdom Collection at Harvard contains quite a number of other manuscripts for future publication, among them apprentice pieces such as "The Mountains" and "Passage to England" and later experiments such as "The Hound of Darkness."

Many critical studies await the alert and perceptive young scholar, among them, studies of Wolfe's relationship to the Romantic poets, Wolfe's place in the American literary tradition, and Wolfe's use of the classics. One especially looks forward to a view of Wolfe's fiction stimulated by Northrop Frye's theory of genre and his theory of myth.

One hopes, finally, for further biographical work by scholarly critics— indeed, too many non-literary investigators have plowed up this ground so far. Here are a few specific needs: a complete investigation of Wolfe's ancestry, a full study of Wolfe's relationship with Aline Bernstein, a study of Wolfe as a teacher and the relation of teaching to his work, a study of Wolfe's reading, an examination of Wolfe's personality and career by an expert in the field of psychology, a psychological consideration of Wolfe's creative process. In fact, work of this sort, plus some of the editorial possibilities mentioned above, will prepare the way for the full-scale Wolfe biography which has been postponed too long.

DAB, XXII, pp. 730–33; *LHUS*, I, pp. 1309–11, *II, 784–86, *Supp*, 213–15.

Aswell, Edward C., "Thomas Wolfe Did Not Kill Maxwell Perkins," *SatR*, XXXIV (Oct 6, 1951), 16–17, 44–46. [Wolfe's change of publishers]

Baker, Carlos, "Thomas Wolfe's Apprenticeship," *Delphian Q*, XXIII (Jan 1940), 20–25, 43. [Wolfe and Carlyle]

*Beebe, Maurice and Leslie A. Field, "Thomas Wolfe Special Number,"*MFS*, XI (1965), 219–328. Contains Richard S. Kennedy, "Thomas Wolfe and the American Experience"; Mark D. Hawthorne, "Thomas Wolfe's Use of the Poetic Fragment"; John S. Hill, "Eugene Gant and the Ghost of Ben"; Larry Rubin, "Thomas Wolfe and the Lost Paradise"; Thomas E. Boyle, "Thomas Wolfe; Theme through Imagery"; Richard Walser, "An Early Wolfe Essay—and the Downfall of a Hero"; Paschal Reeves, "Thomas Wolfe; Notes on Three Characters"; Clyde C. Clements, Jr., "Symbolic Patterns in *You Can't Go Home Again*"; Morris Beja, "Why You Can't Go Home Again: Thomas Wolfe and 'The Escapes of Time and Memory'"; and Maurice Beebe and Leslie A. Field, "Criticism of Thomas Wolfe: A Selected Checklist."

Beach, Joseph Warren, *American Fiction, 1920–1940* (New York, 1941), pp. 173-215.

Budd, Louis J., "The Grotesques of Anderson and Wolfe," *MFS*, V (1959–60), 304–10. [influence of *Winesburg, Ohio*]

Burgum, Edwin Berry, "Thomas Wolfe's Discovery of America," *VQR*, XXII (1946), 421–37. Repr in Burgum, *The Novel and the World's Dilemma* (New York, 1947), pp. 302–21.

*[Cargill, Oscar], "Thomas Wolfe at Washington Square" in *Thomas Wolfe at Washington Square,* ed. Thomas Clark Pollock and Oscar Cargill (New York, 1954), pp. 3–84. [Wolfe as a teacher at N.Y.U.]

Church, Margaret, "Thomas Wolfe: Dark Time," *PMLA,* LXIV (1949), 629–38. Repr in Church, *Time and Reality: Studies in Contemporary Fiction* (Chapel Hill, 1963), pp. 207–26. [Wolfe, Bergson, and Proust; in *Field*]

Cowley, Malcolm, "Thomas Wolfe," *Atlantic,* CC (Nov 1957), 202–12. [Wolfe's unique way of writing and his manic-depressive tendencies]

De Voto, Bernard, "Genius Is Not Enough," *SatR,* XIII (Apr 25, 1936), 3–4, 14–15. Repr in De Voto, *Forays and Rebuttals* (Boston, 1936). [a famous crit attack on Wolfe; in *Field*]

Dykeman, Wilma, *The French Broad,* Rivers of Amer Ser (New York, 1955). [Asheville region]

Fagin, N. Bryllion, "In Search of an American *Cherry Orchard,*" *TQ,* I (1958), 132–41. [on Wolfe's *Mannerhouse*]

Geismar, Maxwell, *Writers in Crisis: The American Novel Between Two Wars* (Boston, 1942), pp. 187–235.

Holman, C. Hugh, " 'The Dark Ruined Helen of His Blood': Thomas Wolfe and the South," in Rubin and Jacobs, *South,* pp. 177–97. [in *Field*]

_____, "Europe as Catalyst for Thomas Wolfe," in Max Schulz ed., *Essays in English and American Literature Presented to Bruce R. McElderry, Jr.* (Athens, Ohio, 1968), pp. 122–37.

*_____, *Thomas Wolfe* (Minneapolis, 1960). Repr in *Seven Modern American Novelists: An Introduction,* ed. William Van O'Connor. [Minn pamph]

*_____, "Thomas Wolfe: A Bibliographical Study," *TSLL,* I (1959), 427–45.

*Johnson, Elmer D., *Of Time and Thomas Wolfe: A Bibliography with a Character Index of His Works* (New York, 1959).

*Kennedy, Richard S., *The Window of Memory: The Literary Career of Thomas Wolfe* (Chapel Hill, 1962).

_____, "Wolfe's *Look Homeward, Angel* as a Novel of Development," *SAQ,* LXIII (1964), 218–26. [in *Field*]

Kennedy, William, "Economic Ideas in Contemporary Literature: The Novels of Thomas Wolfe," *So Econ Jour,* XX (July 1953), 35–50.

Kussy, Bella, "The Vitalist Trend and Thomas Wolfe," *SeR,* L (1942), 306–24.

Lanzinger, Klaus, *Die Epik im Amerikanischen Roman* (Frankfurt am Main, 1965), pp. 27–37, 141–62.

Ledig-Rowohlt, H.M., "Thomas Wolfe in Berlin," *Amer Schol,* XXII (1953), 185–201.

McCoy, George W., "Asheville and Thomas Wolfe," *N.C. Hist R,* XXX (1953), 200–17.

McElderry, Bruce R., Jr., "The Durable Humor of *Look Homeward, Angel,*" *ArizQ,* XI (Summer 1955), 123–28. [in *Field*]

*_____, *Thomas Wolfe* (New York, 1964). [TUSAS]

Muller, Herbert J., *Thomas Wolfe,* Makers of Mod Lit Ser (Norfolk, Conn., 1947). [first extended crit stud]

Nowell, Elizabeth, *Thomas Wolfe: A Biography* (Garden City, N.Y., 1960).

Perkins, Maxwell, "Thomas Wolfe," *Harvard Lib Bull,* I (1947), 269–77. [editing Wolfe's work; in *Field*]

*Preston, George R., Jr., *Thomas Wolfe: A Bibliography* (New York, 1943).

*Pfister, Karin, *Zeit und Wirklichkeit bei Thomas Wolfe* (Heidelberg, 1954). [philos ideas in Wolfe's work from Plato to Spengler]

Raynolds, Robert, *Thomas Wolfe: Memoir of a Friendship* (Austin, Tex, 1965).

*Reeves, George, *Thomas Wolfe et L'Europe* (Paris, 1955). [impact of European life and lit on Wolfe's work]

Reeves, Paschal, "The Humor of Thomas Wolfe," *SFQ*, XXIV (1960), 109–20.

———, *The Negro in the Works of Thomas Wolfe*, Kentucky: Microcards Ser A., No. 84 (Lexington, Ky, 1962).

Ribalow, Harold U., "Of Jews and Thomas Wolfe," *Chicago Jewish Forum*, XIII (Winter 1954–55), 89–99.

Rothman, Nathan, "Thomas Wolfe and James Joyce: A Study in Literary Influence," in *A Southern Vanguard*, ed. Allen Tate (New York, 1947), pp. 52–77.

Rubin, Louis D., Jr., "The Self Recaptured," *KR*, XXV (1963), 393–415. [Wolfe and Proust]

*———, *Thomas Wolfe: The Weather of His Youth* (Baton Rouge, 1955). [analysis of "The Lost Boy," pp. 46–51; analysis of "The Web of Earth," pp. 119–25; discussion of Wolfe and Wordsworth, pp. 54–75]

Schorer, Mark, "Technique as Discovery," *HudR*, I (1948), 67–87. Repr in *Forms of Mod Fict*, ed. William Van O'Connor (Minneapolis, 1948) and elsewhere. [Wolfe as example of failure in technique]

Skipp, Francis E., "The Editing of Look Homeward Angel," *Papers of the Bibl Soc of Amer*, LVII (1963), 1–13.

Stearns, Monroe K., "The Metaphysics of Thomas Wolfe," *Coll Eng*, VI (1945), 193–99.

Styron, William, "The Shade of Thomas Wolfe," *Harper's*, CCXXXVI (Apr 1968), 96–104.

Taylor, Walter Fuller, "Thomas Wolfe and the Middle-Class Tradition," *SAQ*, LII (1953), 543–54.

Turnbull, Andrew, *Thomas Wolfe* (New York, 1968). [biog]

*Voight, Walter, *Die Bildersprache Thomas Wolfes* (Munich, 1960). [classification of Wolfe's imagery]

Volkening, Henry, "Tom Wolfe: Penance No More," *VQR*, XV (1939), 196–215. [Wolfe at New York University]

Watkins, Floyd C., "Rhetoric in Southern Writing II: Wolfe," *GaR*, XII (1958), 79–82. [Wolfe's comic use of rhetoric; in *Field*]

———, "Thomas Wolfe and the Southern Mountaineer," *SAQ*, L (1951), 58–71.

———, *Thomas Wolfe's Characters: Portraits from Life* (Norman, Okla., 1957).

Wheaton, Mabel, and Legette Blythe, *Thomas Wolfe and His Family* (Garden City, N.Y., 1961). [memoir by Wolfe's sister]

Wolfe, Thomas, *Thomas Wolfe's Purdue Speech "Writing and Living,"* ed. William Braswell and Leslie A. Field (Lafayette, Ind., 1964). Includes William Braswell's "Thomas Wolfe Lectures and Takes a Holiday," repr from *Coll Eng*, I (1939), 11–22. [Wolfe's account of his developing soc consciousness; in *Field*]

———, *The Story of a Novel* (New York, 1936). Repr in *The Portable Thomas Wolfe*, ed. Maxwell Geismar (New York, 1936) and elsewhere. [Wolfe's impassioned account of his career up to 1935]

RICHARD S. KENNEDY
Temple University
Philadelphia, Pennsylvania

RICHARD WRIGHT (1908-1960)

Despite the fact that Richard Wright is the author of six books of fiction—*Uncle Tom's Children* (1938), *Native Son* (1940), *The Outsider* (1953), *The Long Dream* (1958), *Eight Men* (1961), and *Lawd Today* (1963)—and of an equal number of non-fictional works—*12 Million Black Voices* (1941), *Black Boy* (1945), *Black Power* (1954), *Color Curtain* (1956), *Pagan Spain* (1957), and *White Man, Listen!* (1957)—his critical reception is virtually polarized around two dates twenty years apart—the publication of *Native Son* in 1940, and his death in 1960. Only on these two occasions was his work the subject of extended serious commentary. *Native Son* was widely and generally enthusiastically reviewed and to this day is regarded by many as not only the best novel by an American Negro but also one of the few pieces of fiction of the 1930s which will endure.

Between 1940 and 1960, Wright's books were reviewed with varying degrees of approval as they appeared; but only infrequently was his fiction discussed in the pages of critical journals. Upon his death, however, a flurry of appreciations appeared, not only by such leading critics as Irving Howe but, more significantly, by novelists such as Nelson Algren, Langston Hughes, and James Baldwin, who made it clear that Wright's work had left an indelible mark on others of his literary generation. But, since 1960, in spite of a burgeoning interest in Negro writing and Negro writers, Wright appears to have fallen back into obscurity. His critical fate at the moment seems to be that he is one of several writers who are discussed in a seemingly endless stream of quasi-critical essays on the modern Negro writer. He is seldom considered as an artist, and his works have very rarely been subjected to any sort of literary analysis. But there are signs that this situation may not last much longer. Two very recent doctoral dissertations and Constance Webb's biography have dealt with Wright's career in such a way as to promise a more sensible and balanced view of his life and fiction.

*LHUS, II, pp. 789, *Supp,* 216.

Algren, Nelson, "Remembering Richard Wright," *Nation*, CXCII (Jan 28, 1961), 85.

Baldwin, James, "Many Thousands Gone," *PartisanR*, XVIII (1951), 665–80. Repr in Baldwin, *Notes of a Native Son* (Boston, 1955), pp. 24–45. [on *Native Son*]

———, "The Survival of Richard Wright," *Reporter*, XXIV (March 16, 1961), 52–55.

Bone, Robert A., "Richard Wright," *The Negro Novel in America* (New Haven, 1958), pp. 140–52. [biog and discussion of *Native Son*]

Brignano, Russell C., "Richard Wright: The Major Themes, Ideas, and Attitudes in His works," *DA*, XXVIII, 666A–67A (Wisconsin).

*Bryer, Jackson R., "Richard Wright (1908–1960): A Selected Checklist of Criticism," *WSCL*, I, (Fall 1960), 22–33.

Burgum, Edwin Berry, "The Art of Richard Wright's Short Stories," *QR of Lit*, I (1944), 198–211. Repr in Burgum, *The Novel and the World's Dilemma* (New York, 1947), pp. 241–59.

Ellison, Ralph, "Richard Wright's Blues," *Antioch R*, V (1945), 198–211. Repr in Ellison, *Shadow and Act* (New York, 1964), pp. 77–94. [on *Black Boy*]

Embree, E. R., "Native Son," *13 Against the Odds* (New York, 1944), pp. 25–46.

*Fabre, Michel, and Edward Margolies, "Richard Wright (1908–1960): A Bibliography," *BB*, XXIV (1965), 131–33, 137. [lists only works by Wright]

Ford, Nick Aaron, "The Ordeal of Richard Wright," *Coll Eng*, XV (1953), 87–94.

French, Warren, *The Social Novel at the End of an Era* (Carbondale, Ill., 1966), pp. 171–80. [*Lawd Today* and *Native Son*]

Gloster, Hugh Morris, "Richard Wright," *Negro Voices in American Fiction* (Chapel Hill, 1948), pp. 222–34. [*Uncle Tom's Children* and *Native Son*]

Hand, Clifford, "The Struggle to Create Life in the Fiction of Richard Wright," in *The Thirties: Fiction, Poetry, Drama*, ed. Warren French (Deland, Fla., 1967), pp. 81–87.

Howe, Irving, "Richard Wright: A Word of Farewell," *New Rep*, CXLIV (Feb 13, 1961), 17–18.

Hughes, Carl Milton, *The Negro Novelist* (New York, 1953), pp. 41–68, 197–206. [*Native Son* and its contemporary reception]

Margolies, Edward L., "A Critical Analysis of the Works of Richard Wright," *DA*, XXVII, 1829A–30A (N.Y.U.).

Scott, Nathan A., Jr., "Search for Beliefs: Fiction of Richard Wright," *U Kan Cy R*, XXIII (1956), 19–24, 131–38.

Webb, Constance, *Richard Wright: A Biography* (New York, 1968).

Widmer, Kingsley, "The Existential Darkness: Richard Wright's *The Outsider*," *WSCL*, I (Fall 1960), 13–21.

JACKSON R. BRYER
University of Maryland
College Park, Maryland

STARK YOUNG (1881-1963)

Although recognized even in his own lifetime as one of America's best drama critics, Stark Young has received comparatively little scholarly attention since his death in 1963. Much of his work is now accessible only in the files of *The New Republic* and *Theatre Arts* magazines. There are, however, in preparation both a volume of his letters and a biography; and the Twayne United States Authors Series will include a critical study of Young's work. For the student, excellent bibliographies of his writings are available in the unpublished dissertations listed below.

The bibliography assembled by Bedford Thurman is particularly good. With the exceptions of *So Red the Rose, Immortal Shadows*, and his translations of Chekhov's plays, most of Young's work is out of print.

LSL, XIII, pp. 6065–69.

Arthos, John, "In Honor of Stark Young," *Shen*, V (Summer 1950), 14–27. [Mainly an estimate of Young's novels]

Bentley, Eric, *In Search of Theatre* (New York, 1953), pp. 8, 94, 172–73, 250–61. [expansion of earlier article, "An American Theatre Critic!" *KR*, XII (1950), 138–47]

Davidson, Donald, intro to Stark Young, *So Red the Rose* (New York, 1953), pp. v–xxxviii. Repr with some shortening in Rubin and Jacobs, *Southern Renascence*, pp. 262–77.

Gilman, Lawrence, "Stark Young," *NoAmerR*, CCXVII (1923), 555–60. [r article on *The Flower in Drama*]

Glasgow, Ellen, "A Memorable Novel of the Old Deep South," *N.Y. Her Trib Bks*, Jul 22, 1934, pp. 1–2. [r article on *So Red the Rose*]

Hussey, Edward, "Stark Young," *NoAmerR*, CCXXI (1925), 763–68. [r article on *Glamour*]

Isaacs, Edith J. R., "The Theatre of Stark Young," *Theatre Arts*, XXVI (1942), 256–65. [an estimate of Young by ed. of best-known theater mag]

*Lumianski, Robert M., "Stark Young and His Dramatic Criticism," Michigan State, 1955. [diss]

Miller, Jim Wayne, "Stark Young, Chekhov and the Method of Indirect Action," *GaR*, XVIII (1964), 98–115.

Payne, L. W., Jr., "A New Southern Poet, Stark Young of Mississippi," *SAQ*, VIII (1909), 316–27. [r article on Young's *The Blind Man at the Window and Other Poems* and *Guenevere, A Poetic Drama*]

Pilkington, John, "Stark Young at the Southern Literary Festival," *U Miss Stud in Eng*, V (1964), 35–42.

Somers, John J., "The Critic as Playwright: A Study of Stark Young's *The Saint*," *Mod Drama*, VII (1965), 446–53.

*Thurman, Bedford, "Stark Young: A Bibliography," Cornell, 1954. [diss]

Wade, John Donald, "Two Souths," *VQR*, X (1934), 616–19. [r article on *So Red the Rose*]

Young, Stark, *The Pavilion* (New York, 1951). [autobiog]

JOHN PILKINGTON
University of Mississippi
Oxford, Mississippi

APPENDIX

SIXTY-EIGHT ADDITIONAL WRITERS
OF THE COLONIAL SOUTH

The lack of accurate information about the writers of the Colonial South is such that it was thought useful to prepare for this volume a supplementary checklist of sixty-eight additional writers, to add to those being treated in the general checklist.

Although I have not given separate entries to many of the early American naturalists, they were important writers of the day. Guides to the writings and achievements of these men (e.g., Dr. Alexander Garden, Dr. John Lining, Dr. John Mitchell) are available in Bell, Guerra, and Hindle, listed in the general checklist for the Colonial period.

In an effort to make the entries for authors as brief as possible, I have used the following abbreviations in addition to those used throughout this volume:

CHAL—William Peterfield Trent *et al*, eds., *The Cambridge History of American Literature*, I (New York, 1917).

Jones—Howard Mumford Jones, *The Literature of Virginia in the Seventeenth Century* (Boston, 1946).

LAP—Kenneth B. Murdock, "The Colonial and Revolutionary Period," in Arthur Hobson Quinn, ed., *The Literature of the American People* (New York, 1951).

Moses—Montrose J. Moses, *The Literature of the South* (New York, 1910).

Tyler—Moses Coit Tyler, *A History of American Literature, 1607–1765* (Ithaca, N.Y., 1949).

GEORGE ALSOP (1638?–*post* 1666)

No accurately printed and thoroughly annotated edition of Alsop's *Character* has been made. A critical chapter and a biographical appendix on Alsop will shortly appear in J. A. Leo Lemay, *A Literary History of Colonial Maryland.*

DAB, I, pp. 227–28; *Hubbell*, pp. 61–62; *LAP*, pp. 24–25; *LHUS*, I, pp. 42–43, *II, 257; *Moses*, pp. 41–44; *Tyler*, pp. 57–61.

Mereness, Newton D., intro to George Alsop, *A Character of the Province of Maryland* (Cleveland, 1902), pp. 5–14.

REVEREND THOMAS BACON (1700–1768)

For a biographical and critical treatment, see Lemay's forthcoming *A Literary History of Colonial Maryland.*

DAB, I, p. 484.

Allen, Ethan, "Rev. Thomas Bacon 1745–1768, Incumbent of St. Peter's Talbot Co., and All Saints, Frederick Co., Maryland," [*AmerQ*] *Church R*, XVII (1865), 430–51.

DR. MARK BANNERMAN (d. 1727)

Jones, Gordon W., "Ramsay the Poet Immortalizes a Virginia Physician," *Va Med Month*, LXXXVII (1960), 642–46.

ARTHUR BLACKAMORE (c. 1679–*post* 1720)

*Davis, Richard Beale, "Arthur Blackamore: The Virginia Colony and the Early English Novel," *VMHB*, LXXV (1967), 22–34.

McBurney, William H., *Four Before Richardson* (Lincoln, Neb., 1963), pp. xvi–xix.

Swem, Earl Greg, ed., *Arthur Blackamore's Expeditio Ultramontana* (Richmond, 1960).

REVEREND JAMES BLAIR (1655–1743)

There has never been a critical assessment of his literary abilities, and there is no adequate biography.

DAB, II, pp. 335–37. *LHUS*, I, pp. 43–44, *II, 76; *Moses*, pp. 50–57; and *Tyler*, pp. 488–91.

*Brydon, George MacLaren, "James Blair, Commissary," *Virginia's Mother Church and the Political Conditions Under Which it Grew*, I (Richmond, 1947), pp. 273-326.

Farish, Hunter Dickinson, intro to Henry Hartwell, James Blair, and Edward Chilton, in *The Present State of Virginia and the College* (Williamsburg, 1940), pp. xiii–lxxiii.

Kammen, Michael G., "Virginia at the Close of the Seventeenth Century: An Appraisal by James Blair and John Locke," *VMHB*, LXXIV (1966), 141–69.

McCulloch, Samuel C., "The Fight to Depose Governor Francis Nicholson: James Blair's Affidavit of June 7, 1704," *JSH*, XII (1946), 403–422.

McCulloch, Samuel C., "James Blair's Plan of 1699 to Reform the Clergy of Virginia," *WMQ*, 3rd ser, IV (1947), 70–86.

Mohler, Samuel R., "Commissary James Blair, Churchman, Educator, and Politician of Colonial Virginia," Chicago, 1941. [diss]

Motley, Daniel Esten, *Life of Commissary James Blair, Founder of William and Mary College* (Baltimore, 1901; Johns Hopkins U Stud in Hist and Pol Sci Ser, XIX, No. 10).

RICHARD BLAND (1710–1776)

Despite Rossiter's excellent study, there is need for a full biography, a bibliography, and a complete edition of Bland's writings.

DAB, II, pp. 354–55.

*Bailyn, Bernard, intro to Richard Bland, *The Colonel Dismounted*, in Bailyn's *Pamphlets of the American Revolution, 1750–1776*, I (Cambridge, Mass., 1965), pp. 293–99, and bibl and notes, pp. 706–12.

Ford, Worthington C., "Washington and 'Centinel X,'" *Penn Mag of Hist and Biog*, XX (1898), 436–42.

Pate, James., "Richard Bland's Inquiry into the Rights of the British Colonies," *WMQ*, 2nd ser, XI (1931), 20–28.

*Rossiter, Clinton, "Richard Bland: The Whig in America," WMQ, 3rd ser, X (1953), 33–79.

Smith, Helen Sublett, "Richard Bland, the Antiquary," Virginia, 1937. [MA thesis]

Tyler, Moses Coit, *The Literary History of the American Revolution, 1763–1783* (New York, 1957), I, 230–31.

ROBERT BOLLING (1738–1775)

The most prolific poet of pre-Revolutionary Virginia, Bolling has never been the subject of even a single scholarly notice. He contributed frequently to the English magazines and his poetry and prose dominated the Virginia gazettes. I am currently preparing an edition of his poetry, based, in part, upon three manuscript volumes of his work at the Huntington Library.

"Observator," "An Account of two Americans of Extraordinary Genius in Poetry and Music," *Columbian Mag*, II (1788), 211–12.

REVEREND JONATHAN BOUCHER (1738–1804)

There is need for a biography, for a bibliography, and for an annotated and indexed edition of his *Reminiscences*.

DAB, II, pp. 473–75; *CHAL*, pp. 138–39; *LAP*, p. 140, *1015.

Chorley, E.C., "Correspondence between the Right Reverend John Skinner, Jr., and the Reverend Jonathan Boucher, 1786," *Hist Mag Prot Episc Ch*, X (1941), 163–75.

Evanson, Philip, "Jonathan Boucher: The Mind of an American Loyalist," *Md Hist Mag*, LVIII (1963), 123–36.

Gummere, Richard M., "Jonathan Boucher, Toryissimus," *Md Hist Mag*, LV (1960), 138–45.

Marshall, R.W., "What Jonathan Boucher Preached," *VMHB*, XLI (1938), 1–12.

Parrington, Vernon L., "Jonathan Boucher: Tory Priest," *Main Currents in American Thought: The Colonial Mind, 1620–1800* (New York, 1927), pp. 218–23.

Read, Allen Walker, "Boucher's Linguistic Pastoral of Colonial Maryland," *Dialect Notes*, VI (1933), 353–63.

Thompson, M.W., "Jonathan Boucher (1738–1804) by Himself," *Blackwood's*, CCXXXI (1932), 315–34.

*Tyler, Moses Coit, *The Literary History of the American Revolution, 1763–1783*, I (New York, 1957), pp. 276–78, 316–28, and bibl, p. 328, n. 2.

Walker, Robert G., "Jonathan Boucher: Champion of the Minority," *WMQ*, 3rd ser, II (1945), 3–14.

THOMAS BURKE (1747?–1783)

Only Burke's poems, surviving in manuscript in the State Department of Archives and History, Raleigh, North Carolina, have been printed. A careful study of the Virginia newspapers of 1765–71 would surely turn up a large number of additional poems. The well known "Stamp Act Repeal," pp. 22–26 in Frank Moore, *Songs and Ballads of the American Revolution* (New York, 1855), is by Burke, as the printing in Walser, pages 32–33, of ll. 35–42, 53–60, 65–70, and 79–95 (under the title "Triumph America"), proves.

DAB, III, pp. 282–83.

Douglass, Elisha P., "Thomas Burke, Disillusioned Democrat," *N.C. Hist R*, XXVI (1949), 150–86.

Sanders, Jennings B., "Thomas Burke in the Continental Congress," *N.C. Hist R*, IX (1932), 22–37.

*Walser, Richard, intro to *The Poems of Governor Thomas Burke of North Carolina* (Raleigh, 1961), pp. 1–13, and "Notes," pp. 60–69.

CHARLES CARROLL (1737–1832)

There is no critical evaluation of Carroll's manifest literary ability.

DAB, III, pp. 522–23.

Hanley, Thomas O'Brien, "Young Mr. Carroll and Montesquieu," *Md Hist Mag*, LXII (1967), 394–418.

Riley, Elihu S., *Correspondence of "First Citizen"—Charles Carroll of Carrollton, and "Antilon"—Daniel Dulany, Jr., 1773, with a History of Governor Eden's Administration in Maryland* (Baltimore, 1902).

*Smith, Ellen H., *Charles Carroll of Carrollton* (Cambridge, Mass., 1942).

LANDON CARTER (1710–1778)

Carter was the most prolific writer of pre-Revolutionary Virginia. There is no bibliography of his published writings (though most of them are cited by Greene in his introduction to Carter's *Diary*: especially p. 7, n. 23; p. 8, n. 26; and p. 24, n. 85), and no critical assessment of his literary abilities. We need a complete edition of his published writings and a complete edition of his correspondence. Carter deserves a full biography.

DAB, III, p. 541.

*Greene, Jack P., intro to *The Diary of Colonel Landon Carter of Sabine Hall, 1752–1778*, 2 vols (Charlottesville, 1965), I, 3–61.

———, "Landon Carter and the Pistole Fee Dispute," *WMQ*, 3rd ser, XIV (1957), 66–69; see also XV (1958), 410.

———, "Landon Carter, Diarist, Essayist and Correspondent," *Manuscripts*, XI (1959), 35–37, 52.

Wineman, Walter Ray, *The Landon Carter Papers in the University of Virginia Library: A Calendar and Biographical Sketch* (Charlottesville, 1962).

REVEREND THOMAS CHASE (1703–1779)

There is no assessment of Chase's abilities as a poet and sermon-writer.

*Beirne, Rosamond Randall, "The Reverend Thomas Chase: Pugnacious Parson," *Md Hist Mag*, LIX (1964), 1–14.

Rightmyer, Nelson Waite, *Maryland's Established Church* (Baltimore, 1956), p. 169.

Wroth, Lawrence C., *A History of Printing in Colonial Maryland, 1686–1776* (Baltimore, 1922).

EBENEZER COOK(E) (1670?–*post* 1732)

Cook spelled his name more frequently without the *e*. A complete edition of his poetry is needed. A biographical and critical treatment will shortly appear in Lemay, *A Literary History of Colonial Maryland*.

DAB, XXI, pp. 189–90. *Hubbell*, pp. 63–65, *926; *LAP*, p. 55, *998–99; *LHUS*, I, pp. 50–51; *Moses*, pp. 46–49; *Tyler*, pp. 483–88.

Jones, Elias, *Revised History of Dorchester County, Maryland* (Baltimore, 1925), pp. 279–90.

Pole, James Talbot, "Ebenezer Cooke and the Maryland Muse," *AL*, III (1931), 296–302.

————, "Ebenezer Cook: The Sot-weed Factor. An Edition," Columbia, 1931. [MA thesis]

Stearns, Bertha Monica, "The Literary Treatment of Bacon's Rebellion in Virginia," *VMHB*, LII (1944), 168–71.

Steiner, Bernard C., ed., *Early Maryland Poetry* (Baltimore, 1900; Md Hist Soc Fund Pub No. 36).

*Van Domelen, John E., "Ebenezer Cook," XXIV (1965–66), 94.

*Wroth, Lawrence C., "The Maryland Muse. By Ebenezer Cooke. A Facsimile, with an introduction," *Amer Antiq Soc Proceed*, n.s., XLIV (1934), 267–335.

JOHN COTTON (c.1643–*post* 1680)

A critical edition of his history and related writings is needed.

Jones, pp. 43–45; *LHUS*, I, pp. 49–50; *Moses*, pp. 45–46; *Tyler*, pp. 61–70.

Basler, Roy P., "Bacon's Epitaph, Made by His Man," *Explicator*, II (1943), 12.

Galinski, Hans, "Kolonialer Literaturbarock in Virginia: Eine Interpretation von *Bacons Epitaph* auf der Grundlage eines Forschungsberichtes," *Festschrift Theodor Spira*, XVIII (1961), 260–308.

Hubbell, Jay B., "John and Ann Cotton of 'Queen's Creek,' Va.," *AL* (1938), 179–201. Repr as "John Cotton: The Poet-Historian of Bacon's Rebellion," *South and Southwest* (Durham, 1965), pp. 205–27.

Schorer, C.E., "One Cotton of Acquia Creek, Husband of Ann Cotton," *AL*, XXII (1950), 342–45.

Stearns, Bertha Monica, "The Literary Treatment of Bacon's Rebellion in Virginia," *VMHB*, LII (1944), 168–71.

Wermuth, Paul C., "Nathaniel Bacon's Poetic Epitaphs," *Va Cavalcade*, VII (1957), 6–8.

REVEREND THOMAS CRADOCK (1718?–1770)

No bibliography or critical evaluation of this poet has been attempted.

Allen, Ethan, "Rev. Thomas Cradock, Rector of St. Thomas' Parish, Baltimore County, Maryland, 1745," *Church Hist*, VII (1854–55), 302–12.

————, *The Garrison Church*, ed. Hobart Smith (New York, 1898).

*Rightmyer, Nelson Waite, *Maryland's Established Church* (Baltimore, 1956). pp. 177–78.

Wroth, Lawrence C., *A History of Printing in Colonial Maryland, 1686–1776* (Baltimore, 1922).

DR. THOMAS DALE (1700–1750)

I am currently editing some correspondence of Dale; and there is need for a full biography, a bibliography, and an edition of his poetry.

Hubbell, pp. 72–73 (reprints a Dale poem as anonymous).

Christy, Miller, "Samuel Dale (1659?–1739), of Braintree, Botanist, and the Dale Family: Some Genealogy and Some Portraits," *The Essex Naturalist*, XIX (1918–21), 49–69.

Law, Robert Adger, "Early American Prologues and Epilogues," *Nation*, XCVIII (1914), 463–64.

――――, "Thomas Dale, An Eighteenth Century Gentleman," *Nation*, CI (1915), 773–74.

――――, "A Diversion of Colonial Gentlemen," *TexR*, II (1916), 79–88.

Seibels, Robert E., "Thomas Dale, M.D., of Charleston, S.C.," *Annals Med Hist*, n.s., III (1931), 50–57.

Waring, Joseph I., "An Incident in Early South Carolina Medicine," *Annals Med Hist*, n.s., X (1938), 608–10.

REVEREND WILLIAM DAWSON (1705?–1752)

There is need for full biographies of both William and Thomas Dawson.

Hubbell, pp. 33–35; *LHUS*, I, p. 52.

*Brydon, George MacLaren, "Commissary William Dawson," in *Virginia's Mother Church and the Political Conditions Under Which It Grew*, II (Philadelphia, 1952), pp. 256–68; also "Commissary Thomas Dawson," pp. 269–87.

*Dean, Harold Lester, "An Identification of the 'Gentleman of Virginia,'" *Papers of Bibl Soc of Amer*, XXXI (1937), 10–20.

THOMAS ATWOOD DIGGES (1741–1821)

*Clark, William Bell, "In Defense of Thomas Digges," *Penn Mag of Hist and Biog*, LXXVII (1953), 381–438.

Elias, Robert H., "The First American Novel," *AL*, XII (1940–41), 419–34. Repr as a foreword to facsimile reproduction of *The Adventures of Alonso* (New York, 1943; Cath Hist Soc Monograph ser, XVIII).

*Kellock, Katharine A., *Colonial Piscataway in Maryland* (Accokeek, Md., 1962), pp. 18–20.

*Parsons, Lynn Hudson, "The Mysterious Mr. Digges," *WMQ*, 3rd ser, XXII (1965), 486–92.

Pursell, Carroll W., Jr., "Thomas Digges and William Pearce: An Example of the Transit of Technology," *WMQ*, 3rd ser, XXI (1964), 551–60.

WILLIAM HENRY DRAYTON (1742–1779)

DAB, V, pp. 448–49.

Bohman, George, "Political Oratory in Pre-Revolutionary America," *Q Jour S*, XXIII (1937), 243–51.

*Dabney, William M. and Marion Dargan, *William Henry Drayton and the American Revolution* (Albuquerque, N.M., 1962).

Tyler, Moses Coit, *The Literary History of the American Revolution, 1763–1783*, I (New York, 1957), 491–93.

DANIEL DULANY SR. (1685–1753) AND JR. (1722–1797)

There is no bibliography of either Dulany, and the literary quarrel of Daniel Dulany, Sr., with Rev. Jacob Henderson has not been examined.

DAB, V, pp. 498–500; *LAP*, p. 141; *LHUS*, I, p. 134.

*Bailyn, Bernard, intro to Dulany's *Considerations on the Propriety of Imposing Taxes*, in Bailyn's *Pamphlets of the American Revolution*, I (Cambridge, Mass., 1965), pp. 599–606, and bibl and notes, pp. 741–46.

*Land, Aubrey C., *The Dulanys of Maryland* (Baltimore, 1955).

Sioussat, St. George L., *The English Statutes in Maryland* (Baltimore, 1903; Johns Hopkins U Stud in Hist and Pol Sci Ser, XXI, Nos. 11–12).

Tyler, Moses Coit, *The Literary History of the American Revolution, 1763–1783*, I (New York, 1957), 101–11.

Wroth, Lawrence C., *A History of Printing in Colonial Maryland, 1686–1776* (Baltimore, 1922).

JOSEPH DUMBLETON (fl. 1741–1750)

The name is probably a pseudonym.

Cohen, Hennig, "The Poems of Joseph Dumbleton, 1740–1750," *BB*, XX (1952), 220.

WILLIAM EDDIS (1738–1825)

There should be a critical edition of Eddis' *Letters from America*, and no evaluation of this excellent writer has appeared.

DAB, VI, pp. 5–6.

Williams, George H., "William Eddis: What the Sources Say," *Md Hist Mag*, LX (1965), 121–31.

PHILIP VICKERS FITHIAN (1747–1776)

Albion, Robert G. and Leonidas Dodson, eds., *Philip Vickers Fithian: Journal, 1775–1776, Written on the Virginia-Pennsylvania Frontier and in the Army Around New York* (Princeton, 1934).

*Farish, Hunter Dickinson, intro to *Journal and Letters of Philip Vickers Fithian, 1773–1774: A Plantation Tutor in the Old Dominion* (Williamsburg, 1943), pp. vii–xlv.

WILLIAM FITZHUGH (1651–1701)

DAB, VI, pp. 438–39; *Jones*, pp. 31–33.

Davis, Richard Beale, "Chesapeake Pattern and Pole-Star: William Fitzhugh in his Plantation World, 1676–1701," *Proceed* of the Amer Philos Soc, CV (1962), 525–29.

*_____, intro to *William Fitzhugh and His Chesapeake World, 1676–1701* (Chapel Hill, 1963), pp. 3–55.

JOHN FOX (c. 1686–*post* 1725)

There is no bibliography of this poet and journalist. In addition to references in

Murdock, there is a long manuscript poem by Fox (in the form of a letter to Thomas Bordley) in the Maryland Historical Society, Baltimore.

*Murdock, Kenneth B., "William Byrd and the Virginia Author of the Wanderer," *Harvard Stud and Notes in Phil and Lit*, XVII (1935), 129–36.

CHRISTOPHER GADSDEN (1724–1805)

DAB, VII, pp. 82–83.
*Walsh, Richard, *The Writings of Christopher Gadsden, 1746–1805* (Columbia, S.C., 1967).

REVEREND ALEXANDER GARDEN (1685?–1756)

Hubbell, pp. 74–75; *Moses*, pp. 82–84; *Tyler*, pp. 513–15.
*Keen, Quentin Bagley, "Problems of a Commissary: The Rev. Alexander Garden of South Carolina," *Hist Mag of Prot Epis Church*, XX (1951), 136–55.
Nelson, Andrew T., "'Enthusiasm' in Carolina, 1740," *SAQ*, XLIV (1945), 397–405.
Pennington, Edgar L., "The Reverend Alexander Garden," *Hist Mag of Prot Epis Church*, II (1933), 178–94; III (1934), 111–19.

CLEMENT HALL (c. 1710–1759)

*Powell, William S., "Clement Hall, Missionary and Author," intro to Hall, *A Collection of Many Christian Experiences, Sentences, and Several Places of Scripture Improved* (Raleigh, 1961), pp. 1–25.
Weeks, Stephen B., "Clement Hall, the First North Carolina Author, and Thomas Godfrey, the First American Dramatist," *Trinity* (N.C.) *Archive*, VI (1893), 330–35.
———, "Clement Hall, the First Native North Carolina Author," Amer Hist Assn, *Annual Report 1895*, pp. 236–38.

DR. ALEXANDER HAMILTON (1712–1756)

Hamilton's brilliant "History of the Tuesday Club" is being edited by Sarah Elizabeth Freeman and Elizabeth Baer, both of Evergreen House, The Johns Hopkins University Library. Hamilton's "Record of the Tuesday Club," at the Maryland Historical Society, Baltimore, although less literary than the "History," is also fascinating; and it too should be edited and published. A biographical and critical chapter on Hamilton will soon appear in Lemay, *A Literary History of Colonial Maryland*.

DAB, VIII, pp. 170–71; *CHAL*, pp. 11–13; *Hubbell*, pp. 67–69, *934; *LAP*, pp. 103–105.
Bridenbaugh, Carl, intro to *Gentleman's Progress: The Itinerarium of Dr. Alexander Hamilton, 1744* (Chapel Hill, 1948), pp. xi–xxxii.
Freeman, Sarah Elizabeth, "The Tuesday Club Medal," *The Numismatist*, LVII (1945), 1313–22.
Friedman, Lee M., "Dr. Hamilton visits Shearith Israel, 1744," *Amer Jewish Hist Soc Pub*, XXXIX (1949), 183–85.
Hare, Robert R., "Electro Vitrifico in Annapolis: Mr. Franklin Visits the Tuesday Club," *Md Hist Mag*, LVIII (1963), 62–66.

Hart, Albert Bushnell, intro to *Hamilton's Itinerarium* (Saint Louis, 1907), pp. ix–xxvii.

Lemay, J. A. Leo, "Franklin's 'Dr. Spence': The Reverend Archibald Spencer (1698?–1760), M.D.," *Md Hist Mag*, LIX (1964), 199–216. [Spencer and Hamilton at the Tuesday Club]

*_____, "Hamilton's Literary History of the *Maryland Gazette*," *WMQ*, 3rd ser, XXIII (1966), 273–85. [*Md Gaz*, June 29, 1748]

Matthews, Albert, "Rattlesnake Colonel," *New Eng Q*, X (1937), 341–45. [origin of the phrase]

Rutledge, Anna Wells, "A Humorous Artist in Colonial Maryland, "*Am Collector*, XVI (Feb 1947), 8–9, 14–15.

_____, "Portraits in Varied Media in the Collections of the Maryland Historical Society," *Md Hist Mag*, XLI (1946), 282–326. [Hamilton's facetious wash drawings]

JOHN HAMMOND (fl. 1640–1660)

For an account of Hammond's role in the literary battles of the 1650s, and for a critical evaluation, see Lemay's forthcoming *Literary History of Colonial Maryland*.

Hubbell, pp. 22–23; *LAP*, pp. 23, *994; *LHUS*, I, pp. 41–42, *II, 257; *Moses*, pp. 39–41; *Tyler*, pp. 53–57.

THOMAS HARIOT (1560–1621)

LHUS, I, pp. 31–32.

Adams, Randolph G., intro to Hariot's *A Brief and True Report of the New Found Land of Virginia* (New York, 1951), pp. ix–xviii.

*Quinn, David Beers, *The Roanoke Voyages, 1584–1590* (2 vols, Cambridge, Eng., 1955; Hakluyt Soc, 2nd ser, vols 104–105).

REDNAP HOWELL (fl. 1765–1770)

Hawks, Francis L., "Battle of Alamance and the War of the Regulation," in William D. Cooke, ed., *Revolutionary History of North Carolina* (Raleigh, 1853).

*Hudson, Arthur P., "Songs of the North Carolina Regulators," *WMQ*, 3rd ser, IV (1947), 470–85.

Tyler, Moses Coit, *The Literary History of the American Revolution, 1763–1783*, II (New York, 1957), pp. 172–73.

JAMES IREDELL (1751–1799)

DAB, IX, pp. 492–93; *CHAL*, p. 148; *Hubbell*, pp. 154–57, *938.

Herndon, Nettie S., "James Iredell," Duke, 1944. [diss]

McRee, Griffith J., *Life and Correspondence of James Iredell*, 2 vols (New York, 1857).

Weeks, Stephen B., "Judge Iredell and the Political Literature of the Revolution," Amer Hist Assn, *Annual Report, 1895*, pp. 236–38.

REVEREND HUGH JONES (1692–1760)

DAB, IX, p. 175; *Hubbell*, pp. 30–31; *Moses*, pp. 62–66; *Tyler*, pp. 495–96.

*Morton, Richard L., editor's intro to Hugh Jones, *The Present State of Virginia* (Chapel Hill, 1956), pp. 3–48.

DR. JAMES KIRKPATRICK (or Kil [l] patrick) (1700–1770)

There is no adequate account of his literary career.

Waring, Joseph I., "James Killpatrick and Smallpox Inoculation in Charlestown," *Annals Med Hist*, n.s., X (1938), 301–308.

Warren, Austin, "To Mr. Pope: Epistles from America," *PMLA*, XLVIII (1933), 61–73. [pp. 64–67 are on Kirkpatrick, though Warren does not know his identity]

HENRY LAURENS (1724–1792)

There is no critical evaluation of his literary ability.

DAB, XI, pp. 32–35.

Tyler, Moses Coit, *The Literary History of the American Revolution, 1763–1783*, II (New York, 1957), 242–45.

JOHN LAWSON (d. 1711)

DAB, XI, pp. 57–58; *Hubbell*, pp. 81–82, *944; *LAP*, pp. 28–30, *995; *CHAL*, p. 26; *LHUS*, I, pp. 46–47, *II, 259; *Moses*, pp. 79–81; *Tyler*, pp. 507–13.

*Diket, A.L., "The Noble Savage Convention as Epitomized in John Lawson's *A New Voyage to Carolina*," *N.C. Hist R*, XLIII (1966), 413–29.

Hudson, Arthur Palmer, "Animal Lore in Lawson's and Brickell's Histories of North Carolina," *MissQ*, XIII (1960), 189–207.

Kirkham, E. Bruce, "The First English Editions of John Lawson's 'Voyage to Carolina': A Bibliographical Study," *Papers of Bibl Soc of Amer*, LXI (1967), 258–65.

*Lefler, Hugh Talmage, intro to John Lawson, *A New Voyage to Carolina* (Chapel Hill, 1967).

Weeks, Stephen B., "John Lawson and his History of Carolina," *Amer Hist Assn*, *Annual Report, 1895*, pp. 224–32.

JOHN LEDERER (fl. 1670–1675)

DAB, XI, pp. 91–92; *Jones*, p. 35; *LHUS*, I, p. 38, *II, 259.

Carrier, Lyman, "The Veracity of John Lederer," *WMQ*, 2nd ser, XIX (1939), 435–45.

*Cumming, William P., "Notes and Comments," *The Discoveries of John Lederer* (Charlottesville, 1958), pp. 69–107, and bibl, pp. 129–35.

Cunz, Dieter, "John Lederer, Significance and Evaluation," *WMQ*, 2nd ser, XXII (1942), 175–87.

Rights, Douglas L., and William P. Cumming, "The Indians of Lederer's *Discoveries*," in Cumming's *The Discoveries of John Lederer* (Charlottesville, 1958), pp. 111–26.

ARTHUR LEE (1740–1792)

There is no bibliography or adequate critical evaluation.

DAB, XI, pp. 96–97, *Hubbell*, pp. 114–17, *944.

*Shipton, Clifford K., "Arthur Lee," in *Biographical Sketches of Those Who Attended Harvard College, 1751–1755* (Boston, 1965; *Sibley's Harvard Graduates*, XIII), pp. 245–60.

Smith, Glen C., "Dr. Arthur Lee: Political Pamphleteer of Pre-Revolutionary Virginia," *Madison Q*, III (1943), 130–37.

Tyler, Moses Coit, *The Literary History of the American Revolution, 1763–1783*, I (New York, 1957), 244–45.

RICHARD HENRY LEE (1732–1794)

DAB, XI, pp. 117–20; *Hubbell*, pp. 110–14, *944; *LHUS*, I, pp. 142–43.

Matthews, John C., "Two Men on a Tax: Richard Henry Lee, Archibald Ritchie, and the Stamp Act," in Darrett B. Rutman, ed., *The Old Dominion: Essays for Thomas Perkins Abernethy* (Charlottesville, 1964), pp. 96–108.

JOHN MARKLAND (1702?–post 1735)

Hubbell, pp. 36–37; *LHUS*, I, 51–52.

*Lemay, J. A. Leo, intro to *A Poem by John Markland of Virginia* (Williamsburg, 1965), pp. 5–12.

Swem, Earl Gregg, intro to Markland, *Typographia* (Roanoke, 1926).

ALEXANDER MARTIN (1740–1807)

A checklist of his writing is the first desiderata.

DAB, XII, 233–34.

[Clarke, Mrs. Mary B.] *Wood Notes; or Carolina Carols: A Collection of North Carolina Poetry*, II (Raleigh, 1854), p. 235.

Silverman, Kenneth, "Two Unpublished Colonial Verses," *Bull N.Y. Pub Lib*, LXXI (1967), 61–63.

JOHN MERCER (1704–1768)

A bibliography and a full biography are needed.

*Davis, Richard Beale, intro to "The 'Dinwiddianae' Poems and Prose," *The Colonial Virginia Satirist* (Philadelphia, 1967), pp. 5–16.

Mulkearn, Lois, *George Mercer Papers, Relating to the Ohio Company of Virginia* (Pittsburgh, 1954).

Stetson, Sarah P., "John Mercer's Notes on Plants," *VMHB*, LXI (1953), 34–44.

HENRY NORWOOD (1615–1689)

Jones, pp. 36–37; *LAP*, pp. 22–23, *994; *Moses*, pp. 36–37.

Harrison, Fairfax, "Henry Norwood (1615–89)," *VMHB*, XXXIII (1925), 1–10.

Tyre, J. H., "Colonel Henry Norwood of Leckhampton, Co. Gloucester," *Trans. Bristol and Gloucestershire Arch Soc*, XLVII (1926), 113–21.

REVEREND GRONOW OWEN (1721–1769)

Hubbell, pp. *59–60.

Gray, Arthur, "Gronow Owen in America," *WMQ*, 2nd ser, XI (1930), 235–40.

GEORGE PERCY (1580–1632)

DAB, XIV, p. 452; *Jones*, pp. 8–9; *Moses*, pp. 24–26; *Tyler*, pp. 35–37.
*Barbour, Philip L., *The Three Worlds of Captain John Smith* (Boston, 1964), pp. 427–28.
Shirley, John W., "George Percy at Jamestown," *VMHB*, LVII (1949), 227–43.

ELIZA (LUCAS) PINCKNEY (1722–1793)

This delightful author has never been the subject of a critical evaluation. A complete edition of her writings, available in the South Carolina Historical Society, is needed.

DAB, XIV, pp. 616–17.

Holbrook, Harriott Pinckney, ed., *The Journal and Letters of Eliza Lucas* (Wormsloe, Ga., 1850).
Nicholas, Edward, *The Hours and the Ages* (New York, 1949), pp. 8–38, *et passim.*
[popular biog approach]
Ravenel, Harriott Horry (Rutledge), *Eliza Pinckney* (New York, 1896).

JOHN PORY (1572–1635)

DAB, XV, pp. 110–11; *CHAL*, pp. 14; *Jones*, pp. 26–28; *LAP* p. 20, p. *993; *Moses*, pp. 32–34; *Tyler*, pp. 43–45.
*James, Sydney V., Jr., *Three Visitors to Early Plymouth* (Plymouth Plantation, Mass., 1963), pp. 3–20, bibl p. 81.
Powell, William S., "John Pory: His Life, Letters and Work," North Carolina, 1947.
[MA thesis]
———, "John Pory on the Death of Sir Walter Raleigh," WMQ, 3rd ser, IX (1952), 532–38.

REVEREND SAMUEL QUINCY (fl. 1730–1751)

Hubbell, pp. 75–76.
Pennington, Edgar L. "The Reverend Samuel Quincy, S.P.G. Missionary," *Ga HistQ*, XI (1927), 157–65.

JAMES REID (fl. 1769)

Davis, Richard Beale, intro to "The Religion of the Bible and Religion of K[ing] W[illiam] County Compared," in *The Colonial Virginia Satirist* (Philadelphia, 1967), pp. 43–45.

JAMES REVEL

Jennings, John M., ed., "The Poor Unhappy Transported Felon's Sorrowful Account of His Fourteen Years Transportation at Virginia in America," *VMHB*, LVI (1948), 180–94.

RICHARD RICH (fl. 1610)

LAP, p. 54.

ROWLAND RUGELEY (1735?–1776)

Although Rugeley published frequently in the English magazines before he emigrated to America (c.1766), and although he published two volumes of poetry, no biographical or critical article has yet appeared. A few references are in the *S.C. Hist and Geneal Mag*, X, 224; XI, 105; XVII, 123; XX, 17; XXI, 114; and XXXIV, 195.

GEORGE RUGGLE (1585–1622)

Neal, Edward D., "George Ruggle, Author of Some Early publications upon the Virginia Colony," *New Eng Hist and Geneal Register*, XXIX (1875), 296–97.

JANET SCHAW (fl. 1774–1776)

Hubbell, pp. 157–59, *958.

REVEREND JOSIAH SMITH (1704–1781)

*Shipton, Clifford K., "Josiah Smith," in *Biographical Sketches of Those Who Attended Harvard College, 1722–1725* (Boston, 1945; *Sibley's Harvard Graduates*), VII, pp. 569–85.

REVEREND WILLIAM STITH (1707–1755)

DAB, XVIII, pp. 34–35; *CHAL*, p. 27; *Hubbell*, 47–48, *259; *LAP*, p. 83; *LHUS*, I, pp. 47–48, *II, p. 259; *Moses*, pp. 78–79; *Tyler, pp. 504–6*.
Tsuruta, Toshiko, "William Stith, Historian of Colonial Virginia," Washington, 1957. [diss]

WILLIAM STRACHEY (1572–1621)

DAB, XVIII, pp. 120–21; *Jones*, pp. 24–27; *Hubbell*, pp. 20–21, *962–63; *LAP*, pp. 20–21, 66–67, *993–94; *Moses*, pp. 26–30; *Tyler*, pp. 37–40.
*Culliford, S.G., *William Strachey 1572–1621* (Charlottesville, 1965).
Sanders, Charles R., "William Strachey, the Virginia Company, and Shakespeare," *VMHB*, LVII (1949), 115–32.
Wright, Louis B., intro to *A Voyage to Virginia in 1609. Two Narratives: Strachey's "True Reportory" and Jourdain's Discovery of the Bermudas* (Charlottesville, 1964), pp. ix–xx.
Wright, Louis B., and Virginia Freund, intro to William Strachey, *The Historie of Travell into Virginia Britania* (London, 1953; Hakluyt Soc, 2nd ser, vol 103), pp. xiii–xxxii.

DR. PATRICK TAILFER (fl. 1735–1745)

Hubbell, pp. 83–86; *LAP,* p. 69; *LHUS,* I, pp. 48–49, *II, p. 260; *Moses,* pp. 84–86; *Tyler,* pp. 515–20.

Ver Steeg, Clarence L., intro to *A True and Historical Narrative of the Colony of Georgia by Pat [rick] Tailfer and Others. With Comments by the Earl of Egmont* (Athens, Ga., 1960), pp. ix–xxxiv.

JOHN THOMAS (1743–1815)

*Kelly, J. Reaney, " 'Tulip Hill, Its History and Its People," *Md Hist Mag,* LX (1965), 349–403, esp pp. 363–66.

HENRY TIMBERLAKE (1730–1765)

DAB, XVIII, pp. 553–54.

Williams, Samuel Cole, intro to Henry Timberlake, *Memoirs, 1756–1765* (Johnson City, Tenn., 1927), pp. 11–17.

BENJAMIN WALLER (1710–1786)

His poetry and literary correspondence, especially the exchanges with Colonel Henry Wood (1696–1757), should be edited and published.

Grigsby, Hugh Blair, *Discourse on the Life and Character of the Hon. Littleton Waller Tazewell* (Norfolk, 1860), p. 9.

Servies, James A., preface to *The Poems of Charles Hansford* (Chapel Hill, 1961), pp. xvii–xix, and p. 78.

CHARLES HENRY WHARTON (1748–1833)

DAB, XX, pp. 26–27.

Tyler, Moses Coit, *The Literary History of the American Revolution, 1763–1783,* II (New York, 1957), 165–69.

REVEREND ALEXANDER WHITAKER (1585–1617)

DAB, XX, pp. 79–80; *LHUS,* I, p. 40, *II, p. 258; *Moses,* pp. 30–32; *Tyler,* pp. 41–43.

*Littleton, William H., "Alexander Whitaker (1585–1617): 'The Apostle of Virginia,' " *Hist Mag of the Prot Epis Church,* XXIX (1961), 325–48.

Porter, Harry Culverwell, "Alexander Whitaker: Cambridge Apostle to Virginia," *WMQ,* 3rd ser, XIV (1957), 317–43.

ANDREW WHITE, S.J. (1579–1656)

A biographical and critical chapter on White will shortly appear in Lemay, *A Literary History of Colonial Maryland.*

DAB, XX, pp. 87–88; *LAP,* pp. 23–24, *994; *Moses,* pp. 37–39; *Tyler.,* p. 53.

Curran, Francis X., "The Mystery ot Andrew White," *Woodstock Letters,* LXXXV (1956), 375–80.

Hughes, Thomas A., *History of the Society of Jesus in North America* (4 vols, London and New York, 1907).

ELIZA (Yonge) WILKINSON (fl. 1770–1783)

Moses, pp. 149–50.

Gilman, Caroline, intro to *Letters of Eliza Wilkinson, during the Invasion and Possession of Charlestown, S.C., by the British* (New York, 1839).

REVEREND CHARLES WOODMASON (1720?–1777?)

The first desiderata is a checklist of his poetry.

Cohen, Hennig, "A Colonial Poem on Indigo Culture," *Agric Hist,* XXX (1956), 41–44.

———, "A Colonial Topographical Poem," *Names,* I (1953), 252–58.

*Hooker, Richard J., intro to *The Carolina Backcountry on the Eve of the Revolution: The Journal and Other Writings of Charles Woodmason, Anglican Itinerant* (Chapel Hill, 1953), pp. xi–xxxix.

*Jones, Claude E., "Charles Woodmason as a Poet," *S.C. Hist Mag,* LIX (1958), 189–194.

Labaree, Leonard W., et al, eds., *The Papers of Benjamin Franklin,* V (New Haven, 1962), 59–62. [repr Woodmason's poem to Franklin, with biog note]

JOHN JOACHIM ZUBLY (1724–1781)

DAB, XX, pp. 660–61; *Hubbell,* pp. 165–66, *974.

*Daniel, Marjorie, "John Joachim Zubly—Georgia Pamphleteer of the Revolution," *Ga Hist Q,* XIX (1935), 1–16.

Tyler, Moses Coit, *The Literary History of the American Revolution, 1763–1783,* I (New York, 1957), pp. 483–86.

J. A. Leo Lemay
University of California
Los Angeles, California